DISCARDED

THE THEME–TOPIC INTERFACE

Pragmatics & Beyond New Series

Editor:
Andreas H. Jucker
(Justus Liebig University, Giessen)

Associate Editors:
Jacob L. Mey
(Odense University)

Herman Parret
(Belgian National Science Foundation, Universities of Louvain and Antwerp)

Jef Verschueren
(Belgian National Science Foundation, University of Antwerp)

Editorial Address:
Justus Liebig University Giessen, English Department
Otto-Behaghel-Strasse 10, D-35394 Giessen, Germany
e-mail: andreas.jucker@anglistik.uni-giessen.de

Editorial Board:
Shoshana Blum-Kulka (*Hebrew University of Jerusalem*)
Chris Butler (*University College of Ripon and York*)
Jean Caron (*Université de Poitiers*); Robyn Carston (*University College London*)
Bruce Fraser (*Boston University*); John Heritage (*University of California at Los Angeles*)
David Holdcroft (*University of Leeds*); Sachiko Ide (*Japan Women's University*)
Catherine Kerbrat-Orecchioni (*University of Lyon 2*)
Claudia de Lemos (*University of Campinas, Brazil*); Marina Sbisà (*University of Trieste*)
Emanuel Schegloff (*University of California at Los Angeles*)
Paul O. Takahara (*Kobe City University of Foreign Studies*)
Sandra Thompson (*University of California at Santa Barbara*)
Teun A. Van Dijk (*University of Amsterdam*); Richard Watts (*University of Berne*)

71

María Ángeles Gómez-González
The Theme–Topic Interface
Evidence from English

THE THEME–TOPIC INTERFACE

EVIDENCE FROM ENGLISH

MARÍA ÁNGELES GÓMEZ-GONZÁLEZ
Universidade de Santiago de Compostela

JOHN BENJAMINS PUBLISHING COMPANY
AMSTERDAM/PHILADELPHIA

∞™ The paper used in this publication meets the minimum requirements of American National Standard for Information Sciences — Permanence of Paper for Printed Library Materials, ANSI Z39.48-1984.

Library of Congress Cataloging-in-Publication Data

Gómez-González, María Á.
  The theme-topic interface : evidence from English / María Ángeles Gómez-González.
    p.   cm. -- (Pragmatics & beyond, ISSN 0922-842X ; new ser. 71)
  Includes bibliographical references and indexes.
  1. English language--Topic and comment. 2. English language--Discourse analysis. 3. English language--Grammar, Generative. 4. English language--Sentences. I. Title. II. Series.
PE1380.G66   2000
425--dc21   00-021725
ISBN 90 272 5086 3 (Eur.) / 1 55619 949 X (US) (alk. paper)   CIP

© 2001 – John Benjamins B.V.
No part of this book may be reproduced in any form, by print, photoprint, microfilm, or any other means, without written permission from the publisher.

John Benjamins Publishing Co. • P.O.Box 75577 • 1070 AN Amsterdam • The Netherlands
John Benjamins North America • P.O.Box 27519 • Philadelphia PA 19118-0519 • USA

To my parents, Cándida González and Isaac Gómez

Thematic patterns are not optional stylistic variants; they are integral part of the meaning of language. Texture is not something that is achieved superimposing an appropriate text form on pre-existing ideational content. The textual component is a component of meaning along with ideational and interpersonal components [...]. The system does not first generate a representation of reality, then encode it as a speech act, and finally recode it as a text [...]. It embodies all these types of meanings in simultaneous networks of options, from each of which derive structures that are mapped onto one another in the course of their lexico-grammatical realization.

[Halliday, M. A. K. *Language as Social Semiotic: The Social Interpretation of Language and Meaning.* 1978: 134]

Table of Contents

List of Tables xiii

List of Figures xv

Abbreviations and Conventions xvii

Acknowledgements xxi

Foreword xxiii

PART I
The Theme–Topic Interface 1

CHAPTER 1
Introduction 3
1.1 Organisation of the book 3
1.2 The nature of the Theme–Topic interface 4

CHAPTER 2
An Evaluation of Three Interpretations of Communicative Categories . 15
2.1 Introduction 15
2.2 The semantic interpretation 16
    2.2.1 Relational aboutness and sentence Topics 17
    2.2.2 Referential aboutness and discourse Topics 25
    2.2.3 Interactive aboutness and speaker's Topic 28
2.3 The informational interpretation 31
    2.3.1 The principles of: FSP, EW, EF and TU 31
    2.3.2 What does "given" mean? 34
        2.3.2.1 Givenness and presupposition 35
        2.3.2.2 Relational givenness vs. referential givenness 35

        2.3.2.3 Recoverability, predictability, shared knowledge,
              identifiability and (assumed) familiarity 37
        2.3.2.4 Activation, accessibility and saliency 40
   2.3.3 Other problems with informational approaches 43
2.4 The syntactic interpretation 49
   2.4.1 The advantage of first mention 49
   2.4.2 Problems with syntactic approaches 52
2.5 Summary 57

PART II
Previous Studies: A Sympathetic Critique 59

CHAPTER 3
The Prague School 61
3.1 Introduction 61
3.2 The informational trend 62
   3.2.1 H. Weil 62
   3.2.2 V. Mathesius 64
   3.2.3 J. Firbas 66
   3.2.4 Ö. Dahl 72
   3.2.5 P. Sgall 75
3.3 The syntactic trend 78
   3.3.1 F. Trávníček 78
   3.3.2 E. Beneš 79
   3.3.3 F. Daneš 80
3.4 Summary 87

CHAPTER 4
Systemic Functional Grammar 89
4.1 Introduction 89
4.2 Characterisation of Theme 94
   4.2.1 A taxonomy of topical Themes 100
        4.2.1.1 Marked vs. unmarked Themes 102
        4.2.1.2 Predicated Themes 104
        4.2.1.3 Thematic equivalents 106
        4.2.1.4 Substitute Themes 107
        4.2.1.5 Reference Theme 108
   4.2.2 Multiple Themes 108
   4.2.3 Interpersonal Themes 109

	4.2.4	Textual Themes	111
	4.2.5	Metaphorical Theme	111
4.3	Troubleshooting		115
	4.3.1	The "double-sided" nature of Theme	115
	4.3.2	Identifying the Theme	126
		4.3.2.1 The first "ideational" element	126
		4.3.2.2 The label "textual Theme"	126
		4.3.2.3 The "structure" imposed by thematic patterns	126
		4.3.2.4 Deriving the "meaning" of Theme	127
		4.3.2.5 Substitute Themes	128
		4.3.2.6 Reference Themes	128
		4.3.2.7 Displaced Themes	128
		4.3.2.8 Initial position	130
	4.3.3	The "separating" stand of the theory	135
4.4	Summary		136

CHAPTER 5
Functional Grammar 139
5.1 Introduction 139
5.2 Topic vs. Focus 143
    5.2.1 GivTop 148
    5.2.2 SubTop 149
    5.2.3 ResTop 150
    5.2.4 NewTop 151
5.3 Theme vs. Tail 153
5.4 Troubleshooting 156
    5.4.1 The semantic criterion of aboutness/relevance 157
    5.4.2 The syntactic criterion of position 158
    5.4.3 The informational criterion of givenness 161
    5.4.4 Topic (and Focus) assignment to one constituent 163
5.5 Summary 169

PART III
A Corpus-Based Analysis of Syntactic Theme in PresE 171

CHAPTER 6
Theory and Methods 173
6.1 An intrinsically functionalist-separating framework 173
6.2 A survey of thematic options 180

6.3	The cognitive salience of the Theme zone		185
6.4	The corpus and the methodology		192
	6.4.1	The LIBMSEC	192
	6.4.2	Some problems of analysis	195
		6.4.2.1 Corpus size	195
		6.4.2.2 Text categories	196
		6.4.2.3 Corpus-based approaches	205
	6.4.3	Statistical methods	207

CHAPTER 7
Results and Discussion ... 211

7.1	Introduction		211
7.2	Non-special Theme constructions		214
	7.2.1	Formal structure and frequencies in LIBMSEC	215
	7.2.2	Discourse function	226
7.3	Marked Theme constructions		229
	7.3.1	Preposings	229
		7.3.1.1 Formal structure and frequencies in LIBMSEC	230
		7.3.1.2 Discourse function	235
	7.3.2	Passive constructions	239
		7.3.2.1 Formal structure and frequencies in LIBMSEC	241
		7.3.2.2 Discourse function	243
7.4	Special Theme constructions		245
	7.4.1	Existential-*there* constructions	257
		7.4.1.1 Formal structure and frequencies in LIBMSEC	257
		7.4.1.2 Discourse function	263
	7.4.2	*It*-Extrapositions	266
		7.4.2.1 Formal structure and frequencies in LIBMSEC	266
		7.4.2.2 Discourse function	271
	7.4.3	Inversions	274
		7.4.3.1 Formal structure and frequencies in LIBMSEC	275
		7.4.3.2 Discourse function	278
	7.4.4	Left detachments	287
		7.4.4.1 Formal structure and frequencies in LIBMSEC	287
		7.4.4.2 Discourse function	292
	7.4.5	Right detachments	297
		7.4.5.1 Formal structure and frequencies in LIBMSEC	297
		7.4.5.2 Discourse function	301

	7.4.6	Cleft constructions 303
		7.4.6.1 Formal structure and frequencies in LIBMSEC 304
		7.4.6.2 Discourse function 312
	7.4.7	Pseudo-cleft constructions 317
		7.4.7.1 Formal structure and frequencies in LIBMSEC 317
		7.4.7.2 Discourse function 323
7.5	Extended multiple Themes 329
	7.5.1	Formal structure and frequencies in LIBMSEC 329
	7.5.2	Discourse function 341

CHAPTER 8
Summary, Conclusions and Further Research 347
8.1 Theoretical conclusions 347
8.2 Corpus-based conclusions 351
8.3 Suggestions for further research 356

Appendix
Data base structure for "A Corpus-based Analysis of Syntactic Theme in PresE" 359

Notes
Chapter 1. The Theme–Topic interface: Introduction 363
Chapter 2. An evaluation of three interpretations of communicative categories 364
Chapter 3. The Prague School 368
Chapter 4. Systemic Functional Grammar 368
Chapter 5. Functional Grammar 372
Chapter 6. A corpus-based analysis of syntactic Theme in PresE: Theory and methods 375
Chapter 7. A corpus-based analysis of syntactic Theme in PresE: Results and discussion 376
Appendix: Data-base structure 380

References 381

Name Index 425

Subject Index 429

List of Tables

Table 1	Some terminology related to the categories of Theme/Topic	6
Table 2	Grammatical devices associated with Theme/Topic	11
Table 3	Trends in the interpretation of aboutness	17
Table 4	The Topic–Subject interface	20
Table 5	Relevance of initial position	50
Table 6	Components of a multiple Theme in SFG	110
Table 7	Summary of principal types of projection	112
Table 8	Summary of principal types of expansion	113
Table 9	Halliday's multiple Theme vs. Downing's thematic frameworks	118
Table 10	Thematic proportionalities within the Theme system complex	120
Table 11	Multiple Theme and textual proportionalities	121
Table 12	Some thematic proportionalities	122
Table 13	Types of "contentless" Subject *it*	124
Table 14	Topic "special treatment" devices in FG	164
Table 15	Theme, Topic and the Given–New contrast	185
Table 16	LIBMSEC Corpus (49.285 words)	192
Table 17	Subjectivity across LIBMSEC texts	197
Table 18	Registers in LIBMSEC	200
Table 19	Incidence of EMT in Fiction	208
Table 20	Incidence of topical and EMTs in LIBMSEC	208
Table 21	Choice of EMT (*yes*-response)	209
Table 22	Choice of non-special Theme (*yes*-response)	217
Table 23	Process types in frontings	217
Table 24	Syntactic function of (non-)special Themes	218
Table 25	Mood in (non-)special Themes	219
Table 26	Incidence of frontings in (non-)special	220
Table 27	± External realizations of (non-)special and (un)marked topical Themes	221
Table 28	Position of topical element in (un)marked EMTs	222
Table 29	Incidence of EMTs in (un)marked Themes	223
Table 30	Type of clause of (non-)special and (un)marked topical Themes	224
Table 31	Type of structure of (non-)special and (un)marked topical Themes	225
Table 32	Ergative functions in (non-)special and (un)marked topical Themes	226

List of Tables

Table 33	Voice in (non-)special Themes	242
Table 34	Special syntactic Themes under analysis	247
Table 35	Incidence of special Themes in LIBMSEC text types	251
Table 36	Incidence and position of logico-conjunctive Themes in special Themes	252
Table 37	Syntactic function of special topical Themes in LIBMSEC	252
Table 38	± External realizations of special topical Themes in LIBMSEC	253
Table 39	+ External realizations of LDs in LIBMSEC	291
Table 40	Falling vs. Rising tones in LDs in LIBMSEC	292
Table 41	+ External realizations of RDs in LIBMSEC	300
Table 42	Falling vs. Rising tones in RDs in LIBMSEC	301
Table 43	Cleft constructions in LIBMSEC	309
Table 44	Falling vs. Rising tones in cleft constructions in LIBMSEC	311
Table 45	Informational classification of cleft constructions in LIBMSEC	313
Table 46	ID/Vl and IR/T constituents of pseudoclefts in LIBMSEC	319
Table 47	Falling vs. Rising tones in pseudoclefts in LIBMSEC	323
Table 48	Choice of EMTs (*yes*-response) in LIBMSEC	332
Table 49	Classification table for choice of EMTs	333
Table 50	Incidence of EMTs in Fiction in LIBMSEC	338
Table 51	Rhetorical purpose of EMTs in LIBMSEC	338
Table 52	Incidence of EMTs in LIBMSEC text types	339
Table 53	Incidence of Beta Themes in EMTs in LIBMSEC	340

List of Figures

Figure 1	Different interpretations of pragmatic/communicative functions	16
Figure 2	Daneš's classification criteria of TPs	82
Figure 3	Daneš's models of thematic progression [my analysis]	83
Figure 4	Thematic progression with a split Theme [my analysis]	84
Figure 5	System network of structural textual options: primary delicacy	91
Figure 6	Texture of clauses as messages	97
Figure 7	Sandwich texture in abstract written discourse	100
Figure 8	Theme in the clause complex	102
Figure 9	The thematic structure of a predicated Theme	105
Figure 10	The thematic structure of a multiple Theme	109
Figure 11	Clauses as topical Theme: congruent and metaphorical versions	115
Figure 12	Theme system in English [my network]	181
Figure 13	Distribution of syntactic Themes across LIBMSEC text-types	212
Figure 14	(Non-)Special Themes in LIBMSEC	216
Figure 15	Special thematic constructions across LIBMSEC text-types	249
Figure 16	Unmarked centripetal array of EMTs	333
Figure 17	(Non-)Extended multiple Themes across LIBMSEC text-types	341
Figure 18	Scopal centripetal relations in unmarked EMTs	343
Figure 19	Major and minor orientations of the Theme zone	344

Abbreviations and Conventions

A	Addressee	Dtho	Diatheme oriented elements
Acc	Accusative	DUM	Dummy element
AdjFI	FI after a preposed adjective	E	Entity
		e	Predication
AdjG	Adjectival Group	ECCs	Extra-Clausal Constituents
AdvG	Adverbial Group	EF	End Focus (Principle)
Agt	Agentive	EMT	Extended multiple Themes
AofQ	Ascriber of Quality	ERCs	Event-Reporting Constructions
B	Bearer of a Quality		
BJ	Boundness Juncture	EXC	Exclamative
C	Core; Linear Ordering; New/Rheme	EXT	Extern
		EW	End Weight (Principle)
CA	Communicative Articulation	f	Predicate
		FBP	Focus-Background Pattern
CB	Contextual Boundness	FG	Functional Grammar
Cb	Backward-looking center	FI	Full Inversions
CD	Communicative Dynamism	Foc	Focus
Cf	Forward-looking center	FSP	Further Specification
CI	Communicative Importance	FUNCT	Syntactic function
CONDSAI	SAI after Conditionals	Giv_F	Assumed Familiarity
COREF	Coreference	$Giv_{I/D}$	Identifiability/Definiteness
CORR-SAI	SAI after a Correlative particle	Giv_K	Shared Knowledge
		Giv_P	Predictability
Cp	Preferred center	Giv_R	Recoverability
CSU	Communicative Sense of an Utterance	GivTop	Given Topic
		GHZ	Gundel, Hedberg & Zacharschi
CWO	Canonical Word Order		
D-Topic	Discourse Topic	IB	Informational Bipartition
Dat	Dative	IC	Intonation Centre
DEC	Declarative	ID	Identified
DS	Discourse Subjects; Deep Structure	IF	Illocutionary Force Operator
Dth	Diatheme		

IFG	Halliday's (1994) *Introduction to Functional Grammar*	Pro-SAI	SAI after a pro-form
		PrPh	Presentation of Phenomenon
IMP	Imperative	PS	Prague School
INT	Interrogative	PSRR	Principle of Separation of Reference and Role
IR	Identifier		
LIPOC	Language Independent Preferred Order of Constituents	Q	Quality (i.e. non copulative verb)
		QFI	FI after a preposed quote
Loc	Locative	R	Relation of Inference; Rheme
MOD	Method of Development		
NG	Nominal group	ResTop	Res Topic
NEGSAI	SAI after negative and restrictive adverbs	Rh	Rheme
		RhPr	Rheme Proper
NewTop	New Topic	RhPro	Rheme Proper oriented elements
NIR	Network of Isotopic Relations		
		S	Given; Sentence; Speaker; Starting point
NOM	Nominalisation		
Nom	nominative	SAI	Subject-Auxiliary Inversions
n.s.	non-significant association		
p	significance level	Set	Setting
P	Pragmatic information, predication; Pretonic segment	SFG	Systemic Functional Grammar
		SoA	State of Affairs
P1	First Intraclausal Constituent	SP	Specific Principle
		Sp	Subject prominent languages
P2	Position Immediate to the Left of the Predication		
		Spec	Specification (i.e. Object);
P3	Position Immediate to the Right of the Predication	SR	Semantic Representation of a sentence
P_A	Addressee's Pragmatic information	SS	Surface Structure
		SubTop	Sub Topic
PCO	Principle of Centripetal Orientation	T	Theme; Token; Tonic segment
PFSP	Principle of Functional Sentence Perspective	TCA	Topic–Comment articulation
Ph	Phenomenon	TCS	Topic–Comment structure
PP	Prepositional Phrase	TFG1, 2	Dik's (1997) *Theory of Functional Grammar* (Vols. I and II)
PPFI	FI after prepositional phrase		
Pr	Presentation (the verb)	Th	Theme
PRED.	Predicated Theme	ThPr	Theme Proper
PresE	Present-day English		

Abbreviations and Conventions

ThPro	Theme Proper oriented elements	Vl	Value
TMEs	Time/Manner exponents	VPFI	FI after a participle
TP	Thematic Progression	WFG	Martin, Mathiessen & Painter (1997) *Working with Functional Grammar*
Tp	Topic prominent languages		
TrPr	Transition Proper	X	entity; proposition
TrPro	Transition Proper oriented elements	x	enhancing expansion; entity
TUP	Task Urgency Principle	Y	Sub Topic
USC	Universidade de Santiago de Compostela		

Orthography

'	projected meaning	ˇ	Tone 4 ((Low) Falling-Rising)
β	Beta Theme (i.e. dependent clause as Theme of a hypotactic clause complex)	χ^2	*"Chi Square"* association test
↓	Drop in pitch	*	Displaced Theme
-	High Level	+	Extending Expansion
α	Hypotaxis (i.e. primary process, dominant constituent)	/	Tone 2 ((High) Rising)
		/	Tone 3 ((Low)Rising)
		=	Elaborating Expansion
β	Hypotaxis (i.e. secondary process, dependent constituent)	\	Tone 1 ((Fall) Falling)
		\	Tone 1 ((High) Falling)
|	Minor tone-group boundary	∧	Tone 5 ((Fall) Rising-Falling)
"	Projected Wording	∧	Tone 5 ((High) Rising-Falling)
↑	Rise in pitch		
Ø	Zero Anaphora; elliptical Theme	_	Low Level
		°	Prominent, but unaccented, syllable
˅	Tone 4 ((High) Falling-Rising)		

Acknowledgements

First, and foremost, I would like to express my gratitude to Teresa Fanego Lema, Christopher S. Butler, J. Lachlan Mackenzie, Angela Downing and Peter C. Collins for years of friendship and support — as well as for illuminating discussions which were crucial to my understanding of this topic. I should also like to mention M. A. K. Halliday, S. C. Dik, M. Berry, P. H. Fries, M. I. M. Matthiessen, M. Hannay, K. Lambrecht, J. S. Gómez-Soliño, T. Jiménez-Juliá, J. M. García-Gallego, B. Samitta and A. Smits, as well as the anonymous reviewers for JB, to whom I am also indebted for their comments and for suggesting a new approach to a number of issues raised in this book. I hereby thank all these scholars for their input and absolve them of any responsibility for what follows. They do not, of course, necessarily agree with me.

My gratitude goes also to Javier Marta-Piñón, to Carmen Cadarso and to the Department of Biostatistics of the University of Santiago de Compostela (USC) for their contributions in the interpretation of the statistical analyses included in this book.

Finally, for years of financial support, I would also like to thank the Xunta de Galicia, grant number PGIDT00PX120402PR and the Spanish Ministry of Education and Science (DGES), grant numbers PB90-0370, PB94-0619, PB97-0507.

Foreword

The meaning and functions of Theme as represented by Michael Halliday have engrossed scholars working within the systemic-functional perspective, channelling and challenging their analytical powers for many years. María de los Ángeles Gómez-González is no exception. But as this volume demonstrates, the scope of her research has not been restricted to the interpretation and analysis of Theme from an exclusively systemic-functional perspective. Rather, the author embarks on an extensive and highly critical overview of those models and variants on the models which include either theme or topic as discourse-pragmatic categories associated with the thematic patterning of the clause.

With a keen critical spirit and untiring zeal, the author exposes the inadequacies, contradictions and vagueness of each of the major theoretical frameworks she scrutinises. Varying degrees of sympathy and approval are also meted out. The inevitable complexity that such an ambitious objective involves, and the daunting burden that the unravelling of such terminological profusion might present to the reader are to a great extent lightened by the author's judicious use of tables and charts. The reader will find these invaluable.

The extensive critical apparatus that occupies Parts I and II of the work leads in Part III to the author's own proposal of syntactic Theme. This proposal, as the author recognises, concurs with views expressed by several systemicists and others, and in fact relies heavily on emendations to the SFG model of Theme put forward by them. But threads are drawn together, parallels and contrasts are established with other functional approaches, and the result is a detailed classification of Theme types and their realizations in the grammar. Quantifications of the results according to text types and extracts from the *Lancaster IBM Spoken English Corpus (LIBMSEC)* presented as supporting illustrations to the proposal make a welcome addition to this part of the study.

To conclude, this is a book that was waiting to be written and that had to be written. Many PhD students, attracted by the thematic structuring of English, have contemplated or perhaps dreamed of attempting such a work, but few have dared to venture beyond the shallows. That María de los Ángeles Gómez-González has dared to plumb the depths is a credit to her, and is a vivid testimony to the perduring inspiration of Michael Halliday's work.

Professor Angela Downing
Universidad Complutense, Madrid

PART I

The Theme–Topic Interface

CHAPTER 1

Introduction

1.1 Organisation of the book

There exists an increasing interest in the study of *information packaging*, that is to say, how information is structurally *realized*, or formally expressed, by syntactic, prosodic, or morphological means to meet the communicative demands of a particular situation.[1] This whole area is all the more a matter of debate owing to the large degree of crosslinguistic diversity, wealth of characterisations and considerable amount of fuzziness implied. How do speakers go about packaging utterances? What are the informational primitives involved in this process? In trying to answer these questions several informational articulations have been put forward in terms of, for example, *Topic* and *Comment*, *Theme* and *Rheme*, *Given* and *New*, *Ground* and *Focus*, *Implicature* and *Presupposition*, to mention but a few.

In this book we shall concentrate on the analysis of two of these information packaging primitives in Present-day English (PresE): the notions of *Theme* and/or *Topic*.[2] This involves first investigating the variegated and confusing usages of these terms and of the categories associated with them, covering a wide range of factors at the intersection of disciplines as diverse as grammar, discourse/text analysis, pragmatics, psycholinguistics, sociolinguistics or computational linguistics. But it also involves trying to introduce an account which (a) captures the insights of previous approaches but circumvents their shortcomings, and (b) proves to be empirically verifiable and operational in natural language.

The book is structured as follows. Part I provides an evaluation of *three dominant interpretations of communicative functions*, i.e. *semantic*, in terms of such concepts as "aboutness" or "relevance", *informational*, invoking the contrast between "given" and "new" information, and *syntactic*, alluding to the "staging" of information. We shall stress the *descriptive potential* and *problems* of these approaches, as well as their primarily *functional orientation*. The discussion may prove revealing in establishing the "correct" categorisation of different phenomena that are sometimes lumped together under the same label. Part II offers a *chronological critique* of the interpretations endorsed by three *functionalist* models, *The Prague School* (PS), *Systemic Functional Grammar* (SFG) and *Functional Grammar* (FG).[3] The analysis is restricted to these three programmes for two reasons. First, this research proceeds within the general *functionalist* paradigm according to which linguistic structures must be explained primarily by reference to their *communicative* roles, that is, by the use to which they are put in the communicative co(n)text in which they occur. And second, this study aims to unravel some of the confusion that has pervaded these hitherto conflicting, or regarded-as-different, functionalist accounts with a view to forging their rapprochement. To this effect, Part III presents a *reassessment of the Theme–Topic interface in natural language*, i.e. the *Lancaster/IBM Spoken English Corpus* (LIBMSEC), and *elicits the formal features, discourse functions, as well as the frequencies of the thematic constructions obtained therefrom*. At the end of Part III, Chapter 8 summarises the new theoretical claims and corpus-based findings of this investigation, making, at the same time, suggestions for further research in this field. The volume closes with a list of bibliographical references.

One way in which the present book can be used is as a *catalogue of approaches* to the object of study, providing extensive bibliography and critical evaluation. It can also be read as a *functional* description of some aspects of PresE grammar as it gives an account of how forms of this language are used in communication, in naturally-occurring spoken texts. But I hope that in either case it will tempt readers to go on to explore in greater depth language as a co-operative enterprise from a communicative perspective.

1.2 The nature of the Theme–Topic interface

Studies in this area have been characterised by terminological profusion and confusion because very different positions have been taken on the appropriate criteria for the definition and identification of the notions of Theme/Topic (and related categories) (Güblig & Raible 1977; Allerton 1978; Brömser 1982; Fries 1984; Schlobinski & Schütze-Coburn 1992; Valldduví & Engdahl 1996). Thus, in addition to *Theme* and *Topic*, many other labels have been invoked either to refer to one and the same concept or to name quite different things, through repeated stages of modification and reinterpretation (Keijsper 1985: 143). Some of these terms are: *object of thought, psychological Subject, Základ, Východisté, Basis, Nucleus, Ground, Foundation, Dictum, Forefront, Figure, Hook, Peg, Onset, Bound Information, Given vs. New (information), Presupposition, Assertion,*

Vorfeld, Point of departure, (Dia)Theme (Proper), Expexegesis, Epitomisation, (Anti)Topic (Proper), Preposing, Extraction, Left/Right Detachment/Dislocation/ Displacement, Extraposition, Afterthought, Tail, Focus, Focus/Y(iddish) Movement, etc. Indeed, as shown in Table 1, the myriad of functions and labels associated with our object of study, and the different elements of structure related to it, reveal the difficulties involved in this type of research and the illusion of reaching a consensus.

This situation, however, should not be exclusively considered the fault of the researchers who have busied themselves with the exploration of the field. Rather, it seems to emerge from the interaction of three factors:

a. the fact that the labels "Theme" and "Topic" have received three different interpretations;
b. the general indeterminacy of functional categories; and
c. the type of framework adopted, which will determine the principles and ultimate goals of the analysis.

The origins of the *Theme–Rheme, Topic–Comment* distinctions can be traced back to classic Greek philosophy (Protagoras, Plato, Aristotle), which characterised human judgement as double (*double judgement*), consisting in first naming an entity (*subject of human judgement*) and then making a statement about it (*predicate of human judgement*). This dichotomy was later on incorporated into linguistics and distinguished from *grammatical Subject* and *Predicate*.[4] While the latter dyad was basically described in morphosyntactic terms (verb agreement, case marking, etc.), *(psycho)logical Subject* and *Predicate* were generally regarded as two language universals involving two complementary issues related to the speaker's thought (or to the process they give rise to in the mind of the addressee):

a. the use of certain referring expressions to locate or access knowledge relevant to interpreting utterances, in the case of (psycho)logical Subject, a discussion reflected in Frege's (1892) *Über Sinn und Bedeutung* (cf. Strawson 1950; Searle 1969); and
b. the existence of conventional linguistic ways of conveying what it is that one judges to be worth saying with respect to that information, and thus being understood by others, in the case of (psycho)logical Predicate, (Paul 1975 [1880]; Høffding 1910).

Focusing on (psycho)logical Subject, the notion was described in relation to three different aspects:

Table 1. *Some terminology related to the categories of Theme/Topic*

Types of Terms	Terms	References
Gradient terms	Given/Known/Salient vs. New/Unknown/Non-Salient (information)	Daneš (1964), Kuno (1972a.b, 1978, 1980), Quirk et al. (1972, 1985), Chafe (1976, 1987, 1994, 1996), Bates (1976), Dahl (1976), Allerton (1978), Prince (1978, 1981a, 1996), Haviland & Clark (1974), Clark & Haviland (1977), Bock & Engelkamp (1978), Deyes (1978), Gundel (1978, 1988, 1994), Morgenthaler (1980), Adamec (1981), Beaugrande & Dressler (1981), Reinhart (1981), Garrod & Sanford (1982), Hupet & Costermans (1982), Copeland & Davis (1983), Lambrecht (1986, 1987a, 1988), Hajicová (1987), Givón (1988, 1992), Tejada Caller (1988), Gundel et al. (1993)
	Bound vs. Free (information)	Sgall (1967, 1974, 1987), Benesová & Sgall (1973), Sgall et al. (1973), Dahl (1974a.b, 1976)
	Dynamic vs. less Dynamic	Firbas (1964, 1974, 1992, 1995), Svoboda (1968, 1974, 1981, 1983), Uhlírová (1969, 1977), Deyes (1978), Chládková (1979), Golková (1983, 1985), Dusková (1985)
Bipolar terms	Theme (vs. Rheme, Focus, Tail)	Mathesius (1939, 1961), Trávnic&ek (1937, 1961, 1962), Beneš (1959, 1968, 1971), Daneš (1960, 1964, 1967, 1970b, 1974b, 1989), Firbas (1964, 1966), Comrie (1972), Enkvist (1974, 1981), Verma (1976), Adjémian (1978), Deyes (1978), Dik (1978, 1980, 1989, 1997), Adamec (1981), Lutz (1981), Morgenthaler (1981), Brömser (1982), Hupet & Costermans (1982), Eiler (1986), Williams (1988), Nwogu & Bloor (1991), Golková (1995)
	Topic (vs. Comment/Focus)	Sapir (1921), Bloomfield (1935), Hockett (1958), Hornby (1972), Dahl (1974), Gundel (1974, 1985, 1988), Barry (1975), Bates (1976), Keenan & Schieffelin (1976), Li & Thompson (1976), Magretta (1977), Schachter (1977), García (1979), Berman (1980), Uwe (1980), Van Dijk (1980), Young (1980), Altman (1981), Kieras (1981), Penelope (1982), Dijk & Kintsch (1983), Fox (1983), Hinds (1983), Bardovi-Harlig (1983), Witte (1983), Silvá Corvalán (1984), Gernsbacher (1985, 1989), Gundel (1988), Van Kuppevelt (1995), García & Joanette (1996)
	Ground/Links/Center(ing) (vs. Figure/Focus)	Bühler (1934), Hovland et al. (1957), Bates (1976), Lutz (1981), Kies (1988), Vallduví (1992, 1996), Grosz, Joshi & Weinstein (1995), Walker & Prince (1996), Portner & Katsuhiko (1998)

Table 1. (*continued*)

Types of Terms	Terms	References
bi-functional terms	Theme/Topic/Ground (Rheme/Comment/Figure) *vs.* Focus/Emphasis	Chomsky (1965, 1972), Halliday (1967a.b, 1970, 1974, 1977, 1979, 1981, 1994), Dezsö (1970), Quirk et al. (1972, 1985), Sgall (1972), Dahl (1974a. b. c, 1987), Hajicová & Sgall (1975, 1987), Chafe (1974, 1976), Jackendoff (1972), Gundel (1974, 1985, 1988), Wierzbicka (1975), Givón (1976, 1979a, 1983, 1988, 1990), Kuno (1969, 1976), Kuno & Kaburaki (1977), Fries (1978, 1982, 1983, 1986, 1987, 1995a. b), Lautamatti (1978), Dik (1978, 1980, 1989, 1997), Young (1980), Fillmore (1981), Reinhart (1981), Davison (1984), Taglicht (1984), Jiménez-Juliá (1981, 1986, 1995), Foley & Van Valin (1984, 1985), Dik (1978, 1980, 1989, 1997), Lambrecht (1986, 1987a, 1988a, 1994), Davidse (1987), Kies (1988), Downing (1991) Schlobinski & Schütze-Coburn (1992), Van Valin (1993), Morris (1998)
Related (psycho) logical terms	Presupposition *vs.* Focus/assertion	Jackendoff (1972), Quirk et al. (1972), Bates (1976), Harries-Delisle (1978), Kuno (1978a), Prince (1978, 1981b), Duranti & Ochs (1979), Atlas & Levinson (1981), Declerk (1984), Lambrecht (1986, 1987a, 1988a, 1994)
	Categorical *vs.* thetic Perspective/empathy	Kuroda (1972, 1984, 1985), Dahl (1974c, 1976), Sasse (1987), Ulrich (1985), Fillmore (1968), Kuno (1976), Dik (1978, 1997), Duranti & Ochs (1979), Zubin (1979)
Related grammatical terms	Predicate/Nucleus *vs.* Argument/Satellite	Reichenbach (1947), Seuren (1969), Dik (1978, 1980, 1989, 1997), Foley & Van Valin (1984, 1985), Van Valin (1993), Hoekstra et al. (1981), de Groot 1981), Bolkestein (1981, 1985b), Dik et al. (1990)

a. contextual relevance;
b. informational status;
c. linearity.

Contextual relevance was invoked as criterial for (psycho)logical Subject status by von der Gabelentz (1869: 378), for example, who interpreted this concept as "what the message is about" and equated it with "the object of speech", i.e. that which the attention of the hearer is directed to, that which the speaker wants the hearer to think of. To quote von der Gabelentz:

> What is a person aiming at when he says something to someone else? He wants to arouse a thought in him. I believe there is a two-fold aim here. Firstly, someone draws another's attention (his thoughts) to something; second, he gets him to think such-and-such about that something. The thing I want my addressee to think about I call *psychological Subject*. [My translation]

Informational criteria were implied in other descriptions such as Høffding's (1910: 88), which associated the distinction between (psycho)logical Subject and Predicate with the contrast between given and new information:

> One will always be able to recognise the logical predicate from the accent [which it bears], whatever place it happens to have from a grammatical point of view. [My translation]

And yet from another perspective focusing on the linear quality of language, Paul (1975 [1880]: 124), among others, characterised psychological Subject "as the idea which appears first in the mind of the speaker" — not necessarily the first element of a linguistic expression. In Paul's words [my translation]:

> The psychological subject is the idea which is present in the consciousness of the speaker/thinker first, and to which a second, the psychological predicate, is connected.

Importantly, at this early stage the assumption was generally accepted that word order reflects the order of importance of the information expressed in sentences, but this phenomenon was analysed from two opposite perspectives. Thus, while von der Gabelentz (1891: 357) and Wundt (1900, Part 2: 363–4), for example, affirmed that words occur in *decreasing* order of conceptual emphasis (if grammatical factors allow freedom of expression), that is to say, the more important the idea, the more stressed it should be, and the more it should move towards the beginning, Paul (1975 [1880]) believed that the prominence of constituents across a sentence normally *increases*, in other words, that the more important the idea is, the more it has to be moved towards the end.

In Chapter 3 it will be shown that the above three aspects of this early notion of (psycho)logical Subject, that is, (a) contextual relevance, (b) informational status, and (c) linearity, were further elaborated and incorporated into modern linguistics by the Prague School. One of its first exponents, Mathesius (1939: 234), defined "the starting point of the utterance" (*východisko*) as "that which is known or at least obvious in the given situation and from which the speaker proceeds", and the core of the utterance (*jádro*) as "that which the speaker states about, or in regard to the starting point of the utterance". But in (1942) Mathesius re-elaborated his notion of "the foundation of the utterance" (*základ, tema*) as "something that is being spoken about in the sentence" and "the core" (*jádro*) as "what the speaker states about this theme".

In Chapter 2 we shall see that corresponding to these three facets of Mathesius's definition, i.e. (a) "what is being spoken about", (b) "that which is known" and (c) "the starting point of the utterance", three dominant interpretations of communicative categories have emerged:

a. *semantic*, suggesting that Theme/Topic establishes a relationship of *aboutness* expressing "what a message is about".
b. *informational*, rendering Theme/Topic as *given information*; and
c. *syntactic*, assuming that Theme/Topic constitutes a *special point of departure* that is associated with *initial position*, i.e. "from which the speaker proceeds".

These three interpretations receive independent treatment in Chapter 2 owing to their complexity and relevance for this study.

The second factor hindering a commonly agreed description of Theme/Topic is of a dual nature. It arises from the general indeterminacy of all functional categories, on the one hand, and from the non-biunique nature of the relationships existing between linguistic forms and linguistic functions, on the other, that is, from the fact that the same linguistic structure may fulfil a variety of functions, and vice versa, the possibility that the same function can be coded by different linguistic constructions. As a result, different approaches to the notions of Theme and Topic have also followed from:

a. a focus upon different aspects of the communication process as identificational criteria (viz. message, speaker/writer, interaction between participants);
b. a focus upon the different elements of structure (viz. entity, proposition, clause, general framework for an entire text or overall discourse);
c. as a corollary, the lack of a clearly defined place in the prevailing linguistic scheme, since our object of study is related to virtually all of the established levels or components of linguistic description:
    i.   Phonology: the intonation patterns of a tone group have been cited as criterial for thematic/topical status;

ii. Morphology: thematic/topical status has been said to be demarcated by inflections or particles;
iii. Syntax: clause organisation has been described as affected by thematic/topical factors;
iv. Lexicon: it has been hypothesised that thematic/topicality relations influence the organisation of and access to entries in a lexicon;
v. Semantics: the categories of Theme and Topic invoke some meaning, or function/purpose;
vi. Pragmatics, or the textual level: the labels "Theme" and "Topic" have been related to the discourse co(n)text.

Furthermore, cross-linguistic investigations have recorded an enormous variation in the particular surface devices used to encode the "point of departure" of a message, "that which is known" and "what a message is about", even if thematicity or topicality have not been the only functions postulated to account for such constructions and even if the actual forms of thematic/topicality marking found in individual languages have not been regarded as unambiguous markers of whatever notion is claimed as Theme or Topic, as illustrated in Table 2 (based on Givón (1983b: 17); cf. Davison (1984: 820)).

The third and last factor is also two-fold, since, although most studies of Theme/Topic (and communicative categories) show some kind of *functionalist* orientation,[5] they vary with respect to (a) their *degree* of functionalism and (b) the *perspective* of the analysis, which can go from *form-to-function* and/or from *function-to form*. Thus, Nichols (1984), for example, distinguishes *three degrees* of functionalism: *conservative, moderate*, and *extreme*. Conservative functionalists are said to add functional explanations to a pre-existing formal model as a separate module (Gundel 1974; Kuno 1978a, 1980; Prince 1978). Moderate functionalists on the other hand share the tenet (denied by Chomsky (1975: 56–7, 1980: 229–30)) that the properties of the structural system of language (i.e. semantic, syntactic, morphological, and phonological rules) must be explained primarily by reference to their communicative role (Halliday 1970a, 1978, 1994). And extreme functionalists regard linguistic structure as merely coded function, denying the existence of purely syntactic constraints, to the extent that "extremists" like Hopper (1991a: 46) claim to be "losing faith in the idea of a language and grammar as stable abstractions" (Hopper & Thompson 1984; Givón 1983a, 1990).

In addition, functionalists adopting a primarily form-to-function approach argue that in order for a constituent to be identified as Theme/Topic (or as any communicative category) it must necessarily have some effect on formal expression. That is, though a constituent may be regarded as thematic/topical on discourse

Table 2. *Grammatical devices associated with Theme/Topic*
Easiest Theme/Topic identification →

Device	Functional Variable	Reference
Zero anaphora, Ellipsis vs. Lexicalisation *The duke has given that teapot to my mother and Ø that vase to my sister*	Given-New Topic-Comment	MacWhinney & Bates (1978), Delis & Slater (1977) Sechehaye (1926), Kuno (1972b)
Clitic Pronouns/verb agreement Unstressed pronouns vs. Stressed/independent Pronouns *He has given that teapot to my aunt*	Topicality Thematisation Givenness Bind events Contrast	Hornby (1972), Kuno (1972b, 1976), Dahl (1974), Gundel (1974, 1988) Mathesius (1939), Firbas (1964, 1974, 1992, 1995) MacWhinney & Bates (1978), Delis & Slater (1977) Osgood (1971), Lesgold (1972) Berman & Szamosi (1972), Gunter (1966)
Left dislocation/detachment/ displacement *The duke, he has given my mother that teapot*	Thematisation Topicality Givenness	Bally (1932), Beneš (1959), Halliday (1967b, 1994), Dik (1978, 1989, 1997), Keenan & Schieffelin (1976), Givón (1976, 1988), Geluykens (1992) Ochs & Schieffelin (1976, 1983), Duranti & Ochs (1979), Prince (1984, 1997)
Definite NG *The duke has given my mother that teapot*	Topicality Givenness	Kuno (1976), Haviland & Clark (1974), van Dijk (1977) Maratsos (1974, 1976), Warden (1976), Chafe (1976)
Right dislocation/displacement/ detachment/Antitopic *He has given my mother that teapot, the duke*	Topicality Thematisation Detopicalisation	Vennemann (1974), Hyman (1975), Hetzron (1975), Givón (1976), Dik (1978, 1989), Geluykens (1987) Travniček (1937), Beneš (1959), Halliday (1967b, 1994), Li & Thompson (1976)
Passivisation *My mother has been given that teapot*	Thematisation Givenness	Halliday (1967b, 1994), Qirk et al. (1972, 1985) Olson & Filby (1972), Wright & Glucksberg (1976)

Table 2. (*continued*)

Device	Functional Variable	Reference
Fronting/Extraction/Topicalisation *That teapot the duke has given to my mother*	Thematisation Topic Givenness Newness Importance Perspective Focus Genericity	Travníček (1937), Beneš (1959), Halliday (1967b, IFG) Dik (1978, 1989), Foley & Van Valin (1984) Grieve & Wales (1973), Bock (1977) Viktor (1917), Dezsö (1970) Lindner (1898), O'Shea (1907) MacWhinney (1975) Leonard & Schwartz (1977) Cadiot (1992)
Cleft/Pseudo-cleft constructions *It is that teapot that the duke has given to my mother/What the duke has to my mother is that teapot*	Thematisation Contrast Given-New 2nd. Topicalis.	Halliday (1967b, IFG), Verma (1976) Chafe (1976), Harries-Delisle (1978), Collins (1985, 1991) Cadiot (1992), Hornby (1972), Clark & Clark (1977), Quirk et al. (1972, 1985) Uwe (1980)
Presentative constructions/Postposition/Extraposition *There is a fallacy in your argument/It is obvious that your argument has a fallacy*	New/Rheme Topic	Halliday (1967b, IFG), Quirk et al. (1972, 1985), Verma (1976) Givón (1983b, 1988)
Most difficult Theme/Topic identification		→

grounds, unless its thematic/topical status receives a special treatment with respect to form, order and prosodic properties, there is no basis for recognising a special clause bound level of description distinct from the semantic and syntactic levels of clause structure. As a result, such messages are analysed as themeless or topicless, or as having no pragmatic function assignment at all (Dik 1989, 1997; Reinhart 1982; Davison 1984; Gundel 1988; Cadiot 1992; Van Valin 1993).

Alternatively, analysts adopting an essentially function-to-form approach assume that Theme/Topic and communicative categories, in general, are universal semantic-cognitive and/or socially motivated primitives. The assumption is that it is inherent in the functionality of language that all messages be endowed with a Theme/Topic (and with communicative functions), either explicitly or implicitly. For this reason, Theme, Topic and communicative categories in general are characterised *notionally* (e.g. "point of departure" of information, the "hook" or "peg" on which the message is hung, etc.) and thematic/topical status is assigned to the clausal/discourse constituents which meet these defining criteria. There is, admittedly, no *a priori* way of delimiting such function-to-form descriptions as they are metaphorical and difficult to apply in a non-circular way, particularly when clauses and other units are examined out of context, and so it happens that different rewordings of communicative categories may be attempted without obtaining unequivocal acceptance.

In closing this introductory remarks, of interest here is the fact that, whatever the interpretation, the characterisations of Theme/Topic (and communicative categories) will be affected by both the degree of functionalism of the approach and by its direction, that is, whether it goes from function-to-form and/ or from form-to-function. As advanced, in this book we shall restrict our analysis to just three models, PS, SFG and FG, here regarded as *moderate functionalist* for two reasons. One, roughly they all share the *moderate* assumption that function only *affects* form, in contrast with the *extreme* functionalist tenet that function *determines* form. And two, although one may prevail over the other depending on the model and on the data under analysis, both function-to-form and form-to-function explanations are resorted to in each programme in order to benefit from the insights of both types of descriptions while surmounting the difficulties posed by extremist positions.[6]

CHAPTER 2

An Evaluation of Three Interpretations of Communicative Categories

2.1 Introduction

In this section we shall analyse three dominant interpretations of communicative categories: (a) *semantic*, invoking such notions as "aboutness" or "relevance"; (b) *informational*, resorting to the given-new distinction; and (c) *syntactic*, related to the "staging" of information in (non-)initial position. It shall be shown that the exact boundaries between these three interpretations are hard to draw because some accounts include aspects of more than one interpretation. More often than not, the tendency has been to identify "what a message is about" with initial position and/or with given information, and vice versa, it has often been claimed that the *function* of message initial position (and word order arrangements in general) or that of the mapping of given/new information is to express "what a message is about".[7]

However, throughout this chapter it shall be explained that these approaches (especially the syntactic and the informational ones) differ radically since they not only do define communicative categories differently, but they also use different criteria for their identification. In the course of our discussion we shall see that, as expounded in Figure 1, semantic interpretations have three main variants, i.e. *relational-referential-interactive* (Section 2.2), and informational accounts two, i.e. *relational-referential* (Section 2.3), in contrast with the relative homogeneity of syntactic analyses (Section 2.4): syntactic and relational analyses are message-centred and are mainly restricted to clause-level analyses, whereas referential and interactive interpretations are context-centred and operate at discourse level.

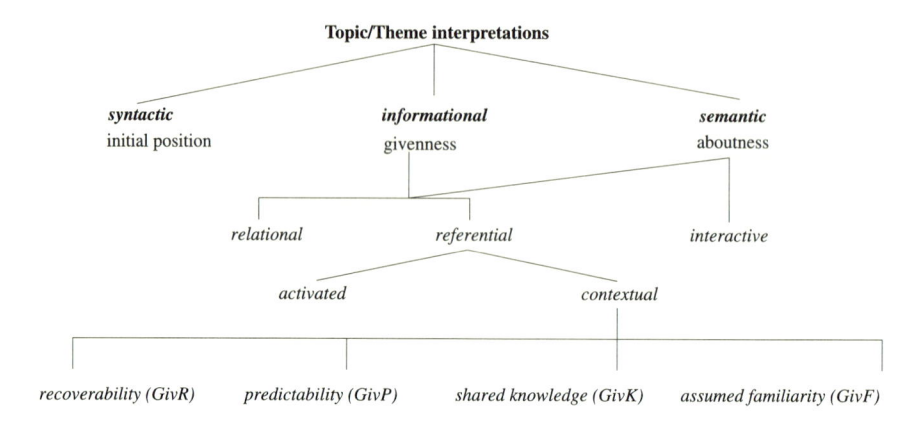

```
                        Topic/Theme interpretations
          ┌───────────────────┼───────────────────┐
     syntactic            informational         semantic
  initial position          givenness           aboutness
                      ┌─────────┼─────────┐         │
                 relational  referential      interactive
                         ┌───────┴───────┐
                     activated       contextual
  ┌──────────────┬──────────────┬──────────────────┬──────────────┐
recoverability (GivR)  predictability (GivP)  shared knowledge (GivK)  assumed familiarity (GivF)
```

Figure 1. *Different interpretations of pragmatic/communicative functions*

2.2 The semantic interpretation

The semantic characterisation has been the most pervasive, if not central, of the three accounts since most linguists (syntacticians, typologists, conversational analysts and the supporters of syntactic and informational approaches) recognise that every language has a common clause type that contains a phrase which represents the thing, object, entity, matter, etc. "about which a statement is made". Emblematic defenders of this view, Li & Thompson (1981: 15, 85) claim that "although it may be an intuitive matter to determine all of the implications of "what the sentence is about", this is essentially a correct characterisation".[8]

Nevertheless, despite its broad appeal, the semantic interpretation faces one significant problem. For one thing, the basis for the identification of "aboutness" has rarely been made explicit, probably because of the inherent vagueness of the notion, and as a result, its specification and that of the categories involved has been highly problematic (Reinhart 1981; Brown & Yule 1983; Pufahl 1992). Its abstract nature admitted, "aboutness" is here claimed to have been approached from basically three different perspectives: (a) *relational,* (b) *referential* and (c) *interactive*, as illustrated in Table 3.

Table 3 indicates that while *relational-semantic accounts are message-centred and refer to analyst-determined clausal aboutness, referential and interactive analyses explore discourse aboutness and are context-centred.* To be more precise, we shall present referential aboutness as an analyst-determined notion

Table 3. *Trends in the interpretation of aboutness*

Message centred interpretation	Context-centred interpretations	
clause level of analysis	discourse level of analysis	
relational interpretation	referential interpretation	interactive interpretation
	contextual activated interpretation interpretation	
sentence Topic utterance entity/proposition in a (complex) clause	discourse Topic discourse entity discourse proposition	speaker's Topic propositional/problem framework saliency/relevance

which may be assessed in roughly two different ways: (a) resorting to the linguistic/situational *context* itself (in the *contextual* variant) or (b) focusing on the interactants' *perception* of this context (in the *activated* variant). But, significantly, it is here suggested that both subtypes of *referential aboutness* turn out to be identified with corresponding versions of *referentially given information* (*contextually given* and *activated information*). By contrast, interactive aboutness represents speakers' discourse perspectives on what is at issue at a given point of discourse, rather than (analysts' perceptions of) contextual incidentals. These three different approaches lead to the identification of different categories, broadly corresponding to what in the literature have been labelled as *sentence Topics*, *discourse Topics* and *speaker's Topics* (less frequently, *Themes*). As already noted, the boundaries between these categories are not clear-cut, but overlap as the same element of structure can be assigned to more that one category, and vice versa, one category may present ample variation, ranging from prototypical to less central members. The three interpretations and their corresponding Topic-types are examined in turn. The discussion will concentrate on raising questions, focusing on problems of analysis and classification (see Gómez-González 1996a, b, 1998d).

2.2.1 *Relational aboutness and sentence Topics*

A classic definition of *sentence Topics* in terms of (relational) aboutness can be found in Hockett (1958: 201) as follows:

> [t]he most general characterisation of predicate constructions is suggested by the terms 'topic' and 'comment': the speaker announces a topic and then says

something about it. Thus *John/ran away*; *That new book by Thomas Guernsey/I haven't read yet*. In English and the familiar languages of Europe, topics are usually also subjects, and comments are predicates: so in *John/ran away*.[9]

Focusing on the announcing or presentative function of the category, another set of definitions specify that sentence Topics "limit the applicability of the main predication to a certain restricted domain", setting "a spatial, temporal or individual framework within which the main predication holds" (Chafe 1976: 50, 1977; Magretta 1977; Thompson 1985: 61; Lowe 1987: 6; Bäcklund 1989: 297; Downing 1991). But all relational-semantic accounts seem to share a common denominator: in all of them sentence Topics are assigned an *anchoring role* with respect to the previous discourse or the hearer's mental world. This anchoring role has been described in psycholinguistic terms and along semantic and/or syntactic lines within the grammar of the clause. Among the psycholinguistic paraphrases that have been put forward stand *frames of reference, cognitive hooks/pegs* on which the message is hung, *links* in the speaker/writer's mind, or *figures* against a *background* of consciousness. By contrast, in other approaches the anchoring role of sentence Topics is viewed as a *perspective taking* device whereby the more closely identified with the speaker an element is, the more likely it is to be topical or topicalised.[11]

The existence of sentence Topics in the aforementioned terms has been invoked to explain clause organisation in (more or less) *Topic-prominent* (Tp) languages in contrast with that of (more or less) *Subject-prominent* (Sp) ones; or more precisely, to elicit the connection between Topics and Subject, roughly taking the former as the origin of the latter. Leaving aside the details of this "evolutionary" process,[12] the difference between Tp and Sp languages has been attributed to a scale from non-grammaticalisation to grammaticalisation. The assumption is that prototypically Tp languages such as Chinese, Labu or Lisu, having a very poor or inexistent morphological structure that marks the syntagmatic value of grammatical units (e.g. agreement, prepositions, etc.), resort to Topic–Comment arrangements to mark such values and rely heavily on the co(n)text for their interpretation. At the other extreme, Sp languages like English grammaticalise transitivity functions to the detriment of the topical dimension and as a result tend to disfavour Topics that do not fit into transitivity patterns (the Topic dimension is almost restricted to single/multiple fronting with/without suprasegmental marking). In the middle, languages such as Japanese exhibit explicit syntactic markers of both the Topic (*wa*) and the transitivity dimensions (*o, ni, de*, etc.).

This simplified typological spectrum has led to the differentiation of *pure Topics* (in Tp languages), *grammaticalised Topics* (in "hybrid" languages) and

Subjects (in Sp languages) in terms of different parameters which here have been narrowed down to four: (a) *separability*, (b) *obligatory referentiality* (*anaphoricity*), (c) *obligatory marker*, and (d) *controller of syntactic processes*, as shown in Table 4 (Shibatini 1991; Jiménez-Juliá 1995).

The first feature, *separability*, alludes to the relative independence of sentence Topics. These, regarded as eminently presentative units, are described as normally *separated from* and *prior to* the main predication, thereby limiting its domain of applicability. Topics may have a close semantic connection with the predication, as in (1a) below, where the Topic is the Agent, or they may have a less direct link, as in (1b) and (1c), which display a whole-to-part relationship and a generic frame of reference-specification relationship, respectively:[13]

(1) a. wǒ xǐhuān chū píngguǒ (Mandarin)
I   like   eat apple
'I like to eat apples.'
b. xiàng bízi cháng (Mandarin)
elephant nose long
'Elephants have long noses.'
c. Gakkoo wa buku ga isogasi-kat-ta (Japanese)
school TOP I   SUBJ busy-PAST
'School, I was busy'

Obligatory referentiality, or anaphoricity, on the other hand, draws on the idea that "what is isolated as topic is a unit of existence and, as such, the existence of the referent of a topic must necessarily be presupposed" (Shibatini 1991: 100). This is the reason why, according to Li & Thompson (1981: 86), (2a) and (2b) below are acceptable constructions, while (2c) is not:

(2) a. gǒu wǒ jǐjīng kàn guo le
dog I already see
'The dog(s) — generic —, I have already seen (them).'
b. nèi zhī gǒu wǒ jǐjīng kàn guo le
that
'That dog, I have already seen (it).'
c. *yi zhi gǒu wǒ jǐjīng kàn guo le
one/a
'A dog, I have already seen (it).'

The third feature, *obligatory mark*, indicates the presence/absence of a mark that identifies a syntagmatic value. This may be interpreted as ascribing a morphological marker to an originally free unit or it may be analysed in a more flexible way (Hopper 1991b). Thus, both the units marked with *wa* in Japanese, as in (3) below — the Japanese equivalent of (1b) above —, and Subjects in inflected

Table 4. *The Topic–Subject Interface*

Functions	Separability	Obligatory Referentiality	Obligatory Mark	Controller of synt. Processes
Topic	+	+	–	–
grammaticalised Topics	+	+	+	(–)
Subjects	–	–	+	+

languages are often taken as grammaticalised Topics. But in most studies it is *initial position* that is regarded as the substance of expression of topical status in both Tp languages (e.g. Chinese) and in those of the "hybrid" type (e.g. Japanese). This is all the more noticeable in cases of concatenated Topics, where the first one is the more general and the subsequent ones, specifications of the first, as expounded in (4a) and (4b):

(3) zoo wa hana ga nagai
     elephant nose long
     'Elephants have long noses.'

(4) a. Zhèi kē shù, huā, yánsè hěn hǎo
         this-CLASS tree flower colour very nice
         'The flowers of this tree have a very nice colour.'
     b. Boku wa natsu   wa genki ga ii ga fuyu wa dame da
         I   summer health good but winter no well is
         'In summer I am in good health, but in winter I am not.'

However, it is also admitted that in both Tp languages and in those of the "hybrid" type there may exist predications that lack a Topic, the so called *topicless* or *thetic sentences*.[14] These are characterised as messages conveying a single unstructured kind of judgement involving only the recognition or rejection of some judgement material, without predicating this judgement of some independently recognised Subject, as in:

a. *impersonal expressions*, that is, events, states, situations or facts in which no referential entity is present and therefore nothing can be said about it;
b. *presentative constructions*, which introduce entities, but fail to report an event about them;
c. any state of affairs presented as a compact whole representing nothing but *new information*.

Thus, in Chinese or Japanese we may find such thetic messages as (5) to (7), or the one in (8), which can be presented with or without a Topic (*wa*), depending on whether or not the initial unit is anaphoric and thereby linked to an identifiable referential context:

(5) hao leng a
very cold
'It is very cold'

(6) hayai desu
early is
'It is early'

(7) genki desu
health is
'I am all right'

(8) kinoo (wa) watashi ga eiga o Tokio de mita
yesterday I FOC/NOM movie ACC LOC saw
'Yesterday I saw a movie in Tokio'

Lastly, the fourth feature of our matrix contrasts the high participation of Subjects with the low involvement of Topics in a number of syntactic processes: (a) *reflexivisation*, (b) *passivisation*, (c) *Equi-NG deletion*, (d) *verbal sequence*, (e) *imperative constructions* (Li & Thompson 1976: 465ff.). Leaving aside whether or not these are effective tests to distinguish Subjects from Topics, they do seem to demonstrate that the relative syntactic independence of the latter hampers their active involvement in predication internal processes.

In light of (some or all) the features discussed so far, (a) *separability*, (b) *obligatory referentiality* (*anaphoricity*), (c) *obligatory marker*, and (d) *controller of syntactic processes*, many accounts of clause organisation distinguish the *transitivity* dimension, which assigns transivity roles (Agent, Patient, etc.) to the elements involved in a predication, from the *Topic*(-Comment) dimension, presenting an entity that limits the domain of applicability of the predication. Accepting the coexistence of the Topic dimension and the transitivity dimension produces a battery of constructive possibilities which range from the complete blending of these two parameters to their absolute separation. In the first case, sentence Topics are mapped onto transitivity elements, which questions the profitability of recognising a separate Topic dimension as there exist morphosyntactic markers that identify transitivity roles. In the second case, in turn, syntactic structures can only be explained by claiming the existence of a topical dimension. In the second part of this book we shall see that this latter dimension is given independent treatment within the *Functional Sentence Perspective* level (FSP) in the PS circle (Chapter 3), the *textual component of meaning* in SFG (Chapter 4) and the *level of pragmatic functions* in FG (Chapter 5).

However, as claimed in Gómez-González (1996a, b, 1998b, c), controversy emerges when one has to *identify* the actual instantiation of (relational) semantic Topic(-Comment) partitions. The conflict seems to reside in the use of two different types of identificational criteria: *syntactic* or (*referential-*) *informational*. In Section 2.3 we shall see that *informational accounts* (e.g. Firbas, FG) take *obligatory marking* and *obligatory referentiality* as the main features of sentence Topics (which crucially alludes to *referential*, rather than to *relational*, *aboutness*). As a result, a referential entity which conveys the non-informative, known, or expected part of utterances/sentence — the sentence Topic (Theme/Comment/ Ground) — is distinguished from the informative, newsy, dominant, or contrary-to-expectation part — the Focus (Comment/Rheme/Figure). Conversely, as shall be explained in more detail in Section 2.4, *syntactic accounts* (e.g. Trávníček, Beneš, Daneš, SFG) focus on (a) the *presentative function* of sentence Topics, (b) their feature of *separability* and (c) the *linear* quality of language. Their conclusion is that sentence Topics (= "what the message/clause is about") occur in *message initial position* or, put differently, that any phrase encoded in a specific left-hand slot must be interpreted as a Topic.

But, before discussing the implications of informational and syntactic approaches independently, let us examine the sequences in (9), (10), (11) and (12)[15] to illustrate the conflicting analyses they produce.

(9) a. John saw the play yesterday.
b. Yesterday John saw the play.
c. The play John saw yesterday.

(10) a. You can define a net in one of two ways, depending on your point of view.
b. There was once an ugly bear who hid from the world.
c. Worst of all was the emasculation of the League of Nations.

(11) a. The boy, I went out with yesterday (vs. *With the boy, I went out with yesterday)
b. As for the student, well, let me see ...
c. As for Paris, the Eiffel Tower is really spectacular.

(12) a. The screen **died** (in reply to "What happened to the screen?");
b. The **screen** died (in reply to "What happened?")

The underlined clause initial elements in (9)–(12) above will be regarded as sentence Topics/Themes by the defenders of the syntactic approach. Adopting a relational-semantic stand, it could be claimed that the aboutness feature of these syntactic Topics/Themes does not reside in their *denotational* force per se, but rather in their providing an *instantiation* to some variable or parameter in an underspecified clausal/utterance context (Gómez-González 1996a, b, 1998b, d, forthcoming). In other words, it could be claimed that the initial items of the aforementioned sequences "instantiate" the speaker's take on the message to be constructed, whether or not they have any referential nominal status. The functional relevance of such syntactic Topics/Themes lies therefore in their *paradigmatic* value, that is, in the contrasts they establish with respect to other potential choices that make up the texture of messages, as well as in their *syntagmatic* relationships, whereby sentence Topics contribute to building up different presuppositions and implicatures, impose different constraints on the interpretation of what follows, raise different expectations on addressees, etc.

Accordingly, it could be said that in (9a–c), (10) and (12) the transitivity and topic dimensions coincide. The Topics/Themes in (9a), (10) and (12) are *unmarked* because they function as *Subjects*, that is, as the expected initial (transitivity/mood) constituent of declarative clauses in PresE. Alternatively, in (9b) and (9c) the Topics are *marked* because some other constituent occupies clause-initial position. In their turn, in order to justify such syntactic structures as those in (11) one needs to resort primarily to a topical (aboutness) dimension (instead of a transitivity dimension), whereby a presentative Topic limits the domain of applicability of the subsequent predication, evoking Chafe's (1976) explanations. In the same vein, but in a wider relational sense, Halliday (1967b, 1994) and Ford & Thompson (1986) identify *propositional sentence Topics* with the initial clause of complex clauses; whereas Tomlin (1985) and Schiffrin (1985, 1992) disregard position and confer such a status to subordinated clauses (*background* events), as opposed to *foreground* events (main clauses).

By contrast, despite individual differences, the supporters of the informational approach would classify (11b) (*The **screen** died*) as a *topicless* or *thetic* construction (see note 15) and (11a) (*The screen–**died***) as a Topic–Comment structure. The main formal difference is argued to be intonational: in (11a), the Topic–Comment structure, nuclear stress falls on the predicate (and a different pitch accent *may be* associated with the Topic); whereas in (11b), the topicless structure, nuclear stress falls on the Subject. Lambrecht (1987a: 366; 1994: 137ff.) explains that what characterises thetic structures (*sentence focus constructions* (SF)) is the absence of a Topic relation between the proposition and that argument which functions as the Topic in Topic–Comment counterparts (*predicate focus* structures (PF)), where some property of an already established discourse referent is pragmatically predicated. Instead, the function of SF structures is to introduce a referentially non-salient or non-individuated, and therefore a non-topical (i.e. relatively inactivated or unidentifiable) NG or event into the universe of discourse (i.e. *entity central* and *event central* thetic sentences, respectively).

Besides, in most (semantic and informational) referential approaches only discourse entities/referents qualify for topical status. This prerequisite automatically excludes from the category of Topic (or Theme) a number of candidates which receive this treatment in syntactic approaches such as: (a) negative and impersonal Subjects actualising non-referential participants, like *You* in (10a) above; (b) fronted circumstantial (including presentative) Adjuncts, like *Yesterday* in (9b); (c) existential-*there*, as in (10b); and (d) fronted Attributes, like *Worst of all* in (10c). Instead, clause level Topics are described as individual participants which (a) are prototypically endowed with the features of referentiality, definiteness and agentivity, and (b) act as Subject or Object on the assumption that both functions are valency-bound to the verb and they may affect the mood structure of clauses. Not involving such syntactic implications, the other syntactic functions (viz. Complements, Attributes or circumstantial Adjuncts) are usually described as Attributes of, and therefore subordinate to, basic clause level Topics (Givón 1983b; Davison 1984; van Oosten 1986; Downing 1991). In this line Huddleston (1984: 58 [my emphasis]) defines Topic as "what the sentence is *primarily* about", the *primarily* being a salutary reminder that a sentence with more than one referring expression (like (13b) and (14b)) could be said to be about the referents of each of them.

(13) a. What did the dog do?
     b. It bit her.
(14) a. What happened to Jenny?
     b. It bit her.

Moreover, if we go beyond simple question-answer sequences, difficulties arise when determining what a sentence is "primarily about". Consider:

(15) Jenny teased the dog. It bit her.

The fact that aboutness is indeterminate here is indicated by the inconclusiveness of the paraphrase-report test (both of the following are possible: *He said of the dog that it bit Jenny*; *He said of Jenny that the dog bit her*). Another test for topichood is also inconclusive: whether the sentence is (or can be) followed by further sentences in which the referent is mentioned ((15) could be followed by, for example, either *It was obviously not used to such treatment*–with the dog as Topic — or by *She ran crying to her mother*–where Jenny is Topic).[16]

In addition, a number of authors insist that none of the posited Topic markers (e.g. Japanese (*-wa*), Tagalog (*-ang*), Korean (*-nun*), etc.) can be simply equated with any existing definition of Topic/Theme. Thus, to illustrate this, Tsutsui (1981: 164) and Kitagawa (1982: 176), for example, provide the examples in (16), where the suffix *-wa* in Japanese (a prototypical Topic marker according to Li & Thompson (1976)) is used to mark: contextually given information (16a), a constituent detached from the clause (16b), and a focus of contrast (16c); whereas Gundel (1988: 218) notes the existence of topical items lacking this particle, as shown in (17). Schachter (1977), Schwartz (1976) and Schachter & Otanes (1972: 81) raise similar points with respect to the *-ang* particle in Tagalog.

(16) a. Boku wa ima san-nen de senkoo wa keizai desu ga ...
I now junior am major economics is but
'I am a junior now and my major is economics but ...'
b. *Taroo wa Hanako ga rede- si-ta.*
Taro Hanako leave- home-do-PAST
'As for Taro, Hanako ran away from home.'
c. *Tom wa ii kedo John wa dame da.*
Tom good but John no good is
'Tom is okay, but John is no good.'

(17) *Hanashi ga hajimaru toki wa eeto mazu otona no hito*
story SUBJ start time TOP well first adult person
tachi ga ippai detekite... sono naka de hitor
SUBJ many appear that among one person
chuugokujin ga nanka no otokonoko ga ... kare wa sosko e
Chinese SUBJ something boy SUBJ he TOP there to
sono omise no toko e itte ... hajime wa tada miteiru ...
that shop place to go first TOP only be looking
'When the story starts [TOP], first a lot of adults appear ... Among (them) one.'

In view of the controversy so far described, a number of writers discard relational-semantic (and syntactic) interpretations of sentence Topics, as well as the hypothesis that this or any other informational categories are structurally encoded in the "information structure" or "textual component" of a language systematically. Instead, the claim is made that communicative categories are essentially *pragmatic*, that is to say, that they must be derived from the semantic, morphosyntactic and phonological properties of individual languages, crucially, *in relation to the co(n)texts* in which they are used (Lyons 1977: 505, Chafe 1976: Comrie 1981: 58; Reinhart 1982: 58; Davison 1984: 806; Huddleston 1988: 158–9, 1991: 99, 101; Schlobinski and Schütze-Coburn 1992).

2.2.2 *Referential aboutness and discourse Topics*

Referential-semantic accounts differ from relational ones in that the former operate at discourse level while the latter work at clause level. An emblematic supporter of referential approaches, Givón (1992: 11) affirms that relational analyses (at clause level) of Topic are seriously flawed since they cause:

> an unfortunate confusion between the facts of the code and the facts of what is being coded. At the level of a single event/state, 'topic' — 'what is talked about' or 'what is important' — is meaningless. This follows by definition from the two fundamental properties that make individual propositions into coherent discourse — the fact that human discourse is both multipropositional and thematically coherent.

Referential-semantic analyses assume that the overwhelming norm in verbally coded human discourse is prototypically about perceptually salient, temporally stable entities, i.e. *referring topical participants*. These are said to establish a relationship of aboutness between individual clauses/utterances and the overall discourse and to be characterised by a tendency to:

a. refer to the preceding (anaphoric) discourse;
b. persist as such in the subsequent (cataphoric) discourse;
c. surface verbally as the nominal arguments of clauses, that is, as grammatical Subject (main Topic) or Object (secondary Topic) (as opposed to all other syntactic roles = non Topic);
d. occur in clause-initial position, though not necessarily so.

Taking the above features into account the notion of "discourse Topic" emerges as:

> the participant most crucially involved in the action sequence of the paragraph; it is the participant most closely associated with the higher-level "Theme" of the paragraph; and finally it is the participant most likely to be coded as the primary topic — or grammatical subject — of the vast majority of sequentially-ordered clauses/sentences comprising the thematic paragraph (Givón 1983b: 8).

In order to identify discourse Topics, referential-semantic analysts resort either to co(n)text, in the *contextual* variant, or to the participants' minds, in the *activated* variant, which leads to the hierarchical ranking of discourse referents in terms of such dimensions as "topicality", "continuity" or "(referential) coherence". (18) below (from Givón 1992) provides one example of such scales of topicality, while (19) illustrates the contextual-semantic identification of discourse Topics in an excerpt taken from Givón (1993: 206 [emphasis in original]):

(18) **Givón's Topic scales**
    a. SUBJECT > DIRECT OBJECT > OTHERS
    b. AGT (Agentive) > DAT (Dative) > ACC (Accusative)
    c. HUMAN > ANIMATE > INANIMATE

(19)   Dear Abby: There's **this guy** I've been going with for near three years. Well, the problem is that he hits me. He started last year. He has done it only four or five times, but each time it was worse than before. Every time he hits me it was because he thought I was flirting (I wasn't). Last time he accused me of coming on to **a friend** of his. First he called me a lot of dirty names, then he punched my face so bad it left me with a black eye and black-and-blue bruises over half of my face. It was very noticeable, so I told my folks that the car I was riding in stopped suddenly and my face hit the windshield. Abby, he's 19 and I'm 17, and already I feel like **an old married lady** who lets her husband push her around. I haven't spoken to him since this happened. He keeps hugging me to give him one more chance. I think I've given him enough chances. Should I keep avoiding him or what?
          Black and Blue.[17]

In addition, in a broader referential sense, instead of *entity* Topics other scholars pursue the notion of *propositional* Topics. *Discourse Topic propositions* are described as "what people have in their heads after reading or listening a text", which consists of the "important" elements, as it were, of the discourse content (Kintsch & Keenan 1973). In a similar vein, the *macro-structure* of a text is characterised as complex proposition entailed by the joint set of propositions expressed by sentences contained in a particular text;[18] whereas the *network approach* suggests a metaphorical tree-structure that expresses relationships among meaning components of texts at two different levels: (a) a *syntactic* one (similar to systemic surface constituency relations) and (b) a *conceptual* one ("substance of"; "reason of", etc.)).[19] Other scholars propose *context-dependent question-based theories*, according to which a (sub)Topic is constituted as the result of a (sub)question and, if no disturbance of the discourse process occurs, a (sub)Topic is closed off when (the speaker assumes) the corresponding (sub)question has been answered satisfactorily. In other words, the Topic of a sentence is determined by the question it answers, whereas a discourse Topic is analysed as a (set of) higher-order sentence topic(s) the actuality of which is continued in discourse as long as subordinated topics arise as the result of subquestioning. To illustrate these broader referential approaches, let us have a look at the question-based proposal in (20), (from Van Kuppevelt 1995: 113):

(20)   A: Late yesterday evening I got a lot of telephone calls.
       Q_1 B: Who called you up?
       A_1 A: John, Peter and Harry called me up.

The assumption in (20) is that the Topic of the dialogue is introduced as the result of the contextual induction of the explicit question Q_1, namely who called up speaker A or the set of persons that may have rung speaker A; while the comment to this Topic is provided by answer A, which replaces the *wh*-constituent in the question and specifies the person asked for, thereby selecting a value from the questioned set of discourse entities (Vennemann 1975; Klein & Von Stutterheim 1987; Van Kuppevelt 1995).

A close scrutiny of referential accounts reveals a number of potential points of conflict that demand some caution on the part of the analysts. It could be adduced, for example, that the postulated scales of topicality/continuity for entity Topics:

a. limit this function to a particular syntactic/semantic category, fundamentally Subject/Agent;
b. leave questions of referent resolution unaddressed since syntactic and semantic constraints on reference are not treated in the degree of detail they deserve;
c. have relative validity because the scales are:
  i. data dependent (they depict at best the coding of protagonists in narratives), and so skew expectations for other data types; and
  ii. by and large based on quantitative analyses.

On the other hand, for some scholars it could also be a problem that none of the propositional-referential interpretations appears to provide a systematic means to identify "the Theme/Topic" of a piece of discourse. Rather, they propose an alternative method of producing a single sentence summary for the text, which can only to a certain extent be objective. As Brown & Yule (1983: 110) remark, "at best, this is a formula for determining, not *the Topic* of a discourse, but the *possible topics* of a discourse." Likewise, Clark & Clark (1977: 164), Allwood, Anderson et al. (1977: 20) challenge the basis of the propositional approach arguing that knowledge does not have to be stored propositionally and that a particular sentence cannot be treated as having a single propositional source. Their point is that a proposition is a partial structuring of what one wishes to communicate, which is part of the verbalisation process and therefore changes in time and is relative to the discourse co(n)text. In view of this criticisms it seems that referential-semantic accounts should work on the clarification of the ambiguities attributed to them.

2.2.3 *Interactive aboutness and speaker's Topic*

For interactive-semantic interpretations aboutness denotes a co(n)text-dependent relationship of *relevance* or *saliency* which is not fixed beforehand, but is continuously negotiated by speakers throughout discourse as a dynamic process;

in other words, it is ranked in the speakers' minds according to *salience/relevance* in a *focus stack* (Section 2.3.2).

According to Sperber & Wilson (1986), "relevance" refers to the contextual effects that the utterance under consideration has on the cognitive environment counterbalanced by the effort which the hearer has to exert in order to process it. From this perspective, Topic "is not an address to store information, but a problem to be treated" (ibid.: 75ff.; Beaugrande & Dressler 1981; de Beaugrande 1992; Yule and Mathis 1992). As a result, interactive aboutness alludes to a *personal* Topic, the *speaker's Topics/Themes*, "what s/he thinks we're talking about" within the general Topic/Theme framework of the conversation as a whole. These are experienced as areas of cognitive/communicative discrepancies, that is, as propositional frames lacking a mutually acceptable specification in some respect, which are given "not in the usual sense of 'having a mutually acceptable reference and manifestness", but rather in the sense of "being a mutually acceptable and manifest problem frame for specification in discourse" (Lötscher 1992: 133).[20]

The dynamics of speaker's Topic grounding is shown in the conversation in (21) below (from Brown & Yule (1983: 88)), where the two participants (L and M) express by means of their personal Topics (usually introduced through first person reference and becoming salient when re-introduced) their personal experience within the Topic framework of the conversation, namely the effect of restoring old buildings:

(21) L: I quite like the way they've done the Mile though + I think it's quite nice
M: yes [^h]^yes
L: the bottom of it anyway
M: it is –it is quite good they've certainly kept within the + em + + preserved it reasonably well or conserved it but we were up in Aberdeen this year for a holiday and we were staying right within the University complex there in Old Aberdeen + and + oh some of the buildings there are beautiful really they are nice + but er Y was quite impressed with it — it's the first holiday we've had up there +
L: I was noticing — I was down by Queen Street or + the bottom of Hanover Street or somewhere + and they've just cleaned up some of the buildings down there + and what a difference it makes +
M: yes I know because there are some beautiful buildings
L: oh it was really nice.

Of interest here are the remarks of Brown & Yule (1983: 83, 90), for example, that Topics/Themes are unlikely to be identified with a part of a sentence, since "it is not sentences that have topics, but speakers". The reason is that "what I think we're talking about" incorporates both what participants take to be the "Topic of conversation" ("What we're talking about") and the individual speaker's version ("the I think"), as s/he makes a conversational contribution. And, while there may be priorities discernible in the choice of elements most likely to be concentrated on within a clause if it is presented in isolation, "such preferences may reflect the rather trivial fact that names are more salient than anything else, in isolation. [...] [Then] It should be apparent that the use of single constructed sentences as the basis for making claims about notions such as 'the topic of discourse' is extremely misleading" (Brown & Yule ibid.).

Indeed, it seems that most interactive approaches avoid, instead of providing answers to, the difficulties inherent in the notion of Theme/Topic. In the first place, they allow for so many types and treatments of Themes/Topics as to render this type of analysis both subjective and virtually useless in accounting for linguistic structure. For one thing, if Themes/Topics are viewed as problem frames to be treated in context-changing utterances, theoretically fewer restrictions have to be made with respect to possible categories for Topics, to the point that within a given proposition any constituent (or the proposition itself) may appear as creating a frame of cognitive/communicative discrepancies calling for treatment. In connection with this, Schank (1977: 424) and Maynard (1980) explain that most discourse analysts, aware of the profusion of topical/thematic candidates, find it more feasible to identify the formal markers of a Theme/Topic shift in discourse, grouped into language-specific coding systems such as:

a. *topic-shift markers* (Duranti & Ochs 1979: 396ff.; Maynard 1980: 266; Button and Casey 1984: 168; Pufahl 1992: 222), or *continuatives* (IFG: 53; Martin 1992a: 164, 218);
b. indentations and paragraphs, the latter being either orthographic or semantic, that is, demarcated by the unity of participants, adverbials changing the setting (time and place) (Grimes 1975: 109; Longacre 1989: 116);
c. genre-specific Topic shift markers, such as changes of place and time in narratives, or changes of direction of the speaker/writer's rationale in philosophical argumentation in written discourse (Grimes 1975: 102; van Oosten 1983; Pufahl 1992);
d. in spoken discourse, *paratones*, or speech paragraphs (Brown 1977: 86; Duncan 1974; Sacks et al. 1974), and *kinesics* (e.g. gaze, body movements, etc.) (Kendon 1967).

Nevertheless, the problem remains that the above Theme/Topic-shift markers represent optional tendencies only. In other words, the question needs to be addressed as to how the analyst can determine the occurrence of a shift in Topic/Theme systematically, as Theme/Topic shift markers may be absent from discourse, or they may not be used as expected.

In sum, the intricacies raised by the numerous and heterogeneous variations of the semantic interpretation have led many scholars to conclude that Theme/Topic in terms of aboutness cannot be regarded as an objectively identifiable *unique* category, but as a clearly *intuitive*, and therefore, subjective concept since "what is being talked about" may be judged differently at different points in discourse, and participants themselves may not have identical views of "what is being talked about" (Kintsch 1974: 124; Brown & Yule 1983: 73; Levinson 1983: x).

2.3 The informational interpretation

The prime concern of informational interpretations is the informational status of the constituents of a message/utterance (mainly NGs). Accordingly, Topic/Theme is typically described as the *Given*, that is, as the part(s) of a message known to the listener, or that the speaker/writer expects the listener to know, or that can be deduced from the co(n)text.[21] Conversely, the part(s) unknown to the listener, or that the speaker/writer believes the listener does not know or cannot deduce from the co(n)text normally represent the *New* or *Focus*.[22] Thus van Dijk (1977: 118) emblematically explains that "each sentence will in principle express the relationship between OLD and NEW information, viz. as TOPIC and COMMENT, respectively" ([emphasis in original]).

2.3.1 *The principles of: FSP, EW, EF and TU*

Informational approaches hypothesise that information in messages tends to display a (*Given*)-towards-*New* movement, and less typically, a New-towards-(Given) flow. These two arrays of information have been accounted for in terms of two principles, which correspond fairly well to the two main perspectives on word order adopted by psycholinguists at the beginning of this century (Section 2.1):

a. *Principle of Functional Sentence Perspective* (PFSP), coined by the PS; and
b. Givón's *Task Urgency Principle* (TUP).

Assigned different labels both within and outside the Prague School, PFSP has been invoked to explain the tendency of languages to place new information (realized by the nucleus of intonation) at the end of the information unit and given information at the beginning.[23] This array of information has been considered to be concomitant with the principles of *End-Focus* (EF) and *End-Weight* (EW).

EF refers to the tendency for the Focus to come towards the end of the intonation unit and has been regarded as a major factor influencing the selection of informational variants (Quirk et al. 1972, 1985: 1361–2). Consider the following question-answer pairs:[24]

(22) a. What did Peter do?
He **locked** Tom in the shed.
b. What happened to Peter?
He was sent to the **headmaster**.

In (22a) the active clause *He locked Tom in the shed* is a more natural response than the corresponding passive *Tom was locked in the shed by him*. Apart from the topical motivation, this is because the sequential arrangement in the grammar of the active matches the non-focal ^ focal ordering of information. The question presupposes that "Peter did something", and this information appropriately precedes the revelation of what that "something" was (namely, locking Tom in the shed). By contrast in (22b) it is entirely natural to use a passive clause as the response. Peter's involvement (as "patient") in some action or event has been established as non-focal, and this matches the grammatical arrangement with his appearing early as subject of the passive construction.

As another example, consider the contrast between (23a) and (23b):

(23) a. Peter sold Beatrice the **microwave oven**
b. Peter sold the microwave oven to **Beatrice**

(23a) is likely to be preferred in a context where it is established that "Peter sold Beatrice something (or some type of oven)" but not that the item in question was the microwave oven. (23b) is more likely in a context where it is established that Peter sold the microwave oven but not that the recipient was Beatrice.

EW on the other hand is the principle by which longer and more complex constituents of the clause (and of other constituents) tend to occur late in the clause (e.g. extraposition, dative-shift, right detachment, etc.) and has also been adduced to explain alternation between informational variants. Compare the examples in (24) and the extraposed alternants in (25):

(24) a. She searched for it in the drawer.
b. She searched for her scarf in the drawer.
c. She searched in the drawer for the new silk scarf that her mother had given her.

(25) a. It is unlikely that he will visit his sister when he travels to Brisbane for a meeting next February.
   b. That he will visit his sister when he travels to Brisbane for a meeting next February is unlikely.

The *for*-phrase is appropriately in non-final position in (24a) and (24b): in (24a) it is "lighter" than the following *in*-phrase, and in (24b) of equal weight. However in (24c) the weight of the *for*-phrase increases considerably, through additional modification of the noun *scarf*, making it preferable to move it into final position. Similarly, (25a) is likely to be preferred over (25b) because it has the long *that*-clause in final rather than initial position in the main clause.

Quirk et al. (1972, 1985) explain that that "heavy" elements are placed last because they are more likely to contain new information; whereas Grice (1975), Langacker (1974:653), Keenan & Schieffelin (1976) and Huddleston (1984: 453) associate this organisation with psychological or processing factors. Grice argues that the PFSP follows from the *maxim of manner*, in particular "be orderly", and therefore is a universal principle of communication: what is Given is logically and conceptually prior to what is New in relation to it; while, roughly, Keenan, Schieffelin, Langacker and Huddleston explain that in texts with good recipient-designs speakers place heavy constituents last in order to facilitate production and comprehension: placed last, heavy constituents do not disrupt the processing of the remainder of the sentence.

Alternatively, according to Givón (1988: 252) speakers' expressions abide by the TUP, i.e. the cognitive notion of *order of attention*: "attend first to the most urgent task".[25] As a result, earlier position in a string is reserved for an information-chunk which is: (a) less predictable and (b) more important. In Givón's words:

> When the topic is *most predictable*, the task of expressing it is *least urgent*. It is then left uncoded (zero), and only the comment is expressed. When the topic is a bit less predictable, but still *more predictable than the comment*, the task of expressing it is thus *less urgent* than that of expressing the comment. The topic thus follows the comment. When the topic is even less predictable, and the task of expressing it is judged *more urgent* than that of expressing the comment, the topic precedes the comment. Finally, when the topic is *least predictable*, and thus the task of expressing it is *most urgent*, the topic is expressed alone [...], while the comment is left uncoded (zero). (1988: 252–3) [emphasis in original]

It is important to note that the principles of FSP, EW, EF, and TU tend to "conspire" to put the Given first and the New last. EW and EF work in tandem, insofar as focal information often needs to be given fuller expression than non-focal; that is, focal information generally requires a longer, "heavier" structure. Conversely, the typically non-focal status of material positioned earlier in the clause (which will often be coextensive with the Topic) is compatible with the use of a relatively short expression (*it*, *this*, *then*, *I*, etc.) which refers to someone or something that is accessible in the context of the discourse. Likewise, according to the PFSP and the TUP, the "most urgent task" of instances of thematisation, fronting, passive (including raisings), left detachment and pseudo-clefts is to move material leftward into a position unmarked for the Given (Creider 1979; Prince 1981a; Davison 1984; Gundel 1985, 1988; Ward 1985); whereas the "most urgent task" of right detachments, *it*-clefts, *there*-structures, presentational structures and extraposed constructions (e.g. *An article {appeared/*disappeared} about the CIA*, Horn 1986: 182) is to place material rightward into rhematic position, the position unmarked for the Focus/New (Jacobs 1975; Ziv 1976; Guéron 1980).

However, the different principles do not always work in harmony in the way described here, making it important to maintain a conceptual and methodological distinction between them. For example, it could be argued that, although given information has been established in the previous discourse and therefore new information is less predictable, yet given information may be either less important than new information (i.e. when the speaker/writer wants to start with given information and focalises new information) or more important (i.e. when the speaker/writer wants to begin with cognitively new information and focalises given information), in which case there would be a conflict between the principles of FSP and TU. In this connection, Gundel (1988) explains that a resolution in favour of *Given–Before New* results in one of the constructions just mentioned *moving material leftward* into a position unmarked for the Given; while resolution in favour of *First Things First* results in one of the structures *placing material rightward* into focal position.[26]

2.3.2   What does "given" mean?

When having to evaluate informational approaches a number of questions spring to mind: how reliably can message/clause elements be identified for any particular informational category or set of categories? In other words, what criteria can be applied to reliably determine the informative status of a specific category? And how is the chosen formulation of Theme/Topic linguistically relevant? How much given information is thematic/topical? Is information status limited to referents, or to noun phrases?

We shall see that two factors lie behind these questions: (a) the fact that the notions of givenness and newness have proved hard to define, which has created a considerable number of conceptual and analytical discrepancies, and (b) the fact that informational interpretations often do not provide operational and empirically verifiable analyses, but rather seem to rest upon rather "subjective" and relatively *ad hoc* assumptions. The first factor is discussed in what follows, while the second one is covered in Section 2.3.3.

2.3.2.1 *Givenness and presupposition*

As already noted by Chafe (1976: 3) and Allerton (1978: 133, 151ff.), for example, *givenness* and *presupposition* must be interpreted as two different concepts, although they have often been used indistinctly in the literature. We have seen that givenness evokes a discourse notion referring to the informational status of the constituents of a message that is determined by the speaker/writer's view of the situational and linguistic co(n)text (including the addressee's communicative needs) and that is indicated by attenuated morpho-syntactic and phonological forms (e.g. pronominalisation, definiteness, lower pitch, weaker stress, etc.). Conversely, presupposition is a logico-semantic notion realized by sentence form which involves a *proposition* (i.e. a potential sentence having the capacity of being true or false), whose assumability is required for the success of the message (Jackendoff 1972: 276–8). And so a proposition may convey Given information, but need not be presupposed (e.g. *It can't be true*, as an answer to *I saw the man*, where *it* stands as given information, but the proposition is not presupposed). Or, vice versa, informationally new items may occur within a presupposition (e.g. *What the duke gave to my aunt was that teapot*, where it is presupposed that the duke gave something to someone ("my aunt'), but the identity of that something is presented as news).

2.3.2.2 *Relational givenness vs. referential givenness*

The given-new contrast has been associated with very different concepts and with varying elements of expression (see endnotes 22 and 23). Here we shall assume that informational accounts fall into one of two main groups:[27]

a. *relational* or *reciprocal*; and
b. *referential* or *denotational*, which in our analysis involves two subtypes:
    i. *contextual*; and
    ii. *activated*.

Relationally, or reciprocally, given information is "given" in relation to the New or Focus, and the latter is "new" in relation to the Given, crucially, within the domain of *individual clauses/utterances*. Accordingly, Gundel (1988: 210), for instance, explains that (cf. Firbas 1964: 272):

... [a]n entity, E, is the Topic [Theme] of a sentence, S, iff in using S the speaker intends to increase the addressee's knowledge about, request information about, or otherwise get the addressee to act with respect to E. [...] A predication, P, is the comment [Rheme] of a sentence, S, iff, in using S the speaker intends P to be assessed relative to the topic of S.

As an example of relational-informational analyses let us have a look at (26) (Vallduví & Engdahl 1996: 463 (3)):

(26) a. What about the pipes? In what condition are they?
The pipes are [$_F$ RUSTY].[28]
b. What about the pipes? What's wrong with them?
The pipes [$_F$ are RUSTY].
c. Why does the water from the tap come out brown?
[$_F$ The PIPES are rusty].
d. I have some rust remover. You have any rusty things?
[$_F$ The PIPES] are rusty.
e. I wonder whether the pipes are rusty.
The pipes [$_F$ ARE] rusty.

From a relational informational perspective, what makes the foci in (26) new or informative is not their denotational force *per se*, but rather the fact that they provide an instantiation to some variable or parameter in an underspecified context. Hence, in (26d) *the pipes* denotes a hearer-known entity (this is structurally realized through the definite article), whose newness derives from its instantiating a parameter in a context establishing that some things are rusty but not which thing(s) are rusty. To demonstrate that such sentences as those in (26) are not interchangeable in any given context despite their semantic equivalence, it is common practice to use the *Q-test*, that is, to set up contexts for them by using appropriate questions that take them as answers; and so each one of the sentences in (26) is an answer to (a) one or more different questions (Sgall et al. 1973; Uhlírová 1977; Hatcher 1965a, b; Grieve & Wales 1973; Daneš 1967).

Alternatively, denotational or referential accounts refer to the *cognitive status* of clause/utterance referents, that is, information about their location in the speakers' memory and attention state, by relating them to the discourse co(n)text in which they occur (in the *contextual* subtype; see Section 2.3.2.3 in this study) or by exploring how the interactants' minds respond to linguistic stimuli (in the *activated* subtype; see Section 2.3.2.4). But before discussing these two types of referential interpretations any further, it is important to note that the relational and the referential dimensions of the given-new contrast should be taken to operate *simultaneously*, yet *independently*, within the attentional structure of discourse. Admittedly, there exist a number of correlations between both dimensions since novel referents tend to appear in the focal segment of an utterance/sentence and conversely familiar referents tend not to be focalised. However, this correlation is incomplete given that items denoting salient, familiar referents — pronouns — can be either focal, as in (27a), or non-focal, as in (27b) (ibid.: 498 (93)), which demonstrates that relational and referential givenness/newness represent two independent dimensions.

(27) a. I like [$_F$ HIM.]
     b. *Him* [$_F$ I LIKE.]

2.3.2.3 *Recoverability, predictability, shared knowledge, identifiability and (assumed) familiarity*

We shall suggest here that *contextual-referential accounts invoke five major readings of givenness (vs. newness)*: (a) *recoverability* (Giv$_R$), (b) *predictability* (Giv$_P$), (c) *shared knowledge* (Giv$_K$), (d) *identifiability* (Giv$_{I/D}$), and (e) *assumed familiarity* (Giv$_F$). Roughly, the first four imply a discrete binary distinction, and the last one a scalar or gradient notion. Recoverability (Giv$_R$) is upheld by Halliday (1967b, 1974, 1977, 1981, 1994) and the co-workers in SFG, for example, who describe new information (New) as what is presented by speakers as not recoverable from the preceding discourse, while Given is "what the speaker is presenting as information that is recoverable from some source or other in the environment — the situation or the preceding text" (Halliday & Hasan 1976: 326), as in // **John** painted the shed yesterday //, where the marked Focus on "John" renders "painted the shed yesterday" recoverable information (Halliday 1967b: 207).

In contrast, for the supporters of Giv$_P$ (predictability) such as de Beaugrande & Dressler (1981) and Kuno (1972a, 1978a, 1981), for example, the Given represents what the addressee expects the speaker/writer is likely to say/write, while the New relates to expressions not following (or not predicted by) these expectations, as in ***John**$_i$ paid Mary and **he**$_i$/Ø bought himself a new coat*, where *he* is predictable from *John* (Prince 1981a: 226 (5)) [emphasis in original]. However, for Haviland & Clark (1974) and Clark & Haviland (1977), emblematic defenders of Giv$_K$ (shared knowledge), the Given is what the speaker "believes the listener already knows and accepts as true" (but is not necessarily thinking about), and the New as that which the speaker "believes the listener does not yet know" (Clark & Haviland 1977: 4). Whether the hearer knows the information directly for having been explicitly told it, e.g. *We got some beer out of the trunk and **it** was warm* (Prince 1981a: 231 (18b)) [emphasis in original]), or indirectly via inference, is immaterial.

Closely related to the latter, Giv$_{I/D}$, that is, identifiability, or definiteness, has been discussed in Hawkins (1978), Chesterman (1991) and Chafe (1996: 37–46) *inter alia*. The latter, for example, explains that speakers treat a referent as identifiable if they judge that the words they use to express it will enable the listener to identify it, which involves three parameters: (a) *shared knowledge* (the speaker judges that knowledge of the referent in question is already shared with the listener, directly or via inference), (b) *adequate categorisation* (the usage of sufficiently identifying language) and (c) *contextual salience* (the identifiable referent must be distinguished from other shared referents that could be categorised in the same way), as illustrated in the following conversation (ibid.: 38 (19)):

(28)[29] a. ... só=,
b. ... what did she dó,
c. the first thíng that
d. ... was to òpen her dráwer,
e. ... and get a .. rúler out,
f. you know.
g. ... She was gonna let me have it,
h. and uh,
i. .. Fàther Jóhn said I've already.. whípped him.
j. ... So she put the .. rúler back.

Focusing on the identifiability of the referent expressed as *the ruler* in (28j), this referent can be assumed to be already shared because of its introduction with the indefinite phrase *a ruler* in (28e), and so it constitutes an example of direct sharing based on prior activation of the referent in question. Besides, the adequate categorisation of this referent is guaranteed by mentioning (a) the ruler-class of referents in (28e) and (b) the pronoun *it* immediately afterwards in (28g) (although in a context involving more than one ruler the speaker would have needed a more elaborate identification like *the ruler she had taken out of her drawer*).

Scalar models of "assumed familiarity" (Giv$_F$) are proposed, for example, by Allerton (1978: 147), Prince (1981a: 233–37), and Gundel, Hedberg & Zacharschi (GHZ) (1993). Allerton distinguishes four degrees of informativity on syntactic and intonational grounds:

a. *New*, in which the speaker/writer makes no assumption about the addressee's knowledge (e.g. *a policeman*, a *bookshop*);
b. *Semi-New*, or information indirectly accessible to the addressee, by delving into the distant past text or the recesses of the mind (e.g. '*the policeman*, '*the bookshop*, (') nuclear fall);
c. *Semi-Given*, that is to say, information directly accessible, mentioned or made obvious in the recent past (e.g. *the policeman, the bookshop*, (/) nuclear rise with a fall on subsequent items);

d. *Given*, or information taken for granted, *the policeman, the bookshop*, non-nuclear).

Prince, on the other hand, proposes a taxonomy with three kinds of Giv$_F$ (although she also resorts to Giv$_S$ in her work on *grounding*, see Section 2.3.2.2.2):
a. *New*, or entities firstly introduced in discourse by the user, are classified into three types:
  i. *Brand-New Unanchored*, when the hearer creates a new independent entity (e.g. *a bus* in *I got on a bus yesterday and the driver was drunk*);
  ii. *Brand New Anchored*, or a newly created entity linked to another entity in the addressee's discourse model (e.g. *A guy I work with* in *A guy I work with says he knows your sister*);
  iii. *Unused*, that is, an entity known to the addressee, but not yet placed in this discourse model (e.g. *Rotten Rizzo* in *Rotten Rizzo can't have a third term*);
b. *Inferrable*, or entities that the speaker/writer assumes her/his addressee can infer through reasoning (e.g. *I got on a bus yesterday and the driver was drunk*, where *the driver* is Inferrable from *a bus*, since buses have drivers), which belong to the *Containing Inferrable* subclass, when what is inferred is a property contained within the Inferrable NG itself (e.g. *Hey, one of these eggs is broken!*, where *one of these eggs* is inferred by a set-member inference from *these eggs*);
c. *Evoked*, or entities that are already present in discourse in two different ways:
  i. *situationally Evoked*, i.e. retrievable from the context (e.g. *you* in *Pardon, would you have change of a quarter?*);
  ii. *textually Evoked*, i.e. recoverable from the linguistic cotext (e.g. *he* in *A guy I work with says he knows your sister*).[30]

Lastly, midway between contextual and activated accounts, GHZ's *Givenness Hierarchy* presents a scale with cognitive statuses ordered from most restrictive (in focus) to least restrictive (type identifiable) with respect to the set of possible referents they include, as shown in (29):

(29) in focus > activated > familiar > uniquely identifiable > referential > type identifiable

{*it*} | {*that*, *this*, *this* N} | {*that* N} {*the* N} {*indefinite this* N} {*a* N}

One of the main premises of GHZ's hierarchy is that different cognitive statuses are signalled by different determiners and pronominal forms which serve as processing signals that assist the addressee in restricting the set of possible referents. Moreover, since it is an implicational scale, the hierarchy predicts that, in using a particular form, a speaker not only signals that the associated cognitive status is met, but also that all lower statuses have been met. For example, the referent of an NG with the definite article *the* in English may be just uniquely identifiable, or it may also be familiar, activated, or in focus; since these statuses all imply uniquely identifiable. As an illustration, consider the contexts in which the referring expressions in (30) can be appropriately used (from Gundel 1996: 145 (14) [emphasis in original]):

(30) I couldn't sleep last night
  a. A **dog next door** kept me awake
  b. **This dog next door** kept me awake
  c. **The dog next door** kept me awake.
  d. **That dog next door** kept me awake.
  e. **This dog/that/this** kept me awake
  f. **It** kept me awake.

According to GHZ, the indefinite article in (30a) signals that the hearer can identify the type of thing described. By contrast, the indefinite determiner *this* in (b) signals not only that the addressee is expected to identify the type of thing described, but that the speaker has a particular dog in mind, whereas the definite article *the* in (c) signals that the hearer is expected to uniquely identify the speaker's intended referent, either on the basis of previous familiarity or from the description itself. The demonstrative determiner *that* in (d) tells the hearer that he is familiar with (already has a mental representation of) the referent and therefore can uniquely identify it, the main difference between (c) and (d) being that the definite article doesn't assume previous familiarity with the referent, but the demonstrative determiner does. Hence, the demonstrative determiner *this* and the pronouns *this and that* in (e) tell the hearer that the referent is activated (readily accessible to consciousness); which would only be appropriate if the referent had recently been mentioned or was in the immediate extralinguistic context.

Finally, the unstressed personal pronoun *it* in (f) tells the hearer that the referent is not only activated, but that his attention is currently focused on it.

2.3.2.4 *Activation, accessibility and saliency*

Accessibility is a notion that is best understood in terms of degrees of activation in consciousness. Hence, Giv_S refers to entity(-ies) which speakers/addressees are not only familiar with, but are actually attending to (thinking of) at the time of utterance, i.e. something the speaker's and the addressee's attention is already focused on. Chafe (1996) distinguishes between: (a) active ideas (those that are in a person's focus of consciousness at the moment), (b) semiactive ideas (those that are in peripheral consciousness, which were in the focus of consciousness for a few moments but which receded from the fully active state) and (c) inactive ideas (those that are neither active nor semiactive, which might be in long-term memory or might never have entered consciousness before). On the basis of these three activation states a given idea is described as one the speaker assumes is already, at this point in the discourse, in the active consciousness of the listener, such as the italicised referents in sequences (b), (g), (i) in (31) ((24) above):

(31) a.   ... só=,
      b.   ... what did she dó,
      c.   the first thíng that
      d.   ... was to òpen her dráwer,
      e.   ... and get a .. rúler out,
      f.   you know.
      g.   ... She was gonna let me have it,
      h.   and uh,
      i.   .. Fàther Jóhn said I've already.. whípped him.
      j.   ... So she put the .. rúler back.

Copeland & Davis (1983) propose the Given–New contrast as composite terms in relation to the variables [±conscious] and [±identifiable], describing Given$_S$ as what the speaker/writer believes to be identifiable and currently thought about by the addressee. Lambrecht (1988a: 146–7; 1994) also uses Copeland & Davis' variables, but places them along a *topic acceptability scale* as follows:

(32) **Lambrecht's (1988a)** *Topic Accessibility Scale*
    Active   most acceptable
    Semi-active   ↑
    Inactive   ↓
    Brand New   least acceptable

The scale in (32) implies that *active* referents [+Identifiable, +Activation] are the *most acceptable* Themes/Topics, followed by *accessible/inferrable* referents [+Identifiable, ±Activation] and *unused* referents [+Identifiable, −Activation], while *Brand-New* referents [−Identifiable, −Activation] stand at the opposite extreme as *least acceptable* Themes/Topics.

The last group of Giv$_S$ accounts represent information states as *filelike data structures*.[31] Some emblematic proposals are: Givón (1988, 1992), Vallduví

(1992), Vallduví & Engdahl (1996), and the *centring theory* advanced by Grosz, Joshi & Weinstein (1995), Walker & Prince (1996), Walker, Joshi & Prince (1997), among others. Givón (1992: 10), for example, understands cognition as a reductive discretising process, that is, a process in which information is discretised as either Given or New, where given (topical) information serves to anchor new information to the already-stored given information. Givón's topicality involves two textual dimensions: *referential accessibility*, i.e. givenness as derived from the cultural knowledge, the speech situation and/or the preceding discourse, and *thematic importance*, i.e. operationalised as the text frequency of referents in subsequent discourse. Referential accessibility and thematic importance correspond to two cognitive domains: *mental storage*, i.e. where a currently inactive node that is already in storage is identified, and *attentional activation*, whereby a file or referent Topic is open, or activated, to receive incoming information.

In this connection, Vallduví & Engdahl (1996) explain that, very roughly, an indefinite NG instructs the hearer to create a new file card (if it denotes a novel referent), while a definite NG instructs the hearer to activate, a dormant, already existing file card (if it denotes a familiar referent). Hence, *links*[32] designate a specific file card in the input file where information update is to be carried out, whereas *tails*[33] encompass ground material indicating that Focus, i.e. the only contribution that (according to the speaker) a message makes to the information state of the hearer at the time of the utterance, is not simply added to the file card designated by the link as a new condition (default mode), but rather that focus must complete or alter a condition that is already there and is designated by the tail (nondefault mode). The *ground*, both link and tail, performs an "ushering" role for the Focus: it guarantees that the update potential of the sentence is "discharged" in the appropriate location (from the speaker's perspective) in the input file. If (the speaker assumes) no usher is needed, a sentence will have no ground, and vice versa, if only some ushering is needed, a sentence may have a link but not a tail, or vice versa. This brings about four *instruction types*, i.e. ways of indicating how the meaning of a message should be "unpacked", included in (33) to (36) (from Vallduví & Engdahl 1996: 470 (15), (16), (17), (18)), which have language-dependent structural realizations:

(33) Tell me about the people in the White House. Anything I should know?
The president [$_F$ hates CHOCOLATE].
a *link-focus instruction*, which designates a locus of update with an addition of a condition on that locus.

(34) And what about the president? How does *he* feel about chocolate?
The president [$_F$ HATES] chocolate-
a *link-focus-tail instruction*, designating a locus of update that points to a

> given condition indicating that the update completes or alters that condition in some way.
>
> (35) The president has a weakness.
> [$_F$ He hates CHOCOLATE].
> an *all-focus instruction*, when no specific file card is designated as a locus of update, but rather a general-situation file card is used.
>
> (36) You shouldn't have brought chocolates for the president.
> [$_F$ He HATES] chocolate][34]
> a *focus-tail instruction*, the locus of update is inferred from previous discourse

Finally, trying to reflect the hearer's inference load when interpreting a message, the centring theory suggests that each utterance U_i in a coherent local sequence of utterances (a discourse segment) $U_i \ldots U_m$, affects the structure of the discourse model in two ways: (a) by evoking a set of discourse entities (file cards) called *Forward-looking centres* (Cf); and (b) by containing a distinguished member, *the Backward-looking centre* (Cb), i.e. an entity that links the current utterance to the previous discourse, so that, if an utterance is discourse-segment initial, then it has no Cb. The modelling of discourse salience is achieved through the determination of the Cb, in combination with a ranking on the set of (Cfs), according to factors which determine discourse salience. The highest ranked element of (Cf) is the *Preferred centre* (Cp), that is, a prediction about the Cb of the following utterance. Sometimes the Cp will be what the previous segment of discourse was about, the Cb, but this is not necessarily the case. Cbs may be changed or shifted producing different types of *centring transitions* (*continue, retain, smooth-shift* and *rough-shift*). The combination of centring constraints, rules and transitions creates a three-step algorithm (in (38)) which makes a set of testable predictions about which interpretations hearers will prefer because they require less processing:

> (38) **Generate** possible Cb-Cf combinations.
> **Filter** by constraints, e.g. contra-indexing, selectional restrictions, centring rules and constraints.
> **Rank** by transition-ordering.

2.3.3 *Other problems with informational approaches*

Besides the conceptual complexity involved, already discussed in Section 2.3.2, informational approaches pose five additional problems. One is that many of these accounts tend to mix up what are in fact two different dimensions, quoting Mathesius's definition, (a) "that which is known or at least obvious in the given situation" and (b) "that [...] from which the speaker proceeds". Fries (1983, 1995a, b) calls these *combining approaches*. The effect is that the informative status of items and their syntactic coding in initial or non-initial position are treated as if they were two different aspects of one and the same phenomenon, the given-new distinction, which leads to a number of misunderstandings. The most typical one is the automatic identification of the first part of a message as Given and the last one as New.[35]

Another issue regards the problematic operationalisation or empirical verification of informational accounts. It has been shown that in this kind of accounts Topic/Theme is not defined directly, but rather is described:

a. in relation to Focus (Rheme, New) at clause/utterance level, in the relational approaches; and, in referential accounts,
b. in relation to such elusive concepts as "recoverability", "predictability", "shared knowledge" and "saliency";
c. as a discrete value along a scale of topicality;
d. as a process of attention activation.

In addition, disputable analyses arise because the three readings of the given-new distinction, relational, contextual and activated, are not independent of each other and have often been used in a loose, non-rigid manner. It seems that all types of givenness qualify for Giv_K, although the reverse is not necessarily the case. Indeed, in order for information to be presented as recoverable, salient or predictable the speaker/writer must assume that the hearer "knows" or can infer a particular thing. Likewise, in order for a referent to be adequately identifiable it must be shared knowledge and contextually salient; and if the speaker/writer assumes some information to be in the consciousness of the addressee, it is also likely to be recoverable and/or predictable from the linguistic or situational context. But the array of knowledge implied by Giv_K is so vast, incorporating both general background knowledge and knowledge arising from the co(n)text, that the concept becomes virtually useless. For one thing, discourse participants tend to have a vast knowledge which is "shared" and this would make any piece of information given.

However, the fact that information is presented as recoverable or predictable by the speaker does not imply that it has to be salient in the addressee's consciousness; in the same way that what the speaker presents as Given or New may not actually be rendered so by the co(n)text. A case in point is (39) (from Prince 1981a: 227 (6a) [emphasis in original]), where the marked foci on *she* and *him* make *insulted* Given, although it does not convey co(n)textually recoverable information:

(39)   John called Mary a Republican and then **she** insulted **him**

On the other hand, Chafe's (1976) and others' requirement that Topics need to be textually or situationally "activated" does not seem to be a necessary condition for topichood, as we see in the case of (40):

(40)   The guy I was telling you about last week, he just won the lottery

(40) appears to be about the referent of the left-detached NG, and yet the referent is not "currently evoked" (the last mention having occurred a week earlier — a salient entity would not normally need such a lengthy description). Corpus based studies have shown that left detachment serves commonly to reintroduce a referent into discourse in this way (Montgomery 1982; Simon-Vandenbergen 1987; Collins 1993; Section 7.4.4 in this book). Exceptions to the weaker shared familiarity requirement (Gundel 1985, 1988) occur with "inferrables", as in (41):

(41)   Can you help me with our visitor's car? The front wheel's caught in the gutter.

Here "the front wheel" is inferrable by logical/plausible reasoning from an already evoked discourse entity, though presumably this Topic is not familiar/previously known to the addressee. Even more problematical for the familiarity criterion are cases where a brand new entity that is familiar only to the speaker — and not to the addressee — seems to be topical, as in:

(42)   My aerobics teacher, she works the class till our bodies ache.

Turning to the criterion of definiteness/identifiability, many writers have noted that specific indefinite expressions can function as Topic expressions, as in:

(43)   A guy I met recently collects beer cans for a hobby

The Subject referent here is "brand-new"/non-identifiable, and yet seems to be topical (insofar as it can be reported via the reporting-paraphrase test: "Peter said of a guy he met recently that he collects beer cans for a hobby"). Notice that the referent in question is introduced by means of an NG containing a modifier which explicitly "anchors" the referent to other entities in the discourse model. As not infrequently happens in discourse, a new referent is introduced, and something is said about them at the same time. These dual functions are more readily distinguishable, arguably, in left-detachment (which Lambrecht (1994) describes as a "Topic promoting" construction); consider the left-detached version of (44):

(44)   A guy I met recently, he collects beer cans for a hobby.

Here, according to Lambrecht (1994), the Subject — and not the *extern* — is the Topic expression. The extern introduces a new entity and "promotes" it; that is, makes it discourse-salient (or "active"), available for subsequent treatment as a Topic. Notice furthermore that what is predicated of the recently-met-guy in the VP (43) and the host clause in (44) is more "informative" (more "communicatively dynamic") than the topical NG, which distinguishes such examples from cases like:

(45)   A guy's at the door.

Sentences like (45) have a "presentational" function ("There's a guy at the door"): they serve to introduce a new referent. The Subject NG in (45) is more informative and, arguably, would not be interpreted as a Topic expression (no left-detached version is available: *A guy, he's at the door*; the reporting-paraphrase test fails: *She said of a guy that he was at the door*).

Activation (Giv_S), in turn, seems to be an inherently unverifiable criterion, its psychological nature being simultaneously its main attraction and its main weakness. For Giv_S definitions assume a knowledge of the workings of memory and attention/consciousness which is hard to verify empirically and as a result there is no easy way of validating whether an element is Giv_S or not. Some vexing questions are: for how long can mental representations be active and eligible for thematic/topical status, if they quickly fade from consciousness unless refreshed by continual mention? Put another way, how long does a referent retain a given status? How can the "silent" mental shift from Given to Accessible be measured and regarded in terms of thematicity and topicality? So far, experimental evidence on cognitive psychology has focused on the way narrative discourse is processed by individual participants, and has provided no conclusive results.[36] Further, although Givón and others hypothesise the same deployment of attention activation for all text types, this issue is for the moment unresolved, since there is virtually no experimental evidence bearing on collaborative discourse that analyses the correlation between grammar and text processing involving interactants jointly.

The question-test (Q-test) has been used to identify topical and focal constituents in a number of activated-informational and semantic approaches, but this test is not without problems, either. It does not determine the *degrees of activation* or givenness of the constituents of a message. In this respect, Daneš (1989: 29) comments that it is doubtful whether "degrees of activation" (abstracting from the opaqueness of this concept itself) can be objectively tested. The same point is made by Weiss (1975: 271ff.), whereas Dressler (1972) observes that it is liable to ambiguous interpretations, because different questions may have the same answer or vice versa. Likewise, Beaugrande (1980: 120) regards the method as artificial and uneconomical, arguing that (a) in natural discourse answers do not normally repeat information which is directly derivable from questions and (b) to apply single questions to individual utterances does not seem to be the easiest and most economical way to determine the Topic or Focus constituents of discourse stretches.

The third difficulty of informational approaches lies in determining how the given-new contrast is realized. Two sets of devices are generally recognised:
a.   syntactic (e.g. pronominalisation, definiteness, etc.);
b.   phonological (i.e. intonation nucleus placement).

Usually, constituent (=syntactic) givenness and news value (=intonational) givenness work together, but they may not always coincide. Hence, the first question is posed as to how to interpret both PFSP and TUP principles (and the categories on which they are based) when syntactic givenness and intonational givenness do not work together. In other words, it is not clear to what extent the given-new status is determined by the syntactic form of sentences (viz. word order, specific givenness/newness markers such as semantically related or repeated lexical units, certain clausal patterns, pro-forms, etc.) or by the effect of placing the "focal stress" on a given constituent, or by a combination of both.

It has been observed, for example, that primary sentence stress, or *Focus*, tends to coincide with the part of the clause/utterance that encodes the Rheme (or the New), although the possibility of a secondary accent on the Theme has also been noted.[37] Likewise, in Part II of this study it shall be shown that, whereas for SFG co-workers it is the speaker that ultimately determines what is to be taken as thematic or rhematic, for FG analysts as well as for many Prague scholars this is determined by the co(n)text, and by intonational givenness within the CD framework.[38]

On the other hand, Reinhart (1982), Gundel (1988), Gundel et al. (1993), Vallduví (1992) and Vallduví & Engdahl (1996), for example, make a distinction between the marking of cognitive status of discourse referents, through the choice of lexical realization of the noun phrase, and the expression of information packaging, structurally realized through syntactic operations, intonational phrasing, and/or morphological marking. However, this picture is not unanimously agreed upon. An alternative account is presented in Givón (1983b,c, 1992), for instance, where both definiteness and word-order permutations are structural reflections of cognitive status ("topicality") of discourse referents, which are hierarchically ranked (starting with the highest degree of topicality and progressively descending) according to their structural realization along the following lines (see Table 2 above):

(46) **Givón's Topicality hierarchy**:
Zero anaphora > weak pronouns > strong pronouns > right-detachment > neutral order (+definite) > left-detachment > Y-movement > clefts > indefinite NGs.[39]

The fourth problem is a corollary of the previous one. Informational accounts tend to restrict their explanatory power mainly to NGs: thematic/topical items are identified with zero anaphora and the (modified) definite, whereas indefinite NGs receive rhematic status. This identification leads to two further debatable issues. One is, if it is true that clauses/utterances may contain more than one Given NG (Givón 1984a, Du Bois 1987, Chafe 1987) and that, generally speaking, only one NG per sentence is perceived as Theme/Topic (Davison 1984: 802; Givón 1992: 42), then it follows that additional criteria apart from that of givenness have to be invoked to select among the potential Themes/Topics. The second is whether or not the commonplace assumption that only Given NGs qualify for Theme/topical status is correct. Allerton (1978: 157), Reinhart (1981: 72), Jordan (1985) and Lötscher (1985) have criticised this assumption in some detail. The latter states that "topicalised elements can be either thematic [referential] [...] or rhematic [non-referential]" in languages such as German, Russian, Japanese, Chinese, French or English, although these languages seem to vary in the ease with which non-referential Topics are expressible (1985: 207–208).

And in closing, a fifth problematic issue could be found when trying to account for clauses/utterances containing new information only (all new clauses, newspaper headlines, titles, etc.). The equation of givenness with Theme/Topic does not seem to be the most elegant way of treating these sequences, because, consisting only of what is newsworthy, they would be devoid of Theme/Topic functions (which in most informational approaches are also glossed semantically as "what the message is about"). To preclude this possibility, Chafe (1987) affirms that all constituents would be good candidates for thematic/topical status, were we to calculate their "activation state" (difficult though it may seem to calculate the degree of activation of some word classes such us conjunctions, adverbs, prepositions etc.). However, if Chafe's procedure were to be adopted, the category of Theme/Topic (and its counterpart) would embody such a vast and heterogeneous territory as to render the concept virtually useless in order to account for the structure of individual messages/utterances/clauses and/or connected discourse.

The problems involved in informational accounts have led Reinhart (1981: 73) and Lutz (1981: 25), among others, to conclude that givenness is neither a sufficient nor the most elegant criterion to explain the phenomenon of thematicity/topicality.

2.4 The syntactic interpretation

Evoking the classic Greek philosophers' theory that human judgement is "double" (see Section 1.2), the supporters of the syntactic interpretation conceive the informational structure of the clause as a *bipartite construct*, consisting of: (a) a *point of departure*, or *syntactic Theme/Topic* ("topos" = "place" in Greek), and (b) the main issue, or *Rheme/Comment*. Further, linking the concept "point of departure" with the *linear quality* of language, i.e. the constraint that words must be ordered into sentences and these into texts according to some organising principle (Lehman 1992) and relying solely on morpho-syntactic structure, the syntactic interpretation roughly equates Theme/Topic with the *leftmost*, or initial, constituent of the clause as a message, the so-called *prefield* (*Vorfeld*) position.

2.4.1 *The advantage of first mention*

Experimental research in psycholinguistics and text linguistics has attested different aspects of the functional relevance of clause/message initial position — as opposed to the non-initial slot —, as illustrated in Table 5.

Function-to-form syntactic approaches assume that message/clause-initial position is a universal category fulfilling a semantico-pragmatic function. An early exponent of this view is Trávníček, who portrays Theme as "the sentence element that links up directly with the object of thought, proceeds from it and opens the sentence thereby" (cited in Firbas 1964: 269); while Halliday (1994: 34) states that "Theme is a function of the CLAUSE AS A MESSAGE […] the point of departure for what the speaker is going to say", iconically realized by the element(s) occupying clause-initial position" [emphasis in original].[40]

Further, elaborating on Chafe's (1976: 53) idea that sentence Topics/Themes "limit the domain of applicability of the main predication to a certain restricted domain […] set[ting] the spatial, temporal or individual framework within which the predication holds", other syntactic analysts point out the *frame-establishing*, the *perspective-marking*, the *orientation* and/or *staging* function of this category. Thus, Magretta (1977: 132) and Vasconcellos (1992) point out that Themes/ Topics serve as the *onset* of the message establishing the primary reference frame or point for the sentence from which the rest of the message unit develops, and in (TFG2: 388) the term "orientation" is used as a superfunction comprising several more specific types of Orientation (temporal, conditional, spatial, etc.) fulfilled by initial constituents (Hannay & Vester 1987; De Vries (1989) on "framing"; Brown & Yule 1983: Chapter 4). And Lowe (1987: 6) observes that the scope of applicability of Topics/Themes may expand over the *ensuing*

Table 5. *Relevance of initial position (based on Bates & MacWhinney 1979)*

Technique	Starting point found to	Reference
Rating	be more 'potent'/'accessible'	Johnson (1967), MacWhinney (1977), Cirilo & Foss (1980), Haberlandt (1980), Haberlandt & Bingham (1982), Aaronson & Ferres (1983), Aaronson & Scarborough (1976), Chang (1980), Givón (1988), Gernsbacher & Hargreaves (1988)
	be drawn larger	Johnson-Laird (1968)
	be more human/animate/concrete	Clark & Begun (1971)
	reflect 'natural order' of our perception of reality/be perceptually or cognitively more salient	Horn (1973), Grimes (1975), Kuno (1975, 1976), Clark & Haviland (1977), Kuno & Kaburaki (1977), Osgood & Bock (1977), Van Dijk (1977), Becker (1980), Fillmore (1981), Mithun (1987), Givón (1983a, 1985, 1988), Downing P. (1995), Downing & Noonan (eds.) (1995)
Elicited production	be large	Johnson-Laird (1968)
	move first	Osgood (1971)
Problem solving	be more easily moved; be constructed first	Huttenlocher & Strauss (1968)
Free recall	be remembered first	Anderson (1963), Clark & Card (1969), Coleman (1965), Kintsch (1974)
Cued Recall	be the best cue	Prentice (1966), Cairns & Kamerman (1975), Marslen-Wilson et al. (1978), Anisfeld & Klenbort (1973)
	aid recall of passive	Schlesinger (1968)
	work best as a cue when active	Blumenthal & Boakes (1968)
	be given information	Bates & MacWhinney (1982), Bock (1982)

Table 5. (*continued*)

Technique	Starting point found to	Reference
Text/clause analysis	be known information and/or connect subsequent sentence with earlier sentences	Green (1980), Ford (1993), Kies (1988), Schiffrin (1985), Thompson (1985)
	be more topic-like that information placed elsewhere in the clause	Montgomery (1982), Ford & Thompson (1986), Haiman (1978), Ramsey (1987), Green (1980)
	perform different discourse functions from final point (initial vs. final adverbials and other elements)	Enkvist (1974: 131), Quirk et al. (1972, 1985), Grimes (1975), Lautamatti (1978), Brömser (1982: 103), Green (1980), Young (1980), Penelope (1982), Gustafsson (1983), Brow & Yule (1983), Collins (1985, 1992), Thompson (1985), Fox (1987b), Geluykens (1987, 1992), Hannay & Vester (1987), Kies (1988), Williams (1988), Bäcklund (1989), Berry (1989, 1992a, 1992b), de Vries (1989), Olsen & Johnson (1988), Hannay (1991, 1994a), Hannay & Vester (1987), Downing (1991), Bolkestein (1992), Martin (1992b), Tyler & Bno (1992), Vasconcellos (1992), Virtanen (1992), Ford (1993), Halliday (1994), Buth (1994), Gómez-González (1994, 1996a, 1998a), Pu & Prideaux (1994), Dik (1997), Dorgeloh (1997), Smits (1998), Mackenzie (1998)

discourse span, i.e. "any unit, usually larger than the sentence, contributing to the topic continuity or discontinuity of texts" (Barry 1975: 3; Lowe 1987; Fries 1987, 1995a, b; Downing 1991; Gómez-González 1998a).

Alternatively, form-to-function syntactic approaches, instead of departing from semantic-cognitive and/or pragmatic-attentional assumptions, characterise Theme/Topic primarily on formal grounds. Accordingly, Van Oosten (1986: 32), for instance, portrays Theme as the initial "non-vocative noun phrase that does not bear any selectional relation to the verb of its clause", whereas Gundel (1985: 86) proposes a wider cross-linguistic description of what she labels as the *syntactic Topic*, invoking the rightmost as well as leftmost NG constituent of the sentence (e.g. *Die Frau da, sie kommt aus Berlin*, ["The woman there she comes from Berlin"] vs. *He's shrewd, that one*, Gundel 1988: 224 [my underlining]). But, importantly, while function-orientated syntactic accounts focus on the functional motivations underlying the choice of different types of Theme, form-orientated descriptions concentrate on their formal marking (i.e. syntactic constraints and/or phonological cues), arguing that, if such formal markers are missing, then no item can be identified as Theme/Topic. Hence, for example, Davison, Gundel, Dik, Foley, Van Valin, Lambrecht and the co-workers within FG pay special attention to whether or not:

a. the rightmost and the leftmost constituents are either clause/core internal or external;
b. these constituents are co-indexed (i.e. whether they refer to another constituent);
c. syntactic Theme slots are empty.

But in all syntactic approaches it remains a moot point whether the rightmost as well as the leftmost clause/utterance predication-internal/external constituent represent functional positions for the Theme/Topic of a message or whether these slots identify such pragmatic/communicative functions. This last remark connects directly with the weaknesses of syntactic interpretations.

2.4.2 *Problems with syntactic approaches*

Syntactic accounts have come in for criticism in four main flanks. The first difficulty lies in how to decide which is the initial constituent of a clause/message. In unplanned (usually spoken) discourse, for example, there exist such phenomena as repetition, hesitation, truncated or elliptical structures and so on, which make it hard to identify syntactic units and hence the borderlines between their thematic/topical constituents. Further, the criteria used to identify syntactic

Themes/Topics are heterogeneous and not necessarily concurrent. Indeed, scholars have invoked as markers of thematic status: (a) phonological criteria (initial tone group), (b) syntactic markers (initial syntactic constituent, either nuclear and peripheral), (c) semantic factors (first semantic role), and/or (d) metafunctional considerations (first constituent fulfilling an experiential, or referential, function).

As a result, depending on the criteria cited, different scholars identify different types of constituents as Theme/Topic (and related categories). Thus, while Enkvist (1974: 131) and Berry (1989, 1992a, 1992b), in the former's words, classify all constituents "from the beginning of a MS (macrosyntagm) up to and including the subject" as part of the Theme, Brömser (1982: 103), Quirk et al. (1972, 1985) and Williams (1988) bar from this category some initial constituents such as: sentence connectors and attitudinal and circumstantial Adjuncts, explaining that they do not fulfil a thematic/topical function. By contrast, Halliday (1994: 56) claims that Theme "extends up to (and includes) the topical Theme", that is to say, the first experiential element, preceded or not by other *textual* and/or *interpersonal Themes*. In this connection Lautamatti (1978), Young (1980), Downing (1991), Vasconcellos (1992) and Gómez-González (1998a) suggest the possibility of recursiveness ("stacking") of several Themes of the same kind, as well as of different levels of syntactic depth, within an all-encompassing metafunctional initial slot. But, while Lautamatti, Downing and Gómez-González dissociate Theme (initial position) from discourse Topic ("what the message is about", usually Subject/Object participants), Young and Vasconcellos distinguish between *minor topical Themes* (i.e. initial Adjuncts) and *major topical Themes* (i.e. other experiential constituents, "often something that has been mentioned before, or something prominent in the situation of utterance", Young ibid.: 147). In contrast, Dik, Foley and Van Valin distinguish the first peripheral slot (viz. a clause initial constituent that is not bound to the predicate) from the first nuclear slot (i.e. the initial constituent that is linked to the predicate).

In this connection, Fries (1978; 1983: 117; 1995b: 1) has pointed out that in order to identify the Theme/Topic of a message, systemic (here "syntactic") accounts, unlike combining approaches, *separate* out the two aspects of Mathesius's (1939: 234) definition, "that which is known or at least obvious in the given situation" and "that [...] from which the speaker proceeds", as two interacting, but distinct choices. Theme (initial position) expresses the "point of departure" of the message, while "that which is known or at least obvious in the given situation" refers to the given-new contrast, which realizes the information structure of messages. Fries's observations would in this way neutralise the criticisms made by informational analysts (Paul, Weil, Mathesius, Firbas, CD supporters, etc.) against syntactic accounts: that clause-initial position may encode not only the Theme/Topic of a message, that is, the Given, but also its Rheme, or the New/Focus; in other words, that thematic/topical status cannot simply be equated with clause initial/final position, since given information may be anywhere in the clause/utterance or it may be absent from it. As Fries has observed and shall be shown in more detail throughout Chapter 4, this criticism does not hold, for in most syntactic (systemic) accounts Theme–Rheme arrangements on the one hand and the given-new contrast on the other represent two independent, though orthogonal choices.[42]

Nevertheless, especially for the defenders of the semantic (referential) perspective (Lyons 1977; Pasch 1982; Hudson 1986; Huddleston 1988), some allegedly "separating" characterisations do seem to distil some "combining" overtones in that they apparently conflate backgrounding (e.g. scene-setting devices) with Themes in the "aboutness" sense ("that with which the clause is concerned"). As already discussed in Section 2.2.2 at some length, this conflation entails that scene-setting devices always give to sentences in which they occur in initial position the status of being about time and place. And for the supporters of the referential-semantic perspective sentence initial temporals or locationals functioning as hooks to the context (or point of departure) are not the concern of the message at all (unless one stretches this concept in what may appear to be a circular manner). Moreover, some of these critical scholars do not only deny that message initial position expresses "what a message is about", but also question its validity as a functional category. Emblematically, Huddleston (1988: 158) explains that "[i]t is not clear that "point of departure" or "starting-point" can sustain an interpretation that is independent of syntactic sequence — that the Theme is the point of departure for the message in a more significant sense than that of being the first element". This problem is exacerbated by the fact that, although predication (internal or external) initial and final position always qualify for thematic/topical status from a syntactic point of view, that is, they always fulfil a syntactic function, the constituents in such positions need not always have a semantic, or referential, correlate (e.g. *it* in English impersonal structures such as *It* is raining, *there* in existential constructions like *There* is a fallacy in your argument, etc.). As a result, the communicative relevance of such allegedly thematic/topical constituents seems to be harder to justify. As already noted in Section 2.2 and will be explained in more detail in Section 4.3.1, this point of conflict could be resolved by arguing that "aboutness" may be treated in three different ways: relationally (in SFG and in other relational-semantic accounts), referentially (in referential-semantic accounts) and interactively (in interactive-semantic accounts).

The second problematic area is that, despite their common highlighting of initial (and final) constituents, syntactic analyses embody a wide range of structurally and communicatively heterogeneous constructions across different languages, as illustrated in (47) below ((a)–(i) from Gundel 1988: 224ff., [my emphasis]) (Altman 1981: 46; Davison 1984; Gundel 1985, 1988):

(47)   a.   Die Frau da, sie kommt aus Berlin.
             'The woman there she come from Berlin.' (left detachment)
      b.   My work, I'm going crazy.
           Double-Subject construction (Chao 1968).
      c.   al sratim ka ele rina mamas meta.   (Hebrew)
           'Movies like that, Rina is really crazy about.'
           Topicalisation, fronting, Y-movement (Berman 1980).
      d.   (To) što menja udivljaet, eto eë mudrost.   (Russian)
           'What surprises me is her wisdom.'
           Cleft construction.
      e.   Your battery seems to be dead.
           Versus It seems that your battery is dead.
           Subject to Subject raising.
      f.   George is difficult to talk to.
           Versus It is difficult to talk to George.
           Object to Subject raising.
      g.   My soup has a fly in it.
           vs. There is a fly in my soup.
           Have constructions.
      h.   He's shrewd, that one.
           Right detachment.
      i.   C'est pour ça qu'il a gagné le prix
           'It's for that that he won the prize.'
           It-cleft.
      j.   I saw the man
           vs. The man was seen
           Subject in active and passive declarative clauses.
      k.   Paul, you can't do that. Vocative.

Numerous studies attest to the diverse communicative status of each or of some of the above syntactic Theme/Topic constructions across different languages. However, it would appear that further research should be undertaken in order to substantiate with *significant* quantitative and qualitative natural evidence the contrast among the different thematic options within and across languages. In other words, syntactic approaches should be able to devise an all-encompassing thematic paradigm which highlights the common and/or the distinctive communicative and structural features of its members and which can be contrasted (cross-)linguistically.

A third debatable issue is, as remarked by Taglicht (1984), whether or not Rheme is a profitable category as attention focuses almost exclusively on the syntactic coding of Theme/Topic. And, lastly, the fourth controversial point of syntactic analyses resides in determining whether Theme–Rheme, Topic–Comment patterns are structural relationships or rather, they underlie non-structural principles of discourse organisation. Indeed, in most syntactic accounts Theme–Rheme, Topic–Comment patterns represent a form of organisation that gives the clause or sentence (less frequently, the group) the status of a communicative event. However, it has also been claimed that the connection between what comes first and what comes last in a message realizes a *non-structural* discourse construct which is communicatively relevant. It deploys a strategy for presenting, or *staging*, information throughout discourse into background, or initial position, and foreground, or final position, surpassing any structural, or grammatical, borderlines (Grimes 1975; IFG; Martin 1992a). Accordingly, Grimes (ibid.: 323) explains:

> Every clause, sentence, paragraph, episode, and discourse is organised around a particular element that is taken as its point of departure. It is as though the speaker presents what he wants to say from a particular perspective.

Grimes's staging metaphor has been widened to apply to processes of linearisation throughout discourse, and so Themes and Rhemes have been argued to extend across clausal boundaries, over paragraphs or even over whole texts. Furthermore, this metaphor has also been invoked to account for various rhetorical devices such as lexical selection, rhyme, alliteration, repetition, markers of emphasis, etc. Thus, for example, Daneš (1964), Adamec (1981), Du Bois (1987) and Martin (1992a, b) invoke the notion of *Hypertheme* (in opposition to that of *Hyper–Rheme*), as the introductory clause or group of clauses (headline(s), title(s), paragraph(s), etc.) established to predict a pattern of Theme selection in following clauses (Anderson et al. 1977). And above the Hyper–Theme, Martin (ibid.) places the *Macro–Theme* (in contrast with the *Macro–Rheme*), which embraces a clause or a combination of clauses predicting one or more Hyper–Theme(s) (e.g. the introductory paragraph of a text, its Table of Contents, etc.).

In sum, it seems that a working description of Theme/Topic in syntactic terms should take into account three main factors:

a. to work out an operational criterion that systematically identifies the initial constituent of a message;
b. to demonstrate that predication external and predication internal clause initial (final) positions have some grammatical relevance, by embodying within the same paradigm the wide range of structurally and communica-

tively heterogeneous constructions that highlight such slots within and across languages;
c. to determine whether the Theme–Rheme pattern is a structural grammatical relationship or a non-structural principle of discourse organisation.

2.5 Summary

In this chapter we have addressed the pros and cons of three dominant interpretations of communicative categories:
a. *semantic* glossing Theme/Topic as "what the message is about" in three different senses:
   i. *relationally*, i.e. a referent entailing a relationship of "aboutness" with respect to a clausal predication;
   ii. *referentially*, that is, the referent that, according to the analysts, establishes a relationship of "aboutness" between individual clauses/utterances and the overall discourse;
   iii. *interactively*, invoking what speakers regard as salient/relevant information within the discourse framework.
b. *informational*, which identifies Theme/Topic with three different types of givenness:
   i. *relational*, representing Theme/Topic as given information in relation to the focal, rhematic or newsworthy part of individual clauses/messages;
   ii. *contextual*, implying that Theme/Topic conveys given information as rendered by the co(n)text, in terms of:
      1. *recoverability* (Giv_R),
      2. *predictability* (Giv_P),
      3. *shared knowledge* (Giv_K),
      4. *assumed familiarity* (Giv_F);
      5. *identifiability*, or *definiteness* ($Giv_{I/D}$)
   iii. *activation* (Giv_S), according to which Theme/Topic is *salient* information in the interactants' minds; and
c. *syntactic*, which equates Theme/Topic with predication-external/internal syntactic initial(/final) position.

We have seen that, although these represent three different kinds of interpretations, semantic glosses in terms of "aboutness" have often been used to account for syntactic and informational communicative notions. And vice versa, different word order arrangements and the different forms of expression of given and new information have also been said to obey "aboutness" relationships. It has been shown that this situation has led to considerable fuzziness and controversy in the field. With regard to semantic approaches, their key concept, "aboutness", has been rendered hard to define and operationalise. In the case of relational-semantic analyses two potentially debatable issues have been spotted: (a) whether or not individual messages/clauses are duplex, that is, consist of a Theme/Topic and a Focus/Rheme; and (b) how to elicit the markers of communicative categories. Likewise, it has been noted that referential interpretations could strengthen their position by substantiating with statistically significant empirical evidence the scales for entity Topics/Themes adduced; whereas interactive interpretations have been encouraged to increase their explanatory potential by suggesting some means to identify speakers' and/or discourse Topics objectively. Considering informational approaches, it has been noted that givenness does not seem to define the category of Topic/Theme unequivocally or independently of other categories, and that referential accounts apparently restrict their explanatory power to NGs. Lastly, it has been suggested that syntactic accounts could strengthen their positions by providing a method to identify the syntactic Theme/Topic of a message and demonstrate its functional relevance by means of statistically significant and natural discourse evidence.

Part II

Previous Studies

A Sympathetic Critique

CHAPTER 3

The Prague School

3.1 Introduction

Prague linguists analyse communicative categories within the level of *Functional Sentence Perspective* (FSP), as opposed to the semantic and the grammatical levels, which study the *static constitutive* (i.e. distinctive and invariant) features of the *sentence*. Treated as a grammatical level since Vachek (1958), FSP sets out to explore the distribution of the elements of the *utterance*, i.e. the minimal communicative unit of languages, in a *dynamic relation* to: (a) the circumstances imposed by extralinguistic reality (i.e. the context, the situation, and the speaker's attitude towards the message and towards the addressee), and (b) the psycholinguistic constraints of communication (i.e. the linear materialisation and linear perception of utterances) (Mathesius 1939: 234; Daneš 1964: 229; Firbas 1966; Novák & Sgall 1968: 292; Novák 1974).

In this chapter we shall see that most PS scholars gloss Theme/Topic along (relational and/or referential) semantic lines, that is, in terms of (clausal) aboutness, echoing Mathesius' notion of *Téma* ("what is being commented upon"). However, when having to identify this category in a message, two main positions emerge. Some claim that the *základ*, or foundation, of a message is given information ("that which is known or at least obvious in the given situation") and thereby subscribe to the informational approach; while others pursue the notion of *Východisté*, i.e. the "point of departure of the message", "that from which the speaker proceeds", the object of study of syntactic accounts. Section 3.2 offers a critical review of the informational trend in the PS, while Section 3.3 evaluates the syntactic one. The main issues raised in this chapter are outlined in Section 3.4.

3.2 The informational trend

This section offers a chronological scrutiny of the following informational PS accounts:

a. Weil (1884), who, despite not being a "member" of the PS, inspired many of their views (Section 3.2.1);
b. Mathesius (1939, 1942, 1947, 1961) (Section 3.2.2);
c. the theory of *communicative dynamism* (CD), proposed by Firbas (1957, 1964, 1974, 1992) (Section 3.2.3); and
d. CD adapted to a *functional-generative framework*, as basically proposed by Dahl (1974b, c, 1976, 1987) and Sgall (1972, 1974, 1975; Sgall et al. 1973, 1980, 1986; Benešová & Sgall 1973; Hajicová & Sgall 1975) (Sections 3.2.4 and 3.2.5).

3.2.1 H. Weil

The ultimate source for the treatments of FSP phenomena in the PS is Weil's (1844) *De L'ordre des mots dans les langues anciennes comparées aux langues modernes*. In this work Weil tried to demonstrate that word order is not only affected by syntactic constraints, but also by the psychological factors involved in interaction between speaker, listener and context in the act of communication. Accordingly, Weil (1884: 29) made a distinction between the *objective movement*, expressed by syntactic relations, and the *natural subjective movement* of thought, that is, a movement from a *point of departure* (*point de départ*), or "the ground upon which the two intelligences meet", which carries known information to both utterer and addressee, towards the *goal of discourse* (*but du discours*), which denotes new information and constitutes the part that develops the statement. This natural movement could also be *pathetic* (*l'ordre pathétique*), in which case messages proceeded from their goal, or unknown information, towards their point of departure, or the knowledge shared by the interlocutors. Messages beginning with a co-ordination in time and/or space or the notion of existence (e.g. *Il y avait un roi*) were regarded as either having no starting point at all or as having an abstract notion (existence, etc.) as the realization of this function (ibid.: 33).

In addition, Weil put forward the theory that languages evolved from showing a dual (syntactic and subjective) movement into a single, or syntactic, one in discourse. His rationale was that the subjective movement prevailed over the objective one in ancient free word order languages such as Latin, so that the *first* lexical item, regardless of its syntactic function, was identified with the point of departure of the sentence (e.g. *Romulus, Rome*, and the idea of founding in *Idem Romulus Romam condidit, Hanc urbem condidit Romulus, Condidit Romam Romulus* (ibid.: 29–30)). By contrast, modern languages (especially Romance languages) would have gradually adapted their objective movement to the subjective flow of ideas in such a way that the point of departure of thought tended to be coded as the grammatical *Subject*, regardless of whether it comes first, medially or finally in the clause.[43] As a result, sequences with no initial Subject, such as those displaying the phenomenon of *inversion*, were regarded by Weil as instances of the natural order showing "the most animated syntax" (id. 37).

Weil's perceptions, however, need to be taken with some caution because no co(n)textual evidence is supplied as to how to: (a) determine what should be taken as given or new information, (b) elicit the factors involved in placing one before the other, or (c) explain why some modern languages show the "unnatural" VSX pattern. Rather, Weil considers sentences in isolation, supplying formal, instead of functional accounts. Moreover, many of Weil's observations seem to be rather *ad hoc*, and with "combining" overtones, as they vary from theory to practice, from one chronological stage to another and from one language to another, without proper justification. The "point of departure" is first identified with given information, regardless of its position or syntactic function. Then it becomes the first lexical item, whatever its informational and syntactic status may be. And later it is coded as the Subject of the sequence, whether it conveys given or new information or comes initially, medially or finally. Obviously, the three criteria do not always identify the same item(s) as point of departure (and thereupon the goal of discourse). But no explanation is provided as to whatever relationships there may be (if any) between/among these three criteria, or about the profitability of distinguishing a *point de départ* from a *but du discours*.

In short, as remarked by Adjémian (1978: 259), Weil did not develop the means to test his intuitions, probably, because these were not conceived as empirically testable hypotheses about language structure, but as descriptive devices useful for understanding the stylistic factors in texts and orations. All in all, however, Weil should be given proper credit for laying the foundations for a theory of information structure or information packaging. He not only showed that both word order and the accentual characteristics of the sentence are intimately connected and influenced by discourse structure; but he also singled out four features that would characterise subsequent approaches to Theme/Topic:

a. to represent one of the two communicative units of the sentence, i.e. the point of departure (as opposed to the goal of discourse);
b. to bear known information (while the goal marks what is unknown);

c. to be thought and expressed before the goal; and
d. to be usually coded by the syntactic function of Subject.

3.2.2 V. Mathesius

Inspired by Weil's natural subjective movement, Mathesius (1939) defined the principle of *Functional Sentence Perspective* (PFSP) as the tendency of utterances to display a Given-before-New array of information and to consist of two communicative units: a *Theme* (*základ*), or "that which is known or at least obvious in the given situation, and from which the speaker proceeds" and a *Rheme* (*jádro*)[44] representing "that which the speaker states about [...] the Theme of the utterance" (1939: 234; cited by Firbas 1964: 268–277, n. 4). Mathesius called the PSFP, illustrated in (48) below (Mathesius 1961: 83), the *objective*, *hearer-oriented* organisation on the assumption that it reflected the movement of thought which eased the information processing of sequences:

(48) Byl jednou | jeden král. | A ten král | mel dva syny.
                    Rheme   Theme   Rheme
'Once upon a time there was a king. The king had two sons.'

Besides the PFSP, and evoking Weil's "pathetic" movement, Mathesius (1961: 156) also recognised a "subjective" movement of human thought, placing the New (Rheme)-before the Given (Theme), in which case "the speaker pays no regard to the hearer, starting with what is most important for himself", as shown in (49) (ibid.: 84):

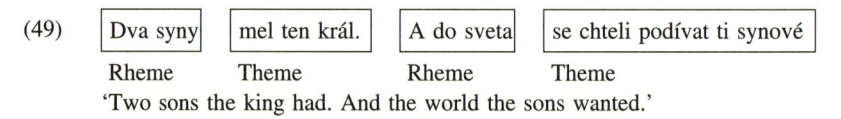

(49) Dva syny | mel ten král. | A do sveta | se chteli podívat ti synové
         Rheme   Theme   Rheme   Theme
'Two sons the king had. And the world the sons wanted.'

And again following Weil's intuitions, Mathesius affirmed that, while (relatively) flexible word order languages complied very easily with the PFSP, (relatively) fixed word order languages did so more restrictedly, their organising criterion being grammar.

Undoubtedly, Mathesius takes a step forward in the functional account of communicative categories and languages. However, his arguments seem to be undermined by the same deficiencies that also pervaded Weil's perceptions. First, Mathesius claims that SVO is the "natural" word order, but he does not comment upon the existence of other word order language types (viz. SXV, VSX; Vennemann 1974), which, according to his explanations, would adhere to an "unnatural" word order (Francis 1966: 149). Neither does he give an explanation of why new information can be placed before given information, if that is not the way in which our ideas flow.

Secondly, Mathesius's analyses show "combining" overtones because he without distinction uses givenness and sentence position, two not necessarily coinciding criteria, to identify the concern of an utterance. Occasionally, in (1939: 171, 1947: 235) Mathesius comments that the notions *point of departure* (*Východisté*), what is being commented upon (*Téma*), and foundation of the message (*základ*), are not necessarily identical. But from 1961 onwards, he returns to the practice he had already chosen in 1939: the term *východiste* is dropped altogether and the terms *Téma* and *základ* (translated as *basis* by Vachek) are synonymously used as cover-terms for: (a) point of departure and given information and (b) the concern of the message. As a consequence, in most of Mathesius's analyses, the category of Theme is described as a *given referential entity* and all-new or thetic sentences as unanalysable or themeless.[45] But this identification runs into two contradictions. The first involves those Themes that designate *new* referential entities (usually at the beginning of narrations) such as (50) below, which Mathesius explains by resorting to the *ad hoc* explanation that the criterion of initial position takes precedence over that of givenness.

(50) | V jedné zemi | panoval král ktéri ... |
Theme Rheme
'In a country there governed a king who ...'

Yet it seems that in instances of the pathetic movement such as (49) above, with a New(Rheme)-before-Given(Theme) organisation, the reverse is the case, in other words, that it is givenness, not position, that determines the thematic or rhematic status of an item. It follows that sentence initial position and givenness are neither simultaneous nor obligatory features of Theme and that Mathesius is inconsistent in simultaneously invoking such criteria in his (1939: 234) definition of the term. Likewise, accepting the existence of "themeless" or "unanalysable" strings contradicts Mathesius's suggestion that messages are materialised and perceived in a linear way, flowing from a point of departure, "a notion that naturally presents itself", towards a goal. According to this hypothesis, all messages should implicitly or explicitly be endowed with a "point of departure" (whether it be the concern of the message or the constituent uttered first) and a "goal" (i.e. the "place" towards which our ideas flow), whatever their referential and informational status may be.

A third and last weakness lies in that Mathesius alludes to the notions of context and Giv$_R$ to identify FSP categories, but his analyses turn out to be virtually subjective because, paradoxically enough, they disregard all contextual domains (viz. the (co)text, the context of situation and the social context) overlooking the intricacies associated with these dimensions (Section 2.3).

3.2.3   J. Firbas

The theory of *communicative dynamism* (CD) was devised to bridge the theoretical gaps opened up by Weil or Mathesius: (a) the treatment of "themeless", "unanalysable" or "groundless" clauses, (b) the possibility that either givenness or sentence position by themselves could identify the Theme or Rheme of a message, and (c) the analysis of decontextualised examples of fundamentally written language. Roughly, CD argues that any linguistic expression (usually independent verbal sentences, but also elliptical sequences and units of lower ranks such as subordinate clauses, phrases, morphemes, submorphemic units, etc.) may constitute a *communicative field* or a *subfield* over which different degrees of "communicative dynamism" are distributed by speakers, pushing the communication forward, as it were, or contributing towards the development of the communication.[46] The "communicative dynamism" of sentence elements is derived from the interplay of three different factors: (a) the *semantic factor*; (b) the *factor of linear modification*; and (c) the *contextual factor*.

The semantic factor assigns degrees of CD in relation to: (a) the logico-semantic pattern of a given sequence; (b) the semantic burden of its constituents; and (c) the syntactic function they fulfil. This factor suggests that messages may present two communicative patterns: the *Presentation Scale*, in (51), or the *Quality Scale*, in (52), corresponding to the thetic-categorical distinction. Messages displaying the Presentation Scale are characterised as introducing a participant in discourse (Ph), i.e. generally the Subject (Agent or affected/effected Goal), towards which the message is oriented and which therefore conveys new information. Alternatively, messages abiding by the Quality Scale ascribe a Quality, Sp-elements or FSP-elements (conveying new information) to the B element, i.e. a context-dependent participant.

(51)   **CD Presentation Scale**
Set(ting) (usually an optional adverbial)–*Pr*(esentation of Phenomenon) (the finite component of the verb) (Pr) (the verb)–*Ph*(enomenon)

(52)   **CD Quality Scale**
Set(ting)–*B*(earer of quality) (usually the Subject)–*AofQ* (Ascriber of a Quality) (copulative verb)/*Q*(uality) (non-copulative verb)–*Sp*(ecification) (Object)–*Fsp*(Further Specification) (Complement).

In the absence of context-independent competitors, the semantic factor also assigns degrees of CD to both word classes and syntactic roles. In the first case, substantives may be assigned a low or a high degree of CD, while verbs are intermediate or highly dynamic. Attributive adjectives on the other hand are considered as more dynamic than predicative ones; initial *-ly* adverbs as exceeding the finite verb in CD; and sentence adverbs as showing an intermediate degree of CD irrespective of sentence position, while pronouns, articles, conjunctions and prepositions, unless contrastive, are rendered non-dynamic. Likewise, decreasing degrees of CD are assigned to syntactic roles as follows: *Complement > Object > Specification* (i.e. obligatory adverbial amplifications of the semantic content of verbs) *> Predicate*. The implication is that Complements are most dynamic because they "develop" the meaning of Subject, Object and Predicate; Objects are more dynamic than Specifications because they "develop" the meaning of Predicate, and so on.

Turning to the second factor, the term *linear modification* is borrowed from Bolinger (1952: 1125), but the concept resembles Mathesius's PFSP, the EFP and the EWP (see Section 2.3.1). It is described as the universal principle by which utterance elements "follow each other according to the amount (degree) of the communicative dynamism they convey, starting with the lowest and gradually passing on to the highest" (Firbas 1962: 136). Accordingly, if two elements follow each other, the one occurring later is assigned the higher degree of CD.

The contextual factor refers to the *recoverability* of items (i.e. Giv_R). But, if Weil or Mathesius handled this notion intuitively, without actually considering the context, in CD recoverability refers to information that irrespective of sentence position is retrievable from the immediately *relevant preceding context* or from the immediately *relevant situational context*. In this connection, Firbas (1986: 67) claims that, on examining the immediately relevant context of sentences, CD also accounts for the communicative structure of the paragraph and for text progression as a whole, a line of research pursued by Deyes (1978), Golková (1987) Dusková (1985), to mention but a few.

The semantic factor, the factor of linear modification and the contextual factor interact in a hierarchical way yielding the *interpretative arrangement*, or communicative importance, of sentence elements, which may be lowered, if affected by context-dependence, or changed, if affected by sentence position. Pace Boguslawski (1977: 203) or Szwedek (1986: 64), who qualify this interpretative arrangement as *sesqui-partitional* or as *tripartitional*, Firbas (1974: 25, 1989, 1992: 97) insists that it is essentially *bipartitional*. Theme (Th) is interpreted along relational-semantic lines, i.e. "what the message is about", as already suggested by Weil or Mathesius, but now it is addressed as the foundation-laying element(s) of the interpretative arrangement carrying the *lowest degree* of CD, which, crucially, "need not necessarily convey known information or such as can be gathered from the verbal or situational context", as implied by relational-informational approaches (Firbas 1966: 272; 1986: 42, 54; 1992: 212–3; Uhlířová 1974: 209–10). Rheme (Rh), in turn, refers to the element(s) conveying the *highest degree* of CD towards which the development of the communication within a distributional field is perspectivised. In between, *transitional element*(s) link these two functions. The qualification "starting point" is intentionally excluded from these definitions because "[t]he described interplay of means of FSP rules out the possibility of permanently linking up certain degrees of CD within certain positions within the linear arrangement, for example, Theme proper with the beginning [...] Rheme proper with the end, of the sentence" (Firbas 1972: 82).

Influenced by Svoboda's (1981, 1983) work, Firbas remarks that the notion "degrees" implies that communicative categories are not *discrete*, but rather constitute a *scale* of CD with the following values: *Transition Proper* (TrPr), *Transition Proper Oriented* elements (TrPro), *Theme Proper* (ThPr), *Theme Proper Oriented* elements (ThPro), *Diatheme Oriented* elements (DTho), *Diatheme* (DTh), *Rheme Proper oriented* elements (RhPro) and *Rheme Proper* (RhPr).

The function of Th is realized by: (a) context-independent or context-dependent B-elements; (b) Set-elements; and (c) intransitive finite verbs (to the exclusion of the TMEs (Time/Manner exponents)) accompanying a context-independent Subject in the absence of a Setting. These items act as *Diathemes* (DTh) if they convey (a) irretrievable information or (b) information that has occurred in the immediately relevant section of the non-thematic layer. But they behave as *Theme Proper* (ThPr) if occurring in the thematic layer of the immediately relevant section. Thus, thematic functions devise a scale, in which the bottom end is taken by ThPr and the upper end by DTh, between them stand Theme Proper Oriented elements (ThPro) and Diatheme Oriented elements (DTho). In addition, thematic elements establish a *hyperthematic string* when several distributional fields share the same context-dependent thematic layer (with the exception of the initial element, which may be context-independent). The following extract (from Firbas 1992: 80) illustrates this scalar analysis of thematic elements (*d* standing for context-dependent information):

(53)   In a steamer chair (Set, DTho), under a manuka tree that grew in the middle of the front grass patch (Set, Dtho), Linda Burnell (B, DTh) dreamed the morning away. (2) She (B, d, TrPr) did nothing. (3) She (B, d, ThPr) looked up at the dark, close dry leaves of the manuka, at the chinks of blue between, (4) and now and again (Set, DTh) a tiny yellowish

lower dropped on her (Set, ThPr). (5) Pretty — (6) yes, <u>if you held one of those flowers on the palm of your hand and looked at it closely</u> (Set, DTh), it (B, d, THPr) was an exquisite small thing. (7) <u>Each pale yellow</u> (B, DTh) petal shone as if each was the careful work of a loving hand. (8) <u>The tiny tongue in the centre</u> (B, DTh) gave it (Set, d, ThPr) the shape of a bell. (9) And <u>when you turned it over</u> (Set, DTh) the outside was a deep bronze colour. (10) But <u>as soon as they flowered</u> (Set, DTh), <u>they</u> (B, d, ThPr) fell and were scattered. [my underlining]

In turn, the Rheme Proper (RhPr) may be expressed by the: (a) Ph-element (if non-initial); (b) the Sp-elements; and (c) the FSP-elements. The other members within the rhematic string show a gradual rise in CD towards the RhPr, in accordance with the linear modification principle. And Transition Proper (TrP) elements serve as a link and as a boundary between the Theme and the Rheme, and may be realized by: (a) invariably the categorical exponents of the verb (i.e. markers of tense, mood, modality, person, number, gender, voice (TMEs)); (b) more often than not, the notional component of the verb; and (c) the elements performing the AofQ-function, the Pr-function and the Q-element of questions. By contrast, Transition Proper Oriented elements (TrPro) are "oriented" towards the TrP through their temporal and modal features and correspond to sentence adverbs or adverbials expressing indefinite time (e.g. *usually*, *naturally*, *of course*).

This scalar perspective allows CD supporters to deny the existence of "themeless", "groundless" or "unanalysable" sequences. Messages with no overt Theme (e.g. *An excellent idea, Entrance, English Department*) or without transitional elements (e.g. *All a mistake*) are analysed in two ways: either retrieving their Th and TrP from an extralinguistic or a linguistic contextual referent, or as consisting of phrasal subfields, with their Heads acting as Themes and their Modifiers as Rhemes. Likewise, thetic sentences like *It rains, There is a man, A man came* derive their interpretative arrangement from the Presentation Scale. They are said to consist of: (a) Rh, the Ph-element(s) (viz. *rain, a man*); (b) Tr, the TMEs (Pr); and (c) Th (viz. *It, There, A man*), which carries the lowest degree of CD on account of the semantic factor (usually expressed by a proform) or as a result of the principle of linear modification (Firbas 1983: 107ff.).

The above represent the CD categories as rendered by non-prosodic factors. But in speech the interpretative arrangement is determined by the *distribution of prosodic prominence* (PP). In most languages PP is *non re-evaluating*, that is to say, it coincides with the non-prosodic interpretative arrangement, because: (a) both abide by the principle of linear modification and therefore point at the same constituent as RhPr (54a); (b) there is an automatic placing of the intonation centre (IC) on the last stressed communicative unit within the field (e.g. *A boy came into the 'room)*; and (c) the speaker normally selects diathematic items (Subject or Adverbials) as the locus of the intonation centre (54b):

(54) a. It should be 'good.
ThrPr + +; Tr 'RhPr   Firbas (1992: 149).
b. The ˋpoor old ^banger /will col'lapse under the 'strain
  ˋ ^DTh/+ '+ ; Tr   'RhPr   (ibid.: 158)

Less commonly, PP is *re-evaluating*, in other words, the prosodic and non-prosodic distribution of degrees of CD do not coincide. The effect is that rhematic elements are *shaded* to a diathematic or to a DTho status, because the IC falls on, or *deshades*, one of the following items: (a) thematic elements (viz. pronominal Subjects or Objects, indefinite Adverbials (e.g. *ever, soon,* etc.), (b) auxiliary verbs, (c) finite verbs expressing emotions (*love, wish, hope,* etc.), (d) emotive predicative adjectives (*sure, sorry, glad,* etc.), (v) intensives (e.g. nouns, adjectives or adverbs expressing a high grade of a quality or a high frequency of a emotion, such as *excellent, always, awfully,* etc.). Prosodic re-evaluation is considered to fulfil primarily an *emotive* function, usually repeating some element (55a), presenting irretrievable information as known information, the so-called *to-be-in-the-know-effect*, (55b), or emphasising either the time, frequency or quality of a phenomenon (55c), or the polarity of the message (55d):

(55) a. [He ˏrang up from /Manchester!] — ^Manchester! [He'd ˋhave to be ^quick/ to ˋget to St. Albans in ˏhalf an ˅hour. ¯It's a ˏhundred and ˏfifty ˋmiles or ˏmore]. [Manchester, Th > RhPr] (ibid. 175)
b. [It's ˋOK for our ˏholiday in ˅Skye, ˏMarjorie. Mum ˅heard from ˏCousin ˏJeannie/ this ˋmorning.] But 'she'd pre ˏfer the ˋlast two ˏweeks in ˏAugust/ rather than the /middle two. [last, Set > RhPr] (ibid.: 177)
c. It'll ˋsoon get to ˏnumber ˏone in the ˏcharts [soon, TrPro > RhPr] (ibid.: 163)
d. You ˋare mean, Simon [are, TrPro > RhPr] (id.)

Other minor uses of re-evaluating PP are to look for a *recapitulatory*, or *summarising*, effect (56) or to remove some *ambiguity*, or *potentiality* (57).

(56) [You /keep such a ˏlot of ˋrubbish in your ˏbag ... — But /this is ˋserious. I really ˋcan't find my ˏnotecase.] It ˋisn't in my ^bag, [I'm ˋsure]. [isn't, TrPro > RhPr] (ibid.: 174)
(57) [I was /talking to Mrs ˋJones/ at the ˋpaper ˏshop/ the ˏother /day [at the paper shop Spec and the other day Set] (ibid.: 181)

Despite its valuable contributions to increasing the explanatory potential of PS accounts (e.g. the analysis of hitherto "unanalysable" sequences as well as written vs. spoken discourse), on closer inspection CD opens up to controversy.[47] For one thing, although it argues for a dynamic, or functional, account of Theme and communicative categories as a result of the interplay of three different factors, semantic, linear and contextual, it turns out that the assignment of such categories is aprioristic, formal and paradigmatic, rather than belonging to the syntagmatic oppositions established by the contextualisation of messages. Let us take the case of Theme, for example. We have seen that thematic status is categorically bound by the logico-semantic factor to B-element(s), Set-element(s), and intransitive finite verbs. This ascription makes one wonder, as Francis (1966: 149) does:

> [o]n what grounds, for example, it is asserted that "provided both the verb and its object convey new information, the object carries a higher degree of CD than the verb regardless of the positions they occupy within the sentence [...].

But Theme is similarly rendered as contextually-bound information (Giv_R), despite Firbas's (1995: 221–2) remark that CD is neither "combining", because a context-independent element can be thematic, nor "separating", because context dependence is not separated from thematicity, nor context independence from rhematicity or thematicity. This identification raises two issues. One is that if messages have to be about their relevant contexts, as the contextual factor suggests, how can communication develop freely towards the attainment of a communicative goal? And more importantly, another problem is posed as to how to determine what counts as retrievable or irretrievable information if no precise account is given of what to be taken as *relevant*, *contextual*, or *retrievable* (cf. Svoboda 1981: 88–9), nor are the problems associated with that kind of givenness solved (Section 2.3).

Firbas (1992: 24) argues that there is no need to answer these questions, for one (or more) of the three factors, semantic, linear or contextual, always remains to remove any possible ambiguity. But this assumption leads to a vicious circle. In order to identify retrievable information we have to go back to the logico-semantic factor, which paradigmatically confers thematic status to B-element(s), Set-element(s) or intransitive finite verbs. But this factor is, in turn, affected by the factor of linear modification (positionally-bound to initial position) and superseded by the distribution of PP in speech (lack of prominence). This practice implies that in the end it is PP that ultimately determines the communicative relevance of items, which reveals the interpretative arrangement to be intonationally bound and turns the label "degrees of CD" into a misnomer (Szwedek 1986: 34; Lötscher 1983: 72–73). Firbas appears to agree with this observation when admitting that as "rhematicity is opposed to non-rhematicity, no distinction is made between thematicity and transitionalness, let alone between various degrees of thematicity or transitionalness" (1992: 203). One could then conclude that the notion "degrees of CD", the major innovation of CD, is seriously questioned, despite the efforts made to demonstrate its profitability (Firbas 1975: 322; Svoboda 1974; Duszak 1983).

In addition, as Szwedek (1986: 64) observes, CD lacks methodological coherence in that categories are not explained within the same parameters. For instance, while Th and Rh are defined primarily with regard to the immediately relevant context, Tr and TrPro are described without invoking contextual factors: the first one links the Th and the Rheme of a message, while the latter expresses indefinite temporal and modal features. Besides, the definitions of communicative functions in general are not accurate or systematic enough. Let us take, for instance, the concept of Diatheme. It can be: (a) the thematic element carrying the highest degree of CD (Svoboda 1981: 5); (b) the temporary centre of the scene, the newly introduced or just chosen quality bearer (ibid.: 42); (c) what was called "the centre of the Theme" (ibid.: 5, 42); (d) whatever is expressed by such devices as ellipsis, pronouns, redundant means, etc. (ibid.: 24, 47). These four descriptions do not seem to involve exactly synonymous definitions (nor of the same type), nor to identify the same items as diathematic.

To conclude, one has the impression that CD leaves the analyst with a batch of different types of Themes, Transitions and Rhemes. These categories are not only difficult to determine, but they also make it hard to say what a text (or a sentence) is about and how this category affects text structure and the grammar of a given language. Furthermore, the profitability of the overall theory remains rather questionable if, as Firbas (1992: 218) responds to Keijsper (1985: 71), it does not attempt to show that the grammatical organisation of sentences (and texts) is the consequence of the fact that some elements are Theme and others Rheme, but simply concludes that some elements are more communicatively dynamic than others. And if this is the case, some questions readily spring to mind. How is it that context independent elements can have any "communicative importance" at all? Is this measure not relative to the context? Or put another way, why should we use the expression "communicative importance" or "communicative dynamism" of linguistic elements, if these turn out to be *a priori* claims based mainly on syntax?

3.2.4   Ö. Dahl

Dahl makes a distinction between the *Topic–Comment structure* (TCS) of utterances, treating the given-new contrast referentially (cognitive status of discourse referents), and their *Focus-Background* pattern (FBP), invoking relational givenness-newness (information update in the speakers' minds) (see Section 2.3.2). TCS consists of two parts, the *Topic*, i.e. where we name or define a set of entities or an individual entity as a definite expression conveying given information (either recoverable from the preceding co(n)text or known to the participants), and the *Comment*, which is a propositional function "predicated" about this set or individual (Dahl 1974b: 75). *Focus* on the other hand is realized prosodically (in English by main sentential stress) and is opposed to Background (information), which relates to the concept of *presupposition*, i.e. a set of propositions associated with a statement, the truth of which is presupposed by both speaker/writer and hearer/reader.

Dahl notes that, although there is often a correlation between Topic and Background, on the one hand, and Comment and Focus, on the other, these are not coterminous concepts. Focus and Comment represent two distinctive types of newness: Comment adds some new information to the development of discourse, while Focus bears sentential stress and may be placed on the Topic or on the Comment. Example (58) (Dahl 1974b: 2 (3)) below shows that these four functions may not coincide [my bold type]:

(58) What does John drink? John   drinks **beer**.
                          Topic   Comment
                          Background Focus

Likewise, two sequences may share the same presupposition, but differ in Topic, or vice versa, as illustrated in (59a, b) below (Dahl 1974b: 6 (15), (16)), which share the presupposition "that the earth is round":

(59) a. John   realized that the earth is round
        Topic   Comment
     b. That the earth is round   was realized by John
        Topic   Comment

Furthermore, Dahl argues that, while all utterances have a Focus, thetic sequences neither exhibit a TCS, nor imply a presupposition. They derive their TCA from their SR by *direct insertion*, that is, from the logico-semantic pattern of the process to be expressed (i.e. the sentence nucleus). In contrast, categorical statements consist of a Comment, described as an *open sentence*, or a quality-ascribing proposition that contains one or more variables, or NG descriptions. The bound, or topical, variable is the Topic and occupies topical, or initial, position. Accordingly, in (1974c: 75) Dahl proposes (60) as the SR of the categorical statement *My brothers are drunkards*:

(60)   LF = D structure: Let A = {x/x is my brother}. Then, for every x such that x is in A, x is a drunkard.

Summarising, Dahl (1974b: 1) distinguishes *neutral descriptions*, involving thetic interpretations (61d), from *categorical statements*, (61a), (61b) and (61c), where something (*is running*) is said "about" the Topic (*John*): (61a) is *not* emphatic, (61b) *is* emphatic, and (61c) presupposes that "someone is running":

(61)   a.   Speaking of John, he is running (Theme)
       b.   John is running, but Mary is not (contrast)
       c.   Who is running? John, is running (exhaustive listing)
       d.   Oh, look! John is running! (neutral description)

Going by Dahl's examples in (58)–(61) (with the exception of (61d)), one has the impression that the criterion of definiteness (and thus of boundness) is abandoned altogether — importantly, without solving the problems raised by that kind of givenness (Section 2.3) — and that Topic is identified with Subject without properly justifying in which aspect(s) the two types of categories are different in order not to be redundant. Indeed, Dahl suggests a major revision of the open sentence hypothesis, arguing that, in order for successful communication to be guaranteed, the existence of a Topic must always be presupposed and, therefore, all statements have to be interpreted as categorical. As a result, instead of two alternative logico-semantic representations, Dahl suggests that the primitive structure of sentences marks the syntactic function of Subject as the item chosen to be Topic, which invalidates the distinction in (61) between thetic (61d) and categorical statements (61a-c). Non-Subject Topics represent a "marked" choice, resulting from the operation of "subject downgrading" or "detopicalisation" rules (such as *There insertion*, etc.), which deprive Subjects of their ordinary privileges: initial position in the sentence, agreement with the verb, being eligible for such operations as Subject Raising, etc.

Then it turns out that in the end Topic becomes whatever syntactic function occupies initial position, a realization criterion allegedly barred from this "autonomous" approach. Furthermore, the model suggests that the surface structure of messages is a reflection of the hierarchical organisation of the underlying structure. Quite contradictorily, however, Dahl has to invoke transformations to derive those surface structures that do not abide by the underlying SR, admitting that that "it is rather hard to state the rules that we would have instead" (1974b: 79). And in (1974a: 20) he points out that the generative-functional proposal provides an explanation for some data only, which renders its supporting evidence and therefore the theory itself not very strong. Probably, behind this weakness lies one paradox, namely: to assume that Topic (Comment,

Focus, or Background) and communicative categories can be formalised into abstract logico-semantic relations and, at the same time, be characterised and expressed as surface structure, or discourse, phenomena, in terms of given and new information.

3.2.5   P. Sgall

Sgall and his associates use two criteria to discern the *Topic–Comment Articulation* (TCA) of a sequence: (a) *contextual boundness* (CB) (resembling Firbas's contextual factor) and (b) *communicative importance* (CI) (based on Firbas's semantic factor). CB renders topical items *contextually bound*, boundness being interpreted in terms of *activation* (G_S) and *shared knowledge* (Giv_K) (Sgall et al. 1980: 155). In other words, topical information is identified with: (a) *foregrounded*, or *activated*, element(s) in a given sequence and (b) the *presupposition*, that is, the rest of the stock of shared knowledge, which is not activated by the given situation itself, but only in the case of a respective quotation or mentioning in the discourse. The mentioning of an element of the stock of shared knowledge brings this element into the foreground of the stock, its foregrounding shading away step by step, though retaining a higher degree of activation than contextually bound elements, known from the situation only. Sgall concludes that the most activated element in the bound segment of the sentence occupies initial position and behaves as the *Topic Proper*. The Q-test is proposed to elicit this category as follows:

> In simple cases we can say immediately on the basis of a possible question [...] which part of the sentence is the topic and which is the comment: the elements that are necessarily present in the question belong to the topic; those that cannot be in the question belong to the comment; the elements that may, but need not necessarily be present in the question belong, according to some views, to the so-called transition. (Sgall et al. 1973: 29)

Two further communicative functions are distinguished, i.e. *Boundness Juncture* (BJ) and *Focus* (or *Comment*). BJ sets up the boundary between Topic and Focus, usually immediately before or after the verb. And Focus signals what is presented as new information, which need not in fact be new information. The scope of Focus may be *neutral*, over the whole sentence, and *marked*, in the other cases (Sgall 1974: 41; Wierzbicka's 1975: 84), establishing the following maxims:

a. in an SR where no participant is contextually bound, for every pair of participants P_j, P_k it holds that if there is a permissible Focus including P_k and not including P_j then S ("deep structure") (P_j, P_k) holds;

b. if C ("linear ordering") (Pi, V) holds, then Pi is contextually bound and outside the Focus (i.e. in the Topic); and alternatively, if C (V, Pi) holds, the Pi is non-bound and included in the Focus; and
c. if Pj and Pk are included in the Focus, then C (Pj, Pk) holds if S (Pj, Pk) also holds.

It must be noted that, while Dahl separated Comment from Focus, Sgall equates these two functions, apparently assuming that presented-as-salient information identifies what is said about the Topic. Besides, Sgall observes that Topic and Focus do not represent co-relational concepts. In other words, the existence of one of these functions is not conditioned by the existence of the other — whether overtly realized or not. Thus, messages may be topicless, i.e. those containing no contextually bound material, but they must always contain a Focus.

In addition, CI establishes the hierarchy in (62) in left-to-right decreasing topicality (Sgall 1974: 33, 37; Sgall et al. 1973: 33):

(62) **Sgall's CI hierarchy**
actor-time/place/manner/instrument-dative-object (of the type ("about what")-objective (patients)-direction-objective complement.

(62) implies that the verb and its accompanying participants usually constitute the bound segment, or Topic, (with the Subject usually as *Theme Proper*), while adverbials represent the non-bound segment, or Focus. Sgall (1974: 41) formulates this factor as follows:

(63) $((a^b_{k1}), ..., (a^b_{kj}), V, (a_{km}), ..., (a_{kn}))$,

where b = bound element, k = CI, $1 \le j$, $j + 1 = m \le n$, $1 \le k_i \le n$, $k_i = k_p$ iff $i = p$, $1 \le i$, $p \le n$. This formula displays the *unmarked* TCA, that is, the (FSP) Given-before-New organisation, which normally occurs in sentences with no contextually bound segments or those in which contextually non-bound elements have a higher degree of CI than the contextually bound elements. Alternatively, *contrastive TCA* takes place when a bound element has a higher CI than some other element that is contextually non-bound, as in *An apple was given to a boy by CHARLES* (Sgall 1974: 28), where the Direct Object has a lower degree of CD, but a higher degree of CI than the Actor. For these cases Sgall reserves the term *topicalisation*. Thus, Sgall (1972: 3–4) distinguishes three layers of TCA:

a. the SR level, the basic distribution of CD determined by the semantic structure of the sentence;
b. the DS level (*deep structure level*), which renders constituents as co(n)textually Known or Unknown as a result of the topicalisation of some of them;

c. the SS level (*surface structure level*), to which belong cases of contrast, or a correction of some misunderstanding concerning a part of the sentence (e.g. slip of the tongue, a fault of perception, an actual error) (cf. Hajicova and Sgall 1975: 24–5).

To relate these three levels, SR, DS and SS, Sgall (ibid.: 11–2) proposes the two rules in (64) be incorporated in the transformational component of GT, or in the transductive component of a "functional" generative transcription:

(64) (A) (Optional) If $i>j$ and x_i precedes y_j, exchange the positions of x_i and y_j, assigning to the head noun of y_j a special mark which can be turned into 'intonation centre' (optionally?) by the phonological component;

(B) (Obligatory, after A if it is present) If $i>j$ and x_i precedes y_j, replace the verb V by $V_{i,j}$, place x_i into the position of x_i, place y_j, into the position of y_j, and assign to the head noun of x_i a special mark indicating that it is an inverted participant.

The similarities between Sgall's tripartitional analysis of Topic–Boundness Juncture-Focus and Firbas's Theme, Transition and Rheme seem clear. But, if CD invokes the actual linear arrangement of items as a determinant of the communicative relevance of Topic and the other categories, Sgall and his associates claim to disregard this factor and invoke just two criteria: (a) the CI of the constituents of the sentence nucleus and (b) their CB, described from a psycholinguistic point of view (*degrees of activation*, Giv_S), from a contextual point of view (Giv_K) and also as a *textual pattern* (Giv_R), that is, the tendency to preserve the same Topic for a sequence of sentences, recency of mention, etc.

However, as argued with regard to Dahl's approach, it turns out that Topic is identified syntactically, that is, with initial position. Accordingly, Sgall explains that in sequences like *An apple was given to a boy by CHARLES*, *An apple* represents the Topic, even if it conveys unbound information and a high degree of CI. Several debatable issues emerge from this characterisation. First, although regarded as a type of "deep" semantic relationship, deterministically bound to syntactic functions, TCA is elicited ultimately by invoking the surface linear ordering (C) of elements, in the first place, and contextual factors in the second place. Second, this priority contradicts the claim that TCA is determined by just the CI and the contextual boundness of elements. Third, if initial position identifies Topic, all messages must contain one, even those conveying no bound information, described as topicless by Sgall. Fourth, if initial position expresses the Topic of a sequence, the Q-test is invalidated as criterial to identify topical status for it merely elicits bound information, posing the problems already discussed in Section 2.3.3. Fifth, the maxims (a) and (b) assigning focal scope seem to run into one contradiction: the same SR (Pj, Pk) holds for a permissible Focus including Pk and not including Pj, and for a permissible Focus including both Pj and Pk. And regarding the rules in (58), Sgall (1972: 13) himself recognises that they leave several issues unresolved such as: (a) various types of verbs and the relationship between their participants; (b) questions of local and temporal setting vs. topic proper, problems of contrastive focus; and (c) the borderline between them and more "normal" cases of TCA.

Finally, as in previous PS accounts, Sgall invokes such terms as "contextual boundness" or "text pattern" to determine the Topic of a sequence, but his examples appear without a co(n)text so that no solution is provided for the issues raised by contextual-informational analyses. It seems then that, as noted by Palková and Palek (1978: 221 endnote 5), the problems so far outlined demand a redefinition of the PS generative-functional approach to FSP phenomena from a textual standpoint. In the following section we shall see that Daneš's work on *thematic progressions* makes a valuable contribution in this area.

3.3 The syntactic trend

In principle most PS syntactic analysts interpret "what an individual clause/ message is about" syntactically, i.e. independently from the context, as one of the speaker/writer's options, that "from which the speaker proceeds". As a result, two layers of structure are posited: word order (related to the linear quality of language) and the Given–New contrast (the axis of information). Mathesius's label *základ* ('the foundation of the message') is discarded in order to avoid the "psychologistic" identification of clause-initial position with given information; while the notions of Given–New (information) are dissociated from the category of Theme, which indicates both "what a sentence is about" (Mathesius's *Téma*) and the "point of departure" of the message (Mathesius's *Východisté*), and is identified with clause-initial position.[49]

In what follows we shall review the work by some exponents of this syntactic trend, namely: Trávníček (1937, 1962, 1964, 1987) (Section 3.3.1), Beneš (1959, 1968, 1971) (Section 3.3.2) and Daneš's (1964, 1970a, b, 1978, 1989) research on *Thematic Progression* (TP) (Section 3.3.3).

3.3.1 F. Trávníček

Trávníček's (1962) revision of Mathesius's perceptions originates the syntactic

PS approach. His criticism revolves around the idea that "what a message is about" cannot be assimilated to given information, as proposed in informational PS accounts, because "the concern of messages" is a hierarchically superior notion which may refer to either given or new information, although it tends to be associated with the lowest degrees of CD within a sentence (Trávníček 1987: 143). Besides, disapproving of the "highly psychological" overtones of informational accounts, Trávníček (1964: 268) explains that their narrowed conception compels to talk about anticipatory Themes, about Themes only seemingly conveying known information, and about sentences that have no Theme at all. Instead, Trávníček suggests that Theme is neither the *psychological subject* of utterances nor given information, but their *point of departure*, their *Východisté*, and to identify this category he resorts to the second part of Mathesius's definition, that is, "(...) from which the speaker proceeds" (1964: 165). Trávníček traces a function-to-form line of realization between the relational-semantic interpretation of Theme and the syntactic Theme, claiming that "[...] the Theme of the sentence is borne out by word order, by the front position" (ibid.: 166). Front position, Trávníček adds, is structurally relevant because it links up directly with the *object of thought* (O), i.e. "a section of reality, taken in by the senses or mediatorially given, which the speaker (writer) has in mind and to which the thought refers" (ibid.: 269), proceeds from it and opens the sentence thereby (Mathesius's *základ* or 'the foundation of the message').

With this latter characterisation Trávníček opens up the door to the "psychological" overtones he wanted to avoid. For claiming that Theme "links up" with the *object of thought* amounts to identifying Theme with "what the speaker has in mind". Besides, Trávníček interprets Given and New as recoverable and unrecoverable information, and front position as the realization of the "aboutness" feature of messages, but he does not address the problems inherent in the notion of recoverability (Section 2.3), neither is initial position properly described or empirically attested. For firstly, Trávníček does not specify what should be understood by "clause-initial position". And secondly, he does not demonstrate that the relevance of clause-initial position, if any, consists in marking what a message is about. Nor does he explain whether different initial constituents achieve identical or different communicative functions. The same deficiencies recur in Beneš's work discussed in turn.

3.3.2 E. Beneš

Beneš's work represents a stepping-stone towards the functional analysis of clause-initial position. The category is freed from the "psychologistic" and difficult-to-test overtones provided by the notion "object of thought" and is also dissociated from the informative category of Given and the syntactic function of Subject. Thus, in his (1959: 205–217) discussion of Trávníček's work Beneš proposes to differentiate between *Basis* (*východisko*) and *Theme*, discarding the "aboutness" feature altogether.

Basis is glossed as the "point of departure" of the utterance, "the opening element of the sentence [which] links up the utterance with the context and the situation, selecting from several possible connections one that becomes the starting point, from which the entire further utterance unfolds and in regard to which it is orientated" (ibid.: 216). In its turn, Theme identifies the element(s) carrying the lowest degree of CD within the sentence, linking up the utterance with the context and making the orientation in the text easier by preserving its logical continuity.

Beneš observes that the choice of Basis is not identified with, but related to, that of givenness (or Newness), and that it depends on the textual structure of discourse. Like Trávníček, he (1959, 1968) notes that the Bases of sentences may be thematic or rhematic, although in most cases sentences begin with elements known from the preceding context, usually their Subjects (thus the confusion between Subject, Basis and Theme). But less frequently, Bases can also be realized by constituents of higher communicative value such as expressions of place, time, condition, purpose, cause, etc., which achieve a condensation of the line of thought by preserving its logical continuity or establishing a sharply drawn link with the preceding context (Beneš 1971).

The functional nature of Beneš's account of Basis/Theme admitted, it raises two issues that recur in other studies adopting a syntactic outlook. One is that although Beneš claims to study utterances, he analyses clauses in isolation without fully explaining what should be taken as Given and New. And the other is that it is not clear whether Basis (= initial vs. non-initial position) is a structural (i.e. clausal, phrasal, group) category or whether it establishes a non-structural (discourse/text) pattern. František Daneš takes up this issue when he formulates the theory of *Thematic Progression* (TP) examined in Section 3.3.3.

3.3.3   F. Daneš

The theory of *Thematic Progression* (TP) produces a substantial expansion of the syntactic PS approach (Daneš 1970a, 1974a, 1974b, 1978, 1989; Uhlířová 1977; Nowakowska 1977; Maynard 1986). Moreover, by showing that the relation between thematic and rhematic material in a text does display regular patterns of development, the PS research on TP constitutes a landmark on the road towards text linguistics, as illustrated by parallel investigations within SFG (see Section 4.2

in this study), and by other authors' research such as Givón (1983b, 1988), van Dijk (1980), van Dijk & Kintsch (1983), Hinds (1983) and Silvá Corvalán (1984), to mention but a few. There exists an importance difference, however. In what follows we shall see that most TP analysts adopt a bottom-up approach, focusing on *decoding* strategies on the assumption that the Theme–Rheme structure of smaller units also applies to the larger ones; whereas the majority of text linguists take a top-down stand, concentrating on *encoding* processes, that is to say, on how what a text is about develops throughout the text.

Daneš distinguishes three different types of notions: (a) the idea of "degrees" of *communicative dynamism*; (b) *informational bipartition* (IB); and (c) *communicative articulation* (CA). The concept of "degrees of" communicative dynamism is not really developed in TP. At most it is admitted that givenness is a graded notion and that newly introduced items show a greater degree of newness than recoverable ones.

IB on the other hand invokes Mathesius's division of an utterance into a starting point (S) and a core (C), which, following Marty (1897: 314) and Heger (1982: 91), are described in terms of *communicative relevance* and *shared knowledge* (Giv$_K$). Accordingly, S stands for information that is "derivable or recoverable [...] from the context, situation and the common knowledge of the speaker and listener" (Daneš 1974b: 109). In contrast, the informational core reflects what speaker/writers present as the *new state of affairs*, that is, the aim of their communicative act. In addition, Daneš emphasises that S and C are *relational* notions showing *bi-directional* relevance; that is to say, they represent the Given and the New, respectively: (a) in regard to the preceding context; (b) with respect to each other; and (c) involving the relation between a specific Theme and Rheme (see endnote 28). From this Daneš deduces that all messages have an (optional) S (either overt or implicit) and an (obligatory) C.

Also interpreted from a relational-semantic perspective, CA consists of Theme and Rheme. Rheme states the purpose of communication (the *communicative sense of an utterance*) and is not identified with a particular clause constituent, but represents a relational category that establishes different types of semantic relationships (e.g. cause, purpose, time, etc.) with respect to its corresponding Theme and the embodying text (Daneš 1974b: 124). Theme on the other hand is claimed to express "what one is talking about" (Mathesius's *Téma*) and to provide a "foundation for the development of discourse" (Mathesius's *Východisté*) by signalling the speaker/writer's choice of "the point of departure" of the utterance, a choice endowed with both *perspective* and *prospective* significance (Hausenblas 1964; Daneš 1974b: 113). From a static standpoint, Theme perspectivises a new utterance against the background of a context, whereas from a dynamic point of view, it announces a point of departure for the further development of discourse.

As already noted by other syntactic analysts, Daneš (1974b: 112) remarks that, unless there is good reason for doing otherwise, speaker/writers select their Themes from the Given, although not all Given information behaves thematically. This suggests that it is not the co(n)text that determines, or dictates, the Theme or Rheme of a message, but the speaker. For this reason Daneš decides to analyse the *thematic progression* (TP) of texts, i.e. the principles underlying speakers' thematic choices and the textual patterns they trace constituting "the skeleton of the plot" (Daneš 1974b: 114). Thus, while Firbas explored the *communicative micro-structure* of the utterance, TP sets out to establish the *macro-structure* of the text involving a *network of isotopic relations* (NIR) that are obtained among *discourse subjects* (DS). DSs are characterised as objects, qualities, processes, states, circumstances, etc. that the "speaker has just in mind when applying a nomination (or deictic) unit in the process of text production in order to introduce/present/mention/re-introduce/recall something" (Daneš 1989: 24). Isotopic relations, in turn, exist when a postcedent DS and an antecedent DS are linked by means of a semantic relation of one of the following types: (a) total identity of Dss; (b) partial identity of Dss; and (c) almost subjective associative relations such as similarity/analogy.

TP are classified according to three kinds of criteria expounded in Figure 2, according to which a contact Thematisation (Rh ($Th_i = Rh_{i-1}$)) is distinguished from a distant Thematisation (U ($Th_i = U_{i-n}$; $n > 1$)), and from a Th derived from the immediately preceding Rh, etc.:

The three criteria in Figure 2 bring about three higher order TP-types: (a) *Simple Linear TP*, (b) *TP with a continuous Theme* and (c) *TP with a derived Theme* (Daneš 1970a: 137ff., 1974a: 118ff., 1978: 190ff.). Simple Linear TPs are characterised by the type of chaining in which each R becomes the T of the next

a. Thematisation concerns a preceding — Theme/Rheme
whole Th-Rh nexus (i.e. an utterance U)
sequence of utterances (a text interval)

b. The thematised content component — is taken over (iterated) from preceding context
is derived from a precedent component

c. The thematised — precedes immediately (a *contact* Thematisation)
precedes at a distance (a *distant* Thematisation)

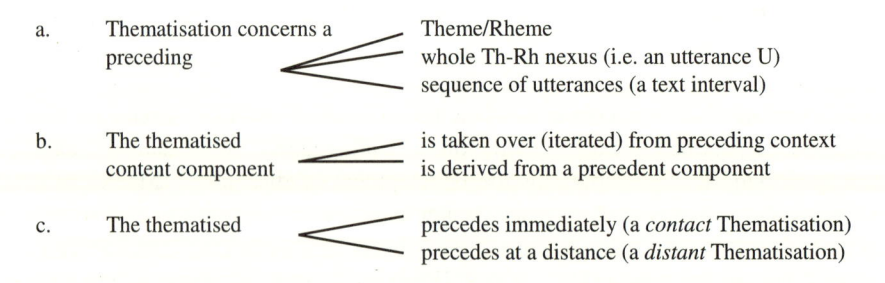

Figure 2. *Daneš's classification criteria of TPs*

Simple linear TP

Text
She said, 'All right. But you must promise two things.
First of all you mustn't eat anyone: it's not allowed.' (SECG02: 34–5)

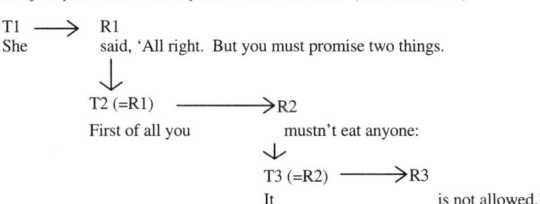

    T1 ⟶ R1
    She   said, 'All right. But you must promise two things.
        ↓
        T2 (=R1) ⟶ R2
        First of all you   mustn't eat anyone:
                ↓
                T3 (=R2) ⟶ R3
                It   is not allowed.'

TP with a continuous (constant) theme

Text
I'd gone to London to do some shopping.
I wanted to get some Christmas presents, and I needed to find some books for my course at college...'.
(SECGO3: 6–9)

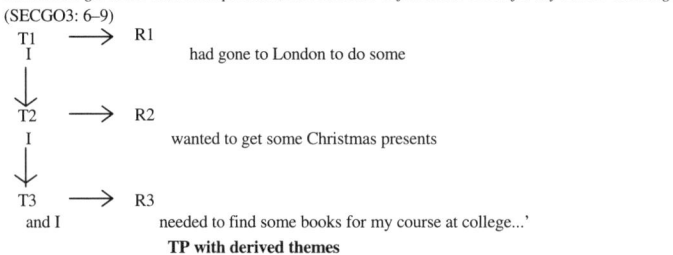

    T1 ⟶ R1
    I   had gone to London to do some
    ↓
    T2 ⟶ R2
    I   wanted to get some Christmas presents
    ↓
    T3 ⟶ R3
    and I   needed to find some books for my course at college...'

TP with derived themes

Text
It was Christmas Eve 1959, and the beginning of another routine flight.
The hostess started preparing the food trays.
A few passengers were trying to get some sleep...' (SECG04: 8–11)

            [T] or hypertheme
        ↙   ↓   ↘
                T3 ⟶ R3
                A few passengers were trying to get some sleep.
    T1 ⟶ R1
    It   was Christmas Eve 1959, and the beginning of another routine flight.
      ↓
    T2 ⟶ R2
    The hostess   started preparing the food trays.

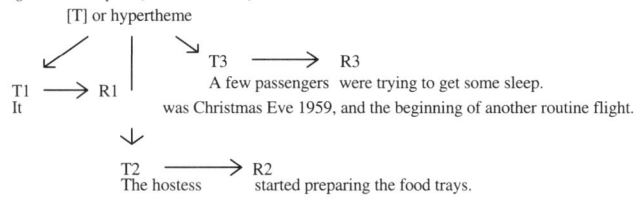

Figure 3. *Daneš's models of thematic progression [my analysis]*

utterance. TPs with a Continuous Theme emerge when one and the same T appears in a series of utterances to which different Rs are linked up. And TPs with a Derived T result when a number of Themes are derived from a higher Theme, or Hypertheme. Figure 3 illustrates these three types of TP with examples taken from the LIBMSEC corpus.

In addition, combinations of higher order TP-types are also recognised in *Expositions of Split Themes* (in Figure 4), for example, where the Themes of

TP with a split rheme

Text

But first, it's worth stressing how the country is dominated by the president, Nicolai Ceausescu. His picture appears everywhere on important occasions, his wife is a member of the top political body, and one of his sons is moving up fast — two others hold important government posts.

(SECA05:23-7)

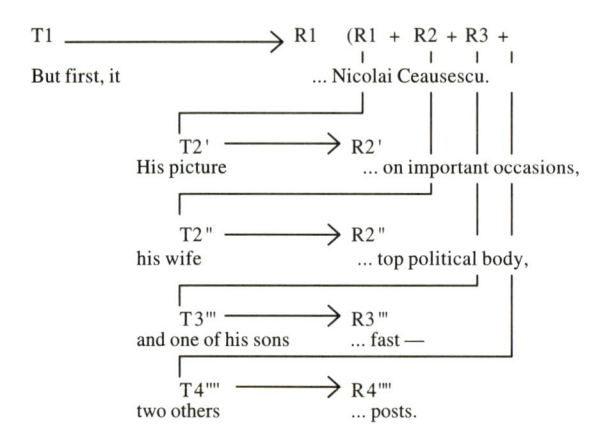

```
T1 ─────────────────→ R1    (R1 + R2 + R3 +
But first, it              ... Nicolai Ceausescu.

         T2' ──────────→ R2'
         His picture           ... on important occasions,

         T2" ──────────→ R2"
         his wife              ... top political body,

         T3'" ─────────→ R3'"
         and one of his sons   ... fast —

         T4"" ─────────→ R4""
         two others            ... posts.
```

Figure 4. *Thematic progression with a split Theme [my analysis]*

consecutive clauses are taken from the Rheme of a preceding clause. Another case is constituted by incomplete or somewhat modified patterns such as the so-called *thematic jumps* involving non-isotopic Themes with omitted links; or those TPs in which both the Theme and the Rheme of a sentence are taken up by the Theme of the following sentence (Morgenthaler 1980: 136).

When trying to apply Daneš's theory to natural texts, one has to face several problems. It turns out, for example, that the identification of Theme is anything but straightforward. For Daneš's semantic conception of CA categories ambiguously switches from relational, i.e. as structural (clausal) function, to contextual, setting up discourse patterns, leaving a number of issues unresolved. To begin with, Daneš (1967: 504) claims to adopt a "separating" perspective dissociating CAs from IBs as follows:

[t]he respective two parts may be defined from two different aspects. (a) Taking for granted that in the act of communication every utterance is, in principle, an enunciation or statement about something, we shall call the respective parts "Topic" or "Theme" (something that one is talking about) and

"Comment" or "Rheme" (what one says about it) [CA]. (b) Following the other line [IB], linking up the utterance with the consituation, we recognise that, as a rule, the Topic contains "old" or "already known" elements, while the Comment conveys the new piece of information.

However, in (1960: 45) and (1964: 228) Daneš mixes up both lines, CAs and IBs, using the terms "Theme" (*thème*) and "Rheme" (*propos*) to identify "the thing already known and spoken about" and "what is said about the Theme, conveying the unknown element of an utterance"; and in (1978: 187–8) he concludes that "as these two aspects coincide in most cases (and/or on the whole), we can reject this distinction [my translation]". In this line, in (1967: 509ff.) Daneš explains that emphatic utterances show a New before Given, or C(Rheme)-T(Theme), organisation, and, not infrequently, he resorts to the same method, the Q-test, both to distinguish *recoverable* and *non-recoverable* information and to ascertain CA and IB articulations. This practice led to identifying Rheme, C and New with the *Wh*-element of the question, and the Theme, S or Given with the rest, as illustrated in the question-answer pairs in (65) and (66):

(65) | What | did he want? |
R/C   T/S

| He | wanted his football |
T/S   R/C

(66) | Who | wanted the football? |
R/C   T/S

| He | wanted the football? |
R/C   T/S

Later, however, Daneš abandons the Q-test, arguing that ascertaining which information is co-textually recoverable or unrecoverable is not exactly the phenomenon involved in the IB of utterances (1989: 27ff.), because different items equally conveying co-textually recoverable information may function as either S or C. This is shown in (67) (Daneš 1989: 27 (1)):

(67)   a.   On Christmas we were expecting our relatives.
        b.   Uncle John came first./
        b′. First came uncle John.

Assuming an unmarked intonation pattern in (67), both *uncle John* and *came first* are contextually bound to *relatives* and *expecting*, but they act as S and C in (67b) and as C and S in (67b′), respectively.

Now turning to CA, Theme is sometimes interpreted syntactically as the clause initial constituent (resembling Beneš's Basis); but it is also singled out "by applying circumlocutions such as *for, as regards, as far as ... is concerned*" (Daneš 1989: 25), a referential, not a relational, identificational criterion, or by invoking informational marks such as a non-terminal intonation contour (e.g. **My brother**, *went to* **Brighton**, *ibid.* [my bold type] implying "as for my brother, he ..."). And, more often than not, the recommendation is to first recognise the Rheme as some information linked to and normally following the element that potentially becomes Theme. Yet, given that any piece of discourse may act as the Theme or the Rheme of any other stretch, it follows that the Theme–Rheme relation transcends the sentential sphere. Furthermore, on studying TP patterns no distinction is made between the distribution of the subject matter in the text and the way in which this subject matter is structured and developed, so that the distinction between the flow of information and the structure of the text is obscured. In other words, CA stops being a clause level structural relation to become a text constructional device. Accordingly, Theme (and Rheme) is no longer a FSP category in its original sense, but alludes to "what a text is about" (and how this is developed).

In addition, Daneš claims that text structure is partially realized by TP, but this claim is not convincingly supported for it is based on the analysis of very short texts. Neither are the relationships examined between the thematic and rhematic elements in TP schemes in detail, nor are workable criteria given for determining a valid relation in such schemes. This raises the question as to whether the TP schemes are refined enough to describe all sorts of texts, whatever length or complexity they may have, or whether much important detail is overlooked through the application of the general patterns to large texts. In sum, further research within the context of TP theory is needed to differentiate systematically the different types and levels of intrasentential relations. At most we are told that these relations are of a *semantic* nature. But this does not seem to be a very helpful characterisation when, once a given Theme has been identified, the analyst has to determine a means of tracing whether subsequent information (across sentence or utterance boundaries) is linked back to the already mentioned thematic element(s). This task is more easily accomplished in writing than in speech, where Theme creation is negotiated in the very process of conversing. In face-to-face interactions speakers introduce, reject, or pick up Themes, which can only be identified retrospectively, after information which may be linked to it is revealed in the other speaker's turn. Admittedly, Daneš contemplates the possibility of interspersed or disconnected TP-types (by complications such as insertions, incomplete or modified form; and combinations obtained by co-ordination, apposition, nominalisation, relative clauses, etc.), but he does not analyse the issue thoroughly. It is not clear, for example, to what degree these disconnections can occur, and if they can, what the function is they fulfil, and how they can affect a given TP pattern.

In conclusion, in order to reinforce the assumption that text structure is partially realized by TP a very careful and detailed examination should be provided of:

a. the defining characteristics of CA articulations and their relations to the parameters involved in FSP;
b. isotopic relations;
c. the quantification of distances between Themes.

Likewise, the TP models derived therefrom should be applied to large natural texts, in order to (a) test the applicability of the method and (b) establish all possible relevant connections between TP patterns and text/register types.

3.4 Summary

In this chapter it has been shown that the PS does not supply truly (moderate) functionalist descriptions of communicative categories or of grammar as a whole for two main reasons. First, functional explanations are restricted to just one level of description, FSP, which in most cases is concerned with isolated independent clauses, rather than with natural language, the intended object of study of functional accounts. And second, no agreement is reached as to the relationships holding within communicative categories and between these and other categories belonging to different levels, for in practice there are no precise boundaries among the three posited grammatical levels.

As a result, a number of discrepancies emerge which turn the PS conception of Theme/Topic into a wild card. Although all Prague scholars seem to subscribe to a (relational or referential) semantic interpretation of this category, as the concern of messages, they disagree in its elicitation. For most advocates of the informational stand Theme/Topic represents given, or recoverable, information (Giv_R). But, while Weil, Mathesius and the co-workers in the generative-functional framework regard thetic messages as unanalysable or themeless, Firbas and the advocates of CD argue that all messages have a Theme, i.e. the element with the lowest degree of CD. Moreover, some of Firbas's examples apart, most PS informational accounts supply no co(n)textual evidence to determine what should be taken as Given or New, or to elicit the factors involved in placing one before the other. Rather, sentences are analysed in isolation and formal, instead of functional, explanations of communicative categories are supplied, which belong to the semantic and/or grammatical levels, rather than to the level of FSP originally devised to study the syntagmatic oppositions established by the contextualisation of messages.

Alternatively, PS syntactic analysts in principle adopt a "separating" perspective, dissociating Theme (initial position) from given information, but these categories are often used interchangeably to such an extent that some conclude that it is not worth keeping these options separate. Besides, although they claim to rely on exclusively morpho-syntactic evidence, some syntactic PS accounts are highly "psychological". And finally a number of debatable issues have been found because relational and referential-semantic treatments of communicative categories, already discussed as two different approaches in Chapter 2, are ambiguously interpolated leaving a number of problematic issues unresolved.

CHAPTER 4

Systemic Functional Grammar

4.1 Introduction

SFG ascribes communicative categories to the *textual component* of languages, as opposed to the *ideational* and *interpersonal* components. The ideational component concerns the expression of experience (processes, entities, qualities, etc.) as well as the logical relations in language (co-ordination, subordination, apposition, modification, etc.). The interpersonal component analyses the speaker's choice of speech role and her/his assessment of the speech event. And the textual component embodies the *text/texture*-creating function of languages, that is to say, the resources languages have to be operationally relevant in real contexts of situation. In contrast with the PS FSP level analysing "texture" relationships *within* the *sentence*,[50] the SFG textual component is claimed to cover both *intra-sentential* and *inter-sentential* relationships (Halliday 1974: 52). Besides, the "separating" idea is adopted that Theme is "the FSP element that is realized by first position, and has nothing to do with previous mention" or with the choices of Given and New (Halliday 1974: 53).[51] The reason adduced is that, although the Given and Theme normally coincide in one wording since languages tend to abide by the Given-before-New principle, speakers may have "good reasons" for doing otherwise (the so-called *good reason principle*). In Halliday's (1967b: 212) words:

> ... while 'given' means 'what you were talking about' (or 'what I was talking about before'), 'Theme' means 'what I am talking about' (or 'what I am talking about now'); and, as any student of rhetoric knows, the two do not necessarily coincide.

Accordingly, SFG *Theme system complex* sets out to discern three concepts coalesced in Mathesius's and most PS definitions:

a. *Theme*, which, corresponding to Mathesius's *Východisté* ("point of departure") and *Téma* ("what is being commented upon"), is ascribed syntactic and semantic accounts;

b. *Identification* (including *cohesion*), which, evoking Mathesius's *základ*, or "the foundation of the message", "what is known from the context", is interpreted from a referential (informational and semantic) perspective (Sections 2.3.2.1, 2.2.2); and
c. *Given* and *New*, which, interpreted as *relational concepts* (Section 2.3.2.2) and evoking material suprasegmentally presented as uninformative and newsworthy, constitute the *information structure* of messages.

These text forming resources are further classified into *non structural* or *cohesive* and *structural*, as shown in (68) below (IFG: 334; Davidse 1987; Driven & Fried 1987; WFG: 54), the latter comprising the simplified *system network*[52] options displayed in Figure 5.

(68) A. STRUCTURAL
   1. thematic structure: Theme & Rheme
   2. information structure and Focus: Given & New
   3. identification (within the noun group and the clause)
 B. COHESIVE (identification)
   1. reference
   2. ellipsis and substitution
   3. conjunction
   4. lexical cohesion

Approached referentially (Section 2.3.2), identification is concerned with *phoricity*, that is, the strategies languages use to get people, places and things into a text and refer to them once there. It operates through relationships of *cohesion* (B) and through *constituency relationships* within the noun group and the clause (A3). Cohesion involves non-structural relationships of *presupposition* (i.e. Giv$_R$) which occur "... where the INTERPRETATION of some element in the discourse is dependent on that of another" (Halliday & Hasan 1976: 4 [emphasis in original]). Five types of cohesive relationships are recognised: *reference, ellipsis, substitution, conjunction* and *lexical cohesion*. Reference retrieves different types of experiential, meaning (e.g. *The little boy had a frog in a jar. It ran away*, Martin 1992a: 99 [3: 4]) [underlining in original]; Allerton's (1978: 145) definite-givenness). Substitution and ellipsis, on the other hand, presuppose *grammatical* functions, rather than referential meanings (Allerton 1978; Leech 1974: 168–9, 194–5). Ellipsis involves systemic features having no realization in structure and therefore having no potentiality of association with information Focus: what is unsaid cannot be otherwise than taken for granted from the co(n)text (e.g. *Will they tack now? — They may*, Martin ibid. 374 [5: 37]). Substitution entails those items which are essentially text-referring like

SYSTEMIC FUNCTIONAL GRAMMAR

```
                                    ┌→ Structural
                      IDENTIFICATION ├→ Non-Structural
                      SYSTEM         │
                                     ├ unmarked
                                     └ marked

                                    ┌→ Tonality
                                    │   ↘ one information unit, two, three,
                                    │                      ┌ Given
                                    │                      │  ↘ initial, non-initial
                      INFORMATION   ├→ Tonicity            │
                      SYSTEM        │                      └ New
                                    │                         ↘ initial, non-initial
THEME SYSTEM          →             │                      ┌ simple
COMPLEX                             │                      │  ↘ + Tone 1, 2, 3, etc.
                                    ├→ Tone                │
major clauses                       │                      └ compound
+Process                            │                         ↘ + Tone 13, 15
+Predicator                         ├ unmarked
+Theme                              └ marked


                                    ┌  Theme
                      THEME         │
                      SYSTEM        │  Rheme
                      →             │
                                    ├ unmarked
                                    └ marked
```

KEY: { = system choices; → structural realization; + insertion

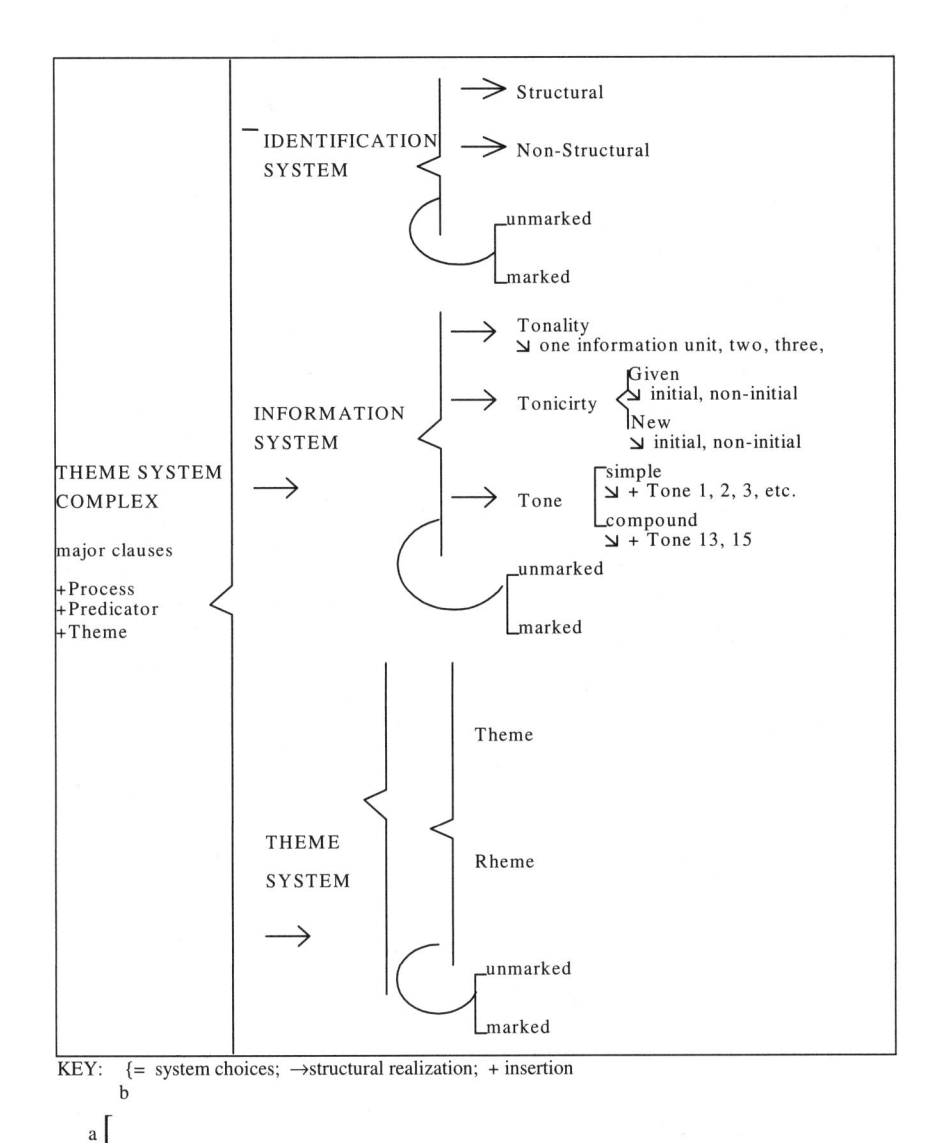

```
    b
a [
    c
```
if *a* (entry condition) then choose *b* or *c* (output features)

Figure 5. *System network of structural textual options: primary delicacy [my network]*

one and *do* (e.g. *Do they tack often enough? — I don't believe they **do***, ibid. [5: 38] [boldtype in original]). Conjunctive items include: (a) *conjunctive* or *discourse Adjuncts*, i.e. adverbial groups or prepositional phrases which tend to occur initially and relate the clause to the preceding text; and (b) *continuatives*, that is, a small set of conjunctions which introduce a new move in discourse (*and, or, nor, but, yet, so then*, etc.) (Section 4.4.4). And, focusing on the way, rather than on the type, of experiential meaning to be recovered, lexical cohesion includes: (a) the repetition of an item; (b) the occurrence of a synonym or an item formed on the same root (e.g. *craft-vessel, vessel-vessels*, etc.); and (c) the occurrence of item from the same lexical set (i.e. co-occurrence, or collocational, group) (e.g. *train, track, baggage-car, rails*, etc.). Turning to structural relations of identification, within the noun group they are assigned to: (a) *Deictics*, indicating whether or not some specific subset of the *Thing*, either a common noun, a proper noun or a (personal) pronoun, is intended (e.g. *this, my, John's, which(ever)*, etc.); (b) *post-Deictics*, or a second Deictic element in the noun group which adds further to the identification of the subset in question (*other, same, different*, etc.); and (c) *Ordinatives* (e.g. *second, subsequent*, etc.), *comparative Epithets*, indicating some quality of a given subset, *Classifiers*, signalling a particular subclass of the Thing in question) and *Qualifiers*, i.e. whatever follows and is embedded within the Thing. And at clause level, structural identifying structures include: (a) cleft clauses or *Theme predicated structures* (Section 4.2.1.2) and pseudo-cleft clauses or *thematic equatives* (Section 4.2.1.3); (b) constructions that create participants (e.g. *have a bath*, etc.); (c) some types of attributes and processes commonly involved in transforming participants (e.g. *wash* and *core* in *Wash and core six cooking apples. Put them into a fireproof dish*, Halliday & Hasan 1976: 2); and (d) appositive structures.

Information structure is interpreted relationally, or reciprocally (Daneš 1974b: 111), in contrast with the referential approach adopted in the analysis of identification (Section 2.3.2). This implies that from a systemic perspective the information structure of a message is not to be derived from the degree of referential/contextual (un)predictability of its constituents, but from the interaction between what is presented as news and not news by the speaker, from the Given–New nexus within the domain of individual clauses/utterances. Thus, the Given, usually expressed by phoric items (i.e. already present in the verbal and/ or situational context) and closely bound up with such cohesive patterns as substitution or reference, is regarded as uninformative or non-prominent in relation to the New, which is presented as not being recoverable from the preceding discourse and to be attended to either as fresh or as contrastive information. But, crucially, in this model the possibility is admitted that any type of information may be presented as the New, i.e. cognitive content, a feature of *Mood*[53] (to confirm an asserted proposition), textual information (in metalinguistic uses), which tends but needs not be new in a contextual or referential sense. The underlying rationale is that the predictions that co(n)textually recoverable information must be presented as Given, or vice versa, that co(n)textually irrecoverable information must be presented as New, have only a *high probability* of being fulfilled for "[i]t is his [the speaker's] decision what to encode as given information and what to encode as new" (Halliday unpub. MS § 21.6).

The marking of material as Given or New involves three simultaneous choices:

a. *Tonality*, whereby speakers package discourse into a linear succession of a number of intonationally realized units of information, or *tone groups*, which may include from one up to a dozen *feet*, i.e. from one up to six/seven syllables, the boundaries of which are determined by either a salient syllable, the one carrying the beat (marked off with a slash "/" before it) or by an initially silent syllable (marked by a caret "^");

b. *Tonicity*, which invokes the speaker's location within the tone group of an optional pretonic segment (P) and an obligatory tonic segment (T), either simple or compound; "information focus assigns the structural function 'new' to a constituent in the information unit, with, optionally, a remainder having the function 'given'" (Halliday 1967b: 211); and

c. *Tone*, or the choice between five possible simple tonic segments (i.e. falling (tone 1 ""), rising (tone 2 "2"), low rising (tone 3 ","), (rising-)falling-rising (tone 4 "%") and (falling-)rising-falling (tone 5 "^") (after the LIBMSEC notational conventions) or a compound tonic segment (viz. tone 13, 53).

Unmarked tonality (in English) consists in tone units being mapped onto clauses, and *unmarked Focus* in the New (or tonic segment) falling on the accented syllable of the *last lexical item* of the tone group, which excludes such *closed systems* as: (a) anaphoric items, referring to what has been mentioned before; (b) situationally-bound elements, which point to the here-&-now of discourse; and (c) non-anaphoric items like verbal auxiliaries and prepositions. As a result, English tone units are said to normally abide by the principles of PFSP, EF and EW (Section 2.3.1), displaying the structure (optional) (*Given*) *followed by New*, which is neither linked to a specific question, nor does it specify the informational status of what is not marked as focal (e.g. // *John painted the* **shed** *yesterday* // does not necessarily imply "what did John paint yesterday?" (or "did John paint the wall?", it may simply imply "what happened?", Halliday 1967b: 208).[54] By contrast, any other placing of the tonic, i.e. on non-final or intrinsically given elements, displays *marked Tonicity* or *marked Focus*, which assigns the function of Given to the remainder of the tone unit and establishes some sort of *contrast*, either with respect to some presupposed information (including a specific question), or in relation to the other members of the system it belongs (if it falls on a non-lexical item (e.g. // ***John** painted the shed yesterday* //, which may imply "who painted the shed yesterday?" (or "did Mary paint ...? or // ***on** the table* //, which means "not under, not beside, etc."), (ibid. 207)).

4.2 Characterisation of Theme

SFG Theme is a direct development of the second leg of Mathesius's definition "that from which the speaker proceeds", a place metaphor, telling us "what the clause as a message is about", a matter metaphor. Although many accounts of SFG Theme refer only to the place metaphor, the matter metaphor ("aboutness") also plays a prominent role, as illustrated by the quotations in (69) ((i)–(vii) Halliday 1967b: 212–213, 236–39; (viii)–(xvi) IFG: 32–43; (xvii)–(xix) ibid.: Appendix 1: 369, 370, 368 [my emphasis])

(69)   a.   'Theme' means 'what I am talking ABOUT' (or 'what I am talking ABOUT now');
           b.   The Theme is what is being talked ABOUT, the point of departure for the clause as a message;
           c.   In a non-polar interrogative, for example, the WH-item is by virtue of its being a WH-item the point of departure for the message; it is precisely what is being talked ABOUT;
           d.   Given that *what did John see?* means 'John saw something and I want to know the identity of that something', the Theme of the message is that there is something the speaker does not know and that he wants to know; the rest of the message is explanatory comment ABOUT this demand: '(as for) what I want to know (it) is the interpretation of the ~something' that John saw';
           e.   These [the Subject in declaratives and the finite verbal element in polar interrogatives] represent, in the unmarked case [i.e. when they are unmarked Theme], 'what the clause is ABOUT';
           f.   There is however a difference between a clause with a predicated Theme and an identifying clause, in the meaning of the highlighting involved. In identification the prominence is cognitive: 'John and nobody else broke the window'; whereas in predication it is thematic: 'John and nobody else is the topic of the sentence';
           g.   The difference between *his earlier novels I've read* and *it's his earlier novels I've read* is again one of the type of prominence: the former

implies the contrast 'but his later ones I know nothing about' [...], whereas the latter is not cognitively contrastive and means simply 'these are the ones I'm talking about';

h. [One of the three broad definitions of the traditional concept of Subject] could be summarised as [...] that which is the CONCERN of the message;

i. The message [in *this teapot my aunt was given by the duke*, where the psychological subject is *this teapot*] is a message CONCERNING the teapot;

j. Psychological Subject meant 'that which is the CONCERN of the message';

k. In *this teapot my aunt was given by the duke*, the psychological subject is *this teapot*. That is to say, it is 'this teapot' that is the CONCERN of the message — that the speaker has taken as point of embarkation of the clause;

l. The Theme [...] is what the message is CONCERNED with: the point of departure for what the speaker is going to say;

m. The Theme is the element which serves as the point of departure of the message; it is that with which the clause is CONCERNED;

n. The Theme is the starting point for the message: it is what the clause is going to be ABOUT;

n. There is a difference in meaning between *a halfpenny is the smallest English coin*, where *a halfpenny* is Theme ('I'll tell you ABOUT a halfpenny'), and *the smallest English coin is a halfpenny*, where *the smallest English coin* is Theme (I'll tell you ABOUT the smallest English coin')

o. So the meaning of *what the duke gave my aunt was that teapot* is something like 'I am going to tell you ABOUT the duke's gift to my aunt [...]'. Contrast this with *the duke gave my aunt that teapot*, where the meaning is 'I am going to tell you something ABOUT the duke';

p. The Theme [...] is *in this job*: 'I'm going to tell you ABOUT the job that has to be done';

q. Clause 2 has a two-part Theme: continuative *now* meaning 'relevant information coming' and topical *silver* meaning 'I'm going to tell you ABOUT silver';

r. Thematic prominence is speaker-oriented: it expresses 'what I am on ABOUT'.

It seems then that in SFG the place and matter metaphors represent two *different*, but *equivalent*, glosses — they are presented in apposition at least three times as shown in (70) (IFG: 32–42) — of the special "special status" assigned to one part of the clause, its Theme, which in combination with "the remainder", or Rheme, gives this unit "the status of a communicative event":

(70) a. In *this teapot my aunt was given by the duke*, the psychological subject is *this teapot*. That is to say, it is 'this teapot' that is the concern of the message — that the speaker has taken as point of embarkation of the clause
b. The Theme [...] is what the message is concerned with: the point of departure for what the speaker is going to say
c. The Theme is the element which serves as the point of departure of the message; it is that with which the clause is concerned.

From the above definitions one could conclude that systemicists draw a function-to-form realization line between a relational-semantic conception of Theme ("what the clause as a message is about") and the category of syntactic Theme ("the point of departure of the clause"). Yet, in (IFG: 38) Halliday avoids a straightforward identification of the semantic gloss with clause-initial position, a syntactic Theme, arguing that the features of "point of departure" and "aboutness" represent a *meaning*, rather than language-dependent *realizations* of that meaning. In other words, Theme is rendered as a potential language universal, a clause functional category or a "principle of organisation", although its expression is language-dependent (e.g. initial position in the clause, the postpositions *-wa*, *-ang*, in Japanese, etc.; Halliday 1970a: 161). The controversy aroused by this characterisation is examined in Section 4.4.2.

Now, to close this descriptive section, let us refer to the function of Theme. In SFG a co-relation is established (in English) between thematic and informative choices, deriving from the partial congruence, or coincidence, between the Given–New and the Theme–Rheme patterns, on the one hand, together with the partial congruence between clause and the tone group, on the other. As noted, this co-relation evokes the PS PFSP (Given-before-New information), which is rephrased as the tendency towards a left to right form of organisation in the information unit, with Given, if present (often an anaphoric or deictic element), mapped on to Theme and thus preceding the New, mapped on to Rheme. These textual patterns are said to assign *wave-like* or *pulse-like* peaks of prominence to the beginning and the end of the clause, as illustrated in Figure 6 (Pike 1982; Pike & Pike 1983; IFG: 337; Halliday 1979; Matthiessen 1988).

Rheme (= last position) is pictured as *hearer-oriented*: it highlights information that is in some respect New. By contrast, Theme (= initial position) is described as a special type of *speaker-oriented deictic element*: it marks the *speaker's angle* on the content of the message. In the subsequent sections we shall see that for systemicists the different types of Themes involve different

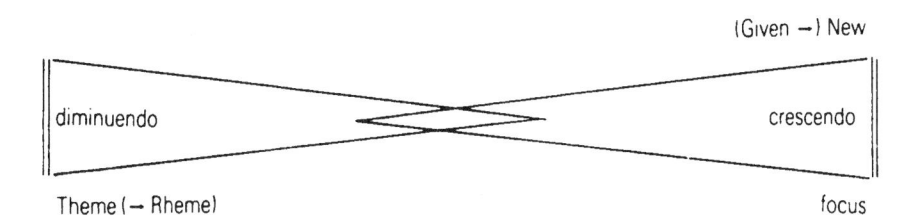

```
                                              (Given →) New
┌─────────────────────────────┐  ┌─────────────────────────────┐
│ diminuendo                   ╲╱                    crescendo │
│                              ╱╲                              │
└─────────────────────────────┘  └─────────────────────────────┘
  Theme (→ Rheme)                                         focus
```

Figure 6. *Texture of clauses as messages*

types of thematic highlighting and set up different *potential domains* or *discourse frameworks* depending on whether Themes are spoken on an independent tone unit or whether they are uttered in the same tone group as the Rheme: in the former case the thematic domain is said to extend over the next tone unit, whereas in the latter it is restricted to the unit in which it occurs (Halliday 1970b: 357; IFG: 187). Thematic (and textual) choices are thus represented as "instrumental" to other grammatical choices, helping texts to be coherent with respect to themselves, that is to say, to be *cohesive*, and to be coherent with respect to their contexts of situation, that is, to be *consistent*, as noted by Halliday (1978: 134):

> [t]hematic patterns are not optional stylistic variants; they are integral part of the meaning of language. Texture is not something that is achieved by superimposing an appropriate text form on pre-existing ideational content. The textual component is a component of meaning along with ideational and interpersonal components [...]. The system does not first generate a representation of reality, then encode it as a speech act, and finally recode it as a text [...]. It embodies all these types of meanings in simultaneous networks of options, from each of which derive structures that are mapped onto one another in the course of their lexicogrammatical realization.

Broadly speaking, the "enabling" potential of SFG Theme is substantiated in five major functional tasks:

a. to provide a framework for the interpretation of the Rheme;
b. to add information which is required for the interpretation of the message;
c. (acting negatively) to co-relate with the principles of EF and EW, helping to build up the *discourse prominence* of (an) item(s): placing an item late in a clause (complex) endows it with the status of new information (in unmarked cases)
d. to contribute to the *Topic continuity* or *discontinuity* of discourse, by either developing or cancelling an assumption which has been established in the previous context; and as a corollary

e. to act as an *orientator* to both the message conveyed by the clause and to the addressee's expectations as to how to understand what is about to come.

From the above it follows that systemicists expand the principle of thematic organisation below and beyond the clause (Halliday 1967b: 199; IFG: 54, 187, 197, 387; Fries 1983; Martin 1992a; WFG: 26ff.). Below the clause, the assumption is that "the principle which puts Theme first is the same as that which puts the Deictic first in the nominal group: start by relating to the speaker in the context of the speech event" (IFG: 187). Thus, such structures as the verbal group and the nominal group are said to show a progression from the element with the greatest specifying potential, the element that fixes the structure in relation to the here-and-now of the speech exchange (viz. the Finite and the Deictic, respectively), towards that which has the least specifying potential, or what is newsworthy (IFG: 197). Above the clause, the thematic principle is found behind the organisation of paragraphs in written and spoken discourse, where the "topic sentence" of a paragraph is nothing other than its Theme (IFG: 54, 387). It is explained that in each particular instance, clause by clause, the choice of Theme is not a haphazard matter, but plays a fundamental part in the way discourse is organised constituting the *method of development* of the text (MOD) (Halliday 1978: 134), which involves one or more of the following parameters: (a) realization type of Theme (viz. ideational, interpersonal and textual); (b) and level of Theme and amount of rank shift; (c) locus of retrieval of Theme (whether the Theme or the Rheme); (d) type of cohesive relations leading to Theme; and (e) distance between thematic material. A number of systemicists have done essential groundwork in the exploration of these parameters opening up three major areas of research.

One involves the study of the *typical thematic selection* of texts, that is, the point of departure most often selected (in terms of Mood, Transitivity, lexical density (i.e. number of lexical items) and grammatical intricacy (i.e. internal structure and degree of nominalisation).[63] A second group of investigations examines *thematic relatedness*, i.e. where Themes come from and how they relate to previous Themes and Rhemes, to the context and to the interactants' minds. One of its major conclusions is that the experiential content of Theme correlates with what is perceived to be the MOD of a text or text segment, that is, if a text is perceived to have a single, simple method of development, then the Themes of the clauses will express meanings which relate to that method of development). In this vein and following Daneš's distinction between Hyper–Themes and Hyper–Rheme (Section 3.3.3) as well as Halliday's claim that the Topic sentences of paragraphs are "nothing other than its Theme", Martin (1992b: 156–7) proposes a hierarchical TP where Theme (and Rheme) is to text as Hyper–Theme (and Hyper–Rheme) is to paragraph, and Hyper–Theme is to paragraph as Theme is to clause (*paragraph* is defined semantically, not orthographically).[64]

The third line of research explores the interaction between Theme (MOD, TP) and *genre*. The rationale behind this group of approaches is that the overall organisation of the text and the type of *register* it belongs to, i.e. the variety (*diatypic variety* in the sense of Gregory 1967) of which a particular text is an instance, determines the choice of Theme in any particular clause or the general pattern of thematic choices (IFG: 103).[65] Three main conclusions can be extracted from this third group of approaches. One is that different patterns of thematic progression correlate with different genres, in other words, patterns of thematic progression do not occur randomly but are sensitive to genre. For instance, it has been suggested that narrative and expository texts normally show the same topical Themes (lexico-referentially expressed) throughout stretches of discourse; while in instructions or argumentations Themes are typically extracted from the Rheme of the preceding clause.[66]

Another set of investigations pursue the notion that the experiential content of Themes correlates with different genres. Among the claims made in this direction is the belief that that dialogues have the pronouns *I* (speaker), *you* (addressee), and the Finite or Wh-word (in interrogative clauses) as most recurrent topical Themes.[67] Lastly, other approaches predict that since the meanings of Theme–Rheme and Given–New differ, the two sets of categories will respond to different forces and will contain different types of information as a text progresses through its various stages. In this connection, Martin (1992a: 381–492) observes that since Theme is speaker-oriented ("what the speaker is on about") and New is listener-oriented ("news to the listener"), it follows that the two categories must produce different communicative results. In a similar vein, drawing on Linde & Labov (1965) and Horvath (1985), Fries (1983: 135) concludes that the choices of New look backward, gathering up the meanings which have accumulated to elaborate a text's field, developing discourse in experiential terms, while the choices of Theme project forward, scaffolding the text with respect to its *rhetorical purpose* (IFG: 61, 67, 336, 387).[68] These perceptions are substantiated in the theory of *sandwich texture*, outlined in Figure 7 (Martin 1992b: 172).

Figure 7 symbolises that TP takes thematic meaning and harmonises it by means of cohesion structuring it in terms of concentric layers of structure in a text, i.e. Macro–Theme, Hyper–Theme and clause Theme. Each layer predicts a subset of the next layer, in order to give addressees something to come back to, an orientation, a perspective, a point of view (Downing 1995: 148).

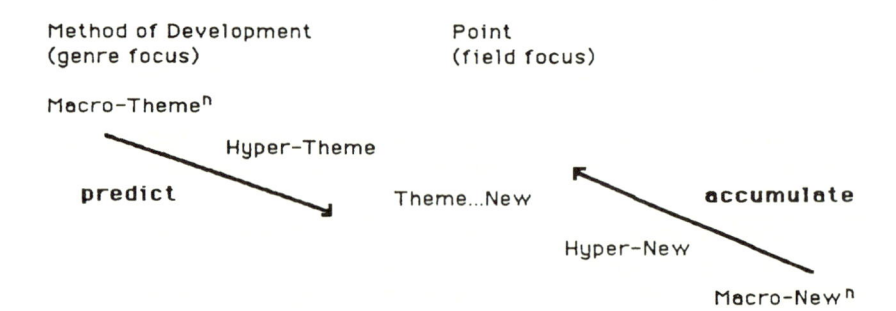

```
Method of Development              Point
(genre focus)                      (field focus)

Macro-Theme ⁿ
         ╲      Hyper-Theme
  predict  ╲                                    accumulate
            ╲___,  Theme...New      ↖
                                      ╲
                              Hyper-New ╲
                                         ╲
                                          Macro-New ⁿ
```

Figure 7. *Sandwich texture in abstract written discourse*

4.2.1   *A taxonomy of topical Themes*

According to SFG, in English topical Theme is iconically realized by the element(s) occupying clause-initial position, extending up to (and including) the first *transitivity constituent*[55] in the clause, that is to say: a "participant" (<u>George Bernard Shaw</u> *was born in Dublin.* <u>The house</u> *was gloomy and uninviting*), a "circumstance", giving information about time, place, manner, cause, etc. (<u>In 1876</u>, *Shaw joined his mother and sister in London,* <u>On the upper floor of such premises</u>, *a tall person cannot stand erect.*), and, occasionally, it might also be process (<u>Says Mr Smith</u>: *"It's too early to draw any conclusions yet."*) (IFG: 56; WFG: 24;). This element constitutes the *topical*, or cognitive, Theme, which is identified in this way by Halliday for two main reasons. One is:

> [...] the overwhelming effect whereby, when the clause was divided into two tone groups, two information units, the boundary between the two came at the point that I have identified. So the hypothesis was, if the clause is two information units, then the overwhelming probability is that the boundary will fall between the Theme and the Rheme. [Personal communication, *Seminar on Systemic Functional Linguistics*, Córdoba May 5–7, 1993]

The second identification criterion adduced is that Themes tend to be "picked up", or announced explicitly, by means of some special expression like *as for* ..., *with regard to* ..., *about* ... (e.g. <u>As for my aunt</u>, *the duke has given her that teapot,* <u>About that teapot</u> — *my aunt was given it by the duke*, IFG: 39). In addition, Theme predication (it + be ..., e.g. <u>It is my father</u> *who rang*) is used to identify topical Themes (Section 4.4.1.2); and in the case of "longer Themes" two further identification tests are proposed: (a) to replace the expression with a pronoun (e.g. <u>Mice, elephants and humans/they</u> *are some of the animals we know*); and (b) to make the expression non-thematic (e.g. in <u>From house to house</u> *I went my way*: *I went my way from house to house*, the alternation involves *from house to house* as a whole, not only say *from house*).

At the level of form, a topical Theme may be a single syntactic constituent, typically a nominal group, but it may also be an adverbial group, a prepositional phrase, a verbal group, or a clause (e.g. *The Queen of Hearts she made some tarts, if the duke gives anything to my aunt it'll be that teapot*, IFG: 39, 56). Likewise topical Themes may be a complex of single elements linked by a relationship of *paratactic or hypotactic expansion* or *projection*[56] (e.g. *The Walrus and the Carpenter were walking close at hand, Tom, Tom, the piper's son stole a pig and away did run*, ibid.: 40) or by a relationship of *embedding*[57] (a) *embedded wh-clauses* (e.g. [[*What he ate that night*]][58] *gave him terrible heartburn, What he said is nonsense,*), (b) *embedded non-finite clauses* (e.g. *Doing twenty sit-ups a day will improve your tummy muscles, To err is human ǁ to forgive (is) divine,*), or (c) *embedded that-clauses* (e.g. *The fact*) [[*that the food might not be fresh*]] *didn't occur to the*m).

In addition, a special treatment is given to the initial clause (Theme$_1$) of clause complexes. These are claimed to be usually the Head (or dominant) clauses (*alpha (α) Themes*), or less frequently, the Modifying (dependent) clauses (*beta (β) Themes*). Compare the following:

(71) a. *Were you lonely in Paris*, [[*when I was in the concentration camp?*]]
      b. *When I was in the concentration camp*, [[*were you lonely in Paris?*]]

(71a) is regarded as displaying an unmarked ordering (main clause^modifying clause). Alternatively, in (71b) (modifying clause^main clause) the *when*-clause provides a marked Theme orienting the context for the question *Were you lonely in Paris?* (IFG: 56–57). Besides, since both Themes$_1$ and Rhemes$_1$ are realized by clauses, a further layer of Theme$_2$–Rheme$_2$ patterns may be recognised, i.e. Themes and Rhemes structuring the component clauses of clause complexes, as shown in the alternative thematic analyses in Figure 8 (IFG: 57).

But recognising two layers of thematic structure poses the problem of where to ascribe the thematic material, either to Theme$_1$ or to Theme$_2$ (e.g. but honestly Mary *if winter comes* $_{βTheme}$ can spring be far behind?, ibid.: 57). To solve the problem the intonation pattern of a sequence is suggested to demarcate its *thematic scope*: the information preceding the topical Theme is part of Theme$_1$ if spoken on a separate tone group, and, if not, it belongs to Theme$_2$ (Halliday 1967b; see Sections 4.4.1.1 and 4.5.1 in this book).

Paratactically related complexes on the other hand are rendered as lacking sentence level Themes on the assumption that they are not reversible (*John came* and *Bill left* vs. *And Bill left, John came**). They are said to have the thematic

If	winter	comes	can	spring	be far behind
Theme₁			Rheme₁		
structural	topical	Rheme₂	Finite	topical	Rheme₃
Theme₂			Theme₃		

Figure 8. *Theme in the clause complex*

structure of simple sentences, though implying different types of semantic relations (between them, rather than within them) that fit into the pattern of ordering of information extending throughout a passage or a text. Embedded clauses, in turn, reflect the thematic structure of dependent finite clauses, but their thematic contribution is discarded on the grounds that they are not immediate constituents of the clause, but act within the structure of a nominal group.

The above describe prototypical realizations of topical Themes. *Minor clauses*, however, are set aside as having no Theme–Rheme structure because they do not have any verb and therefore do not select either for Mood or Transitivity. This is the case of *greetings* (e.g. *Hallo, Bye-bye*), *exclamations* (e.g. *Good Shit!*) or *minimal conversational moves* (e.g. *Oh*). Sequences may also consist only of Rheme when Themes can be retrieved by different types of referential cohesion. This is the case of (i) *elliptical clauses* (e.g. He roared in fury ‖ *and* ( ) struggled with all his might, WFG: 29) and (ii) *non-finite clause without a Subject*, which are backgrounded for interpersonal reasons (e.g. *to fetch her poor dog a bone* in *Old Mother Hubbard went to the cupboard to fetch her poor dog a bone*, or *eating his Christmas pie* in *Little Jack Horner sat in the corner eating his Christmas pie*) (WFG: 28; IFG: 62; Davies 1998).

4.2.1.1 *Marked vs. unmarked Themes*

The intersection of the system of Theme with the system of Mood specifies the marked or unmarked thematic status of declaratives, interrogatives, exclamatives and imperatives (Halliday 1967b: 213; IFG: 43; see endnote 54 in this book). From this description it follows that the unmarked topical Theme of English declarative clauses conflates with Subject (e.g. *Little Bo-peep has lost her sheep*, IFG: 43), with a WH-element in exclamatives (e.g. *how cheerfully he seems to grin*, ibid.: 47), and in interrogatives with: (i) the Finite verb (carrying the expression of polarity) plus the Subject, in yes/no questions (e.g. *can you find me an acre of land?*, ibid.: 48); or (ii) the WH-element (including the group or phrase in which it occurs), in WH-questions (*who killed Cock Robin?*, ibid.). In their turn, the unmarked Theme of imperatives is identified with: (i) *you* (e.g. *you keep quiet*, IFG: 47); (ii) *do* (e.g. *do take care*, ibid.); (iii) *don't* or *let's (not)* in negative imperatives (e.g. *don't [you] argue*, ibid.); or (iv) Predicator (e.g. *keep quiet*, ibid.).[59]

By contrast, any other clause initial mood element realizes a *marked topical Theme*, as in the following examples:

(72)   merrily we roll along (ibid.: 46)

(73)   this responsibility we accept wholly (ibid.: 45)

(74)   yesterday did John see the play? (Halliday 1967a: 214)

Marked Themes are said to: (a) be explicitly foregrounded as a point of departure for the message; (b) add some sort of contrast; and (c) be frequently marked off in speech by being spoken on a separate tone group (e.g. // 4 *in* **England** // *1 they drive on the* **left** //, // 1 *in England they drive on the* **left** // and // 13 *they drive on the* **left** *in* **England** //, 1967b: 239).

With regard the feature (c) Halliday (1967b: 214) observes that there is a difference in scope between Themes spoken on a separate intonation unit and those embodied in the same information unit as the Rheme. The latter are claimed to be usually marked Themes (typically circumstantial Adjuncts or such items as *only*, *either*, etc.) uttered on tone 3 or tone 4 and sometimes reinforced by a silent ictus (e.g. // 4 ***that*** // *1 I don't know* //, ibid.). The underlying rationale is that the domain of the Themes spoken in a separate tone group extends over and/or are presupposed in the next information unit (e.g. // ***John*** // // *saw the play and* **liked** *it* //, which implies a following clause presupposing *John* as subject, ibid.: 220). In contrast, Themes spoken within the same tone group as the Rheme restrict their domain over the information unit in which they themselves occur. Consider Halliday's (ibid.) examples:

(75)   a.   // these **houses** // my grandfather sold and *the rest of his property* he left to **me** //

         b.   // **John** // saw the play and *Mary* went to the **concert** //,

(75) is adduced to show that the difference in thematic domains is a relevant distinction for it may render sequences acceptable or unacceptable: (75a) is considered unacceptable because the intonational presupposition does not correspond with the semantic and syntactic structure of the sequence; by contrast, the unacceptability of (75b) resides in that the domain of *these houses* extends over the following information unit, but has no function within the second clause.

In addition, the markedness of a Theme is also associated to the *system of voice*.[60] The assumption behind is that by choosing passive sequences speakers dissociate the roles of Actor and Theme while leaving the Theme unmarked, which at the same time allows for: (a) the *Goal* (*Beneficiary*, *Range*, or some other "indirect" participant such as a Complement to a preposition, which gives location-/manner-passives) to be infused with thematic prominence signalling what the message is about; (b) the Agent either to be non-thematic or not specified at all (usually when unknown or pronominal); and (c) the unmarked Focus to fall on a constituent other than the Goal (Halliday 1967b: 215; IFG: 169), as shown in the active and passive sequences in (76a) and (76b) below (WFG: 24):

(76) a. Peter Piper picked a peck of pickled peppers (unmarked Theme/ Subject + Rheme)
b. A peck of pickled pepper was picked by Peter Piper (unmarked Theme/Subject + Rheme).

4.2.1.2 *Predicated Themes*

Predicated Theme constructions (e.g. *it was [wasn't] John* who broke the window) are said to single out one experiential element to serve as both Theme and New, making explicit the assertion that the Rheme ("who broke the window") is (or is not) valid for this particular Theme ("John") (IFG 3.7).

Formally, predicated Theme constructions are characterised as creating a local structure by means of predication (*it was/is* ...) so that the predicated element becomes the unmarked information Focus of the predicated construct (// it was **John** // ...), selecting for polarity independently from the matrix predication (e.g. *it is/isn't John* who broke/didn't break the window), but probably not for tense (although in speech there seems to be a tense assimilation). This thematic pattern may be interpreted in two ways, that is, as a Theme$_1$ or as showing a Theme$_2$-Rheme$_2$ pattern, as illustrated in Figure 9 (IFG: 60):

Semantically, predicated Theme constructions are considered *identifying* constructs because they establish a relationship of identification between two entities: one that is to be identified, the *Identified* (ID), and another that identifies it, or the *Identifier* (IR). The unmarked order is ID followed by IR, but these constituents can appear the other way round. The functions of Identified and Identifier are conflated with those of *Value* (Vl) and *Token* (T), which show different degrees of abstraction, but the same degree of generalisation: Vl indicates how an entity is valued, referring to its function, meaning or status, while the T defines how it is recognised, specifying its form, target or holder. The conflation of these four functions can go either way, i.e. either the Token or Value can serve as the Identifier.

In addition, in SFG both predicated Themes and thematic equatives are

	It	was his teacher	who	persuaded him to continue
(a) local thematic structure	Theme	Rheme	Theme	Rheme
(b) thematic structure of a predicated Theme	Theme		Rheme	

Figure 9. *The thematic structure of a predicated Theme*

classified as identifying structures of the *encoding* type. The assumption is that the identification proceeds by *encoding*, mapping the IR onto the T, as opposed to *decoding* identifying constructions, in which the identification proceeds by decoding conflating IR and Vl. Accordingly, in predicated Theme constructions, the functions of IR/T are mapped onto the topical Theme ("John was the one who broke the window"), whereas the Rheme represents the IR/V, or what is at issue ("who broke the window").

Systemicists affirm that any element with a representational function can be marked off by predication and take on the status of a predicated Theme, with the exception of: (a) processes, which stand as a highly restricted option; (b) the V in an equative relation (e.g. in *it's the leader* that's John, *the leader* can only be interpreted as the Identifier "this is how John can be recognised"); and (c) the Identified element, blocked by the structural make-up of identifying sequences. As a result, in contrast with marked Themes, predicated Themes are characterised as not cognitively contrastive, as meaning simply "these are the ones I'm talking about", as to be more likely to constitute one information unit (with tone 1 or 13) and as demanding a question that questions the identity of the Theme (e.g. *is it his earlier novels you've read?*).

A further opposition is established between predicated Themes (e.g. *it was John who*) and presentational structures (e.g. *there was John who ...*) on the one hand, and marked predicated Themes (e.g. *John it was who ...*), on the other (Halliday 1967b: 238). The assumption is that through predication a Theme is uniquely specified ("John and no other") while with *there* it is simply described ("John, possibly among others"), which is in keeping with the Hallidayan analysis of *it* and *there* as the cataphoric forms of the definite and indefinite article, respectively. Conversely, marked predicated Themes are said to be used (especially in speech) to explicitly assert the thematic status of the topical Theme, *it* remaining non-anaphoric and thus contrasting with its anaphoric pronominal Counterpart.

4.2.1.3 *Thematic equatives*

Thematic equatives are described as the option whereby any message may be organised into a number of possible arrangements of a two part identifying structure of the form "x equals y", through the nominalisation of one set of its elements, typically of the WH-type (or noun head (substitute) form such as the place, the reason, etc.), which regularly, though not obligatorily, includes all elements in the clause except one (e.g. <u>what John saw</u> was the play, Halliday 1967b: 223).[61]

As encoding equatives, the nominalisation element of the equative represents the function complex ID/Vl, while the WH-item acts as the IR/T (e.g. in <u>what John saw</u> was the play, *the play* is the IR/T corresponding to *what* in the presupposed question "What did John see?"). Alternatively, in the *demonstrative* type (e.g. *that's what I meant*, Halliday 1967b: 226) the IR/T function is realized by a phoric (demonstrative) pronoun or a (deictic) adverb, i.e. *her/his/now* (near-speaker-oriented, inclusive of addressee) or *there/that/then* (far not speaker-oriented, past time), whose reference may be either situational or textual (either anaphoric or cataphoric).

The IR/T may fulfil a variety of functions with respect to the nominalisation: Subject (e.g. <u>the one who painted the shed last week</u> $_{ID/Vl}$ was John $_{IR/T}$, ibid.: 224); Complement (e.g. <u>what John painted last week</u> $_{ID/Vl}$ was the shed $_{IR/T}$, ibid.); Adjunct (<u>when John painted the shed</u> $_{ID/Vl}$ was last week $_{IR/T}$; <u>now</u> $_{IR/T}$ is when he's supposed to be here $_{ID/V}$, ibid.: 433); or even Predicator (e.g. <u>what John did to the shed last week</u> $_{ID/Vl}$ was (to) paint it $_{IR/T}$, ibid., in which case the nominalisation must contain a substitute verb, in addition to the finite element if present).

ID/Vl and IR/T may occur in either sequence, but, irrespective of the sequence, the unmarked Focus falls on the IR/T, which is in keeping with this category functioning as that with which something is to be identified. Thus, a thematic equative typically displays the series ID/Vl/Given/Theme^IR/T/New/Rheme (e.g. // what John saw$_{ID/Vl/Given/Theme}$ *was the play* $_{IR/T/New/Rheme}$ //) or that of IR/T/New/Theme^ID/Vl/Given/Rheme (e.g. // *the play* $_{IR/T/New/Theme}$ *was what John saw* //$_{ID/Vl/Given/Rheme}$).

In cases of unmarked tonality the thematic equative is mapped onto one information unit. But thematic equatives may also bee packed in two information units reflecting the two part syntagmatic foregrounding of IR/ID. The boundary between the information units is at the end of the Theme so that both the ID/Vl (typically marked by Tone 1 or Tone 4) and the IR/T carry the information Focus (e.g. // <u>the one who painted the **shed** last week</u> // was **John** // or // **John** // was the one that painted the **shed** last week //, ibid.: 226). In turn, in thematic equatives of the demonstrative type the locus of the information Focus depends on the type of reference of the demonstrative. It is claimed that demonstratives are normally non-focal when anaphoric (// *that's what I meant* //), because what is referred to anaphorically is Given, and focal otherwise since what is referred to situationally or cataphorically is New (// ***that's** what I want* //, ibid.: 231, where *that* refers to something in the situation, unless anaphorically contrastive).

As to their function, thematic equatives are said to highlight *cognitive prominence exclusively identifying* a participant, circumstance, attribute or process by its participation in the process described in a given message (e.g. in <u>what John saw</u> was the play, "the play" (and nothing else) is the exclusive goal of John's perception), the polarity and modality (but not the speech function) of the identification being independent of those of the main clause. And so, the IR fulfils some sort of anaphoric function (particularly in the demonstrative type), integrating the clause into the discourse through the identification of the defined participant (process or circumstance) with one that has been mentioned before. By contrast, in Theme predication (e.g. <u>it was the play</u> that John saw) the type of prominence is described as fundamentally *textual* or *thematic*: Theme is given explicit prominence by *exclusion* ("the play and nothing else" is under consideration). This argument is based on the fact that while almost everything can be predicated and thus become the Theme of a message, not all messages have identifying equivalents (e.g. <u>it was in spite of the cold</u> that he went swimming, which has no thematic equative Counterpart).

4.2.1.4 *Substitute Themes*

Substitute Themes are presented as a special kind of "afterthoughts" whereby an element which would otherwise appear as unmarked Theme is assigned to clause-final position (e.g. *they don't seem to match, <u>these colours</u>*, Halliday 1967b: 239). In other words, a substitute Theme reverses the normal sequence Theme–Rheme, introducing a delayed Theme after the remainder of the message. The meaning is, as it were, "first I'll say what I have to say and then I'll remind you what I'm talking about."

It is argued that substitute Themes tend to function as the Subject of the sequence. This referent is substituted in the modal constituent by a concord pronoun, which refers cataphorically to the delayed Theme and which at the same time has anaphoric overtones, given that the typical context for a substitute clause is one in which the delayed Theme is partially recoverable from the co(n)text. According to Halliday (1967b) substitute Themes display three variants, i.e. (a) *they don't seem to match, <u>these colours</u>*; (b) *they don't seem to match, <u>these colours don't</u>*; (c) *they don't seem to match don't, <u>these colours</u>*, normally exhibiting a compound tone, typically 13, with the delayed Theme bearing the minor tonic marking information as either New, but subsidiary, or Given, but to be noted (e.g. // 13 *they don't seem to* **match** *these* **colours** //).

4.2.1.5 *Reference Theme*
Restricted to declarative clauses with a nominal Theme (marked or unmarked), reference Themes (e.g. *Britain it's all roads*, Halliday 1967b: 241) are analysed as a form of pronominal anaphora within the clause. The substitute Theme tends to be placed on a separate information unit and may "picked up" by an anaphoric pronoun later in the clause (typically by reference but sometimes only by lexical cohesion), which specifies separately its transitivity role in the clause. The function assigned to this construction is that of announcing the Theme independently from the structure of the rest of the clause (as opposed to being built into it), sometimes as a form of reprise for a long Theme, but more frequently as a means to introduce and provide the setting for the message.

4.2.2   *Multiple Themes*

In (IFG: 55) it is explained that speaker/writers choose a *multiple Theme* when they place one or several *textual* and/or *interpersonal* items before a simple topical Theme (e.g. *Well, but then, Ann, surely, wouldn't the best idea be to join the group?*), as expounded in Figure 10 (Lautamatti 1978; Martin 1995: 255 endnote 5; WFG: 27):

The assumption is that, although the elements fulfilling an interpersonal and/or textual function before a topical Theme do not exhaust the thematic potential of a clause because they are not representational, they do contribute something to the point of departure chosen for the clause. But while textual and interpersonal Themes are optional, all messages must contain a topical Theme, either implicit in the co(n)text or explicitly stated (IFG: 53). Table 6 sets out the components of a multiple Theme proposed in (IFG: 48ff.).

The topical Theme marks the end of the Theme: non-ideational elements are part of the Theme if and only if they precede the topicalTheme, so that unmarked multiple Themes display the series (textual) ^ (interpersonal) ^ topical. Any other arrangement yields a marked multiple Theme and thus conveys some additional semantic feature. Although it is admitted that Themes may "stack" within the clause initial slot showing thematic depth (i.e. different types of logico-semantic and tactic relationships), it is also claimed that there is no further thematic structure within the topical Theme whereas further structure is allowed within the textual and interpersonal components (Halliday 1967b; IFG). The textual component may contain continuative, structural and/or conjunctive

Well	but	then	Ann	surely	wouldn't	the best idea	be to join the group
continuative	structural	conjunctive	Vocative	modal	finite	Subject participant	
textual			interpersonal			topical	
Theme							Rheme

Figure 10. *The thematic structure of a multiple Theme*

Themes, while the interpersonal element may embody vocative, modal, and finite Themes (IFG: 53). Interpersonal and textual Themes are given independent treatment in Sections 4.2.3 and 4.2.4. respectively.

4.2.3 *Interpersonal Themes*

In SFG interpersonal Themes are described as clause initial items used by speaker/writers to exchange roles in rhetorical interactions with their addressee(s) (statements, questions, offers, etc.) and to express their own angle on the matter, that is, accompanying degrees of *modalisation* (i.e. probability and usually) or *modulation* (i.e. inclination and obligation).

The interpersonal part of the Theme, if present, includes one or more of the following five kinds of items: (a) the *Finite*, typically realized by an auxiliary verb, its presence in thematic position signals that a response is expected (*Should they be doing that? Are you coming?, Don't touch that!*); (b) a *Wh-element*, signalling that an "answer" is required from the addressees, although it is also a topical Theme (participant/circumstance in the clause) (*Why can't you come over tonight?*); (c) a *Vocative*, identifying the addressee in the exchange (*Mr Wolf, Mr. Wolf, may we cross your golden waters?*); (d) an *Adjunct*, typically realized by an adverb providing the *speaker's comment, assessment or attitude* towards the message (*Sadly, it doesn't look like the old places will be around much longer*); and (e) first and second person *"mental" clauses* which express the speaker's opinion or seek the addressee's (*I should think there would probably be some of them that you'll never see*; *I don't suppose you need Old English and Anglo-Saxon*). The instances of group (e) are regarded as *"interpersonal metaphors"* of *modality*, in other words, they are compared with Adjuncts like *probably* and treated as interpersonal Themes (WFG: 25; IFG: 58, 354–63; Section 4.2.5 below).

Table 6. *Components of a multiple Theme in SFG*

Metafunction	Component of Theme	Examples
textual	continuative	*Yes, no, well, oh, now*
	structural	
	Conjunction	
	co-ordinator	*And, or, nor, neither, but, yet, so, then*
	subordinator	*When, because, though, if, even if, given that*
	WH-relative	
	Definite	*which, who, that, whose, when, where, why, how*
	Indefinite	*whatever, whichever, whoever, whosoever, whenever*
	conjunctive Adjunct	
	Elaborating	
	Appositive 'i.e. e.g.'	*that is, in other words, for instance*
	Corrective 'rather'	*or rather, at least, to be precise*
	Dismissive 'in any case'	*in any case, anyway, leaving that aside*
	Summative 'in short'	*briefly, to sum up, in conclusion*
	Verifactive 'actually'	*actually, in fact, as a matter of fact*
	Extending	
	Additive 'and'	*also, moreover, in addition, besides*
	Adversative 'but'	*on the other hand, however, conversely*
	Variative 'instead'	*instead, alternatively*
	Enhancing	
	Temporal 'then'	*meanwhile, before that, later on, next, soon, finally*
	Comparative 'likewise'	*likewise, in the same way*
	Causal 'so'	*therefore, for this reason, as a result, with this in mind*
	Conditional '(if) ... then'	*in that case, under the circumstances*
	Concessive 'yet'	*nevertheless, despite that*
	Respective 'as to that'	*in this respect, as far as that's concerned*
interpersonal	Vocative	*Oh, soldier, soldier, won't you marry me*
	modal Adjunct	
	Mood	
	Probability 'how likely?'	*probably, possibly, certainly*
	'how obvious?'	*perhaps, maybe, of course, surely, obviously*
	usually 'how often?'	*usually, sometimes, always, never*
	'how typical?'	*for the most part, seldom, often*
	opinion 'I think'	*in my opinion, from my point of view, personally*
	comment	
	Admissive 'I admit'	*frankly, to be honest, to tell you the truth*
	Assertive 'I assure you'	*honestly, really, believe me, seriously*
	Presumptive 'how presumptive'	*evidently, apparently, no doubt, presumably*
	Desiderative 'how desirable?'	*(un)fortunately, to my delight, luckily*
	Tentative 'how constant?'	*initially, tentatively, looking back on it*
	Validative 'how valid?'	*broadly speaking, in general terms, on the whole*
	Evaluative 'how sensible?'	*wisely, understandably, foolishly, by mistake*
	Predictive 'how expected?'	*to my surprise, as expected, amazingly*
	Finite	*Oh, soldier, soldier, won't you marry me*
	WH-interrogative	*who killed Cock Robin?*
experiential	topical (Subj., Compl., Circumst. Adj.)	*who killed Cock Robin?*

4.2.4 Textual Themes

Associated with a *linking function* textual Themes include: (a) *structural conjunctions*, (b) *relatives*, (c) *conjunctives* and (d) *continuatives*. The claim is made that almost always these items are given thematic prominence, coming before any interpersonal Themes, because they "have, as the language evolved, as it were migrated to the front of the clause and stayed there" (IFG: 51; WFG 25–26). Structural conjunctions may link two clauses *paratactically*, when allowing a branching structure, i.e. ellipsis within the clause complex (e.g. *John arrived <u>but</u> Mary didn't*), or *hypotactically* marking one clause as dependent on another (e.g. *<u>We</u> were walking into the ring, <u>when suddenly an Alsatian</u> leapt over the wall*), involving at the same time the logico-semantic relations of *projection* or *expansion*. Tables 7 and 8 provide a summary of the principle types of projection and expansion recognised in SFG, respectively (IFG: 270; 328–9; Martin 1992a: 174).

Relatives (either pronouns or adverbs), on the other hand, relating a dependent clause to another clause, also serve as topical Themes since they serve to specify a participant or a transitivity role (e.g. *We heard Professor Smith's lecture, <u>which</u> was a great disappointment*, WFG: 26). Conjunctives in turn provide a cohesive link (usually internal (endophoric)) back to previous discourse (e.g. *<u>Furthermore this alternative</u> would be far too costly*), which may or may not be thematic depending on whether they occur first in the clause (e.g. *later* is thematic in *<u>Later the state-owned Taiwan Cooperative Bank</u> took over Changhua*; but it is not thematic in *<u>He</u> later offered a brief, televised apology*, WFG: 26). Lastly, continuatives introduce a new move in discourse in order to: (i) punctuate an exchange (e.g. *<u>Well there</u> was a little bit of bakelite before the war, wasn't there?*) and (ii) stage or develop discourse turns (e.g. *now*, *all right*, *okay*) (Halliday & Hasan 1976: 267–71; Martin 1992a: 218ff.).

4.2.5 Metaphorical Theme

Halliday (IFG: 41) notes that more often in writing than in speech β Themes tend to express *grammatical metaphors*, typically of the ideational type by means of *nominalisations*, "whereby any element or group of elements takes on the function of a nominal group in the clause" (e.g. *<u>what the duke gave my aunt</u> was that teapot*, ibid.: 58).

But metaphorical Themes can also express interpersonal metaphors involving modalisations or modulations (WFG: 68–70). Instances of thematic subjective modalisations are achieved through *first person*,[62] present tense "mental" processes of *cognition* (e.g. *I think, I reckon, I suspect*) or "relational" processes of *cognitive state* (*I'm sure, convinced, uncertain, ...*); whereas thematic objective

Table 7. *Summary of principal types of projection*

Project process (quotes and reports)	Rank:	Clause complex			Nominal group		
	Orientation: Taxis: Speech function	Quote Paratactic	Report 1 2	Hypotactic α β	Embedded ‖ :	Fact as Postmodifier	As Head
Verbal (Locution "Projected wording")	Proposition	"1. 2 'It is so,' he said	"1. 2 It was so, he said	α "β. He said that it was so	his assertion that it was so	the saying that it is so ↑	(it is said) that it is so ↑
	Proposal	"1! 2 'Do so!' he told them	"1! 2 They should do so, he told them	α "β! He told them to do so	his order to them to do so ‖'	the stipulation to do so ↑	(it is stipulated) to do so ↑
Mental ('idea' Projected meaning)	Proposition	'1. 2 'It is so,' she knew	'1. 2 It was so, she knew	α 'β. She knew that it was so	her knowledge that it was so ‖'	the fact that it is so ↑	that it is so ↑
	Proposal	'1! 2 'Do so!', she said to herself	'1! 2 She would do so, she decided	α 'β! She decided that she would do so	her decision to do so ‖'	the need to do so ↑	to do so ↑
		'direct'	'free indirect'	'indirect'	indirect qualifying	impersonal qualifying	impersonal

↑ = same as on left

Table 8. *Summary of principal types of expansion*

type of expansion			functional relationship with which expansion is combined	COHESION between clause complexes (non-structural)	INTERDEPENDENCY between clauses in a clause complex	
					paratactic	hypotactic
(=) ELABORATION	apposition		expository exemplificatory	In other words For example	that is	which, who / non-finite clause /
	clarification		various types	Or rather, Anyway, Actually &c.	at least	NON-DEFINING RELATIVE CLAUSE
(+) EXTENSION	addition		positive negative adversative	Also Neither However	and nor but	while whereas / besides without
	variation		replacive subtractive alternative	On the contrary Otherwise Alternatively	only or	except that if not ... then / besides other than
(x) ENHANCEMENT	spatio-temporal	place	extent point(s)	There	there	as far as where(ver)	
		time	extent point(s) prior subsequent various complex types	Throughout Simultaneously Previously Next Finally, At once, Meanwhile &c.	now then	while when(ever) before, until after, since as soon as &c.	while, in when, on before, until after, since
	manner		means quality comparison	Thus Likewise	so	as, as if	by like, as if
	causal-conditional	cause	reason result purpose insurance	Therefore Consequently To that end	so, for thus	because in order that in case	with, by as a result of (so as) to, for in case of
		condition	positive negative concessive	In that case Otherwise Nevertheless	then otherwise though	if, as long as unless although	if, in event of without despite
	matter		respective	In this respect			
class of item	that is being related: by which relationship is realized			clause(complex): prepositional phrase or adverb	independent clause: conjunction	finite or non-finite dependent clause: conjunction, preposition, or relative (noun)	

Table 8. *(continued)*

EMBEDDING of clause as Modifier in nominal group	CIRCUMSTAN-TIATION in clause (as process)	PHASE, CONATION &c. in verbal group complex (TENSE, VOICE in verbal group)		ATTRIBUTION or IDENTIFICATION as relational process in clause
which, who; [non-finite] that [clause] DEFINING RELATIVE CLAUSE	as ROLE	PASSIVE VOICE is (vⁿ)	PHASE (a) TIME start, keep (b) REALITY seem, turn out	INTENSIVE 'is' ⊖
whose, of which DEFINING RELATIVE CLAUSE (POSSESSIVE)	with, including without ACCOMPANIMENT instead of except (for)	PAST TENSE has (vⁿ) OBLIGA-TION has td (v°)	CONATION & POTEN-TIALITY try; succeed; can, learn	POSSESSIVE 'has' ⊕
DEFINING RELATIVE CLAUSE (CIRCUMSTANTIAL) (a) CIRCUMSTANCE AS HEAD place (where/that) time (when/that) reason (why/that) &c. (b) CIRCUMSTANCE AS MODIFIER [HEAD] where/at which [noun] when/on which for which about which &c.	for PLACE at, in for at, on before TIME after during &c. by, with (adverb) MANNER like because of CAUSE for in case of in the event of in default of despite CONDITION about MATTER	PRESENT TENSE is (at) (vⁿ) EXPECT-ATION is to (v°)	MODULA-TION (a) TIME begin by (b) MANNER venture hesitate (c) CAUSE happen, remember	CIRCUMSTANTIAL 'is at' (a) CIRCUMSTANCE AS PROCESS occupies, follows, causes concerns &c. (b) CIRCUMSTANCE AS PARTICIPANT is at, in, on, before, like, because of, about &c. ⊗
finite or non-finite rankshifted clause: relative (noun, adverb, or prepositional phrase)	propositional phrase: preposition	verbal group: auxiliary	verbal group complex: verb	nominal group: verb or preposition

modalisations are deployed through *nominalisations of probability and usuality*, construing them either as a quality (adjective) or a thing (noun) (e.g. *it is likely, there is no possibility*). In contrast, thematic subjective metaphorical modulations involve first-person, present-tense mental processes of *affection* (e.g. *I want, I need, I'd like, I'd hate*); whereas their objective counterparts are regularly made explicit through nominalisations of *inclination* and *obligation*, construing these either as a quality or a thing (e.g. *it's permissible, it's compulsory*, the intention/ desire/determination, etc.).

Figure 11 (IFG: 58) illustrates the congruent and the metaphorical representations of a topical Theme, which although potentially *co-representational*, i.e. they represent the same piece of reality (and in this respect form a set of metaphoric variants of an experiential kind), are regarded as not synonymous (Martin 1992a; Halliday & Martin 1993).

I	don't believe	that pudding	ever will be cooked
Theme	Rheme	Theme	Rheme
interpersonal (modal)		topical	
Theme			Rheme

Figure 11. *Clauses as topical Theme: congruent and metaphorical versions*

4.3 Troubleshooting

This section addresses three aspects of SFG Theme that have been challenged or disagreed upon: (a) the "double-sided" nature of the category of "topical Theme" (Section 4.3.1); (b) the identification of the Theme of a message (Section 4.3.2); and (iii) the "separating" standpoint of the theory as a whole (Section 4.3.3) (see Gómez-González 1996a, b, 1998a, b, d, forthcoming).

4.3.1 *The "double-sided" nature of Theme*

The supposedly "double-sided" nature of SFG Theme has been debated by many scholars, both within and outside the systemic literature.[69] We have seen that in this model two metaphors are used as two *different*, but *equivalent*, glosses of topical Theme: (a) the spatial metaphor, or "the point of departure of an English clause as a message" (realized by the first experiential/interpersonal element), and (b) the matter metaphor, or "what a clause is about" (Section 4.2, quotations in (69) and (70)). Most criticisms emerge from the assumption that these two glosses, "starting point" and "aboutness", in fact invoke two distinct notions which tend to, but need not, coincide in one wording. As a result, unlike Halliday and his co-workers in SFG, the defenders of this "dissociating" view, exclude from *topical status* the clause initial constituents listed in (77) below (see examples (9), (10), (11), (12), Section 2.2.1):

(77) a. *non-referential participants* such as negative Subjects (i.e. *nothing, nowhere*, etc.) and impersonal Subjects (e.g. *You can define a net in one of two ways, depending on your point of view*, Downing 1990: 123);

b. *Fronted circumstantial* Adjuncts (including presentative Adjuncts) (e.g. *At seventeen, he announces ...*, ibid.: 124);

c. *There* in *existential constructions* (e.g. *There was once an ugly bear who hid from the world*, ibid.: 126);

d. *Fronted Attributes* (e.g. *Worst of all was the emasculation of the League of Nations*, ibid.: 127).

However, while "dissociating" authors like Huddleston (1988, 1991, 1992) or Hudson (1986), for example, divest clause-initial position of any grammatical relevance and understand Topic as an intuitive referent that can only be inferred from the co(n)text; others, like Fries (1983, 1987), Downing (1991) or Downing & Locke (1992), argue for the functional validity of both notions (see Section 2.2.1 above, examples (13), (14) and (15)).

Emblematically, Downing (1991) describes Theme as the clause initial slot that may set three different kinds of *frameworks*, depending on two syntactic criteria, [± Participant], [± nuclear constituent], and three semantic parameters [± experiential meaning] [± spatial] and [± temporal meaning], as expounded in Table 9 (Bäcklund 1989: 297; Thompson 1985: 61; Lowe 1987: 6; Section 2.4.1 above):

a. *individual frameworks*, i.e. initial participants, attributes or processes (e.g. <u>The Gauls</u> *sacked Rome*, Downing 1991: 123) [my emphasis]);

b. *circumstantial frameworks*, i.e. initial Adjuncts that pertain to one of the following types:

i. *temporal*, i.e. an initial temporal Adjunct which may refer to the previous context (e.g. <u>Until that time</u> *they had waged war, and generally unsuccessful war, with the Etrusca*ns, ibid.: 133) or not (e.g. <u>For two hundred years</u> *the Roman soldier-farmers had struggled for freedom and a share in the government of their state*, ibid.: 132);

ii. *spatial*, i.e. initial spatial Adjunct (e.g. <u>In the East long before the time of Buddha there had been ascetics</u> ..., ibid.: 134);
iii. *situational*, realized by items other than participants, attributes, processes, or by spatio-temporals (viz. participant-tied V-en dependent clauses like <u>Thwarted in the West</u>, *Stalin turned East* (ibid.: 135); participant-tied V-ing dependent situation clauses <u>like *Now, starting from his colony of Albania*</u>, *he decided to conquer Greece* (ibid.: 137) [my emphasis] or V-to-infinitive purpose clauses and conditional initiators and other contingencies.[71]
c. *discourse frameworks*, equivalent to Halliday's textual and interpersonal Themes plus a new category, that of *relational Themes* (e.g. *legally, consumer-wise, from the point of view of sales*, etc.), which "present the clausal message from the point of view of something else related to it" (1991: 124).[72]

Besides, adhering to van Oosten's (1986) analysis, Downing & Locke (1992) distinguish between *superordinate*, or text level, *Topics* (i.e. "what a text is about"), and *clause level Topics* (i.e. "what a clause is about"). Superordinate Topics are defined as *cognitive schemata* (referring to the organisation of thoughts into schemes of things) that compress the Topic of a whole text into a single proposition e.g. titles of books, articles, lectures, etc., whereas clause level Topics are identified with Subject and Object participants which contribute to building up text level Topics. The other syntactic functions, i.e. Complements, Attributes or circumstantial Adjuncts, are described as *Attributes* of, and therefore subordinate to, basic clause level Topics.[73]

Importantly, this description leaves out from "topical" status the initial constituents listed in (77) above, regarded as "topical Themes" in SFG (Davison 1984: 827). The reason is that from this standpoint only initial Subjects and Objects can behave as Topics and hence be properly labelled as "topical" Themes. For Downing and Locke, for example, the devices comprised in (77) represent some of the means available in English to mark *Topic discontinuity* in discourse, that is, to introduce *new* clause level Topics, providing emphatic points of departure and/or infusing with rhematic (EW) and/or focal (EF) prominence an element (the NewTopic) that otherwise would not receive this type of prominence.[74]

In my opinion, these conflicting positions can be reconciled by accepting the view that "aboutness" may be approached from three different perspectives, *relational*, *referential* and *interactive*, which pursue different phenomena, yield different results and pose different analytical and theoretical problems, as

Table 9. *Halliday's multiple Theme vs. Downing's thematic frameworks [my Table]*

Halliday's multiple Theme	Downing's thematic frameworks				
Metafunctions	Framework	Particip.	Nuclear	Experient.	Theme
Ideational	Individual	+	+	+	participant (Subj., Obj.,
		−	−	+	Compl., *as for.* elements)
		−	+	−	attribute
					process
	Circumst.				
	Spatial	−	−	+	Place Adjunct
	Temporal	−	−	+	Time Adjunct
	Situational	−	−	+	other Adjuncts (e.g. Participant-tied V-en clauses, participant-tied V-ing dependent situation clauses, to-infinitive clauses, etc.)
Textual	Discourse	−	−	−	Conjunctive Themes, continuatives, conjunctions, relatives and relational Themes
	Logical				
Interpersonal	Subjective	−	−	−	Modal Themes

discussed at some length in Chapter 2 above. Roughly we have explained that *relational aboutness* refers to an *analyst-determined* and *message-centred (clausal)* notion, whereas *referential* and *interactive aboutness* evoke two distinct *context-centred* categories. My assumption is that most interpretations of Topic allude either to *referential aboutness*, i.e. a relationship of aboutness established between a clause/utterance referent and the overall discourse (*discourse Topics*), or to *interactive aboutness*, representing speakers' discourse perspectives on what is at issue at a given point of discourse, rather than (analysts' perceptions of) contextual incidentals (*speaker's Topics*).

Alternatively, the aboutness feature of SFG (topical) Theme seems to distil a *relational* character. SFG analyses apparently rest on the relational assumption that, as a result of the linear quality of language, "what a message is about" is iconically coded by predication-external/internal message initial experiential/transitivity position, i.e. a participant, an attribute, a circumstance or a process, in relation to a clausal predication, or Rheme (as noted with regard to (9), (10), (11) and (12) in Section 2.2.1 above). Indeed, a relational account of the "aboutness" feature of Theme fits in well with both such psycholinguistic expressions as the "point of departure/point of embarkation of the clause as a message", or "the hook/peg on which the message is hung", and with the deictic and frame-establishing potential assigned to this category. By signalling which transitivity role acts as the Theme ("point of departure") of a given process, the speaker is determining from which "semantic perspective" that particular process is to be viewed. And by choosing one particular starting point, whether multiple or non-multiple, marked or unmarked, congruent or metaphorical, the speaker is making a meaningful textual choice because these constructions involve different means of packaging information.

Besides, a relational interpretation of thematic "aboutness" (as setting the speaker's angle on the experience being constructed) lends itself to the interpersonally-oriented systemic accounts that the function of unmarked thematic patterns of declarative, interrogative, imperative or exclamative messages is to expresses their Mood, or purpose, while marked Themes occur when an element other than the expected one for each mood pattern has been *preposed*, or *fronted*, to clause-initial position. Incidentally, the claim that Theme expresses the mood of messages also satisfies the objection that it is rather counterintuitive that question-answer pairs more often than not imply a change of Theme. In short, as shown in Table 10 (based on IFG: 37ff.), from a relational perspective the *valeur*, or paradigmatic value, of thematic choices is established "relationally", that is, in relation to the *proportionalities*[75] or relationships in which they participate with respect to:

a. the Rheme within the clause;
b. the Given and the New within the Theme system complex;
c. cohesive relationships, within the textual component;
d. grammar as a whole; and
e. discourse it all its dimensions, that is, *register*, *genre* and *ideology* (comprising various aspects of cultural diversity such as ethnicity, class, gender, generation, etc.).

In keeping with this a clause like *And perhaps he's right* could be claimed to be simultaneously "about" *and*, *perhaps* and *he* in that these items stand within the thematic domain for the speaker's choice of, for example, one of the proportionalities included in Table 11.

Likewise, an account of Theme in terms of relational aboutness could be reconciled with such examples as those in (77) above, regarded as topicless in many referential accounts, answering at the same time such demands as Huddleston's (1988, 1991), for instance, who asks for a reconciliation of the IFG account of Theme in terms of the matter metaphor. As advanced in Section 2.2.1, sequences like those in (77), e.g. *Nothing will satisfy you*, *You could buy a bar of chocolate like this for 6d before the War* and *There is a fallacy in your argument*,

Table 10. *Thematic proportionalities within the Theme system complex*

Theme system complex			Examples		
Theme system			Information system		
multiple	special	marked	marked tonality	marked tonicity	marked tone
−	−	−	−	−	−	//1 *the duke* has given my aunt that **teapot**//
−	−	+	−	−	−	//1 *the duke* surely has given my aunt that **teapot**
−	−	+	+	+	−	//4 *that* **teapot**// //1 the duke has given my **aunt**//
−	+	−	−	+	−	//5 *what the* **duke** *gave to my aunt* was that teapot//
−	+	+	−	+	−	//4 *the* **teapot** it was that the duke gave to my aunt//
−	+	−	−	−	−	//1 *it was that* **teapot** that the duke gave to my aunt//
−	+	−	−	−	−	//13 *the duke* has given it to my **aunt** that **teapot**//
−	+	−	+	−	−	//4 *that* **teapot**// //1 the duke has given it to my **aunt**//

could be said to "be about" and have "as point of departure" *nothing*, impersonal *you* or *there*, for example, because these items express the speaker's experiential/interpersonal onset of the message to be constructed, whether or not they are endowed with referential nominal status. The functional relevance of these points of departure lies in the contrasts they establish with respect to other thematic (and rhematic) choices in given co(n)texts, as expounded in Table 12:

Drawing on this issue, Matthiessen and Martin (1991: 43–8) explain that negative Themes such as *Nothing* contrast with positive Themes (e.g. *something, somebody, everybody, etc.*) and with rhematic instances, thematizing the polarity of the clause (except that the negative feature is restricted to the Theme) as well as a participant, which (when the participant is not Subject) leads to Finite preceding Subject (e.g. <u>Nowhere</u> *would you get a better offer*, ibid.: 44). Matthiessen and Martin also observe that items such as *nothing* and *you* in (77) above,

Table 11. *Multiple Theme and textual proportionalities*

Clause	Theme		
	textual	interpersonal	topical
And perhaps he's right	1	2	3
And he perhaps is right	1	0	2
Perhaps he is right	0	1	2
He perhaps is right	0	0	1

discarded from topical status by the "as for" test applied in many referential analyses, get topical status when picked out by other thematic markers such as *speaking of*, or even by *as for* itself in specific contexts and/or usages, as expounded in (78) (ibid.: 47):

(78) a. Speaking of nothing, have you paid the phone bill yet? [my emphasis]
b. You and Henry have very different personalities. Henry is slow and deliberate. He tends to plan things well in advance and consult with everybody who might be affected. He will only start projects if there is a very definite purpose. Sometimes that can be a disadvantage. As for you, you always act on impulse. [my emphasis]

Moreover, Martin & Mathiessen (1991) note that *as for* (or similar) constructions cannot be used as a "test" of thematic status (even if they are used in this way in (IFG: 39)), but as explicit markers of thematic status of specific referential Themes, which:

a. typically function as Subjects;
b. convey given information;
c. play an experiential role in the ideational structure of the clause;
d. introduce an elaboration of some aspect of a general statement made earlier in the text (usually the second or later in a series);
e. either question or leave out from thematic status items that do behave as Themes (IFG: 39; Matthiessen & Martin 1991: 46).

Other cases in point are *It*-Themes (*ambient it*; *non-representational it* and *anticipatory it*) and instances of postponed (or discontinuous) Themes, which, acting negatively, endow with EF and/or EW prominence items that otherwise would not get this type of discourse prominence, easing, at the same time, the information processing of the sequence(s), as also claimed by Downing & Locke, for example, defenders of the dissociation of syntactic Theme (relational aboutness) and Topic (referential aboutness).

Table 12. *Some thematic proportionalities*

Theme	Markedness	Samples
Non-special Themes		
Theme-Mood	unmarked	You could buy a bar of chocolate like this for 6d before the War
	–	Nothing will satisfy you
	–	Your argument has a fallacy
	marked	A bar of chocolate like this you could buy for 6d before the War
	–	You nothing will satisfy
	–	A fallacy your argument has
Theme-Transitivity	unmarked	A bar of chocolate like this could be bought for 6d before the War
	–	You will not be satisfied
	marked	Before the war a bar of chocolate like this could be bought for 6d
special Themes		
Theme-Predication	unmarked	It was a bar of chocolate like this that you could buy for 6d before the War
	–	It is you that nothing satisfies
	–	It is your argument that has a fallacy
	marked	Before the war it was a bar of chocolate like this that you could buy for 6d
	–	You it is that nothing satisfies
	–	Your argument it is that has a fallacy
Theme-Identification	unmarked	What you could buy for 6d before the War was a bar of chocolate like this
	–	Who nothing satisfies is you
	–	What has a fallacy is your argument
	marked	A bar of chocolate like this was what you could buy for 6d before the War
	–	You are who nothing satisfies
	–	A fallacy is what your argument has
Theme-Reference	unmarked	As to chocolate, you could buy a bar like this for 6d before the War
	–	As for being satisfied, nothing satisfies you
	–	Regarding your argument, it has a fallacy
	marked	As to chocolate, before the war you could buy a bar like this for 6d
	–	Regarding your argument, a fallacy it has

Table 12. *(continued)*

Theme	Markedness	Samples
Theme-Substitution	unmarked	You could buy it for 6d before the War, a bar of chocolate like this
	–	it has a fallacy, your argument
	marked	This you could buy for 6d before the War, a bar of chocolate like this
	–	A fallacy it has, your argument
Existential Theme	unmarked	There was a bar of chocolate that you could buy for 6d before the War
	–	There is nothing that satisfies you
	–	There is a fallacy in your argument
	marked	Before the War there was a bar of chocolate that you could buy for 6d
	–	In your argument there is a fallacy

As shown in Table 13, (WFG: 31–34) analyses the three different uses of *it*-Themes as instances of unmarked Subject Themes.

Ambient *it* is portrayed as a perfectly regular unmarked topical Theme in that it serves as a participant in the transitivity structure of the clause.[76] In contrast, non-representational *it*, i.e. in "meteorological" clauses and in the "impersonal" use of *it*, presents itself as a rather peculiar kind of topical Theme because: (a) it does not represent a phenomenon of experience and does not serve a participant role (e.g. unless metaphorically, we would not say *what is it doing? — It's raining, what's raining*); (b) it is not open to such transitivity oriented thematic strategies as Theme-predication (**it was it that rained*) or marked absolute Themes (**as for it, it is said that he is very wealthy*); and (c) *it* cannot be picked up textually by reference (if we say *it rained yesterday and it's snowing today*, the second *it* does not refer back to the first). Yet systemicists treat non-representational *it* as unmarked topical Theme because it orients the mood selection of the clause (*it [is]: is it*) and because it contrasts with marked topical Themes in the same way as prototypical, representational unmarked topical Themes do, as shown in the alternants in (79) (WFG: 33):

(79) a. Henry is swimming today : Today Henry is swimming.
     b. It is raining today : Today it is raining
     c. It is said nowadays that this substance is harmless
     d. Nowadays it is said that this substance is harmless

Table 13. *Types of 'contentless' Subject* it

type	subtype/use	example	agnate example
i. ambient *it*		it's hot	The room's hot
ii. non-representational *it*	meteorological *it*	it's raining	(rain's falling)
	impersonal projection *it*	it is said that he's a decent fellow it seems that he's a decent fellow	they say that he's a decent fellow: it is said to be the case that he's a decent fellow it seems to be the case that he's a decent fellow
iii. anticipatory *it*	in mental and relational clauses with postposition	it worries us that he has disappeared it is irrelevant that she's a woman	the fact worries us that he has disappeared : (the fact) that he has disappeared worries us the fact is irrelevant that she is a woman : (the fact) that she's a woman is irrelevant
	in Theme predication	it was the dog that died	the one that died was the dog : the dog died

Similarly, the anticipatory *it* occurring in *mental and relational* clauses that anticipates an embedded clause occurring later in the structure has a thematic variant where the embedded clause is Theme (e.g. *it worries me that he's not doing his homework* vs. *that he's not doing his homework worries me*); while the anticipatory *it* of *predicated Themes* is said to show thematic agnation with non-predicated versions (e.g. *It was **Rabbit** who saw Piglet first* : *Rabbit saw Piglet first*, WFG: 28).

There-structures, on the other hand, are described as ideally designed for introducing participants as unmarked news at the end of the clause (e.g. *There's always a long queue*, *There was trouble at the mill*, *There might come a time...*, WFG: 34; Martin 1992b). In the systemic literature one can read that, not indicating location, existential *there* functions as unmarked Subject Theme because it gives the mood choice (of declarative or interrogative) of the sequence, even if it does not realize a participant. Existential *there* functions simply to map the meaning "existence" onto Theme which acts as an anticipatory framework signalling that something is coming, namely a new participant in a story, which is often picked up referentially and thematically in the subsequent discourse. In other words, the point of departure is precisely the fact that a participant (such as *a long queue or trouble at the mill*) is to be introduced. So although *there* does not itself function as a participant (or circumstance) it is still regarded as topical Theme.

Finally, by distinguishing three interpretations of aboutness, it could be argued that Huddleston's or Downing's Topic (coding interactive and referential aboutness, respectively) and Halliday's Theme (invoking clause relational aboutness), for example, represent distinct choices that do not need to coalesce, but may interplay in discourse, as expounded in (80):

(80) a. She broke it)
b. What about the battery?
c. It was OK
d. There was nothing wrong with it
e. I had to replace it

Topic (context dependent): *she, it, she broke it, the battery* (in referential and interactive approaches).

Theme: *she, what about, it, there* (in relational and syntactic accounts).

The analysis in (80) shows that these apparently irreconcilable perspectives can be reconciled, taking heed at the same time of the systemicists' warning against the danger of a direct "translatability" across the notions of Theme in SFG and Topic in formal grammars (IFG: 38, 52; Martin & Matthiessen 1991; Hasan & Fries 1995b: xxix–xxx). Besides, it could be concluded that systemicists are consistent in treating the matter metaphor ("aboutness") and spatial metaphor ("point of departure") as two different aspects of Theme, i.e. the relational "semantic" (in the aboutness sense) and the psycholinguistic and syntactic, respectively.

By recognising this "double-sided" nature of Theme, relational-semantic ("aboutness") and syntactic ("point of departure"), we can do justice to the more global implications of the SFG notion of Theme while avoiding two negative side-effects. One is the "reductive distortion" of this category to the notion of "aboutness", as implied in referential criticisms. And the other is that we are consistent with SFG descriptions of Theme in terms of both the spatial and matter metaphors (Section 4.2, quotations in (69) and (70)), instead of contradictorily forcing ourselves to admit that one (e.g. "starting point") takes precedence over or neutralises the other, as apparently distilled from, for example, Matthiessen & Martin (1991) explanations. Indeed, if aboutness is dismissed, how could one, for instance, explicate such thematic constructions as Theme substitution (e.g. *they don't seem to match, these colours*) or Theme reference (e.g. *Britain it's all roads*), or Theme predication (e.g. *it was John who broke the window*) or thematic equatives (e.g. *what John saw was the play*)? Or vice versa, if the notion of "point of departure" is abandoned, how could one highlight the multifunctional nature of the Theme (vs. Rheme) zone in terms of, for example, consistency, relative weight, or iconicity of its realization at clause level, beyond and below the clause — in terms of syntactic sequence as what comes first, whether it be transitivity, interpersonal and/or textual elements, vs. what comes last?

4.3.2 Identifying the Theme

Despite the possible benefits of assuming a relational interpretation of the aboutness feature of SFG Theme, it seems that three issues remain moot points in the identification of this category. These shall be treated in the following sections: (a) six aspects of terminology (Sections 4.3.2.1–6); (b) the notion of "displaced Theme" (Section 4.3.2.7); and (c) initial position as a criterion to identify Theme (Section 4.3.2.8).

4.3.2.1 *The first "ideational" element*
It seems that "first ideational element" is an inaccurate identification of Theme given that this category embodies items fulfilling both a logical and an experiential metafunction, when only the latter are considered to be really topical. A more adequate description for topical Theme would perhaps be the first experiential/transitivity constituent of the message.

4.3.2.2 *The label "textual Theme"*
Similarly, the label textual Theme appears to be both tautological, since the category of Theme in its broadest sense is a textual notion, and inexact for it refers to initial items fulfilling a logical metafunction. Textual Theme might therefore be more accurately relabelled either as conjunctive or as logical Theme.

4.3.2.3 *The "structure" imposed by thematic patterns*
It seems that Huddleston (1991: 106) is right to observe that "constituency is not the appropriate concept for the strings that Halliday labels [multiple] Theme", since, as shown throughout this chapter, systemicists insist that the Theme system comprises non-constructional, non-discrete categories, assigning wave-like, or pulse-like, peaks of prominence to the beginning and end of the English clause. If this premise is to be accepted, it is only reasonable to believe that systemic expositions do lack some rigour when, for example, talking about the "structure" of the multiple Theme, about the order of "elements" within it, about the marked or unmarked nature of its "constituents", and when representing multiple Themes as layered constituent structures.

Going by SFG descriptions, the fact that elements fulfilling a logical and/or an interpersonal function may precede the first experiential/interpersonal item should not be taken as a constructional argument for three reasons. To begin with, as already noted, textual patterns are described as non-constructional. Secondly, if different metafunctions are said to have different patterns of realization, then it follows that the different kinds of Theme (viz. experiential/ transitivity, interpersonal and logical) should also impose different patterns and/ or vary with respect to their scope of influence. Furthermore, if the mappings of the three metafunctions are *simultaneous*, as remarked by Halliday (1978: 134), it does not seem to be very consistent to dissociate the three metafunctions arguing for three kinds of Theme.

None of these issues seem to have yet been discussed in the degree of detail they deserve. At most, it has been suggested that elements fulfilling a specific metafunction may fall outside the patterns of organisation imposed by that particular metafunction, in the same way that items not fulfilling a specific metafunction may be inside or outside the structural patterns that metafunction imposes (e.g. comment and conjunctive Adjuncts are said fall outside the Mood-Residue, although they are interpersonal and textual in function, respectively (IFG: 84). But, crucially enough, these two possibilities equally undermine the SFG tenet that linguistic structures consist of multifunctional constituents. Similarly, it remains to be explained how a thematic item may fulfil a conjunctive and/or interpersonal and/or experiential/interpersonal function, all of them described as different types of *constituency* multivariate relationships, and at the same time impose *non-constructional* patterns in discourse.

4.3.2.4 *Deriving the "meaning" of Theme*

Bazel (1973: 201) and Huddleston (1991: 105) remark that to derive the meaning of Theme from the meaning of the construction as a whole would represent a massive shift in the concept of SFG Theme that has never been properly acknowledged. I think, however, that enough evidence has been presented throughout this chapter in favour of the opposite. It has been shown that SFG Theme derives its functional potential "relationally", i.e. from its relation with that of Rheme (an entity plays the role of Theme because there is another playing the role of a rhematic predication). Halliday himself states this explicitly when describing the thematic structure of subjectless imperatives (e.g. *Keep quiet*):

> [s]trictly speaking, these have no explicit Theme; the meaning "I want you to", which might have been thematized, by analogy with those above [Subject imperatives], or with the interrogative, is realized simply by the *form* of the clause." (1985a: 49) [my emphasis])

4.3.2.5 *Substitute Themes*

In Section 7.4.5 below we shall see that, although often treated together in the systemic literature, a distinction should be made between substitute Themes or "right detached" elements (RDs) and "afterthoughts", since the two are structurally and functionally radically different (Lambrecht 1994). Roughly, the differences between these two constructions can be summarised along three parameters. First, RDs are upward bounded, afterthoughts are not. This is evident in such examples as *I learned he$_i$ was there John$_i$ from the newspaper* vs. **I learned he$_i$ was there from the newspaper John$_i$*. Note the ungrammaticality on the RD and not on the vocative reading and compare the wellformedness of *I learned he$_i$ was there from the newspaper, John$_i$, I mean*, which is acceptable in the afterthought and non-vocative reading.

Secondly, RDs display a necessary coreference between the final NG and its intra-clausal correlate, afterthoughts need not, since they may (and in fact they do) correct the referent assignment, so the clause internal NG need not be pronominal nor coreferential with the external NG. Accordingly, sequences like *I learned he$_i$ was there from the newspaper, John$_i$, I mean*, with coreference, or e.g. *Bill$_i$ is here, John$_j$ I mean in fact*, with no coreference, display afterthought structure and intonation. Finally, intonational distinctions may be evident between them as well. In light of this, conflating (RDs) and afterthoughts seems an oversimplification.

4.3.2.6 *Reference Themes*

There are those who distinguish as for NG ... pro ... as a non-left detached construction from NG initial constructions as *left detachments* (LDs). With respect to the latter, perhaps, more emphasis should be laid on the fact that LD, or reference Themes, are not part of the clause, but rather are *external* constituents *attached* to the clause. Thus, for example, the RD element does not behave as a clause-initial constituent. An indication of this is that fronting over it is impossible, unlike over clause-initial constituents elsewhere. Rather, fronting takes place in such instances to a position clause initially, immediately following the LD constituent. Relevant examples are e.g. **Last year, Rosa$_i$ she$_i$ lost 20 pounds and this year ...* vs. *Rosa$_i$, last year she$_i$ lost 20 pounds and this year*. This will become more evident in Section 7.4.4 below where the form and function of LD are addressed in more detail.

4.3.2.7 *Displaced Themes*

The SFG suggestion that topical Themes may be "displaced" apparently conceals a third terminological and conceptual drawback (Downing 1991; Gómez-González

1996a, b, forthcoming). In a note at the end of a textual analysis in (IFG: 64) the category of displaced Theme (marked off with an asterisk "*") is described as Themes that would be unmarked in the ensuing clause, if the existing marked topicalTheme was reworded as a dependent clause, as Robert in (81):

(81) *Apart from a need to create his own identity «having been well and truly trained and educated and, indeed, used by his father for so long, emotionally and practically» Robert* felt that at twenty the last thing he wanted to do was to join a family firm in Newcastle.*

The claim is made that if this example was reworded more *congruently*[77] as *Besides needing to create his own identity, Robert ...*, then in the ensuing clause *Robert* becomes an unmarked Theme.

It seems to me, however, that the notion of a "displaced Theme" is unnecessary, not to say inconsistent with SFG theses. First, the idea of a displaced, or non-initial topical Theme, violates the systemic description of this category as extending up to (and including) the first experiential/transitivity element (IFG: 56; WFG: 24). Hence, on not being initial, it follows that "displaced" transitivity constituents cannot be regarded as thematic. And second, the identification of a displaced Theme as that which "would be unmarked Theme in the ensuing clause, if the existing marked topical Theme was reworded as a dependent clause", is so vague that virtually all marked Themes could be considered to precede a displaced Theme. This would imply a shift in the theory that, to my knowledge, has never been intended. Rather, the account of displaced Themes is restricted to just three examples of different types of marked (Adjunct) Themes as illustrated in (82) (IFG: 64–5), which reveals the account of this category as *ad hoc* and somewhat inconsistent:

(82) a. <u>Apart from a need to create his own identity «having been well and truly trained and educated and, indeed, used by his father for so long, emotionally and practically» Robert</u>* felt that at twenty the last thing he wanted to do was to join a family firm in Newcastle.
  b. <u>For all his integrity and high principles, Robert</u>* pulled a slightly fast one over his father and business partners.
  c. <u>In a letter [written to Longridge] on 7 June, eleven days before Robert's departure, George</u>* sounds distinctly miserable, even bitter, «though trying hard to hide it,» at the prospect of travelling to Liverpool in time to see e.g. Robert off.

Indeed, if it could be admitted that the topical Themes in (82a) and (82b) do display some sort of semantic dependency on *Robert*, which could support the analysis of this constituent as a "displaced" Theme, that is not the case in (82c), where an independent place Adjunct is also analysed as "displacing" the topical Theme. This could be a consistent analysis if, SFG Theme was interpreted referentially, which would restrict this category to referential participants. But, this does not seem to be the case for elsewhere initial circumstances are presented as a central type of marked topical Theme, which apparently indicates that SFG adopts a relational-syntactic interpretation of this category.[78]

4.3.2.8 *Initial position*
A more serious allegation is whether or not Halliday demonstrates, i.e. gives some type of evidence, empirical, grammatical or semantic, or only asserts, that the topical Theme is the cut-off point between Theme, and whether or not there is a single invariant meaning attaching to this category (Hudson 1986: 798; Taglicht 1984: 14; Huddleston 1988, 1991, 1992). Not infrequently, the reader does have the impression that SFG descriptions in this connection are somewhat vague. The lack of explicitness appears to stem from a two-fold source:

a. the systemicists' belief that functional categories are inherently *ineffable*, i.e. they cannot be defined (IFG: 38; Halliday's personal communication in *Seminar on Systemic Functional Linguistics*, Córdoba May 5–7, 1993); and
b. the nature of the textual metafunction in particular.

As a result we can find some rather obscure explanations in the systemic literature. We are told, for example, that grammatical categories are much more general than lexical ones and that accordingly it is impossible to lexicalise grammatical categories just as it is impossible to grammaticalise lexical ones. Likewise, one can read that since the textual metafunction is not representational and therefore cannot be turned back on itself to represent itself, the category of Theme (and textual categories in general) must be articulated in terms of metaphors, involving (motion through) abstract space such as *point of departure* (or *topic basis, peg* [as a location for meaning], *framework foreground/background, transition, guidepost, flow of information*) (Halliday 1984; Halliday & Martin 1993; Matthiessen & Bateman 1991; Matthiessen 1988, 1992, 1995; Martin & Matthiessen 1991; Hasan & Fries 1995a, b). Further, we are explained that these metaphors are "ideational" translations of textual meanings, not "semantic" interpretations, whatever that means (Martin 1995: 255 endnote 9; Hasan & Fries 1995b: xxv).

Be that as it may, of importance here is the fact that, probably under the influence of PS syntactic analysts, five different, and, in my view, not necessarily concurrent, accounts of Theme are proposed in SFG (Gómez-González 1996a, forthcoming):

a. a *psycholinguistic notion*, i.e. "psychological Subject", or the "object of thought", as opposed to the notions of: (i) the grammatical Subject, or the one of whom a statement is predicated, and (ii) the logical Subject, the one "who is said to have carried out the process that the clause represents" (IFG: 32);
b. the *spatial metaphor*, i.e. "point of departure/takeoff point" or "the point of embarkation of the clause"; in other words, "what I, the speaker, choose to take as my point of departure" (1967a: 200, 205; 1994: 299;), "the peg on which the message is hung" (1970a: 161), "the heading to what I am saying" (ibid.: 163) (see Section 4.4, quotations in (70) above);
c. the *matter metaphor*, i.e. "aboutness/concern", glossed as "the concern of the message"; "what is being talked about" [...] "what I am talking about" (or "what I am talking about now" (1967a: 212); "that with which the clause is concerned" (IFG: 37) (see Section 4.4, quotations in (69) and (70) above);
d. a *realizational statement*, i.e. initial position, "[a]s a general guide, [...] that element which comes in first position in the clause" (IFG: 38);
e. a *functional description*, that is to say, "one element in a particular functional configuration which, taken as a whole, organizes the clause as a message" (IFG: 38).

Halliday readily abandons gloss (a), psychological Subject, arguing that there is no way of knowing "what the speaker has in her/his mind at the moment of speaking" (personal communication, *Seminar on Systemic Functional Linguistics*, Córdoba May 5–7, 1993). Instead, as already explained in Section 4.2, systemicists use the matter and spatial metaphors as two different, but equivalent, glosses of Theme, which opens up the debate already discussed in Section 4.3.1 above. We are then left with (d) and (e), but, importantly enough, these two criteria do not necessarily involve the same notions because it is argued that clause-initial position represents a *criterion of identification*, not a *functional definition* of Theme. The underlying rationale is that clause-initial position is the expression of Theme in languages such as English, whereas in other languages this category may be coded morphologically and/or it may be placed in other positions.

However, the argumentation that leads to the conclusion that initial position is the expression of Theme in PresE seems to be circular and tautological. In (IFG: 39) we are told that clause-initial position is the "natural" position for Theme provided that: (a) in any given language the message is organised as a Theme–Rheme structure, and (b) this structure is expressed by the sequence in which the elements occur in the clause. The first proviso implies that there may be languages lacking the Theme–Rheme patterns, which contravenes the SFG assumption that these patterns are universal principles of organisation instrumental to the ideational and interpersonal meanings (see Section 4.4.2).

The second proviso, on the other hand, suggests that Theme–Rheme patterns may or may not be expressed by the sequence in which these functions occur, which apparently depends on whether or not a language displays morphological cues that mark the thematic status of items. This assumption stumbles over two problems. The first is that, as advanced in Section 2.2.1, for many analysts none of the postulated Topic markers (e.g. Japanese (*-wa*), Tagalog (*-ang*), and Korean (*-nun*)) can be simply equated with any existing definition of Topic/Theme, while all languages do display a syntactic Theme, that is, predication external/internal initial position, its intrinsic functional relevance being language-dependent. As a corollary, regardless of the grammatical structure of languages, one can conclude that the initial slot position remains a communicatively important zone from a relational-semantic and/or a syntactic perspective. In other words, as already noted in Section 4.3.1, it may be concluded (and systemicists should have done so in order to be consistent with their own arguments) that, deriving from staging, or the linear quality of language, the initial zone codes relational-semantic "aboutness" (the speaker's point of departure setting her/his angle on the experience being constructed) syntactically across different languages, although the relevance of this position varies in accordance with the morpho-syntactic structure of specific languages.

In fact, systemicists seem to share this view when admitting that the effects of linearisation are not only restricted to the Theme of clauses, but they also operate below and above this unit, even if, contradictorily enough, minor clauses or "little texts", both instances of texts in any case, are deprived of any thematic structure (IFG: 392–97). In other words, the effects of thematisation should be acknowledged at *all* levels of *delicacy* (i.e. degree of detail) crosslinguistically, instead of restricting them to PresE clauses. This accords well with Halliday's (1964a: 16) and Martin's (1981: 22) observation that:

> ... the scale of delicacy [...] has proved of value in textual analysis because it provides a variable cut-off point for description: the analyst can go as far as he wishes for his own purpose in depth of detail and then stop.

Once the functional relevance of the Theme zone has been acknowledged, a further problem is posed as to how to identify it since SFG resorts to three different cues of thematic status: (a) semantic cues, the initial experiential function, (b) syntactic cues, the initial transitivity element, and (c) phonological cues, the initial tone group, which, as shall be shown, seem inaccurate and not necessarily coterminous criteria.

First, if Themes may "stack" within a metafunctional slot, then there may be more than just one constituent in this and/or the previous functional slots, linked by any type of tactic and logico-semantic relationships. In this connection, Halliday (1967b, 1968, IFG) allows for the *iterative use* of topical Themes, but, importantly enough, based on his observation of English, he notes that marked Themes either conflate with Adjuncts or with Complements, but not with both. However, it is not hard to imagine messages where more than one marked topical Themes occur such that they conflate with distinct mood functions (e.g. *Last year in LA those same shoes I...*, Hasan and Fries 1995b: (3iii) xxxv). Moreover, recursiveness or stacking within the Theme zone makes it hard to identify the borderline between the Theme and the Rheme of a message.

Two cases in point within the SFG framework are Berry (1989, 1992a, 1992b, 1995) and Matthiessen (1992). Unlike Halliday, these two scholars treat as thematic everything that precedes the verb of the main clause, which may mean including more than the first ideational element within this category. Berry further distinguishes between *interactional* thematisation and Topic-based, or *informational*, thematisation. The former foregrounds the interactiveness of the discourse by referring to interactants, whereas the latter foregrounds the organisation of the content by referring to aspects of Topic. Informational Themes are further classified into *current*, i.e. Subject referents that are the same as in the immediately preceding main clause, and *displaced*, Subject referents that are not referred to in the immediately preceding main clause (Martin 1986; and endnote 31, this investigation). In turn, Young (1980), and Vasconcellos (1992) make a distinction between *minor Themes* (Adjunct/textual) and *major Themes* (participants) in the following terms:

> [t]he notion of a major theme is useful because it helps to establish the point at which the rheme begins. In other words, nothing comes between it and the rheme, which is the rest of the unit. The theme ends abruptly, and this makes sense, because its function is specific and finite; once the theme's job is done, other systems of the language take over. Even though themes can stack, there is no progression of salience; each theme slot has a specific function. The rightmost slot is for the major theme, which is the cognitive "hook" on which the rest of the message is hung; the next is for minor themes that create the setting; and the leftmost slot is for themes that link the unit as a whole to the rest of the discourse. The slots do follow a progression from cognitive to non-cognitive and, within non-cognitive, from discoursal to interpersonal. Within adjuncts, the non-cognitive precede the cognitive, and both types can be stacked. The stacked cognitive adjuncts must be either of different subtypes (time, place, manner, cause) or in a logical sequence within the same subtype. [...] The

pattern *conjunction > adjunct > major theme* is more general than Halliday's order classes for English. (Vasconcellos 1992:157 [emphasis in original])

Likewise, as already noted in Section 4.3.1 above, Downing (1991) does not only dissociate the categories of (discourse and clause level) Topic, interpreted referentially, and Theme, interpreted syntactically as clause-initial position, she also suggests that first experiential elements need not represent the cut off point between Theme and Rheme. Downing postulates the possibility of having recursive textual, interpersonal and ideational elements extending up to (and including) the clause level Topic (1991:127), as shown in (84) (Downing's (10) [my emphasis]):

(84)
1. ideational — Towards the end of his life, (1)
2. ideational (+ Topic) — Freud (2) concluded that (3)
3. structural — he (4) was not a great man,
4. ideational (+ Topic) — but (5) he (6) had discovered
5. structural — great things. Arguably (7),
6. ideational (+ Topic) — the reverse (8) might be true.
7. modal
8. ideational (+ Topic)

But the question is posed that, if, as suggested by Halliday, recursive Themes are phonologically coded by tone concord or tone sequences, then it follows that thematic elements do not need to belong to the same information unit either. Furthermore, in spoken (especially spontaneous) speech all sorts of pauses and hesitations could be regarded as legitimate Themes in that they act as the psychological "crutch" on which the speaker relies to continue her/his discourse. Taking this into account, some scholars like Trager and Smith (1951), Henderson (1974), Goldman-Eisler (1972) and Romero Trillo (1994) suggest that the basic unit for the thematic analysis of speech is not the grammatical clause, but the *Phonemic Clause*, i.e. "a phonologically marked macrosegment which contains one and only one primary stress and ends in a terminal juncture" (Trager & Smith (1951) in Boomer (1965:149).

In addition, as suggested by Taglicht (1984:23) in relation to Halliday's remark that everything after the marked Theme is Rheme, it could be argued that the latter category also displays its own thematic structure. As a result, Rhemes could be considered as either unmarked or marked (e.g. end shifted Subject/constituent, final item separated by a partition from item that would precede it, if it were part of the unmarked Rheme). And, discontinuous participants would also be excluded from thematic status (e.g. *A problem has arisen that we need your advice on*). Be that as it may, systemicists acknowledge that analyses of Rheme are indeed deficient, probably on account of the unmarked correlation between Rheme, New and heavy elements, which accordingly are more difficult to systematise. Difficulties notwithstanding, this is an area that deserves further study.

4.3.3 The "separating" stand of the theory

The last trend of criticism questions the SFG allegedly "separating" treatment of the choices comprised within the textual component. In this line Daneš (1974b: 110–1) affirms that he cannot see how the speaker can make her/his addressee interpret as New information that is already recoverable, and regards Halliday's notions of Given and Rheme unclear and indirectly defined. Likewise, Firbas (1974) and Brazil et al. (1980: 112) complain that Halliday's description of the terms "recoverable" or "given" is too vague. Chafe (1976: 38) on the other hand believes that Halliday mixes up the psycholinguistic notion of Given with that of Focus (understood as contrastive), while Allerton (1978: 156–7) affirms that Halliday seems to confuse Theme and Given.

Despite these critical remarks, it is to be hoped that enough evidence has been provided throughout this chapter that one of the major achievements of SFG lies precisely in the untangling of three different sets of categories and levels of analysis that have been or are still confused in other models: (a) Identification (referential coherence and referential aboutness); (b) Information structure (Given and New interpreted as relational concepts) and (c) Theme–Rheme patterns ("point of departure"/"relational aboutness" related to the staging of information).[79]

In line with this "separating" spirit, in (1967b: 217) Halliday affirms that "thematisation is independent of what has gone before". This statement, however, has also provoked critical reactions on the part of Daneš (1964: 109, 1974b: 108–109), even if he has made similar statements (Section 2.3.3 above), Kuno (1975: 326 endnote 1) and Firbas (1974: 25), among others. Thus, Daneš emblematically comments that:

> ... such a conclusion appears very doubtful in the light of the fact that the choice of the Themes of particular utterances can hardly be fortuitous, unmotivated and without any structural connection to the text. In fact, even a superficial observation of texts reveals a certain patterning; this statement also corresponds to our intuitive expectation that the progression of the presentation of subject matter must necessarily be governed by some regularities, must be patterned.

This type of criticism loses sight of the separating nuance with which Halliday uses the notion of *context-independence*, invoked to dissociate Theme from Given. Theme is described as "context-independent" in the sense that it is a structural category of the clause as a message, while Given is related to the notion of co(n)text (Giv$_R$), a semantic, non-constructional construct (Jiménez Juliá 1986: 65). Halliday himself explains that the choice of Theme is independent of the context in the sense that it is neither necessarily pre-selected by any previous or high level choice nor it is determined by the preceding clause: the context gives you information about discourse as a whole, but it does not enable you to predict the Theme of each individual clause (personal communication, *Seminar on Systemic Functional Linguistics*, Córdoba May 5–7, 1993).

Elsewhere, however in (1967c: 205) [my emphasis]), Halliday admits that thematic choices are co(n)textually constrained because "the speaker has *within certain limits* the option of selecting any element in the clause as thematic". It could be argued then that these "certain limits" are imposed by the *system* of the language, which, in its turn, are affected by the *co(n)text* in which language is used. Hence we can to a certain extent predict that given types of co(n)texts will demand specific types/classes of Theme. Or put differently, only if they are explained as paradigmatic choices standing in co(n)textual opposition, can thematic proportionalities constitute a plausible system within the textual component of languages. Consequently, Theme, in this general and broadest sense, as Halliday himself explains, is concerned not only with "what is being said", carrying forward the development of the text as a whole contributing to its MOD and TP (1994: 64–67; 368–391), but also with "what has gone before in the discourse" (1967b: 199), as well as with, as suggested by the notion of *intertextuality*, texts of similar kinds, since the semantic and syntactic structures of sentences and discourses reflect basic categories and structures of our cognitive models of reality (cf. van Dijk 1987: 173; Lemke 1985; de Beaugrande and Dressler 1981).

4.4 Summary

In this section it has been shown that SFG separates out three different notions coalesced in other accounts: (a) identification; (b) given information; and (c) Theme. In addition, we have analysed three controverted areas related to the notion of SFG Theme: (a) the supposedly double-sided nature of topical Theme; (b) the identification of this category and (c) the "separating" nature of the account. It has been argued that whereas most scholars' notion of Topic alludes to different versions of either interactive aboutness or referential aboutness, in SFG thematic aboutness lends itself to relational interpretations. In other words, it entails a syntactically coded relation between an entity/proposition, or syntactic Theme, and a clausal (complex) predication, or Rheme, which derives from the linear quality of language. Hence, "what a message is about" can be said to be iconically coded by message initial transitivity/mood position, the syntactic Theme, cross-linguistically, the functional relevance of this category depending on the morphosyntactic features of each language in particular.

As a result, two main conclusions have been drawn. It has been argued that, despite the criticisms that SFG coalesces two different categories, i.e. Topic ("what a message is about") and Theme ("point of departure" of the clause as a message), systemic are perfectly consistent in treating the matter and spatial metaphors as two different aspects of Theme, i.e. the relational-semantic and the psycholinguistic-syntactic. This amounts to saying that the "aboutness" feature of: (a) thetic clauses, (b) those having a non-referential item as Theme (e.g. *Nothing will satisfy you*, *You could buy a bar of chocolate like this for 6d before the War*, *There is a fallacy in your argument*, etc.), (c) different choices of Mood, and (d) all sorts of Themes in general, is to be derived from the proportionalities their containing messages participate in, in terms of the grammar and the discourse co(n)texts in which they appear.

Nevertheless, it has been noted that systemic expositions are vague at times, fundamentally on the definition of topical Theme, textual Theme and displaced Theme. Thus, it has been suggested that topical Themes be identified with the first experiential/transitivity constituent of the clause as a message, rather than with the first ideational element. The category of textual Theme has been relabelled either as logical or as conjunctive Theme, and the category of displaced Theme has been said to violate the systemic portrayal of topical Theme. A potential inconsistency has also been found in claiming that textual patterns are non-constructional whilst talking about the "structure" of the multiple Theme and about the marked or unmarked nature of its "constituents". Lastly, it has been concluded that the "separating" stand of the theory must be strengthened because at times the notions of "point of departure" and "what a clause is about" seem to be confused with: (a) given information, and (b) the referential and/or the interactive semantic notions of "what text/discourse is about".

Chapter 5

Functional Grammar

5.1 Introduction

FG makes a distinction between the rules that govern the *constitution* of linguistic expressions (i.e. semantic, syntactic, morphological, and phonological rules) and *pragmatic functions*. These specify the informational status of the constituents of the predication in relation to the wider *communicative setting*, that is to say, in terms of the Speaker's (S) estimate of the Addressee's (A) *pragmatic information* (P), or A's *general, situational*, and *contextual* full body of knowledge and feelings at the moment of speaking (TFG1: Ch. 13, pp. 263–87).[80]

From this description a three-fold implication follows. First, pragmatic functions are concerned with a *dynamic quantity*, i.e. one that can vary in time: the speaker's estimate of the pragmatic information of the addressee (($P_A)_S$). Second, pragmatic categories are *speaker-determined*, that is, they are mediated through S's (the Speaker's) estimate of P_A (the Addressee's pragmatic information). And third, pragmatic rules belong to the generative apparatus of grammar itself as systemic aspects co-determining the form and semantics of linguistic expressions, as against utterance facets, the full weight of which can only be determined within one specific situation. As a corollary, pragmatic functions are assigned to the fully specified *underlying structure* of the clause, which is input to a set of *expression rules* determining the form, constituent order and prosodic properties of the clause.

In addition, contrasting with the *function-to-form type* of reasoning posited by PS and SFG co-workers, for example, as well as by previous FG formulations (where pragmatic functions were allocated to the constituents allegedly meeting their defining criteria),[81] the current version of FG adopts a *form-to-function orientation* (Section 1.2). For the claim is made that pragmatic functions are assigned to those constituents that display *special treatment*, i.e. salient morphosyntactic formal, ordering and prosodic properties, the informational significance of which is sought in the subsequent discourse setting.[82]

The "special treatment" requirement underscores three further features of pragmatic functions. First, it implies that pragmatic functions are assigned by *clause*, while topical and focal referents are determined by *discourse* (which may be longer than a clause). Secondly, it contends that, regardless of discourse or psychological considerations, if the coding of both intra-clausal and extraclausal pragmatic functions is missing from the underlying structure of the clause, then there is no basis for recognising a special clause-bound level of pragmatic organisation distinct from the semantic and syntactic levels of clause structure. And thirdly, the "special treatment" requirement serves as the basis to distinguish between *extra-clausal* pragmatic functions (ECCs), in (85A) below, on the one hand, and *clause-internal* ones, in (85B), on the other (based on TFG2: 379–409, 1989: 264):

(85)[83]   A   EXTRA-CLAUSAL (ECCs) [my italics])
1. *Interaction management* ECCs (e.g. I'm afraid, *Peter* [Address], that you're going a bit too fast, Dik 1989: 265)
   a. *Greetings* and *leave-takings*
   b. *Summons*
   c. *Addresses*
2. *Attitude specification* ECCs (e.g. *Damn it*, TFGII: 386).
3. *Discourse executors* (e.g. It's rather hot in here, *isn't it*? [Tag, Illocutionary Modifier], Dik 1989: 265):
   a. *Responses*
   b. *Tags*
4. *Discourse organisers*, classified into (e.g. *Well*, ladies and gentlemen, shall be start the game, ibid.: 387):
   a. *Boundary markers*:
      i. *Initiators*
      ii. *Shifters*
      iii. *Push* and *Pop markers*
      iv. *Finalizers*
   b. *Orientators* (e.g. *As for the students* [Theme], they won't be invited, ibid.: 264; He's a nice chap, *your brother;* John gave that book to a girl, *in the library*, Dik 1978: 153):
      i. *Condition*
      ii. *Setting*
      iii. *Theme*
      iv. *Tails*

   B   CLAUSE INTERNAL [my emphasis]
1. *Focus* (e.g. **Mary** John love, John love FM **Mary**, be **Mary** who John love, Dik 1989: 278–9);

2. *Topic* (e.g. Yesterday I got a phone call from *the tax inspector* (NewTop). *He/The man/The joker* (GivTop) wanted me to come to *his* (GivTop) office, and *he/Ø* (GivTop) gave me the impression that I was in for some trouble, Dik's (ibid.: 271).

Formally, ECCs are described as not belonging to the clause proper on the grounds of the three following features:

a. they are typically "bracketed off" from the clause by pause-like inflections in the intonation pattern and thus they may precede, interrupt, or follow the clause proper;
b. they are not sensitive to the clause-internal grammatical rules, although they may participate in relations of coreference, parallelism (i.e. same case marking), or antithesis (e.g. negative Tag with positive clause) with the clause they are associated with;
c. they are not essential to the integrity of the internal structure of the clause: if left out, the remaining clause structure is complete and grammatical.

And, functionally, ECCs are ascribed a three-fold role: (a) commenting on the content of the clause proper; (b) "managing" verbal interactions; and (c) organising the content of the expression, in relation to the context in which it occurs.

Interaction management ECCs are related to the creation and maintenance of the interactional conditions, including:

a. *Greetings and leave-takings*, through which the speaker acknowledges the presence of an addressee and signals that it is available for communication (e.g. *Hello!*, *Good day sir*, could I ask you a question, TFG: 384);
b. *Summonses* to draw the attention of some addressee (e.g. *Hey there*, what's your name, ibid.);
c. *Addresses*, including proper names accompanied by titles, functions, or references to the relation between A and S (e.g. *John*, could you give me a hand please?, ibid.: 385), special Address particles (e.g. *O Lord*, help me in my misery, ibid.), the vocative case, minimal responses (*hm, mm, mhm*, etc. ibid.: 386), politeness expressions (e.g. *Excuse me, Sir*, could I have a word with you, ibid.).

Attitude specification ECCs on the other hand symbolise the speaker's emotional state (e.g. *Ouch, my finger!*, ibid.); whereas discourse executors comprise:

a. *Responses*, or ECCs produced as a reaction to what the other participant says (e.g. *yes*, *no*, *perhaps*, *it is*, etc. ibid.: 406).
b. *Tags*, i.e. ECCs that occur outside the clause proper and are typically set off from it by a prosodic break (e.g. Open the door, *will you?*, ibid. 407).

The last type of ECCs, *discourse organisers*, are used to secure a proper organisation and a proper receipt of the discourse proper, by means of *boundary markers* and *orientation devices*. Boundary markers mark the beginning, end and internal articulation of (a) the discourse as a whole, (b) the different constituent discourse episodes or (c) the "moves" which make up the episodes. They are further classified into:

a. *Initiators*, preceding the clause and usually occurring in utterance initial position, they serve to open up a new discourse, episode or a conversation (e.g. *well*).
b. *Topic Shifters*, occurring at the beginning of an utterance, the speaker uses them to indicate the introduction of a NewTop (e.g. *by the way*).
c. *Push and Pop markers*, which indicate that a subsection, subroutine, or subsequence within a unit is entered or left;
d. *Finalizers*, which round off (a Topic) of conversation (e.g. *Okay, and how about you, anyway*).

As regards orientation devices, they are aimed at anchoring the dynamic and cumulative discourse model built up by A as discourse proceeds and may be of include four different kinds:

a. *Conditions*, which are said to introduce a discourse (episode) or speech act by means of typically a ECC conditional subordinate clause, the validity of its information being limited to a world of which the condition is true (e.g. *if you promise to stop crying*, then you may have a sweet, TFG2: 395);
b. *Setting* specifications, which typically occur discourse initially (when there is no antecedent expectation pattern) and are defined by the parameters of the speaker, addressee, time of speaking and place of speaking, that is, her/his *deictic centre*; they may be integrated into the clause or occupy the preclausal Orientation position (e.g. *In Paris, in the beginning of spring*, John felt awful, TFG2: 397);
c. *Theme*; and
d. *Tail*.

The ECCs of Theme and Tail receive independent treatment in Section 5.3 below owing to their wider repercussions for the FG pragmatic module and for this study. The same applies to the intraclausal category of Topic and its subtypes (vs. that of Focus and its subtypes), which are analysed in turn.

5.2 Topic vs. Focus

The informational status of linguistic expressions is determined in relation to the dimensions of *topicality* and *focality*, involving a restricted universal set of grammatically relevant distinctions that are realized by means of language-dependent markers. Topicality "concerns the status of those entities 'about' which information is to be provided or requested in the discourse", and focality "attaches to those pieces of information which are the most important or salient with respect to the modifications which S [...] wishes to effect in P [...], and with respect to the further development of the discourse" (TFG 1: 312).

Hence, the status of Focus is attached to those pieces of information which represent the "relatively" most important or salient information (Dik 1978: 19; see TFG 1 for a taxonomy of Focus types). But, importantly, unlike in SFG, for example, in FG the category of Focus is not equated with stress or accentuation for two reasons (Gussenhoven 1983, 1985; Gussenhoven et al. 1987, Baart 1987). The first is that for FG co-workers accentual prominence may not only be used to mark a Focus, but it may also:

a. mark topical elements (i.e. NewTop, contrastive GivenTop, SubTops, ResTops);
b. help express personal emotions (viz. introvert or extrovert personal emotions);
c. create conventionalised pragmatic effects (e.g. (im)politeness, arrogance, modesty, sarcasm, etc.) when falling on operators at the π_4 level (see Section 2.2.3 above on Firbas's contrast between re-evaluating and non-re-evaluating PP).

Likewise, it is noted that constituents identified as focal by morphosyntactic means, in (a) to (d) below, may not simultaneously receive special prosodic marking (Dik 1989: 278–9):

a. Q-test applied to Question-Answer pairs on the assumption that in questions the Focus falls on the Q-word, whereas in answers (and, by analogy, in declaratives) it is placed on the expression(s) which provide(s) the actual answer to the question posed) (see Section 2.3.2);
b. special positions (e.g. **Mary** John love);
c. special Focus particles (e.g. John love FM **Mary**);
d. special Focus constructions (e.g. be **Mary** who John love).

Some sort of "trade off" among focalising devices is recognised so that it is argued that, when the Focus is marked morpho-syntactically, this category needs not be marked prosodically, and if it is so marked, it gets a weaker prominence.

Alternatively, the dimension of topicality is assessed in relation to one set of *pragmatic states* (i.e. mental representations of entities in a discourse). These are determined by the psychological factor of *consciousness* and thus refer to the speaker's assumptions about the statuses of the mental representations of discourse referents in the addressee's mind (in both the *short-term memory* and the *long-term memory*) at the time of an utterance, namely: *identifiability* and *activation* (Chafe 1987; in this study Sections 2.3.2).

Identifiability accounts for the difference between referents for which the speaker assumes a *file* has already been opened in the discourse register and those for which such a *file* does not yet exist (Chafe 1976). What counts for the linguistic expression of this cognitive distinction is whether or not the speaker is able to pick a referent out from among all those which can be designated with a particular linguistic expression and identify it as the one which the speaker has in mind, provided that, given the appropriate discourse context, a referent is more or less permanently stored in the long-term memory of the speaker/hearer and can be retrieved without difficulty at any particular time. A referent may be identifiable either because it has been mentioned in a discourse (i.e. *anaphoric reference*) or because it is either visible/salient in the speech setting or because it is "inalienably possessed" or otherwise anchored in the individuality of one of the interlocutors (i.e. *deictic reference*, e.g. *those ugly pictures* or *the woman in the green hat over there, your left leg or my sister's second ex-husband*). All instances of identifiability and their expression by a single grammatical category assume the existence of a so-called cognitive *schema*, or *frame*, that is:

> ... any system of concepts related in such a way that to understand any of them you have to understand the whole structure in which it fits; when one of the things in such a structure is introduced into a text, or into a conversation, all of the others are automatically made available. (Fillmore 1982: 111)

Activation on the other hand evokes Chafe's (1987: 22) idea "that our minds contain very large amounts of knowledge or information, and that only a very small amount of this information can be focused on, or be "active" at any one time". Accordingly, when stored in the short term memory, a topical referent is depicted as displaying one of the three following degrees of activation:

a. *active*, designating "currently lit up" (mental representations of) referents that are "in a person's focus of consciousness at a particular moment";
b. *semiactive* (or *accessible*), that is, mental representations of referents that are in a person's peripheral consciousness and of which a person has a background awareness, but one that is not being directly focused on as a result of three factors:

i.   *deactivation* from an earlier state (i.e. *textually accessible*);
ii. *inference* from a cognitive schema or frame, that is, from some other active or accessible element in the universe of discourse (i.e. *inferentially accessible*)
iii. *presence* in the text-external world referent (i.e. *situationally accessible*)

c. *unused*, or *inactive*, referring to mental representations of referents that are "currently in a person's long-term memory, neither focally nor peripherally active".

The various terms in the systems of identifiability and activation are summarised in the diagram in (86), while (87) lists alternative labels for the above six values of identifiability/activation:

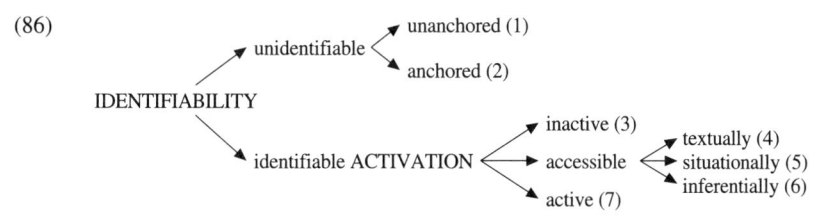

(86)
```
                          ┌─ unanchored (1)
              ┌─ unidentifiable
              │           └─ anchored (2)
IDENTIFIABILITY
              │                          ┌─ inactive (3)      ┌─ textually (4)
              └─ identifiable ACTIVATION ─┼─ accessible ──────┼─ situationally (5)
                                         │                   └─ inferentially (6)
                                         └─ active (7)
```

(87) (1) unidentifiable/brand-new
     (2) unidentifiable anchored/brand-new anchored
     (3) inactive/unused
     (4) textually accessible
     (5) situationally accessible
     (6) inferentially accessible
     (7) active/given

The parameters of activation and identifiability interact in a predictable way defining four cognitive statuses of discourse referents:

a. *Identifiable Active* (Given$_S$)
b. *Identifiable Semi-Active* (Given$_{F/K}$, echoing Prince's (1981a) Inferrables, i.e. entities that the speaker/writer assumes her/his addressee can infer through reasoning);
c. *Identifiable Inactive* (or Unused, which Prince (ibid.) defines as an entity known to the addressee, but not yet placed in this discourse model);
d. *Unidentifiable* (evoking Prince's (ibid.) Brand New, or entities firstly introduced in discourse by the user).

These four cognitive statuses are placed along Lambrecht's (1988a: 147; 1994: 165) *scale of Topic acceptability* in (88) (see (32) above, Section 2.3.2):

(88)   **Lambrecht's *Topic Accessibility Scale***
   Active   most acceptable
   Semi-active   ↑
   Inactive   ↓
   Brand New   least acceptable

The scale of topicality in (88) reinterprets the Given-before-New principle cognitively. It implies that utterances are more likely to be about Active referents than about Brand-New referents, because the former are already in the forefront of the addressee's consciousness and hence can be retrieved more easily, as shown in (89), (90) and (91) (Dik's (1978: 151) (71), (72) [my emphasis]) (even if these could not be valid analyses in the later versions of the model)):

(89)   a.   **Who** ate *the fish*? (eat$_V$ (Q$_x$: animate (x$_j$))$_{AgSubjFoc}$ (dx$_i$: fish (x$_i$))$_{GoObjTop}$
       b.   **John** ate *the fish*. (eat$_V$ (dx$_j$: John (x$_j$))$_{AgSubjFoc}$ (dx$_i$: fish (x$_i$))$_{GoObjTop}$
(90)   a.   **Who** is the one who ate *the fish*? (be$_V$ (dx$_i$: animate (x$_i$): eat$_V$ (x$_i$)$_{AgSubj}$ (dx$_j$: fish (x$_j$))$_{GoObjTop}$)$_\emptyset$ (Qx$_k$)$_{\emptyset Foc}$)
       b.   **John** is the one who ate *the fish*. (be$_V$ (dx$_k$: John (x$_k$))$_{AgSubjFoc}$: eat$_V$ (dx$_j$: fish (x$_j$))$_{GoObjTop}$)
(91)   a.   **Who** is it who ate *the fish*? (be$_V$ (dx$_i$: animate (x$_i$): eat$_V$ (x$_i$)$_{AgSubj}$ (dx$_j$: fish (x$_j$))$_{GoObjTop}$)$_\emptyset$ (Qx$_k$)$_{\emptyset Foc}$)
       b.   It is **John** who ate *the fish*. (be$_V$ (dx$_k$: John (x$_k$))$_{AgSubjFoc}$: eat$_V$ (dx$_j$: fish (x$_j$))$_{GoObjTop}$)

In contrast, Brand-New referents are only marginally acceptable as Topics on the grounds that if the addressee cannot identify the referent of a Topic, neither can s/he assess whether what is predicated about that referent holds.

Topic is thus described as *the* entity about which the predication predicates something, in relation to the overall discourse and as processed by the speaker/decoder's mind. Three important features follow from this description. The first is that no more than *one* Topic per predication is allowed. The second is that this function can only be assigned to *terms* (i.e. discourse referents/participants, mainly Subjects or Objects). And thirdly, topical elements are endowed with different degrees of referential accessibility, the topicality of which is derived from the cognitive status implied in the Topic Accessibility Scale in (88) above. Accordingly, a distinction is drawn between: (a) *Given Topics* (GivTop), associated with Active discourse referents (Section 5.2.1); (b) *SubTopics* (SubTop), assigned only to Semi-Active referents (Section 5.2.2); (c) *Resumed*

Topics (ResTop), identified with Semi-Active referents assumed to be still in peripheral consciousness (Section 5.2.3); and (d) *New Topics*, which may be assigned to either Unused or to Brand-New referents (NewTop) (Section 5.2.4). These four subtypes of Topic share two features:

a. they are necessarily identifiable as such by their formal characteristics, which in turn are assumed to correlate with the different cognitive statuses their referents have in the S's mind; and
b. they are not in a one to one correspondence with the four degrees of activation of discourse referents, in other words, they cannot be automatically assigned to the discourse referents of a particular cognitive status.

Before describing these subtypes of Topic independently, it should be stressed that their characterisation in terms of feature (b) suggests that in FG the correspondence between the two sets of notions, topichood–focushood and Given–New, is in principle presented as *incomplete*, as also implied by two other FG tenets:

a. that the functions of Topic and Focus are only assigned to certain constituents — those singled out for "special treatment";
b. that Focus is a hierarchical, rather than a discrete, notion (i.e. the *relatively* most salient information), which does not prevent Topic and Focus from coinciding in the same term, in the same way that not being assigned Focus function is not a sufficient condition for a constituent to be identified as Topic, and vice versa (Hannay 1983: 214ff.).[89]

As a result, pragmatic function assignment in FG allows for a wide range of analytical possibilities that would be unacceptable or unaccountable in other informational approaches, such as clauses/utterances:

a. with hybrid pragmatic functions to designate:
    i. focal elements falling on active discourse referents:
        1. in instances of contrast (Sonia and Joyce came to help me. **Sonia** worked **like mad**, but **Joyce** was **horribly slow**. Siewierska (1991: 174 (43) [my emphasis]);
        2. in cases of emphasis (e.g. I heard that Peter got married. **Peter's** married. How amazing! I don't believe it!, ibid.: (44) [my emphasis]);
        3. when the Focus falls on the whole predication, that is, when the Focus falls on the illocutionary point of the predication, the truth value in the case of an assertion or the force of a request, promise, greeting, warning, etc., (e.g. Dali **did** design the bottle, **Do** sit down, I **do** promise to be there, Do **not** be late, ibid.: (45)) [my emphasis]):

ii. topical elements which are referentially New (e.g. NewTop as in There emerged *a problem*, ibid.: 169 [my emphasis]);
b. with neither Topic nor Focus (i.e. all new thetic clauses, as in answers to questions like "What happened?");
c. with a Topic and without a Focus (i.e. presentative clauses such as There appeared *a band of poachers with automatic weapons*, In the heart of the tusk there was *a corroded bullet*, ibid. 176 (48a, b) [my emphasis]);
d. with a Focus and with no Topic, i.e. when there is no term in the Given part of the predication (e.g. **Anna** has complained. **Ted** has complained and **Lyn** and **Elaine** have complained too, in response to Who has complained?, ibid. (49a, b) [my emphasis]).

5.2.1 *GivTop*

GivTop is associated with active discourse referents, that is, entities which may be inferred from the previous cotext, as exemplified in (92) (Dik 1989: 271 (19) [my emphasis])):

(92) Yesterday I got a phone call from the tax inspector (NewTop). He/The man/The joker (GivTop) wanted me to come to his office, and he/Ø (GivTop) gave me the impression that I was in for some trouble.

GivTops are said to contribute to building up discourse Topics (D-TOPs) on the assumption that whether or not an utterance Topic becomes a D-Topic depends to a large extent on whether or not it is pursued or elaborated on as a GivTop in the following discourse (Dik ibid.: 270). The underlying rationale is that once an entity has been introduced into the discourse by means of a previous NewTop, SubTop or ResTop, it can be treated as a Given Topic (GivTop) in the subsequent discourse, where it must be "kept alive" through repeated reference. Formally, GivTops are described as being signalled by the following devices:

a. *anaphoric reference*, which, as exemplified in (89) above, may be established via:
   i. anaphoric (independent, bound or clitic) personal or possessive pronouns;
   ii. terms specifying the class to which the GivTop belongs to;
   iii. an Epithet qualifying the GivTop;
   iv. zero anaphora (Ø);[85]
b. *syntactic parallelism*, which refers to the tendency of GivTops to reappear in similar syntactic positions in subsequent predications;[86]
c. *switch reference*, or a Topic (dis)continuity device which marks whether or

not there is a shift to a different Topic in the verb (e.g. De Vries's (1985) analysis of Wambon);
d. *obviative*, that is, a grammatical distinction coded in third person participants (nouns, pronouns or cross-referential elements of the predicate) between *proximate* (i.e. the GivTop of a discourse) and (*second/further*) *obviative* (equated with NewTops) (e.g. Bloomfield's (1962: 38) study of Menomini);
e. lack of accentual prominence.

At this stage it is worth noting that unlike Comrie (1981) or Givón (1979a, 1984a), who describe Subjects as grammaticalised Topics, Dik (1989: 216–217) claims to agree with De Vries (1985) that, despite their strong correlation, Subject and GivTop represent two distinct notions: whereas the GivTop determines the *contextual* perspective from which the discourse is organised, the Subject determines the perspective from which the SoA is presented. Although it is natural for the two kinds of perspective to coincide, because speakers tend to reflect in the sentence-grammar the dominant contextual perspective of the discourse, this is not necessarily the case because:

a. a GivTop may be a non-Subject (e.g. A. *What happened to the demonstrators?* B. *Well, the police* (Subj) *removed them* (Obj-GivTop) *from the platform* [my emphasis]), and vice versa, the Subject may be a non-Given Topic (e.g. *Who* (Subj-Focus) *removed the demonstrators? The police* (Subj-Focus) *did* [my emphasis]);
b. Subject, and syntactic functions in general, are not considered to be universally valid in FG, in contrast with pragmatic functions and semantic ones, which are taken to play a role in the structural organisation of the clause in all languages; consequently, it follows that a language may not have Subject/Object assignment (languages lacking passive and dative constructions), but still GivTop remains a relevant pragmatic function;
c. in some languages (e.g. Maranao) Subject assignment and pragmatic function assignment represent two distinct processes: the former is restricted to the more central members of the predication, whereas the latter applies to peripheral terms.

5.2.2 *SubTop*

SubTops are defined as Topics which may be legitimately inferred from GivTops on the basis of our knowledge of what is normally the case in the world and are called in full "SubTops of the GivTop" (Dik 1989: 275). Close to Hawkins'

(1978: 123–130) *associate anaphora*, Clark & Haviland's (1977) *bridging assumptions* or Prince's (1981a) and Chafe's (1987) *inferrables*, Hannay (1985b: 53) symbolises the feature of inferrability of SubTops with the formula in (93):

(93)   if Y R X

where a *relationship of inference* (R) (viz. part of, member of, subset of, instance of, copy of, aspect of, opposite of, projection of, associated with) is implied between an entity X that has been activated in the given setting (or it is assumed to be so by the Speaker) and a *SubTopic* (Y). As mentioned, Haviland and Clark (1974, 1977) call R a *bridging assumption*, and demonstrate by psycholinguistic means that the processing of SubTops takes more time than that of GivTops. Two cases in point are contained in (94) (my emphasis):

(94)   a.   Mary got some beer out of the car. The beer was warm.
       b.   Mary got some picnic supplies out of the car. The beer was warm.

Whereas in (94a) *the beer* is a GivTop (it is an active referent directly retrievable from the previous context), in (94b) it acts as a *SubTop*: the sequence is given coherence by means of the A's inference relation/bridging assumption "the beer must have been among the picnic supplies", which takes more time and processing effort.

The existence of R as a necessary precondition for felicitous Subtopicality entails that this function is assigned only to inferrable referents which the speaker considers or treats as semi-active. In contrast, Unused Inferrables fall within the scope of the Focus function. Siewierska (1991: 158) illustrates this point with the two readings of (95) (her (16)) below:

(95)   We are having a wonderful time in the department. The boss is away.

where *the boss* may be interpreted as either SubTop (if the primary stress falls on *away*) or as Focus (if it gets a primary stress). Lastly, compared to GivTop, SubTopic is said to typically have a greater degree of accentual prominence for two reasons. The first is that unlike GivTop, SubTops have not been mentioned as such and so their individual identity is in this sense New. And the second motivation is that SubTops may have something "new" or something "contrastive" about them, as there may be other potential SubTops of the same GivTop (e.g. in (94), for example, *the beer* is only one of the picnic supplies).

5.2.3   *ResTop*

A Resumed Topic (ResTop) is said to revive or re-establish an entity that has been introduced into the discourse, and therefore is still in peripheral consciousness, but that has not been mentioned for some time (after several Topics have been introduced and discourse has been about one of these). Dik (1989: 277) mentions the three following devices as typical markers of a ResTop, as illustrated in (96) below (his (33) [my emphasis]):

a. some indication that a shift is made from one GivTop to another (e.g. *now*);
b. a strong form of anaphoric reference (e.g. *John's sister Mary*);
c. an explicit or implicit indication of previous mention (e.g. *who I mentioned before*)

(96) John had a brother Peter and a sister Mary. Peter ... [considerable episode about Peter]. Now, John's sister Mary, who I mentioned before ...

In addition, Dik explains that ResTops typically get a degree of accentual prominence, since they act as "reminders" of entities which may have shaded into the background of the A's pragmatic information, whereas Siewierska (1991: 160) remarks that ResTop is one of the functions typically associated with Theme.

5.2.4 *NewTop*

NewTop is the most controversial of FG Topic types, characterised as a hybrid function that combines the dimensions of topicality and focality. The topicality of NewTops is said to lie in their introducing an entity into the discourse, which is going to be taken up again subsequently, while their focal status resides in the very act of introducing such an entity into the discourse, which hence designates the more salient piece of information. Described in this way, NewTop ceases to meet the "aboutness" sentence/predication-based condition of FG dimension of topicality, unlike the other three Topic functions, to become a discourse notion. In other words, NewTops do not present the entity about which the predication predicates something in the given setting, but present a referent which is to constitute a future Topic of discourse. Samples of *NewTops* are included in the *presentative thetic clauses* in (97) (from Siewierska (1991: 161 (19)), as opposed to the *all new thetic clauses* in (98) (her (18)) [my emphasis]:

(97) a. There's a man at the door.
b. There's been several whites killed at X junction.
c. There occurred a strange accident.
d. In the garden sat Mary and her sister.
(98) a. A tiger chased a tourist.
b. A man just got run over by a car.

All-new clauses like (98) are described as containing no (New) Top on the assumption that their primary purpose is not to present a referent, but to establish an event that is more likely to be continued with utterances containing none of its referents as Topics. This kind of all-new event messages do not receive one single treatment in FG. They have been analysed as having Focus assigned to each constituent of the predication (cf. De Jong 1981), as falling outside the scope of pragmatic functions altogether in order not to deprive the notion of Focus of most of its substance (cf. Dik et al. 1981), or as being related to the discourse-based notions of *saliency* and *cohesiveness*, in contrast with sentence-level-based categories (Bolkestein 1985a, b).

Conversely, the presentative clauses in (97) are endowed with a NewTop fulfilling a *presentative function*, or a form of "appearing on the scene" (Hannay 1985b: 171). They manifest "expletive", "dummy" pronouns (i.e. existentials in (a), (b), (c)) or adverbials (i.e. locative-existentials (d)), taking the position which would otherwise be occupied by the Subject, while the NewTop is assigned to the immediately post-verbal position, for it is expected to be taken up again by the follow-up clauses that this type of construction tends to co-occur with.[87] Dik (1978: 184–87; 1980: 220) posits (99c) below to account for English (existential) presentative constructions, as opposed to (99a) and (99b), which represent the functional patterns of English declaratives, and of Q-word questions and inversions triggered by initial negative elements respectively (P1 = initial intraclausal constituent):

(99)   a. P_1 S V_f V_i O X
        b. P_1 V_f S V_i O X
        c. P_1 V_f V_i S X

Yet Dik (ibid.: 187) and Hannay (1985b: 47) recognise that presentative constructions do not always comply with (99c), as in (100) below [my emphasis]:

(100)   a.   Yesterday there was <u>an accident</u>.
         b.   At night there arrived <u>three horsemen</u>.

where *there* is said to occur not in P1, but in the pattern position of the Subject in the declarative pattern.

Whereas Hannay (1985b) restricts the NewTop function to just presentative thetic clauses (e.g. those in (97) above), Dik (1989: 268–9) distinguishes three further NewTop markers (TFG 1: 315–316 [my emphasis]):

a.   an explicit meta-linguistic device expressing what the ensuing discourse is going to be about (e.g. *I'm going to tell you a story about* an elephant called Jumbo);
b.   placement in the object or second argument position (e.g. *In the circus we saw* <u>an elephant called Jumbo</u>);

c. predicates designating a form of "appearing on the scene" (*Suddenly, right before our very eyes, there appeared, ...*).

To these devices, De Vries (1989: 66–71) adds the possibility of morphologically marking the NewTop (e.g. Wambon), which Siewierska (1991: 171) claims to be affected by the referential properties of the discourse referents as determined by such parameters as definiteness, genericity, specificity, individuation and presupposition.[88] Likewise, Siewierska (1991, ibid.) remarks that NewTops may also occur predication-externally, that is, separated from the predication by a short disjuncture, as in (101) (her (40b)):

(101) Evo   kave eve   na   alive   komatmbo.
       that man TOP   pause-marker yesterday die:3SG:PAST
       'That man, yesterday he died.'

Functionally, NewTop are attributed three properties cross-linguistically:

a. a strong preference for taking a relatively late position in the clause, which is in keeping with their introducing future Topics of discourse, and which Dik (1989: 179) postulates as one of the factors responsible for the difference between the expression of a GivTop and a NewTop (e.g. *The dog is in the garden* (Pres {(the garden)$_{Loc}$} (ds1xi: dog$_N$(xi))$_{\emptyset SubGivTop}$) vs. *There is a dog in the garden* (Pres {(the garden)$_{Loc}$} (is1x$_i$: dog$_N$(xi))$_{\emptyset SubjNewTop}$), [my emphasis]:
b. a tendency to take the form of an indefinite term, implying that typically S has no reason to assume that A is aware of the identity of the entity the NewTop refers to; this is, however, not a necessary condition, for, less frequently, NewTops have also been reported to introduce definite terms (e.g. *There is the dog in the garden*, Dik ibid.), the effect being, as Dik puts it, "I am now introducing an entity which, though new to this turn in the discourse, is well-known to you";
c. a propensity to capture the most prominent accent of the expression.

5.3 Theme vs. Tail

Theme is functionally described as presenting an entity or sets of entities that the subsequent predication is going to bear upon (e.g. *That guy, is he friend of yours?*, *That trunk, put it in the car*, *As for the students, they won't be invited*, Dik 1978: 132 [my emphasis]). Dik (ibid.: 140) explains that Barry's (1975) definition of "Topic" would be quite appropriate for his interpretation of Theme:

... topic has the function of specifying the *relevant universe of discourse* (frame of reference, domain of referentiality) of its comment; the range of things with respect to which it makes sense to assert that comment.[90]

Formally, Theme displays the following four characteristics:

a. it is offset from the main predication (typically to its left) prosodically, by a short disjuncture;
b. it often appears in absolute form, i.e. without any overt case marking (e.g. *The boy, I went out with yesterday* vs. **With the boy, I went out with yesterday*), although in some languages such as Russian it can bear the case-marking corresponding to its coreferential pronoun;
c. it lies outside the performative modalities of the main predication (viz. declarative, imperative and interrogative);
d. as a corollary, it is capable of having interrogative modality (e.g. *My brother? I haven't seen him for years*, ibid.: 135 [my emphasis]).

It is argued that Theme may be connected with the predication *only* via the pragmatic relation of *relevance* (x_i) in the Gricean sense ("Make your contribution relevant in terms of the existing topic framework"), in which case Theme is considered to be co-dependent upon the pragmatic information available to both S and A (e.g. *As for Paris, the Eiffel Tower is really spectacular*, Ross (1970: 231 endnote 20), quoted in Dik's 1978: 137 (35a) [my emphasis]). In other cases, the pragmatic relation (x_i) is also paralleled by a language-dependent structural relationship between Theme and Predication: some languages tend to always express it by means of pronominal elements, others leave it unexplicit (e.g. *That man, I hate him* vs. *That man, I hate*, ibid.: 140). To suit both possibilities, Dik (ibid.: 138) proposes the following schema:

(102) (x_i) $_{Theme}$, $(\emptyset \ldots (x_i) \ldots)$ $_{Predication}$

(102) symbolises that "if the Theme x_i corresponds to a term variable x_i in the predication, then the relevance of the relationship between Theme and Predication is reduced to the relevance of pronouncing the predication $\emptyset \ldots$ Theme/x_i ..., where this latter formula indicates the result of inserting the Theme constituent into the position marked by the corresponding variable in the Predication" (TFG 2: 394; Dik 1978: 138).

Crucially, the predication is chosen in such a way that the antecedently given Theme constituent fits its selection restrictions, which seems to be consonant with the way Ss actually construct Theme–Predication combinations (e.g. *As for my friend John, he is crazy about bronze statues* vs. **As for bronze statues, they are crazy about my friend John*, Dik 1989: 137 (32b) and (33b), respectively [my emphasis]). As a result, Theme structures are characterised as a two step strategy, as it were: (a) here is something with respect to which I am going to produce a predication; (b) here is the predication, of crosslinguistic validity, though with language-dependent degrees of grammaticalisation. This device tends to be used when the S does not have a clear idea what sort of predication s/he is going to produce, as illustrated by the fact that hesitation phenomena frequently occur between the Theme and the Predication (e.g. *As for the student, well, let me see ...* ibid.: 136 [my emphasis]).

In those cases in which there is a more direct relation between Theme and the predication, that is to say, when the Theme is *resumed* within the clause, or when a language requires a cross-referential element in any main verb corresponding to a certain function in the clause, the difference between a Theme and a (preposed) Topic may be slight. Consider (103) and (104) (TFG: 395):

(103) a. That man, I hate Ø.
      b. That man I hate.
(104) a. That man, he-hates me.
      b. That man he-hates me.

In FG the difference between the (a) and (b) counterparts in (103) and (104) is considered to be only presentational, by means of the prosodic break (Dik 1978: 142; TFG2: 395, 403–405), their frequency and communicative contexts being language-dependent. In this connection the evolutionary theory is mentioned that the grammaticalisation process could be interpreted in terms of a gradual demarking of an original marked construction with either a Topic-shifted constituent (Theme), or an afterthought-Topic (Tail) (see Section 2.2.1 and endnote 13 in this study).

In turn, Tail constituents are formally described as a mirror-image of Theme constituents: they are set off from the main predication, typically to its right, by means of a break in the intonation pattern (symbolised by means of a comma) (e.g. *He's a nice chap, your brother, I like John very much, your brother I mean, John gave that book to a girl, in the library*, Dik 1978: 153 [my emphasis]), as represented in the schema in (105) below:

(105)   Predication, $(x_j)_{Tail}$

The schema in (105) indicates that Tails should be interpretable as "afterthoughts" to the predication, that is to say, as further specifications, modifications or corrections of (parts of) the predication. As was the case with Theme, all languages are assumed to have Predication-Tail constructions, although to a different degree of grammaticalisation. Characteristically, Tails tend to have the same semantic and (possibly) syntactic function marker of the constituent they refer to cross-linguistically (e.g. *We gave the book to him yesterday, to your brother* vs. **We gave the book to him yesterday, your brother*, Dik ibid.: (88a, b) [my emphasis]). There seems to be only one exception to this tendency: those Tails realized by extensions of the predicates (i.e. by satellites in apposition) (e.g. *John gave that book to a girl, in the library*, ibid., 153 (85) [my emphasis]).

Although their typical position is after the clause, as an "afterthought", providing some additional information, FG Tails may also occur as parenthetical insertions within the clause, set off from it by prosodic breaks or commas, or they may even follow Themes, as illustrated in (106) (TFG2: 402, (71), (73)):

(106) a. I saw John hand it — the money I mean — to the girl.
b. John — your brother I mean — what's his name?

The functional description of Tails is completed (TFG2: 403) by alluding to Geluykens (1987), who establishes the following points:

a. Tails are especially used in unplanned spoken conversation;
b. they may represent a conversational repair strategy: S, after having produced a pronominal element in the body of the clause, fearing that the reference may not be clear, adds more explicit information;
c. the repair is most often "self-initiated";
d. it is usually preceded by a short pause;
e. it is often accompanied by a metacommunicative expression such as *I mean*.
f. the strategy is typically used when the speaker believes that the reference may not be clear, which occurs above all when:
   i. the pronominal element in the clause might be taken as co-referential to more than one entity in the preceding discourse;
   ii. when the referent is "inferrable" (SubTop) rather than explicitly mentioned and the speaker is not certain that the addressee has established the appropriate "bridging assumptions".

5.4 Troubleshooting

In this section we shall discuss whether or not FG succeeds in dissociating and handling the notions coalesced in Mathesius's (1939: 234) definition of Theme: (a) Topic (= Mathesius's *Téma* ("what is being commented upon")); (b) Theme vs. Tail (= Mathesius's *Východisté* ("point of departure")); and (c) Given (= Mathesius's *základ* ("psychological Subject" and/or "given information"). We shall address two major weaknesses that, to my opinion, hamper a functionally "adequate" characterisation of pragmatic functions as they are presented within the FG programme (see Gómez-González 1996a, 1998c):

a. the inconsistencies emerging from an equivocal use of the three functional interpretations explained in Chapter 2, i.e. syntactic, informational and semantic, without solving the problems posited by such accounts;[91] and, as a corollary,
b. the debatable functional adequacy of the analysis.[92]

For space constraints this critique will concentrate on just four points stemming from the two issues above: (a) the weaknesses implicit in the semantic FG characterisation of pragmatic functions in terms of relevance or "aboutness" (Section 5.4.1); (b) the ambiguities derived from resorting to position, a syntactic identificational criterion, for the same purpose (Section 5.4.2); (c) the problems posed by the informational rationale that topicality and focality must be related to givenness and to newness, respectively (Section 5.4.3); and (d) the profitability of the methods suggested for Topic and Focus assignment (Section 5.4.4).

5.4.1 *The semantic criterion of aboutness/relevance*

We have seen that in FG the assignment of Theme, Tail and Topic is explained along the *referential-semantic* dimensions of relevance in the Gricean sense, that is to say, in terms of "aboutness" and "salience" (Dik 1989: 267; Hannay 1985a). Resembling Chafe's (1987) or Givón's (1983b, c) conception (see Section 2.2.2 in this book), FG Topic is only assigned to the *terms* that stand in a relation of *aboutness* or that are *referentially* linked to an entity or group of entities in some "mental world" that show the property of topicality (Dik 1989: 46, 266–7, n. 5; Brown & Yule 1983: 71). Further, Topic is described as the *predication-internal* entity (a syntactic identificational criterion) *about which* the predication predicates something, *in relation to Focus*, a relational-semantic criterion (in Bolkestein 1998) or with regard to the overall *discourse* as processed by the *speaker/ decoder's mind*, a referential semantic and informational notion (in most FG descriptions). Likewise, Focus denotes some element of the predication that predicates something *about* the Topic (Dik 1978: 130); whereas Theme and Tail are rendered as *predication-external* entities that also involve a relationship of aboutness: Theme presents to the left and external to the predication an entity or set of entities that the subsequent predication is going to bear upon, while Tails are "afterthoughts" bearing upon and set off from (typically to its right) the main predication.

Going by these descriptions one could draw the conclusion that, though treated as different categories, FG *Topic, Theme* and arguably *Tail* are in fact rendered *as different realizations* (predication internal or clause external) *of one and the same hierarchically superior pragmatic function*: their use presupposes *manifest relevance* ("aboutness"), a notion related to the dimension of discourse topicality. Jiménez-Juliá (1981: 342), for example, also raises this issue as follows [my translation]:

> Dik's extra-clausal pragmatic functions do not have in fact a different pragmatic content, rather they are mere cases of thematisation realized by means of a syntactic device of apposition, which partly explains the independence of these elements.'[93]

According to Jiménez-Juliá this situation might be due to the FG co-workers' reaction against the generativists' practice of deriving very different structures from the same phenomenon, while overlooking the lack of one-to-one correspondence between linguistic form and function. Be that as it may, this first debatable issue seems to indicate that communicative functions should be assessed from the uses to which they are put, i.e. from a top-down function-to-form perspective, rather than from their morpho-syntactic expression, i.e. from a bottom-up form-to-function approach; or, adopting an intermediate position, from both perspectives simultaneously, pursuing a matching of communicative functions with language-specific formal and behavioural properties. Whether or not this is the intention of FG co-workers needs further clarification, not to mention the problems posed by semantic accounts already discussed in Section 2.2 above.

5.4.2 *The syntactic criterion of position*

In FG the "separating" principle is insisted upon that the syntactic and informative axes should be kept apart, in other words, that pragmatic positions should not be equated with given or new information (nor therefore with pragmatic functions), while recognising some sort of correspondence between the two (Prince 1984; De Schutter 1985, 1987). As a result, three positions are considered to be pragmatically relevant on a cross-linguistic basis: *P1, P2* and *P3*.[84] P1 is described as the first intraclausal constituent of the clause on the assumptions that:

a. for every finite clause, P1 *must be filled*, which also applies to non-finite clauses containing designated categories, such as *while washing the dishes,* ... (Dik 1989: 362);
b. P1 may contain no more than *one* constituent of the clause, and this constituent is always the first intraclausal constituent (or the only constituent

of clauses containing one constituent);
c. generally, the *presence/absence* of a *comma/pause* after candidates for P1 placement has been taken as indicative of P2 (extraclausal)/P1 (intra-clausal) status respectively;
d. clause co-ordinators such as *and*, *but*, *so* and *for* are analysed as being interclausal, and as such not occupying any position in the clausal pattern;
e. it is occupied by constituents which: (i) either must be placed there (e.g. in English Q-words, subordinators, relative pronouns); (ii) or, if that is not the case, fulfil the pragmatic functions of Topic (with the exception of NewTop) and Focus (Dik (1978: 178).

On the other hand, P2 names the position to the immediate left of the predication (which unlike P1 may accept more than one constituent) and is closely aligned with the pragmatic function of Theme. Lastly, P3 identifies the position to the immediate right of the predication and is related to the pragmatic function of Tail. FG concentrates on P1 on the basis that this is a universally relevant position used for special purposes, including the placement of constituents with Topic or Focus function in accordance with the *Principle of Pragmatic Highlighting* (Dik 1989: 343; TFG1: 420–424; Mackenzie 1998).

Nevertheless, it seems that, rather than exploring the interactions between pragmatic locations and pragmatic functions, FG analysts are apparently more preoccupied with the former as the "special treatment" given to the latter, to the extent that in the end they seem to be one and the same thing (see endnote 82). Thus, when faced with having to give operational criteria for identifying Theme and Tail constituents, most FG co-workers disregard "aboutness" and plump for P2- and P3-positioning respectively, a clearly syntactic identification criterion. A case in point is the FG claim that the dependencies between these extraclausal and the Predication run from left (P2) to right (P3), echoing the linear processing of information, i.e. from the Theme (P2) through the Predication to the Tail (P3), as shown in the formula in (107) (Dik 1989: 130):

(107) $(x_i)_{Theme}$, Predication, $(x_j)_{Tail}$

But, arguably, FG accounts show a number of moot points inherited from this syntactic stand. Consider, for example, the form-to-function criterion of "special treatment" used to distinguish between predication-external and predication-internal pragmatic functions and between P2 and P3 on the one hand and P1 on the other, that is: the presence/absence of a comma or a pause before or after the predication. We have seen that this criterion does not always invoke functionally distinct categories (integrated Theme and Tail constituents). Now we suggest that its formal characterisation needs further refinement. For one thing, it seems that there may be many factors at work in determining comma/pause placement, not in the least hesitation phenomena and personal style, which need spelling out. A further problem is posed by the fact that (in English at least) what may be seen as intra-clausal constituents in semantic terms (e.g. Adjuncts) are very often presented as if they were clause-external; and vice versa, what appears to be typically extraclausal in semantic terms (e.g. Adjuncts) are not infrequently integrated into the clause.

Probably because of these circumstances in many investigations (both outside and within the FG framework) the distinction between predication-external and predication-internal items is *not* treated as *discrete*. Thus, Siewierska (1991: 160, 171) comments that ResTops and NewTops can be associated with Theme, when in principle FG presents these as mutually exclusive pragmatic functions. Likewise, De Groot (1981: 87) argues that in Hungarian there are ambiguous Topic/Theme constructions, i.e. some Themes must be viewed as being incorporated into the predication (108a) and (108b), and constructions containing "special Themes or Topics with the function to emphasise the Focus" (108c):

(108) a. A pék könyvet adott Marínak
the baker-NOM book-ACC gave-he Mary-DAT
'The baker (Topic) gave Mary a book.'
b. A pék, neki nem adtam semmit
the baker-NOM he-DAT not gave-I nothing-ACC
'The baker? (Theme) To him I didn't give anything'.
c. A péknek annak nem adtam semmit
the baker-DAT that-DAT not gave-I nothing-ACC
'To the baker I didn't give anything.'

Another case in point is De Vries's (1989: 66–71) observation that in Wambon (or in Modern Standard Arabic or in English) some (New) Tops may occur predication-externally, i.e. they are separated from the predication by a short disjuncture. Yet he specifically argues against recognising a separate predication-external (P_2) pragmatic function for such Topics, claiming that the presence of a pause has no bearing on the form of the predication. Instead, De Vries decides to assign two potential structural realizations to (New) Top, a predication-internal and a predication-external one. His assumption is that, given that NewTop is identified by the presence of special particles/constructions rather than positionally, and that P_2 is a structural location, there is no reason why NewTops cannot be associated with more than one location. In sum, the analytical fuzziness involved and its repercussions for the pragmatic module of FG reveals a need to clarify how to determine what is precisely extra- and intra-clausal and why.

In this connection, Bolkestein (1998), for example, argues that the presence/

absence of intonational integration at the beginning and/or end of the clause implies the presence/absence of corresponding Topic–Focus spans or message peaks, as illustrated in (109a) (109b) (Hannay's (1994a) (21) (23)) and (110) below (Bolkestein's 1998 (1)):

(109)   a.   John first cooked the onions, very slowly.
         b.   John first cooked the onions very slowly.

(110)   UNFORTUNATELY, he has GONE

Whereas in (109b) there is only one Topic–Focus span, in the double constructions (109a) and (110) the addressee is invited to give separate focal emphasis to both "cooking the onions" and to the fact that John did so slowly (in (109)), and to one state of affairs (his leaving) and to S's attitude towards the content of this message in (110).

The above examples indicate that there exists indeed a vast richness of ECCs both in terms of function (e.g. orientational messages, vocatives, attitudinal markers, circumstantial specifications, etc.), syntactic realization (ranging from subordinate clauses to non-verbal clauses, all the way down to simple adverbials and dislocated elements) and volumewise (one clause may contain two or more ECCs constituents), which is not well reflected by simply postulating a single P2 or P3 placement. Conscious of this simplification, Hannay (1994a) proposes to replace P2 by an *orientation field*, as shown in (111) below, which houses a variety of grammatical structures performing a variety of orientational functions with different functional loads awaiting further analysis.[94]

(111)   orientation field   core   elaboration field
         basic order for   P1 S Vf Vi O X
         orientational expressions
         ← orientation zone →

5.4.3   *The informational criterion of givenness*

In Section 5.4.1 we have discussed the problems posed by the *referential-semantic* dimension of FG pragmatic functions. Now we shall examine the difficulties found when resorting to *referential-informational criteria* to identify the category of Topic (and Focus). For, as shown in Section 5.2 above, the dimensions of *topicality* and *focality* involve *given* and *new* information, respectively, even if the correspondence between the notions of topichood-focushood and givenness-newness is presented as incomplete.

Firstly, it could be adduced that FG descriptions do show some "combining" overtones, especially in its characterisation of Focus, where syntactic and informational factors, in principle described as belonging to different dimensions, are said to realize the same category. This same observation is made by Jiménez-Juliá (1981: 340) as follows:

> ... but in considering that the informative unit consists of syntactic constituents, without making any distinction between the structure of information and the structure of the sentence, [Dik (1978)] does not distinguish the different nature of the syntactic and the non syntactic devices that express pragmatic functions, either. Indeed, the realizations of Focus are several: intonation, constituent order, specific morphemes or special constructions [...], but none of them in particular [...]. Dik mixes up, then, a device that belongs to the structure of information (i.e. intonation), with another one that is inherently syntactic (i.e. constituent ordering); and so, that which is recoverable from the context (elicited via the structural device of the *WH-Question*) and that which is 'focused' by the Speaker at a given moment (intonation Focus) are treated as the same pragmatic element. [My translation]

In addition, the nature of the relationship of relevance posited between (a) the subject matter of discourse (D-Topic), (b) the terms conveying "what the clause is about" (Topic) and (c) the concept of $Given_{R/S/F/K}$ (Dik 1989: 266) is left unspecified, which could lead to a confusion of the three sets of notions. We are told that the first presentation of a D-Topic is a NewTop, and that an entity so introduced becomes a GivTop if reintroduced. An entity which is mentioned, temporarily neglected and later revived is a ResTop; and an entity inferred from other entities is labelled as SubTop. This classification distils a three-fold "combining" implication.

First, although presented as different, it treats sentence Topics (a linguistic category) and D-Topics (a cognitive category) as non-distinct: the former subcategorise the latter, which could serve as a basis for the further identification of Themes and Tails as clause-external D-Topics. Second, it assumes that only entities qualify for sentential topical or D-topical status, when a person's pragmatic information includes also the properties of those entities, relations between different entities, SoAs (higher-order entities) in which those entities play a role, etc., organised in general knowledge structures relating to particular kinds of entities and events, and constructed on the basis of prior or simultaneous experience. And third, with the exception of inactivated/unidentifiable NewTops, considered as a subcategory of Focus, i.e. *Presentative Focus* (Mackenzie & Keizer 1991 [1990]: 194; Hannay 1985b: 171; 1991 [1990]: 138),[95] Top status ends up being assigned to *given information* as determined by the speakers, that is, to an/the entity which the interactants are thinking of at the time of utterance (Giv_S). This is demonstrated by the fact that the four different subtypes of

Topics, NewTops, GivTops, SubTops and ResTops, are placed along Lambrecht's *scale of Topic acceptability* in (88), which suggests that the more active the entity, the more likely it is to become Topic, since it is already in the forefront of the addressee's consciousness and therefore can be retrieved more easily.

But it seems that the assignment of Topic-functions does not admit of easy empirical verification for a number of reasons. The first is that givenness is an elusive notion that can be judged differently depending on:

a. what is presented as New, in the relational approach, at individual clause/ utterance/single speech act level; or
b. in connected discourse, the context and cotext, or
c. the interactants' minds, according to activated interpretations.

The third position (c) seems to be the stand adopted in FG. However, on closer inspection, activated givenness (Giv_S) appears to be used within this framework invoking four versions of contextual givenness, namely: (i) recoverability (Giv_R), (ii) shared knowledge (Giv_K), (iii) assumed familiarity (Giv_F) and (iv) predictability (Giv_P). The negative implications of using these different notions in a loose manner as well as the problems posed by Giv_S itself have already been discussed in Section 2.3.3 above. Now it suffices to mention some observations made in this direction within FG.

Thus, Mackenzie & Keizer (1991: 187) argue, for example, that not all GivTops need to be contextually given, or introduced into the discourse by means of a NewTop, but can also be situationally given (Situationally GivTops) or generally given (Generally GivTops) (e.g. *Watch out! The ceiling is caving in!*). Similarly, it seems that not all inferrable elements are inferred from a GivTop or fulfil a SubTopic function. For many inferrable elements may also act as NewTops. These may be new at contextual level but given or inferrable with regard to the addressee's general or situational pragmatic information (e.g. *–What did you see in the circus? –Well, there was an elephant that amazed us with his tricks...*).

5.4.4 *Topic (and Focus) assignment to one constituent*

We have already analysed the problems posed by resorting to the notions of aboutness, initial position and to the given-new contrast to characterise pragmatic functions in FG. Now let us concentrate on the difficulties derived when trying to apply the "special treatment" criteria to assign such functions. The "special treatment" requirement involves the following: (a) the devices in Table 14; (b) prosodic contour; (c) the Q-test; and (d) placement in P1.

After considering the devices included in Table 14, one may formulate a number of questions. One may wonder, for example, why GivTops receive the same special treatment as ResTops (apart from the latter's strong anaphoric reference or indication that the entity has been mentioned before), which in turn demands further specification of two issues. One is for how long a referent must not be mentioned in order to get ResTop status. And secondly, it seems that the "special treatment" devices assigning ResTop status need reworking because, if they are indeed what they are intended to be, then many instances of Topic Resumption will not qualify for the FG ResTop function (i.e. a ResTop need not be marked by explicit/strong anaphoric reference). And vice versa, cases that could abide by the ResTop "special treatment requirement" will not perform this function (e.g. *Now* does not necessarily indicate Topic resumption, but may suggest a change of Topic in general). In other words, as Mackenzie & Keizer conclude, ResTop isn't relevant for English, but it might be for some other

Table 14. *Topic "special treatment" devices in FG*

Topic types	Device
GivTop	(i) anaphoric reference (viz. anaphoric (independent, bound or clitic) personal or possessive pronouns, Epithet, zero anaphora (Ø); (ii) syntactic parallelism (iii) switch reference (iv) obviative
SubTop	(i) if Y R X, a relationship of inference (R) (viz. part of, member of, subset of, instance of, copy of, aspect of, opposite of, projection of, associated with) is implied between an activated entity X and a Sub-Topic (Y).
ResTop	(i) some indication that a shift is made from one GivTop to another (e.g. *now*); (ii) a strong form of anaphorical reference (e.g. *John's sister Mary*); (iii) an explicit or implicit indication of previous mention (e.g. *who I mentioned before*)
NewTop	(i) presentative thetic clauses (e.g. In the garden sat *Mary and her sister*); (ii) an explicit meta-linguistic device expressing what the ensuing discourse is going to be about (e.g. I'm going to tell you a story about *an elephant called Jumbo*); (iii) placement in the object or second argument position (e.g. In the circus we saw *an elephant called Jumbo*)

language (Dik's examples are in quasi-English (what he says about *now* is not a claim about English *now*)).

In addition, a revision of the definition of SubTops is also desirable, for it would appear that this kind of Topic may not only be inferrable from GivTops, as implied, but also they may refer to the contextual, situational or general pragmatic information and be expressed by means of either deictic pronouns or full expressions. This suggests that the open-ended list of bridging relations proposed for SubTops by Hannay (1985a: 53) and Dik (1989: 276), for instance, should be further specified in a principled way. Or else the *reductio ad absurdum* could follow that all terms in congruent discourse qualify for SubTop status: they all have to be relevant to (and hence be inferred from) the context in which they are used. And finally, the category of NewTop should also be described in more detail because: (a) it embodies such vaguely defined constructions as explicit meta-linguistic devices expressing "what the ensuing discourse is going to be about" (which poses the question as to whether such is not also the case for all the other Topic types singled out for "special treatment"); and (b) it involves placement in the object or second argument position (which, unless typified in a principled way, seems to imply that all objects/second arguments should bear topical status, when in practice that is not the case).

In sum, the need for a revision of FG Topic types leads us to the issue of how to determine which item gets topical status from the mass of given information. Some questions the analyst must face are: (a) how the most topical element could be isolated from the other contextually bound elements; (b) what precisely makes an intended referent identifiable in a given context and situation; (c) how one is to distinguish between various degrees of identifiability. In what follows we shall see that neither the "one term only" restriction, nor phoric reference, prosodic prominence, the Q-/or similar tests, nor P1-placement appear to provide conclusive answers to these question.

Some authors point out some exceptions to the "one term only" restriction, while others authors disagree with this restriction altogether, arguing that predicates or all types of information may be Topics or topicalised just as well (De Groot 1981; Siewierska 1988: 73ff.). Besides, the term restriction does not state clearly which one is Topic and which one is not in contexts where there is more than one candidate for Topic assignment. As to phoric reference, the grammatical means used for maintaining Topic continuity cross-linguistically, it need not indicate topichood, either: phoric items can be used to refer to contextually given or inferable entities which need not be Topics, as in (112) below (Brown & Yule 1983: 183 [emphasis in original]):

(112) There was a car approaching the junction, but the driver didn't stop <u>at the give way sign</u>

Prosodic prominence, in its turn, seems to be equally vague. GivTops are described as lacking prosodic prominence (unless contrasted to some other Topic, in which case such prominence does not distinguish them from Focus elements). Conversely, SubTops and ResTops are allowed to show some degree of accentual prominence, but this prominence is only "typical", and applies only to spoken language.[96] A systemic elaboration of Sgall's (1975) Q-test is suggested to bring us nearer to the solution of this problem. However, in Section 2.3.3 above, we noted that the efficiency of this test is rather questionable basically because (a) it merely elicits bound information and (b) it proves to be an artificial and an uneconomical technique (De Beaugrande 1980: 120; Dressler 1972).

We are forced then to turn to the last "special treatment" device to mark the function of Topic, namely: P1-placement rules, a separating identification criteria. In an attempt to account for positioning constituents in P1, Dik (1980: 21) proposes (15), three strictly ordered P1-placement R-rules (cf. Siewierska 1991: 220):

(113) **P1-placement rules**[97]
(R1) P1-constituent → P1
(R2) GivTopic, SubTop, Focus → P1
(R3) X → P1

These rules do not take account of the facts that:

a. some languages may lack a clearly demarcated P_1 position (although no language lacks an initial position, of course);
b. as Hannay (1991: 135; 1993) points out, even if it has been decided that P1 will always be filled, it is not stipulated the conditions under which:
   i. a Topic as opposed to a Focus constituent is placed there, at least in PresE (e.g. *John and Bill came to see me. JOHN was NICE, but BILL was rather BORing*, where "the constituents John and Bill [the second instance] are emphasised [and so qualify for Focus status], although they have already been introduced and may thus be assumed to be Given Topics to A", Dik (1989: 278 (34)) [capitals in original]);
   ii. there is a singular or a multiple filling of P1 (as in the case of clause initial function words, relative pronouns or non-Subject constituents, which demand that either the singular filling assumption be revised or the designated categories be reanalysed as not belonging to P1 in the functional pattern).

In sum, it seems that the P1-placement expression rules in (113) leave a number of issues unresolved.[98] To increase the explanatory potential of these rules Mackenzie & Keizer (1991: 213) propose their reformulation in the following terms:

(114) **Expression rules for English P1-placement**
[R1] If a clause consists of one constituent only, this constituent must be placed in P1.
[R2] If a clause consists of more that one constituent, one of which is a P1-constituent (question word, subordinator, relative pronoun), place this P1-constituent in P1.
[R3] Else, if a clause is interrogative, (yes–no question) or imperative, place V_f in P1.
[R4] Else, if a clause contains a constituent with Focus function, place this Focus constituent in P1. (Alternatively, Focus constituents may be given special treatment by means of prosodic prominence, parallelism, or any combination of these focalising devices.)
[R5] Else, place$_{\sigma 2}$-satellite (i.e. level 2 satellites) in P1 (optional)
[R6] Else, place constituent with Subject function (including dummy it) in P1 (unmarked case).

The rules in (114) seem to suggest that all kinds of word order variations may result from one and the same underlying structure, which opens up a number of important issues, such as:

a. that word order cannot be controlled by the grammar itself, probably because R4 is insufficiently elaborated;
b. that R4 and R5 appear to underestimate the specific pragmatic status of level 2 satellites in clause-initial position;
c. that fronted items may involve both focality or topicality, which leads to the question of whether to accept multiple or single assignment of pragmatic functions to a constituent; and as a corollary, if the former possibility is accepted, whether a constituent must have features of all the functions it fulfils, or, if only one pragmatic function can be ascribed to a constituent, then the decision has to be made as to which one of the competing pragmatic functions is relevant.

In order to resolve some of this controversy, Mackenzie & Keizer argue that, as topical elements may appear in P1 only if other elements have not been chosen, and given that Focus assignment is enough to guarantee that the placement rules work to produce the appropriate ordering of constituents, Topic assignment in English can be dispensed with. But it seems that, if this solution is adopted, a number of useful distinctions are missed out. Consider, for example, the difference between constructions having Subjects in P1 and those with non-initial Subjects (e.g. extrapositions, frontings, etc.), generally explained as having an aboutness-motivation or a strongly marked topical flavour, which demands the function of Topic be retained.

In an attempt to circumvent this problem, Mackenzie (1998) proposes an *incremental functional grammar*, assuming that the succession of discourse utterances as well as their internal structure results from an incremental, left-to-right build-up. This hypothesis entails that every utterance begins with a P1 position, which is seen as the position of the first increment, the first subact, of the utterance, the one that co-determines which increment or increment can follow. Thus, linking up with dynamic-functionalist psycholinguistic research into starting points (see Section 2.4.1 in this study), the global utterance structure in (115) is proposed, where either Topic or Focus may occur in P1, as shown in (116):

(115)   P1   Rest
(116)   a.   Topic–Focus   as in *He* **left.**
        b.   Focus–Focus   as in **John** **left** (but Mary didn't).
        c.   Focus–0   as in **John** did.

(116) indicates that P1 may be used for placing the Topic (a), or the Focus in (b) and (c). The fundamental purpose of filling the "Rest", or some of it, is to indicate the clause type explicitly or *analytically*. Mackenzie claims that by choosing an analytical mode the S offers the A an explicit clue to the intended illocution, as illustrated in the English example in (117):

(117)   a.   DECL: Subj > P1   John left
        b.   INTERR: Vf > P1   Did John leave?
        c.   IMP: Vi > P1   *Leave* now!

(117) symbolises that in English clause type is regularly marked, every else being equal, by the filling of P1, an hypothesis that seems to be compatible with SFG perceptions on Theme markedness (see Section 4.2.1 in this study). But P1 is also relevant for the explanation of "minimal utterances" or "holistic" expressions, which, according to Mackenzie, will minimally consist of a P1 Focus-item that ensures the illocutionary status of the sequence (e.g. **When? Why? Pity!** as reactions to e.g. *John left*).

Hannay (1991, 1998) on the other hand proposes a *system of message modes*, *Grounding*, *Reaction* and *Neutral*, which constrain in a top-down fashion what pragmatic functions may be assigned within the predication. Thus, in Hannay's terms the sequences in (116) and (117) above reflect different message modes, belonging as they do in different contexts and answering to different intentions. But, despite the advantages of the message modes hypothesis, notably the provision of an interface between the grammatical description of linguistic expression and a broader description of language outside grammar, there exist a number of matters related to the theory that need to be addressed in more detail, for example:

a. the precise relation between the individual message modes and the various cognitive principles proposed in the literature for explaining word order tendencies (e.g. the principles of FSP, EW, EF, TU);
b. the speaker's motivation for placing a particular constituent initially;
c. how listeners interpret initial constituents.

In sum the above discussion leads us to conclude that FG could benefit from a clarification of the notions and identificational criteria espoused to account for pragmatic functions and/or for pragmatic positions, paying due attention to the relationship between pragmatic functions and pragmatic positions, as well as to the status conferred to both. Besides, when undertaking this task, in order to satisfy the criteria of pragmatic adequacy, psychological adequacy and typological adequacy, FG analysts should surmount the theoretical gap existing between the speaker's dynamic forward-looking view of verbal interaction and the static backward-looking perspective adopted by many FG analysts, preoccupied with instances of pragmatic function assignment. This necessity could be viewed as an argument against the assignment of pragmatic functions in the derivation of the layered structure of the clause. Instead it seems to point to the creation of a pragmatic module that does full justice to discourse phenomena "as the all-encompassing framework within which semantics and syntax must be studied" (Dik 1989: 7; Hannay & Bolkestein (eds.) 1998).

5.5 Summary

In this chapter we have outlined the FG model of pragmatic functions focusing on Topic, Theme and Tail. Theme presents to the left and external to the predication an entity or sets of entities that the subsequent predication is going to bear upon. Tail constituents are set off from the main predication, typically to its right, as "afterthoughts", or further modifications of the predication. And Topic represents *the* predication-internal entity about which the predication predicates something, comprising four subtypes, i.e. New Topics, Given Topic, SubTopic, and Resumed Topic. These are placed along a Scale of Topic acceptability on the assumption that utterances are more likely to be about Active referents than about Brand New referents, because the former are already in the forefront of the addressee's consciousness and therefore can be retrieved more easily.

A number of problems have been addressed emerging from using in a loose manner syntactic, informational and semantic criteria for the assignment of pragmatic functions. It has been argued that, though presented as different categories, going by FG explanations, Theme, Topic and possibly Tail seem to be three different realizations of one and the same, hierarchically superior, pragmatic function, related to the dimension of topicality. We have also analysed the difficulties involved in determining the formal and functional differences involved in P1 and P2 placement, as well as the intricacies associated with the activated semantic FG notion of Topic, identified with salient information (Giv_S). Finally, we have sketched a number of problems found when having to apply the "special treatment" requirement to identify pragmatic functions, involving (a) the "one term only" restriction, (b) anaphoric reference, (c) prosodic prominence, (d) the Q-/or similar tests, and (e) P1 placement.

Part III

A Corpus-Based Analysis of Syntactic Theme in PresE

CHAPTER 6

Theory and Methods

6.1 An intrinsically functionalist-separating framework

Parts I and II of this research have emphasised that there seems to be *no universal definition* of Theme/Topic that covers all instances and solves all the problems of the three aspects ascribed to these terms, i.e. semantic, informational and syntactic. It has been shown that the PS analyses of FSP phenomena tend to be restricted to one level of description only and are often based on extrinsically functionalist assumptions made about contrived and decontextualised examples (Chapter 3). In addition, both generative-functional PS descriptions (Sections 3.2.4 and 3.2.5) and FG accounts (Chapter 5) have been claimed to share an apparently paradoxical assumption: to consider communicative categories as universal pragmatic categories, dealing with the syntagmatic relationships established by the contextualisation of messages, and at the same time, to formalise them into a "relatively autonomous" system, restricted to specific categories, or to sequences receiving a "special treatment", which represent pragmatic functions as abstract logico-semantic relations devoid of their claimed universality. Likewise, with regard to SFG, some problems have been discussed basically in relation to the conception of Theme as the "starting point of the clause" (expressing "what the clause is about") and the treatment of clause-initial position as a language-specific (PresE) identificational criterion (Chapter 4).

With these provisos, Part III of this investigation sets out to explore the *functional relevance of syntactic Theme*, or *clause-initial position*, out of the conviction that the initial slot has inherent *cognitive salience*, in both fixed word-order languages such as English and in flexible word order languages. This seems a good start to narrow down our territory of analysis, when a global approach seems unattainable, by providing an observable criterion of identification that can at the same time be related to both informational and semantic accounts. That is to say, we can observe the interaction of clause initial/non-initial positions with the mapping of given and new information and, simultaneously, investigate the kind of aboutness relationship entailed by the *Theme zone* (Hannay 1994a, b; Mackenzie 1998; Smits 1998), i.e. relational, referential and interactive (Chapter 2). We can thus determine the "orientation" of the Theme zone, on the basis of both the nature of the relationship its elements have with each other, on the one hand, and the nature of the relationship they establish with both the preceding and subsequent co(n)text, on the other. In this light it seems only fair to conclude that the syntactic approach profiles itself as the most elegant and profitable way to *reconcile* hitherto conflicting, or regarded-as-different, (moderate functionalist) accounts of Theme/Topic.

In addition, what follows intends to circumvent or provide solutions for the three main problems encountered in syntactic accounts (Section 2.4.2):

a. to work out an operational criterion that systematically identifies the initial constituent of a clause as a message;
b. to demonstrate that predication (external and internal) clause-initial positions have some grammatical relevance, by embodying within the same paradigm the wide range of structurally and communicatively heterogeneous constructions that highlight such slots;
c. to determine whether the Theme–Rheme pattern is a structural grammatical relationship or a non-structural principle of discourse organisation.

As a first step, we shall adopt an *intrinsically functionalist* perspective. This implies, to begin with, that the scope of our analysis is restricted to *major clauses*.[99] Accordingly, although the decision of what to put first in minor clauses, groups, phrases, sentences, paragraphs, texts, etc., is also presumed to be a meaningful one, to assess the functional relevance of such decisions lies beyond the scope of this study. The second implication is that we shall distinguish the three layers of clause structure — levels of meaning — as posited in SFG (Section 4.1): *ideational* (clause as a representation), *interpersonal* (clause as an exchange) and *textual* (clause as a message), which are regarded as *complementary*, not in competition. Importantly, however, our results will support the existence of upward or increasing scopal relations between the experiential/ representational level, the interpersonal level and the textual/rhetorical level, as implied in the *layering hypothesis* proposed in e.g. FG or RRG (Hengeveld 1989; Fortescue et al. 1992; Van Valin Jr. 1993; Vet 1998). For it will be shown that the level at which thematic items function in the clause plays a role when a language user opts for a particular thematic organisation (Section 7.5).

Besides, this investigation adopts a "separating" standpoint that equally has SFG reverberations (Section 4.1). And so we shall distinguish two levels of description within the textual component of languages:

a. the non-structural, or co(n)textual, level; and
b. the structural level, which comprises:
   i. Information structure;
   ii. Theme–Rheme patterns.

Parts I and II have shown that the merging of these levels of analysis may lead to a number of misrepresentations or problematic issues that can be avoided by recognising their different domains. Thus in Chapter 2, it has been claimed that while syntactic accounts of Theme/Topic are pretty homogenous, both semantic and informational approaches have two major variants: referential or contextual, at level (a), and relational, at level (b). By way of illustration, Chapter 3 explains that many Prague scholars succumb to inaccuracies when assimilating the relational-semantic interpretation of Theme/Topic (i.e. "what the rhematic predication is about") with co(n)textually given information (at level (a)), and yet analysing clauses in isolation. As concerns SFG descriptions, though in principle "separating", it has been argued that they sporadically show "combining" overtones when coalescing "what a clause as a message is about" with: (a) given information or with (b) "what text/discourse is about" or "what is at issue" (Section 4.3.3; endnote 79). And within the FG model the mixture of levels recurs because Topic is assigned a level (a) referential-semantic interpretation of (i.e. clause referent entailing a relationship of "aboutness" with the co(n)text), although it is presented as a non-obligatory level (bii) category. As a result, FG take pains to distinguish discourse Topics (D-Topics) from sentence Topics (i.e. lexical or pronominal Topic Expressions), without providing a clear criterion to identify the latter. For sentence Topics are ultimately described in terms of given information ($Giv_{S/K}$), but no definite answer is given to such questions as for how long mental representations can be active and eligible for thematic/topical status, how different degrees of activation and accessibility can be measured and regarded in terms of topicality, etc.

In order to avoid the referred mismatches, in this study non-structural co(n)textual relationships are taken to embody not only *cohesive relationships*, as implied in SFG, but also the referential or contextual dimensions of syntactic, semantic, and informational approaches. As a result, the analysis of how information is "staged" throughout *texts* or *paragraphs* into different points of departure and continuations corresponds here to the co(n)textual dimension and therefore lies beyond the focus of this investigation, namely: to explore Theme–Rheme patterns in major clauses. The same holds for the "semantic" notions of discourse Topic, speaker's Topics, as well as for the denotational and referential informational accounts in terms of Giv_R, Giv_P, Giv_K, $Giv_{D/I}$, $Give_F$,

Giv$_S$ and related notions. At this stage we shall not proceed any further into the theoretical primitives and problems of analysis involved in each of these notions since they have already been discussed at some length in Chapter 2.

Of more importance for our purposes now is to retain a constant and narrowly defined view of such key notions as Topic and givenness (vs. newness) for they will be resorted to in what follows. With regard to the category of discourse Topic, it will be interpreted in cognitive terms as:

> a prominent conceptualisation which acts as a kind of cognitive anchoring point; other [...] conceptualisations are brought into the discourse by virtue of their perceived ties to the reference point. (Kemmer 1995: 58)

The given-new contrast, on the other hand, in its referential dimension, or referring to the cognitive status of discourse referents, will be interpreted in terms of *recoverability* (Giv$_R$) and will be differentiated from such logico-semantic notions as presupposition, implicature, etc. (Section 2.3.2). Space constraints oblige to a sketchy presentation. Referentially speaking, *new information* refers to information that is presented by speakers as not recoverable from the co(n)text, and that it can be either *fresh* or *contrastive* (IFG; Halliday & Hasan 1976). Freshness or not recoverable information is associated with intonational and syntactic prominence (the latter involving nonbackgrounding through anaphora, deixis, and so forth). Contrastiveness in turn refers to recoverable, but to be attended to, information. This is typically realized by special syntactic constructions (preposings, inversions, clefting, and the like) and by marked information Focus or by nucleus choice, typically a falling-rising Nucleus in English declarative clauses. Alternatively, Giv$_R$ designates two kinds of recoverable information that is retrieved from the co(n)text: *stale* and *inferrable*. Staleness designates given information that is recoverable directly (e.g. in cases of repetition, ellipsis, substitution), and which is consistently associated with intonational non-salience, and often with syntactic non-salience. By contrast, inferrability, as noted by Prince (1981a), implies an indirect form of recovery of the "antecedent", by inference (e.g. relationships of synonymy, hyponymy, hyperonymy, etc.). Typically, what happens with inferrability is that there is an intonational Nucleus in a recoverable constituent and at the same time there is little evidence that information is being presented "for noting". The scalar degrees of informativity of the four categories defined may be represented in terms of the following system network:

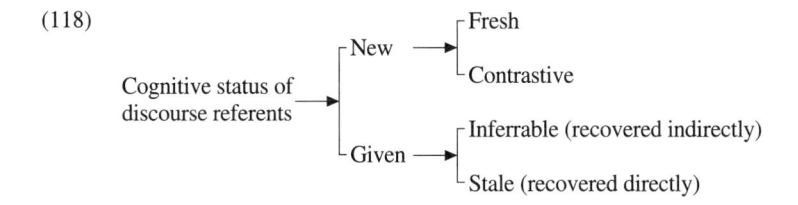

(118) Cognitive status of discourse referents
- New
  - Fresh
  - Contrastive
- Given
  - Inferrable (recovered indirectly)
  - Stale (recovered directly)

In addition, drawing on Collins (1992), the categories in (118) are cross-classified by the parameters of *similarity* and *opposition*, and by the variables of *field*, *tenor* and *mode*,[100] depending on the kind of relationship established with their "antecedents". Accordingly, Giv$_R$ may invoke co(n)textually similar or opposite referents, which may be derived straightforwardly or "co-operatively" with regard to the variables of field, tenor and mode, each of these variables being typically associated with one of the major process types in Halliday's system of transitivity (see endnote 53).

Thus, Field-Giv$_R$ is related to material/existential processes (e.g., *do*, *happen*) and designates experiential meaning retrieved from the setting of relevant actions and events within which the language is happening. In turn, Tenor-Giv$_R$ alludes to recovered interpersonal meaning (i.e. the speaker/writer's emotions, reactions, and so on), and is associated with mental processes (e.g. *worry*, *amaze*) and related "subjective" constructions (e.g. *be amazing*, *be interesting*). Finally, Mode-Giv$_R$ evokes the meaning recovered metalinguistically (i.e. from the mode of communication itself, including channel, genre and rhetorical purpose) for the purpose of clarifying it, interpreting it, commenting upon it, etc. Mode-Giv$_R$ is generally associated with "reconstructed" antecedents through projecting (typically verbal) processes (e.g. *say*, *mean*).

This study adopts the textual-recoverability approach to givenness on the assumption that we can proceed a good way without having to resort to such "inaccessible" notions as consciousness or knowledge. Instead, in order to determine the recoverability of an item, we shall let circumstances decide how far back the one should go. This procedure facilitates a degree of flexibility (barred from other approaches such as Givón's (1983b, c) *quantitative* analysis, for example, suggesting twenty clauses back as the upper limit), which makes allowances for the *interactional aspects* of language such as:

a. the possibility that an item may be present and therefore may be recoverable in purely informational terms but its referent may not be taken as recoverable by discourse participants (first mention does not guarantee successful introduction of a referent);

b. the evidence that the amount and quality (i.e. whether of a similar or of a different nature) of preceding material affects the recoverability of an item;
c. the circumstance that the measurement of units (i.e. clauses) is not always an easy task, especially in speech usually replete with unfinished clauses, pauses, repetitions, false starts, differences of speech rates, etc., made by more than one participant;
d. the fact that the progression of discourse (especially if unplanned) is not always linear, but tends to switch from one issue to the next.

The points outlined seem to indicate that the recoverability status of a referent does not depend solely on its having been previously mentioned within some rigid quantitative boundaries.

Likewise, also relevant for the analysis to follow is the addressee-oriented discourse notion of *current focus of (listener's/reader's) attention* with its "management" performed by various devices (among which word order and intonation Focus). A *focus of attention* represents a particular prominent activation status, achieved through some kind of signal or *instruction* which triggers the activation or focusing of formerly non-activated (or semi-activated) referents. In this sense, the sentence focus constitutes the *current focus* of attention, in contrast with previous *displaced focus/-i* of attention (Section 2.3.2; endnote 31).

Turning now to *structural textual resources*, these are here interpreted as speaker's/writer's *relational* or *reciprocal* choices at clause level, in the case of Theme–Rheme, or within information units, in the case of non-focal vs. focal information. As already explained (Section 4.1), the latter dyad concerns the "relational" contrast between material that is presented as *suprasegmentally uninformative* and that which is rendered *suprasegmentally informative* in terms of *marked* and *unmarked Focus*. Roughly, in the unmarked case the intonational Focus (or tonic segment) coincides with final position (the accented syllable of the last lexical item of the tone group), which allows the maximum amount of material to be presented as focal. Alternatively, marked (information) Focus involves any other placing of the tonic, i.e. on non-final or intrinsically given elements, and tends to be associated with constructions that affect the linear order, and therefore the thematic structure, of message, typically when the speaker requires special emphasis, usually in order to express a contrast or to make a correction.

Within this framework, in what follows the category of syntactic Theme will be described in three ways, as required in intrinsically functionalist models: (a) by the relations to other features at the same level of analysis; (b) by their downward relations with their realizations at the level of form; and (c) by upward relations with aspects of our knowledge of the universe (Halliday 1979;

Fawcett 1980; Halliday's personal communication in *Seminar on Systemic Functional Linguistics*, Córdoba May 5–7, 1993). Our aim is to subsume the functional relevance of thematic phenomena in more general terms in order to identify the *contextual conditions* of their usage. We cannot really seek to do justice to the abundant literature on the Theme–Topic interface (Parts I and II), but we will at least provide some answers to a number of issues awaiting further discussion, as demanded by a number of authors:

> To ascertain the discourse contexts of functional categories is an important study. [...] To combine systemic studies with theoretical studies is, I think, absolutely essential. You must look at functional categories in terms of their place in the grammar as a whole, which is always my demand: from the same level, from below and from above. But then you want to back this up with so much discourse evidence as you can and I think it very likely that you will be able to find features that are significant. But you won't be able to find that kind of single label which captures the discourse function of some unique category. But I'm sure you will be able to say something about it. I think it's terribly important to do this. (Halliday, personal communication, *Seminar on Systemic Functional Linguistics*, Córdoba, May 5–7, 1993] It
>
> [...] it seems reasonable to ask whether the semantic value of all these various categories of theme is the same so far as their function in the economy of textual organisation is concerned? While there is a discussion of the local meaning of equative and predicated Themes, and remarks will also be found on the local meaning of marked Theme [...], the question of whether or not they function variably within the economy of discourse has, to the best of our knowledge, not been addressed by SF linguists. As for the Themes meta-functionally classified, only sporadic remarks [...] have been made about the relevance of some category of Theme [...] to some specific aspect of textual organisation. [...] These studies are, in fact, simply indicative not providing any firm hypothesis about the role of metafunctionally differentiated subcategories of Theme in textual organisation. Again, one might ask if multiple theme selection is systematically different in its textual function from simple [non-multiple] theme selection? (Hasan & Fries 1995b: xxxii)

Thus, focusing on the LIBMSEC corpus, Chapter 7 offers significant quantitative and qualitative evidence that *subjectivity* plays an important role in thematic constructions. It will be shown that, contextualised, thematic choices are *interpersonally* oriented textual choices, establishing *point of view* in discourse and acting as *discourse markers*, helping texts be *cohesive* and *consistent*. Sections 6.2 and 6.3 address this characterisation of syntactic Themes in more detail, which is further developed and attested in Chapter 7 by exploiting the material and methods described in Section 6.4.

6.2 A survey of thematic options

In keeping with the intrinsically functionalist-separating framework outlined so far, syntactic Theme is here identified with the leftmost, or initial, transitivity/mood position in the clause, i.e. a participant, an attribute, a circumstance or a process acting as Subject, Object/Complement or Adjunct, since every clausal constituent having an experiential function is bound to conflate with an interpersonal function as well (see endnotes 54 and 56). This element may be realized predication *externally* or *internally*. In the former case Themes occupy P2 or P3, using FG terminology (Section 5.1), in which means that they: (a) are separated off from the main predication by one or several disjunctures (i.e. tone group boundaries, silent ictus, pauses), (b) lie outside the modality of the main predication, and (c) tend to occur in the *absolute* form, i.e. without any overt case marking (e.g. *That teapot, the duke has given it to my aunt*). In contrast, clause internal topical Themes occur in P1 (Section 5.4.2), i.e. initial intraclausal experiential position (e.g. *The duke has given that teapot to my aunt*).

In this context, the status of PresE as an SVO (Greenberg 1966), grammatical (Thompson 1978), or rigid word order (Givón 1988) language provides two crucial prerequisites for an analysis of Theme–Rheme patterns in this language: first, word order is largely determined by syntactic functions, and second, reordering options within and between clauses (in complex clauses), which, though also following pragmatic principles, simultaneously bear an additional meaning of deviation or *markedness*.

In the paradigmatically-based framework adopted here, markedness refers to *probabilities of choice* (Davison 1984: 833; Kies 1988: 73 endnote 2) within a language *semiotic system*, that is to say, a systematic *resource for meaning*, a *meaning potential* consisting of *metastable open systems*, i.e. systems that persist only through constant change (Halliday 1989). The underlying rationale is that systems tend towards one or other of just two types of choices: (a) *equiprobable* (i.e. 0.5/0.5) or (b) *skew* (e.g. 0.9/0.1). Equiprobable choices have no unmarked term, while the skew ones have one of their terms marked: the less probable. With this in mind, the system of Theme is here represented as consisting of *skew choices*. On the basis of the three levels of clause analysis, experiential, interpersonal and textual, "we shall refer to the mapping of Theme and Subject as the **UNMARKED THEME** of a declarative. The Subject is the element that is chosen as Theme unless there is good reason for choosing something else (IFG: 43 [emphasis in original])" (Section 4.2.1).

This argument for a *motivated choice* will be developed throughout the subsequent sections as the principal source of the semantics of Theme. It rests on the *optionality* of thematic choices, on the one hand, and on their *context-dependence*, on the other. In this study, the argument for a motivated choice involves the existence of a choice between: (a) *classes* and *types* of Theme;[101] (b) *non-special* vs. *special thematic* constructions; and (c) *unmarked* vs. *marked* Theme–Rheme patterns, as expounded in Figure 12.

The parameter of internal structure motivates the distinction between two *subtypes* of syntactic Themes:

a. *simple* vs. *complex*, which refers to whether or not Themes involve hypotactic, paratactic or embedded relationships of projection and expansion (see Tables 7 and 8), as illustrated in (119):

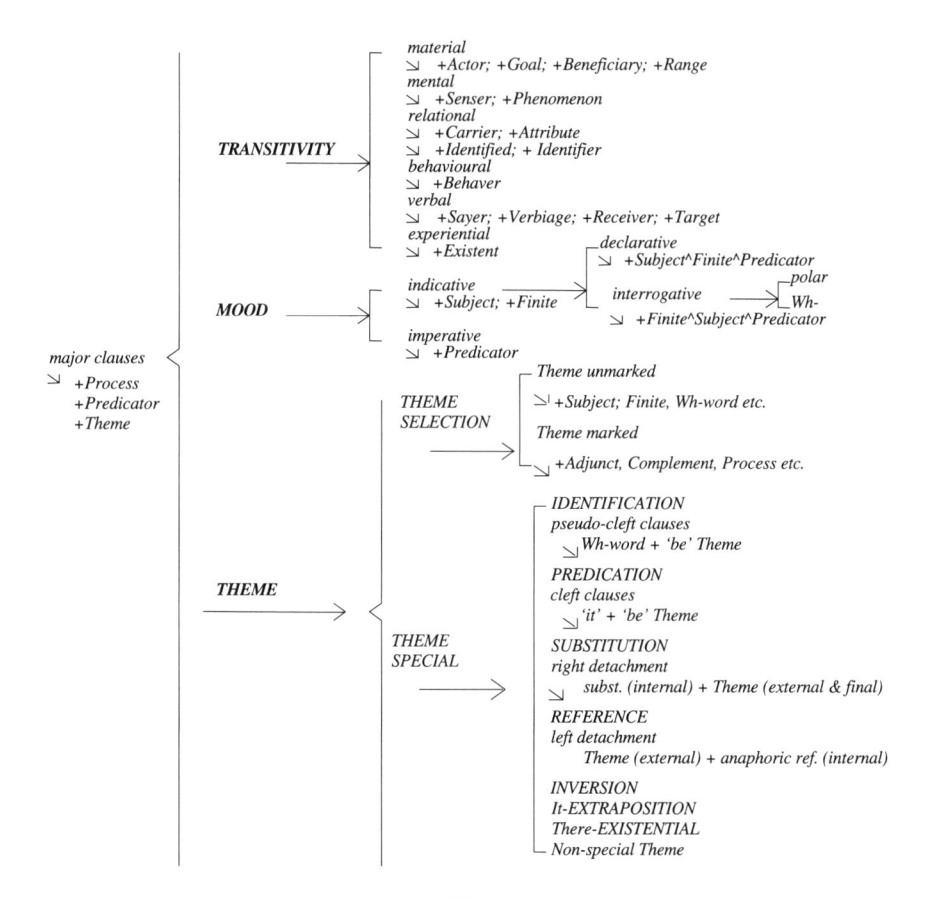

```
                                 material
                                    ↘ +Actor; +Goal; +Beneficiary; +Range
                                 mental
                                    ↘ +Senser; +Phenomenon
                                 relational
                                    ↘ +Carrier; +Attribute
                  TRANSITIVITY →    ↘ +Identified; + Identifier
                                 behavioural
                                    ↘ +Behaver
                                 verbal
                                    ↘ +Sayer; +Verbiage; +Receiver; +Target
                                 experiential
                                    ↘ +Existent
                                                      declarative
                                                         ↘ +Subject^Finite^Predicator
                                 indicative                                          ┌polar
                  MOOD →         ↘ +Subject; +Finite   interrogative ─────→          └Wh-
                                                         ↘ +Finite^Subject^Predicator
                                 imperative
                                    ↘ +Predicator
major clauses                                  ┌ Theme unmarked
  ↘ +Process                                   │   ↘ +Subject; Finite, Wh-word etc.
    +Predicator            THEME                │ Theme marked
    +Theme                 SELECTION →           │
                                                └ ↘ +Adjunct, Complement, Process etc.
                                     ┌ IDENTIFICATION
                                     │   pseudo-cleft clauses
                                     │       ↘ Wh-word + 'be' Theme
                                     │ PREDICATION
                  THEME →            │   cleft clauses
                                     │       ↘ 'it' + 'be' Theme
                          THEME      │ SUBSTITUTION
                          SPECIAL →  │   right detachment
                                     │       ↘ subst. (internal) + Theme (external & final)
                                     │ REFERENCE
                                     │   left detachment
                                     │       Theme (external) + anaphoric ref. (internal)
                                     │ INVERSION
                                     │ It-EXTRAPOSITION
                                     │ There-EXISTENTIAL
                                     └ Non-special Theme
```

Figure 12. *Theme in English [my network]*[102]

(119) a. | in ⁻eighteen _ninety-/four | when we were /founded | ⁻counting our _Reverend /Mother | we were \six | (LIBMSECHPT02: 20–22) (complex marked (preposed) topical Theme displaying hypotactic elaboration vs. *Counting our _Reverend /Mother we were six in eighteen ninety-four, when we were founded*)

b. | in a \brief | 'twenty \minute | a/ppearance | which it\self 'spoke \volumes | a'bout Pre/toria's | 'growing im\patience | with the Na'mibian /problem | ⁻President /Botha | 'signed the ⁻formal 'procla/mation | es\tablishing the ⁻new 'interim /government | 'uttered a \few 'words of enᵛcouragement | and 'then ∧ 'promptly \left | to 'fly _back to South \Africa | 'leaving ⁻those | ⁻internal /leaders | who've ⁻come to\gether | to ᵛform a new 'government | to _get \on with it | (LIBMSECAPT09: 22–28) (complex marked (preposed) topical Theme displaying hypotactic elaboration vs. where the non-fronted equivalent would be unacceptable owing to processing and EW/EF factors)

b. *non-special* vs. *special Themes*, the latter being topical Themes marked off by means of special syntactic constructions, restricted in this study to seven subtypes of word order arrangements: (i) *clefting* (Section 7.4.6), (ii) *pseudo-clefting* (Section 7.4.7), (iii) *left detachment* (Section 7.4.4), (iv) *right detachments* (Section 7.4.5), (v) *It-extrapositions* (Section 7.4.2), (vi) *inversions* (Section 7.4.3), and (vii) *existential-there constructions* (Section 7.4.1). (120) below includes one example of each subtype, respectively:

(120) a. It was a con⁻tinuing be_lief in \providence|/which sus⁻tained | °Voltaire's \deism | (LIBMSECDPT02: 137) (vs. *Voltaire's deism was sustained by a continuing belief in providence*)

b. | \what they should ᵛteach is ᵛinner re\sourcefulness | (LIBMSECGPT05: 105) (vs. *inner resourcefulness should be taught*)

c. | the \badminton and the \weightlifting they suffered \badly from the lack of the ⁻Asians | (LIBMSECJPT01: 173) (vs. *the badminton and the weightlifting suffered \badly from the lack of the Asians*)

d. | I _know we take *this* for \granted | in ᵛEngland | that | \oh I'll just go \home for the week\end | (LIBMSECJPT06: 452) (vs. *I know we take for granted in England that oh I'll just go home for the weekend*)

e. | it was e\nough | to ex⁻pose the \crisis | in the \relevance of \art | ↓how/ever | °Dada ⁻did put _forward _some | °positive pro\posals | (LIBMSECDPT1: 119) (vs. *to expose the crisis in the relevance of art was enough*).

f. | above the _slogan | ⁻Dada ist _politisch | was ⁻George °Grosz' | _Germany | a °winter's \tale | (LIBMSECDPT01: 051) (vs. *George Grosz' Germany, a winter's tale was above the slogan 'Dada ist politisch'*)

g. | ↑there's \also a danger of \communal violence in the ⁻areas | _bordering the Tamil \north |(LIBMSECAPT01: 034) (vs. *a danger of communal violence also exists in the areas bordering the Tamil north*)

In addition, the recognition of three metafunctions determines the distinction between two *classes* of syntactic Themes, i.e. *non-multiple* vs. *extended multiple Themes* (EMTs) (Section 7.5). In the latter case topical Themes are preceded and/or followed by textual and/or interpersonal elements, as shown in (121) below:

(121) | ↑and in ⁻Mara\dona | without \doubt | they °had the \star of the ∧ °compe°tition | (LIBMSECJPT01: 065) (vs. *and without doubt they had the star of the competition in Maradona*)

Finally, the feature of markedness contrasts *unmarked* Theme–Rheme patterns displaying a *canonical word order* (CWO) with *marked* ones, in terms of: (a) Mood, (b) Voice, (c) relative order of main and dependent clauses in complex clauses, and (d) the relative ordering of topical and/or textual and/or interpersonal elements within the Theme zone. Examples of marked Themes are included in (122) below:

(122) a. | ⁻one figure inci°dentally | you \may find \useful | (LIBMSECFPT02: 064) (vs. *incidentally you may find one figure useful*)
b. | to ˅see | where ⁻this argument ⁄leads ᵦ | ⁻let's con°sider _export prohi\bitions | (LIBMSECPTC01: 336–339) (vs. *let's consider export prohibitions to see where this argument leads*)
c. | more ˅typically how°ever | it's ⁻not ⁄governments | but °business \enterprises ∧ which °ship the °imports |(LIBMSECCPT01: 473) (vs. *however, (more typically), it's not governments, but business enterprises which (more typically) ship the imports (more typically)*).

Although inspired by the SFG model (Section 4.2), this survey of thematic options outlined so far involves *a new approach to unmarked Themes* (Section 7.2) and *marked Themes* (Section 7.3) in the light of: (a) a reformulation of *special Themes* (Section 7.4), and (b) a new category, i.e. *extended multiple Themes* (EMTs) (Section 7.5). Besides, the SFG notions of metaphorical and displaced Themes will be abandoned, and textual Themes will be relabelled as *logical* or *logico-conjunctive Themes*[103] on the assumption that (a) the latter is a more appropriate term to designate an initial item fulfilling a logical or a conjunctive function (although logical and conjunctive elements may also occur within the Rheme), and (b) all classes of Themes realize a textual function (Section 4.3.2).

The metaphorical realizations of the different types of syntactic Themes are not explored here to circumvent the difficulties involved in such a task. Halliday (IFG: 345) himself seems to be very sceptical of the possibility of formalising the differences between congruent and non-congruent realizations of metafunctional choices. Likewise, the reasons to dispense with Halliday's notion of displaced topical Theme were explicated at length elsewhere (Section 4.2.1) and can now be summarised as follows:

a. displaced Theme violates the conception of syntactic topical Theme as the first experiential/transitivity element (or the last one in substitute syntactic topical Themes);
b. it mistakenly implies that all marked syntactic topical Themes precede a displaced topical Theme.

Now, turning to the second aspect of the argument for a *motivated choice*, the assumption that speakers may have "good reasons" for choosing a particular thematic option implies that such "good reasons" must be determined *against the background of a co(n)text*. This is the rationale underlying our adoption of a *corpus-based approach* in order to explore the *textual* and *interpersonal* semantics (and, at some later stage, also the experiential semantics) of thematic options: how do they affect the texture of messages? What do speakers want to do with them?

In this connection, Kies (1988: 74) observes that marked options are: (a) comparatively lower frequency of occurrence, (b) comparatively higher structural complexity; and (c) more restricted distribution in definable environments (Givón's (1993: 178) condition of "discourse distribution"). However, it should be borne in mind that marked patterns are not always less frequent — less expected from the addressee's point of view — than their unmarked counterparts, for they are affected by such factors as text type (Siewierska 1988: 12), or by matters of position and context (Mithun 1987: 313). For instance, it has been claimed that discourse-initial sentences belong to highly marked situations and therefore give rise to the so-called *markedness reversal*, i.e. to a local affinity with marked constructions (Fox 1987b; Pu & Prideaux 1994). This suggests that in order to determine the probabilities of a thematic choice one must take into account not only *global probabilities*, or the terms of all the systems of a language, but also *local probabilities*, which are the effect of "what's done before in discourse" (i.e. *transitional probabilities*), and which affect the probability of "what's going on in discourse" (i.e. *conditional probabilities*). Section 6.4 describes the material and methods used in this corpus-based investigation, as well as its inherent limitations and problems of analysis.

6.3 The cognitive salience of the Theme zone

The thematic options outlined in Section 6.2 above have a common core, namely the premise that *syntactic Theme* or the clause-initial slot is a functional category of crosslinguistic validity (although with language-dependent significance), deriving its functional relevance from the *linearisation* constraint of natural languages, that is to say, the fact that "signs cannot but follow each other in the chain, whether or not they bear a direct grammatical relation" (Lehman 1992: 398). The inherent cognitive salience of the Theme zone has already been attested by abundant experimental research in psycholinguistics and (text) linguistics (Section 2.4.1). In this study further evidence shall be provided that *the Theme zone constitutes an orientation zone in natural language (PresE), giving orientation or anchoring for what is to follow in the background of a co(n)text* (Thompson 1985, Ramsey 1987, Ford 1993). A positional choice in discourse, the clause-initial slot is here conceived as a special "deictic" with both *backward-looking* and *forward-looking* discourse relevance, helping texts to cohesive and consistent (Hausenblas 1964; Daneš 1974b; Section 3.3.3 above). Furthermore, the relevance of this category is considered to be *intrinsically functional* in that it can be elicited in terms of its relationships from above the linguistic system, from below it and at the same level of description. Thus, at the same

Table 15. *Theme, Topic and the Given–New contrast*

Category	Structural	Unit	Function		
Topic	–	Text	"what a text is about" in the case of discourse Topic "what speakers are talking about" in the case of speaker's Topic		
Given/New	+	Tone unit	to present something as "news"		
				from above	related to the MD, the TP and the genre of texts
Theme	+	Clause (complex)	to act as an *orientation zone*	at the same level	related to Rheme, and the mapping of Given and New
				from below	clause initial experiential/transitivity position

(semantic) level, Theme indicates a term in a proportional relationship with respect to Rheme and the Given–New contrast, as shown in Table 15.

It is in this light that one can suggest, for example, that acting negatively in presentative messages (e.g. *There was once an ugly bear who hid from the world*) and in impersonal event-reporting clauses (e.g. *It's raining*), Theme contributes (in unmarked cases) to place a heavy item late in a clause and thereby endowing it with the status of New information (Sections 2.2.1, 4.3.1). And in broader terms, it can be concluded that, as a result of the interaction with other categories such as Given–New, presupposition, Focus, cohesion, reference, Topic or Rheme, individual con(n)text-dependent thematic choices affect the dynamics of discourse, imposing a left to right wave-like movement that has been associated with the principles of FSP, TU, EF, EW.

From above the linguistic system, that is, taking into account its upward involvement with textual proportionalities, abundant research (Sections 2.4.1, 5.4.2) has shown that syntactic Theme:

a. affects/is affected by the Topic discontinuity or the Topic continuity of texts, cancelling an assumption which has been established in the previous context (viz. a situation which is no longer true, a temporal or locational setting etc. or elaborating a previously referred to item);
b. orients both the message conveyed by the clause (complex) and the addressee's expectations with respect to the preceding and the following co(n)texts;
c. affects/is affected by the MOD, the TP and the genre of texts.

And from below, as explained, for instance, in Section 6.2 above, the category of syntactic Theme can be characterised by its realization at the level of form in relation to the parameters of e.g. (a) internal structure, (b) the metafunctions and (c) markedness.

It is because of their *backward-looking potential* that syntactic Themes provide a *link between the clause they instantiate and what has come before*. In this sense, a plausible iconic relation can be established between Theme choices as *strategy* or *discourse markers* and the level of text organisation. Although the notion of "discourse markers" has been usually applied to (conversational) spoken language meaning "sequentially dependent elements which bracket units of talk" (Schiffrin 1987: 31), here this kind of function is also attributed to Theme choices: their "bracketing" — or structuring — contribution to discourse will be shown to arise out of the functional potential of re-ordering within the English word order system and out of the discourse slot in which they are used (Schiffrin 1987: 317). It follows that, as a marker of discourse structure, the Theme zone involves some kind of localisation, upon which rests its "deictic" presentative flavour having endophoric or exophoric, single or multiple, orientation.

Another reason to treat Theme choices as discourse markers is that their *varying textual functions make them more or less suitable for specific genres or text types*. Thus, in Chapter 7 it will be shown that the usage and frequency of different classes and types of Theme in LIBMSEC varies along a scale from factual descriptive registers such as reports and lectures to the rhetorical persuasive registers, such as propaganda charity appeals or religious services. Roughly, we shall see that Theme choices acting as digression markers are prone to occur in informative or descriptive texts, contributing to virtually building up this discourse type in terms of structure; whereas more interpersonal kind of texts, such as argumentations and expositions, are more likely to contain subjectively oriented Themes, more often expressing a direct comment or an evaluation (where an evaluating or commenting attitude is not established beforehand or would not be expected overall), and simultaneously demarcating constitutive subparts of argumentation and exposition.

Besides, the *use of specific classes and types of Theme* will also be related to three different *speaker's attitudes*: the speaker as *experiencer*, as *architect* (of discourse structure), and as *commentator* (Section 6.4.2.2). It will be shown, for example, that when a text deals with an actual description of states from the outside world, Theme choices also fulfil a descriptive function contributing to producing an effect of *displaced immediacy*: a descriptive structure reproduces relations from an actual scene being evoked, which will be taken as an instruction to "view" the scene mentally, building up organisational parts, or commenting on the content expressed. Alternatively, in the case of non-descriptive textual functions, Theme choices tend to build up more abstract descriptive structures, organising discourse along relations between discourse entities following a principle of "similarity" (Giora 1990: 303).

There is a common core in what has been said so far on *the usage and function of Theme–Rheme patterns* in actual discourse: *they profile themselves as carriers of interpersonal meaning*, which justifies their treatment both as *discourse markers* and as *markers* of *interpersonal meaning*. It can be argued that the interpersonal orientation of Theme–Rheme patterns lies in that, through them, the speaker/writer is "doing something to the listener or reader" (Halliday 1985a: 53), whereby a direct outflow of the presence of both the speaker and speaker-addressee-relations is created in the text. It will be shown that starting points:

> [...] give *interpersonal* information on the ensuing discourse, such as indicating its illocutionary force [...], or setting the mood [...] or giving an evaluation of the importance or reliability of the information in the ensuing discourse (Lowe 1987: 7 [my emphasis])

In keeping with this, in Chapter 7 we shall see that *Theme choices* are *subjective speaker's choices* that obey not only to *textual reasons* (in terms of the *thematic* and *information* structure of the clause), but also to *interpersonal motivations* (affecting the meaning of the clause as an *exchange*).

We have already mentioned one aspect of the subjectivity of Theme choices: the fact that they reflect different speaker attitudes in different text types. In addition, and in close connection with this, *marked* and *special Themes* (vs. unmarked and non-special ones) will be shown *to carry an added subjectivity* in that they show a word order or syntactic pattern that is deviant from the norm causing an effect that clearly goes beyond their ideational meaning (Sections 7.3 and 7.4). The underlying rationale is that the ideational content of marked and special Theme constructions is roughly equivalent in truth-conditions to that of their unmarked or non-special counterparts, so that the level of meaning of the clause as representation of experience is not substantially affected. Under these circumstances and under the conditions of PresE grammaticalised word order system, in Chapter 7 our corpus-based results will show that the choice of a marked or special Theme, as opposed to their unmarked and non-special counterparts, involves a semiotic process whereby extra-meaning bearing a component of *emotivity* is added as a result of two main factors: (a) the *expressive syntax* of these constructions (Weil's "animated syntax", Section 3.2.1 above), and (b) a principle that could be paraphrased in terms of *Grice's* (1975) *maxim of quantity*. Thus, Banfield (1982), for example, explains that it is because of their "expressive syntax" that constructions like inversions are excluded from embedded clauses, and that this restriction can be applied to other addressee-oriented and exclusively expressive linguistic items, such as exclamations, subjectless imperatives, addressee-oriented adverbials and the like.

On the other hand, Grice's (1975) maxim of quantity could be adduced to explain that, generally speaking, the choice of marked or special Theme–Rheme patterns involves the breaking of expectations about the use of an unmarked sentence pattern concerning "normal" discourse conditions, so that the hearer/reader is licensed to infer that something that goes beyond the meaning of the unmarked or non-special counterpart is meant by the speaker. Put another way, the choice of marked, special or extended multiple Themes, in contrast with unmarked and non-special ones, requires an instruction which attracts special attention to them so that "the cost of an extra, perceptible [...] signal is indeed worth incurring only when there is a need to prevent the hearer from coming to a likely — but erroneous — conclusion" (Garcia 1994: 334, 338; Stein 1995).

The assumption is that the "natural" salience of the clause-initial position makes a constituent placed there apt to participate in a dynamic discourse process whereby it serves as the *reference point*[104] for the preceding and subsequent discourse, independently of its actual discourse-status since "any — known or unknown — referent may be put on stage" (Stein 1995: 136). More precisely, given that, as already noted, the Theme zone may be occupied by entities or by constituents that *are "relational" rather than "nominal" in character, syntactic Themes establish a frame of reference in discourse, which serves as a "search domain", or framework, in which the subsequent predication is integrated, linking the ongoing discourse to the co(n)textual ground, and by reference to which the subsequent discourse can be anchored and construed* (Section 2.2.1, endnote 10). It is in this "relational" sense that we re-address a number of apparently conflicting views raised in this connection by previous accounts, such as:

a. what I take to be the systemicists' contradiction of regarding Theme as a *universal category*, i.e. "the *point of departure/starting point*" of the clause as a message, and yet claiming that "initial experiential position" is the expression of Theme in some languages only; and
b. the FSP and FG analyses questioning the assumptions that:
   i. clauses as messages are bipartite (i.e. provided with Theme and Rheme);
   ii. thematic/topical "aboutness" is systematically marked;
   iii. all messages have a Theme.

It seems that these points of conflict can be reconciled by considering that syntactic Themes entail *relational*, or *reciprocal*, relationships (Sections 2.2.1 and 4.3.1 above). This implies that the "aboutness" feature of syntactic Themes, whether they be participants, attributes, circumstances or processes, does not reside in their referential status *per se*, but rather in their establishing a relation with a Rheme in the background of a discourse co(n)text. In other words, the Theme zone states "what a clause is about" in the sense that it "stages", or "presents", providing a "framework" for, the predication. In sum, *the functional relevance of the Theme zone is here regarded as "relational rather than nominal in character, i.e. it profiles a relationship instead of a thing"* in the sense that is serves "to introduce an element into the scene" that has a bearing on the subsequent discourse, normally to become a new focus of attention" (Langacker 1993: 26), which underlines the hypothesis that clause "beginning elements have a wider semantic range than elements towards the end" (Bolinger 1952: 117).

Thus, in Chapter 7 we shall see that *Theme (and Rheme) choices*, whether multiple or non-multiple, marked or unmarked, special or non-special, do have an effect on the *addressee-side* (one of *hearer/reader-involvement*): they *give an instruction about the addressee's current focus of attention*, or about the *emphasis to be attached to individual discourse items* (Hannay's (1991, 1998) "message modes", Section 5.4.4 above; Lambrecht's (1994) "allosentences"; Vallduví & Engdahl's (1996) "instruction types"). Indeed, in the absence of a concrete descriptive purpose, addressees are *instructed* to perform a *continuation* or a *change* in her/his *focus of attention* within the discourse organisation. In other words, exploiting their *forward looking potential*, Theme choices establish a *viewpoint* and determine a *perspective* on the experience being constructed, which affects the *focus management* (i.e. "camera movement", perspective or viewpoint) of discourse, structuring it into separate units or episodes. These instructions may involve an invitation for a *dynamic viewing*, creating expectations and tension that go beyond a mere focus management task, or they may imply a *static viewing*, representing discourse markers typical of a descriptive kind of progression within a text.

Thus, in the subsequent sections it will be shown that unmarked and non-special Themes tend to correlate with discourse expectations conveying instructions of continuity of discourse participants, of referential predictability and of foregrounded or in discourse focus material, while marked and special thematic constructions are generally used when "normal" discourse expectations fail to be met, pointing to instructions of topic shifts, of backgrounded (or de-focused) material, of digressions or turns within the structure of the text (Fox 1985; Givón 1985b, 1987, 1988). The same holds for a *change of perspective*: while sameness in form usually reflects a constant perspective, any deviation from a norm is apt to signal a departure from it, and is thereby a natural symptom of topic change, subjective viewpoint, or change in focus of attention (Garcia 1994: 337). In this connection, Langacker's (1990) examples below may prove illustrative:

(123) a. The tree is in front of the house.
      b. In front of the house is a tree.

Langacker claims that a sentence like (123a) is "appropriate only if the tree is in the viewer's line of sight" (p. 6), i.e., if the location is defined in relation to the viewer, although it may remain unclear whether the side where the tree stands is the front or the back side of the house. Alternatively, in (123b) no such potential ambiguity arises: the viewpoint from where the phenomenon is seen is moved to the house, the location of the tree defined in relation to it. By using an inversion, the speaker thus moves her/his own position from where s/he views a phenomenon to the location designated by the referent of the NG in the fronted constituent. Relational information thereby becomes what Langacker calls a *profiled relationship*: it forms the starting-point of a presentative construction, which may be static, in the case of, for example, temporal or locative relations, dynamic, e.g. in the case of directional relations.

In addition, Langacker (1990) explains that a *perspective*, or a point of view, may be performed *subjectively* or *objectively*. He claims that in the *optimal viewing arrangement* the subject, i.e. the speaker/viewer, is only implicit, he is non-salient and "offstage" and hence *subjectively construed*. Consider, for instance, (124) and (125) below (Dorgeloh 1997: 107, (76), (78a)), where the speaker remains subjective and "offstage", assuming the viewpoint of the fronted constituent which is a part of the conceptual scene:

(124) Next come the Gerinan Expressionists and the paintings of Nolde and Munch, in particular, have been carefully selected to indicate the important role that this School played in the formation of 20th century art. (LOB, sc.writ.)

(125) These are shocking figures, but even more shocking is the fact that at least half the people behind these crimes will go undetected. (LOB, ed.).

By contrast, if, as in (126), some part of the *ground*, e.g. the speaker and/or the hearer, is put "onstage" or *profiled* (Langacker 1990: 10), the ground itself becomes salient, *objectively* construed, with the result that "the inherent asymmetry diminishes between a perceiving individual and the entity perceived" (Langacker 1990: 7) (cf. Kuno's (1987) "empathy").[105]

(126) The women were standing in the background. Behind them were the children, who were […]. (Dorgeloh 1997: 104 [emphasis in original])

In (126) there exists an effect of "staged activity" or "camera movement": the speaker starts from the viewpoint of the fronted PP, i.e. of the referent which it contains, and from this new vantage point focuses *the children*.

To sum up, the above leads to conclude that one means of marking a constituent as the focus of discourse is by bringing it to the front position and/or by resorting to special Theme–Rheme arrangements, thereby expressing directly that — and how — the speaker is affected by this item. Since this active instruction via word order choice and special syntactic constructions implies that "the speaker or writer [is] doing something to the listener or reader by means of language" (Halliday 1985a: 53), Theme choices can be plausibly analysed as involving a combination of ideational, textual and interpersonal meaning.

6.4 The corpus and the methodology

6.4.1 The LIBMSEC

The *Lancaster IBM Spoken English Corpus* (LIBMSEC) is a machine-readable corpus of natural spoken British English compiled at the University of Lancaster in 1984. It contains 49,285 words broken down into ten textual categories of spoken PresBE (Table 16): (a) Commentary (A); (b) News broadcast (B); (c) Lecture Type I — aimed at a general audience (C); (d) Lecture Type II — aimed at restricted audience (D); (e) Religious broadcast (E); (f) Magazine style reporting (F); (g) Fiction (G); (h) Poetry (H); (i) Dialogue (J); (j) Propaganda (K).[106]

Table 16. LIBMSEC *Corpus (49.285 words)*

Text	Category	Date[107]	Length min: LIBMSEC	#Speakers	#Words	% Words
A01–A12	Commentary	11–24–84 06–22–85	64: 30	12	9.066	18.4
B01–B04	News Broadcasts	11–24–84 01–14–86	29: 12	15	5.235	10.6
C01	Lecture Type I General audience	11–20–85	30: 00	1	4.471	9.1
D01–D03	Lecture Type II Open University Audience	– –	57: 00	3	7.451	15.1
E01–E02	Religious Broadcast	11–26–85 11–27–85	11: 18	2	1.503	3.1
F01–F04	Magazine-style reporting	11–24–84 12– –86	25: 30	14	4.710	9.6
G01–G05	Fiction	06–25–85 01–28–87 01–26–86	46: 25	5	7.299	14.8
H01–H05	Poetry	11–26–86	9: 00	5	1.292	2.6
J01–J06	Dialogue	– –82 12– –86 03–11–87	37: 28	9	6.826	13.8
K01–K02	Propaganda	01–18–87 01–25–87	8: 41	2	1.432	2.9

Three reasons justify the choice of LIBMSEC as the corpus for this investigation. One is its relatively small size as compared to other tagged machine-readable corpora, which makes it suitable for a manual (clause by clause) analysis of syntactic Themes across different textual categories, given that our characterisation of syntactic Themes precludes any kind of automatic data searching. Indeed, the available text retrieval programs cannot automatically find instances of syntactic Themes because these are not characterised by one specific element in itself, but by the specific Theme–Rheme combination in which a particular thematic option occurs.

The second advantage of LIBMSEC is that all the texts are in the *spoken mode*. This will allow us to observe how segmental and suprasegmental factors work together to achieve the desired communicative effects, and how, as a result of real-time production constraints, spoken language tends to show a *high interdependence with the context of situation*, expressed by: (a) features of *intonation* and *rhythm*, (b) a *low lexical density* (or proportion of content words to the total discourse), and (c) a high degree of *grammatical complexity* (subordination) (Halliday 1979). We can see for example, how *changes in intonation* (a) indicate different attitudes and moods, and (b) mark grammatical structures like questions or commands while simultaneously helping to establish a rhythm by drawing attention to grammatical boundaries in utterances. Similarly, one can observe how *pitch variations*, *loudness*, *pace*, *silence* and *pauses*, as well as *vocal effects* (e.g. throat-clearing or coughing) allow speakers to reinforce their attitudes and responses as in real speech situations.

Nevertheless, it should be noted that the LIBMSEC does not offer a wide range of varieties of spoken English, but is restricted to the *language of radio broadcasting*. Even though each kind of (LIBMSEC) programme has its own distinctive lexical, grammatical and prosodic features, the language of radio broadcasts as a whole can be characterised as *not spontaneous*, but *planned* and *formal*, as a mix of *spoken and written language* (Abercrombie 1963; Gregory 1967: 192). Like written language, it is polished and edited, yet it is usually delivered as though it is spontaneous speech. Because it is written to be "read" aloud to a very diverse audience that normally will listen to the linguistic codes only once as the programme is transmitted, the language is *easy to articulate*, *fluent* and *understandable*, concerning *carefully organised* texts, often made up of short, uncomplicated units so that maximum use can be made of the timeslot allocated in the programming schedule. Indeed, people who work regularly in the medium of television or radio learn to speak in a way that emulates the spontaneous spoken word even if they are reading aloud. Where ordinary people appear in programmes, editing often has eliminated all the false starts, hesitations and repetitions which are characteristic of spontaneous informal conversation, although, admittedly, there exist examples of truly spontaneous speech (unprepared answers in a Dialogues or live Commentaries) and of language that is written with no attempt to reflect spontaneous speech (in Fiction or Religious Services).

The *structure* of each programme depends upon its type — one-off programmes are self-contained, whereas serial programmes run from episode to episode. The *opening* and *closing* of the News, for example, always follow a predefined pattern. They usually start with a formal greeting, an indication of the specific programme being broadcast and the newsreader's name; and they end with a summary of the main news and a formal closing (e.g. *and that's all we have time for... [...] from..., goodnight*), with intonation patterns also indicating to the audience that the programme is beginning or coming to an end. Following a pre-defined schedule, Topic shifts in News are generally smooth and rarely challenged (as they might in informal conversations), and Topic ends are equally carefully organised, since they are subject to time constraints. If time is running out, presenters may have to break off a discussion by explicitly reminding participants that the programme is about to end or that something different will soon be introduced (e.g. phrases like *and I'm afraid I'll have to stop you there...* or *and we'll have to leave it here* ..., adverbials like *lastly...* or with non-finite clauses like *to conclude...*); or the audience may be left with a cliff-hanger for continuation in he next programme or a neat summary which finalises the issues covered.

Alternatively, other programmes such as Commentaries and Dialogues are structured around a very organised form of *turn-taking* despite possible interruptions, overlaps or digressions, which requires participants to behave according to certain "rules" in order to guarantee effective communication. In these "informal" contexts the *end of a Topic* can be identified by phrases like *by the way... and incidentally...* or clauses like *that reminds me...* and *to change the subject...* may be used to bring one topic to an end and establish a new one. New Topics can reintroduce material that cropped up earlier in the exchange but in a new form (e.g. *as I was saying before* ...), by relating a new Topic to the old one (e.g. *speaking of which* ...); or taking a completely new direction (e.g. *let's talk about something else...*). Interruptions may he seen to bring a topic to its end before its natural conclusion. After a digression, an attempt may be made to revive the old Topic (e.g. *where was I?*), or the new Topic may be allowed to replace it because it is seen as more interesting. This kind of *topic management*, however, is unlikely to take place in a formal speech context (e.g. Lectures, News/ Financial reports or Religious services), where the topic is usually predefined and particular speakers are dominant.

The lexis of the LIBMSEC texts is also directly linked to the content of each programme. Religious Services, Poetry and Lectures, for instance, are subject-specific texts and their language reflects this; others, like Fiction or Dialogues, are based on ordinary informal interaction and the language is therefore far more wide-ranging. The same holds for the *grammar* of the texts. The more serious the context, the more likely the grammar is to be both formal and complex. And conversely, where a broadcast is imitating the structures of informal conversation, even if the structure of broadcasted interactions is quite tightly defined with participants following the expected patterns of behaviour, the grammatical structures are more likely to be straightforward and the utterances are more likely to be incomplete, with a higher amount of (a) *conversational repairs* (in the case of e.g. misunderstood questions in an interview; participants talking simultaneously in a debate; unexpected silences in a discussion) and (b) *adjacency pairs*, i.e. recognisable structural patterns that have a logical connection following each other and are produced by different speakers (e.g. questions and answers, greetings, commands and responses).

Lastly, the semiotic process described in Sections 6.2 and 6.3 gives ample reason to assume a substantial communicative function for the choice of syntactic Themes and therefore makes it worthwhile to consider their distribution in a corpus, as well. Chapter 7 will show that LIBMSEC provides a useful survey of the distribution of different thematic choices over different kinds of texts and in particular it allows for relating the patterns of usage to functional text characteristics. The distribution of different classes and types of Theme–Rheme constructs over the LIBMSEC genres, and with that the degree to which these constructions are relatively more or less expected, confirms the existence of genre conventions and at the same time justifies treating Themes as *markers* of *discourse/subjectivity.*

6.4.2   *Some problems of analysis*

Despite the strengths of the LIBMSEC in particular (Section 6.4.1), and of corpus-based approaches, in general (e.g. total accountability, eclecticism, samples of natural written and/or spoken natural material representing a whole range of usage, objectivity, etc.) (Svartvik & Quirk 1980), this corpus work on Theme–Rheme patterns, as compared to morphological or lexical features, has encountered a number of problems, which are enumerated in turn.

6.4.2.1 *Corpus size*
The first problem concerning the LIBMSEC is that owing to its small size it did not contain examples of all (sub)types and (sub)classes of syntactic Themes postulated above (Section 6.2). This made it occasionally necessary to resort to

made-up examples or to tokens taken from the relevant literature. Besides, to obtain more representative figures, the categories (C) and (D), *Lecture Types I and II*, had to be subsumed under the cover-term *Lecture*, and, occasionally, all the LIBMSEC texts were grouped in two, i.e. *Fiction* (viz. Poetry and Fiction) and *non-Fiction* (viz. Commentary, News Broadcast, Lecture, Religion, Magazine, Dialogue and Propaganda).

6.4.2.2 *Text categories*

The second shortcoming resides in the tenor relationships (i.e. socially meaningful participant relationships) of the LIBMSEC. Admittedly, the relative status of a programme and its audience is directly linked to the relationship created between them, which inevitably affects the linguistic and prosodic choices made. The LIBMSEC broadcasters sometimes use "experts" who are in the role of advisers or educators (Lectures, live Commentaries); or they may use ordinary people as an integral part of the programme in order to let the audience participate (Dialogues); or they may simply reproduce everyday life (News). Yet, all in all tenor relationships in LIBMSEC are fairly restricted. They concern formal vs. informal interactions between active, well-defined speakers and a passive, undefined audience, which does not seem to offer a wide range of variables to justify Theme choices from a tenor perspective. At most Taylor & Knolls (1988: 5ff.) explain in the manual of information accompanying LIBMSEC that (a) "the style of the main newsreaders is more formal than that of the reporters", (b) fiction texts are "aimed at an adult audience", (c) dialogues are "of varying degrees of informality", (d) speakers have an (RP) pronunciation and (e) they are mostly males (70%), especially in News and Commentary.

Another weakness involves, as pointed out, the *mode* of LIBMSEC texts, restricted to the language of broadcasting. This precludes the possibility of contrasting the different means whereby Theme–Rheme patterns perform in written vs. spoken discourse such orientation or anchoring tasks as the marking of relative salience or prominence of discourse entities, the indication of topic changes or the expression of emotions and attitudes. Under these circumstances it was felt necessary to resort to further variables in order to obtain more delicate information about text types in LIBMSEC. One means of doing this was to organise the LIBMSEC categories in Table 16 in terms of *decreasing subjectivity* as follows and as shown in Table 17:

> Propaganda (including Religious Broadcasts), Dialogues, Essays (Fiction/Poetry) > Commentaries > Lectures > Reportages (news, magazine)

Table 17. *Subjectivity across LIBMSEC texts*

	Text	Field	Mode	
↑	K	Propaganda Charity appeals	Persuasive	To exhort
	E	Religion Religious services	Instructive	To exhort
	J	Dialogue Dialogues	Argumentative	To discuss
− Subjectivity +	H	Poetry Poems	Narrative (poetry)	to entertain
	G	Fiction Stories	Narrative (fiction)	to entertain
	A	Commentaries	Argumentative Narrative	to comment to inform
↓	C	University Lecture I	Expositive	to teach
	D	University Lecture II	Expositive	to teach
	B	News Reports	Narrative (report)	to inform
	F	Magazine financial Reports	Narrative (report)	to inform

This ordering corresponds to an intuitive characterisation on the assumption that most speakers would consider propagandistic or dialogic texts, (fiction or poetry) essays, and commentaries as more subjective kinds of texts than lectures or (press) reportages. Hence, at one extreme lie Propaganda, Dialogues and Essays, on the assumption that these LIBMSEC text-types show a comparatively higher degree of subjectivity. Dialogues, leading to discussions about specific topics, represent *argumentative* discourse. By contrast, Religious broadcasts and Propanda have a common rhetorical purpose: *to exhort*, the former belonging to the *instructive* genre, and the latter to *persuasive* discourse.

Religious broadcasts in LIBMSEC are restricted to *liturgical forms*, i.e. chants, thanksgivings, invocations, petitions, hymns and psalms written to be read or sung. They are a distinctive form of religious language adopting the form of a polite plea addressed to the deity. They seek to *persuade* people to believe and to act in a certain moral way (*conative function*), but they also have an *expressive* function since they are partly concerned with an expression of feelings, prescribing a specific attitude to life. Religious broadcasts make use of a formal language which retains archaic linguistic features, but since its main use is in public group contexts, it is still accessible to the intended audience. *Formulaic utterances*, i.e. formal phrases and idioms (e.g. *Let there be ... Let us pray...*) and *antithesis* (e.g. *heaven and hell, sin and forgiveness, and death and resurrection*) are very common. There are also frequent instances of *the naming of the godhead* (e.g. *Almighty God, most merciful Father, Lord, our heavenly Father*), the central concept of any religion, and of *first person plurals*, which reflects the public, group nature of worships. The *present tense* is also recurrent, concerning rarely interrogative clauses, but frequently *declaratives* and *imperatives*, and a relatively high amount of *subjunctive* processes. Modal verbs are equally common, implying contrasts in speaker attitudes and often conveying a certainty in future time or to mark a spiritual command which should be followed (e.g. I and the ˉKing will _answer them | ˅truly | I ˋsay [...]| 'then he will 'say to 'those at his ˋleft 'hand | LIBMSECE02).

Fiction and Poetry on the other hand are instances of the *narrative* genre aimed at *entertaining*. Although wide-ranging, above all these texts offer opportunities for authors to experiment, to manipulate language in order to create the best possible effects so that the author can influence the addressee. The dominant function of language is therefore *poetic*, and because literature deals with human emotions and states of mind, the *expressive* function is also very important. But authors can do much more than entertaining through their creation of an imaginary world. Narrative prose, for example, can implicitly raise the addressee's awareness about an issue or about the world in general, and can thus educate and inform (*referential* function). Likewise, poetry has a wide range of functions: it can *entertain*, *arouse emotions* and *provoke thought*; it can *describe*, *evaluate* or *inform*.

As a result, the first, third, intrusive or unintrusive, reliable or unreliable, narrator may recreate not only events, but also the thoughts and opinions of the characters in a fictional world. Thus, in Fiction and Poetry in LIBMSEC *interior monologues* (in which the author orders and patterns the exposition in order to mirror a character's thoughts) alternate with passages reflecting the *stream of consciousness*, in which syntax is manipulated to show the complexity of the human mind, how chaotic and jumbled thoughts often are. Likewise, instances of *direct speech* (e.g. an exact copy of the precise words spoken, allowing characters to speak for themselves), whereby the speaker's point of view is given prominence, co-occur with instances of *indirect* and *free indirect speech*. In the former the person who is reporting the conversation intervenes as an interpreter by selecting what someone has said, normally using a subordinate *that* clause.

Alternatively, the free indirect speech merges the approach of both direct and indirect speech: the main reporting clause (e.g. *he said that ...*) is omitted; it uses the same third person pronouns and past tense as indirect speech, but reproduces the actual words spoken more accurately. The free indirect speech may be used to create irony because it gives the addressee the flavour of characters' words, while keeping the narrator in a position where he or she can intervene; or it can also be used to direct addressees' sympathy away from certain characters or to indicate changes in the role of a character. As to the lexis, it may be simple or complicated, formal or colloquial, descriptive or evaluative. Depending upon the author's intentions, the connotations of the words chosen will build up a particular viewpoint of the fictional world.

The category of *Commentaries* on the other hand represents a hybrid midway text-type whose rhetorical purpose is primarily *argumentative* and subsidiarily *narrative* (*exposition*). Generally speaking, commenting on a topic implies sticking to it for a stretch of a text (or for the whole of it), so that there exist fewer potential topic changes as compared with other genres. Also, the number of procedural uses is relatively lower for two reasons. One is that argumentation is a matter of facts and conclusions so that a visual impact reading is least likely to be adequate. And, secondly, comments presuppose a certain level of previous knowledge, which makes them only selectively contain informative (narrative or descriptive) passages. In this latter case, "indirect" uses of narration and description are put into the service of the function of argumentation.

Turning to *Lectures*, these are here characterised as representing informational *exposition* (e.g. economics, mathematics, etc.). Given that, in Lectures (and in scientific writing in general), dealing with a certain topic usually requires its discussion in some detail, they show fewer topic changes than other genres. Also, visual impact readings are generally less suitable in scientific texts because the nature of the argument is often highly abstract.

Finally, in the "objective" extreme of our subjectivity scale are (news and magazine) *Reportages*. These are regarded as instances of reference or representative *narrative* discourse, differing from Fiction in being information-oriented texts generally dealing with actual events. Typically, reportages contain *static* viewing in the form of description, either serving procedural ends, i.e. primarily creating a visual impact reading, or functioning as a real focus management device within the discourse organisation making use of marked informational Focus. Importantly, however, it should be noted that, even though news reportages are in principle considered to present information in a neutral and unbiased form, because news stories are selected and presented in a certain way, there will always be evidence of subjectivity. The subjective bias of news broadcasts may be recognised in many ways: certain stories are included at the expense of others; priority is given to some stories by placing them first in the running order; words are chosen to convey the intended message in a way that suits the particular media institution; and the images which accompany television news can be chosen to influence the audience emotively rather than intellectually. All this underscores the fact that the news does not present us with reality, but with a view of events which has been ordered and reconstructed.

Table 18. *Registers in LIBMSEC*

	Text	Field	Tenor	Mode of presentation: Spoken language	Channel radio	Genre	rhetorical purpose
↑ Subjectivity +	K	Propaganda charity appeals	Formal	Language in action	− feedback + aural − visual	Persuasive	to exhort
	E	Religion Religious services	Formal	Language in action Construction	=	Instructive	to exhort
	J	Dialogue Dialogues	Informal	Language in action	= + feedback	Argumentative	to discuss
	H	Poetry Poems	Formal	Reconstruction	=	Narrative (poetry)	to entertain
	G	Fiction Stories	Informal	Reconstruction	=	Narrative (fiction)	to entertain
Subjectivity −	A	Commentaries	Informal	Reconstruction	=	Argumentative Narrative	to comment to inform
	C	University Lecture I	Formal	Construction	=	Expositive	to teach
	D	University Lecture II	Formal	Construction	=	Expositive	to teach
↓	B	News Reports	Formal	Reconstruction	=	Narrative (report)	to inform
	F	Magazine financial Reports	Formal	Construction (constructed language that is reconstructed)	=	Narrative (report)	to inform

An additional mode variable was taken into account according to Martin's (1984b, c) two kinds of physical distance: *addressee-proximity* and *content-proximity*, as shown in Table 18. These are two basic situational properties that can be related to the factors of "copresence" and "interaction" of language producer and receiver, which together define the property of *situatedness* (Chafe 1994: 44f.), reflecting "the closeness language has to the immediate and social situation in which it is produced and received" (p. 44).

Addressee-proximity comprises three variables: ±*aural*, ±*visual* and ±*feedback*, i.e. the presence/absence of addressee's response. In its turn, content-proximity concerns the values of: (a) *language in action*, i.e. language used as a means to interact in or act upon reality (as in Charity Appeals, etc.); (b) *reconstruction*, i.e. language employed to monitor reality (as in e.g. reports or commentaries) or recreate it (e.g. in Poetry, Fiction stories); and (c) *construction*, i.e. language that creates a "new", usually highly specialised, reality (e.g. in Lectures on economics, etc.).

Parallel to the these three variables comprised under the content proximity dimension, i.e. language in action, construction and reconstruction, we shall distinguish three different *speaker attitudes* in discourse: the speaker as a *experiencer*, as an *architect* (of discourse structure) and as a *reporter*.

As a *reporter* the speaker may inform about his/or her own situation or about displaced matters. In news broadcasts, for example, information is typically treated as events, not as displaced experience. The reason is that it is rarely the journalist's own experience that he has to report, because what has originally been immediate experience is usually shifted through a number of intermediaries (the so-called "informed sources" such as agencies, eyewitness reports, statements by official organs). Depending on the extent to which the reporter processes the material obtained into a discourse organisation of her/his own, her/his role as speaker varies in kind. Be that as it may, in reportages information is normally presented as chunks of experience that are shaped according to the needs of the addressees, following the principle of increasing specification, in contrast with the continuous nature of immediate experience (Lüger 1983). As a corollary, events are usually strongly reduced and very selectively treated, and *deictic* elements, locating "an experience in space and time, and also with respect to a self" (Chafe 1994: 205), are reduced to a minimum. The effect is that the reporter presents information as displaced events, but s/he is not displaced in her/his consciousness, and so s/he uses immediate speech with a location in space and time that is recognisably different from the events being talked about. The excerpt in (127) below, gives us an example of a reconstructive text (News), where the speaker adopts the role of a reporter:

(127) BBC ′News | at ˏeight o'clock on ⁻Saturday the 'twenty-fourth of Noˎvember | ⁻this is 'Brian ˏPerkins | a ˋthousand 'people were led to ˋsafety after being ˋtrapped by a ⁻fire | in the ⁻London ˎUnderground last 'night | ˏmany had to 'walk along the ⁻track to the 'nearest ˎstation | Mr ˋEnoch 'Powell | has ⁻praised Mrs ᵛThatcher | for ⁻standing ˏfirm at the ˏAnglo-'Irish ˋsummit | the ⁻Overseas Deᵥvelopment 'Minister | is ˏvisiting Ethiᵛopia this week'end | to 'see the 'famine reˋlief ope'ration | ⁻high winds | and ⁻heavy ᵥseas | have been causing 'further ⁻problems | in the ᵛsouthern 'part of 'Britain | leaving ⁻homes 'flooded | and ˏroads ˎblocked | a ⁻big ˎrescue ope'ration was ⁻mounted in central ˏLondon | 'late last ⁻night | after a ᵛfire | at ⁻Oxford ˏCircus ˋUnderground 'Station | the e⁻mergency ˏservices were ⁻hampered by ˏthick ˎsmoke | which 'spread ᵛquickly through the 'station | and into ᵛtunnels | where 'five ˋtrains were cut ˋoff | ˋsome 'passengers were ˋstranded for two ˋhours | ↓and ˋthen had to be ˋguided on ↑ˋfoot along the ˋtrack | (LIBMSECB01013 [my emphasis]))

In turn, when the speaker behaves as an *experiencer*, s/he focuses on her/his immediate experience, which is characterised by (a) temporal continuity, i.e., the order of presentation in the text is identical to the order of occurrence of the represented events, (b) richness of detail, which would be irrelevant in reports, and (c) the use of deictic expressions, which emphasise the eyewitness nature of the mode. Likewise, the speaker may also adopt the position of a displaced consciousness with the effect of displaced immediacy, in which case s/he shifts her/his ground back in time, from the current to a previous — or pretended — position as an experiencer (Chafe 1994: 226ff.). As already noted, going by Langacker's (1990) work on subjectivity, this can be done in two alternative ways: objectively, when the speaker is objectively put "onstage", or subjectively, if the speaker remains off the scene expressed via language. To illustrate an objective construal of the speaker's ground, consider (128) below:

(128) | the 'world ⁻cup | *we*'ll be⁻gin | with ᵛMexico | and 'Martin ˎFookes | well ′Martin | as a 'compeˏtition | did it live ⁻up to your expecˎtations | [change of speaker: Martin Fookes] well I reˎcall 'saying at the ˋtime | *that I* 'think the ˋgood 'outweighed the ˎbad | we ˋcertainly 'did have some ˋdire matches in ˬ ˏMexico | and 'one that 'comes to ˏmind is | Moˋrocco a'gainst West ˋGermany | where 'we were ˬ ⁻all ˎpraying | for the ⁻final 'whistle to ˎgo | but a⁻gainst ˏthat | we had some ˋexcellent 'matches | ˋFrance a'gainst the 'Soviet ⁻Union | 'finished 1-⁻/¹ | an in⁻credible game | be'tween ⁻Belgium | and the 'Soviet 'Union '4-ˏ₃ | and ˋFrance a'gainst Braˎzil | de'cided on ˎpenalties | ⁻those were the ˋhighlights I 'felt | of the 'World ˎCup | and of ⁻course | the ˋfinal itˎself | was ˋexcellent | (LIBMSECJ01037)

In the passage in (128), Martin Fookes focuses on his own displaced experience, showing the maintenance of relative continuity, a richness of subjective details and the switching to the past tense. It does, however, not involve displacement of *self*, because the ground is construed objectively by first person pronouns. By contrast, (129) displays displaced immediacy emerging from a subjective construal of the ground:

>   (129) | but ˋfirst it's worth 'stressing how the _country is ᵥdominated | by the ˋpresident | _Nico'lai Ceauᵥse'scu | his ᵛpicture aˈppears ᵢeverywhere on imˈportant oᵢccasions | his ᵢwife | is a ᵢmember | of the ˰ _top poˈlitical ᵢbody | and ˋone of his ᵥsons | is ˉmoving up ᵢfast | two ᵢothers | hold imˈportant _government ᵢposts | ˋCeau'sescu's ᵢspeech | to the ˰ ˋCommu- nist 'Party ᵥCongress | 'lasted ˉfour and a 'half ᵢhours | and drew ˉforty-ᵢ three | _standing oᵥvations | on 'each oᵢccasion | an aˉppropriate ˋslogan was ᵢshouted | ˉeach _time | Ceauˋsescu | was the ᵢfirst 'word of the ᵢslo- gan | ᵛmuch of the 'speech | conˈsisted of a ᵥeulogy | of Ru_mania's ᵢprogress | of the _Party's conᵢcern | for the 'people's ᵢliving 'standards | and the ˰ ˉnew ᵢheights | of 'civiliᵢsation | which Ru_mania had ᵢreached | ˉoutᵢside | 'people _queued for an ᵢhour | in the _slush for baᵢnanas | ᵢfar 'longer for ᵥmeat | and had ᵢtrudged 'past shop ᵛwindows | where ᵢsuits 'cost ᵢtwo-'thirds of a _month's ᵢincome | at 'every ᵛroad interˈsection | stood ˉtwo ˋpolicemen | ᵢsuppleˈmented by ciᵥvilians | who ˋhanded out diˈrections to ᵢthose | who ᵢmight be 'thinking of _taking a 'wrong ᵢturn- ing | (LIBMSECA0505)

In the passage in (129) the speaker's ground is construed subjectively: he remains 'offstage' to empathise with the discourse world established, which facilitates displacement of self. The speaker focuses first on the figure of Ceausescu (his power, his family, his speech), switching from the present tense to the past tense. Then, the camera angle shifts to its location, from the interior of the Congress, to what happened *outside* and *at every road intersection*, whereby the speaker produces a real-world vivid account of the situation in Rumania at that time.

Lastly, as an *architect (of discourse organisation)* the speaker generally performs an analytical task, inviting the addressee into the immediacy of the speaker's organisation of discourse. Instead of involving a physically existent, immediate or displaced, experience, in this mode addressees are invited into a "constructed" or "made-up" experience. In other words, they are taken into the speaker's mind, into her/his own reasoning about how s/he sees, relates and evaluates the textual relations among topics which s/he builds up when organis- ing her/his discourse necessarily under the constraints of linearisation. To illustrate this, consider the passage in (130):

(130) ↑let's re⁀turn | to our 'philo‿sophes | ↑in par‿ticular to Vol\taire | now ⁻Vol⁀taire | was ⁻not a ⁄Christian | in 'any _orthodox \sense | in ˇhis view | the ⁄rituals | ⁄priests | and ˇdoctrines of 'Christi'anity | ↑had _fostered ⁄hatred | and exˇtremism | \rather than com⌣passion | and 'toleˇration | ⁄yet | un\til his 'death in 'seventeen 'seventy-⁄eight | ↑he re⁀tained | a be_lief in ⁀God | 'though Vol\taire's 'God | the \God of a ⌣deist | ↑was 'one that \most Christians ^ would 'scarcely have ⁀recognised | ˇdeists | were 'people who be⁀lieved | in 'God as a cre⁀ator | but ⁻unlike the ˇtheists | a ⌣similar 'name | but a \very \different ⁄school | ⁄deists | re_jected ^ reve⁀lation | ↑ˇNewton for e'xample | was a ⁀theist | 'Volˇtaire | was a ⁀deist | (LIBMSED02019)

In this excerpt, the speaker directs the addressee's attention with a firm pulse throughout the text by means of such overt "architectural" directions as: *let's...*, *now...*, expressions of contrasts (e.g. *rather than compassion and toleration, unlike the theists*), with illustrative exemplifications (e.g. *Newton, for example, was a theist... Voltaire was a deist*), or with parenthetical (explicative) comments (e.g. *but unlike the theists, a similar name but a very different school, deists rejected revelation*). Moreover, as a descriptive passage, in (130) there is no prototypical sequence inherent to the content to be expressed that can serve as a basis for defining the order in which information can be selected for mention and linearised in the text, which allows for a more abstract local or temporal orientation (switches from direct speech, or quotations, to the time of the description) or for one that is an entirely non-locative property. By contrast, in narratives, the conceptualisation of events normally corresponds to their actual unfolding in time, to the actual chronology of events.

Summarising, we shall see that when the speaker behaves as an experiencer or as a reporter, typically in active and in reconstructive texts, thematic choices tend to be used to reproduce an effect of *immediacy* or one of *displacement*, i.e. a type of discourse in which the consciousness of language producers and receivers focuses on "experience that is *displaced from* the immediate environment in which the possessor of the mind is located" (Chafe 1992: 231 [my emphasis]).[108] Alternatively, Theme choices may also be used to build up organisational parts of discourse, typically in constructive texts in which the speaker often adopts the role of an architect, or they may be used in to comment on the content expressed, mainly in opinionative texts. These three speaker's roles expressed by Theme–Rheme patterns, with corresponding effects on the addressee-side, underline their interpersonal character.

However, in closing this section, the necessity should be stressed of not oversimplifying the correlation between text-types, speaker roles and choices of different classes and types of Theme–Rheme constructions. Admittedly, it would go too far to suggest that a very neat, in the sense of a predictable, picture of Theme choices based on the affinities established between speakers' roles and text-types. For one thing, speakers' roles do not have to stick to a specific attitude, but may change within the course of a text. As a result, we can speak of sub-genres or subtext-types. Thus, in reports, for example, although reporters tend to report on displaced experience, they may also behave as experiencers of immediate experience, sometimes explicitly marked as an "eyewitness report" or, alternatively, by mentioning of the name and location of the correspondent. On the other hand, it must also be taken into account that speakers' attitudes are not only expressed through Theme–Rheme patterns, our object of analysis, but they may also be expressed by a range of additional devices (intonation, modality, polarity, lexicon, etc.).

6.4.2.3 *Corpus-based approaches*

Corpus texts are running texts and, as such, are frequently composed of various passages with characteristic sequences of syntactic phenomena. Thus, if one treats corpus texts as "randomised" samples, i.e. as collections of clauses which are in principle unrelated, one neglects that different classes and types of Themes (and Rheme) are not randomly distributed, but vary largely in consecutive stretches of individual texts, occurring in clusters or having an uneven distribution. With respect to this, throughout Chapter 7 we shall discuss individual text passages as providing the appropriate context for the types and classes of Theme recognised in this investigation (under the heading *Discourse function*) following their formal and quantitative analysis (sections on *Formal structure and frequency in LIBMSEC*).

In addition, as argued by Jucker (1992), it should be noted that syntactic phenomena do not easily lend themselves to the type of analysis proposed here, that is, a choice-based analysis resting on paradigmatic relations between linguistic variables. The rationale underlying this corpus-based analysis it that it is useful to investigate the differences between: (a) Topical vs. EMTs, (b) marked vs. unmarked Themes and (c) special vs. non-special Themes. This means that we shall not reveal the mean square of occurrence of a particular class or type of Theme (e.g. inversion, frontings, etc.) in isolation, as a single phenomenon. Instead, *relative frequencies of occurrence and discourse functions will be elicited by relating each class or type of Theme to the total number found in LIBMSEC, as well as to the other alternative Theme–Rheme constructions*, applying the statistical methods described in Section 6.4.3 to the 27 variables considered in this investigation (*Appendix I*).

In this connection, as normally happens in taxonomic analyses, two main problems were encountered involving the classification of syntactic Themes. On the one hand, it sometimes happened that a token did not meet all the defining criteria of a given type of Theme, and therefore the notion of *peripheral member* was resorted to, as opposed to *central* or *prototypical members*.[109] This is the case of e.g. peripheral non-special, special and extended multiple Theme constructions (Sections 7.2, 7.3, 7.4, 7.5) or elliptical constructions (e.g. <u>And the weather</u> — *northern areas will have bright intervals and showers which will be heavy in place*, LIBMSECBPT03: 109–110).

On the other hand, it also happened that some tokens shared the features of two or more different types of Themes, in which case the assignment corresponds to the features regarded as "heaviest". This is the case deictic elements such as *now*, for example, which can be analysed, depending on the context, as (enhancing) textual Themes (e.g. <u>Now</u>, *Babylonian astronomy began much later than Babylonian mathematics*, LIBMSECDPT03: 170) or as preposed topical Themes (e.g. <u>and now, with England in Australia for the Ashes series</u>, *Botham looks like being at least a batsman in the England side, if not a bowler, for years to come*, LIBMSECFPT04: 075). Two further instances involve the interpersonal or topical character of: (a) *expressions of frequency* and (b) *question words* (WFG: 29–30; IFG: 49, 54, 89, 357–360.). Expressions of frequency ("usuality" Adjuncts) such as *sometimes, often, usually*, etc. are regarded as interpersonal rather than as experiential in nature (unlike other expressions of temporal location/extent such as *in the mornings, on Saturdays*, etc.). The assumption is that only topical elements can undergo the *predication test* (Section 4.3.1) and therefore successfully function as predicated Themes (e.g. <u>On Saturdays</u> *we used to go jogging*, <u>It was on Saturdays</u> *we used to go jogging, On Saturdays* is topical Theme). Conversely, interpersonal Themes trigger doubtful sequences (e.g. <u>Usually</u> *Jeremy is too drunk (to drive home)* *<u>It is usually</u> *that Jeremy is too drunk, Usually* is not topical Theme). In their turn, interrogative "*Wh*-items" (*Where, Why, When, How*) are considered to be both interpersonal and topical, both in direct and indirect (reported) *wh*-interrogative clauses (Table 6). This is because they play a role both in the interpersonal structure of the clause — as the *Wh*-function — and in the transitivity structure of the clause, as participant or circumstance (e.g. *Who* (interp/top. Theme) *would even know who* (interp/top. Theme) *you were?*). Fortunately, however, such fuzzy, or borderline, cases were not numerous enough to be statistically significant.

To round off this section, it should be borne in mind that the range of possible options relevant for the analysis of Theme–Rheme patterns is ultimately wider than the 27 variables considered in this study (*Appendix I*), including, for instance, other thematic constructions (e.g. alternating complementation frames, postpositioning of Complements or of phrasal dependants, etc.), as well as further variables (e.g. ± animacy, ± definiteness, other text types, other modes, other languages, other periods of time, etc.). But this leads to a complexity which lies well beyond the reach of this investigation, and which reveals the alleged "total accountability" of corpus studies as only relative.

6.4.3 *Statistical methods*

In order to locate syntactic Theme tokens in major clauses within LIBMSEC (which was done manually clause by clause), a data-base was devised that contained 27 variables all relevant for the identification and production of the hypothesised types and classes of Theme. These features are listed in *Appendix I*. Pauses and tone group boundaries were also taken into account since they were thought to provide evidence for a predication external realization of syntactic Themes, as well as for the locus of informational Focus and choice of Tone.

The analysis of the variables above was implemented by means of the statistical computer package *SPSS* (licence University of Santiago de Compostela (USC)), running the following three statistical tests: (a) the *"Chi Square" association test* (χ^2), (b) the *Fisher's Exact test*, and (c) the *Stepwise Logistic Regression procedure*. These methods were all appropriate to exploit the kind of data I had, that is to say, raw frequencies of *categorical*, or *nominal*, variables, which involved a process of classification of different tokens into categories based upon some definite characteristics that allocated them to one and only one cell. As the details of the development of the three tests are somewhat complicated (Agresti 1990) and, in any case, the resulting arithmetic may be performed by software packages such as SPSS, I will only offer a cursory explanation of what each test does, giving three examples from LIBMSEC.

Both the χ^2 and the Fisher's Exact Tests seek for *significant associations*, or meaningful relationships, between two variables, in which case the *significance level*, or probability of error, *p* must be < 0.05 (5%). Tables 19 and 20 below illustrate the type of results obtained by the Fisher's Exact test and the χ^2 test, respectively: the former displays 2×2 tables only, whereas the latter does not have such a constraint.[110]

Lastly, the third statistical test mentioned above, namely the Stepwise Logistic Regression procedure, detects the variables that can affect a binary outcome variable, i.e. one involving a "yes"/"no" response, as illustrated in Table 21.

The regression analysis estimates the *odds*, or higher probability of occurrence, of the *yes*-response over the *no*-response, distinguishing the subset of

Table 19. *Incidence of EMTs in Fiction*

LIBMSEC text	Topical Theme	EMT	Row Total[8]
Fiction	698	321	1019
	29.1	19.3	25.1
Non-fiction	1700	1339	3039
	70.9	80.7	74.9
Column Total	2398	1660	4058
	59.1	40.9	100.0

Fisher's Exact Test significance: .00000
Missing observations: 39

Table 20. *Incidence of topical and EMTs in* LIBMSEC

LIBMSEC text types	Topical Themes	EMTs	Row Total
Commentary	374	262	636
	15.6	15.8	15.7
News reports	287	107	394
	12.0	6.4	9.7
Lecture	439	286	725
	18.3	17.2	17.9
Religion	63	55	118
	2.6	3.3	2.9
Magazine	147	154	301
	6.1	9.3	7.4
Fiction	650	282	932
	27.1	17.0	23.0
Poetry	48	39	87
	2.0	2.3	2.1
Dialogue	327	412	739
	13.6	24.8	18.2
Propaganda	63	63	126
	2.6	3.8	3.1
Column Total	2398	1660	4058
	59.1	40.9	100.0

Chi-Square test significance
Pearson .0000
Likelihood Ratio .0000
Linear-by-Linear Association .0000
Minimum Expected Frequency 35.589
Number of Missing observations: 39

Table 21. *Choice of EMTs* (yes-*response*)

Variables	B	S.E.	Wald statistic	Degree of freedom	Signif.	R	Exp (B)
Posit. Topical Theme			369.9322	2	.0000	.2616	
Position 1	3.5513	.1869	360.8518	1	.0000	.2591	34.8576
Position 2	3.5799	.7022	25.9920	1	.0000	.0670	35.8694
Posit. Logico-Conjunct. Theme			267.1264	3	.0000	.2210	
Position 1	2.5688	.2007					13.0498
Position 2	4.4756	.5953	163.8311	1	.0000	.1740	87.8465
Position 3	3.7863	.3992	56.5290	1	.0000	.1010	44.0920
			89.9385	1	.0000	.1282	
Posit.Interp. Theme			84.7763	3	.0000	.1214	
Position 1							
Position 2	1.9816	.2521	61.8021	1	.0000	.1058	7.2540
Position 3	1.9586	.5673	11.9205	1	.0006	.0431	7.0891
	2.2816	.5078	20.1858	1	.0000	.0583	9.7919
Type of Text			39.0980	9	.0000	.0628	
Commentary	−1.1787	.2945	16.0141	1	.0001	−.0512	.3077
News Broad.	.1042	.3176	.1076	1	.7429	.0000	1.1098
Lecture	− .3036	.2632	1.3307	1	.2487	.0000	.7381
Religious Broad.	.0866	.4488	.0372	1	.8470	.0000	1.0904
Magazine	− .1599	.3074	.2707	1	.6028	.0000	.8522
Fiction	−1.0023	.2390	17.5877	1	.0000	−.0540	.3670
Poetry	.2256	.4730	.2275	1	.6334	.0000	1.2531
Dialogue	− .1058	.2427	.1899	1	.6630	.0000	.8996
Propaganda	− .4850	.4699	1.0655	1	.3020	.0000	.6157
β Theme			11.6904	5	.0393	.0178	
Spatio-Temp.	− .0052	.5322	.0001	1	.9922	.0000	.9948
Manner	.8099	.6351	1.6264	1	.2022	.0000	2.2477
Cause	− .4136	1.1126	.1382	1	.7101	.0000	.6612
Goal	− .4245	.6624	.4107	1	.5216	.0000	.6541
Condition	1.3487	.4332	9.6927	1	.0019	.0379	3.8524

significant variables from those having no effect on the response variable "step by step", i.e. in decreasing degree of potential influence. For example, Table 21 shows the results of search to determine which variables (and in which order) affect the choice of an EMT (the *yes*-response). As expounded in the Table, the Stepwise Logistic Regression technique selected only five variables as significant for the choice of an EMT (in decreasing potential of influence): (a) position of topical Theme, (b) position of logico-conjunctive Theme, (c) position of interpersonal Theme, (d) LIBMSEC text type, and (e) β Theme (i.e. thematic dependent clause). These results are explained in Chapter 7.

CHAPTER 7

Results and Discussion

7.1 Introduction

After hand-searching the entire LIBMSEC, 4,097 tokens of syntactic Themes in major clauses were obtained, whose distribution is shown in Figure 13 (representing mean squares).

Figure 13 shows that *Fiction contains the highest amount of overt syntactic Themes, followed by Dialogue, Lecture, Commentary, News Broadcasts, Magazine, Propaganda, Religious Broadcasts and Poetry*. Curiously enough, Commentary and Lecture are the largest text types and yet have fewer explicit syntactic Themes than Fiction and Dialogue, coming third and fourth in size, respectively. Conversely, in News Broadcasts, Magazine, Propaganda and Religious Broadcasts the ratio of Themes is proportional to the texts' size, but in Poetry again it is relatively poor. The genre and rhetorical purpose of the texts could explain these results. The high frequency of overt Themes in Dialogues, Magazine, Propaganda and Religious Broadcasts could be said to result from the architectural labour of the speaker, seeking to express the basis of his/her arguments and points of view clearly under real-time production constraints such as interruptions, silences, quick questions/answers, etc. Likewise, it could be claimed that in Fiction syntactic Themes provide frameworks to guide addressees throughout the fictional reality created for them; whereas Lectures and Commentaries, dealing with specialised topics and aimed at specialised audiences, tend to add rhematic information to the same thematic framework across clause boundaries, and so they display a lower proportion of overt syntactic Themes. The same could be applied to Poetry, probably as a result of the creative prerogatives allowed to speakers in this genre (cf. Goatly 1995). All in all, however, the distribution of syntactic Themes is consequent upon the LIBMSEC texts' rhetorical mode of presentation: the largest type, reconstruction (viz. Commentary, News, Fiction, Poetry) contains the highest percentage of explicit tokens (50.8%), as opposed to 27.9% appearing in construction (viz. Lecture, Religion, Magazine)

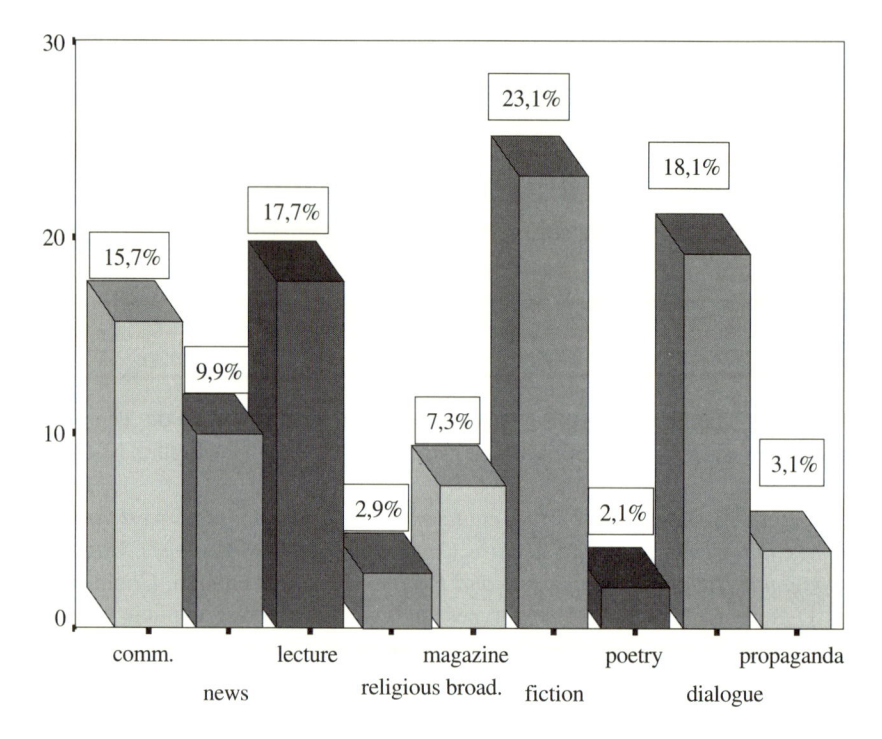

Figure 13. *Distribution of syntactic Themes across LIBMSEC text-types*

and 21.2% in language in action (viz. Dialogue, Propaganda), second and third textual groups in terms of size, respectively.

Elliptical topical Themes amount to 315: 288 (*81.1%*) of *the anaphoric type* as in (131), and 27 (18.9%) of the *exophoric presentative type* as in (132a) and (132b):

(131) | Steve 'Annett | °talked to ˇsome of the °passengers | as ˇthey arrived | on the ⁻platform at Piccaˇdilly °station | ᵁthey'd been °stranded | for °two \hours | and Ø had ⁻walked about °half a \mile along the \tunnels | ↓and \then Ø had to be \guided on ↑\foot along the \track [interview by Steve Annett is omitted] (LIBMSECBPT01: 032–6).

(132) a. | °finally Ø the °headlines a⁻gain | (LIBMSECBPT02: 196)
       b. |Ø_BBC ʹNews | at _eight o'clock on ⁻Saturday the °twenty-fourth of No\vember | (LIBMSECBPT01: 005).

(132a) illustrates two instances of (anaphorically) elliptical Themes (Ø) contained in paratactically extending clauses. These establish cohesive ties with their typically definite and immediately preceding cotextual given (Giv_R) field antecedents (*some passengers*). In contrast, the Themes in (132b) are omitted because they convey information referring to the rhetorical context of situation. In accordance with a pre-established scheme, elliptical Themes typically appear at the beginning and at the end of News reports in order to locate the news, presenting the discourse Rheme, what is "news", so to speak: the time, the speakers' names and the headlines.

With regard to tactic relationships, *my results confirm the grammatical intricacy of the spoken mode*: major clauses in LIBMSEC are typically complex (39.9%), of which 21.3% were hypotactic and 18.6% paratactic. Second in frequency are *simple clauses* (34.3%) often used to produce an emphatic or striking effect. The Themes of embedded clauses were disregarded in this study, on the assumption that they contribute to developing the Theme–Rheme patterns of the clauses they are embedded in (most previous studies have only analysed the Theme of main clauses, e.g. Brown & Yule 1983; Fries 1983; IFG: 62; Berry 1995; Martin 1995). In hypotactic clauses, on the other hand, projections (6.4%) are less frequent than expansions (14.9%), within which enhancings (10.8%) are more popular than elaborations (3.9%) or extensions (0.2%) (see endnote 56). Similarly, paratactic clause complexes belong less commonly to the projecting type (2%) than to the expansion type (16%), which typically extend previous clauses (13.5%), rather than enhance them (2.3%) or elaborate them (1%). In other words, *hypotactic clause complexes in LIBMSEC favour enhancing expansions, while extensions are more common in paratactic complex clauses.*

In terms of Mood, LIBMSEC prototypically consists of *declaratives* (67.1%) typically fulfilling an *expository or descriptive purpose*, but *interrogatives* (4.1%), *imperatives* (2.3%) and *exclamatives* (0.7%) are also used to vary the pace, change the focus or produce some emotive effect: they tend to make direct addresses to the participants, inviting judgements or opinions on events and characters or suggesting a specific course of action; furthermore, such addresses are often marked by a change from simple past tense to simple present. The remaining 25.8%, comprising dependent and rankshifted clauses, was classified as "missing" (i.e. discarded) in terms of the Mood variable.

In addition, the relative frequency of the different types of processes was also analysed out of the conviction that verbs not only tell the addressee about the kinds of actions and processes occurring; their transitivity or ergativity patterns also influence the selection of items more likely to be thematised. The most recurrent processes in LIBMSEC are *material* (39.6%), the events being presented "dynamically" (normally in objective informative texts causing an "eyewitness" impact), or *relational* (31.9%), implying a "synoptic" interpretation of reality (mostly in subjective registers) (Halliday 1977; Francis 1989a: 203; Ravelli 1995). In other words, while the use of stative verbs suggests that the speaker's interest lies in description, whether it be of setting or states of mind, dynamic verbs place an emphasis on what is happening, implying that the speaker is more interested in action than in contemplation. *Verbal* and *mental processes* are also relatively frequent in Reports, Dialogues and Fiction (14.2% vs. 10.3%), causing an effect of (displaced) immediacy. Instances of (free) indirect and direct speech are often interpolated in these text types either to direct addressees' sympathy towards or away from certain participants or to indicate changes in the role of one, imbuing the passage with real-life vividness. In turn, existential and behavioural ones are comparatively infrequent (3.3% and 0.8%). This seems to indicate that in LIBMSEC the existence or behaviour of discourse referents was hardly ever at issue.

Interestingly, it was also observed that, irrespective of their type, *processes typically select affirmative, rather than negative, polarity* (94.5% vs. 5.5%), and *the active, rather than the passive, voice* (92% vs. 8%). These findings suggest that speakers tend to report *on what does happen or is, rather than on what does/is not, focusing on the agents of these processes, rather than on their patients*. This accords well with the rhetorical purpose of LIBMSEC radio-broadcasts, since most of them are devised to report current information, or to demand some positive action upon reality, or to provoke some kind of reaction on the part of the audience.

Section 7.2 describes the frequencies, the formal features and the discourse functions of unmarked non-special Theme constructions in LIBMSEC, whereas Section 7.3 deals with marked options in terms of Mood and Voice, that is, with instances of preposings (Section 7.3.1) and the Themes of passive processes (Section 7.3.2). Section 7.4 analyses special thematic constructs, including: (a) existential *there*-constructions (Section 7.4.1), (b) *It*-extrapositions (Section 7.4.2), (c) inversions (Section 7.4.3), (d) left detachments (Section 7.4.4), (e) right detachments (Section 7.4.5), (f) cleft constructions (Section 7.4.6) and (g) pseudo-cleft constructions (Section 7.4.7). Finally, Section 7.5 addresses the category of EMTs.

7.2 Non-special Theme constructions

In the conciliatory spirit of this investigation, our characterisation of unmarked non-special thematic constructions is compatible with previous accounts such as e.g.: Hannay's (1991 [1990]) description of the *Topic mode* in FG, i.e. a message mode whereby Topic is placed in P1 and Focus at a later stage in the linguistic expression; or Vallduví & Engdahl's (1996) *link-focus* or *link-focus-tail* instruction types, the former designating a locus of update with an addition of a condition on that locus, and the latter a locus of update that points to a given condition indicating that the update completes or alters that condition in some way.

However, what in referential approaches were previously regarded as topicless/themeless constructions will be here treated as having a Theme, that is to say: Hannay's (1991 [1990]) *All New Mode* messages, i.e. messages consisting of new information only; or Vallduví & Engdahl's (1996) *all-focus instructions*, in which no specific file card is designated as a locus of update, but rather a general-situation file card is used. The reason is that, as elsewhere explained (Sections 2.2.1, 4.3.1, 6.3 above), syntactic Themes are regarded as being *relational* rather than *nominal* in character, that is to say, they are considered *to profile a relationship* instead of a thing, in the sense that they constitute *an orientation zone* in discourse, a framework, with both backward- and forward-looking potential, involving relevance for the preceding context as well as for what is to follow, independently of their informational or focal status (Mackenzie 1998; Section 5.4.4 above).

7.2.1 Formal structure and frequencies in LIBMSEC

In LIBMSEC *non-special thematic constructions represent the unmarked* option, i.e. they are more frequent and therefore presumably less co(n)textually constrained than special ones: 89.3% vs. 10.7%, respectively. Figure 14 shows that this percentage of occurrence of both types of constructions remains the same across the LIBMSEC texts. This indicates that, *whatever the type of text, non-special Themes remain a more frequent choice than special ones*. This was confirmed by the results of the Chi-Square test: $p = 0.144\%$, n.s.

Furthermore, our results confirm that, formally speaking, *overt non-special Themes tend to be realized by nominal groups* occupying *P1 position* in *simple clauses* or in the *dependent clause of hypotactically complex clauses, normally involving material* or *relational processes*. Besides, they tend to be *unmarked* in terms of *Mood* and *Voice*, i.e. they correspond to the initial transitivity/mood constituent demanded by each active mood pattern (usually *Agent/Subject*) in keeping with the *CWO* (Canonical Word Order) *of PresE declaratives*. Indeed, according to the results obtained by the logistic regression analysis in Table 22, non-special thematic constructions can be characterised according to six significant variables (in decreasing order of influence): (a) type of *process*; (b) *mood function*; (c) their ± *external realization*; (d) *type of clause*; (e) the *structure* of topical Themes; and (f) their *transitivity* function.

216   THE THEME–TOPIC INTERFACE

```
30

20

10

0
     commentaries      lectures       magazine       poetry      propaganda
            news         religious        fiction       dialogue
                       broadcasts
     ■ Non-special thematic constructions    □ Special thematic constructions
```

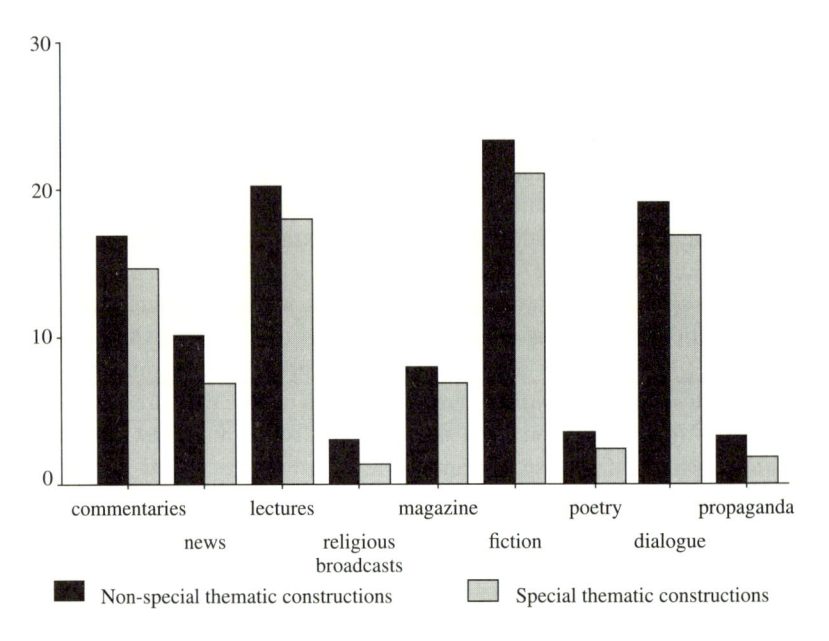

Figure 14. *Non-special vs. special topical Themes in* LIBMSEC

The above results were confirmed by both the Chi-Square Test and the Fisher's Exact Test. The predominant feature was the type of *process*, according to which non-special thematic Themes constructions seem to be associated primarily with *material* and *mental processes*. Likewise, *unmarked Themes*, whether in special or non-special thematic construction, also show an association with *relational* and *material* processes, as expounded in Table 23.

This feature is illustrated in the reportage in (133) and the description in (134):

(133) | a ˈthousand ˈpeople were led to ˈsafety after being ˈtrapped by a ˉfire | in the ˉLondon ˌUnderground last ˈnight | _many had to ˈwalk along the ˉtrack to the ˈnearest ˌstation | Mr ˈEnoch ˊPowell | has ˉpraised Mrs ˇThatcher | for ˉstanding _firm at the _Anglo-ˈIrish ˈsummit | the ˉOverseas Deˌvelopment ˈMinister | is _visiting Ethiˇopia this weekˈend | to ˈsee the ˈfamine reˈlief opeˈration | ˉhigh winds | and ˉheavy ˌseas | have been causing ˈfurther ˉproblems | in the ˇsouthern ˈpart of ˈBritain | leaving ˉhomes ˈflooded | and _roads ˌblocked | a ˉbig ˌrescue opeˈration was ˉmounted in central _London | ˈlate last ˉnight | after a ˇfire | at ˉOxford _Circus ˈUnderground ˈStation | the eˉmergency _services were ˉhampered by _thick ˌsmoke | which ˈspread ˇquickly through the ˈstation | (LIBMSECBPT01:013)

Table 22. *Choice of non-special Theme (yes-response)*

Explanatory variables in decreasing order of significance as established by the Stepwise Logistic Regression Procedure	Wald statistic	Degree of freedom	Significance
Type of process	148.0333	5	.0000
Syntactic function of topical Theme	50.9317	3	.0000
± External realization of topical Theme	34.2748	1	.0000
Type of clause	75.9118	4	.0000
Structure of topical Theme	15.6048	6	.0160
Transitivity function of topical Theme	10.1989	3	.0169

Table 23. *Process types in frontings*

Process type	Unmarked topical Theme	Marked/fronted topical Theme	Row Total
material	1345	277	1622
	39.9	38.4	39.6
relational	1141	165	1306
	33.8	22.9	31.9
mental	471	109	580
	14	15.1	14.2
verbal	292	110	422
	8.7	18.0	10.3
existential	104	30	134
	3.1	4.2	3.3
behavioural	22	11	33
	0.7	1.8	0.8
Column Total	3375	722	4097
	82.4	17.6	100.0

Chi-Square significance: .00000
Missing observations: 0

(134) | arriving in ˬ °Bucha/rest | on a ⁻grey No°vember after/noon | is ⁻pretty /much | as one _might ex\pect | a °light /rain was | °turning into /snow | the /plane | \taxied °past | °serried /ranks | of anti-/aircraft °guns | and the \dozen or °so /passengers | from the _Austrian /Airlines °plane | were \bussed °into a \totally un°heated _airport \building | eᵛventually | it was °my /turn | to be in_spected by the immi\gration o°fficial | who \gazed at me | from his _little \booth | but ᵛhere | °things took an unex\pected °turn | you are ⁻here for the /Congress ˬ he °asked | /yes ˬ I °said | he ⁻then went

ₒut | to °call a _large poˋlice-officer °over | the °officer ᵛbellowed °at me | °over _various ˌbarricades | ↑you have °inviˈtation | I have a ᴵᵛvisa | ⁻no ˌvisa | you have °inviˈtation | ˌno ₓ I °said |(LIBMSECAPT05: 000–036)

Acting as a reporter the speaker in the excerpt in (133) uses mostly non-special Theme-constructions concerning material processes in the past tense. Information is thereby presented as displaced events, making use of a very selective camera angle which rapidly shifts from one chunk of experience to another following the principle of informative economy, in contrast with the continuous and detailed nature of an immediate experience. Alternatively, (134) involves mainly material and relational processes, in which the unmarked Themes contribute to presenting different details of a typical autumn afternoon in Bucharest. In turn, marked Themes are used at the end of in (134) to signal a change in the progressions of discourse, a switch of discourse focus, from a general to a specific odd event (*here*, which involves a material process), and from reported to direct speech (signalled by projected Themes of the subsequent verbal processes), which involves a change from displaced to immediate discourse perspective.

Concerning the second significant variable, *mood function*, the results of the χ^2 test reported in Table 24 *represent thematic Subjects as the prototypical Theme of PresE clauses*, whether occurring in special or non-special thematic constructions. This finding can be seen as a concomitant of the fact *that declaratives represent the unmarked choice of Mood in* LIBMSEC, followed by interrogatives, imperatives and exclamatives, as illustrated in Table 25.

Table 25 presents *Subject Themes* as especially frequent in non-special

Table 24. *Syntactic function of non-special vs. special Themes*

Syntactic function	Non-special Theme	Special Theme	Row Total
Subject	3064	284	3348
	86.6	64.5	84.2
Adjunct	333	41	374
	9.4	9.3	9.4
Finite/Predicator	86	43	129
	2.5	9.7	3.2
Complement	54	72	126
	1.5	16.3	3.1
Column Total	3537	440	3977
	88.9	11.1	100.0

Chi-Square significance: .0000
Missing cases (i.e. number of cases in the database which are irrelevant to this particular comparison): 120

Table 25. *Mood in special vs. special Themes*

Mood	Non-special Theme	Special Themes	Row Total
Declarative	2754	364	3118
	75.3	82.7	76.1
Exclamative	24	4	28
	.7	.9	.7
Interrogative	147	21	168
	4.0	4.8	4.1
Imperative	86	9	95
	2.4	2.0	2.3
Missing	646	42	688
(dependent/rankshifted clauses)	17.7	9.5	16.8
Column Total	3378	710	4097
	82.6	17.4	100

Chi-Square Significance: .00000
Missing cases: 0

thematic constructions, while thematic Adjuncts, Predicators and Complements are reported as more numerous in declarative sequences and in special Theme constructions. These results indicate two things. First, *they confirm the existence of a scale of thematic freedom in PresE depending on the Mood and tactic status of the message* (IFG: 61). At one end of the scale lie independent major declarative clauses, which show the greatest thematic freedom, as opposed to other supposedly more constrained choices of Mood and tactic relationships: 83.5% of frontings in LIBMSEC occurred in declaratives. But, the further one moves from this end more the thematic options are restricted by structural pressures from other parts of the grammar that are themselves thematic in origin. Thus, dependent finite clauses (with the exception of WH-clauses, in which the WH-element fulfils the two functions) typically consists of a conjunction as a structural Theme (Table 6), followed by a topical Theme, while non-finite clauses tend to have a preposition as structural Theme, followed by the Subject as the topical Theme, although they may as well consist only of a Rheme, deriving their Themes from the co(n)text. Exclamative, interrogative or imperative structures, on the other hand, embodying the thematic principle in their unmarked structural make-up, leave only highly marked alternative options or no alternative at all. However, as exemplified in (135) below, our findings report imperatives as having more marked topical Themes than interrogatives (12.6% vs. 3.3%), *contra* the hypothesis put forward in IFG that the former, as more constrained Mood choices than questions, should have fewer marked Themes.

(135) | to ˇsee | where ⁻this argument ˌleads ᵦ | ⁻let's con°sider _export prohi\bi-tions | (LIBMSECPTC01: 336–339)

The second conclusion that can be extracted from our results in Table 24, also confirmed by the Fisher's Exact test in Table 26, is that *there exists a significant association between choices of unmarked Themes in terms of Mood and the occurrence of non-special Theme constructions*. In other words, *unmarked Themes are more frequently found in non-special thematic constructions, whereas the special ones contain a higher amount of frontings or preposings*, although the latter remains a marked choice in both construction types. On the one hand, this finding underlines that marked and special Theme constructions have a common core: a nuance of subjectivity (Sections 7.3 and 7.4). On the other hand, the results seem to indicate that preposings are highly constrained choices in non-special thematic constructions. Conversely, special constructs, being syntactically marked, reveal themselves as productive devices embodying in their structural make-up precisely that thematic effect: to bring to the fore, to front position, by means of different strategies, a constituent that according to CWO patterns should not be there, in order to satisfy a variety of co(n)textual conditions (Section 7.4).

Table 26. *Incidence of frontings in non-special vs. special Themes*

Mood markedness	Non-special Themes	Special Themes	Row Total
Unmarked	3074	301	3375
	84.1	68.4	82.4
Marked (frontings)	583	139	722
	15.9	31.6	17.6
Column Total	3657	440	4097
	89.3	31.6	100.0

Fisher's Exact Test Significance: .00000
Missing observations: 0

As an example observe (136a) and (136b) below, where Subject or unmarked non-special Themes co-occur with an inversion and a left detachment, both bringing a constituent to front position and thereby breaking the expectations of the declarative CWO of both constructions (Section 7.4). Alternatively, (136c) exemplifies the choice of a fronted non-special Theme (Section 7.3):

(136) a. ↑they just co\llapsed ˄ said the °radio °operator | *I* \don't feel ˇtoo good | my\self | can ˇyou °land the °plane | said the ˌdoctor | ↑\me | ↑\no | ˌ√I'm not a °pilot | we've \got to re\vive them ˄ he re°plied |

the ˎplane's on °auto°matic ˌpilot | we're ˋOK for a ˇcouple of °hours | °I don't ˌknow ˄ said the °doctor | they ¯could be ˌout | for a ¯long ˌtime | ¯I'd better ˌcontact | °ground conˋtrol ˄ said the °radio °operator | (LIBMSECGPT04: 033–035)

b. | ˋas for the ˋrich | in ¯this ˌworld | ˋcharge them ˋnot to be ˋhaughty | or ¯high ˌminded | ˋnor to set their ¯hopes on unˇcertain °riches | but on ˋGod | who ˋrichly ˇfurnishes us | with ˋeverything to enˋjoy | they are to °do ˋgood | to be _rich in good ˌdeeds | ˋliberal | and ˋgenerous | (LIBMSECEPT02: 044)

c. | ¯there in the _shadowy ˇcentre |Ø a ¯tiny ˌnest | and ˋon it ˋfacing us Ø a ˋbright-°eyed ˋbird ˋsitting | she has ¯five ˌeggs | ¯shaped and _speckled most ˋdaintily | but ˋthis she ˋcannot ˋknow | (LIBMSECHPT04: 027)

Let us now turn to the third feature affecting the choice of a non-special vs. a special Theme, that is, its ± *external realization*. Table 27 shows that, *though representing the unmarked option in both thematic constructions, the incidence of predication-internal* (P1) (including elliptical) *realizations is higher in non-special than in special constructions, and it is consistently associated with unmarked topical Themes, whereas in frontings predication-external* (P2) *realizations represents the unmarked option*. To illustrate this claim, let us consider (137):

(137) | ¯I was ˌhungry ˄ said the °lion | I could ¯easily have ˋeaten him | only I'd ˋpromised you | ˋand his ˋmother ˌwouldn't have ˋliked it ˄ said the little °girl | (LIBMSECGPT01: 165–66)

In (137) above there are two instances of marked special constructions, two inverted special Themes bringing quotations or Verbiages to front position, *I was angry* and *his mother wouldn't have liked it*, both of which are separated from the

Table 27. ± *External realization of (non-)special and (un)marked topical Themes*

Realization of topical Theme	Non-special Theme	Special Theme	Unmarked Theme	Fronted Theme	Row Total[111]
Internal	3083	323	3092	314	3406
	87.2	73.4	90.8	43.4	85.6
External	454	117	163	408	571
	12.8	26.6	19.2	56.6	14.4
Column Total	3537	440	3255	722	3977
	88.9	11.1	81.8	18.2	100.0

Fisher's Exact Test Significance: .00000
Missing observations: 120

rhematic projecting predication by tone boundaries and typographically by commas. In contrast, the other four instances of unmarked non-special Themes involving *I* and *his mother* are not marked off from their Rhemes. Section 7.2.2 relates the fact that unmarked non-special Themes are not normally separated from their Rhemes to their tendency to display a (Given$_R$)-before-New array of information and to have no conventional implicatures associated with them. Conversely, in Sections 7.2 and 7.3 it will be shown that the special syntactic prominence of marked and particularly of special Themes, often reinforced suprasegmentally by means of a tone group boundary and an intonational Focus scope, satisfies "special" discourse conditions.

In addition, the results of the χ^2 test in Table 28 *indicate that topical Themes occupying the second and third slots of EMTs have a higher tendency to be unmarked*, or put differently, *that topical Themes in EMTs do not easily lend themselves to a process of fronting* ((138a), (138b)). These conclusion was confirmed by the results of the Fisher's Exact Test in Table 29.

(138) a. | and of ⁻course | the \final it\self | was \excellent | °Argen/tina | /coasting a°long there | ⁻two goals _up | through ⁻Brown and Val_da-no | (LIBMSECJPT01: 048–050)

b. | /possibly | his °new /pessimism was a re°sult of the great \earth-quake | of °seventeen °fifty-\five | which on \All °Saints °Day of ^all °days | had ⁻left | the ⁻great | ⁻Catholic °city of _Lisbon | a \ruin | (LIBMSECDPT02: 145)

Furthermore, the Fisher's Exact Test and the χ^2 Test reported that *logico-conjunctive Themes tend to co-occur with unmarked, rather than with preposed,*

Table 28. *Position of topical element in (un)marked EMTs*

Position of topical element in EMTs	Unmarked	Marked	Row Total
Initial	1940	509	2449
	59.6	70.5	61.6
Medial	1243	198	1441
	38.2	27.4	36.2
Final	72	15	87
	2.2	2.1	2.2
Column Total	3255	722	3977
	81.8	18.2	100.0

Chi-Square Test significance: .00000
Missing observations: 120

Table 29. *Incidence of EMTs in (un)marked Themes*

Class of Theme	Unmarked	Fronting	Row Total
Non-extended multiple	1921	477	2398
	57.6	66.1	59.1
Extended multiple	1415	245	1660
	42.4	33.9	40.9
Column Total	3336	722	4058
	82.2	17.8	100.0

Fisher's Exact Test significance: .00001
Missing observations: 39

topical Themes (78.7% vs. 69.6%). This is exemplified in (139) below, where most instances of structural Themes precede either overt or elliptical unmarked non-special topical Themes:

(139) I they ˈunderstood that he was a ˈforeigner I ⁻strayed from his _own ˌbeach I ↑and they pro_ceeded to forˈget him I ↓but ˈhe was ˈhappy I ˈhe was ˈwith them I ↑they be⁻gan ˌdiving I a⁻gain and a_gain from a ⁻high _point into a ⁻well of ˌblue °sea I between ⁻rough °pointed ˈrocks I ˈafter they had ˌdived I and Ø⁻come ˌup ₚI they ⁻swam aˌround I Ø ᵛhauled themselves °up I and Ø⁻waited their _turn to _dive aˈgain I they were ᵛbig °boys I ˈmen I to ˌGerry I ˈhe °dived I and ⁻they ˈwatched him I and ⁻when he _swam a°round to °take his ˌplace ₚI they °made ˈway for him I (LIBMSECGPT01: 068–76)

Turning now to the fourth relevant variable, *type of clause*, Table 30 shows that a high ratio of *unmarked* and *non-special Themes* appears in *simple clauses* or in the *dependent clause* of hypotactic complex clauses, which is evidenced in the extracts in (140a) and (140b) (LIBMSECGPT04).

(140) a. I °as we drove ˌon I towards ⁻Suchiˌtoto ₚI we could ⁻see I ⁻over to the ˌleft I the ˈsun I be°ginning to ˌset I °over the ˈcraggy I ⁻always ᵛawe-inspiring I ˈmountain of Juˌcuapa I
b. I we ⁻drove ˌon I a ˈjet aˈpeared aˌbove I diˈrectly aˈbove I it ˈheld its tra⁻jectory for ˈone ˈminute I ⁻flashes ˌburst I from its ˌwings I and ⁻rockets exˌploded I ⁻safely beˌhind us I our ᵛdriver I the ˈNew ˈYork ᵛTimes ˈman I ⁻pressed his acˌcelerator I and ˌducked I his ᵛeyes I ˈpeering ˈover the ˌdashboard I ⁻more ˈrockets I or perˈhaps ˈmore ˌbombs I ⁻landed beˌhind I what ˈseemed like ⁻hours ᵛlater I we ⁻reached the ˈarmy ˌcheckpoint I ˈsix ˈmiles ˈdown the ˌroad I a ˈlittle ˈfurther ˌon I a ˈtown I where there was a ˌfair I ˈgoing ˌon I a ⁻big

Table 30. *Type of clause of (non-)special and (un)marked topical Themes*

Clause	Non-special Theme	Special Theme	Unmarked Theme	Marked Theme	Row Total
Simple	1268	133	1198	203	1401
	34.8	30.2	35.6	28.1	34.3
Paratactic complex	664	98	596	166	762
	18.2	22.3	17.7	23.0	18.6
Hypotactic complex	794	76	621	249	870
	21.8	17.3	18.4	34.5	21.3
Rankshifted	270	86	307	49	356
	7.4	19.5	9.1	6.8	8.7
Dependent	652	47	644	55	699
	17.9	10.7	17.9	7.6	17.1
Column Total	3648	440	3366	722	4088
	89.2	10.8	82.3	17.7	100

Chi-Square significance: .0000
Missing cases: 9

ˇwheel | was ˌspinning | ˋchildren 'ate ˇpopcorn | and ˋcandyfloss | ˋfairground 'music ˉfilled the ˌair |

It should be admitted, however, that if the two contingency tables included in Table 30 are looked at individually, the correspondence postulated above is not so clear. First, the highest percentage of frontings presents itself in hypotactic complex clauses (triggered by fronted β Themes, i.e. initial dependent clause in a clause complex). And second, for unmarked Themes the percentages of dependent, hypotactic and paratactic clauses are very similar.

With regard to the *structure of the topical Theme* in special vs. non-special constructions, *a further correlation has been found between non-special and unmarked Themes, on the one hand, and special and marked ones, on the other*, as shown in Table 31. The findings reported in Table 31 demonstrate that *non-special Themes tend to be realized by nominal expressions* (i.e. pronouns, common nouns, proper nouns). More precisely, *unmarked topical Themes are typically pronominal, less frequently nominal, and seldom rankshifted clauses*. However, in contrast to what is claimed elsewhere (IFG: 43), probably because most of LIBMSEC is not conversational, the findings do not point to first person pronominal Themes as the most popular choice, but to *third person ones* (21.9%), as exemplified in the sequences in (141) below, followed by *first person* (10.8%), *demonstrative pronouns* (6.5%), *second person pronouns* (6.1%), *relative pronouns* (4.2% each), *indefinite pronouns* (1%) and *Numeratives* (0.4%).

Table 31. *Type of structure of (non-)special and (un)marked topical Themes*

Structure	Non-special Theme	Special Theme	Unmarked Theme	Marked Theme	Row Total (see fn. 85)	
common noun	1155	41	1069	127	1196	
	32.7	9.3	32.8	30.1	30.1	
proper noun	250	7	240	17	257	↑ 3463
	7.1	1.6	7.4	2.4	6.5	↓ 87.1
pronoun	1757	253	1849	161	2010	
	49.5	57.5	56.8	22.3	50.5	
adjective group	5	3	0	8	8	
	.1	.7	.0	1.0	.2	
adverbial group	48	9	7	50	57	
	1.4	2.0	.2	6.9	1.4	
prepositional phrase	213	40	28	225	253	
	6.0	9.1	.9	31.2	6.4	
verb phrase	86	45	17	122	135	
	2.5	10.3	.5	16.3	3.4	
rankshifted Clause	19	33	44	8	52	
	.5	7.5	1.4	1.1	1.3	
Continuatives		9		9	9	
(Interp. Themes)		2.0		1.2	.2	
Column Total	3537	440	3255	722	3977	
	88.9	11.1	81.8	18.2	100.0	

Chi-Square significance: .0000
Missing cases: 120

(141) a. | when ↑he °sought the ad_vice | of ⁻Youth\aid | which is an ⁻organi-°sation | which °helps °young ⁻unemployed \people | /so | he ⁻got the /money | he ⁻found a /job | °albeit a ⁻part-ˇtime °job | *he* ⁻started /work | *he* ⁻stopped °claiming /benefit | and as he \said °somewhat ˇruefully_β| he \now had a ˇlittle °money | and to \look | for a \better 'job | (LIBMSECPT01: 046)
b. [RG] and ⁻what did he \think of °Saudi A°rabia | (LIBMSECJPT06: 012)

Finally, let us consider the sixth significant variable under consideration: the *transitivity function* of the topical Theme and its concomitant, i.e. the *choice of voice*, in special vs. non-special constructions. Table 32 shows that *both special and particularly non-special Themes tend to be realized by Agents and therefore to be prototypically unmarked in terms of voice (active)*.

Non-special Agent Themes had a higher frequency of Actors (29% vs. 5.9%),

Table 32. *Ergative functions in (non-)special thematic constructions*

Ergative function	Non-special Theme	Special Theme	Row Total
Process	89	41	130
	2.3	9.3	3.3
Agent	2749	286	3035
	77.7	65.9	76.4
Medium	321	68	389
	9.0	15.5	9.7
Beneficiary	43	3	46
	1.1	.7	1.1
Range	3	42	3
	0.8	8.6	.1
Circumstance	332		374
	9.1		9.4
Column Total	3537	440	3977
	88.9	11.1	100.0

Chi-Square significance: .0000
Missing cases: 120

Sensers (11.7% vs. 2.0%), Behavers (0.7%), Sayers (7.8% vs. 0.5%) and Carriers (26.8% vs. 21.8%); while in the special type the predominant role was Existent (28.4% vs. 0.1%) and Token (7.3% vs. 1.7%). Witness to this (142) below, where a circumstantial β Theme (i.e. initial dependent clause in a clause complex) in the first unstressed presentative *there*-construction establishes a temporal framework for the two subsequent Agent non-special pronominal Themes:

(142) I when ᵛI've been through °Athens airport I and ˋthat's about °two dozen ˋtimes in the past °two ᵛyears ᵦI there's ᵛnever been more than ⁻one se͜vcu-rity man on °duty I and ⁻he's ˎfrequently reading a ˋnewspaper I or ⁻chat-ting with _other ˋairport °staff I he ˋseldom I °seems to be keeping an ˋeye I on the teleˋvision °screens I (LIBMSECAPT08: 24–28)

7.2.2   Discourse function

By choosing non-special thematic choices, speakers syntacticise the clausal thematic role and reference in one wording: *generally the initial predication internal (P1) transitivity/mood constituent* (including cases of ellipsis) *in the clause*, notably, with the exception of *complex beginnings*, which entail the *recursive* use of different kinds of *tactic and logico-semantic relationships* expressed *in different intonational, and therefore predication external, groups*.

These unmarked P1 realizations contravene a basic communicative principle, that is to say, the *Principle of Separation of Reference and Role* (PSRR), which can be described as follows:

> ... the grammatical principle whereby the lexical representation of a topic referent takes place separately from the designation of the referent's role as an argument in a proposition [which is often reflected in the syntax of spoken (and to a certain extent in written) sentences]. [...] The communicative motivation of this principle can be captured in the form of a simple pragmatic maxim: "Do not introduce a referent and talk about it in the same clause." There are two processing reasons for adhering to this maxim, one speaker-oriented, one hearer-oriented. From the speaker's point of view, it is easier to construct a complex sentence if the lexical introduction of a non-active topic referent is done independently of the syntactic expression of the proposition about the referent. [...] From the hearer's point of view, it is easier to decode a message about a topic if the task of assessing the topic referent can be performed independently of the task of interpreting the proposition in which the topic is an argument. (Lambrecht 1994: 185–191).

The consistency of our results underline the hypothesis that unmarked non-special thematic constructions violate the PSRR as a result of *language users' unconscious inclination to impose a presuppositional structure on isolated clauses*, because (a) clauses are the primary units of information in coherent discourse and (b) information normally relies on presuppositions concerning a communicative co(n)text.

Hypotactic clause complexes in LIBMSEC *were also found to normally display an unmarked "logical" organisation: Head^Dependent* clause. This organisation reflects the basic communicative principle whereby dependants are expected to succeed the referents they depend on. However, under special circumstances, this "logical" array can also be overridden by the principles of EF and EW, whereby the longer and more informative clause, regardless of its tactic status, comes last (Section 7.3.2).

The above leads us to conclude that *unmarked non-special thematic constructions are usually associated with a presupposition of existence, which favours their displaying a (Given-before)-New, Head^Dependent array of information in accordance the principles of EF, EW, FSP and TU*. These features highlight both the textual make-up of unmarked Theme choices, contributing to underlining the coherence of a text, and their interpersonal orientation, since such choices have corresponding effects on the addressee's side. Generally, unmarked non-special Theme constructions convey no *conventional implicatures*, i.e. different conventional meanings, as opposed to "literal" meanings (Grice 1975; Harnish 1976). Their most "urgent" task is therefore to instruct for "sameness", that is to say, for: (a) *Topic continuity*, the *maintenance* of which is typically done by keeping the same Theme as the preceding clause, while its *progression* normally involves selecting a constituent from the preceding Rheme; and (b) *continuity of discourse perspective*.

In LIBMSEC unmarked non-special Themes normally become discourse Topics as a result of their participation in TPs with a continuous Theme (Daneš 1974b: 118; Section 3.3.3 above). That is to say, what texts are about (typically the Agents of processes) is normally repeated, extended or detailed throughout the paragraph(s) in clause-initial position entailing cohesive relationships (Giv_R) of substitution, reference or ellipsis. Consider (143) below as an illustration:

(143) Topic: Mr Norman Willis in the miners' conflict
⁻General _Secretary of the °TU/C I ↓Mr Norman /Willis I has said the \Coal °Board's ᵛstrategy I of _trying to \lure miners ⁻back to _work by ⁻offering ᵛbonuses I will ˌfail I he ⁻told ˌminers I ↓at a °meeting in /Chatham in ᵛKent last °night I that the ⁻board should i_nitiate new dis\cussions with the ⁻mineworkers' ˌunion I in an ⁻effort to ˌend the dis°pute I ↓he said the ⁻TU⁻C I ↓would be getting an °extra ⁻quarter of a °million \pounds I to \help °striking \miners I Mr ⁻Willis was warmly a\pplauded I as he a\rrived at the °meeting I the ᵛlast °time I he a_ddressed striking /miners I ↓in South /Wales I _earlier this °month I he was \jeered I and a ⁻hangman's ˌnoose I was ⁻dangled in ˌfront of him I. (LIBMSECBPT01: 54–63)

In addition, the findings reported *unmarked non-special Theme constructions as comparatively more objective than special ones*. It was observed that non-special Themes tend to concern relational or material processes whereby synoptic or dynamic pictures of reality are provided. Moreover, non-special Themes normally have a nominal expression and are often preceded by logico-conjunctive Themes (especially by the structural kind), the most "objective" sub-class of Theme (31.4% vs. 26.1%). This picture accords well with the LIBMSEC text-types in which a higher proportion of unmarked Themes were found to occur: informal texts representing language in action (22.8% vs. 13.6% fronted ones), that is, especially in (J) Dialogues (19.7% vs. 10.5%), and also in (K) Propaganda (3.1% vs. 3.0%). Subject to real time communication constraints, Dialogues as instances of informal and unplanned discourse normally demand less processing time and therefore a lesser degree of structural complexity than constructive or reconstructive texts. Unmarked thematic choices as prototypical instantiations of Theme–Rheme patterns that are for this reason assumed to be less co(n)textually unconstrained are particularly well suited for these co(n)textual conditions, where speakers normally behave as actors and therefore cannot count on the monitoring and displacing resources available in reports nor are they expected to guide addressees through intricate comments, arguments or descriptions. In spite of their inherent subjectivity, the "unmarked" textual conditions of "active" texts underline straightforward reflections of the interactants' immediate experiences, and it is this rhetorical purpose that constitutes the communicative core of unmarked Theme choices and therefore explains their higher relative frequency in dialogic texts.

7.3 Marked Theme constructions

In this section it will be shown that, unlike their unmarked counterparts, marked Theme constructions depart from CWO active mood patterns. *Their effect will be shown to be one of subjectivity or emotivity implying conventional implicatures, that is to say, conventional meanings (as opposed to what they "literally" mean) that are part of the linguistic system and that arise whenever such constructions are used.* It will be shown that the "most urgent task" in frontings (in terms of Mood and Transitivity) is to instruct addressees to *"re-orientate" the structure of the text in some way or another when "normal" discourse expectations fail to be met, pointing to specific discourse instructions that normally entail a change of perspective, of focus of attention, or a subjective viewpoint.*

Once more, this analysis of marked thematic constructions is compatible with previous accounts presented in other models, such as: (a) Hannay's (1991 [1990]) (i) *Reaction mode*, expressed by messages placing the Focus constituent in P1, or (ii) a subtype of the *Presentative mode*, situating a STager (e.g. a scene-setting (spatial or temporal) adverbial or dummy element) in P1; or (b) Lambrecht's (1986, 1987, 1988a, b, 1994) description of (i) *Topicalisations*, characterised as marked types of Topic–Comment constructions, (ii) *Background-Establishing constructions*, having a pragmatically presupposed proposition acting as a scene-setting Topic for another proposition, and (iii) cases of fronted *Identificational constructions*, in which the assertion has the purpose of establishing a relation between an argument and a previously evoked open proposition.

7.3.1 *Preposings*

Syntactically, preposings can be characterised as "those sentences in which a phrasal constituent is moved leftward to sentence-initial position" (Ward 1988: 2).

Going by this description, preposings can be related to inversions (FI) in that in both there is a non-canonical constituent in clause-initial position, but they differ in the relative position of Subject and process, as shown in (144) and (145) below:

(144) | ⁻one figure inci°dentally | you ˎmay find ˎuseful | (LIBMSECFPT02: 064)

(145) |beˉhind Shaᵛron | is the Is_raeli ˎgovernment | (LIBMSECAPT03: 045)

In (144) a Complement (*one figure*) is preposed while the Subject remains in preverbal position. By contrast, the inversion in (145) moves a place Adjunct to initial position and locates the Subject in postverbal position. Moreover, while some inversions have a preposed counterpart, most preposings are constructions that could not be subject to inversion: they occur with transitive verbs, with negation or with pronoun Subjects. Preposing is therefore a separate construction, rather than underlying an (derived or direct) alternative to inversion (FI) (Section 7.4.3).

Another thematic construction with which preposing could be related is left detachment, since in both a constituent is moved to front position. Nevertheless, they differ in that the latter also involves the requisite of a coindexed proform in the CWO slot (Section 7.4.4), a condition which preposings lack.

7.3.1.1 *Formal structure and frequencies in LIBMSEC*

As already noted, in our corpus preposings were more frequently found in special thematic constructions than in non-special ones (Table 30 above), probably as a result of three factors. One is that 51.9% of the cleft constructions in LIBMSEC shift a circumstantial Adjunct to thematic position, as expounded in (146) below:

(146) | it was with ˎjust this °grave emˎbarassed in°spection that ˎshe re°warded him | (LIBMSECGPT01: 103)

Besides, 48.2% of the left dislocated ones also front to external initial position a referent fulfilling a different function than the expected one for each mood pattern, which is exemplified in (147):

(147) | ↑⁻as for the ˌhijack | °interest in ˌthat | °focuses on the ⁻military ˌprison | at Atˎlit | which ˎdoesn't °actually ᵛlook much like a °prison | at ˌall | (LIBMSECAPT07: 016)

Lastly, the third factor explaining the frequency of marked Themes in terms of Mood in special constructs in LIBMSEC is that many of them are triggered by inversions in verbal processes, displaying the marked pattern: projected Verbiage ^ projecting process ^ Subject/Sayer, as illustrated in (148) below:

(148) a. | we're ˌall going to ˋdie ₐ 'screamed a 'man | ⁻even the ˋhostesses 'looked 'worried | *as* ˋ*panic* be'gan to ˋspread through the 'plane | [...]| ˋthat was ᵛnearly | a ⁻perfect ˋlanding | ⁻well ˌdone ₐ 'shouted the con'trol 'tower | ˋthanks ₐ said the 'man | any 'chance of a ⁄job | (LIBMSECGPT04: 165–66)
　　　 b. | °go aˌway ₐ said the °lion | you ˋmight knock my ˋfriend °over | ⁻go aˌway | ˋshan't ₐ said Jack °Tall | (G02: 139–141)

This third factor also explains that *verbal* and *mental* processes appear third and fourth in terms of frequency in LIBMSEC preposings, preceded by (in this order) *material* and *relational* processes, and followed by *existential* processes (Table 23). In addition the Fisher's Exact Test and the χ^2 Test selected five more variables as significant: (a)/(b) *mood/transitivity function* of topical Theme; (c) its *structure*; (d) its ± *external realization*; and (e) *type of clause*. As the reader will remember, these variables were also selected as significant by the logistic regression procedure for the choice of non-special thematic constructions representing in that case the unmarked option.

Going by our results reported in Table 24, in LIBMSEC *circumstantial Adjunct* is the *prototypical* function fulfilled by *fronted Themes*. Some instances are included in (149)–(152):

(149)　*circumstance of accompaniment/Adjunct*
　　　 | wiˋthout our a⁻bility to _hear | we would be ˋcut off from ⁻many of our _everyday acˋtivities | (LIBMSECKPT02: 10–1) (PP)

(150)　*temporal circumstance/Adjunct*
　　　 a. ^going to the ᵥshore | on the ˋfirst 'morning of the ᵛholidayᵦ | the ⁻young ᵥEnglish boy | ⁻stopped at a _turning of the ᵥpath | and ⁻looked _down at a ⁻wild and _rocky ˌbay | and ᵛthen | 'over to the ˌcrowded ˋbeach | (LIBMSECGPT01: 6–9) (Beta Theme1: *-ing* clause ^ PP)
　　　 b. | ˌyet | un'til his _death in ⁻seventeen seventy-_eight | ↑he re_tained | a be_lief in ˌGod | though Volˋtaire's 'God | the ⁻God of a ᵥdeist | was ˋone that ᵛmost 'Christians | would _scarcely have ˋrecognised | (LIBMSECDPT02: 130–133) (Adv. Group^PP)
　　　 c. |'next ˌmorning | when it was ˋtime for the rouˋtine of ⁄swimming and ˌsunbathing | his ⁻mother said | ↑are you ᵥtired of the 'usual beach 'Gerry | would you _like to go _somewhere ᵥelse | (LIBMSECGPT01: 23–25) (NG^Dependent clause)
　　　 d. | ˌalso in °19°80 | °following the °second ᵥoil °crisis | the ᵛthen | ˋLiberal °government of ᵛCanada | a_dopted | a _compre°hensive | _National ˌEnergy °Programme | (LIBMSECCPT01: 297–310) (PP ^ *-ing* clause)

e. | in °197₍₃ | the °year in °which it was ˏlaunched | with such ˏfanfare | the °estimated ˏshare | of U_nited °States ˏenergy con°sumption | suᵥpplied | ᵛby do°mestic °sources | was °8_5 per ˋcent | in °19⁄⁸0 | when the ᵛauthors of °Project Inde°pendence | had enˏvisaged | that it would °be a°pproaching ᵛ100 per cent | it ⁻was in _fact | °8ˋ6 per °cent | °as for the °19ᵛ80 | °US syn°thetic ⁄fuel °target | of °500°000 _barrels | of ˏoil e°quivalent | per ˏday | by °198₍₇ | the ⁻likely ˋout- come | in ⁻that _year | is ˋsomething | ˋvery °much ᵛlower |_(LIBMSECCPT01: 297–310) (PP^NG; PP^Dependent clause; PP)

(151) spatial circumstance/Adjunct
a. | at ˏClacton | it _took some 'five ˋhours | to get _Nemo out of the ˏwater | and _into the ˋlorry | (LIBMSECBPT02: 179–180) (PP)
b. |at a ᵛnews 'conference | ˋafter their 'instaᵥllation | the ⁻party ᵛlead- ers | ⁻clearly be_trayed | the ⁻differences beˏtween them | (LIBMSECAPT09: 35–44) (PP ^ PP)
c. | in Mr ⁻Howell's _world | in the ⁻world of his ˏpredecessors | ⁻and his suᵥccessors | and their o⁻fficial adˏvisers | ˋno other ˋpractical ˋpossibility | eˏxists | (LIBMSECCPT01: 115–117) (PP ^PP)

(152) manner circumstance/Adjunct
a. | he ⁻gained the ˏsurface | ⁻clambered about the _stones that ⁻littered the 'barrier 'rock until he 'found a ˋbig one | and with ⁻this in his ˏarms | ⁻let himself _down over the _side of the ˋrock | (LIBMSECGPT01: 148–151) (PP)
b. | there were ˋno such moments of ˏglory | for _Severiano Balleˋsteros | by his ⁻own awesome 'standards | ↑it was a medi ˋocre 'season | but he _still topped the _order of ˋmerit | (LIBMSECFPT04: 130–132) (PP)

Conversely, *preposed Complements*, as in (153) and (154), stand as the most *highly marked option*, whereas *fronted Predicators* are third in frequency as a result of their generally acting as Theme2 of complex reporting clauses (normally inverted Theme1 triggered by the preposing of a quote), as illustrated in (148) above.

(153) a. | she has ⁻five ˏeggs | ⁻shaped and _speckled most ˋdaintily | but ˋthis she ˋcannot ˋknow | (LIBMSECHPT04: 26–29) (NG)
b. | _no ˋthis she 'cannot ˋknow | ⁻nor indeed ˋanything that ˋwe call 'knowledge | ⁻nor such 'love and ˋhope as ours | (LIBMSECHPT04: 31–32) (NG)
c. | the ⁻flow'rs we _knew we ˋwelcome aˋgain in their ˋturns | ˏprim- rose | aˏnemone | ˏdaffodil and ᵥtulip | ⁻blossom of _cherry | ⁻blos- som of _pear and ˋapple | ⁻iris and ˏcolumbine | and ⁻now the °white ˏcistus | (LIBMSECHPT04: 11–14) (NG)

(154) a. |more im˅portant how'ever | is that the ⁻biblical _writers
them˅selves | ⁻thought that e_vents that ˅followed natural 'laws |
could ⁻still be re_garded as mi'raculous | (LIBMSECAPT01: 47–49)
(AdjG)
b. | ˅second | was a ⁻talent of 'boundless 'prospect | from the 'Basque
country | ⁻Jose Ma_ria O'lazabal | (LIBMSECFPT04: 132–134) (AdjG)

In keeping with these results and considering now their transitivity function, *preposed Themes in* LIBMSEC *tend to perform the role of Circumstance* (40.4%). Within this group, circumstances expressing condition were the most frequent (30.7% β Themes in non-special Theme constructions vs. 19.2% β Themes in special Theme constructions), followed by those of place or time (28.3% β Themes in the former type vs. 15.4% in the latter). Illustrations of these occur in (149)–(152) above. Second in frequency, *preposed Mediums* (10.3 %) were more frequent in special than in non-special thematic constructions. These were typically: (a) Attributes (7.7% vs. 0.2% non-special), (b) Verbiages (4.3% vs. 0.8%) and (c) Values (2.3% vs. 0.8%). In contrast, Medium non-special Themes had a higher number of Goals (6% vs. 0.7% in special Theme constructions), Ranges (100%) and Phenomena (1.2% vs. 0.5%). As a further illustration of the transitivity roles performed by preposed Themes consider (155) below, which contains instances of initial: (a) Circumstances (*for this*), (b) Goal Mediums (*he, which, his task*), and (c) circumstantial Tokens (*It was about this time…, it's no coincidence*), in contrast with unmarked Actor/Senser Agents (*who, we*):

(155) | ↑for ˅this | 'Voltaire ˅must take | ↓much 'credit | though he was 'greatly 'helped | by the ˅French New°tonians | ↓like /Maupertuis | and ˅d'Alembert | who ⁻treated the _more mathe˅matical aspects of New°tonian phi°losophy | ↑which Vol˅taire | _tended to ig'nore | his 'task was ˅also made °easier | by an °admi˅ration for °England | that was _then widely 'felt | in 'France | ↓we should re^member that it was about ˅this time | that ˅Montesquieu | con⁻ceived his re/spect for /English /parliamentary de'mocracy | and it's 'no co'incidence | that from the ⁻seventeen /twenties | ⁻French _views on the re'lationship be'tween ⁻science | and re/ligion | ↑also be⁻gan to re_flect | ⁻English 'influence (LIBMSECDPT02: 083–87)

With regard to their structural realization, *preposed topical Themes showed a tendency to be realized by non-nominal expressions* (Table 31). More specifically, in LIBMSEC the *prototypical fronted Theme is a PP*, or less frequently, *an adverbial group* (AdvG), as in (149)–(152) above, *a nominal group* (NG), an *adjectival group* (AdjG), as in (153) and (154) above, or a *Continuative element* or some type of *conjunctive or modal Adjunct*, which usually represent locutions or ideas in projections (mainly in special (inverted) Theme constructions, e.g. (148)).

To the above should be added 264 instances of preposed Themes realized by *enhancing and projected clauses in complex clauses*, representing 6.6% of the overall Themes in LIBMSEC and 16% of the complex clauses, which explains the high incidence of special and fronted Themes in paratactic clauses (normally corresponding to the pattern: the projected ^ projecting type) (Table 30, examples in (148) above).

The majority of these marked β Themes (80.3%) (i.e. initial dependent clause in a clause complex) involve enhancing relationships such as conditional (30.7% in non-special Theme constructions vs. 19.2% in special ones), spatio-temporal (28.3% vs. 15.4%), manner (11.3% vs. 7.7%) or cause (6.1% vs. 1.9%), as illustrated in (156a–d), respectively:

(156) a. | had I ˅not spoken any °Arabic_β| then their °attitude towards this °strange ˅foreign woman | ˋmight have been totally ˋdifferent |
(LIBMSECJPT06: 480–482)
b. | ˋafter they had ˏdived | and ˉcome ˏup _β| they ˉswam a˅round | ˅hauled themselves °up | and ˉwaited their _turn to _dive aˋgain |
(LIBMSECGPT04: 72–74)
c. | and as ˋChris °Poole reˋminds us_β | ˉone ˊhorse | °played a sigˉnificant ˏpart | in °making the ˉyear | ˉso ˏmemorable | [change of speaker: Chris Poole] | (LIBMSECFPT04: 247–248)
d. | and as ˋfootball is the °world's most ˅popular °sport | and as it proˊvided us with the °year's ˅centrepiece | the °world cup _β| we'll beˉgin | with ˅Mexico | and °Martin ˏFookes | (LIBMSECJPT01: 32–34)

Besides, through the logistic regression technique it was found that choices of *β Themes* in LIBMSEC are directly affected by (in descending order of influence): (a) the type of *process*, (b) the *function* of the *β* Theme and (c) its predication *external/internal* realization. According to the data, *β Themes normally have predication-external realizations* (72.3% vs. 27.3%), and they tend to be triggered by *material, relational* or *verbal* processes, expressing *conditions, spatio-temporal information*, circumstances of *manner* or *cause*, or *Verbiages/Complements*.

Considering now the last relevant variable for the characterisation of preposings, the results reported in Table 29 show that, though globally representing the marked option, *most instances of preposings* involve *predication-external (P2) realizations* (71.5% vs. 28.5% of clause-internal (P1) ones), whereas this tendency is reversed in unmarked Themes (19.2% vs. 90.8%). In all the instances of preposings in (149)–(152), (154) and (156) above, Themes are separated from the rhematic predication, in contrast with P1 realizations of unmarked Themes. By contrast, in (153) above, and in (157) and (158) below preposings are realized predication-internally:

(157) *temporal circumstance/Adjunct*
  a. ⁻after lunch Miss ˋDobson 'phoned | she ˋsaid that ⁻Western ⌄Video 'Systems | had to ˋcancel their 'last ˋorder | because their ˋcustomers had changed their ˋminds | (LIBMSECJPT05: 87–89)
  b. | ˋsix 'months beˊfore I re'called | ⁻sixty ˋsoldiers | were ₍lured | 'down that ₍road | ⁻by the gue₍rrillas | and 'all ˋsixty | were ˋwiped ₍out | (LIBMSECAPT04: 52–53)
  c. so between ˋMarch and Sepˋtember there is no ˋschooling as such | (LIBMSECJPT06: 223)

(158) *spatial circumstance/Adjunct*
  a. | ⁻down he 'went until he 'touched the wall of ˋrock a'gain | but the ˋsalt was so ˋpainful in his ˋeyes | that he ₍could not ˋsee | (LIBMSECGPT01: 120)
  b. | in Afghaniˋstan they were mainly ˋSunni as ˋwell just like in the Su⁻dan | (LIBMSECJPT06: 393)
  c. | in ⁻some places _sea defences were ⁻breached | and 'many _roads have been ⁻blocked | by ⁻flood water | and _fallen ˋtrees | 'Laurie Marˋgolis re₍ports | (LIBMSECAPT13: 121–122)

The discourse effects of (predication-external and predication-internal) realizations of frontings are treated in turn.

7.3.1.2 *Discourse function*

Preposings share with inversions (FI) the way in which they exploit the clause-initial position as a marker *of discourse recoverability* and as a *strategy marker* in discourse. According to Ward (1990: 760), the co(n)textual conditions of preposing are highly restricted:

> [...] preposing serves two simultaneous discourse functions: first, it marks the entity represented by the preposed constituent as being anaphorically related to the other discourse entities via a salient (partially ordered) set relation [...]; and second, preposing involves instantiation of a salient OPEN PROPOSITION [...] ([emphasis in original])

Put differently, the front-shifted item establishes a link to previously established discourse units and thereby marks a whole proposition as recoverable at a given point in discourse. As shall be shown in Section 7.4.3 below, the latter part of these discourse conditions is in clear contrast to the function of FI, which requires no recoverable information in the sense of an open proposition in order to be felicitous (Ward & Birner 1994). In sum, *preposing is a comparatively local phenomenon that links a new proposition to prior discourse.* The requirements in terms of recoverability are absolute rather than relative, with consequences for its discourse positioning: preposings are generally barred from discourse-initial contexts, while inversions are not (only if the postponed constituent is also discourse-new) (e.g. *In a little white house lived two rabbits* vs. **In a little white house two rabbits lived*, Ward & Birner 1994: (13a) (13b)).

Drawing on Prince (1981b), Ward (1988) in his book-length study of preposings distinguishes between "topicalisation"/"Topic preposing" (where the governing clause contains the focal element so that the construction shows extended multiple accented syllables: on the preposed constituent and on the non-preposed Focus), and "Focus-preposing" (where the preposed constituent is focal and therefore bears the single accented syllable of the utterance). Text-based studies of so-called "topicalisation"/"Topic preposing" often comment upon the "topic-preserving" role of the construction: it serves to maintain the flow of discourse by maintaining a currently "salient/evoked" entity (whereas left-detachment generally redirects the flow of the discourse — because the Topic entity does not have "salient/evoked" status, speakers need to make amends, as it were, for presenting it as topical by selecting a construction which strongly foregrounds the current focus of attention). The preposings in (153) above, now renumbered (159), could correspond to this description:

(159) a. | she has ⁻five ˌeggs | ⁻shaped and _speckled most ˈdaintily | but ˈthis she ˈcannot ˈknow | (LIBMSECHPT04: 26–29)
   b. | _no ˈthis she 'cannot ˈknow | ⁻nor indeed ˈanything that ˈwe call 'knowledge | ⁻nor such 'love and ˈhope as ours | (LIBMSECHPT04: 31–32)
   c. | the ⁻flow'rs we _knew we ˈwelcome aˈgain in their ˈturns | ˌprim-rose | aˌnemone | ˌdaffodil and ˌtulip | ⁻blossom of _cherry | ⁻blossom of _pear and ˈapple | ⁻iris and ˌcolumbine | and ⁻now the °white ˌcistus | (H04: 11–14)

However, such descriptions as the above in terms of "entities", contravene our characterisation of Themes as "relational", rather than "nominal" in character (Section 6.2), and are hard to apply to instances of preposed non-referring expressions (e.g. qualities, dummy elements, etc.) or to circumstantial Adjuncts. Besides, our data show that: (a) most preposed items are recoverable/salient at that point of discourse; and (b) both the preposed element, whether it be predication-internal or predication-external, and the rhematic predication normally serve as (one or more) loci for and therefore are under the scope of intonational Focus. Under these circumstances, it seems that a (clear-cut) distinction between alleged "Topic" vs. "Focus" preposings needs reworking with the support of further empirical study of the question.

It seems safer to conclude that frontings have a common core: *their* *referents typically convey Giv$_R$ information, which constrains the use of fronted Themes to specific co(n)texts and disfavours indefinite and non-specific realizations* (Kuno 1972a, b; Gundel 1974; Chafe 1976; Prince 1981b, 1984; Hankamer 1979; Feinstein 1980; Davison 1984: 814; Ward & Birner 1994). Hence, typically realized by definite and specific expressions, fronted referents convey information that is co(n)textually recoverable, either directly (stale information) or indirectly (via inference), involving relationships of opposition or similarity in relation to the field, the tenor or the mode of the discourse situation. The referents of preposed elements function as anaphoric discourse bridges that entail a recoverable circumstance to frame a subsequent predication, or summarise or describe the discourse referent with which they stand in an (inferrable/stale) identity relationship, or represent "entified" qualities of preceding and/or following referents. Discourse evidence of this has been provided by the instances of preposings offered throughout Section 7.3.1.1.

Now let us analyse the interpersonal dimension of preposings. Though infrequent in our corpus ((153), (159) above), *fronted entities (Complement NGs) seem to support the hypothesis that they instruct for Topic continuity in discourse* (through pronouns or nominal groups referring to persons or things, events or situations just mentioned). Alternatively, *the interactional component of the scene-setting textual function of initial adverbials*, by far the most recurrent type of preposing in our corpus, *resides in their guiding and shifting the addressee's attention in the development of discourse, foregrounding background information, highlighting extended turns, or modifying speaker-recipient roles*.[112] To be more precise, adverbial preposing acts as a *discourse/strategy marker* that marks typically *minor boundaries between textual units*. Directly relating to previous discourse and to the next proposition, they contribute to marking *normally minor textual shifts*, in contrast with FI which tends to signal major shifts (Virtanen 1992: 108). It follows that by breaking CWO patterns, preposings constitute discourse-organising strategies that participate in the chain of expectations arising in a text/speech. In this light and going by the records of adverbial frontings presented so far, one can conclude that initial e.g. conditional, temporal, spatial or purpose clauses raise addressees' expectations that what is conditioned will be presented, that some new event or participant will be introduced, or that a goal will be fulfilled, normally over the subsequent minor textual span sharing a common spatio-temporal location.

Though subservient to the principles of EW and EF, whereby the longer and more informative clause, regardless of its tactic status, comes last, the discourse expectations raised by the Dependent ^ Head marked organisations of hypotactic complex clauses also reflects an *iconic organisation*, i.e. a function of language in use, underlining one or several of the following four factors (Downing & Locke 1992; Goatly 1995: 189):

a. *to mark the temporal reference of the two clauses*, that is, that the temporal reference of the dependent clause is located before, or at least not posterior to, that of the dominant clause, as in (160);

(160) I ˋafter they had ˏdived I and ⁻come ˏup ᵦI they ⁻swam aˏround I ˇhauled themselves °up I and ⁻waited their _turn to _dive aˋgain I (LIBMSECGPT01: 072–74) (Sequence in Time)

b. *to highlight the non-factual nature of the subordinate clause*, especially in conditional clauses, so that by placing it in front of the apodosis speakers avoid the apodosis being interpreted as a factual statement, while this resort is not necessary when the protasis does not indicate non-factuality overtly, as in (161):

(161) a. I ↓if °verdicts go against ⁻Time and °CBˇS ᵦI °both pre-ˋeminent in their ˇfields I the ˋimpact on ˇlesser °news organisations I ˏcan be exˏpected to be _far-ˋreaching I (LIBMSECAPT03: 056–58) (non-Factuality)
b. I and ⁻this is ˋfortunate I because if the ˋtarget had been ˏreached ᵦI the ⁻costs in°volved I would have been iˇnordinately I ˏhigh I_(LIBMSECCPT01: 310)

c. *to iconically mirror cause-effect relationships between the two clauses* since cause precedes effect (at least in our conceptualisation of the world), as in (162):

(162) a. I ↓and as a ˋseven per cent °increase in the basic ˋpension for a ˋsingle person is °two pounds ˇfifty ᵦI they'd see ˋvirtually ↑ˋno rise at ˋall I in their _income I in Noˏvember I [Change of speaker: Vincent Duggleby] (LIBMSECFPT02: 4852) (Cause-Effect)
b. I to °get a free ˋpass on the Soutˏhampton to °Cowes ˇferry ᵦI an inˆvestor in the ˏSouthampton ˏIsle of °Wight and ˋSouth of °England ˇPacket °Company I ˋneeds to buy °shares worth more than ⁻seven _thousand ˋfive hundred ˋpounds I (LIBMSECFPT01: 041–44) (Purpose/Goal-Effect)

d. *to abide by the principle of FSP*, i.e. the Given-before-New principle, so that dependent clauses typically act as pivotal points in the local organisation of a text: they not only limit the frame of reference for subsequent discourse, but they also establish a common ground with respect to alternative disjuncts and/or the preceding discourse in a limited number of ways, i.e. by repeating or assuming an early claim, by offering a contrast, by providing exemplification, by opening up new possibilities whose consequences were to be explored, as in (163).

(163) [change of speaker: Kevin Geary] going °back to the West \Indies | where we \started ᵦ| they didn't have it ᵛall their own °way | (LIBMSECFPT04: 82–83) (Summative/Common Ground).

Considering now the overall distribution of frontings across the LIBMSEC text types, the findings indicate that, contra Quirk & Greenbaum (1973) or Feinstein (1980), but in line with Leech & Svartvik (1975), *preposings are most common in formal and planned texts, i.e. reconstructive texts* (53.7% vs. 50.2% unmarked ones) *and constructive texts* (32.7% vs. 26.9%) (cf. Ghadessy 1993, 1995; Goatly 1995). The reason why frontings are frequent in reportages, the most objective text-type in our subjectivity scale, seems to be that through this thematic choice reporters can move the camera angle of discourse, either serving procedural ends, i.e. primarily creating a visual impact processing of what is reported, or functioning as a real focus management device within the discourse organisation making use of marked informational Focus. Alternatively, in reconstructive texts the effects of preposings are basically the same, but their rhetorical purpose changes. Usually playing the role of "architects", in reconstructive texts speakers need to prepose discourse elements (typically adverbials) to invite their audience into the immediacy of their made-up organisation of discourse, i.e. the way in which their mind relates and evaluates the textual relations among the topics developed throughout the text. Finally, their nuance of "emotivity" or "subjectivity" could explain that the highest ratio of frontings has been found in three "subjective" texts: (E) Religious Services (5.7% vs. 2.3% non-fronted Themes) and (H) Poetry (4.3% vs. 1.7%), (A) Commentaries (19.1% vs. 14.9%), as opposed to the other less skewed percentages: (G) Fiction (23.8% vs. 23% without frontings (C, D) Lecture (18.4% vs. 17.5%), (F) Magazine (8.6% vs. 7.1%).

7.3.2 *Passive constructions*

Active and passive are grammatically distinct clause constructions differing in the typical correspondence between Subject and (the semantic role of) Actor in the case of the active, and between Subject and Patient in the case of the passive (Siewierska 1984; Downing 1996):

(164) a. Tom painted the fence (active)[113]
b. The fence was painted by Tom (passive)

A language-particular definition of the passive for PresE might draw informally on derivational concepts as follows:

a. demote Subject of active to a *by*-PP in passive;[114]
b. convert active Object into passive Subject;
c. add catenative *be* as superordinate to the original verb, which in turn becomes a past participle and whose inflectional properties are transferred to *be* (except for any person-number properties, which are determined by agreement with the passive Subject).

Passive clauses may be subordinate. A distinction should be made between passives lacking catenative *be* or *get*, usually referred to as *bare passives* (e.g. *painted by Tom* in (165) below), from those which, like main clauses, have *be* or *get*, often called *expanded passives* (e.g. (164) above and *be(en) painted by Tom* in (166) below):

(165) a. Fences *painted by Tom* attract a good deal of attention
b. I want this fence *painted by Tom*.
(166) a. The fence *had been painted by Tom*.
b. The fence appeared to *be painted by Tom*.

On an auxiliaries-as-catenatives analysis (in which *have* would, like *appear*, be a non-argument-taking catenative) we shall need to further distinguish between passives of the "direct" type in (165) from the sentences in (166) which are only "indirectly" passive. That is, while they have active alternants — *Tom had painted the fence and The fence appeared to be painted by Tom* — it is strictly speaking only the embedded clause that is passive.

Although lying beyond the reach of this investigation, any purportedly comprehensive description of active-passive alternation will need to address the challenging issue of how to account for the various restrictions on such alternation. For instance, there are various types of active transitive clauses that do not have passive counterparts. Consider (167), showing transitive clauses with obligatorily reflexive object (a); clauses with catenative *want*, *like*, *hate*, etc. (b); clauses with verbs having a logically "symmetrical" meaning, like *equal* in (c); clauses with various other verbs of stative meaning (d):

(167) a. John perjured himself — *John was perjured by himself.
b. Everyone wanted Sue to leave — *Sue was wanted by everyone to leave
c. Two times three equals six — *Six is equalled by two times three
d. John has three sons — *Three sons are had by John

Conversely, not all passive clauses have active counterparts (e.g. *He was said by his parents to have been a docile child* ~ **His parents said him to have been a docile child*). As is the case with most grammatical categories, so with the passive construction we find that there is a prototype, shading out into more and more marginal subtypes. These non-prototypical passives include: (a) *Agentless passives* (e.g. *Trespassers will be prosecuted*), some being obligatorily agentless (e.g. *Tom was taken ill*), which are textually more frequent than "agented" passives; (b) *passives of ditransitives*, where normally the indirect Object becomes passive Subject (e.g. *We were given a warm welcome by Bill*), but in some dialects and with some verbs the direct Object can become passive Subject (e.g. *A warm welcome was given to us by Bill*); (c) *Passives with stranded prepositions* in which the Complement of preposition becomes passive subject (e.g. *Your application has been dealt with by the committee*); (d) *Get passives* (*She's getting married soon*), where *get* rather than *be* is the superordinate catenative, are largely restricted to informal style, and to cases where the Subject referent is not a patient but intends, and assumes some responsibility for, the action, and are associated with adversative or beneficial implicatures (e.g. *She got injured* vs. *She got rewarded*); and (e) *Bare passives without (intransitive) get* or *be*. We may have Objects of transitive catenative verbs such as *see, hear, have, get, want, order* (e.g. [*He wanted it*] *destroyed*); also Modifiers in NG structures (e.g. [*Did you* come across any bones] *buried in the garden?*); or Object, Complements or peripheral dependants in NGs or clauses (e.g. *Warned to double their commitment*$_{\beta Theme}$, [*the researchers finally recognised the need for an intense effort*]).

7.3.2.1 *Formal structure and frequencies in LIBMSEC*

The results reported in Table 33 show that *most passive processes in LIBMSEC are expressed by means of non-special thematic constructions, while special ones have a higher tendency to involve active processes*. In other words, *non-special thematic constructions represent the unmarked choice in terms of voice selection*, that is, they allow for a greater freedom of choice.

Indeed, the structural and functional realizations of the Themes of passive processes were found to correspond fairly well with those of non-special Themes. The former also tend to: (a) act as *Subjects* (88.1% vs. 83.7% in active processes), or as *circumstantial Adjuncts* (10.6% vs. 9.5%), and less likely, as *Objects/Complements* (0.9% vs. 3.0% in active processes); and (b) be expressed by *common noun groups* (58.1% vs. 27.6% in the active voice) or by *prepositional phrases* (8.8% vs. 6.2%). The excerpts in (168) below illustrate the prototypical structure and transitivity/mood function of non-special Themes in passive processes:

Table 33. *Voice in (non-)special Themes*

Voice	Non-special Theme	Special Theme	Row Total
Active	3341	427	3768
	91.4	97.0	92.0
Passive	316	13	329
	8.6	3.0	8.0
Column Total	3657	440	4097
	89.3	10.7	100.0

Fisher's Exact Test significance: .00003
Missing observations: 0

(168) a. | ⁻they gave _names | to the °unit _fractions | from the _ordinal ₍numbers | one ᵛthird for e°xample | could be ⁻written out in ₍words | as ⁻to ₍triton | or it ⁻might be a ̀bbreviated to ₍to | just ⁻T ₍O | ⁻followed by the °letter ₍gamma | °repre°senting ₍three | with ᵛon | ⁻O ₍N | as a ˋsuper°script | ᵛlater | ⁻unit ₍fractions were °repre°sented | ⁻simply by the ˋletter | or ₍letters | of the de₍nominator | _followed by an ˋaccent | ⁻one ₍third | °would ₍ °thus °just be °written as ₍ °gamma ˋdash | (LIBMSECDPT03: 195–7)

b. | in ⁻some places _sea defences were ⁻breached | and °many _roads have been ⁻blocked | by ⁻flood water | and _fallen ˋtrees | (LIBMSECBPT01: 121–122)

Besides, although the difference in percentages was small and, as a consequence, the Fisher's Exact test reported a non-significant association between the choice of an unmarked or marked Theme and that of an active or passive process ($p = .05020$, n.s.), it was observed that, as happened in non-special thematic constructions, *the Themes of passive processes have a higher tendency to be unmarked than those of active ones* (86.3% vs. 82.0). And vice versa, like special Themes, *the Themes of active processes involve more cases of frontings than those of passive ones* (18% vs. 13.7%). From these results it can be inferred that *the active voice represents a less thematically constrained choice than the passive one, which validates our treatment of the latter as the marked choice*: only 0.3% of passives in LIBMSEC occurred in interrogatives, the rest were all declaratives and only in material processes were they more numerous than active ones (73.3% vs. 36.7%). Interestingly enough, my findings report as possible the combination of marked voice, or passive, with marked Theme, elsewhere excluded as ungrammatical (Halliday 1967b), as demonstrated in (169) below:

(169) | when the Is/raelis | were °picking _people ͺup | ↑they *were a*ʹ*rrested* in South ͵Lebanon | for any ᵛnumber of °reasons | as the Is/raelis | _scrambled to ͵leave | and ʹwere at °first /held | at the ᵛAnsar °prison °camp | which _Israel ʹused | in _South ͵Lebanon | ⁻with the /pullback | _that *was* ͵*closed* | and more than a ⁻thousand /Shi'ites | *were _moved* to At'lit | (LIBMSECAPT07: 034)

Finally, modal Adjuncts were found to co-occur more frequently with the topical Theme of passive processes than with those of active processes (90% vs. 43%), the latter being more recurrently accompanied by all other types of interpersonal Themes. This is exemplified in (170) below:

(170) | ʹSpain | °funnily e/nough | was °repre°sented in all ʹthree Euro°pean /finals | (LIBMSECJPT01: 097)

7.3.2.2 *Discourse function*

The use of passivised Themes is strongly *motivated by the principle of TU, in this case, the speakers' desire to infuse texts with objectivity, as well as by the principles of EF and EW, and by the unmarked correspondence between Subject and Theme, their referents being normally profiled as the current focus of discourse, and their dissociation from the role of Actor*. This can be explicit in the Rheme owing to its "heavy" or informative weight. In turn, so-called "*agentless passives*" may, furthermore, be motivated by the *speaker's not knowing the identity of the Agent-referent, wishing to conceal it, considering it unimportant*, or the like.

According to the data, *the Themes of passive clauses act as textual devices* whereby, *in seeking objectivity, speakers tend to construct different types of reality, concentrating on the referents affected by it, rather than on those responsible for it*. For in LIBMSEC the passive voice predominates over the active one in constructive texts (42.9% vs. 26.6%), while the reverse is the case in both reconstructive and action-like texts (48.9% vs. 51% and 8.2% vs. 22.3%, respectively). More specifically, in Lectures passives are twice as common as actives (35.6% vs. 16.1%), while the latter are only one or two percentage points higher in Magazine and Religious Broadcasts (7.5% vs. 6.1% and 3.1% vs. 1.2%, respectively). Furthermore, passives are the unmarked choice in informative reconstructive texts such as Commentaries (20.4% vs. 15.3%) and News Broadcasts (25.2% vs. 8.6%), but the opposite is the case in more subjective genres such as Fiction (2.7% vs. 24.9%) and Poetry (0.6% vs. 2.3%). As for language in action texts, the focus centres on direct speech participants, usually the initiators of processes, hence the prototypical choice of the active voice in Dialogues and Propaganda (19.1% vs. 7.0% and 3.3% vs. 1.2%, respectively).

On the basis of these results one can conclude that *the grounds for passive messages are constructed "subjectively"*, to use Langacker's (1990) terminology, that is to say, *speakers remain off the scene expressed via language, sympathising with the participants in the scene and facilitating displacement of self.* An illustration is included in the extract in (171) below, where the speaker uses the passive voice to "empathise": (a) with the contents of an encyclopaedia; (b) her/his role as a narrator; and (c) Descartes and Cartesian thought:

(171) ↑like ˬmost encyclo'paedias | it *was ˌwritten* to con_vey ˋtruths | but ˉtruths *a_rrived at* in the ˉonly _way that the ˉphilo_sophes thought it ˇpossible to ac'quire certain 'knowledge | by ˉreason | and exˌperience | [...] | and in the ˇrest of this 'talk | I *shall be* ˇ*chiefly con'cerned* | with the diˋversity | ˉrather than the ˬunity | of ˌFrench | En_lightenment ˋthought | [...] ↑during the 'first _quarter of the eighteenth ˌcentury | ˉFrench _natural phi_losophy | was 'almost _totally Carˌtesian |[...] | and its poˋsition *was made* ˋall the ˇmore se'cure | by the _large _measure of aˇpproval | that it had _won with'in the Catholic ˋchurch | ˌtrue | it *was 'still o*ˇ*pposed* | by ˋDescartes' most imˇplacable 'enemies | the ˋJesuits | [...] quite ˬsuddenly | in the ˉlate seventeen ˌtwenties | Carˉtesian phiˌlosophy in ˌFrance | *beˉgan to be* ˬ*challenged* | [...] ↑ˉsince the sixteen ˬeighties in 'England | ˉDescartes' ˌphysics | and his psyˌchology | *had been* ˉ*so se*ˇ*verely a'ttacked* | ↓by ˉNewton | and ˉLocke | that ˉby the _early ˇeighteenth 'century | Carˇtesianism 'there | *was _almost* | ˋ*totally* | *aˋbandoned* | ↑Volˌtaire | who was in ˇexile in 'England | from 'seventeen twenty-ˉsix | to 'seventeen twenty-ˉeight | ↓obˉserved the _changes in English phiˋlosophy | and *was _duly im_pressed* | by 'Newton's ˉsplendid ˬfuneral | in ˉWestminster _Abbey | in _seventeen twenty-ˋseven | a 'man whose ˇpall | *was 'borne* by ˇdukes | and ˇearls | was _clearly of exˋceptional imˋportance | (LIBMD02019)

In addition, in LIBMSEC *the passive voice has the effect of thematising prototypically Subject/Medium common nouns or, less typically, Adjunct/Circumstance prepositional phrases of declarative material processes.* This claim supports the view that the passive voice enables speaker/writers to dissociate the roles of Actor and Theme while leaving the Theme unmarked, which at the same time allows for:

a. the Agent either to be non-thematic or not specified at all;
b. the unmarked Focus to fall on a constituent other than the Goal (Halliday 1967b: 215, 1994: 169).

Indeed, my findings corroborate the hypothesis that in most cases speakers choose the passive voice with two main purposes: *either to ensure that the phrase describing the Agent is at the end rather than at the beginning of the clause and thus can display end Focus and end Weight*, as in most instances of passive constructions in (171) above and the one included in (172) below, *or to omit the Agent phrase*, because its referent is inferrable from the co(n)text or because it is unknown, as in some of the tokens of passive Themes in (171) above and the two occurring in (173) below:

(172) and he was su⌄pported in this °view | by the ⁻first repre_sentatives of a ⁻school of ⌄British theo°logians | who re⁻lied on the _use of ⁻natural ˌreason | ⌄rather than reve°lation | for their _knowledge | of \God | (LIBMSECDPT02: 098)

(173) a. | a °major se⁻curity reˌview | has been °ordered at the ⌄state de°partment | in /Washington | after a /gunman | ⁻entered the ˌbuilding | ⁻shot °dead his ˌmother | who ↓⌄worked °there | and _then °killed himˌself | ⁻BB_C | (LIBMSECBPT02: 011–014)

b. | the \last re°porter to be ˌkilled °here | ⁻back in \March | was ⁻shot \dead | in a ˌcrossfire | ⁻on that ˌroad | (LIBMSECAPT04: 015)

On other occasions, the use of the passive implies that the event described has a particular effect on the speaker or on some other explicitly mentioned affected person. This explains the relative frequency of thematic modal Adjuncts in this voice (90% vs. 43% in the active), with which speakers, empathising with the experience being construed, express their opinions about it, as in (171) above or in (174):

(174) | ↑⁻not surˌprisingly | the ˌtendency to ⌄think in these °terms | has been \strengthened in ˌrecent °years | ↑by de_velopments | on °inter_national ˌenergy °markets | (LIBMSECCPT01: 261–26)

7.4 Special Theme constructions

In this study special thematic constructions are classified into seven *prototypical* types:

a. *Existential-there* constructions (e.g. *There is a teapot (at home) that the duke has given to my aunt*) (Section 7.4.1);
b. *it-Extrapositions* (e.g. *It is strange that the duke gave to my aunt that teapot*) (Section 7.4.2);
c. *inversions* (e.g. *Here is the teapot that the duke has given to my aunt*) (Section 7.4.3);
d. *left detachments* (e.g. *As for that teapot, the duke has given it to my aunt*) (Section 7.4.4).

e. *right detachments* (e.g. *The duke has given it to my aunt, that teapot*) (Section 7.4.5);
f. *cleft clauses* (e.g. *It was that teapot that the duke gave to my aunt*) (Section 7.4.6);
g. *pseudo-cleft clauses* (e.g. *What the duke gave my aunt was that teapot*) (Section 7.4.7).

The first and second parts of this study have shown that previous moderate functionalist models have also invoked (some or all of) the above special thematic constructions. However, we have seen that these structures either have not received intrinsically functionalist accounts or have not been described systematically according to homogeneous criteria. These will be the aims of Section 7.4. Its subsections will systematise the formal structure of the seven types of special Theme constructions in terms of eight features, as expounded in Table 34:

a. [±COREF], i.e. the presence vs. absence of an item marking a coreference relationship between the Theme and the rest of the clause predication (viz. an anaphoric, a clitic, an agreement expression, etc.) in the Rheme;
b. [±PAUSE], i.e. the presence vs. absence of prosodic pause or silent ictus to the left or to the right of the clausal predication;
c. [±FUNCT], i.e. the presence vs. absence of syntactic function within the dominant, or main, predication;
d. [±NOM], i.e. the presence vs. absence of a nominalisation in an encoding equative clause;
e. [±PRED], i.e. the presence vs. absence of a Predicated Theme in an encoding equative clause.
f. [±DUM], i.e. the presence vs. absence of a dummy element, or Subject slot filler;
g. [±EXT], i.e. the presence vs. absence of an element external to the structure of the main clause predication.
h. [.], i.e. feature which is not relevant for the formal characterisation of a prototypical type of topical Theme.

We will not be concerned with whether these seven types of special thematic constructions are base-generated or derived from "simpler" linguistic units. Neither will the grammaticality, acceptability or generative power of such sequences be evaluated as artificially produced isolated constructs, although this has been a continuous preoccupation among generativists and strict moderate functionalist linguists.[115]

Rather, we shall concentrate on the *textual* and *interpersonal* semantics of

Table 34. *Special syntactic Themes under analysis*

Types		Coref	Pause init.	Pause fin.	Funct	Nom	Pred	Dum	Examples
equative +ext	Cleft	+	.	.	+	–	+	+	*It was that teapot* that the duke gave to my aunt.
	Pseudo-cleft	+	.	.	+	+	–	–	*What the duke gave my aunt* was that teapot.
non-equative –ext	*It*-Extraposition	–	–	–	+	–	–	+	*It is strange* that the duke gave to my aunt that teapot
	Existential-there	–	.	.	+	–	–	+	*There* is a teapot (at home) that the duke has given to my aunt
	Inversion	–	–	–	+	–	–	–	*Here* is the teapot that the duke has given to my aunt
non-equative ext	Right Disloc.	+	–	+	+	.	.	–	The duke has given it to my aunt, *that teapot*
	Left Disloc.	+	+	–	+	.	.	–	*As for that teapot*, the duke has given it to my aunt.

these construction types: how do they affect the texture of messages? What do speakers want to do with them? However, a complete description of special thematic constructions will also have to involve, at some later stage, the consideration of other thematic constructs (e.g. alternating complementation frames, such as *Mary pleases me* vs. *I like Mary*, postpositioning of Object, such as *They pronounced guilty everyone of the accused*, postpositioning of phrasal dependent, such as *The time had come to decorate the house for Christmas*), as well as the elucidation of the experiential semantics of these constructs: what interpretation of experience do they express?

Hence, following the intuition that "[t]hematic patterns are not optional stylistic variants; they are an integral part of the meaning of language" (Halliday 1978: 134), we shall assume that thematic proportionalities constitute a plausible system within the textual component of a language, only if they are explained as *motivated choices*, that is, as paradigmatic choices standing in co(n)textual opposition. Section 7.4 brings this underlying rationale to the fore exploring the frequencies, the formal structure and discourse motivations of the special Theme constructions found in LIBMSEC, as opposed to non-special ones already described in Section 7.2 above. It will be shown that just as different mood patterns express different speech functions and different transitivity patterns code experience in different ways, special Theme–Rheme constructions satisfy specific discourse needs that make them appropriate for specific discourse co(n)texts only. It will be argued that special thematic constructions are interpersonally oriented textual devices that establish speaker's/writer's point of view in discourse, instructing addressees to adopt a specific course of action.

In LIBMSEC special Theme constructions represent the marked option: 10.7% vs. 89.3% non-special Themes. Figure 15 shows that the most recurrent special type is the unstressed *there*-existential construction (176 instances, 4.3%), followed by *It*-Subject Extrapositions (105 tokens, 2.6%), Subject-Predicator inversions (79 cases, 1.9%), *It*-clefts and left detachments (27 and 29 examples, respectively, representing 0.7% each), and pseudo-clefts and right detachments (13 and 11 tokens respectively, coming up to 0.3% each of them).

Going by the results of the logistic regression technique, in what follows special Theme constructions will be characterised in relation to the following six variables (in decreasing order of effect): (a) the *type of process*, (b) the *Mood function* of the topical Theme, (c) its ± *predication-external* realization, (d) *type of clause*; (e) the *structure* of topical Theme; and (f) its *transitivity* function. The findings indicate that special Themes:

a. tend to involve *relational processes* (36.1% vs. 31.4% in non-special ones), *verbal* processes (30% vs. 0.1%) or *existential* processes (11.8% vs. 10.1%),

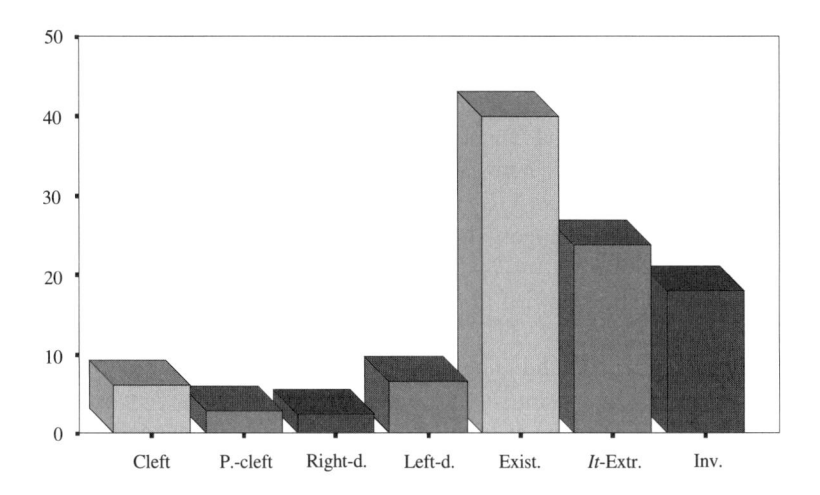

Figure 15. *Special thematic constructions across LIBMSEC text-types*

which suggests that, typically, special Theme constructions either give *synoptic* pictures of reality or provide speakers' individual reports on it, through the use of verbal processes;
b. *have a lower tendency to behave as Subjects and therefore a higher proportion of preposings than non-special thematic constructions*;
c. have a higher ratio *of predication-external realizations* than non-special ones;
d. tend to appear in *complex clauses or in simple clauses*;
e. have a higher ratio of *pronominal, verbal, prepositional, clausal, adverbial* or *Continuative realizations* (in this order of frequency) than non-special Theme constructions;
f. are *less prone to behave as Agents and therefore more likely to be marked in terms of transitivity than non-special thematic constructions.*

A general discussion of these claims and the statistical evidence supporting them, as well as the discourse instructions obtained therefrom will occupy us in what follows, whereas the subsequent subsections are devoted to provide individual analyses of each of the seven types of special thematic constructions posited in this investigation.

Concerning the type of process, our findings indicate that *existential-there-constructions, inversions, it-Subject Extrapositions, right and left detachments, cleft and pseudo-cleft clauses tend to cluster around relational processes*, which, rather than simply presenting reality, give subjective synoptic views of it, (a) thematising interpersonal meaning, (b) guaranteeing the right identification of a given referent by cancelling or reinforcing a previous presupposition made about it, and (c) thematising an Attribute of a rhematic referent. In the following subsections, the subjective usages of special Theme constructions will be related to different kinds of conventional implicatures. *At this stage it suffices to say that the variable of process selection underlines the subjective orientation of special Theme constructions*, a claim which supported by two further statistical findings. The first is that, as shown in Table 35, *special Themes normally occur in "subjective" texts*, i.e. texts in which speakers had to either *reconstruct reality*, such as in *Fiction* (21.1%) or in *Commentaries* (11.4%), or act upon it as in *Dialogue* (19.3%).

Likewise, it was found that *the majority of interpersonal Themes* (in LIBMSEC) *co-occur with special Themes, especially with modal Adjuncts* (4.8% vs. 3.9% in non-special Themes) and Finites (3.6% vs. 1.6%) although this tendency is less clear in *there*-existential constructions and *it*-extrapositions. Consider (175), where *of course*, the only instance of interpersonal Theme, introduces the only example of special Theme construction of the excerpt:

(175) | ↑\some Free ᵛChurch people | °feel that in ᵛpractice | the _Anglicans go it a\lone whenever they °can | an ⁻article in this week's °Baptist ᵛTimes | asks \what °bishop wants to conᵛfer | ↑when _he can have a ⸝camera | and a ⸝microphone | ⸝all to him\self | ↓when the ⁻Church of °England's General ᵛSynod | can \now get so much atᵛtention from the °press ₐ| the ⁻role of the \British Council of ᵛChurches | ⁻seems to _fade into the \background | ↑of course \what concerns °church \leaders | ⁻isn't neces⸝sarily | ⁻what °worries ordinary \churchgoers | (LIBMSECAPT01: 025–28)

Pointing to the same effect, Table 36 demonstrates that *special thematic constructions in LIBMSEC as a whole are not normally accompanied by logico-conjunctive Themes, the most objective class of Theme*. Co-occurrences of logico-conjunctive and special topical Themes are most frequent only in left dislocated and pseudo-cleft constructions: in the former logico-conjunctive Themes normally appear in initial position (i.e. before a topical and/or an interpersonal Theme) while in the latter they generally occur in medial position (i.e. after a topical or an interpersonal Theme) or in final position (i.e. after both a topical and an interpersonal Theme).

Turning to the second formal feature, as reported in Table 24 and in Table 37, *special Themes in LIBMSEC have a greater amount of frontings than non-special thematic constructions, although, globally, in both unmarked Subject Theme is the most recurrent choice. Most special thematic constructions are again declaratives* (93%), followed by 4.8% interrogatives (mainly *there*-constructions,

Table 35. *Incidence of special Themes in LIBMSEC text types*

Type of text	Cleft	P-cleft	Right detach	Left detach	Exist	It-extr.	Invers	Row Total
Reconstructive	8	7	3	13	80	45	62	218
	29.6	53.8	27.3	44.8	45.5	42.9	78.5	49.5
Constructive	14	5	1	7	54	35	13	129
	51.9	38.5	9.1	24.1	30.5	33.3	16.5	29.3
Language in action	5	1	7	9	42	25	4	93
	18.5	7.7	63.6	31.0	23.9	23.8	5.1	21.1
Column Total	27	13	11	29	176	105	79	440
	6.1	3.0	2.5	6.6	40.0	23.9	18.0	100.0

Chi-Square significance: .00000
Number of missing observations (i.e. non-special Theme constructions): 3657

it-Subject Extrapositions and Inversions), 2% imperatives (detachments) and 0.9% exclamatives (*there*-constructions and *it*-Subject extrapositions). But, interestingly enough, *marked special Themes in* LIBMSEC *are not only more numerous than marked non-special ones, they also show a reversed distribution. For in special thematic constructions it is Complement that represents the most recurrent marked choice and circumstantial Adjunct the most highly marked one,* while it was the other way round in marked non-special Theme constructions. This finding seems to suggest that *special Themes are participant-centred, i.e. they tend to highlight participants rather than processes or circumstances, whereas marked non-special Theme constructions are normally non-participant centred*

Moreover, it was observed that *the tendency of special topical Themes to co-occur with interpersonal Themes is even higher when the former are marked than when they are unmarked*, since *many marked special Themes are accompanied by mainly modal Adjuncts* (52.6 vs. 44.3% in non-special Themes) (176a) or by Vocatives (22.8% vs. 9.4%) (176b):

(176) a. | ′perhaps | with the di/visions | that have °opened ′up | ,and | with ⁻all the re°crimi\nation | the \Pale°stinian ˌmovement | °thought there was ⁻little ,hope | for a °PN_C at ,all | (LIBMSECAPT02: 036–38)
b. | so ⁻Father | in the ⁻mystery of your ᵛprovidence | we ⁻trust that in ,this | we shall ⁻find our ᵛown °peace | and ⁻life e_ternal | through ⁻Jesus ˌChrist | ⁻our ,Lord | aˌmen | (LIBMSECEPT02: 061).

With regard to ± predication external realizations of special Themes, *it was found that external special Themes are three times as common as non-external ones* (73.4% vs. 26.6%), *especially in the case of detachments and extrapositions,*

Table 36. *Incidence and position of logico-conjunctive Themes in special Themes*

Position of logico-conjunct. Theme	Cleft	P-cleft	Right detach	Left detach	Exist.	It-extr.	Invers	Row Total
Ø	15	7	6	11	106	64	54	263
	55.6	53.8	54.5	37.9	60.2	61.1	68.4	59.8
initial	11	3	5	16	67	40	24	166
	40.7	23.1	45.5	55.2	38.1	38.1	30.4	37.7
medial	1	1		1	1			6
	3.7	7.7		3.4	1.7			1.4
final		2		1		1	1	5
		15.4		3.4		3.0	1.3	1.1
Column Total	27	13	11	29	176	105	79	440
	6.1	3.0	2.5	6.6	40.0	23.9	18.0	100.0

Chi-Square significance: .00000
Number of missing observations: 3657

which indicates that the special syntactic prominence of special Themes is normally suprasegmentally reinforced by means of a tone group boundary, whereby such P2 slots have their own intonational Focus being simultaneously brought into discourse focus. This is shown by the results of the Chi-Square Test in Table 38 and the special thematic constructions included in the excerpts in (175) and (176) above.

Table 37. *Syntactic function of special topical Themes in LIBMSEC*

Syntactic function of topical Theme	Cleft	P-cleft	Right detach	Left detach	Exist.	It-extrap	Invers	Row Total
Subject	13	13	8	15	136	99		284
	48.1	100.0	72.7	51.7	77.3	94.5		64.5
Finit./Pred.	1		1		1		40	43
	3.7		9.1		.6		50.6	9.8
Compl.	4		1	10	25		32	72
	14.8		9.1	29.0	14.2		40.5	16.3
Circ. Adjunct	9		1	4	14	6	7	41
	33.3		9.1	19.3	8.0	5.7	8.9	9.7
Column Total	27	13	11	29	176	105	79	440
	6.1	3.0	2.5	6.6	40.0	23.9	18.0	100.0

Chi-Square significance: .00000
Number of missing observations: 3657

Table 38. ± *External realizations of special topical Themes in* LIBMSEC

Realization of topical Theme	Cleft	P-cleft	Right detach	Left detach	Exist	It-extrap	Invers	Row Total
External	21	10	6	28	147	102	32	350
	77.8	76.9	54.5	96.6	83.5	97.1	40.5	79.5
Internal	6	3	5	1	29	3	47	90
	22.2	23.1	45.5	3.4	16.5	2.9	59.5	20.5
Column Total	27	13	11	29	176	105	79	440
	6.1	3.0	2.5	6.6	40.0	23.9	18.0	100.0

Chi-Square significance: .00000
Number of missing observations: 3657

The fourth formal feature of *special Theme constructions underscores their tendency to occur in either simple clauses or in complex clauses*. It is their "animated syntax" (Section 6.2) that probably explains the restrictions that hold for embedded and dependent constructions. Their absence from these structurally marked type of clauses can be related to the expressive kind of meaning carried by special constructions. Indeed, in LIBMSEC a majority of right detachments (54.5%) and existential-*there* constructions (40.3%) appear in simple clauses, while the remaining special Theme constructions occur mainly in complex clauses.

Moving on to the structural realizations of special topical Themes, Table 31 indicates that, *although most special Themes are expressed by nominal groups* (63.4%), *they lend themselves to non-nominal expressions more easily than the non-special ones: verb phrases* (10.2%), *clauses* (7.6%), *prepositional phrases* (9.1%), *adverbial groups* (2%), or *Continuatives* (2%), while *adjectival groups* (0.7%) represent the most peripheral realizations. Significantly, verbal, prepositional, clausal, Continuative, but above all, *pronominal realizations are more common in special Theme constructions than in the non-special type*. This result can be related to the fact that most instances of existential and extraposed constructions have a pronoun as their Theme, i.e. *there* and *it*, respectively, as exemplified in excerpt (177) below, where, in contrast, all non-special syntactic Themes are realized by nominal noun groups:

(177) [interview by Steve Annett is omitted] the ˅fire caused \chaos on the \tube system | ˅scores of °trains | on \three lines were \halted | because the \power | ↓had to be turned \off | and for \hours ˅road traffic | had to con⁻tend with di˅versions | because of \street °closures | [change of

> speaker: Brian Perkins] ⁻London °Regional ⁻Transport | say that \so far this ⁻morning | only ⁻tube trains on the ᵛCentral °Line | are \stopping at Oxford \Circus | ⁻Bakeloo Line °trains are °running ⁻through the °station without ₍stopping | there's \no service on the Vicᵛtoria °Line | between Vic_toria and \Warren Street | (LIBMSECAPT13: O42–44)

Conversely, β Themes, i.e. those realized by dependent clauses, are infrequent as realizations of special Themes (19.7% vs. 80.3% non-special ones). In most cases, they act as Verbiages/Direct Objects in inverted Theme constructions (55.8%), as in (178), or as Conditional (19.2%) or Spatio-Temporal (15.4%) Adjuncts:

> (178) | \why don't we ⁻play | like the \others |_β the lion °asked | (LIBMSECG02: 091)

Concerning the sixth significant association, our results show that *active and special Theme constructions are more prone to have frontings and non-nominal realizations than passive and non-special ones* (i.e. Object/Complements (3.0% in active special clauses vs. 0.9% in passive ones) or Finite/Predicators (3.7% vs. 0.3%)). But special passive Themes have a high amount of Mediums, concerning attributive/identifying relational or verbal processes acting as Attributes (7.7% vs. 0.2% in non-special ones), Values (2.3% vs. 0.8%) or Verbiages (4.3% vs. 0.8%). The same applies to processes (9.3% vs. 2.3%) and circumstances expressing matter (100%).

So far we have discussed the formal tendencies of special Theme constructions; let us now summarise their corresponding communicative effects. In the subsequent sections different special thematic constructions will be shown to convey different *conventional implicatures*, that is to say, different conventional meanings (as opposed to what they "literally" mean) that naturally arise as a result of the varying devices whereby constituents are brought to front position within the grammaticalised word order system of PresE. Grammaticalisation reduces the speaker's choice, so that, only when there is still the option of meaningfully deviating from the word order norm, are those meanings of a speaker-based, hence subjective, nature. Only then can they be attributed to a Gricean mechanism of quantity, as suggested above, and ultimately have the status of implicatures (Section 6.2).

Structurally, most special Theme constructions considered here have a corresponding CWO non-special version. Yet, the actual *use* of each of them is often far from being a choice; under many contextual conditions the use of special theme constructions is almost unacceptable, while only others, quite specific ones, make the choice in favour of a particular special thematic construct really preferable. Our corpus-based findings have *already identified the general contextual conditions of usage of special Theme constructions vs. non-special ones: they cluster around subjective texts, a finding which confirms the existence of genre conventions in that respect and at the same time justifies treating special Themes as markers of subjectivity.*

In the subsequent sections this claim will be further developed and seen from the perspective of each of the seven types of thematic constructions considered in this investigation. *Generally speaking, however, it can be argued that the conventional implicatures carried by special thematic constructions depart from a two-fold common core.* On the one hand, special Theme constructions *involve movements in information packaging.* Thus, in contrast to the canonical varieties, inversions (like preposings) and left detachments display a leftward movement within the clause which has a substantial effect, whereas a different effect arises from a rightward movement in right detachments, existential-*there* constructions and extrapositions (Section 2.3.1). On the other hand, special Theme *constructions can be related to the presence/absence of an existential presupposition*, or a *presuppositional set*, in discourse, which, if present, is questioned, contradicted or highlighted (see Section 2.3.2.1 above).

Furthermore, *special thematic constructions bring about different kinds of thematic and/or rhematic highlighting by exploiting the PSRR differently* (Lambrecht 1994; Section 7.2.2 in this study). Indeed, *it will be shown that both left and right detachments abide by the PSRR*: their selection of syntactic topical Theme, the lexical representation of the clause thematic referent, takes place separately from and outside the designation of the referent's role as an argument in the proposition that presupposes the existence of such a referent, to its left in left detachments and to its right in right detachments. *Left detachments will be shown to represent a conventionalised grammatical construction that acts as discourse Topic switch device*, establishing a contrast or parallelism with respect to the previous cotext or introducing a new participant in discourse. The reversal of the PSRR is displayed *by right dislocated constructions*, which will be said to convey the conventionalised meaning *of an implicit request to put the propositional information "on hold" until what the proposition is about is uttered in P3*, on the assumption that the preceding coreferential pronominal expression did not suffice to ensure its understanding.

In turn, *cleft and pseudocleft constructions*, although they fuse the role and reference of the syntactic topical Theme in one wording and therefore violate the PSRR, will be *described as displaying conventionalised forms of thematic highlighting with respect to a presupposition of existence.* It will be argued that, while *cleft Themes establish an implicature of exhaustiveness*, or exclusive contrast, with respect to the previous or subsequent presupposition, *pseudocleft ones identify a participant, circumstance* or *emphasise a process in a presupposed state of affairs*.

On the other hand, *inversions, there-existential constructions and Subject-It-extrapositions will be accounted for as primarily presentative constructs*. Like frontings, *inversions serve to place recoverable, particularly inferrable, elements clause-initially, which, in English, are exempt from Subject status* and are thereby unexpected in their discourse role of departure *creating an effect of emotivity, typically over major discourse shifts*. This effect is also contributed to by the marked position of the Subject, which is thereby signalled to be unexpected as well, and which means that in principle some other potential referent should have been more likely or expected. The *presentative* nature of inversions resides in *their foregrounding of the speaker's syntactic point of departure*, which (a) usually receives *intonational prominence*, (b) *precedes a clausal presupposition*, and (c) serves *a variety of communicative purposes* (viz. to solve problems of encoding, to act as a spatio-temporal framework-setting device for the introduction of new participants in discourse, to establish a cohesive tie, to create an effect of emphasis).

Alternatively, *there-existential* constructions and Subject *it*-extrapositions lack a presupposition of existence and, not infrequently, violate the PSRR. Roughly, if unmarked, the two constructs have an initial so-called "dummy" Subject expression that is not infused with discourse prominence but merely builds up to the rhematic predication in Focus. Acting negatively, both special, and in this sense somehow "prominent", Themes contribute to two different types of rhematic highlighting as a concomitant of the principles of EF and EW.

We shall see that in the unmarked cases *existential-there constructions* tend to place in *P1 a Stager*, i.e. scene-setting spatial or temporal adverbials, which acts as a *presentative device that*, in combination with BE or other existential processes, *creates an existential/presentational framework, bringing to rhematic and End Focus position a "heavier" (lexically and informatively) Existent*. This element is introduced into the discourse generally to be developed as Topic over the ensuing discourse stage (Firbas's *presentation scale*, Section 3.2.3 above; Hannay's (1991) *there-existential* mode, Section 5.4.4 in this book; Lambrecht's (1994) presentative thetic constructions).

In turn, prototypical *it-extrapositions thematise speakers' objectified modality and modulation value scales* (viz. "possibility-probability-certainty" or "permission-desire-requirement") by means of a thematic predicative structure, with the dummy pronoun *it* as unmarked Theme replacing "heavier" subordinate nominal clauses that are extraposed to rhematic and focal position (Hannay's (1991 [1990]: 144) *Neutral mode*; Lambrecht's (1994) thetic constructions).

The following sections explore the formal and discourse-functional features, as well as the frequencies, of each of the seven types of special Theme–Rheme constructs posited in this investigation, in relation to the eight features suggested at the beginning of this section, i.e. [±COREF], [±PAUSE], [±FUNCT], [±NOM], [±PRED], [±DUM], [±EXT], [.]. Section 7.4.1 examines Subject *It*-Extrapositions and Section 7.4.2 Inversions. Presentative *there*-constructions are discussed in Section 7.4.3, while Left and Right detachments are covered in Sections 7.4.4 and 7.4.5, respectively. Last come the analyses of cleft and pseudo-cleft constructions, in Sections 7.4.6 and 7.4.7.

7.4.1   *Existential*-there *constructions*

This section discusses the frequencies, the formal characteristics and the communicative properties of existential-*there* constructions (e.g. *There is a teapot (at home) that the duke has given to my aunt*), displaying the features [−EXTERN, −COREF, −in./fin. PAUSE, +FUNCT, −NOM, −PRED, +DUM]. 176 tokens were found in LIBMSEC, constituting 40% of its special Themes and 4.3% of all the syntactic Themes found in the corpus. Although regarded as themeless or topicless in other moderate functionalist accounts, existential-*there* constructions are here classified as tokens of special Theme constructions (different from inversions) in view of their having two different Subjects, namely: (a) *There*, an (almost) empty syntactic Subject and (b) the *Existent*, or semantic Subject, as shall be shown in turn.

7.4.1.1 *Formal structure and frequencies in* LIBMSEC
Prototypically, existential *there*-constructions display the pattern *Subject^Process ^Existent^(Extension)* (Hannay 1985b). The function of syntactic Subject is realized by *unstressed, non-locative* [+DUM] *there*. Existential *there* fulfils the usual requirements for Subject in PresE (except for pronominalisation and agreement): (a) unlike the preposed locative of a locative inversion (Birner 1992: 38), it inverts with the operator in interrogatives (e.g. *Is there anybody home?* (including interrogative tags, as in *There's nobody home, is there?*); (b) it may enter into agreement with the verb (e.g. *There's three people away today*); and (c) it occurs in pre-verbal position. In addition, in contrast with "strong" locative or "deictic" *there*, existential, or "expletive", *there*: (a) is typically *unstressed* (Hartvigson & Jacobsen 1974: 62); (b) is not a copy or anticipation of adverbials of place, direction, etc. (Erdmann 1990: 60); and (c) from a synchronic perspective, it does not have the meaning of "location" at all (Bolinger 1977: 91), but "simply postulates the existence of some entities" (Quirk et al. 1985: 1406) and may contain no locative information at all.

The process of existential-*there* constructions is typically realized by *be*, but it may also be realized by a small set of intransitive verbs mainly denoting arrival or appearance (e.g. *follow, remain, appear,* etc.). The *Existent* (Hannay 1985b), on the other hand, represents the "displaced" semantic, or notional, Subject. For, as Hannay (ibid.: 193) remarks, *there* acts as a presentative-existential place-holder, which has "the positional properties associated with the Subject but does not constitute the Subject term itself". This latter function is fulfilled by the Existent, whose existence or, alternatively, whose spatio-temporal location is predicated in the existential clause (complex). Crucially, as happens in Subject/Process inversions, the placement of *there* in unmarked Subject position involves a process of postponement and thereby is endowed with *cataphoric potential*: it points to and triggers the shifting of the Existent to postverbal Complement position, where typically it is postmodified or followed by an Extension and therefore carries end-Weight and end-Focus.

What follows the "displaced" semantic Subject, or Existent, I shall call, again following Hannay (1985b), the *Extension*. This is an *ad hoc* term which is not intended to name a syntactic function, but designates an optional Qualifier, Complement and/or Adjunct that either postmodifies the Existent or complements the existential process itself. Consider the range of existential unstressed *there*-constructions included in (179) below:

(179) a. ↑mean^vwhile | a ⁻browse through the ^vcurrent 'perks 'list | ↓is a re'minder that *there* \are ^vone or 'two | u^vnusual con'cessions | that ^vdon't hit the 'headlines | like re_duced 'cross-'channel \ferry 'fares | (LIBMSECFPT01: 033)

b. | ↑*there's* \also a danger of \communal violence in the ⁻areas | _bor-dering the Tamil \north | where °tensions are _still running ⁻high | ⁻following the \massacre | of nearly _one hundred and fifty ci^vvilians | in the _mainly Sinhalese \town of Anuradha\pura last °month |(LIBMSECAPT01: 034)

c. | but ⁻even if eco°nomic °change were more pre^vdictable ₆| ↑*there* would re\main | ⁻basic objections | from the ^vorthodox °point of °view | to the ^vkinds | of au⁻tarchic policies | ⁻which are a͵ssociated | with e^vssentialism | and the _fortress men\tality | ↑in par^vticular | (LIBMSECCPT01: 315)

In (179a) *there's* presents a "heavy" Existent, *one or two unusual concessions* with the Extension postmodifying it in the form of a relative clause (*that don't hit the headlines...*). By contrast, (b) also contains both Existent and Extension, but these are realized as two independent syntactic units: the "light" non-human entity Existent, *danger of communal violence*, and the "heavy" locative Extension of the existential process, *in the areas bordering Tamil... month.* In (c), in turn, the Existent, *basic objections*, is introduced by *there remain*, rather than by *there be*. Roughly the difference between these two process constructions lies in that, whereas *there + Be* presents states of entities or affairs, *there + other* existential processes highlight the actions in which the referents are involved.

In LIBMSEC *there + be constructions are far more common than those consisting of intransitive verbs denoting arrival or appearance* (e.g. *remain*, and *appear*, etc.) (99% vs. 1%). And within *existential processes* other than *there + be*, the *there-less type*, such as those in (180) below, *is much more popular than that introduced by there*, as in (181), (95% vs. 5%):

(180) a. | ↑the ˋnephew of Miss ˋWorld organiser Julia ˇMorley | has aˉppeared in °court in ˏLondon | accused of ˋblackmailing her ˉhusband ˇEric Morley | for ˉtwenty thousand ˏpounds | (LIBMSECBPT03: 103–5)

b. | ↑now the ˉquestion aˏrises as to just ˇwhy the E°gyptians | °chose the par°ticular combiˇnations of °unit °fractions | ˏfound in the _two-to-ˋn table | (LIBMSECDPT03: 078)

c. | ˇsuddenly | °armed _men a°ppeared on all ˋsides |(LIBMSECJPT02: 014)

(181) a. | but ˉeven if eco'nomic 'change were more preˇdictable | ↑there would reˏmain | ˉbasic obˏjections | from the ˇorthodox 'point of 'view | to the ˇkinds | of auˉtarchic ˏpolicies | ˉwhich are aˏssociated | with eˇssentialism | and the _fortress menˋtality | ↑in parˇticular ||(LIBMSECCPT17)

b. | and ˉthere _stood | a ˋlion | ˉblocking her ˏway | ||(LIBMSECGPT02)

It can be claimed that both *there*-less constructions, such as those in (180) above, and *there*-containing ones, as in (181), are "existential" constructions in that they express that something has happened/come into existence, even if these two types of constructions are not strictly equivalent (in terms of definiteness, for example, as in *?There has appeared in court the nephew of ...* vs. (180a) above (IFG: 142–44).[116]

In LIBMSEC *there-less existential constructions tend to be declaratives having unmarked* (Subject) *Themes*, normally expressed by means of *simple definite or generic indefinite NGs*, usually accompanied by an *Extension*, which often gets some sort of *prosodic highlighting*. Accordingly, as their predicates are normally communicatively "heavier" than their Themes, *there*-less existentials can be said to abide by the principles of FSP, EW and EF (all their predicates receive some sort of prosodic highlighting). This is especially illustrated in (180b) above, where the Theme of the existential process, *the question*, a discontinuous definite and therefore Giv_R Head of a noun group, receives thematic relevance, whereas its informationally heavier tail, *as to just why Egyptians ... gets* rhematic, end-Focus and end-Weight highlighting.

Turning now to *there-containing existential constructions*, in LIBMSEC *those containing an Extension element prevail over the Extension-less type* (93% vs. 7%). *Extensions* (in italics) in our corpus display *five patterns*, as reproduced in (186)–(190) below. The excerpts in (186) illustrate the prototype, consisting of a *finite clause Extension* (*that* or relative clauses) postmodifying the event/entity Existent (56%):

(186) a. | there was a ⁻very ⁻very 'high proba\bility | *that the ⁻body | ⁻was 'that of ⸜Mengele | the _odds a⁻gainst he 'said | were ⁻astro⸝nomical |* (LIBMSECBPT020:92–093)

b. ⁻once u°pon a ⸝time | there was a ⁻little ⸜girl | *who didn't* ⱽ*like going to* °*school* | (LIBMSECGPT02: 006)

Second in frequency are existential *there*-constructions containing *spatio-temporal locative Extensions*, normally realized by an PP (30%), as in (187):

(187) a. | there were \three of us *in the* ⸝*car* | \all °rather ⸝nervous | (LIBMSECAPT04: 018)

b. | but there's been \no 'communal violence *to* '*speak of in Co**lombo and the* *south for two* *years* | ⸝*unlike in the _mixed 'Tamil 'Muslim and* *Sinhalese areas* | *in the* *east* | *where _getting on for ⁻one hundred people* *died in recent* *clashes* | *in which the e_lite police co**mmandos* | *were* *also involved* | ↑there's \also a danger of \communal violence *in the ⁻areas* | *_bordering the Tamil* *north* | *where 'tensions are _still running ⁻high* | | (LIBMSECAPT12:009)

The displaced subject NP may either be *substantive* (as in (187a)), with *be* accordingly having a *stative meaning*, or it may be *dynamic* (with *be* accordingly meaning "occur, take place" (as in (187b)). With the dynamic type, existential formation is obligatory (**A danger of communal violence also is ...*; **No communal violence to speak of is in Colombo...*).

The third most frequent existential *there*-pattern is realized by *non-finite V-infinitive/present/past participial Extensions* (7%), as in (188), respectively:

(188) a. | ↑⁻is there °going to be a ⱽsimilar co\llapse | of South ⸝African °willpower | *to con*°*tinue* ⱽ*governing the* °*territory* | (LIBMSECAPT09: 077)

b. ⁻well | I was \on my \way to °visit a \village near the °front \line | I \came round a \bend in the ⱽroad | and °there was a \tree *lying a**cross the road* | (LIBMSECJPT02: 013)

c. on ⁻top of a ⱼhill | over⌄looking °Windhoek | there is °one of the ⁻many eⱼxamples | of °German ⌄architecture | °dotted aⱼround | this °capital ⸜city | °South West ⱼAfrica | °once having been ⸝ruled | by ⌄ⱼGermany | °until its deⵁfeat | in the ⸍first world ⸜war | since ⱼwhen | the ⱼterritory | has been ⸍run by South ⸜Africa | (LIBMSECAPT09: 006)

Last in frequency are Complement Extensions (5.3%), as in (189), and other *circumstantial Extensions* (1%), as in (190):

(189) | there were ⸝no such moments of ⱼglory | *for ⸍Severiano Balle⸝steros* | (LIBMSECFPT04: 130).

(190) | there was no ⱼfraternising | ⱼobviously | *with* ⌄*female* °*teachers* | ⸝*even with* °*Euro*⌄*pean teachers* | (LIBMSECJPT06: 014–16);

Alternatively, *the predicate of Extension-less type consists simply of an NG or a nominal clause Existent* (underlined), which tends to convey co(n)textually Giv_R *information*, referring to either an *entity* (70%), as in (191a) below and the first two examples of (191c), or to an *event* (30%), as in (191b):

(191) a. | ⸝isn't there °anybody⸍else ⌃ he °asked | (LIBMSECGPT04: 066)
       b. ⁻two goals ⸍up | through ⁻Brown and Val⸍dano | and °then the °West ⁻Germans came °back | through ⸍Rummenigge | and ⸍Voller | just a ⁻few minutes to ⸍go | and ⸝then there was °*that fan*⁻*tastic* ⸝*climax* | [live commentary omitted] (LIBMSECJPT01: 052)
       c. ↑but there's ⸍*no* ⸝*motive* sir |[change of speaker] *there* ⌄*may have* °*been Ø*| I ⁻mean | there ⸝was °*that* ⌄*scandal* | *with the* ⌄ⱼ*property* °*company* | (LIBMSECJPT03: 120)

The examples in (191) are often called "bare existentials" (Quirk et al. 1985) in that there is no extension nor a non-existential counterpart (**Isn't anybody else*, **And then that fantastic climax was*…). The type includes "ontological" sentences (e.g. *There is a God*), where, even though logically-speaking existence implies location the locative component is very vague/general (here = "on earth" or "in heaven").

Instances of *both unmarked and marked there-constructions* in LIBMSEC amounted to 80% and 20%, respectively. *Marked Themes were more common in the Extension-containing type than in the Extensionless variant* (92% vs. 8%). One example of each is reproduced in (192) and (193) below, respectively, which shows that marked Themes are normally separated from the rest of the clause by a tone group boundary.

(192) [Change of speaker: Clive Small] _here in ⸍Washington | in Bei⸍rut | ⁻and in Je⌄rusalem | there's ⌄no °hint | that ⁻any _diplomatic ⱼmove | has

⁻broken | the ⁻three way ˎdeadlock | and oˉfficials | ⁻give the imᵛpression | that they ⁻may be _in | for a ᵛlong | ⁻contest of ˎwills | (LIBMSECBPT02: 057–60)

(193) | ⁻like at ᵛall °party °conferences | °round the ˎᵥworld | there's a parˉticular _atmosphere | of °camaˎrade°rie | but it ⁻does ˏseem | that ᵥthis °meeting | ˎis | a _little bit ˎspecial | ʹperhaps | with the diᵥvisions | that have °opened ʹup | ˏand | with ⁻all the re°crimiʹnation | (LIBMSECAPT02: 033)

Also, it was observed that *most marked Themes in existential-there constructions in* LIBMSEC *belong to the β-type*, i.e. Themes realized by dependent clauses. In fact, they represent 28.8% of the overall amount of β Themes found in special Themes in LIBMSEC (being outnumbered only by those found in inversions (50%)). Normally they promote to initial position *temporal Adjuncts* (38%) or *spatial Adjuncts* (22%), and less frequently, manner Adjuncts or conditional(-concessive) clauses (17% each), or accompaniment Adjuncts or the Existent itself (2% each). Consider (194) containing an example of each type:

(194) a. | when ᵛI've been through °Athens airport | and ʹthat's about °two dozen ʹtimes in the past °two ᵛyears |_β there's ᵛnever been more than ⁻one seᵥcurity man on °duty | (LIBMSECAPT08: 024) (Marked time Adjunct Theme)

b. ↑in the orˉnate ʹoffices | of the °Kremlin ˏpalace | which °houses the °central comᵥmittee of the °Communist °party | in the ʹministry ʹbuildings | throughout ʹMoscow | and ↑in the °tiny com_mittee °rooms | of the _party through°out the °fifteen reᵥpublics |_β there ᵛis we're °told | a ʹnew °tempo of ˎwork | (LIBMSECAPT11: 006) (Marked place Adjunct Theme)

c. | ʹjust as there are ʹno pre°cisely de°fined _national ᵥneeds | that °have to be ˏmet | reˉgardless of ᵥcost |_β ᵛso | there are °no oveˉrriding reˏquirements | for ⁻unintе°rrupted suˏpply | which can be iˉdentified | in ⁻central buˏreaucracies | ↑and _used | as a _basis for ˎpolicies | (LIBMSECCPT01: 331) (Marked manner Adjunct β Theme containing an unstressed *There*-Theme2)

d. | if a ʹpolit°buro ʹmember | is in ˎtrouble with the ʹbottle | and is being ⁻punished | by °losing his ᵛinfluence |_β ↑what _chance is ˏthere | for Iʹvan | or ʹIgor | or Naˎtasha | who've ᵛsimilar °problems | and °regularly °fail to °turn up for °work as a reˎsult | (LIBMSECAPT11: 051–54) (Marked conditional β Theme)

e. | ↑ˉis there °going to be a ᵛsimilar co°llapse | of South ᵥAfrican °willpower | to con°tinue ᵛgoverning the °territory | ˏweariness | fruˏstration | and a deʹsire to get ᵥout | there _certainly ˎis | but ᵛnot | at _any ˎprice | and ᵛcertainly °not to °make way | for an °unchecked

\SWAPO ˌgovernment I in ˌWindhoek I (LIBMSECAPT09: 077)
(Marked Existent Theme)

Another remarkable finding is that, *whether marked or unmarked, there-Themes in LIBMSEC occur in simple clauses* (40.3%) or in *hypotactic or paratactic complex clauses* (27% and 26.5%), *generally displaying affirmative, rather than negative polarity* (93.2% vs. 6.8%).

Besides, *our results reported two meaningful parallelisms between there-constructions and it-extrapositions*. The two constructions have a tendency to co-occur with the same class of Themes and also in similar text types. *Both of them favour simple Themes* (97% vs. 3% in the case of *there-constructions*) and *disfavour extended multiple ones* (59.1% vs. 40.9% in the case of *there-constructions*). In existential-*there constructions* interpersonal Themes are particularly infrequent (9%), of which 4.5% are modal Adjuncts, 2.8% Finites, 1.1% interrogative or exclamative pronouns and 0.6% Vocatives. By contrast, logico-conjunctive Themes are slightly more popular (39.8%), especially the structural type (29%), followed by conjunctive Adjuncts (6.8%) and continuative elements (4%). *Likewise, both existential-there constructions and it-extrapositions show a tendency to appear mainly* in *reconstructive texts* (45.5% in the case of *there-constructions*): 18.8% in Commentaries, 13.6% in Fiction and 11.4% in News, in contrast with the lower percentages found in constructive texts (30.7%) and particularly in active texts (23.8%).

7.4.1.2 Discourse function
Roughly, it shall be claimed here that existential or unstressed or expletive *there introduces a distinct type of presentative construction*, which neither serves to set up a specific location in the addressee's model (in contrast with inversions), nor points to a real or imagined location (in contrast to inversions with demonstrative deictics, i.e. *here*, *there*) (Drubig 1988: 93). The underlying rationale is that *the interpersonal dimension of existential-there constructions does not reside in their transmitting the notion of the existence or the non-existence of something, but rather in their conveying an instruction to present something on the scene*. In this light, the claim is made that *there* is not semantically empty, but "brings something into awareness": it brings a piece of knowledge into consciousness, whenever the verb itself fails to accomplish such task (Bolinger 1977; Downing & Locke 1992). Its functional relevance can be derived from its difference with respect to stressed or deictic *there* as follows:

[...E]xpletive *there* cannot by definition carry the focus and effect a shift in the center of attention [...]. Therefore, expletive *there*, much like a definite anaphoric pronoun, can only pick up its reference from the context: it refers back to whatever has been established as the relevant scene or reference situation in the preceding context, possibly further narrowed down by a fronted scene-setting adverb. (Drubig 1988: 93)

In this connection, Davidse (1997) claims that there exist systematic grammatico-semantic differences between so-called *cardinal* and *enumerative* existential-*there* constructions, although both are concerned with a quantitative approach, the one cardinal, the other ordinal, to instantiations of a more general type. Cardinal existentials have cardinally quantified Existents, whereas enumerative existentials typically have proportionally quantified Existents. Cardinal existentials quantify the instantiation of the "designated by the type specification in the Existent NG" (p. 34) (as in (191a) above, *there were three of us in the car, all rather nervous*). By contrast, enumerative existentials name or enumerate instances of a contextually implied type, which must be matched by the superordinate types projected by the Existent NGs (as in (195b) above, *two goals up through Brown and Valdano and then the West Germans came back, through Rummenigge and Voller, just a few minutes to go and then there was that fantastic climax*). Davidse remarks that if cardinal existentials contain circumstances of time or place, these deictically delineate the instantiation under discussion (*e.g. But there's little sign of life in the seven blocks of flats*, LIBMSECAPT06:009). Alternatively, in enumerative sequences Extensions tend to function as postmodifier to the Existent NG, as shown in (195) below:

(195) | the reᵛdeeming 'features | in_clude the re˴silience | of the ˴people | the Ru˴manians | are a ˋLatin 'race | and there's ˬsometimes | a ⁻lightness of ˴touch | '*not seen else*ˋ*where* | *in 'this part of the* ˴*world* | (LIBMSECAPT05:052)

In addition, *pace* the largely accepted claim that only indefinite NPs Existents occur in existential *there-be* constructions, the examples presented so far demonstrate that *especially the enumerative and extensionless type, but also some subtypes of cardinal existentials have definite Existent NGs*. These results seem to suggest that, rather than being *indefinite*, the Existent of existential *there-be* constructions normally contain "*weak*" determiners (i.e. expressions of non-quantification or cardinality) and tend to refer to a *non-anaphoric, non-unique and specific* piece of information (Rando & Napoli 1978; Milsark 1979; Aniya 1992).

As in cases of Subject Extrapositions and Subject/Process inversions, *the usage of existential-there constructions underscores the principles of EW, EF* and *FSP* (i.e. Given-before-New principle). It has been observed that, in keeping with the EWP the rhematic part of *there*-constructions in LIBMSEC is lexically and informatively four times heavier than the thematic part (8 vs. 2). In many cases the latter consists only of the relatively empty *there*, and as a result, Rhemes are more prone to be the locus of one or several focal stress(es) (more often than not they were realized in more than one tone group). This array of information contributes to facilitating the processing of *there*-constructions: placed last, heavy rhematic constituents do not disturb the processing of the thematic part, which at the same time provides an existential-presentational framework for grounding the most informative material.

This tendency, however, is occasionally contravened when marked Themes are used, which, as the reader will remember, are much more frequent in the Extension-containing *there*-constructions. Although marked Themes very rarely surpass in lexical density their corresponding Rhemes, they are still wordy and contain one (or more) focal stress(es). The marked Themes of existential-*there* constructions usually fulfil a connective function. Generally conveying Giv_R information, they tend to ground the Existent with respect to the previous discourse by (a) setting up a spatio-temporal reference, as in (194a) and (194b) above, or a manner or conditional framework, as in (194c) and (194d), or (b) by establishing a contrast with respect to a definite set of referents, as in (194e).

To sum up, *existential-there-constructions act as presentative devices*. Though almost semantically empty, *there* functions as an unmarked Subject Theme in order to ensure PresE SV declarative word order. At the same time, *there* fulfils the textual function of presenting in the scene of discourse and within the Rheme, cataphorically referring to it, an Existent (an event or entity) in order to instantiate *cardinal* or *enumerative* quantifications at a given point in discourse. As a consequence, the Existent is moved from initial to post-verbal position, where it typically carries unmarked end-Focus (Falling Tone) and end-Weight. Besides, the choice of *There + be* as an existential process has the effect of expressing a situation or event as if it were a state, or in systemic terms, as a Thing. By contrast, the real process tends to be reduced to a participle or to an infinitive, as in e.g. (188) and (190) above.

The functional features of *There*-constructions outlined hitherto explain their recurrent use in informative and descriptive reconstructive texts. Existential-*there*-constructions allow mainly news-readers, columnists and commentators to locate a cardinal or an enumerative quantification of entities and situations with respect to the previous co(n)texts, presenting them in the scene of discourse and within clausal Rhemes and thereby getting unmarked end-Focus and end-Weight. At the same time, the side-effect is often caused of silencing the agency of a process, which imbues these constructions with a depersonalised quality. This permits speakers to avoid claims about the responsibility for the assertion in question, which is often necessary in objective constructive and reconstructive texts.

On the other hand, the relative scarcity of existential-*there* constructions in active and specialised texts can be justified in processing terms. Existential-*there* constructions bring about the "delay" of the notional Subject until the end of the construct. By doing so, the addressee's short-term memory is put under strain and the process of comprehension becomes slower. Obviously, this is an undesired effect for scientific and dialogic texts, seeking to get a specialised message through to the audience or pursuing an immediate response, which justifies the relative absence of existential-*there* constructions from these text types.

7.4.2   It-*Extrapositions*

Let us examine the formal features and communicative properties of extraposed Themes, defined here as [−EXTERN, −COREF, −in./fin. PAUSE, +FUNCT, −NOM, −PRED, +DUM] (e.g. *It is strange*$_{Theme1}$ *that the duke gave my aunt that teapot*). 105 tokens were analysed, representing 23.9% of the special Themes and 2.6% of the overall syntactic Themes in LIBMSEC.

7.4.2.1 Formal structure and frequencies in LIBMSEC
Prototypical extrapositions move a rankshifted nominal clause out of Subject position in the dominant clause to the right of its predicate, replacing it with the dummy pronoun *it* (Huddleston 1984: 451–2; McCawley 1988: 95; Collins, 1994: 2; Gómez-González 1997). As a result, the main clause, with [+DUM] *It* as its Subject Theme2, becomes the Theme1 of the whole clause complex and the extraposed one its Rheme1. Extrapositions may be obligatory as in constructions with *it is a fact* or when the extraposed clause itself contains a subordinate clause and the type of subordination is the same at both levels (e.g. **To avoid the speculation that for Richard Gardiner Casey to approve his son's wish to serve in what was expected to be a short war while using his own influence to minimise the dangers to be faced by his son would have been in character is difficult*, Collins ibid.). Similarly, extraposition is obligatory with certain verbs that take finite clause Subjects (e.g. *appear, seem, chance, happen*), and certain verbs that take infinitival clause Subjects (e.g. *remain, be hoped, be intended, be said*). But on other occasions extrapositions are blocked by grammatical factors, such as, for example, when a dominant predicate contains another clause as Complement (e.g. *That he hasn't replied shows he's not reliable*. ?*It shows he's not reliable that he hasn't replied*) or an identified predicate Complement (e.g. *How we can get back in is the main problem*. **It is the main problem how we can get back in*).

Besides, under certain restrictive conditions extrapositions may also involve the shifting of units other than nominal clauses, such as prepositional phrases or noun phrases that are semantically equivalent to subordinate interrogatives, typically containing *the* and a restrictive relative clause (e.g. *It's extraordinary the amount of energy our leader has*, *It's extraordinary how much energy our leader has*) (Collins 1994; McCawley 1988: 96). But for the sake of simplicity these marginal cases have not been included in this category. Also barred from this analysis are those cases of extrapositions moving a constituent out of Complement position over another Complement in the dominant clause replacing it with the dummy *it* as in (196):

(196) | ˅Israel | was °making *it* aˋbundantly ˅clear to°wards the °end of the °week | *that the re⁻maining ⸝Shi'ites* | ⁻*were to be re⸝leased* | ˋ*anyway* | °*not as* °*any* °*conse*°*quence of the* ′*hijack* | *but* ˋ*purely as a* °*function of the* ⁻*level of* ⸝*trouble* | *in* _*South* ⸝*Lebanon* | (LIBMSECA07: 044)

The assumption is that extrapositions like (196) affect the Rheme, rather than the Theme, of dominant clauses in clause complexes. Be that as it may, the question remains that the phenomenon of extraposition must be differentiated from three superficially similar clausal structures:

a. *impersonal sequences* having neutral *it* as Subject Theme (e.g. *It was getting dark*, LIBMSECAPT04: 072, *It is now ten past eight*, LIBMSECBPT02: 205);
b. *identifying constructions* having a generic anaphoric *it* as Subject ID/VL (Identified/Value) (e.g. *It could have been an outsider*, LIBMSECJPT03: 023);
c. *right-detachments* (Section 7.4.5 below), where, typically, a NG is shifted outside, and to the right of, the main clause, and where the pronoun *it*, if present, is referential (cataphoric), in contrast with its non-referential anticipatory nature in the extraposed construction (e.g. *It is nice, the rose*).

The first two cases are here regarded as having non-special unmarked Themes, and as constructions that place within their Rhemes the unmarked locus of focal stress, the information which is "newsworthy". By contrast, right-detachments and extrapositions are treated as different instances of special Themes, because both imply a process of substitution of the Theme and its shifting to the right of the main predicator.

Admittedly, the identificational criteria of extrapositions, i.e. substitution of Theme by a dummy element and right-shifting and rankshifting of a nominal clause, do not suffice to differentiate all instances of this type of special Theme construction from right detachments. Firstly, they apply to prototypes only. Secondly, extraposed clauses exhibit varying degrees of nominalisation. And thirdly, in a given context, the status of an introductory *it*, i.e. whether referential or not, may be ambivalent — especially given the fact that the primary function of detachments is to disambiguate this ambivalence. This would leave us only with the criterion of prosody, whereby prototypical right-dislocated clauses would be expected to be spoken with a compound intonation Nucleus and extrapositions to have a simple Nucleus. However, in practice, this difference is again anything but clear-cut, for in many tokens of Subject extrapositions there is a tone group boundary separating the Head from the extraposed clause (Quirk et al. 1985: 1393).

With these provisos, Subject extrapositions are here considered as a special type of Theme construction in their own right. In LIBMSEC the typical *It-Theme of these constructions refers to finite nominal that-clauses* (54%), of which 93% are *declaratives* with or without *that*, as in (197a) and (197b), and a minority of interrogatives, as in (197c).

(197) a. | but it ⁻does ₍seem | that ᵥthis °meeting | ᵢis | a _little bit ₍special | (LIBMSECAPT02: 035)
       b. ₍well | they ᵛsearched me | of ᵛcourse I ᵛdidn't have any ʹweapons | just a ᵛcamera | ↑it's ʹfunny they let me ᵛkeep it | (LIBMSECBPT03: 026)
       c. | or ⁻could it ₍be | that °when you look ⁻back | at the ⁻sporting _year | ᵛ198⁻6 | °etched inᵛdelibly on your ⁻memory | will be the ⁻frighteningly | dra⁻matic ₍moment | when °Nigel ⁻Mansell's | ᵛtyre °burst | at ⁻200 °miles an ₍hour | to deᵛny him | the °World _Motor Racing ᵛChampionship | or °those _classic enᵛcounters | be°tween °Dancing ʹBrave | and ⁻Shahraᵛstani |(LIBMSECJ01: 014–20)

Alternatively, non-finite *infinitival*, e.g. (198), or *gerundial clauses*, e.g. (199), are *more peripheral* (39% and 7%, respectively):

(198) | and it is ᵛvery ᵛdifficult | to °work | ↓under conᵛditions like ᵛthat | when the ᵛtemperature's °what | _fifty degrees ʹcentigrade sometimes | (LIBMSECJPT06: 228)

(199) | it's ᵛnot a °bit of ᵛgood | ᵛmooching aᵥbout | and ᵛmoaning | and °saying ₐ ⁻this ᵥweather | ⁻what a ᵥclimate ₐ and °so on | °this is ↑ᵛ (LIBMSECGPT05: 009)

The percentages given above suggest that, nominal finite and infinitival clauses extrapose more freely than gerundials (Collins 1994: 11). The fact that, like noun phrases, *-ing* clauses are generally resistant to being extraposed confirms that the latter are more highly nominalised than finite or infinitival clauses (they also invert more readily with the operator in interrogatives and can take a possessive expression as a Subject). Quirk et al. (1985: 1393) claim that gerundial extraposed clauses are uncommon outside informal speech and Huddleston (1984: 452) remarks that they are more acceptable when both the *-ing* clause and the matrix clause are relatively short, which is the case of the tokens found in LIBMSEC: the lexical density, i.e. proportion of content words, of their Themes and Rhemes is 3.5–7, respectively.

Subject extraposed infinitival clauses in LIBMSEC are normally introduced by to (96%) (e.g. (198) above) *and occasionally by for* (4%) (e.g. (200) below)[117]:

(200) I you °see ˋthey worked at the °Hotel ᵥHilton I °and it was ˋin their ᵛinterests I for them to ˋlearn °English I so the ˋcompany ᵛsponsored them I to _come I and have _lessons with ᵥme I ᵥso I I (LIBMSECJ06: 102)

As to *the matrix predicate*, it generally shows the *Subject-Predicator-Subject Complement pattern* (71%), with the Complement most commonly realized as an AdjG (54%), as in (201a), and less often as a NG (37%), as in (201b), or as an AdvG (9%) as (201c):

(201) a. [change of speaker: Kevin Geary] ʹwell I our reʹview I is ˉalmost comᵥplete ᵢnow I but it's ˉreally I only °right and ᵥproper I that the ˉold °year I should go _out with a ˋbang I and °heavyweight ʹboxing I (LIBMSECFPT04: 286)
b. I it's a ᵛuseful re°minder I that ᵛsome °scientists I °find _Don ʹCupitt I °unscienᵥtific I the deˉbate I goes ᵥon I (LIBMSECAPT01: 77)
c. I it was eʹnough I to exˉpose the ᵥcrisis I in the ˋrelevance of ˋart I ↓howʹever I °Dada ˉdid put _forward _some I °positive proˋposals I (LIBMSECDPT1: 119)

The second most common type of extraposed pattern (20%) is *Subject-Predicator* (the predicator being passive (6.7%) or active (93.3%), e.g. (202a) and (202b), the latter being occasionally modified by an Adjunct).

(202) a. I ↑it's ˋbeen °widely suᵥggested °here I that the °great imˋbalance in ᵛthis ex°change I °might have ˋprompted the °Beirut ᵢhijackers I into ᵛthinking I they could ᵥforce °Israel I into reᵢleasing I _more °Arab ᵢprisoners I (LIBMSECPT04: 041)
b. lˋeastern block ˋinfluence inᵛside UNESCO I is now ˉtoo ˋgreat I ↓the _government beˉlieves I and reʹform from in°side is imˋpossible I so it ˋseems the °widespread ᵛpressure to stay in I has been reᵢsisted I (LIBMSECBPT03: 087)

In this type non-extraposed counterparts are normally not available (*?That the great imbalance in this exchange might have prompted the Beirut hijackers into thinking they could force Israel into releasing more Arab prisoners* has been widely suggested; *That widespread pressure to stay in has been resisted* seems).

The third pattern is *Subject-Predicator-Object/Complement* (5%), as in (203), where a Range is acting as Complement), and the fourth is *Subject-Predicator-Indirect Object* (3%), as in (204):

(203) | the °Nova °Park E⃮lysee in ᵛParis | °costs ⁻three ₍thousand | °nine hundred _pounds | a ₍day | ⃮whereas it ᵛonly °costs | °six hundred and °fifteen ↑⃮dollars a °day | to °stay in the ⃮world's most ex°pensive ᵛhospital | °needless to °say in °Cali⃮fornia | (LIBMSECFPT03: 079)

(204) | it was ⃮then pointed ᵛout to the °officer | by a ᵥFrench °journalist | that the Al⃮gerian ᵥwar was °lost in ⃮Paris | ⃮not in Al₍giers | (LIBMSECAPT09: 075)

Two reasons suggest themselves for the infrequency of these last two types of extrapositions. First, *the matrix predicates displaying patterns three and four* are normally, though not always (e.g. *costs* in (198) above), *of a dynamic*, rather than of a stative, nature, and so *they are more likely to favour animate non-verbal Subjects than clausal* (especially finite) *ones*, the latter being the typical Subject of *It*-Subject extrapositions. The second reason is the effect of the principles of EW and/or EF. The predicates associated with these two patterns, i.e. material or verbal, are normally "heavier" and more informative than those in the first two patterns, i.e. relational or mental, and therefore the pressure for extraposition is weaker.

Finally, moving on to the extraposed clause itself, as already mentioned earlier in this section, it always acts as the Subject of the main clause and so collaborates in displaying an unmarked mood pattern in prototypical extrapositions. However, *there also exist some peripheral instances of marked Subject extrapositions* in LIBMSEC (10.5%), i.e. extrapositions with fronted topical Themes. In some cases these result from the presence of a β Theme (i.e. a dependent clause preceding the dominant clause of the extraposed construction) (33%), as in (205a), or from the fronting of an Adjunct before the dummy Subject *It* (67%), as in (205b), where *neither*, at the same time, triggers the phenomenon of Subject/Process inversion:

(205) a. | but al↑⁻though °Fine _Gael and _Labour | ᵛhave lost °ground to the oppo°sition | it's ↑⁻far from ₍clear | that _Fianna °Fail would ₍sweep the ᵥboard | if it were _called to⃮morrow |(LIBMSECBPT02: 138–41)

b. | °neither in Hong ₍Kong | nor °anywhere ⃮else | does it ⁻make _sense to ᵛspecify | as an ⁻aim of ₍policy | ⁻on the ₍basis of ⁻soap-ope₍ratic ⁻intu₍ition a₍lone | a par°ticular ₍ratio of do⁻mestic pro°duction | to ⁻total con₍sumption | (LIBMSECCPT01: 240–3)

7.4.2.2 *Discourse function*

Extraposition is undoubtedly motivated primarily by the principles of EW, EF and FSP, but few have commented on their thematic prominence, that is to say, the complementary pressure to front expressions conveying a range of objective modalities expressing (a) judgements: fascinating, true, clear, etc; (b) deontic conditions: better, necessary, desirable, etc; (c) potentiality: possible, impossible, etc; case: etc.; (d) ease, difficult, hard, etc; or (e) usuality: customary, usual, common, etc.). Thus, while the principles of EF, EW and the FSP explain the end-positioning of material in extrapositions, thematic prominence accounts for their initialisations, both being "urgent tasks" in these constructions. The fact that in PresE Subject clauses tend to be moved to the right reflects two things: (a) a strong tendency to avoid long units at the beginning of clauses (i.e. EWP); and (b) a preference for the "Given-before-New" ordering of information (i.e. FSPP). This tendencies are attested by my findings in LIBMSEC in that:

a. extraposed clauses are "heavier" (i.e. have a higher lexical density, cf. Francis 1989a, Collins 1984) than dominant predicates (8.6 vs. 3.6);
b. there is a more even distribution of weight between the rankshifted and the dominant predicate in non-extraposed sentences;
c. dominant predicates are generally heavier in non-extraposed than in extraposed constructions;
d. clauses with clausal Subject in initial position followed by a comparatively light matrix predicate are disfavoured.

In addition to the EWP, extrapositions in LIBMSEC reflect the FSPP, that is, a Given-before-New array of information. Informatively speaking, in most cases the newsworthy bit of information is placed in the extraposed clause, that is, within the Rheme1 of the clause complex and thus is marked as New, getting unmarked focal stress. As an example consider (206) below:

(206) | it's °quite ′likely | that a`nother old °timer | the Prime ′Minister | Mr `Tikhanov | will re_tire ,soon | and be re,placed | by a °young ′technocrat | ↑with the _Gorbachev ,style | the `phrase that ,struck °me with ˇmost °force | in his °recent ′speech | was `when he was °talking a°bout the ¯need | for a °psychoˇlogical °change | from _top to ,bottom | in _Soviet so,ciety | and he ˇpushed this °thought a°gain this °week | when he ′called | the °heads of °all the state ˇmedia °organi°sations | °in for a `pep talk | it was `their ˇjob he °said | to ex`pose in,adequacies in the ′system | by °changing _people's per,ceptions | (LIBMSECAPT11: 025–40)

In (206) above the thematic matrix clause "it's quite likely" is informatively poor as compared with the information coded in the rhematic extraposed clause, where it is announced that the current Prime Minister of the Soviet Union, Mr. Tikhanov (expressed by a definite proper noun whose referent is contextually inferrable), may be replaced by a young technocrat, who is presented as New (indefinite expression with focal stress) and whose referent was up to that point in discourse New, to become Topic over the subsequent discourse span. In contrast, when the Theme2–Rheme2 pattern of a Subject rankshifted clause in a clause complex encodes recoverable information the tendency is for it to remain in initial position, rather than to be extraposed to the rhematic slot. Importantly enough, however, it seems that the newness of extraposed clauses does not reside in the individual informative status of one particular constituent, but rather in the structure itself, that is to say, in the predicative link established between the Theme1 and the Rheme1 of the construct. This link usually conveys unrecoverable, or new, information, while the referents of the participants and circumstances of Extrapositions themselves are often presented as recoverable (i.e. realized by definite, deictic or pronominal forms, especially in infinitival clauses).

It only remains to analyse the discourse relevance, if any, of the thematic matrix clause in Subject Extrapositions. My findings in LIBMSEC confirm my prediction that, *as instances of special Theme constructions, Subject extrapositions code some sort of interpersonal meaning*. The clausal Theme of Subject extrapositions normally seeks the communicative effect of *enabling speakers to express an "objectified", or depersonalised, modality or modulation* (they were introduced by impersonal *it*) on the ensuing Rheme and/or discourse. Indeed, LIBMSEC speakers choose extrapositions in two capacities:

a. in 15% of all cases, to *project some meaning or wording in order to avoid an unqualified claim* (e.g. *it seems that...*) or to ascribe to an unspecified source the responsibility for an assertion (e.g. *it is said that...*);
b. in the remaining 85%, *to thematise their camera angle*, or *point of view*, along different values of typically *modality*, as in the instances under (i) below, or less commonly of *modulation*, the tokens listed under (ii):
    i.   *modality* (57%), when assessing the likelihood or usuality of an event or when predicating the ease or difficulty of an action, as in:
         1. ± *possible* (32%):
         (207) | the ˈstudents are ˈreally at | an ˈall-time ˈlow | and it's ˈvery ˈdifficult to ˈmotivate them | ˇinto | into ˌstudies aˈgain | (LIBMSECJPT06: 273)
         2. ± *probable* (24%)
         (208) | ↑it may _well ˈbe | that ˉoil and ˌgas | will be ˈso ˚much ˈmore ˚valuable in the ˌfuture | even aˇllowing | for the ˌinterest ˚factor | that ˚has to be ˌtaken into aˌccount | ˌin such ˚calcuˌlations | ↑that _governments | should

\'limit pro°duction ᵛnow | and °possibly ᵥalso en°courage \'imports |(LIBMSECCPT01: 425)

3.   ± *certain* (44%)

(209) | it's been _taken for \'granted | what\'ever the ⬆\'party in ⁻office | ⬇that the ⁻Secretary of State for ⁾Energy | \'or in\'deed the ⁻Cabinet it\'self | must de⁻termine the _size | of the ⁻nuclear power ⁾programme | the _choice of re⁾actor | ⁻and the appropriate ᵥstructure | for the ⁻nuclear ᵥindustry | (LIBMSECCPT01: 117)

ii.   *modulation* (23%), when imposing a requisite or asserting the desirability of an action, as in:

1.   ± *desirable* (92%)

(210) | it's just a \'pity | °Greg ᵛNorman | doesn't ᵥqualify | [change of speaker: Kevin Geary] (LIBMSECFPT04: 142)

2.   ± *required* (8%)

(211) | but it was \'part of the Muslim ⁻law _there that the ⁻women | _wore | °those | ⁻things to cover them_selves | (LIBMSECJPT06: 363–4)

In addition, in LIBMSEC *matrix predicates of Subject extrapositions displaying the patterns Subject-Predicator and Subject-Predicator-Complement* normally involve some sort of *projection or modulation of finite extraposed clauses*. Generally, the latter express facts, and so their factual nature make them liable to be projected or judged. In turn, when these two matrix predicate patterns extrapose infinitival clauses, they normally concern different values of thematic modality, as in (206) above. This result fits well with the action-like nature of infinitives, since degrees of possibility, probability or certainty are congruently applied to actions, rather than to facts. Likewise, the findings corroborate Mair's (1990: 25) claim that infinitival Subject clauses are only extraposed by predicates expressing some physical process, rather than by those used to judge the truth or likelihood of specific propositions or events, which would rather extrapose fact-like finite clauses.

Summarising, the results indicate that *Subject extrapositions act in two capacities: an objective and a subjective one*. On the one hand, they can serve the semantic role of "objectifying" a modality, that is to say, they are used as a way of either averting the responsibility for an assertion or of claiming objective necessity or certainty for what in fact could be regarded a matter of opinion. And, on the other hand, Subject extrapositions fulfil the communicative role of *foregrounding the modal expression thematically, by placing it in a clause superordinate to, and preceding, that expressing the rhematic and newsworthy proposition*. The soundness of suggesting this objective and subjective usage for this type of special constructions is corroborated *by the classes of Themes they tend to co-occur with in* LIBMSEC *and* by *their distribution across the different text types.* When used *objectively*, Subject Extrapositions have *a tendency to involve just topical Themes* (66%), or, less frequently (34%), EMTs concerning logico-conjunctive Themes (28% Structural, 5.7% Conjunctive Adjuncts and 1.9% Continuatives). Only *10% co-occur with interpersonal* Themes (4% modal Adjuncts, 6% Vocatives), *which are used to reinforce the "subjective" orientation of some extrapositions.*

In addition, *Subject extrapositions appear mainly in reconstructive texts* (42.9%). Some of these texts *are in principle fairly objective*, such as some (A) Commentaries (17.1%) or (B) News reports (13.3%), *but others more subjective*, as in (G) Fiction (12.4%) (and also some (A) Commentaries). It can be argued that Subject extrapositions are popular in reconstructive texts because they allow news readers to move away from any responsibility for what they were reporting, whereas commentators and fictional characters use them to foreground their perspective on the reality they are monitoring. This is not the case of constructive texts, where lecturers or financial columnists, for example, are devoted to transmitting their professional expertise to their audiences as objectively as possible. Yet, not infrequently (33%), even in this textual type Subject Extrapositions come in handy to project and thus depersonalise some general statement, hope, feelings, etc. and/or to avoid an unqualified claim, as in (C, D) Lecture (17.1%), (F) Magazine (15.2%) and (E) Religious Broadcasts (1%). The same rationale explains the rather frequent use of Subject extrapositions in (J) Dialogue (23.8%). But no less important is the speaker's intention to highlight the modulation and/or modalisation of facts and acts as the relevant concern of her/his collaborative addressee.

In conclusion, Subject-extrapositions constitute a semantic region where the three metafunctions overlap, the textual, the ideational and the interpersonal. Crucially, as Downing (1986: 174) observes, these constructions "are not the speaker's comments on the process but form part of the content of the clause itself", and for this reason Whittaker (1995: 112) suggests that Subject-extrapositions should be called *Evaluative Ideational Themes.*

7.4.3 *Inversions*

Inversions (e.g. *Here is the teapot that the duke has given to my aunt*), prototypically displaying the features [–EXTERN, –COREF, –in./fin. PAUSE, +FUNCT, –NOM, –PRED, –DUM], are the third group in terms of frequency of special thematic construction found in the LIBMSEC. They totalled 79 tokens, representing

18% of the special Themes and 1.9% of the overall amount of syntactic Themes classified in this analysis.

7.4.3.1 *Formal structure and frequencies in* LIBMSEC

The phenomenon of inversion is understood very broadly here. The definition follows Green (1982: 120), who characterises inversions as "those declarative constructions where the subject follows part or all of its verb phrase" (Bolinger 1977; Dorgeloh 1997). The description covers *full inversions* (FIs) and *Subject-Auxiliary inversions* (SAIs), which, besides involving the fronting of a constituent X and thereby becoming a marked Theme in terms of Mood, also trigger the placement of the Subject in postverbal position, either after the main verb (Predicator), in the case of FIs, or after an auxiliary (Finite), in the case of SAIs. Though in many respects different, FI and SAI are here treated jointly on the assumption that both represent *marked* alternatives to the basic PresE CWO and/or preposing variants.[118] For, with a few exceptions, the element placed clause-initially could canonically stand elsewhere in the clause.

LIBMSEC contains both inversion types, amounting to 86%, FIs, and 14%, SAIs, which renders *SAI as the marked type*. In our corpus, SAIs appear in the following environments:

a. after *negative* and *restrictive adverbials* such as *only*, *hardly*, *never*, as well as after negative Direct Object preposing (NEGSAI) (72%), as in:

(212) a. | ⁻only when the government in'sisted | on ⁻all Sri Lankans having ˇvisas | be'fore arriving in ˇBritain | did the ˬmessage | be_gin to sink ˋin | (LIBMSECAPT01: 062)
b. | ⁻Youthˏaid | I can a'ssure you | is a ˇvery °tightly °run | ˋcharity | it never °wastes a ˋpenny | it gets _nothing from ˏgovernment | °nor would it ˋwant to | (LIBMSECKPT01: 068)

b. *Pro-SAI*, introduced by such pro-forms as *so*, *such*, *thus* (13.5%), as in:

(213) | yet ⁻so for _us would ⁻beauty ˋstill be °meaningless | ⁻mortal and ˏmeaningless | (LIBMSECHPT04: 051)

c. in counterfactual *conditional clauses* after suppressed "if" (CONDSAI) (11.5%),[119] as in:

(214) | had I ˇnot spoken any °Arabic | then their °attitude towards this °strange ˇforeign woman | ˋmight have been totally ˋdifferent | (LIBMSECJ06PT04: 081)

d. inversion in *correlative constructions* in clauses linked by e.g. *so/such ...that, more/-er/less... than* (CORR-SAI) (3%) (Quirk et al. 1985: 999ff.) as in:

(215) | °such is the in⁻cestuous \nature | of Na°mibian ᵥpolitics | *and* °so a\ppar-ent | the ⁻self-im\portance | of °some of its pracᵥtitioners | that ⁻those inᵛvolved in the new °government | \obviously °find it ᵥdifficult | to °rise aᵛbove | the °level of _small town ᵥpolitics | (LIBMSECAPT09: 044)

Alternatively, FIs display the following patterns:

a. inversion *after preposed quote* (QFI) (47%),[120] as in:

(216) | ↑\this underᵛstanding say the °scientists | ᵛis in °fact | °unscien\tific | ↓and the °reason 'is they °say | that ᵛnatural laws | do ᵛnot °cause | or dic_tate e\vents | (LIBMSECAPT01: 059)

b. inversion after (AdvG, PP) *spatio-directio-temporal expressions* (41%), comprising full lexical AdvGs/PPs, as in (212), here classified as either *lexical-presentative* or *lexical-predicative FIs*, and *deictics* (e.g. *there, next, first and then*, etc.), referred to as *deictic presentative FIs*, e.g.:

(217) a. | be⁻hind Shaᵛron | is the Is_raeli \government | (LIBMSECAPT03: 045)
b. | and be⁻neath her _breast | \cherishes the di⁻vine \life | (LIBMSECHPT04: 059)
c. | on the ⁻walls were inter_spersed 'large \placards | 'bearing \slogans | (LIBMSECDPT01: 049)
d. | ↑beᵛfore him | will be _gathered ⁻all the ᵥnations | and he will \separate them | 'one from a\nother | as a ᵥshepherd | ᵛseparates | a \sheep from the \goats | (LIBMSECEPT01: 031)

(218) a. | ↑here's a ᵥrecent illu'stration | from the ⱼEuropean Co⫽mmission | in \Brussels | (LIBMSECCPT01: 022)
b. |\here's a good ⱼjob | ⁻Saudi A\rabia| (LIBMSECJPT06: 006)

c. inversion after (*past/present*) *participles* (VPFI) (6%), as in (219):

(219) | ᵛcoupled with °this | is the ᵛmilitary °effort | °aimed at de\stroying °SWAPO's °armed ⱼwing | and ᵛforcing the °organi°sation | to °come to the neᵥgotiating °table | as °just aᵛnother | Na_mibian ᵥparty | (LIBMSECAPT09: 064)

d. inversion after *preposed AdjGs* (AdjFI) (3%), as in (220):

(220) | more imᵛportant how°ever | is that the ⁻biblical _writers themᵛselves | ⁻thought that e_vents that ᵛfollowed natural °laws | could ⁻still be re_garded as mi\raculous | (LIBMSECAPT01: 047–49)

In PresE the various inversion types differ from each other in *their degree of grammaticalisation*. Although there exist substantial differences among some of them (especially among *Adv-, PP- and Adj-Is*), a detailed analysis of the various FI types, as opposed to the SAI subtypes, lies beyond the scope of this investigation. For our purposes it suffices to say that SAI types occur obligatorily with semantically heavy or affective constituents, revealing themselves as grammaticalised prominence or affect-marking constructions. In the case of constituents optionally followed by SAI, a special meaning effect is created, i.e., additional prominence is given to them, by virtue of being followed by inversion. The issue of the degree of grammaticalisation of the different inversion types will be taken up again in Section 7.4.3.2, when discussing their discourse function and relationships with corresponding CWO counterparts.

Our results report inversions as normally occurring *in declarative paratactic complex clauses of the projecting type (quotes)* (62%) or *in simple clauses* (21.5%), rather than in hypotactically complex (7.6%), rankshifted (6.3%) or dependent (2.5%) clauses. Besides both FIs and SAIs are prone to concern *active*, rather than passive, processes (98.7% vs. 1.3%) and to have *simple* vs. complex (89.9% vs. 9.1%) and *non-extended multiple Themes* (74.7% vs. 25.3%).

These findings show that *owing to its "expressive syntax" inversion is a highly constrained thematic choice which is, if not strictly excluded from embedded clauses, a predominantly declarative main clause phenomenon*. Further symptoms of their expressive syntax are the absence of: (a) compound tenses in inversions, which also "testifies to the "Presentative" or initiating nature of these constructions" (Stein 1995: 138); (b) transitive verbs, which "have too much content" (Schmidt 1980: 295) themselves; and (c) internal causal adverbial clauses.

A further feature obtained is the tendency of inversions to concern *verbal* and *relational* processes, predominating over material or mental ones (60.8% and 16.5% vs. 13.9% and 8.9%, respectively). The reason is that verbal processes often trigger QFIs, and relational processes most instances of SAIs and the remaining FIs, possibly with the exception of NEGSAI, CONDSAI, and directional FIs, which have a higher proportion of material and mental processes. As a corollary, the Themes of LIBMSEC inversions tend to be Direct C./Verbiages (57%), or circumstantial Adjuncts (33%). The former are normally realized by clauses, thematising a participant's whole turn in a conversation. But not infrequently, thematic Direct C./Verbiages just consist of projected logico-conjunctive Themes (i.e. continuatives and/or conjunctive Adjuncts) and/or Vocatives, such as e.g. *well, Ah!, Oh dear, Noil*, but they tend to be developed after the main reporting clause. The excerpts in (221) below include examples of each subtype of Direct C./Verbiages Themes in QFIs:

(221) a. |↑you °simply °have to be ˰ °philo\sophical a°bout it ˰ said °Mr °Henshaw | ⁻rubbing the ₍window | and re⁻garding | a ⁻rural ₍landscape | diᵛssolved | in ₍rain | (LIBMSECGPT05: 006)
b. | pre₍cisely ˰ said °Mr °Henshaw | that's e⁻xactly what I ₍mean | the \happiest \days of their ⁻lives | and they just ⁻roll ₍over | (LIBMSECGPT05: 056)
c. | \Noil | said the little °girl | his ⁻name is ᵥNoil | (LIBMSECGPT02: 073)

Circumstantial Adjuncts, on the other hand, realized by AdvGs or PPs, have an overwhelming tendency to express *place* (93.5%), as in (222a) below, less frequently time (3.5%), as in (222b), and only residually, angle (3%), as in (213) above. This confirms the hypothesis that adverbials of place in general have higher frequencies as specifications than adverbials of time (Firbas 1979: 43).

(222) a. | above the _slogan | ⁻Dada ist _politisch | was ⁻George °Grosz' | _Germany | a °winter's \tale | (LIBMSECDPT01: 051)
b. | ⁻only when the government in\sisted | on ⁻all Sri Lankans having \visas | be\fore arriving in ᵛBritain | did the ᵥmessage | be_gin to sink \in | (LIBMSECAPT01: 062)

The more peripheral cases are VPFIs (8%), as in (223):

(223) a. | ↑⁻stuck onto the _head is a \tape-°measure | sug°gesting that ⁻man | the ⁻measure of ⁻all ₍things | is ⁻now him⁻self re₍duced | to a ₍cypher | (LIBMSECDPT01: 188)
b. | ⁻shut again till ₍April | ⁻stands her little ₍hutment | ⁻peeping over _daisies | ⁻Michaelmas and ⁻mauve | ⁻lock'd is the ᵥElsan | in its ⁻brick a₍butment | ⁻lock'd the little ₍pantry | ⁻dead the little ₍stove | (LIBMSECHPT01: 011–12)

In sum, whatever the pattern they belong to, or whatever the structure, the function and the class of Theme, both FIs and SAIs involve a three-fold process:

a. the fronting, or thematisation, of a constituent different from the expected one in each Mood/Transitivity pattern (usually in declaratives);
b. the postverbal placement of the Subject participant;
c. an emphatic arrangement of information.

Section 7.4.3.2 shows that these three features of inversions trigger specific discourse effects limiting the use of these constructions to specific discourse co(n)texts.

7.4.3.2 *Discourse function*

We shall see that the *discourse function of inversions results from the combination of four factors*: (a) their *presentative function*; (b) their *behaviour as information-packaging devices*, thereby endowed with *a linking function*; (c) their *intonational Focus-* and *discourse focus-marking effect*, in accordance with the principles of EW, EF and FSP; and (d) their role as *markers of subjectivity and discourse structure*.

Behind this four-fold functionality lies the natural/cognitive prominence of the Theme zone, as inversions share with other special constructions the highlighting of initially placed constituents in non-canonical sequences, albeit with not exactly the same discourse meaning. While existential-*there* constructions constitute a more freely available and grammaticalised presentative device than inversions, preposings are much more local in their effect; and left-detachments are, like FIs and SAIs, concerned with reference and the negotiation of topic entities in discourse, but they reveal themselves as basically conversational strategies.

Our results in LIBMSEC report that most inversions are tied up to particular discourse conditions provided by: (a) mainly formal *reconstructive texts*, as shown by the percentages *Fiction* (60.8%), Lecture (13.9%), Commentaries (11.4%), (B) News Broadcasts (6.3%), Dialogue (3.8%), Poetry (1.3%) and Religious Broadcasts (1.3%); and (b) *circumstances of displacement*, i.e. a type of discourse in which the consciousness of language producers and receivers focuses on experience that is *displaced from* the immediate environment of the speaker's mind. The effect is normally one of subjective topic construal whereby a point of reference is created, permitting the speaker to stay out of the text and to nonetheless adopt a perspective from within it (Section 6.3.2.2).

Birner (1994: 234) characterises the informational motivation of inversions in sufficiently general terms to cover all the instances of recognised here as follows:

> an information-packaging mechanism, allowing the presentation of relatively familiar information before a comparatively unfamiliar logical subject.

Let us first consider the "presentational" role of the various inversion types implied in Birner's definition. QFI remains an optional strategy of presentation because the QFI pattern, Quotation^Process^Subject, has a very close equivalent, the preposed pattern Quotation^Subject^Process. The choice seems to depend on the relative informativeness and weight of the final element. Subjects normally precede processes when they are realized by pro-forms, whereas the inverted type is preferred when Subjects are full lexical forms, whether or not qualified by hypotactic and/or paratactic extensions or elaborations. But both patterns seek the same communicative effect. Under conditions of displacement, mostly in Fiction, QFIs and their preposed counterparts present or stage changes from the spatio-temporal setting of the narration to the spatio-temporal framework of the quote, in order to introduce speech-act participants (or their views) directly and/or insert relevant background information about them. By resorting to the direct or free indirect speech effect of preposed quotes, narrators construe the discourse ground or point of reference subjectively. As a result, the speaker-narrator remains in the background as a mere reporter, to empathise with the participants, giving the impression that it is the participants themselves that interact directly or express their own perspectives on discourse, all to the overall effect of real-time, real-world vividness. Consider (224) as an example:

(224) | at ᵛplaytime | the ⁻little ₍girl | and the ₍lion | went °into the ᵛplayground |
⁻all the ₋children | stopped ₍playing | to ᵛstare at the ₍lion | ᵛthen they °went on ᵛplaying a°gain | the ⁻little ₍girl | ⁻stood in a ₍corner of the ₍playground | with the ᵛlion | be₍side her|
ᵛwhy don't we ₋play	like the ᵛothers ₎ the °lion °asked
the ⁻little ₋girl ₋said	I don't ᵛlike ₍playing	be°cause some of the ᵛbig boys	are so ᵛbig	and ₍rough	they ⁻knock you ᵛover	without ᵛmeaning to.
the ₍lion	ᵛgrowled ᵛ| they °wouldn't knock ᴵᵛme over ₍₎ he °said.
there's ⁻one ₍big ᵛboy	the ᵛvery ₍biggest ₎ said the ᵛlittle °girl	his ᵛname is °Jack ₍Tall	he ⁻knocks me ₍over	on ᵛpurpose'.
°which is ₍he ₎ said the °lion	⁻point him ₍out to °me.
the ⁻little ₍girl	ᵛpointed °out Jack ₍Tall	to the ₍lion.
₍ah ₎ said the °lion	so ᵛthat's °Jack °Tall	(LIBMSECGPT02)

Now, let us turn to the presentative prototype of FI, the construction after *deictic adverbs*, from which the mechanism of inversion following *fully specified lexical constituents is functionally derived*. There has been enough specialisation to warrant recognising *deictic presentational FI as constituting a semi-grammaticalised construction*. The deictic hasn't been "subjectivalised" as much as existential-*there*, for example. It can't invert (e.g. *Here is your change* vs. **Is here your change?*), or act as Subject in non-finite clauses (e.g. **I'd like here to be your change*), and yet it can enter into agreement with the verb in informal usage (e.g. *Here's your tickets*). When the post-verbal NP is a case-marked pronoun it may be accusative (e.g. *Here's me on the mountain*), suggesting that it is the deictic element that functions as Subject.

A sign of the not-fully-grammaticalised nature of the deictic presentative FIs is that often there are no real truth-conditional equivalents with comparable CWO patterns, as shown by the semantic difference between examples like *Here comes the bus* and *The bus comes here*, or *There goes John* and *John goes there*, or those cases in which there is no acceptable non-presentational alternant (e.g. *There goes my last opportunity to meet her* **My last opportunity to meet her goes there*).

This suggests that the meaning of the deictic adverbs in FIs has been grammaticalised into a *textual metaphor* (of the originally situational presentative prototype), thereby expressing different locations (*textual* vs. *situational, internal/endophoric* vs. *external/exophoric*, Halliday & Hasan 1976: 241) or different truth-conditions than a corresponding CWO clause.

Indeed, it is the *external-internal opposition* in combination with the contrast between a *presentative scale* vs. a *quality scale* reading of the predication, to use CD terminology (Section 3.2.3, (51) and (52)), that makes the truth-conditional effect of FIs following deictic adverbs, in opposition to adverbs in final position, more explicit. Where both orderings are grammatical, the adverbs in fact refer to different locations. Although also depending on the location of the speaker, *CWO spatio-temporal deictics* perform an objectively given, *external* or *situation-based*, reference, specifying a physical location or a property belonging to the outside world. In other words, they get a *quality scale reading* whereby "the adverbial element performs the dynamic function of expressing a specification [...]; [...] [it] completes the development of the communication within the sentence" (Firbas 1986: 48f.), attributing to the Subject a (transient) quality, with the adverb as a specification and at the same time the unmarked sentence Focus (in unmarked conditions).

By contrast, *deictic presentative FIs* express speaker-based discourse organisation and typically produce a meaning of *internal deixis* that is anchored within the text or within the speech event itself as a "shared perceptual field", and therefore is subjectively given. The presentative nature of these constructions lies in that the adverbial starting points performing the dynamic function of expressing the setting (Firbas 1986: 48). Summarising, *deictic FIs render a presentational scale reading*. They constitute a bi-focal construct whereby a scene is set, conveying an instruction to retrieve from elsewhere (situational or textual context) the information for locating discourse entities, and a discourse entity is subsequently introduced (Halliday & Hasan 1976; Firbas 1986). The intention is to raise expectations for subsequent discourse: the presentative construction, by virtue of introducing an entity by (subjective) reference to the co(n)text itself, the Subject, which has also not been in discourse focus before, becomes the new Focus and is thereby put "onstage", suggesting some higher-level topical status, raising expectations of further elaboration in the subsequent discourse. As an illustration of these capacities of deictic FIs, behold (225) and (226), containing instances of *here* and *there*:

(225) a. | here's the _news °read by David \Geary | (LIBMSECBPT03: 005) (vs. CWO *David Geary is here*)

b. ⁻here for eˌxample | is the ˋthen °President of the U_nited ˌStates | ʹRichard ˌNixon | in an A⁻ddress to the ˌNation | in Noˋvember °19°7ˇ3 | ⁻launching the ˌprogramme | ˌknown | as _Project Indeˋpendence | (LIBMSECCPT01: 265) (vs. CWO ?*The then president..., for example, is here*)

c. | also ˌhere in its ˌplace | on the ⁻DIYE ˌstage | is ˌMr Micawber's diˋchotomy | (LIBMSECCPT01: 166) (vs. CWO *Mr Micawber's dichotomy is also here...*)

(226) and ˇthere | on the ˌtable | where my ˇnewspaper had been | was ˌmy ˌpacket of ˋbiscuits | (LIBMSECGPT03: 046–47) (vs. CWO *And my packet of biscuits was there ...*)

After locative, directional, or temporal adverbials *lexical presentative FIs* work in a similar way. But, while the deictic adverbs followed by FI must be interpreted relative to the point in discourse at which they occur, the Themes of presentative lexical FIs in fact *construct a new setting* as a physical stage or *ground* (Drubig 1988: 81), typically by specifying a new location in relation to the previous ground. Several examples are in (227):

(227) | ↑⁻turn ˌnow | to the °first ˋplate | the ˇphotograph | is a ⁻partial ˌview | of the ⁻First Inter_national °Dada ˋFair |[...] ↑a⁻mong the _hundred and °seventy-four exˋhibits | ˋlisted in the ˇcatalogue | ⁻were | °photomon'tage | ˌphoto°graphs | reʹliefs | ʹcollage | ʹpaintings | conʹstructions | ʹdolls and ˌdummies | on the ⁻walls were inter_spersed °large ˋplacards | °bearing ˋslogans | ↑in ⁻plate ˌone | you can see ⁻two °large ˌpaintings on the °walls | ˋboth now ˋlost | a⁻bove the _slogan | ⁻Dada ist _politisch | was ⁻George °Grosz' | _Germany | a °winter's ˋtale | ↑⁻Grosz had ˇfinished this | in °nineteen-nineˌteen | and ˇlater | ⁻wrote in his autobiˌography | ↑my _mood was °turned into a ⁻large po°litical ˌpicture | ↑in the ˌcentre _sat the e⁻ternal _German ˋbourgeois | ˋfat and ˋfearful | at his ⁻slightly °wobbly ˌtable | beʹlow | [...]| ⁻covering the _head of the ˇleft-hand °war cripple | is a ˋcollage °painting by ⁻Grosz | ⁻called re⁻member °uncle ˌAugust | (LIBMSECDPT01: 045–160)

The extract in (227) describes Plate 1, a photograph of a partial view of the First International Dada Fair in 1920. It contains seven FIs, whereby the addressee is invited to start from the introductory lexical information as the physical stage or the ground, and then something is brought figuratively before her/his eyes: different sections of the photograph, viz. the catalogue, the walls, the overall plate, the section that is above the slogan "Dada ist politisch", and the centre and lower part of the picture. The effect is one of "staged activity" (Bolinger 1977: 94), which produces rather drastic changes in perspective, even if all refer to one and the same Plate.

Some of the FIs included in (222) and (212a–c) above, however, could be regarded as "squishy" transitions between the *lexical presentative* and *lexical predicative types*. The former are more *verbal-dynamic*, involving *real frames of reference* (directions and spatio-temporal locations), while the latter are more *adjectival-static* in kind, generally used to *anchor predicates* (properties). In other words, *predicative* lexical FIs combine an existential scale reading with a statement inherently ascriptive in kind, in which a quality or property is specified by the rhematic predication attributed to the Subject. The token of AdjFI in (220) above, now reproduced as (228a) along with (228b), and those of VPFIs reproduced in (218) and (223) above, now included in (229), could be taken as more prototypical instances of the lexical predicative FI, where in addition to the use of static verb or copular *be*, as Dorgeloh (1997: 81) puts it:

> there is a combined effect of complex lexical information provided by the PP [...] and of apparent absence of discourse familiarity [...] and most clearly so in cases of abstract, at best non-locative, meaning [...].

(228) a. | more imᵛportant how°ever | is that the ⁻biblical _writers themᵛselves | ⁻thought that e_vents that ᵛfollowed natural °laws | could ⁻still be re_garded as miʳaculous | (LIBMSECAPT01: 047–49)

b. | and ⁻ louder _clang the _waves | aʻlong the ⸝coast | (LIBMSECHPT02: 35) 047–49)

(229) a. | ᵛcoupled with °this | is the ᵛmilitary °effort | °aimed at deˋstroying °SWAPO's °armed ⸝wing | and ᵛforcing the °organi°sation | to °come to the ne⸝gotiating °table | as °just aᵛnother | Na_mibian ⸝party | (LIBMSECAPT09: 064)

b. | ↑⁻stuck onto the _head is a ˋtape-°measure | sug°gesting that ⁻man | the ⁻measure of ⁻all ⸝things | is ⁻now him⁻self re⸝duced | to a ⸝cypher | (LIBMSECDPT01: 188)

c. | ⁻shut again till ⸝April | ⁻stands her little ⸝hutment | ⁻peeping over _daisies | ⁻Michaelmas and ⁻mauve | ⁻lock'd is the ⸝Elsan | in its ⁻brick a⸝butment | ⁻*lock'd* the little ⸝pantry | ⁻dead the little ⸝stove | (LIBMSECHPT01: 011–12)

The reason to classify AdjFIs and VPFIs as primarily predicative-lexical is that front-shifted AdjPs and participle forms in fact behave quite similarly. In a CWO clause containing a past participle, an agent can always be added, at least potentially, but it cannot occur if the participle is fronted; this is a clear clue that the verb in VPFI has lost part of its verbal meaning and is in principle *predicative* in kind (Svartvik 1966: 132ff.). Further support for the predicative nature of VPFIs is that, unlike their CWO counterparts, fronted present participles lack "the implicature of imperfectiveness" due to the absence of a competing preterit form, leaving a rather static, property like meaning (Ward & Birner 1992: 578).

A different lexical grounding mechanism is typically displayed by *SAIs*, involving pro-forms (PRO-SAI), correlative constructions (CORR-SAI) and NEGSAIs. This type I shall globally call the *anaphoric/cataphoric type*, following Dorgeloh (1997: 89ff.). In the prototypical anaphoric/cataphoric SAI the pro-forms followed by inversion refer back to an entire predication (e.g. *so*) or to some referent, including or excluding it from the same predication (e.g. *nor/ neither*). The result is a bi-focal construction like all other FIs, but pronominal and correlative elements construct inversions which are "deictic" in a somewhat broader sense, constituting especially close syntacticised units (Quirk et al. 1985: 1381). They convey an instruction to link sentences anaphorically or cataphorically — the majority of them with almost obligatory SAI — and/or attach particular prominence to the constituents initially placed. In the latter case, the constituents are either "inherently" prominent and are automatically followed by SAI, or they are, by means of AuxSV order, signalled to be so. Consider the tokens of anaphoric/cataphoric SAIs included in (230), to which could be added the aforementioned in (212), (213), and (215) above:

(230) a. | 'neither in Hong /Kong | nor 'anywhere \else | does it ⁻make _sense to ˅specify | as an ⁻aim of ,policy | ⁻on the ,basis of ⁻soap-ope,ratic ⁻intu,ition a,lone | a par'ticular ,ratio of do⁻mestic pro'duction | to ⁻total con\sumption | (LIBMSECCPT012: 40–043)

b. | so \not only has 'Beirut \airport this ,year | _witnessed a ⁻member of its own se˅curity staff | ˅hijacking an 'aircraft | as a \protest about low ˅pay | it's \also been the 'scene of ˅one 'hijack | ⁻where | after \posing for \photographs at the 'side of the /aircraft | the \hijackers 'blew it ⁻up | (LIBMSECAPT08: 041)

Approaching inversions now as information packaging devices, the evidence presented so far clearly shows, as noted in Birner's (1994) characterisation above, that the Subject referent does not need to be "brand new", but merely less salient/familiar than the fronted element. This is clearly the case in anaphoric/ cataphoric inversions, where the fronted element typically fulfils a connective function (Quirk et al. 1985: 1381). Similarly, unambiguously local (deictic or lexical) points of departure prototypically introduce non-salient discourse entities (though more so than the fronted deictic) and the predication corresponds to a presentative-scale reading. Not surprisingly, the verbs in this construction are "informationally light", which according to Levin & Rappaport (1994) is a requirement of (locative) inversion, thus enabling end-Focus to be readily associated with the Subject. In the absence of Subject postposing, EF would be associated, inappropriately, with the verb and the result would be, to use Quirk et al. (1985: 1379)'s words, "bathetic or misleading" (e.g. *More important are the moral objections* vs. (?) *More important the moral objections **are***). The same holds for lexical FIs and SAIs. But, interestingly, since the Themes of lexical FIs are heavier than those of the deictic type and since SAIs often constitute a grammaticalised clause linkage of complex constructions, the two types make a stronger case for the recognition of a double Focus: the marked "heavy" Themes move an informational Focus to the front (in LIBMSEC normally uttered on a high level) and at the same time, the Subject, which would not be in focus in CWO counterparts, also acquires focal status (in LIBMSEC usually with Falling tones) and is thereby put "onstage".

In this connection, Quirk et al. (1985: 1410–11) seem to suggest that the EF (end-Focus) motivation is a more important consideration for FI than the "presentational" role that it sometimes has. They compare instances of the inversion construction (e.g. *On the doorstep was a parcel* vs. *On the doorstep was my uncle*) with instances of the existential construction having a fronted locative expression (e.g. *On the doorstep there was a parcel* vs. ?*On the doorstep there was my uncle*). After contrasting the frequency of definite NPs like *my uncle*, and indefinite NPs like *a parcel*, Quirk et al. find that while the numbers are fairly balanced for inversion, with the existential construction indefinites far outweigh definites. Their conclusion is that "whereas the AVS construction without *there* is motivated by the wish to achieve end-focus, the *there*-construction has the more general "presentative" function". Our results in LIBMSEC also confirm that inversions tend to conform with the principles of EW, EF and FSP, putting heavy and informative material last. With the exception of reporting inversions, in all other subtypes Rhemes were twice as heavy as Themes, with an average lexical density of 5 vs. 2.5. And even quotations in LIBMSEC seem to generally abide by this tendency since, when reporting clauses are heavy (comprising such items as adverbs, co-ordinate verbs or clauses, mention of the addressee, etc.), quotations are normally projected after their projecting clauses, thereby contributing to increasing their weight and newsworthiness.

Here, however, I should like to demonstrate that, in order to explicate the communicative relevance of inversions, the factors of EF, EW, FSP, as well as their presentational capacity should be regarded as complementary, not in competition. To these should be added a further component that has already been mentioned: the added *subjectivity of inversions*, that is to say, *their interpersonal and textual "subjective speaker-oriented" meaning*. This *emphatic* meaning is triggered by their breaking CWO expectations, resulting in a process whereby "meanings become increasingly based in the speaker's subjective belief state/ attitude toward [...] what the speaker is talking about" (Traugott 1995: 31). It is in this sense that all inversion types can be considered as instances of subjectivisation, or subjectification.

In this line, we have already seen how inversions produce a perspective in discourse, which creates an effect of focus management in discourse. It has also been shown that inversions often provide subjective Topic construals, creating their own point of reference that reflects the viewpoint of a discourse entity (either from the co(n)text or created as a reference point), and expressing at the same time the speaker's subjectivity and his/her presence within the respective universe of discourse. This effect of displaced immediacy is typical of descriptive discourse's usually following a principle of "similarity", which Giora (1990: 303) claims to be the categorical structure of all non-narrative texts (Fiction). But in other types of discourse, inversions function as discourse markers inducing a change in focus within the discourse organisation or providing informative and evaluative background.

Thus, the occurrence of lexical FIs in the excerpt in (236) above allowed us to illustrate their *procedural* or *descriptive* use, imbued with a "eyewitness" flavour. Indeed, there we could see how FIs can be used to create a visual impact, and at the same time, they all introduce topic entities which are further treated in the following discourse; thus, the locative relations expressed in the fronted constituents are also constitutive for the structure of the entire passage. Alternatively, constrained by rigid time-slots and schedules, the inversions found in News or in constructive texts (Lectures), e.g. (218a), (225) above, follow the principle of "increasing specification": they collaborate to include the most crucial information typically at the absolute beginning, or at least at the beginning of each paragraph.

The above underscores the labour of inversions as *discourse markers*. They generally signal *major textual shifts* in contrast with the minor shifts of preposings, structuring the discourse into separate sub-parts. Either they add a temporary perspective of immediacy to the information about a scene or event from the outside world (generally in narrations such as Fiction); or they mark a digression from the mainly descriptive progression, providing informative or evaluative background (e.g. News) or initiating constitutive sub-parts of argumentation and exposition in the more interpersonal (argumentative, explanatory) discourse types (e.g. Dialogues, Commentaries, Lectures).

But, in the absence of a concrete descriptive purpose, inversions can be regarded as discourse markers with also an addressee-oriented subjectivity: they constitute instructions to perform *a change in her/his focus within the discourse organisation*. Generally speaking, FIs trigger a presentative mechanism that rests upon their exploitation of the Theme zone as a kind of localisation, and it is for this reason that they can be regarded as emblematic discourse markers (Section 6.2.2). By contrast, the various SAI types reflect an overall subjective attitude on the part of the speaker, expressing that (and how) he/she is affected by the item fronted or how s/he relates predications to each other, where an evaluating or commenting attitude is not established beforehand or would not be expected overall.

To conclude, the discourse functions so far outlined explicate the distribution of inversions across the LIBMSEC text-types. As mentioned at the beginning of this section, inversions seem to be the more linked to literary styles or to relatively vivid accounts of an event (Fiction, Poetry, Religion), in which case they normally instruct for *dynamic viewing*, creating expectations and tension that go beyond a mere focus management task performed by FI. Alternatively, inversions have also been found in text-types more interpersonal in kind, i.e. in expository and argumentative discourse (Commentaries, Dialogues, Lectures, News), in which case they generally rest on *static viewing*, representing discourse markers typical of a descriptive kind of progression within a text. In terms of the speaker roles, inversions in LIBMSEC can reflect the speaker as the architect of discourse structure and, more commonly, as the commentator on the events involved: the construction is a marker of (parts of) the argumentation and an expression of the speaker's own explanation or argumentation.

7.4.4 Left detachments

This section studies the frequencies, the formal structure and the discourse function of "left detachments"[121] in LIBMSEC (e.g. *As for that teapot, the duke has given it to my aunt*), prototypically displaying the features [+EXTERN, +COREF, +IN. PAUSE, +FUNCT, NOM, PRED, –DUM]. They amounted to 29 tokens, representing 6.6% of the special Themes and 0.7% of the overall Themes in LIBMSEC.

7.4.4.1 *Formal structure and frequencies in LIBMSEC*
Typically LDs consist of a LD Theme, i.e. a predication external topical Theme that lies outside and to the left of the performative modalities of the main predication, often appearing with no case marking, which is re-entered in the subsequent clause internal structure via pronominal reference (COREF). The key feature of LDs is therefore to contain a COREF clause-internal pro-form that is *anaphoric*, i.e. that refers back to, the extern topical Theme. This anaphoric reference involves a transition from specific to generic reference because the referent of the topical Theme is semantically more fully specified than that of the

COREF element, and so identifies the precise referential status of the latter. This characterisation reveals that the predominant feature of LDs is *semantic*, rather than syntactic: there exists a requisite of coreferentiality between a "bare" NG, i.e. an NG which is not the argument in another clause, and a "complete" clause "complete" in the sense that all the argument slots of the verbal predicate are filled (Geluykens 1992: 19).

The requisite of (+strict COREF) serves to distinguish LDs proper from constructions labelled here as *quasi-LDs*, in this study classified as instances of preposings. Although formally they resemble LDs, quasi-LDs do not display a relationship of strict coreference but one of lexical cohesion (i.e. repetition, synonymy, superordination or hyponymy), as shown in (231) below:

(231) a. °and | the ′weather | ⱽnorthern areas will have ʾbright intervals and \showers | which will be ⱽheavy in places | ʾrain in some ⱽsouthern areas will clear a°way | ↓but ¯further rain is likely to\morrow | (LIBMSECBPT03: 109–10)

b. | as to ⱽlarge states | being ¯necessarily more suʾccessful on the con°temporary economic ₍scene | ʾthis notion is hard to ʾreconcile with the ′fact | that in ⱽEurope | it's two ⱽsmall countries | ＿Sweden and ⱽSwitzerland | ʾwhich by conⱽventional tests | are ₍possibly the ₍most eco₍nomically adʾvanced | (LIBMSECCPT01: 058)

In (231a) *the weather* establishes a relationship of lexical cohesion with (i.e. it is superordinate to) *northern areas, rain,* and *but further rain*; while in (231b) *the notion* is synonymous with the extern constituent *as to large states ... scene*. But neither Q-LD can be said to contain a relationship of strict coreference since there exist no pronominal elements which might qualify as the COREF. Similar examples to (231) are supplied by some authors (e.g. Lambrecht 1994) in support of the contention that the relationship between a detached NP and the host clause is not grammatical but pragmatic (i.e. describable in terms of "aboutness", "relevance", and the like). Here instead the lack of such a grammatical relationship will lead us to exclude such examples from the construction.

Again, barred from LD status in this study are discourse sequences of the type in (232) (Geluykens 1992):

(232) A: You know Steve
B: oh yeah quite an extraordinary fellow
A: he likes beans

It is highly likely that the LD construction has evolved in the language via grammaticalisation of the discourse processes at work in such sequences (introduction of referent > acknowledgement by interlocutor > formulation of proposition) (Section 2.2.1 above), but here they will not regarded as instances of LDs (all taking place within the same speaker's turn).

Another type of sentence that does not qualify is that with a non-referential (depictive) left-positioned NP, as in:

(233)   The bastard, he's taken my chair

(233) informs us that the referent of *he* has taken the speaker's chair, and that on this account the speaker considers him to be a bastard (not **the** bastard).

COREF elements in LIBMSEC *mostly represent core arguments of the clause*, i.e. *Subject* (51.7%) or *Complement* (29%) (including Complement to prepositions), which tend to act as Agents (48.3%) or Mediums (32.4%), as in (234):

(234) a. I a °forty-year-old Pales\tinian I who'd been a \fighter °most of his \life I with a ⱽLibyan-°backed °group I o\pposing °Mr \Arafat I the ⱽone in °fact I that °helped to ⱽforce the °PLO °leader I \out of °Tripoli last ⱽyear I \he's °here I (LIBMSECAPT02: 51–52)
b. I po⁻tatoes in the _garden I but ⁻nobody to _bake *them* I ⁻fungus in the \living room I and ⁻water in the \coke I (LIBMSECHPT01: 018)

A minority of COREFs in LIBMSEC however are realized by spatio-temporal Adjuncts (19.3%), as expounded in (235):

(235) ah that's \totally unlike Su\dan I because °obviously Suⱽdan is I °by and large a ⱽMuslim country I and of course ⱽthere you I don't have ⱽvery many °holidays I but I the month of ⱽRamadan I when people are ⁻fasting I from \sunrise to sun⁻set I every °day I then \very little work \does get done I (LIBMSECJPT06: 299–301)

No samples were found of COREFs performing other transitivity or mood functions. There were no examples, either, of COREFs included within larger constituents, such as, for instance, a possessive within an NG (e.g. *Steve, his mother likes beans* or *Steve, I like his mother*, Geluykens 1992: 20, (25) (26) [my underlining]).

In LIBMSEC LDs show a tendency to be *unmarked*, both in terms of Mood and Transitivity. Out of 93.1% declaratives and 6.9% imperatives, 51.7% were unmarked (i.e. with Subject COREFs), while 48.3% were marked ones (i.e. with non-Subject COREFs). To this latter type belong all instances of imperatives such as (236) below:

(236) I \as for the \rich I in ⁻this \ⱽworld I \charge *them* \not to be \haughty I or ⁻high \minded I \nor to set their ⁻hopes on unⱽcertain °riches I but on \God I who \richly ⱽfurnishes us I with \everything to en\joy I (LIBMSECE0244–46)

Likewise, *100% of LDs in* LIBMSEC *concern active processes, and therefore are also unmarked in terms of voice.*

As for the typical constituents appearing as *LD Themes, no record was obtained of gerundial or infinitival constructions* (e.g. <u>Eating beans</u>, *Steve likes that,* <u>To eat beans,</u> *Steve likes that,* Geluykens ibid.: 21, (38) (39)), which involve some degree of nominalisation:

(237)   a.   <u>Leaking budget documents</u>, it's now common practice
         b.   <u>To give up now</u>, it /that wouldn't serve any useful purpose
         c.   ^(?)<u>That Australia could become a Republic by the year 2000</u>, it's not totally impossible

Table 39 shows that in LIBMSEC *most LD Themes are NGs* (65%, consisting of 58.3% common nouns and 6.7% proper names), followed by *PPs* (31%, of which 30% are preceded by the periphrasis *as for* and 1% postmodified by an embedded clause), and by AdvGs (4%). See (238) for examples of these realizational tendencies:

(238)   a. | the ˋbadminton and the ˋweightlifting *they* suffered ˋbadly from the lack of the ⁻Asians | (LIBMSECJPT01: 173)
         b. |ah | Saˋmantha | I wonder what ˋ*she* °wants | (LIBMSECJPT05: 05111)
         c. | ↑⁻as for the ˌhijack | °interest in ˌ*that* | °focusses on the ⁻military ˌprison | at Atˋlit | which ˋdoesn't °actually ˅look much like a °prison | at ˌall | (LIBMSECAPT07: 016–17)
         d. | and in Afghaniˌstan | what they ˌwear | *it* ⁻has this small ˋgrille-like ⁻feature over the ˌeyes | so that ⁻you can see _out and | ⁻other people of °course can't see ˋin | (LIBMSECJPT06: 340–43)
         e.   and he ⁻knew that ˋnow | ⁻this ˌmoment | when his ⁻nose had °only just °stopped ˌbleeding | when his ⁻head was still ⁻sore and ˋthrobbing | ˋ*this* | was the ⁻moment when he would ˌtry | (LIBMSECGPT01: 208–21)

Table 39 shows that *LDs in* LIBMSEC *favour non-extended multiple Themes.* Furthermore, it was found that, if realized *by prepositional phrases, LD non-extended multiple Themes tend to be simple*, whereas if they have *nominal or adverbial expressions*, they are *generally complex*, involving a logico-semantic relationship of elaboration. Overall, however, *all LD Themes in* LIBMSEC *are characterised by a relatively high lexical density.* In their turn, *extended multiple LD Themes tend to consist of logico-conjunctive, rather than of interpersonal, Themes* (viz. appositive conjunctive Adjuncts or Continuatives), which either precede or follow the left extern topical Theme. As illustrations, consider the tokens in (239):

Table 39. + *External realizations of LDs in* LIBMSEC

Structure	Lexical density (lexical items per Theme)	Grammatical intricacy	Class of topical Theme		Multiple Theme	
			simple	complex	simple	complex
Common group. 17 48.3	9.4	Hypotactic/rankshifted elaboration/enhancing	3	9	2	3
Proper noun 2 6.9	2.0	paratactic elaboration			1	1
Adverbial group 1 3.4	19.0	paratactic elaboration				1
Prepositional phrase 9 31.0	3.6	—		7		2
Total of Classes of Theme			10 34.0	9 31.0	5 17.5	5 17.5
				65.0		35.0

(239) a. | that ˈform I °mentioned ˌearlier for e°xample | *it* ˇshould have a°llowed us | ˌvall to be °present | for the hi°storic °opening ˌsession | on _Thursday ˌnight | which ˇboth °sides | ˈdesperately °wanted reˌported | as °much in ʹEurope | and the U°nited ˌStates | as ˌanywhere | (LIBMSECAPT02: 63–65)

b. | ˌno | I ˈdon't think ˈthat's a very °good iˌdea | ↑°er ˆ °Addis ʹAbaba | an ʹEnglish co°mmunity °school | ↓I ˌdon't think I'd like ˌvthat very °much |(LIBMSECJPT06: 046–48)

Exploring now whether or not the LD Theme is separated suprasegmentally (and typographically) from the clausal predication, only 3.5% of the LDs in LIBMSEC have no tone group boundary between the two, as in (240a). *In most cases (96.5%) LD constructions display the features [+IN. PAUSE] and [+EXTERN]*. That is to say, they have either a tone group boundary (93.1%), as in (240b), or a pause (3.4%), as in (240c), between the LD Theme and the clausal predication, so that both elements have at least one separate nuclear accent:

(240) a. | the ˈbadminton and the ˈweightlifting *they* suffered ˈbadly from the lack of the ⁻Asians | (LIBMSECJPT01: 173)

b. | ⌈two ˈdoctors | who ⁻happened to be _driving °through the ˇarea | ⁻*both* ˇstopped | and ⁻did what they ˈcould | to _help the ˇinjured | until ˇambulances aˈrrived | (LIBMSECBPT02: 107–09)

c. | °one of the ↑ˈpassengers | I ˈoverheard ˇ*him* saying | that ˇhe'd been a °pilot | in the ˈwar | I'll ˈget him | (LIBMSECGPT04: 056)

Table 40. *Falling vs. Rising tones in LDs in LIBMSEC*

Tone mark	End tone of LD Theme	Tone on left external topical Theme itself	Row Total
Falling tone	2	22	24
	8.3	76	55.8
Rising tone	11	3	14
	88.5	10.3	31.1
other: no nucleus, level	1	4	5
	4.2	13.7	7.1
Column Total	14	29	43
	32.8	67.2	100

The tokens in (240) demonstrate that typically the tonality and tonicity patterns of LDs in LIBMSEC corroborate the special status of this type of syntactic Theme as both external and New: it is normally spoken in a separate tone group and hence gets focal stress. To determine the choice of tone in this type of special Theme constructions, the relevant pitch movement was considered to be marked by the tone of the LD Theme itself and by the end tone of the left external constituent. The resulting choices of tone within LDs in LIBMSEC are rendered in Table 40.

Table 40 demonstrates that *most LD Themes are endowed with the feature of finality: a majority of them are uttered with just a falling tone on the external topical Theme, while a minority has an additional, generally rising, end tone.* In the following section all these formal characteristics of LDs are analysed from the perspective of their discourse function and distribution across the LIBMSEC text-types, which reveals LDs as a collaborative discourse device.

7.4.4.2 Discourse function
Their distribution in our corpus shows clearly *that LDs are primarily a conversational phenomenon.* In line with this Geluykens (1992: 153) observes that this construction is not only more frequent in conversational as opposed to spoken/non-conversational and written discourse, but "its functioning in other discourse types is to a large extent a reflection of its conversational functions" (p. 153).

In LIBMSEC LDs are most common in category (J) Dialogue (31%), followed by (A) Commentary (17.2%), (C) and (D) Lecture (13.8%), and (G) Fiction (13.8%). With the exception of Lecture, *all these text types share the common denominator of having an informal tenor that results in a fairly unplanned discourse.* This is mainly used to act upon reality, promoting discussion in argumentative discourse, or to reconstruct reality in the guise of narrative reports. In its turn, the relatively high ratio of LDs in *Lecture*, a formal and constructive text, results from the *desire for clarity demanded by this expositive genre*. It must also be recalled, however, that this text type is second in size in LIBMSEC containing 7.7% of its overall syntactic Themes tokens, and therefore it is more likely to comprise a higher amount of different types and classes of this category. In contrast, LDs are more infrequent in the remaining textual types, which are more formal in tenor and smaller in size. Thus, LDs do not occur in Propaganda, and are scarce in Magazine (3.4%), News and Religious Broadcasts (6.9% in both) and Poetry (6.9%).

As to discourse function, LDs reveal themselves (as well as the instances of quasi-LDs) as *participant/circumstance-(re)introducing devices*: they either reintroduce or introduce the referents of the LD topical Themes in discourse, which in LIBMSEC tend to be Subject Carriers (41%), Sensers (21%), Actors or Complement Goals (38%). Analysing their backward, or cohesive, potential, the majority of these items are Giv$_R$ (72.3%), of which 37.9% are directly Recoverable and 34.4% Inferrable. Accordingly, *these results indicate that LDs tend to re-introduce a participant or circumstance in discourse*, as exemplified in (242) below:

(242) a. | ˋI'd like to go and have a ⁻look at those ˋrocks | down ˋthere | she _gave the idea her aˋttention | it was a ˋwild °looking ᵛplace | and there was ⁻no one ˋthere | but she _said | of ↑ˋcourse °Gerry | ↓°when you've had eᵛnough | °come to the ˋbig °beach | ᵛor | ⁻just go ⁻straight °back to the ˋvilla | if you ˋlike | she ⁻walked aˋway | that ⁻bare ᵛarm | ⁻now °slightly ˋreddened | from ˋyesterday's ᵛsun | ˋswinging | he was an ⁻only ˋchild | e⁻leven years ˋold | ⁻she was a ˋwidow | she was deˋtermined to be ˋneither poᵛssessive | nor ˋlacking in deˋvotion | she went ᵥworrying | °off to her ᵢbeach | ˋas for ᵛGerry | ˋonce *he* °saw that his ˋmother had ˋgained her ᵛbeach | he be⁻gan the _steep de_scent to the ᵢbay | (LIBMSECGPT01: 037–9)

b. | ⁻shut again till ᵢApril | ⁻stands her little ᵢhutment | ⁻peeping over _daisies | ⁻Michaelmas and ⁻mauve | ⁻lock'd is the ᵥElsan | in its ⁻brick aᵢbutment | ⁻lock'd the little ᵢpantry | ⁻dead the little ᵢstove | ⁻keys with Mr ᵥGroombridge | but ⁻nobody will ᵢtake *them* | to her ⁻lonely _cottage | (LIBMSECHP01: 016).

In fact, only 27.7% of all LDs in LIBMSEC bring up new referents, such as, for example, (243) below:

(243) ⁻Black Sepˋtember | the °bloody ʹbattles | in ⁻nineteen-ᵛseventy | between the Jor°danian ᵥarmy | and the _PLᵥO | a ⁻physical _clash | °leading to ₐ re°grettable eᵥvents | as °King Hu_ssein °put it | in his ⁻opening aᵢddress |

on _Thursday ˌnight | °bringing out ⁻old _ghosts | in the ⁻hope | that they'd ˌthen be °laid _finally to ˌrest | ˈthings °do ˌchange in °this part of the °world | in the °most unbeˇlievable | ˌways | a °forty-year-old Palesˈtinian | who'd been a ˈfighter °most of his ˌlife | with a ˇLibyan-°backed °group | oˈpposing °Mr ˌArafat | the ˇone in °fact | that °helped to ˇforce the °PLO °leader | ˈout of °Tripoli last ˇyear | ˌhe's °here | (LIBMSECAPT02: 51–52).

My findings, therefore, confirm Lambrecht's (1981: 60) prediction that the referents of LD Themes "must have been mentioned in previous discourse or be salient parts of the situational context of the discourse or be otherwise recoverable". And conversely, the results contradict Geluykens (1992: 53), who claims that the referents of most LD Themes are "highly irrecoverable; this explains why introduction and acknowledgement of the REF is felt to be necessary".

The findings support Geluykens's view that LD Themes "introduce" and "require the acknowledgement of their REF". However, it seems that these features do not necessarily imply that the referents of LD Themes have to be "highly irrecoverable". Rather, they could underscore the second utility of LDs, namely, to act as Topic-switching devices. In other words, as shown in the figures and excerpts presented so far, most LDs do not act as mere referent-tracking devices, as claimed by Geluykens, because the referent of most LD Themes are already clear from the preceding co(n)text. With the exception of absolutely initial LDs (i.e. those having no previous cotext), what most of these constructions seem to do is *to redirect the flow of discourse by reintroducing a "lapsed Topic"* (in cognitive terms, an "inactive but accessible" referent) *as a LD Theme, which is "promoted" in the host clause for the purposes of saying something new about it* (Lambrecht 1981: 64; Duranti & Ochs 1979: 394). This hypothesis is strengthened by the fact in our corpus the majority of LD Themes appear at the beginning of speakers' turns or between discourse stages in order to let addressees assimilate that a change in the progression of discourse is to take place. This change normally implies that the referents of LD Themes are going to be further developed over the subsequent discourse span as "direct" (i.e. co(n)textually recoverable) or as "indirect" (i.e. inferrable) discourse Topics.

This discourse capacity of LDs stresses again the linking, i.e. backward-looking, function of the sentence-initial position, as well as the creation of expectations for subsequent discourse. Likewise, it also shows that the assumed information-status of discourse entities does not in fact follow any absolute standard, but rather reflects the speaker's assumptions. Thus, in (242a) above, for example, the referent of the LD Theme, *Gerry*, Senser and Actor Subject of the two subsequent clauses respectively, is recoverable both contextually as a proper noun and cotextually (it is mentioned at the beginning of the excerpt and throughout the text). However, its being picked up by *as for* marks an explicit switch in the camera angle of discourse, which, after having focused on his mother over the previous discourse span, returns to *Gerry*. In (242b) above in turn the switch is smoother, changing from *her little hutment* (Subject/Carrier) to a hyponym of it, *keys*, which acts as Object/Goal of the subsequent clause. Lastly, the wordy LD Theme in (243) above makes the thread of discourse descend from a bird's-eye view, depicting a general situation of conflict between the Jordanian and Palestinian armies, to the top-down individual point of view of one Palestinian who took part in that hostility.

We have seen that on a few occasions the referents of LD Themes provide spatio-temporal circumstantial frameworks. The effect is that a contrast or parallelism takes place between a previous state of affairs and the one taking place after the LD Theme, over the subsequent discourse span (i.e. until a new spatio-temporal framework is established), as in (238d–e) above, or in (244) below:

(244) [Heather Kempson] ᵛyes | but ⁻life in Su_dan is ⁻very very \different to | ⁻life in ᵛthis country | a \lot of children | ᵛfinish °school | ⁻after they've done °six years \primary | in \any case | I su⁻ppose the children who _come | from the | mainly ᵛrural districts but | the \whole of Su\dan is | a ᵛrural district | I suppose ₍they must | _do some work in the ᵛfields | [Rita Green]_yes ↑I | I just para\llel that situ°ation | with \China where | as ⁻soon as the ₍children are | out of ⁻school | or they have a ⁻holiday | \if they're from the \countryside and | ↓still °eighty per°cent of the people ↑⁻work | ᵛin the °country | *then* | they i\mmediately go into ⁻working | (LIBMSECJPT06: 244–46)

In (244) both Heather Kempson and Rita Green use an LD to refer to countryside children who go working, but while the former speaker is speaking about Sudan the latter refers to China.

No record was found of what Geluykens (1992: 83–96) calls *non-referent introducing* LDs. Geluykens claims that, formally, these LDs end in a rising pitch movement signalling both syntactic and interactional incompleteness (completeness is not achieved until +COREF pronoun is uttered), and that functionally, they fulfil the following functions:

a. *contrast*, in which the referent of the LD Theme expresses the second member of a set of opposites which are contrasted with one another and which are not necessarily made topical in the subsequent discourse, as in e.g. yes — mhm* I can't get away from it. but this I really like # / **this other one**! #. by/ contrast it's — **I'm / not 'sure !what it: 'is**#, ibid.: 86 (5) [emphasis in original];

b. *listing*, as above but establishing a contrast among more than two members of a set, as in e.g. B: mhm# — / **les ! Enfants 'du 'Paradis # / what about 'that #**, ibid.: 91 (18) [emphasis in original];
c. *condition*, expressing a conditional relationship between the syntactic Theme and the subsequent clause, as in e.g. B: [...] but **if you /don't drift: out till 'three in the: '/morning #. #/ this is all 1 'right #**, ibid.: 92 (22) [emphasis in original];
d. *emotion*, whereby the speaker places some attitudinal emphasis on the referent of the LD Theme which is not central to the development of discourse, as in e.g. A: [...] # — **"/dear old :Sandy :'/Paterson # ooh I want to !'see him #** now I wonder if he's in today, ibid.: 95 (32) [emphasis in original];
e. *summary*, in which the syntactic Theme summarises some aspect of the preceding discourse, as in A: look. it's **/N**'looking # . per/**N**'cussing #. well it's. **/N' looking #/'feeling#. per/ 'cussing # ?oscul'tation#. they're the/four 'things # that a ((/doctor 'syll syll#))**, ibid.: 93 (29) [emphasis in original];

According to Geluykens, the referents of LD Themes in non-referent introducing left detachments are not really "introduced" (or New), but establish a (contrastive, emotive, conditional, summative) link with the preceding discourse.

Be that as it may, the findings confirm that *LDs are an interactional phenomenon that reflects a co-operative effort between speaker and hearer in the following stages* (Geluykens 1992: 40):

a. Stage 1, *Referent introduction*;
(b. Stage 2, *Acknowledgement*)
c. Stage 3, *Establishment*.

To illustrate these three stages, let us reconsider example (234) above: | *that* *form I* °*mentioned* *earlier for e*°*xample* | *it* ⱽ*should have a*°*llowed us* | ᵥ*all to be* °*present* ... In Stage 1 the referent of the LD Theme, *that* *form*, is introduced. As in our example, this item may be modified by some elaborative material, *I mentioned earlier*, and generally, it receives some form of prosodic, or focal, highlighting, which indicates that the referent of the LD Theme is presented as important information. In the majority of cases, as in our example, the LD Theme ends in a falling pitch movement, representing this stage as a complete utterance in its own right. Speakers may decide to include Stage 2 to give their addressees a chance to acknowledge (or reject) the referent *after* it is uttered. This stage may be verbal, or explicit, in which case there is a turn intervening, usually made by the addressee. Or it may be non-verbal, or implicit, i.e. when there exists only a prosodic break or a pause after the Theme within the same turn, as in almost all examples of LDs in LIBMSEC. In (234) stage 2 is realized by both the presence of a tone group boundary and by the occurrence of a logico-conjunctive Theme, *for example*. Finally, in Stage 3 speakers reword the referent of the LD Theme as a pronominal (the COREF), *it* in our example, plus an entire proposition, e.g. "*it* ˅should have a°llowed us …". In our study all instances of LDs have Stage 3 in the same turn as Stages 1 and 2, for locations of Stage 3 in subsequent turns (made by the speaker or her/his addressee) have not been considered to constitute LDs in the sense adopted here.

7.4.5 Right detachments

This section examines the frequencies, the formal structure and the discourse motivation of "right detachments" (RDs)[122] in LIBMSEC (e.g. *The duke has given it to my aunt, that teapot*), prototypically displaying the features of [+EXTERN, +COREF, +FIN. PAUSE, +FUNCT, NOM, PRED, −DUM]. 11 tokens were found, representing 2.5% of the special Themes and 0.27% of the overall Themes in LIBMSEC. This percentage renders RDs the scarcest type of special thematic constructions in LIBMSEC, which precludes an exhaustive treatment of the construct.

7.4.5.1 *Formal structure and frequencies in LIBMSEC*

Mirror images of LDs, prototypical RDs consist of a right extern, or non-argument, (or rhematic) element, therefore lying outside the performative modalities of the main predication and often appearing in absolute form, which has already been entered in the preceding clause-internal predication via pronominal reference (COREF). Hence, as happened with LDs, the distinctive feature of RDs is to contain a clause internal COREF or pro-form that is *cataphoric*, i.e. that announces the RD element. The latter, being semantically more complete, identifies the precise referential status of the COREF and marks an implicit *newsworthy transition from generic to specific reference that occupies non-initial (or rhematic) position and typically gets focal highlighting*. As in LDs, the requisite of (+strict COREF) bars from RD status the following three constructions:

a. those described by Dik (1978: 155) as Tails realized by extensions of the predicates (i.e. by satellites in apposition), which have no previous COREF element (e.g. John gave that book to a girl, *in the library*, ibid.)
b. "afterthoughts", whereby speakers correct or specify the previously unclear Subject referent of the main predication, as in (245) below:

(245) a. ᵛmy only °inex… ₐ ex°perience in °teaching ₐ °children is in Indoˋnesia (LIBMSECJPT06: 087)
   b. ˋno | not ᵛreally | *it* was | *the* ˋ*tobe* was | ᵛmore or less | uniˋversal | and it was ˋawfully ˋhot | ᵛmost of them were made of ˋnylon | and imˋported | which ˋI found ˋvery °very ˋstrange | (LIBMSECJPT06: 350)
   c. cases of quasi-RD, which formally resemble RDs, but which, instead of strict coreference display relationships of lexical cohesion (i.e. repetition, synonym, superordination, hyponymy) in the form of a elaborating apposition (e.g. I like all sorts of literature, *short stories, in particular*, where *literature* is not coreferential with, but a hyperonym of, *short stories*).

In LIBMSEC *the COREF element of RDs tends to be realized by third person singular neutral pronouns (27.3%), by demonstrative pronouns (27.3%), or by interrogative Wh-pronouns (27.3%),* while the first person objective pronoun *me* is more peripheral (18.1%), as illustrated in excerpts (246) below:

(246) a. | as ⁻one of the ˌslogans in the °exhibition ˋhad *it* | ⁻art is ˌdead | °long live the ma_chine art of ᵛTatlin | (LIBMSECDPT01: 109)
   b. | and you ⁻can't beˋlieve | I _know we take *this* for ˋgranted | in ᵛEngland | that | ˋoh I'll just go ˋhome for the weekˋend | (LIBMSECJPT06: 452)
   c. ˌyes | I su°ppose you ˌcould | they're °paying ˌ*what* | a ´hundred pounds ex°penses | (LIBMSECJPT06: 064–66)
   d. | ˋso | ⁻if you'd ⌄like to send a do°nation | ⁻send it to ˌ*me* | ˌSusan ˌHampshire | the ⁻Commonwealth So_ciety for the ˌDeaf | ⁻Susan ⌄Hampshire | the ⁻Commonwealth So_ciety for the ˌDeaf | ⁻one o ˌfive | ᵛGower Street | ⁻one o °five ˌGower Street | ⁻London | ⁻WC_1ᵛE | ⁻6AˌH | ˋLondon | ⁻W_C⁻1_E | ⁻6_AˋH | (LIBMSECKPT02: 059)

In terms of Mood, unlike in LDs, *the majority of COREFs in RDs refer to constituents that, if initial, would constitute marked Themes*, i.e. (transitivity/mood) constituents that are normally non-initial in each mood pattern (63.6% vs. 36.4% unmarked ones), in 73% declaratives, 9% interrogatives and 18% imperatives. One possible explanation for the abundance of "marked" RDs could be *the fact that they occupy a "marked", or non-initial, position after the main predication*, or less likely, *a medial position after a previous COREF item*. Thus, neither the COREF nor the RD element in all imperatives and in 62.5% declaratives realizes the function expected for the initial element of these two mood patterns in PresE (i.e. Subject/Predicator and Subject, respectively), as illustrated in (246d) and (246b–c) above, respectively.

In connection with (246c) above, it should be noted that LIBMSEC contains two further examples of this clause type, namely: *a blend of declarative and interrogative, which turns the predication into a peremptory question, and its RD Theme into its peremptory answer*. Following Halliday (1967b: 214), these have been regarded as declarative clauses; but here they have been classified as instances of *marked special Theme–Rheme constructs*, because (a) the RD element occurs to the right of the clausal predication, generally separated from it by a preceding falling tone (tone 1), and (b) in the three examples found neither the COREF nor the RD element realizes the function demanded for the Theme of the declarative pattern in PresE, i.e. Subject.

Conversely, in the remaining 37.5% of the declaratives and in (247) below, the only interrogative token, both the COREF and the RD element are "unmarked":

(247) | ↑there's a ⁻line of harbour _lights | at Peri\vale | *is it* ⁻rounding rough Pen_tire | in a ⁻flood of °sunset _fire | the ⁻little fleet of °trawlers under °sail | (LIBMSECHPT03: 026)

where the COREF *it* refers back to *a line of harbour lights at Perivale* and, at the same time, it anticipates its non-metaphorical referent expression *the little fleet of trawlers under sail*.

In terms of transitivity, *most COREF and RD elements are also "marked"* (64% vs. 36% unmarked ones): normally *Beneficiaries* (29%) of a *material process*, as in (246d) above, the *Range* or a *Circumstance* in also a *material process* (14% for both), as in (246c) above and (248a) below, the Attribute of a relational process (29%), as in (248b), or the Phenomenon of a mental process (14%) as in (248c).

(248)   a. | and it \is ⁻very \difficult ∧ to °work ∧ under con°ditions like °*that* | when the °temperature's \what | /⁵0 de°grees °centigrade | /sometimes | (LIBMSECJPT06: 229)
        b. | as ⁻one of the \slogans in the °exhibition \had *it* | ⁻art is \dead | °long live the ma_chine art of \Tatlin | (LIBMSECDPT01: 109)
        c.   [RG]| and you ⁻can't be\lieve | I _know we take *this* for \granted | in ᵛEngland | that | \oh I'll just go \home for the week\end | (LIBMSECJPT06: 452)

From the point of view of their realization, *the majority of RD elements in LIBMSEC are NGs* (54%), of which 36% are *common nouns* and 18% *proper names*, followed by paratactic finite clauses (46%), expressing a logico-semantic relationship of elaboration or manner enhancing, witness (246) above and Table 41.

Table 41. + *External realizations of RDs in* LIBMSEC

Structure	Lexical density (lexical items per Theme)	Grammatical intricacy	Topical Theme		Extended multiple Theme	
			simple	complex	simple	complex
common group 4 3 36.0		Hypotactic elaboration/ enhancing	2	5	2	2
proper noun 2 21 18.0		Paratactic elaboration				
clause 5 46.0	7.8	paratactic/hypotactic elaboration/enhancing	18.0	46.0	18.0	18.0
Total of Classes of Theme			64.0		36.0	

Table 41 above shows that, *like LDs, most RDs in* LIBMSEC *favour complex non-extended multiple RD constituents* (64% vs. 36% extended multiple) expressing a logico-semantic relationship of elaboration or enhancing. *As for lexical density, RD elements are "heavier" than their LD counterparts.* This is in conformity with the principles of EF and EW, two of the main factors responsible for the communicative make-up of these constructions (Section 7.4.5.2). As to *extended multiple RD constituents, they are mostly realized by structural logico-conjunctive items* (viz. relative adverbs) heading the right external transitivity constituent, or by *entreaty modal Adjuncts*, such as *please*, that announce the following request and precede a Finite, as in (249) below:

(249)   I ˅either °way I ⁻please I will you °send a do⁻nation to ˎme I ⁻Brian ˎRedhead I °at ˏ ⁻Youthˎaid I it's ⁻all one ˎword I ⁻Youthˎaid I ⁻9 I ˎPoland ˏ °Street I ⁻9 I ˎPoland ˏ °Street I ⁻London I ˎW1ˏV I ⁻3 I °DˎG I ⁻London I ˎW1 I ⁻V for _Victor I ⁻3 I ⁻D for _David I ⁻G for ˎGeorge I
(LIBMSECKPT01: 077)

Finally, the last formal feature of RDs reported by our findings is that *all instances display the features [+EXTERN] and [+FIN. PAUSE]*. In other words, as expounded in Table 42, the RD element and its COREF are always uttered into two different tone groups, being separated by either a pause (9%), or in most cases, by a tone group boundary (91%), as in (250) below:

(250)   I and you ⁻can't beˎlieve I I _know we take *this* for ˎgranted I in ˅England I that I ˎoh I'll just go ˎhome for the weekˎend I (LIBMSECJPT06: 452)

Table 42. *Falling vs. Rising tones in RDs in* LIBMSEC

Tone mark	End tone of predion	Tone on right external topical Theme	End tone of right external topical Theme
Falling tone	8	6	4
	73.0	55.5	36.3
Rising tone	2	4	—
	18.1	35.5	
Other: no nucleus, level	1	1	2
	9.0	9.0	1.8

The figures in Table 42 above show that *in most RDs the predications containing the COREF element are endowed with the feature of finality* (73% of falling tones vs. 27.1% non-falling). This formal characteristic collaborate to mark the special status of *RD items as both external-rhematic and informationally New*, i.e. in the scope of an intonational Focus. These are also highlighted by falling tones (55.5% vs. 44.5% rising tones, of which 36% have also a subsequent falling end tone). Importantly enough, my findings contradict Quirk et al. (1985: 1417) and Ziv (1994: 639), who claim that RDs constitute a single contour (fall plus rise), with no pause preceding the right external constituent and should therefore be distinguished from "afterthoughts", which do have this pause or prosodic break and therefore get focal stress. Section 7.4.5.2 demonstrates that the formal characteristics of RDs outlined so far are once more the reflection of specific communicative needs that underscore the collaborative nature of discourse.

7.4.5.2 *Discourse function*

The distribution of RDs across the ten LIBMSEC text types echoes that of LDs in that both are *most common in conversational and interactive text types* (56% in Dialogue, and 17% in Propaganda, as opposed to only 9% appearing in Commentary, Lecture and Poetry). *These statistics confirm that RDs, like LDs, are conversational phenomena. Both constructions are employed in informal, relatively spontaneous discourse to act upon reality*, either *promoting discussion in argumentative texts* or *encouraging collaboration in persuasive texts*. Furthermore, leaving the text type aside, all RDs in LIBMSEC share a common functional denominator, namely, *they convey the conventionalised meaning of an implicit request to put the thematic propositional information "on hold" until the identity of the COREF element is revealed by the referent of the RD element*. Besides, the latter, being semantically more fully specified than the former, marks *an implicit transition from generic to specific reference* on the assumption that the preceding coreferential pronominal thematic expression does not suffice to ensure understanding of what the proposition is about (Lambrecht 1994). *The newsworthiness of these transitions is formally reinforced by the non-initial (or rhematic) placement of the RD element and by its normally getting prosodic highlighting* (with its own focal span).

Considering now *the backward-looking potential of RD items, all of them are reported as invoking Giv_R referents*: 54.5% are directly recovered from the immediately preceding cotext, and 45.5% are inferrable from a linguistically preceding or situational referent. *This indicates that RDs identify and reintroduce into discourse a referent that is situationally or linguistically recoverable.* As in LDs, this is normally done in a two/three-stage process, but in a reverse order, which also obeys the PSRR. That is to say, RD constructions keep the role and reference of their Topics separated: the mood and transitivity role is performed within the proposition by the COREF, while its referent is fully specified by the expression of the RD constituent. Accordingly, the COREF is incorporated into the proposition in Stage 1, while optionally Stage 2, realized by pauses or tone group boundaries, again acts as an implicit instruction to the addressee to search their linguistic or situational surroundings for the appropriate recoverable entities and to attend to them. Finally, in Stage 3 the referent of the COREF element is specified *after* the clausal predication and normally within the same turn, which prompts a switch from generic to specific reference.

RDs function as explicative "re-introducers" of referents in discourse. For this reason RDs tend to appear at the beginning of turns, paragraphs or texts, and RD constituents generally have a fully informative referential expression. This is normally a proper noun, or a clausal (relative) or nominal description, which is highlighted as New, or as communicatively important information. To exemplify this process, let us examine one last token of RD:

(251) ˌhm ǀ ˈah ǀ ˈhere's one for ˈcyprus ǀ but ˌthat's °teaching ˈchildren a°gain ǀ
[RG]
↑have you ˇever taught °children ǀ
[HK]
⁻only ˌonce ǀ °that was in ˈLondon ǀ in a ˈprivate °school ǀ
[RG]
did you /like it ǀ
[HK]
ˇyes ǀ it was ˈmore or °less a ˈprivate ˌlesson ǀ I had ˈtwo young Iˇtalian °brothers ǀ I °used to °take them ˰ °down to the ˌmarket ǀ and °get them to °do ˌshopping °for me ǀ and ᴺthey seemed to °like it ǀ and their ˈEnglish ˰

> °actually im°proved | as ˻well | °much to my sur/prise | I ˻don't know whether | ˇI had ˏ any e°ffect | or ˏ °whether it was °just because they were °living in ˏ ¯London it˻self |
> [RG]
> ˻well *that* ¯makes a big ˻difference | ˻doesn't it | when you're °actually ˻living in the °country where | you °have to °learn the °target ˏlanguage ||
> ˇmy only °inex… ˏ ex°perience in °teaching ˏ °children is in Indo˻nesia | ˻I had to °teach some °Indonesian ˻girls | in the after˻noon | and I ¯must ad˻mit | they were ˻very ˏquiet | (LIBMSECJPT06: 086–87)

(251) reproduces an excerpt of a dialogue between Heather Kempson and Rita Green, who are discussing their own and some of their acquaintances' experiences as teachers. Starting from an ad for a teaching post in Cyprus, Heather recalls, at Rita's request, her experience as a private English teacher in London. Then, Rita's turn commences with a RD constituent, separated off from the main predication by a previous prosodic break after an echo question. The COREF is realized by a demonstrative deictic *that*. By using *that*, Rita establishes a cohesive link with Heather's last statement and, at the same time, she subscribes to it, making it into a general assertion. Besides, this RD serves as a bridge between Heather's teaching in London and Rita's experience in Indonesia, the discourse Topic of the subsequent discourse span.

In sum, *rather than "afterthoughts" to the predication*, as claimed by Dik (1989) or Geluykens (1987), among others, *RDs are here analysed as explicative referent re-introducing devices in mainly conversational discourse: they reintroduce discourse referents shifting the camera angle of discourse from generic to specific reference*. The side effect is that *most RDs obey the principles of EF and EW: the majority of RD constituents are communicatively "heavy"* (lexically and prosodically as focal information) *and are also endowed with a forward-looking potential as discourse Topics, in that they are usually developed over the ensuing discourse span*.

7.4.6 *Cleft constructions*

Now let us discuss the frequencies, the formal structure and the discourse function of "cleft constructions"[123] (e.g. *It was that teapot that the duke gave to my aunt*) prototypically featured here as [+EXTERN, +IDENT., +COREF, +in PAUSE, +FUN, −NOM, +PRED, +DUM]. 27 tokens have been found, representing 6.1% of all special topical Themes and 0.7% of the total amount of syntactic Themes in our corpus.

7.4.6.1 *Formal structure and frequencies in LIBMSEC*
Although the structure of the cleft construction is often not clear-cut, its prototypical or unmarked declarative pattern could be represented as follows (Prince 1978: 883 fn 1):

(252)

It	Process: be	C_i*[124]	wh- prep. + wh-. that Ø	C-C_i
1	2	3	4	
ǀ it	was	a con⁻tinuing be_lief in ˈprovidence	ǀwhich sus⁻tained ǀ	

°Voltaire's ˌdeism ǀ (LIBMSECDPT02: 137)

In (252) constituents 1, 2 and 3 constitute the *Head clause*, a special case of identifying construction, *it was a continuing belief in providence*, and constituent 4, the dependent clause, *which sustained Voltaire's deism*. There are several ways in which the Head behaves like an ordinary clause. It can be subordinated:

(253) He claimed that it was a continuing belief in providence which sustained Voltaire's deism.

And it may be interrogative or exclamative, and occur with fronted complement:

(254) a. Was it a continuing belief in providence which sustained Voltaire's deism?
b. How surprising it was that a continuing belief in providence sustained Voltaire's deism!
c. A continuing belief in providence it was which sustained Voltaire's deism.

Now, focusing on the constituents of the Head clause, *It*, or constituent 1, can be interpreted either as (a) a non-referential dummy element merely filling the Subject slot, or (b) a third person singular neuter pronoun Subject that refers cataphorically to the presupposition of existence conveyed by constituent 4, i.e. the subsequent relative clause. Constituent 2, the relational process *be*, "cleaves" the clausal message *into a non-reversible identifying pattern*, consisting of *Identifier-Token*, i.e. constituent 3, and *Identified-Value*, i.e. constituent 4. Constituent 3, here called the *predicated Theme* or *highlighted element* (C_i), represents *any* Constituent which acts as the Subject Complement of *It* and also as Identifier/Token of the identifying structure built up by the Head clause. It is called "highlighted element" because this constituent receives rhematic highlighting, both syntactically, by means of a thematic relational predication (*it + be* ... in clause-initial position), and prosodically, by normally getting EF (especially if the predication in which it is contained is spoken in a separate tone group.

The Head clause tends to involve an *intensive identification* (i.e. involving a relationship of the type "X is Y"), but it may also express *circumstantial or possessive identification* (i.e. implying logical relationships of the type "X has Y" or "X is in Y", respectively). Taglicht (1984: 57) observes that there are two possible variants of the *possessive type*: a head noun postmodified by a possessive of-prepositional phrase as Predicated Theme and a non-possessive relative construction, which are typically found in formal discourse, e.g. (255) below:

(255) a. a°place's /universe | °worked \perfectly °well wi°thout a °God | °and as a ma⁻terialist | he \therefore °saw ⁻no ˌreason | for \postu°lating di°vine acˌtivity | it's \in the °writings of La̸place | at the ˌᵥend of the °century | that we \see the °culmi⁻nation | of the tra⁻dition | of °atheistic ma⁻terialist _thought | °which had been de°veloping ᵛin France | \since a°bout ⁻seventeen ˌfifty| (LIBMSECDPT02: 225)
b. a nominative or accusative possessive pronoun/adjective or Head noun as Predicated Theme and *whose* as the relative pronoun (e.g. It is Laplace in whose writings at the ˌᵥend of the °century | we \see the °culmi⁻nation | of the tra⁻dition | of °atheistic ma⁻terialist _thought|).

However, the two possessive types are not totally synonymous. Whereas in (255a) the predicated Theme identifies where we can see the culmination of the tradition of atheistic materialist thought, its alternative in (255b) highlights the possessor.

In its turn, the *relative clause* of *it*-cleft constructions *is structurally similar to a restrictive relative* in being introduced by a relative phrase (*who*, *that*, etc.) or by zero. However, *there are four notable differences*.[125]

a. unlike in standard relatives, *wh*-forms are relatively rare except where the *wh*-word is *who, whom* and *whose* (although less so than Quirk et al. (1985: 1397) claim), in comparison with the higher frequency of *that*-and zero realizations, which are a rather habitual device in (spoken) clefts to highlight non-ideational items such as tense, modality, aspect and polarity (e.g. *It's not that Mervyn's totally unreliable*, where merely polarity is highlighted, Collins 1992: (27)]);[126]
b. the relative clause does not need to agree in person with its antecedent, i.e. the predicated Theme (e.g. *If there's trouble, it won't be me that starts it*, ibid. (9)),[127] which can be of any word class, e.g. a PP or finite clause (e.g. *It's in Chicago that he lives, It was because he was out of breath that he stopped*);
c. the relative clause cannot readily be tagged (e.g. ?*It's the duke that gave my aunt that teapot, didn't he?*); and

d. "[t]he *wh* word cannot, or can scarcely, follow a preposition or longer sequence: we would use (23iii) ["*It was Ed* that she was referring to"] or (iv) "*It was to Ed* that she was referring"] rather than "*?It was Ed* to whom she was referring" (Huddleston 1984: 460 [my italics]).

These four features are illustrated by the relative constituent of the cleft construction included in (257) below:

(257) ↓they ⁻looked ↓down | \gravely | \frowning | ⁻he _knew the ↓frown | at ⁻moments of ↓failure | when he ⁻clowned to °claim his \mother's a°ttention | <u>it was with \just this °grave em\barrassed in°spection</u> that \she re°warded him | the \rock | \lately \weighted with \boys | (LIBMSECGPT01: 103)

In (257) *that* refers back to a prepositional instrument Circumstantial *with \just this °grave em\barrassed in°spection*. In cases like this one, Quirk et al. (1985: 1387) explain that the relative pronoun does not have a "strict pronominal status" (**it was with \just this °grave em\barrassed in°spection* which \she re°warded him).

In view of the evidence presented so far supporting their (non-restrictive) idiosyncrasy, we shall regard the relative constituent of cleft constructions as *manifesting subordination of the non-embedded type* (Huddleston 1984). In other words, we shall regard the relative clause as *an immediate constituent of the sentence as a whole* (rather than as forming a constituent with its antecedent). The implication is that the referent of the predicated Theme reveals the identity of the relative constituent as a dominant coreferential entity (in a hypotactic construct), rather than as being restricted in meaning by the relative Qualifier (implying rankshifting), and so the relative constituent, resembling the non-restrictive type of relatives, elaborates its antecedent (to use Hallidayan terminology) as information that is separate from, and secondary to, the remainder of the dominant clause.[128]

As is often the case in spoken discourse, in LIBMSEC tokens of clefts were found where the unmarked pattern in (252) above is altered by language processing or co(n)textual constraints such as ellipsis, repetition, interruptions, side-tracking, disruptions, incomprehensibility, inaudibility etc. This is exemplified in the excerpts in (262) below:

(262) a. [change of speaker: Martin Fookes] ↓yes it \was | em ₍ ⁻they sur↓prised me | \greatly | (LIBMSECJPT01: 035) (Interruption)
b. <u>but it's not \just a re\vising of the \past</u> | which \worries many ob\servers of these two °trials | <u>it's the impli↙cations for the \future Ø|</u> (LIBMSECAPT01: 072) (Ellipsis of the relative constituent in the second *It*–cleft 'which worries many observers');

c. ˋwell | ˋas it worked ᵛout in °fact | ˋthey didn't °pay themᵛselves | it was the ˋcompany that | they ˋworked °for | you °see ˋthey worked at the °Hotel ˌHilton | °and it was ˋin their ᵛinterests | for them to ˋlearn °English | so the ˋcompany ᵛsponsored them | to _come | and have _lessons with ˌme | ˌso I | I ˉwasn't ˌreally exᵛploiting them | but I ˋused to °make them ˌpay | whether they ˉcame or ˌnot | (LIBMSECJPT06: 100) (Ellipsis of the relative constituent of the second *It*–cleft "that paid them");

Interruption is illustrated in (262a), where apparently Martin Fookes is introducing his turn with an *It + be*-cleft, but he interrupts it abruptly with a continuative and replaces it with a non-special Theme–Rheme pattern. In turn, (262) (b-c) contain two cases of ellipsis. In both the relative constituents are elided as they are directly retrievable from the previous cotext.

Following Plötz (1972: 37) and Collins (1991: 47), the type of *it*-clefts represented by the last two examples is distinguished from non-cleft copular constructions where *it* refers anaphorically to either a general notion (e.g. "problem", "thing", "question", etc.) or to an animate (usually human) referent, as in (263) (from Collins ibid. (67)), where *it* is anaphoric in that it reveals the identify of the Agent of the contextually previous phone call:

(263) The word put an idea into his head, and he hurried through to the lounge and went to the phone. He dialled a Streatham number, and in a few moments was gratified to hear Conquest's clear voice.
"It's me, sir — Fred," panted the porter. "Something's happened, sir."
(LOB N05, 178)

Likewise, *it*-clefts with no overt predicated Theme (e.g. *It's not* that Mervyn's totally unreliable vs. *Mervyn's* not totally unreliable) have been distinguished from extrapositions of nominal clauses (e.g. *It is true* that Mervyn's totally unreliable vs. *That Mervyn's totally unreliable* is not true) (Collins 1992: 35),. This distinction, however, is not always easy to make mainly because cleft clauses do not necessarily have an uncleft counterpart, neither do all extraposed clauses show a non-extraposed alternative. In addition, clefts (and pseudocleft) constructions are distinguished from constructionally similar (intensive, circumstantial or possessive) *attributive constructions* (where an attribute is ascribed to an entity) also containing relative clauses. Consider (264):

(264) | ↑in ˌfact | ᵛeight out of the °top °ten °listeners' port°folios | °have ˋmoney in Hong ˌKong | *and* ˋ*as it's a* ˌᵛ*volatile* °*market* | *which has* °*taken a* ᵛ*tumble* °*recently* | the °field's °still ˉwide ˌopen | as the °compe°tition enters its °last °few ˌmonths | (LIBMSECFPT03: 09)

(264) could lend itself to an identifying interpretation ("what has taken a tumble recently is a volatile market"), or to an attributive class-member reading ("the market which has taken a tumble recently is volatile"), in which case the Subject *it* would be coreferential with *market*. Declerck (1983: 18) and Collins (1992: 41) regard this type of construction as borderline cleft clauses on account of their sharing some characteristics with standard attributive sentences such as the admission of comparison and modification of degree, and the possibility that the highlighted element is preceded by *no* or *not a*.

Finally, note has also been taken of Jespersen's (1965 [1927]: 89) differentiation of cleft constructions and *such proverbial attributive constructions* as those in (265):

(265) a. It is a poor heart that never rejoices.
 b. It is an ill bird that fouls its own nest.
 c. It is a long lane that has no turning.

Rather than a relation of identity between two entities (e.g. "That which never rejoices" and "a poor heart"), these clauses establish an attributive class-member relationship ("The heart that never rejoices is poor"), because the relative clauses, rather than identifying their referents, belong to the restrictive type qualifying non-specific noun phrase antecedents (viz. *hearts*, *birds* and *lanes*). As a result, the structures in (265) involve a conditional interpretation (e.g. "if a heart never rejoices it is a poor heart"), which is absent in the idiosyncratic relative clause of clefts. Furthermore, unlike the dummy *it* of clefts, the *it* of these proverbial clauses seems to have some referential flavour. Supporting evidence is provided by the fact that in earlier English and in PresE *he*, *she* and *it* alternate as the Subject of this type of construction, so that variants like *He is a poor heart that never rejoices* can in fact be found (Declerck 1983: 15).

Table 43 summarises the structure, lexical density, grammatical intricacy, Mood/Transitivity roles and classes of clefts in LIBMSEC. These involve mainly *material or mental processes* (63% and 22.2%, respectively), in *active declarative* clauses (96.3% vs. 3.7%). Besides, Table 43 shows that the predicated Themes of clefts in LIBMSEC have a *lexical density of 7.1 and tends to have simple rather than complex expressions* (56% vs. 44%). 48.1% of all *predicated Themes* are realized by *NGs*, which generally are identified by *comparatively heavier relative clauses* (lexical density of 8.5). 40.7% of the nominal Predicated Themes are *common nouns*, which are generally qualified by appositive or hypotactic relationships of elaboration, expansion and enhancing, as in (266a) below, while 7.4% are expressed by *demonstrative pronouns* (i.e. *this* and *that*), as in (266b). Next come *predicated prepositional phrases* (37%), which are also identified by

Table 43. *Cleft constructions in LIBMSEC*

Structure	Lexical density. Theme-relat CL		Gram. intricacy	Transitivity mood function	Topical Theme simpl compl	Ext mult Theme simpl compl
NG 11 40.7	3	7.1	Paratactic/hypo-tactic Elaboration Extension Enhancement	Carrier/Subject 1 3.7 Actor/Subject 7 25.9 Beneficiary/Subject 2 7.4 Phenomenon/Subject 1 3.7	8………4 29.0 14.0	8…………7 29.0 27.0
PP 10 37.0	2.7	8.2	Hypotactic projection Hypotactic elaboration	Circumstantial Adjunct 10 37.0		
Adv.P. 3 11.0	1	10.0	–	Circumstantial Adjunct 3 11.0		
Pronoun 2 7.4	1	8.5	–	Goal/Subject 1 3.7 Actor/Subject 1 3.7		
Clause 1 3.9	8	12.0	Hypotactic enhancement	Circumstantial Adjunct 1 3.9		
Total of Classes of Theme					44.0	56.0

equally heavy relatives (8.2), as illustrated in (266c). More peripheral are the cases of predicated AdvGs (11%) or *dependent clauses* (3.9%). These last two types of clefts are accompanied by still heavier relative clauses (10, 12, respectively), as exemplified in (266) (d-e), respectively:

(266) a. | in ˎany case | it's ˎnot the ˇgovernments of these °countries | through conˋcerted action among themˇselves | that have a°chieved rapidly increasing ˌshares | in ex°panding world ˌmarkets | ˋthis has been the ˇwork | of ˌindividual ˋenterprises |(LIBMSECCPT01: 073)
b. | the ⁻first _two were a°dapted from ˋfuturism | the ˇlast | ˇcollage | ˋcame from ˇcubism | but it was ⁻this which _Berlin °Dada transˋformed | into the ⁻new ˌmedium | of °photomonˋtage | as ˋHuelsenbeck ˋwrote | (LIBMSECDPT01: 126)
c. | it is ⁻through this ↑ˋcraving | that ˋsome have ˋwandered aˋway from the ↑ˇfaith | and ˋpierced their ˋhearts with ˋmany ˋpangs | (LIBMSECEPT02: 030)
d. | but it's eˇspecially °relevant | in the ˌenergy °field | be_cause | it's ˇhere | in parˌticular | that ⁻risks | are in⁻evitable | and the °possible ⁻consequences of diˇsturbance | are _still ˌserious |(LIBMSECCPT01: 518)
e. | it's °only when you °stop to ˋthink about | all the ˋfeasts | laid ˋon for us | by the ˌworld's | ˋsportsmen and ˌwomen | that you ˇrealize | that °198ˇ6 | was ↑in_deed | a ⁻vintage ˌyear | for some ˋhugely enˇjoyable | _overinˋdulgence | (LIBMSECJPT01: 022–24)

In terms of Mood, 51.9% of *cleft Themes are marked*, acting as circumstantial *Adjuncts* (43% spatial, 43% temporal, 14% instrumental). These are realized by prepositional, adverbial and clausal structures, whereas the unmarked ones have nominal expressions (48.1%). In this connection, it should be noted that marked circumstantial cleft Themes have been obtained by two slightly different criteria. In 65% of cases a Circumstance, rather than a Subject referent, realizes the highlighted element and therefore receives Theme1 highlighting within the *it*-cleft clause, as in, for example, (265c–e) above. In contrast, 35% of marked *it*-clefts are triggered by a fronted Circumstance, as in (267) below, where *in recent months* acts as the marked circumstantial (temporal) Theme of the cleft:

(267) | in ⁻recent _months | it's ˋmen who've ˇbenefited | from the °slackening ˋpace | of _unemˋployment | but °now ˋthis seems to be °helping ˋwomen as ˋwell | (LIBMSECBTP03: 032–34)

In any case, *the high frequency of marked Themes strengthens the view of cleft constructions as flexible thematic devices, because in most other thematic constructions marked non-nominal Themes represent fewer and supposedly more constrained choices. The same applies to the idiosyncratic relative constituent of it-clefts.* As already noted, unlike standard relatives, the relative element of clefts allows for all types of constituents as their antecedents, either human or non-human, and in LIBMSEC they tend to be headed by *that* (63%), rather than by *wh*-forms (37%).

Turning to their structural realization, Table 43 shows that, unlike RDs and LDs, a large proportion of predicated Themes are extended multiple (56% vs. 44% non-extended multiple). 11% of them are realized by a modal Adjunct (268b), while 45% result from the presence of a logico-conjunctive Theme: 29.6% Structural, 11.1% Conjunctive Adjuncts, 4.3% Continuatives, as in (268a).

(268) a. well ˈlet's turn our aˈttention °now | to ˈnorth of the ˇborder | where alˈthough it was er | ˋCeltic and Aberˆˋdeen | who °ended °up with the ˈtrophies | the ˈstory was ˇreally a°bout °Martin | the ˏ ˋdesperate ˏluck | of poor ⁻Heart of Midˈlothian | (LIBMSECJPT01: 038)
b. | °how_ever to | ˇeveryone's sur°prise | it was the | Chiˇnese cavalry | that _dashed in and | ˈsaved a few ˈscalps | ˇhurriedly | (LIBMSECAPT12: 015)

In its turn, Table 44 reports on whether or not the highlighted element of *it*-clefts is separated off into a different tone group and so marks prosodically the "cleavage" of the construction into Identifier/Token (IR/T) and Identified/Value (ID/Vl).

Table 44. *Falling vs. Rising tones in cleft constructions in* LIBMSEC

Tone mark	Tone on pred. Top. Theme	End tone of pred. Top. Theme	Pause/tone group boundary +	−
falling tone	11	1	19	8
rising tone	14	8	70.3	29.7
other: no nucleus, level	2	1		

Table 44 shows that most cleft Themes in our corpus have unmarked tonality and tonicity (Halliday 1967: 229ff.; Hornby 1971). On the one hand, the results confirm that most cleft Themes display the features [+EXTERN] and [+IN. PAUSE]. That is to say, most of these constructions mark the "cleavage" of the construction into clausal thematic IR/T vs. clausal rhematic ID/Vl. Accordingly, the Tonic typically falls on the last lexical item of each clausal constituent, and the highlighted element gets intonational prominence and is signalled as New. Furthermore, the present results report 73% as rising tones (which usually express contrast and/or incompleteness) and 23% as falling tones (which indicate completeness), so that the unmarked prosodic contour of *it*-clefts in LIBMSEC is: a rising nuclear tone in the highlighted element followed by a fall within the relative clause.

The functional motivation of the formal claims so far enumerated about *it*-clefts are evaluated in Section 7.4.6.2, where the discourse behaviour of these constructions is examined.

7.4.6.2 *Discourse function*

The formal features so far outlined reveal *it-clefts to be thematic and focal build-up devices*. Being non-reversible identifying structures, the emphasis of cleft constructions lies in the predication of a topical Theme. Through this mechanism a local clause structure is created for *the intonation Nucleus to typically fall on unmarked clause-final position*, i.e. *the highlighted element*. At the same time, the *predicative structure allows for a thematic flexibility that is paradigmatic in orientation*. In other words, since non-referential *it* ties its Complement to no particular category it provides a device to thematise almost any item. As a consequence, there are a wide range of elements highlighted in clefts (e.g. prepositional phrases with no *wh*-item equivalent or the zero realizations of the predicated Theme), which could not be compatible with more ideational types of highlighting, such as those of pseudo-clefts, RDs or LDs.

In addition, *the syntactic functions promoted by it-clefts could also be explained in the light of their inherently textual prominence* (IFG: 58ff.; Collins 1992). *It*-clefts imbue with thematic and intonational prominence the syntactic functions least likely to receive these two kinds of prominence, that is, either the Subject (unmarked Theme), or those functions most likely to be placed within the Rheme, namely different types of circumstantial Adjuncts (marked Themes). Besides, by placing normally a rising nuclear tone in the highlighted element itself speakers can provide this constituent with a contrastive flavour and, at the same time, emphasise that the construction is incomplete. *The contrast conveyed by clefts involves a relationship of identity between two elements: the highlighted element and the presupposition of existence encoded in the rhematic relative clause*, so that the construction is congruently marked as incomplete until the rhematic Identified/Value is uttered.

From the above it follows that *it*-clefts are typically "newness-oriented" and so can be exploited by speakers as a means of directing their addressee's attention towards a particular interpretation of information. This tendency is ratified by the patterns displayed by the backward-looking potential of the Themes and the relative clauses of the *it*-clefts in LIBMSEC, which are contained in Table 45.

Table 45 shows that the first pattern of cleft outnumbers patterns 2 and 3 (63% vs. 18.5%, respectively). Pattern 1 is regarded as the unmarked one on the assumption that, as most predicated Themes in LIBMSEC have a tone group of their own and get focal stress (on the highlighted element), they are likely to

Table 45. *Informational classification of cleft constructions in LIBMSEC*

Markedness	Types	Predicated Theme	Relative clause	LIBMSEC # %
Unmarked	1a	New	Given	5
	1b	Contrastive	Given	8
	1c	New	Inferrable	2
	1d	Contrastive	Inferrable	2
	Total			17
				63.0
Marked	2	Given	New	5
	Total			5
				18.5
	3a	New	New	1
	3b	Contrastive	New	4
	Total			5
				18.5
Total				27
				100

convey either non-recoverable information or contrastive information. In the latter case predicated Themes establish a contrast with respect to the members of a definite set, whether reinforced or not by contrastive focal stress (in Halliday's sense). In contrast, the relative clause is associated with givenness because of its hypotactic status. That is to say, because of its being subordinated to the impersonal *it + be* thematic predication, the relative clause is imbued with a hedged, reportive flavour that presents it as logically presupposed. Patterns 2 and 3, on the other hand, can be regarded as marked deviations from the expected pattern. The excerpts in (269), (270), and (271) include samples of the variations of each pattern, respectively.

(269) *Type 1*
    a. *New–Given*
        | as to ˇlarge states | being ⁻necessarily more suˋccessful on the con°temporary economic ˏscene | ˋthis notion is hard to ˋreconcile with the ˊfact | that in ˇEurope | it's two ˇsmall countries | _Sweden and ˇSwitzerland | ˋwhich by conˇventional tests | are ˏpossibly the ˏmost ecoˏnomically adˋvanced (LIBMSECCTP01: 053)

b. *Contrastive–Given*
   | aˇnother °reason | is that ˌunre°flecting ˇcentralism | ⁻conjures °up a ˌpicture | in which imports | are ⁻always ˌbought | diˇrectly | from °chronically ⁻unreˌliable | _foreign ˌgovernments | more ˇtypically how°ever | it's ⁻not ˌgovernments | but °business ˋenterprises ₍ₐ₎ which °ship the °imports | (C01473)

c. *New–Inferrable*
   well ˋlet's turn our aˋttention °now | to ˋnorth of the ˇborder | where alˋthough it was er | ˋCeltic and AberↃˋdeen | who °ended °up with the ˋtrophies | the ˋstory was ˇreally a°bout °Martin | the ₍ₐ₎ ˋdesperate ˌluck | of poor ⁻Heart of Midˋlothian | (LIBMSECJPT01: 038)

d. *Contrastive–Inferrable*
   (⁻why | you're not exˇpecting any °post are you | you ˋtold them not to ˇforward any | ⁻well _naturally I | ˋmade exˊceptions | there is this _Asian ˊcrisis | I'm ˋsure the °paper can manage without you for °three ˇweeks | if you ˋwant something to ˇdo | you can | ⁻knead this ˋdough | ˋI don't want °anything to ˊdo | it's the ˋrest of this °household that should con°cern ˋyou | (LIBMSECGPT05: 116)

(270)   *Type 2: Given–New*
ninety-_five-year-old °Fonte⁻nelle | °published an ˋessay deˇfending Car°tesian °vortices | as ⁻late as °seventeen fifty-ˋtwo | but at ˋleast a ˋdecade before ˇthen | ˋmost °French philosophers had alˋready aˇbandoned | the ˋspeculative °physics of Des⁻cartes | in _favour of the °more | experiˋmentally based °physics | of ˋNewton |(…)| ↓we should re^member that it was about ˇthis time | that ˇMontesquieu | con⁻ceived his reˌspect for ˌEnglish ˌparliamentary deˋmocracy |(LIBMSECDPT02: 089)

(271)   *Type 3*
a. *New–New*
   well you _had to °ask your | Foreign Aˇffairs Office | that ⁻means you had to go to somebody ˋin your university and ask ˇthem | and if they a⁻greed | then you could go °down to the poˇlice station | and ⁻they would give you a ˋpermit | to _travel | to a ⁻certain place which you °named | on a _certain _day | by a ⁻certain type of ˋtransport | in ⁻other _words they wanted to °know the e⁻xact ˌdetails | of ⁻where you would _be at any given ˋtime | now I ˋthink it was in Ocˋtober eighty-ˋtwo that °policy suddenly ˋchanged| (LIBMSECJPT06: 447)

b. *Contrastive–New*
   | Meˋnata is °now ⁻happily _using her ⁻new ˌhearing aid at ˋschool | it is in preˋcisely ˋthese ˌareas | that the ⁻Commonwealth Soˌciety for the ˌDeaf | has been ⁻working for the _past twenty-five ˋyears | aˋssisting ˌparents to °set up ˌschools for the °deaf | and enˌcouraging the ˌtraining for ⁻teachers | of the ⁻deaf | providing ⁻much needed eˌquipment | and aˋbove _all | coˋoperating with ⁻government deˌpartments

| and ˈlocal ˅voluntary organi°sations | to run ˈsurveys to iˈdentify the ˈcauses | and ˈprevalence | of ˌdeafness | (LIBMSECKPT02: 033)

The referents of the complex Predicated Theme in (269a), *Sweden and Switzerland*, are not recoverable from the previous co(n)text, whereas the existence of economically advanced countries, presupposed in the subsequent relative clause, is already cotextually present, though predicated about large states. In (269b) the complex predicated Theme establishes a contrast between *governments* and *business enterprises*, which is reflected by the paratactic relationship of replacive extension linking them, whereas the content of the relative clause "which ship the imports" is directly retrievable from the immediately preceding "imports are always bought directly from chronically unreliable foreign governments". Moving on to (269c), the referents of the topical Theme "ˈCeltic and Aber↑ˈdeen |" are introduced in discourse for the first time and thus are New, but the meaning conveyed by the relative clause "who ended up with the trophies" is inferrable from the previous cotext, in which different speakers have been discussing the victories of different football teams in the league championships of Great Britain and the rest of Europe. In (269d), the last subtype of the first pattern, the predicated Theme is contrastive since the speaker contrasts *the rest of this household* with his wife's preoccupations about whether or not he is busy or expecting the newspaper, while the fact that this lady is concerned, the content of the relative clause, is inferrable from the way she is questioning her husband. Moving on to (270), *this time* is unmistakably Giv$_R$ because of the anaphoric deictic *this*, but the information contained in the relative clause ("that Montesquieu conceived his respect for English parliamentary democracy") is New. Finally, in (271), both Theme and Rheme distil some sort of newness. In the first, the predicated Theme encodes a newly introduced date, *October eighty-two*, in which a new situation with respect to the previous state of affairs suddenly took place, which is coded in the relative clause. In the second, the predicated Theme is contrastive, which is signalled by the anaphoric deictic *these* that gets contrastive stress, but the wordy relative clause (containing three hypotactic non-finite clauses expressing a relationship of elaboration) conveys information that is Fresh, or not yet addressed in discourse.

In addition to this, it was observed that *it*-clefts constitute a textual proportionality, in that like pseudo-clefts, they *all share an implicature of exclusiveness*, or *exhaustiveness, which is absent from uncleft sequences*, and which is often explicitly asserted by such words as *only, precisely*, etc. within the predicated Themes. The implication is that only the referents of the highlighted element, and nobody or nothing else, represent the Identifier/Token with respect to a

Identified/Value mapped on the presupposition coded in the subsequent relative clause. *It follows that the exclusiveness feature conveyed by clefts (and pseudo-clefts) is a matter of their texture, i.e. an inference warranted by the identifying construction itself, rather than a part of their ideational component.* That is to say, the exclusiveness feature of clefts is brought about by the coalescence of Theme and Identifier, and, in unmarked instances, of New, in the same wording. That this exclusiveness feature of clefts is of a textual nature is proved by the fact that it is not affected by such grammatical processes as negation or interrogation, which do affect ideational meaning such as the one asserted in uncleft sequences by words like *only* (e.g. *The duke* didn't only give my aunt that teapot vs. *It is not that teapot* that the duke gave to my aunt, in the former the implicature is contradicted, but in the latter it is retained).

The three communicative properties mentioned so far, i.e. *their acting as thematic build-up devices of paradigmatic flexibility, their being newness-oriented and their sharing an implicature of exhaustiveness*, in principle make *it*-clefts particularly suitable constructions for *argumentative or persuasive formal discourse*. Indeed, their structural *similarity to impersonal constructions (it is thought that..., it is said that...,* etc.) imbues predicated Themes with a depersonalised quality and formality that is well suited for argumentative or persuasive formal discourse, and often inadequate or uncommon in informal unpremeditated texts. The same idea suggests itself when considering that when using Type 1 and 3 cleft constructions speakers are forced to present news at the outset, which indicates that these constructions tend to be encoded with much of their content "pre-formulated", rather than be subject to capricious or spontaneous intuitions. On the other hand, the defining features of persuasive or argumentative texts, where some information is taken as known or presupposed in contrast with what is presented as New, coincide in the main with the communicative purpose of clefts and *also explain the relative frequency of extended multiple and negative predicated Themes of the type it is not ...,* (14.8% vs. 0% RDs, 3.4% LDs, 6.8% *There*-existential, 6.7% *it*-extraposition, 7.6% Inversion).

These claims made about the discourse behaviour of *it*-clefts are confirmed by their distribution across the ten LIBMSEC text-types. They are most frequent in (C, D) Lecture (33.3%), (A) Commentary (18.5%), (J) Dialogue (14.8%) and (F) Magazine (11.1%). Types (C, D, A, F) are formal in tenor and are employed to construct an abstract reality (viz. economics, philosophy, finance in (C, D, F)) or to reconstruct current reality (A). For these textual types the hedged, reportive flavour imbued by the impersonal associations of the *It* + BE thematic predication is particularly suitable. In turn, though informal in tenor, (J) Dialogue also favours the use of *it*-clefts because of its argumentative nature and its aim to discuss. In contrast, *it*-clefts do not appear in Poetry, and are sparse in News, Propaganda (3.7% in each), Religious Broadcasts and Fiction (7.4% in each). None of these texts have the function of giving opinions. Rather they either seek to direct action upon reality or pursue the entertainment of some sort of fiction. It seems that the depersonalised quality of clefts or the processing effort they require make this type of construction inadequate to fulfil these two purposes. Finally, their infrequency in News is only predictable. As in this type of reports everything is expected to be "news", so there is not much place for the presuppositions conveyed by most relatives or some of the Themes of *it*-clefts.

7.4.7 Pseudo-cleft constructions

We turn now to consider the formal structure and discourse function of "pseudo-cleft" constructions or "*wh*-clefts"[129] (e.g. *What the duke gave my aunt was that teapot*), prototypically featured in this study as [+EXTERN, +IDENT, +COREF, +in./fin. PAUSE, +FUN, +NOM, −PRED, −DUM]. 16 tokens of these have been found, representing 3% of both all the Themes and the special thematic constructions in this corpus.

7.4.7.1 Formal structure and frequencies in LIBMSEC

The term "pseudo-cleft" suggests, quite rightly, that despite its resemblance in a number of respects to the cleft construction, it is not to be described in an analogous fashion. The main reason is that there are pseudo-clefts that are not relatable to a more elementary, non-cleft, source:

(272) a. What John likes about European cars is their responsiveness.
      b. *John likes about European cars their responsiveness.
(273) a. What happened to Tom was that he lost his way in the dark.
      b. *That he lost his way in the dark happened to Tom.

Another reason for preferring a "direct" rather than "transformational" description of pseudo-clefts is that the former enables the construction to be related to other semantically-related cases of the specifying be construction. Compare:

(274) a. What I want is a long holiday
      b. The thing I want is a long holiday
      c. All I want is a long holiday

The clauses in (274b) and (274c), which have a NG rather than a fused relative as Subject, could not be plausibly accounted for in terms of a "cleaving" operation. If no such operation is posited in the description of (274a) then all these clauses can receive similar treatment. Identifying-be constructions with an identified NG headed by *all*, as in (274c) above, express a component of exclusiveness which is not asserted in (a) or (b). They may be related to identifying clauses with an identified noun phrase having thing as head and only as premodifier:

(275)   The only thing I want is a long holiday.

In line with this, clauses like (274b), and sometimes (274c), are often included in the class of pseudo-clefts by functional grammarians, who note the systematic relationship between the relative items *what, who, when, where, why and how* on the one hand, and the pro-forms *thing, one, time, place, reason,* and *way* respectively on the other. The semantic parallels are persuasive with the reversed construction:

(276)   a.   This is what/the thing you need.
        b.   That's who/the one who stole your purse.
        c.   That's when/the time when the trouble began.
        d.   This is where/the place where I live.
        e.   That is why/the reason he failed.
        f.   This is how/the way the cover should be removed.

Here, however, in the spirit of Prince (1978), a pseudo-cleft involves the *nominalisation of one set of its elements by means of a rankshifted nominalised fused-relative clause* (i.e. a nominalisation of the *wh*-type fused with preceding proform Head), constituent 1 in (277) below, which is typically introduced by the relative pronoun *what*, or less frequently by *who, where, when, why* or *how*.[130] Regularly, though not obligatorily, the fused relative includes all elements in the clause except one (C-C$_i$ or "clause minus Constituent$_i$"), which is called the *highlighted* or *emphasised constituent/element*:

(277)
                    wh- C–C^i Process: ^{be} C$_i$
                        1   2   3
    | ˈwhat they should ˇteach is ˇinner reˈsourcefulness I(LIBMSECGPT05: 105),

(277) displays the *"basic" pseudo-cleft pattern* (1^2^3), where *the fused relative is Subject* and the *highlighted element Subject Complement. 84.6% pseudo-clefts in* LIBMSEC *display this basic pattern*. By contrast, *15.4% show the pattern 3 2 1* and are called *"reversed" pseudo-clefts*: the *fused relative is Subject Complement* and *the highlighted element Subject*, which tends to be a *demonstrative pronoun* (*that, this*), as in (278a) below, or less frequently a NG, as in (278b), the reversed counterpart of (277):

(278) a. | ↑I _think they're 'still in ˈbed | preˌcisely ˏsaid 'Mr 'Henshaw | that's e⁻xactly what I ˌmean | the ˈhappiest ˈdays of their ⁻lives | and they just ⁻roll ˌover | when ˈI was a 'lad in the ⁻country | it was ˈup with the ⁻lark | and ⁻on with the ˈwellies | (LIBMSECGPT05: 057)
   b. Inner resourcefulness is what they should teach.

As in clefts, the relational process *be* entails a *encoding identifying structure* between the fused relative and the highlighted element, whereby the message is organised into a *two-part (now) reversible identifying structure of the form "x equals y" or "y equals x"* (Section 4.2.1.3). Thus, in *basic pseudo-clefts, the Subject relative clause* is mapped onto (a) *the semantic function of ID/Vl* (Identified/Value), (b) the textual function of *Theme*, and (c) the logico-semantic function of *presupposition*. In its turn, the *Subject Complement highlighted element* (C$_i$) realizes (a) the semantic function of *IR/T* (Identifier/Token) and (b) textual function of *Rheme*. In reversed pseudo-clefts this pattern is reversed. In other words, the IR/T highlighted element is Subject and Theme, while the ID/VL fused relative clause is Subject Complement and Rheme.

Table 46 illustrates the formal features of the IR/T and the ID/Vl constituents of thematic equatives in LIBMSEC. The statistics above show that, compared to *it*-clefts *wh-clefts highlight a narrower range of IR/T units than clefts*, i.e. they tend to be *restricted to nominal structures invoking non-human referents*. This substantiates the hypothesis that clefts and pseudoclefts involve two different

Table 46. *ID/Vl. and IR/T constituents of pseudoclefts in LIBMSEC*

Type of identification	ID/VL		IR/VL	
	Fused relative Type	lexical density	Structure	lexical density
intensive	*what*-13 81.2	4	demonstrative pr. finite clause non-finite clause NG	1 10.5 6.5 2
circumstantial place	*where*- 1 6.2	8	*-ing* clause	19
circumstantial reason	*why*- 1 6.2	17	demonstrative pr.	1
circumstantial manner	*how*- 1 6.2	5	demonstrative pr.	1

types of thematic prominence, with a greater pressure being exerted in pseudo-clefts for a nominal highlighted element (Halliday 1967a; unpub. MS, § 22.13). Human noun phrases are normally excluded (although quite acceptable in clefts) because the fused relative of pseudo-clefts does not normally allow *who*. Compare:

(279)   a.   <u>It was Margaret</u> who found it
        b.   *Who found it was Margaret

The only exceptions are reversed pseudo-clefts with a demonstrative as Subject and cases where a human NG is used non-referentially.

(280)   a.   <u>That's</u> who I met
        b.   <u>What he is</u> a poor loser

69.2% of pseudo-clefts in our corpus *emphasise finite noun clauses* (vs. 7.6% of the *non-finite type*), and in more peripheral instances, *NGs* (23.2%), either third person demonstrative pronouns or common nouns. Tokens of clausal pseudo-cleft highlighting are included in (281), NGs highlighted elements in (277) above, and demonstrative (reversed) realizations in (282) below:

(281)   a.   we ˅have un°fortunately | to re/ly | on the °semi-o/fficial | _Moscow ˋrumour ma°chine | ˋthis de°livers the ʹgoods | in a vaˉriety of ͵ways | by °casual re/marks | at °diplo°matic reˉceptions | °nods and ˋwinks from o⁻fficials | and ↑a_pocryphal ͵stories | <u>ˋwhat it's °telling ˋme at the ˅moment</u> is | that ͵Gorbachev | is in˅deed | ⁻slowly but ͵surely | ˅isolating | ⁻those who o͵ppose him | (LIBMSECAPT11: 35–7)
        b. | °Western ͵governments | have °taken ͵action | ⁻individually ˅and co°llectively | _both to re°duce de/pendence | on im°ported ͵oil | ͵and | to pro°vide for an e˅mergency | °should it a͵rise | ↑in par͵ticular | they have °made conˉsiderable ˅progress | _some of it °quite ͵recent | in ͵freeing | in˅ternal °markets | for ⁻energy ͵products | <u>⁻where they've ͵failed to °act | ͵largely be°cause of the ˅dominance | of mi͵staken eco°nomic ˅notions</u> | is in e͵stablishing | and °making ac͵ceptable | the ⁻principle | that ⁻even in _times of per°ceived ͵scarcity | °energy °markets should be a°llowed to _function ͵freely | and °prices should re_flect | °willingness to ͵pay |(LIBMSECCPT01: 524–6)
        c. | oh ˋcheers | the ˋweather | oh no _no | doesn't bother ˋme | I _simply don't ˋnotice it | <u>no ˋwhat bothers ˋme</u> | is my ⁻restless ˋfamily | can't ͵settle to °anything | (LIBMSECGPT05: 131–3)

(282) a. | and there's the ˎdoctor I _came a°cross | who I'd °interviewed in _Tripoli | ᵛduring the °fighting last De°cember | in a _makeshift ˎhospital | in a _school ˎbasement | ˎhe now °works in ˎCairo | and ˬsays | only ᵛhalf °jokingly | the ˬnext PN°C | _could be ˎthere | ˎthat's how °fast things ˎchange| (LIBMSECAPT02: 61)

b. | ˎthen | the ⁻value to the eˌconomy | of a ⁻barrel of ˌoil | 'sold ᵛon that 'market | is a _hundred ˎdollars | since ˌthis is | 'what do_mestic con'sumers in ˌgeneral | would be ⁻willing to ˌpay | for the ˎimports | that it _makes ˎpossible | (LIBMSECCPT01: 399)

c. | well ˎlet's now °turn our aˎttention to ↑ᵛcricket | and once ˎmore it's been a ⁻year when °test ^matches | and the uˎbiquitous ⁻one day inter⁻nationals | proˎliferated around the ⁻world | and that's ⁻why it was ᵛalso a year | when our °cricket re⁻porter | Chris ⁻Florence | had to _buy a ⁻jumbo-sized ᵛrecord book | to keep ˎtrack of it °all | [change of speaker: Chris Florence] (LIBMSECFPT04: 12)

Other periphereal realizations of the highlighted element are: PPs, as in (281b) above, and, though absent from our corpus, also AdjGs (280b) and AdvGs (283) below, the first two only if the fused relative is introduced by *where*, *when*, or *how*:

(283) How she dances is gracefully

Syntactically, in addition to the Subject, Direct Complement and Adjunct functions which are most commonly assumed by the relative element within the fused relative, as in (279a), (278), (283) above, one can also find the functions of Complement of a preposition, as in (281b) above, Subject Complement, as in (280b) and Complement of *do* (284) below:

(284) What John did was wash his car

The type of pseudo-cleft illustrated in (284) has no cleft analogue (**It was wash his car that John did*). The complement of *do* which is relativised may be a non-finite construction of the infinitival type (with or without *to*), the *-ing* type or the *-en* type:

(285) a. What they did was (to) collect evidence
b. What they're doing is collecting evidence
c. What they've done is collected evidence

Besides, Table 46 above and the examples presented so far show that *wh-clefts tend to imply an identification relationship of the intensive type* (81.2%), while instances of *circumstantial identification are more peripheral* (18.8%) the possessive type does not occur in our corpus *and tends to be restricted to reversed pseudo-clefts of the demonstrative type*, e.g. (282a, c) vs. (281b) above. This seems to indicate that *pseudo-clefts with a fused relative clause introduced by a wh-item other than what are more commonly reversed than basic*, and usually *have demonstrative this or that as subject/highlighted element*.

A further feature of *pseudo-clefts reflected in Table 46 is that they abide by the principles of EF and EW*. This tendency is especially noticeable in instances of the demonstrative reversed type where the Rhemes far outweigh their Themes, but instances of the non-reversed type largely conform to the two principles as well.

In addition, *most pseudo-clefts have EMTs* (84.8%, vs. 7.6%), undoubtedly because the *wh*-element of fused relatives by itself realizes that class of Theme, but thematic continuatives (7.7%), conjunctive Adjuncts (23.1%) and modal Adjuncts (15.4%) have also been found. Consider:

(286) a. | ⸜one at ⸜least | °Wieland ᵛHerzfelde | was a ⁻member of the _newly-formed °German ⸜communist °party | and his ⁻brother John _Heartfield was in °close ⸜sympathy | as was °George ⸜Grosz | ↑this _certainly ⸜coloured the political ⸜spectrum of °Dada | but ⁻has I _think to be °kept to some extent ⸜separate | from the _movement it⸜self | what I ᵛam suggesting there°fore | is that ⁻Berlin _Dada con°sisted of a ⁻hetero_genous °group of ⁻writers and ₁artists | whose ⸜coming together ⁻constituted | a ⁻brief a_lliance between ⁻radical ₁politics | and _radical aes⸜thetics | (LIBMSECDPT01: 027–9)

b. | the ⸜weather | oh no _no | doesn't bother ⸜me | I _simply don't ⸜notice it | no ⸜what bothers ⸜me | is my ⁻restless ⸜family | can't ₁settle to °anything | (LIBMSECGPT05: 132)

(287) | ↑of course ⸜what concerns °church ⸜leaders | ⁻isn't neces/sarily | ⁻what °worries ordinary ⸜churchgoers | even ⁻less the _general ⸜public | (LIBMSECAPT01: 28)

Finally, Table 47 summarises the prosodic contour of *wh*-clefts in LIBMSEC. The Table shows that *the prosodic patterns of prototypical and reversed pseudo-clefts do not coincide*. As in the case of prototypical clefts, *the thematic fused relatives of most non-reversed pseudo-clefts display the features of [+EXTERN] and [+IN. PAUSE], having unmarked tonality and tonicity*. In other words, they are realized in two tone groups (82% vs. 8% in a single one), marking the cleavage of ID/VL$_{Theme}$-IR/T$_{Rheme}$ and imbuing both constituents with the focal prominence of the New element in unmarked final tone unit position (Halliday 1967: 226). Moreover, most *wh*-Themes have a Falling-Rising pattern, whereas their Rhemes, i.e. the highlighted element, present the opposite, Rising-Falling. *The Falling-Rising nuclei within the wh-Themes endow these constituents with a flavour of contrastiveness and incompleteness*. As remarked about *it*-clefts, these tonal

Table 47. *Falling vs. Rising tones in pseudoclefts in LIBMSEC*

tone mark	tone on WH-Theme	end tone of WH-Theme	tone on C_i Rheme	Pause/Tone group. bound. +	Pause/Tone group. bound. −
Non-reversed					
Falling tone	6 55.0	3 27.0	16 100	14 87.5	2 12.5
Rising tone	1 9.0	6 55.0			
other: no nucleus, level	4 36.0	1 9.0			
Reversed					
falling tone	2 50.0		4 100	2 50	2 50
rising tone					
Other: no nucleus, level	2 50.0	4 100			

effects enhance at the same time the bi-member quality of pseudo-clefts, as reversible identifying structures, while preserving the unmarked correspondence between the IR and the New.

In contrast, *demonstrative reversed pseudo-clefts in our corpus have a comparatively higher number of single tone group realizations*. In two cases the demonstrative IR/T receives focal prominence and is signalled as contrastively New, e.g. (282a, b), whereas in two other instances it does not get prosodic highlighting, e.g. (278a) (282c). But in all cases there is one (or more) nuclear (Rising)-Falling tone within the Rheme, which marks this constituent as the informative point of the clause. Now Section 7.4.7.2 explicates the discourse relevance of the segmental and suprasegmental make-up of pseudo-clefts so far described.

7.4.7.2 Discourse function
The *pseudo-cleft construction is a thematic bracketing device which enables the speaker to select almost any element or group of elements as the Theme*. Consider the few possibilities included in (288) below:

(288) a. What Ted did was give Sam a cigar
       b. What Ted did with the cigar was offer it to Sam
       c. What happened to Sam was that Ted offered him a cigar
       d. A cigar was what Ted gave Sam (reversed pseudo-cleft)
       e. Give Sam a cigar was what Ted did (reversed pseudo-cleft)

In terms of their thematic structure reversed pseudo-clefts are similar to clefts. Compare:

(289) a. A cigar was what Ted gave Sam
 b. It was a cigar that Ted gave Sam

There is nevertheless, a subtle difference in the type of thematic prominence ascribed to the highlighted element, *a cigar*, by the two constructions. In (a) *A cigar* is highlighted in terms of its participation (as the "Goal") in a process of giving, giving it prominence of a "conceptual" kind, whereas in (b) the (superordinate) clause in which *a cigar* serves as Complement is concerned solely with the identity of the cigar, giving it prominence of a "textual" kind.

Indeed, *the evidence presented so far suggests that pseudo-clefts function as thematic build-up devices of an ideational, participant-like flavour*. In contrast with the textual prominence of clefts, the ideational prominence of the dominant clause of *wh*-clefts can be negated or questioned, or both (e.g. What they should teach isn't inner resourcefulness, Is inner resourcefulness what they should teach, where the Range status of *inner resourcefulness* is questioned or negated). *The (unmarked) Theme of pseudo-clefts highlights the involvement of a participant or the attendance of a circumstance in a given state of affairs by means of a relational process*. This mechanism allows for *a thematic flexibility that is syntagmatic in orientation*. In other words, the ideational prominence of pseudo-clefts emerges from establishing a direct reversible equation between two segments that enable all possible distributions of these two elements into Theme and Rheme. These are presented as two entities, a fused relative clause and its Complement in the unmarked cases. The latter, acting as the IR/T of normally a *what*-fused relative clause, is more likely to be nominal and to fulfil participant-related functions (hence the relative absence of prepositional and adverbial realizations, which are fairly common in *It*-clefts). Significantly enough, the preference of pseudo-clefts for participant-related functions appears to override the pressure to maintain the word order patterns of non-cleft versions. This is most obvious in reversed pseudo-clefts of the demonstrative type which have thematic *this* and *that* acting as circumstantial identifiers, rather than the adjuncts *here*, *there* or *then*.

Besides their *syntagmatic flexibility*, two further key features characterise the communicative function of pseudo-clefts: (a) their *interpersonal flavour* and (b) their *givenness-orientation* (Collins 1992). These emerge from the tension derived from the unmarked mapping of (a) Subject, (b) the ID/VL, (c) Theme and (d) a presupposition onto the same wording. Hence, besides allowing for the incorporation of (an) element(s) with an ideational function within the Rheme and the New, the fused relative clause combines the speaker orientation of

Theme, on the one hand, and the listener orientation of Giv_R, on the other. The information conveyed by the relative clause is backgrounded syntactically, by its rankshifted status, and logically, by coding a presupposition which is assumed to be true by the speaker. Thus, through its thematic highlighting, the fused relative clause generates a strong feeling in the addressee that s/he was expected to accept or to infer the relevance of the proposition presupposed by it (as non-controversially recoverable), paying attention, at the same time, to the segment that gets prosodic highlighting.

Pseudo-clefts therefore offer speakers a means of specifying precisely the background knowledge to which the addressee is expected to have access before announcing the message itself. The source for this background knowledge (Giv_R) could be cotextual (viz. directly/indirectly opposite/similar inferable from/to the preceding text) or it could be contextually retrieved from the field, tenor or mode of the discourse situation. In 50% of all cases the relative clauses of non-reversed pseudo-clefts in LIBMSEC code information which is indirectly opposite to their preceding cotexts, as in (290a). 25% have contextual tenor-antecedents, as in (290b), 12.5% situational mode-antecedents, as in (290c), and 12.5% are indirectly similar to their preceding cotexts, as illustrated in (290d):

(290) a. *cotextual indirectly opposite*
| ˅making your own is °simply | ⁻doing something to °fill in the ˋtime | like _half these °daft ˋyouth opportunity °projects they ⁻foist off on the ˎyoung | building ˎwalls | no one ˎneeds | making ˋfoot°paths | we never ˋwalk on | what they should ˅teach is ˅inner reˋsourcefulness | ah this is a ˋrestless gene°ration it ⁻cannot sit _still | if we were _all to sit ˋquietly for an °hour every ˅morning we might ⁻change the ˋworld | (LIBMSECGPT05: 105)

b. *contextual tenor-antecedent*
↑by comˋparison in Afghaniˋstan | the ⁻women _there had to ⁻wear | the ˋveil | from °head to ˋtoe | e⁻specially the women from _outside | the ˋcapital | ⁻only my ˋstudents there were a°llowed to wear European ˋdress | so that | if I went ˋout into the ˋvillages just outˋside the °capital | I would ⁻always find the °women ˋcovered in the | what was called the 'chadaˋree' | ˋcovered from ⁻head | to ˎtoe | in fact ⁻I | °tried one of them ˎon | just to ⁻see what it was ⁻really ˋlike | to be beˋhind one of those °things | and in Afghaniˋstan | what they ˎwear | it ⁻has this small ˋgrille-like ⁻feature over the ˎeyes | so that ⁻you can see _out and | ⁻other people of °course can't see ˋin | but what was really quite aˋmusing is that the ˋwomen who ˅wore them | would ⁻often _wear ˋvery nice ˋshoes | at the ˋbottom | to sort of ⁻show that they | were ˋtrying to be | more ˋWesternised even though

their ˋhusbands and ˋfamily didn't aˋllow them | ↑did ⁻you have that | ↑situ°ation at all | outˊside the main °cities | (LIBMSECJPT06: 343)

c. *contextual mode-antecedent*
ˋone at ˋleast | °Wieland ˇHerzfelde | was a ⁻member of the _newly-formed °German ˋcommunist °party | and his ⁻brother John _Heartfield was in °close ˋsympathy | as was °George ˋGrosz | ↑this _certainly ˋcoloured the political ˋspectrum of °Dada | but ⁻has I _think to be °kept to some extent ˋseparate | from the _movement itˋself | what I ˇam suggesting there°fore | is that ⁻Berlin _Dada con°sisted of a ⁻hetero_genous °group of ⁻writers and ˌartists | whose ˋcoming together ⁻constituted | a ⁻brief a_lliance between ⁻radical ˌpolitics | and _radical aesˋthetics | (LIBMSECDPT01: 029)

d. *cotextually indirectly similar*
we ˇhave un°fortunately | to reˌly | on the °semi-oˌfficial | _Moscow ˋrumour ma°chine | ˋthis de°livers the ˊgoods | in a va⁻riety of ˌways | by °casual reˌmarks | at °diplo°matic re⁻ceptions | °nods and ˋwinks from o⁻fficials | and ↑a_pocryphal ˌstories | ˋwhat it's °telling ˋme at the ˇmoment is | that ˌGorbachev | is inˇdeed | ⁻slowly but ˌsurely | ˇisolating | ⁻those who oˌppose him |(LIBMSECAPT11: 037)

In (290a) the speaker's opinion about *what they should teach* contrasts indirectly with the preceding cotext, where he has been explaining the objectives of *youth opportunity projects*. In turn, the recoverability of *but what was really quite amusing* in (290b) is speaker-centred. The speaker presents impersonally his previously unmentioned thoughts about women's costumes in Afghanistan (i.e. his amusement or surprise) as "shared background knowledge" and as the relevant concern of the collaborative addressee. In contrast, in (290c) the speaker's *what I'm suggesting therefore* invokes the mode of his discourse: it acts as a metalinguistic clarification of his previous discourse that is assumed to be comprehended by the collaborative discourse participants. Finally, the Theme of the pseudo-cleft in (290d) encodes information that is indirectly similar to the previous cotext through generic to specific inferencing: the preceding paragraph dwells on the way the semi-official Moscow rumour machine delivers information, while *what it's telling me at the moment* particularises how the speaker interprets this information.

All these examples underscore the fourth and last feature of pseudo-clefts, namely the fact that, as in *it*-clefts, their identifying structure has the effect of an added *implicature of exhaustiveness*. In other words, *pseudo-cleft constructions assert both crucialness and exclusiveness of the Theme by establishing an explicit contrast either with respect to the preceding co(n)text* (directly or inferentially) or, less commonly, *with regard to the cataphoric cotext* (i.e. with what one might expect). *In informational terms the newness of pseudo-cleft Themes is also contrastive, rather than Fresh*, because the Focus, if present, falls upon an item that was Giv$_R$. As a result of this contrastive effect, *wh-clefts act as discourse markers whereby the camera angle of discourse is directed towards the Theme itself and deviated from the other items to which this category is compared*. This factor explicates the fact that pseudo-clefts tend to be used at *turning points* in discourse with the following capacities:

a. to *announce a change of Topic*, as in (290a, d) above;
b. to *repair the old ("wrong") Topic with a new ("right") one*, as in (291) below;

   (291) | oh ˈcheers | the ˈweather | oh no _no | doesn't bother ˈme | I _simply don't ˈnotice it | no ˈwhat bothers ˈme | is my ⁻restless ˈfamily | can't ˌsettle to °anything | we've ˈrented this ˈcottage in the ᵛcountry | for ˈpeace and ˈquiet | and ˈall they do is ˈwander about | _fiddling with ˈthis | _fiddling with ˈthat | and ˈfighting | (LIBMSECGPT05: 132)

c. to provide *a summary or Topic statement* for the entire text or for a stretch of text, as in (290c) above;
d. *to advance opinions*, or perspectives, with respect to some co(n)textually present Topic, as in (290b) above.

By contrast, *reversed pseudo-clefts are comparatively "newness oriented"*: more often uttered on a single tone group than non-reversed ones, their Focus is more likely to fall upon the rhematic and more informative relative clause ID/Vl, as compared to the thematic IR/T demonstrative pronouns. Consider the four tokens found reproduced below as (292):

   (292) a. | ↑I _think they're 'still in ˈbed | preˌcisely ˌsaid 'Mr 'Henshaw | that's e⁻xactly what I ˌmean | the ˈhappiest ˈdays of their ⁻lives | and they just ⁻roll ˌover | when ˈI was a 'lad in the ⁻country | it was ˈup with the ⁻lark | and ⁻on with the ˈwellies | (LIBMSECGPT05: 057)
   b. | well ˈlet's now °turn our aˈttention to ↑ᵛcricket | and once ˈmore it's been a ⁻year when °test ^matches | and the uˈbiquitous ⁻one day inter⁻nationals | proˈliferated around the ⁻world | and that's ⁻why it was ᵛalso a year | when our °cricket re⁻porter | Chris ⁻Florence | had to _buy a ⁻jumbo-sized ᵛrecord book | to keep ˈtrack of it °all | [change of speaker: Chris Florence] (LIBMSECFPT04: 12)
   c. | ˌthen | the ⁻value to the eˌconomy | of a ⁻barrel of ˌoil | 'sold ᵛon that 'market | is a _hundred ˈdollars | since ˌthis is | 'what do_mestic conˈsumers in ˌgeneral | would be ⁻willing to ˌpay | for the ˈimports | that it _makes ˌpossible | (LIBMSECCPT01: 399)

d. | and there's the \doctor I _came a°cross | who I'd °interviewed in _Tripoli | ᵛduring the °fighting last De°cember | in a _makeshift ₍hospital | in a _school ₍basement | ᵛhe now °works in ₍Cairo | and ᵥsays | only ᵛhalf °jokingly | the ᵥnext PN°C | _could be ₍there | \that's how °fast things ₍change| (LIBMSECAPT02: 61)

In (292) all the thematic demonstratives exhibit "anaphoric text reference" within the pseudo-clefts: a deictically recoverable stretch of discourse is represented as Theme and offered as specifying, or exclusively identifying, the referent of the rhematic relative clause (Halliday 1967b: 232; Halliday & Hasan 1976: 52–3). In the first two cases the Theme is naturally non-focal because it is non-contrastively anaphoric, whereas in the other two a marked contrast is established with the preceding text owing to the emotional state and emphatic tone of the speaker. In (292a) Mr Henshaw's reversed pseudo-cleft corroborates the opinion of his interlocutor just advanced: *that* is anaphoric in this sense but it is also cataphoric in that it grounds Mr Henshaw's own opinion which is to be developed within the fused relative clause. Likewise, in (292b) the word *also* is an important cue to removing any possible topical contrast with the previous cotext. Rather, by creating a cohesive tie its Theme insists on the preceding idea, that cricket test matches and one day internationals proliferated in that year. Conversely, in (292c) and (292d) *this* and *that* are emphatically anaphorically contrastive: they refer back to the previous discourse stretch to emphasise (a) what domestic consumers will be willing to pay, in (292c), or (b) the rapidity of events in Tripoli at wartime, in (292d).

Reversed pseudoclefts have been found to normally occur at the end of stages in discourse. The low informativity and internal referencing summative function of their Themes convert these constructions into text-structuring devices especially suited to marking (stage) endings. When used in this way reversed pseudo-clefts tend to have little informational content (e.g. they are clichés, repetitions, generalisations), but they insist on or summarise the idea developed throughout the stage or text. Consistent with this text structuring role, reversed pseudo-clefts lack the interpersonal flavour ascribed to the non-reversed type, which derives from the association of Theme and presupposition. *Unless they are contrastive, reversed pseudo-cleft Themes do not draw any attention to themselves but provide a cohesive framework with which to develop the rhematic presupposition conveyed by the relative clause.*

One final remark should be made regarding *the distribution of pseudo-clefts across* LIBMSEC *text-types. It is similar to that of it-clefts*: 38.5% in Commentary, 30.8% in Lecture, 15.4% in Fiction, and 7.7% in Magazine and Dialogue. These results suggest that *pseudo-clefts normally cluster around opinionative texts*.

Generally, speakers use them to identify their views or situate the thread of discourse with respect to some co(n)textual presupposition, when recreating reality (Commentaries), when creating it (Lecture, Fiction, Magazine) or when acting upon it (Dialogue). But significantly enough, pseudo-clefts are only half as frequent as *it*-clefts in performing these tasks, probably because of their interpersonal flavour, which makes their frequent use inadequate for the formality of most texts in our corpus.

7.5 Extended multiple Themes

What follows characterises the frequencies, the formal features and the discourse motivations of extended multiple Themes (EMTS) in LIBMSEC. This involves first describing this category, and then analysing the results obtained by the application of different statistical tests to the tokens of EMTs found in the corpus. The findings reveal a list of textual patterns derived from the co-occurrence of topical and/or interpersonal and/or logico-conjunctive items within the Theme zone, whereby the discourse motivations behind such patterns can be elicited. *It will be shown that the unmarked display of EMTs is (logico-conjunctive) ^ (interpersonal) ^ topical ^ (interpersonal) ^ (logico-conjunctive)*. This organisation will be said to abide by the *principle of Centripetal Organisation* (Dik 1989: 342), which, in turn, is explained according to the *layering hypothesis* (as proposed in FG or RRG by e.g. Hengeveld 1989; Fortescue et al. 1992; Van Valin Jr. 1993; Vet 1998;) *arguing for a scopal, rather than a parallel or "comparatively independent" organisation of the metafunctions* (as claimed in SFG).

7.5.1 Formal structure and frequencies in LIBMSEC

The notion of *EMTs* radically modifies the premises inherent in the SFG conception of multiple Theme in four main respects (Section 4.3.2 above; Gómez-González 1998a). First, while in SFG multiple Themes occur only when one or several textual and/or interpersonal items are placed *before* a *simple* topical Theme, here the category of *EMTs is proposed as a cover-term for topical Themes co-occurring with pre-topical and/or post-topical textual and/or interpersonal elements*, as shown in (293) in turn:

(293) a. | ↑\this of °course was \not because the \government \failed in its su°pposed \duty as pro^vvider | ↑but ₗlargely | because _energy prices rose con^vsiderably | in reₗlation to \other prices |(LSECCPT01: 199)

b. | Wes\`tmorland for e°xample | became par\`ticularly ˅passionate | when \`talking about the °influence ⁻television re˅porting from Viet°nam | had \`had on the ˅White °House | in the °late \`sixties | (LSECAPT03: 030)

The implication is that post-topical interpersonal and/or textual elements can equally be regarded as metafunctional boundaries that separate off the Theme from the Rheme in a clausal predication. Further evidence for this analysis lies in the fact that the Theme–Rheme separation is often reinforced suprasegmentally, by means of one or more of the following three devices:

a. *Tone sequence*, i.e. two or more instances of the same tone marking paratactic or hypotactic elaboration, as in (294):

(294) and he ⁻knew that \`now | ⁻this ˌmoment | when his ⁻nose had °only just °stopped ˌbleeding | when his ⁻head was still ⁻sore and \`throbbing | \`this | was the ⁻moment when he would ˌtry | (LSECGPT01: 208–21) (Tone 1 sequence);

b. *Tone concord*, i.e. 1–1, 3–1 and 4–1, the unmarked realizations of Themes involving a relationship of cohesion, parataxis and hypotaxis respectively, as in (295):

(295) ah that's \`totally unlike Su˅dan | because °obviously Su˅dan is | °by and large a ˅Muslim country | and of course ˅there you | don't have ˅very many °holidays | but | the month of ˅Ramadan | when people are ⁻fasting | from \`sunrise to sun⁻set | every °day | then \`very little work \`does get done | (LSECJPT06: 299–301) (4–1 Tone concord: hypotaxis)

c. *a Tone group boundary*, as in (296):

(296) | ˌwhat for e°xample | is he ⁻doing to en°sure that \`his grip on ˌpower | is ˅strong e°nough | to _make the °necessary ˌchanges | (LSECAPT11: 031)

The examples in (295) and (296) above illustrate a second claim: that in EMTs, *not only textual and interpersonal elements*, as claimed in IFG, *but also topical ones, may be complex*. This claim is based on the observation that topical, interpersonal and textual items can be equally used recursively within (or outside) EMTs, by entailing different kinds of logico-semantic and tactic relationships (viz. paratactic, hypotactic or rankshifted expansions or projections). Some examples follow:

(297) a. | ´perhaps | with the diˌvisions | that have °opened ´up | ˌand | with ⁻all the re°crimiˊnation | the ˅Pale°stinian ˌmovement | °thought there was ⁻little ˌhope | for a °PN_C at ˌall | (LSECAPT02: 036) (EMT with a Complex Marked Topical Theme).

b. | perhaps ˻she though so ˅small | of so ˻quick-°perishing ˅beauty | is ⁻none the ˻less | a ˻part of °His immortal °dream | and be⁻neath her _breast | ˻cherishes the di⁻vine ˻life | (LSECHPT04: 036) (EMT with a complex Unmarked Topical Theme).
c. | ₎often | though not ˅always | the ˻case for self-su°fficiency is ˅argued | with ⁻reference to a °country's °need to en_sure se˅curity | by ⁻minimising de₎pendence on ₎foreign ˻sources |(LSECCPT01: 249) (EMT with a complex Interpersonal Theme).
d. | em | and al°though I have °ample ↑˻time to get through the °work I ˻want to get through I have a˻nother problem | in that | the °students just cannot ↑˻concentrate for twenty °weeks | (LSECJPT06: 261) (EMT with a complex Textual (or Logico-Conjunctive) Theme).

Thirdly, as already noted (Section 4.3.2), while in SFG topical Themes are described as clause initial items fulfilling an *ideational* function, here they are characterised as playing an *experiential/transitivity* role. The reason is that the ideational metafunction comprises both experiential and logico-conjunctive items, when only the former qualify for topical status, that is to say clause-initial: (a) *processes* (phenomena to which a specification of time may be attached); (b) *participants* (i.e. the linguistic representations of non-human, inanimate, abstract entities, as well as human beings, involved in the situations); and (c) any possible attending *circumstance(s)* (or qualities/attributes) of the whole situation or of the participant(s). In the same vein, the label *textual Theme* has been replaced by that of *logico-conjunctive Theme*, which, considering that all classes of Theme are textual in nature, seems to be a more appropriate term to designate an initial item fulfilling a logico-conjunctive and/or a conjunctive function (although logico-conjunctive and conjunctive elements may also occur within the Rheme).

Our results report *EMTs as the marked option*, i.e. a less frequent and therefore presumably more constrained choice than non-multiple Themes (40.9% vs. 59.1% non-extended multiple ones). *Most EMTs (86.7%) involve the presence of a logico-conjunctive Theme, while only 13.7% result from the appearance of a thematic interpersonal element.* Within logico-conjunctive Themes, *structural items are the most frequent* (77%), followed by *conjunctive Adjuncts* (13.5%) and *Continuatives* (9.4%). In turn, *modal Adjuncts outweigh the other sub-classes of interpersonal Themes* (45.6%), as opposed to scarcer realizations of: interrogative/exclamative pronouns (22.3%), Finites (20.6%), and Vocatives (11.5%).

As illustrated in Table 48, the logistic regression technique reports five variables as significant for the choice of a EMT (in decreasing order of effect): (a) *position of topical Theme*, (b) *position of logico-conjunctive* Theme, (c) *position of interpersonal Theme*, (d) LIBMSEC *text-type* and (e) *the presence of a β Theme*.

Table 48. *Choice of EMTs (yes-response) in* LIBMSEC

Variables	B	S.E.	Wald statistic	Degree of freedom	Signif.	R	Exp (B)
Posit. Topical Theme			369.9322	2	**.0000**	**.2616**	
Position 1	3.5513	.1869	360.8518	1	.0000	.2591	34.8576
Position 2	3.5799	.7022	25.9920	1	.0000	.0670	35.8694
Posit. Logico-conjunct. Theme			267.1264	3	**.0000**	**.2210**	
Position 1	2.5688	.2007	163.8311	1	.0000	.1740	13.0498
Position 2	4.4756	.5953	56.5290	1	.0000	.1010	87.8465
Position 3	3.7863	.3992	89.9385	1	.0000	.1282	44.0920
Posit.Interp. Theme			84.7763	3	**.0000**	**.1214**	
Position 1	1.9816	.2521	61.8021	1	.0000	.1058	7.2540
Position 2	1.9586	.5673	11.9205	1	.0006	.0431	7.0891
Position 3	2.2816	.5078	20.1858	1	.0000	.0583	9.7919
Type of Text			39.0980	9	**.0000**	**.0628**	
Commentary	−1.1787	.2945	16.0141	1	.0001	−.0512	.3077
News Broad.	.1042	.3176	.1076	1	.7429	.0000	1.1098
Lecture	− .3036	.2632	1.3307	1	.2487	.0000	.7381
Religious Broad.	.0866	.4488	.0372	1	.8470	.0000	1.0904
Magazine	− .1599	.3074	.2707	1	.6028	.0000	.8522
Fiction	−1.0023	.2390	17.5877	1	.0000	−.0540	.3670
Poetry	.2256	.4730	.2275	1	.6334	.0000	1.2531
Dialogue	− .1058	.2427	.1899	1	.6630	.0000	.8996
Propaganda	− .4850	.4699	1.0655	1	.3020	.0000	.6157
β Theme			11.6904	5	**.0393**	**.0178**	
Spatio-Temp.	− .0052	.5322	.0001	1	.9922	.0000	.9948
Manner	.8099	.6351	1.6264	1	.2022	.0000	2.2477
Cause	− .4136	1.1126	.1382	1	.7101	.0000	.6612
Goal	− .4245	.6624	.4107	1	.5216	.0000	.6541
Condition	1.3487	.4332	9.6927	1	.0019	.0379	3.8524

The significance of these five variables is further corroborated in Table 49.

Table 49 demonstrates that, considering only the values of the five significant variables selected by the regression analysis, 94.49% cases of EMTs are rightly predicted to be extended multiple, while only 5.51% are incorrectly regarded as non-extended multiple. By the same token, 91.58% instances of non-extended multiple Themes are correctly classified as non-extended multiple, whereas just 8.42% are wrongly analysed as extended multiple. In the light of the consistency of these results, EMTs shall be characterised firstly in relation to the five variables selected by the logistic regression technique.

Table 49. *Classification table for choice of EMTs (yes-response)*

Observed variables	Predicted non-multiple Theme	Predicted multiple Theme	Percent correct
Non-multiple Theme	2247	131	94.49%
Multiple Theme	134	1458	91.58%
		Overall	93.32%

It seems that the selection of the first three variables, i.e. (a) *position of topical Theme*, (b) *position of logico-conjunctive Theme* and (c) *position of interpersonal Theme*, is self-evident because for there to be a EMT a topical Theme (variable (a) and therefore the most important one) has to co-occur with a logico-conjunctive and/or an interpersonal Theme (variables (b) and (c)). Likewise, it could be argued that logico-conjunctive Themes are reported as statistically "more significant" than interpersonal ones because the former are more numerous in LIBMSEC than the latter. However, the fact that it is *the position of the three classes of Theme that is selected as most significant for the choice of a EMT profiles itself as a most revealing finding*. It seems to support the hypothesis that *the unmarked array of EMTs abides by the principle of Centripetal Orientation* (PCO), i.e. ordering determined by the relative distance from the Head of a constituent, possibly with mirror image relations (Dik 1989: 342). The PCO will lead us to suggest that, rather than the pattern (textual) ^ (interpersonal) ^ topical as proposed in e.g. SFG, *unmarked EMTs display a centripetal organisation of the type (logico-conjunctive) ^ (interpersonal) ^ topical ^ (interpersonal) ^ (logico-conjunctive)*, i.e. unmarked hierarchical relations between y (logico-conjunctive Themes) and x (interpersonal Themes) with respect to H (topical Themes, the Nucleus or Head, of EMTs), as illustrated in Figure 16.

Figure 16 represents y and x as arranged in the unmarked cases in relation to their scope of influence, suggesting that x tends to occupy position 1 and y

```
                        ─── y ───
                     ─── x ───
     2        1           H           1         2
(logico-conjunct.)^(interpersonal)^ topical ^(interpersonal)^(logico-conjunct.)
     y        x           H           y         x
```

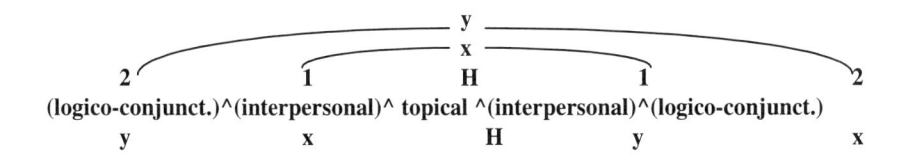

Figure 16. *Unmarked centripetal array of EMTs*

position 2 because the former is in the scope of the latter. This organisation is described as "centripetal" on the assumption that both y and x pivot on H, which represents the pivotal, or "obligatory", element of the construct, lying within the scope of the other two elements. Topical Themes (H) are described as the "pivots" of EMTs because:

a. they tend to appear in medial position, i.e. either before or after a logico-conjunctive and/or an interpersonal Theme, whereby topical Themes can be said to "attract" the other two classes of Themes towards themselves;
b. interpersonal Themes (x) tend to occupy position 1, which implies their outer scope with respect to topical Themes and their inner scope in relation to logico-conjunctive ones;
c. most logico-conjunctive Themes (y) occur in position 2, which suggests the outer scope of this class as compared to both interpersonal and topical Themes.

This hypothesis is supported by the figures obtained in this field research. According to our findings, logico-conjunctive Themes have the highest ratio of position 1 realizations (96.2%), while topical elements display the lowest percentage of position 1 realizations (10.1%), but a very high rate of second places, i.e. after a logico-conjunctive or an interpersonal Theme (84.7%), and a minority of third slot realizations, i.e. after both a logico-conjunctive and an interpersonal Theme (5.2%). In their turn, although they also have a high ratio of initial realizations (56.7%), interpersonal Themes are second more rarely than topical Themes, but more frequently so than logico-conjunctive Themes (36.5%), and they come third, i.e. after a logico-conjunctive and a topical Theme, in more cases than the other two classes (6.4%). In the light of these positional tendencies one can conclude that the unmarked EMTs is, as already noted, "centripetal" with logico-conjunctive Themes appearing either in pretopical or post-topical position 2, depending on whether they precede or follow the topical Theme, whereas, with the same provisos, interpersonal Themes occupy either pre- or post-topical position 1. To illustrate their centripetal arrangement, consider the *unmarked high-low patterns* listed in (298), *where a logical and/or an interpersonal element precedes a topical one in the Theme zone*, and the *unmarked low-high patterns* included in (299), *where a topical element is followed by an interpersonal and/or logical item within the thematic slot*; both unmarked patterns amount to 94.9% of EMTs. Alternatively, marked extended arrangements such as (300) represent the remaining 5.1%.

(298) *Unmarked high-low patterns: logico-conjunctive and/or interpersonal Themes preceding topical ones* (66.6%):
1. *Logico-conjunctive^topical*, as in:
   a. | for ex_ample | ˈI had ˉtwo Japanese ˋcooks ₍ whom I °used to °teach | (LIBMSECDPT03: 223)
   b. | after ˋall | °who needs teleᵛvision °drama | ˉwhen you can _see the °real ˋthing | (LIBMSECAPT03: 062)
   c. | howˋever | ˈsuch is the inˉcestuous ˋnature | of Naˈmibian ᵥpolitics | and ˈso aˋpparent | the ˉself-imˋportance | of ˈsome of its pracᵥtitioners | that ˉthose inᵛvolved in the new ˈgovern-ment | ˋobviously ˈfind it ᵥdifficult | to ˈrise aᵛbove | the ˈlevel of _small town ᵥpolitics |(LIBMSECAPT09)
2. *Interpersonal^topical*, as in:
   d. | ᵛFather | ˉhelp us to ᵥwalk | in your ↓_son's _footsteps | reˉmembering | ˉhis _self-for_getting | huᵥmility | his ˋlove for °all ᵥpeople | his comˋpassion for the ᵥfallen | his for↓ˋbearance with the misᵥtaken | and his ↓ˋpatience with the ᵥslow | and his forˉgiveness | of ˉall ˋthose | who ˋhurt him | (LIBMSECEPT01: 059)
   e. | °heavenly Father | whose ˋwill is ˋgood and _perfect | we beᵢlieve and _trust | that ˉyou _will | ˉonly what is for the ˉtrue _happiness | of ˉyour ᵥpeople | (LIBMSECEPT01: 060–62)
   f. | of ᵥcourse | °why °God should have °chosen to creᵛate such an im°perfect °world | was a ˋmystery | (LIBMSECDPT02: 154)
3. *Logico-conjunctive^interpersonal^topical*, as in:
   g. | because of course ˋtravelling in the Suˋdan is extremely ˋdifficult | for ˉone thing | there are no ˉroads | and for a_nother the | public ˋtransport system is °very very | °poor | (LIBMSECPTJ06: 304)
   h. | and of ˉcourse this ᵥmeant that there was | no ᵢalcohol | (LIBMSECJPT06: 377–9)
4. *Topical ^Logico-conjunctive^Logico-conjunctive^Topical (complex)*
   i. | the ˉblueprint itᵢself howˈever | and Mr ᵥGorbachev's ˈblunt exhorᵛtations | do ˉnot in them_selves | ˋchange the ˈpetrifiᵥca-tion that's set ˈin | through ˉfifteen ᵥyears | of ˈPresident ˈBrezhnev's ˈrule | and the ˈhelter ˈskelter ᵢmonths | of ˉsickness | and ˈindeᵥcision | which aˈffected _two of his sucᵥcessors |

(299) *Unmarked low-high patterns: Logico-conjunctive and/or interpersonal Themes following topical ones* (28.3%):
4. *Topical^logico-conjunctive*, as in:
   j. | ᵢwhat for e°xample | is he ˉdoing to en°sure that ˋhis grip on ᵥpower | is ᵛstrong e°nough | to _make the °necessary ᵥchanges | (LIBMSECAPT11: 031)

k. | ⁻here for eˌxample | is the ˋthen °President of the U_nited ˌStates | 'Richard ˌNixon | in an A⁻ddress to the ˌNation | in Noˋvember °19°7ᵛ3 | ⁻launching the ˌprogramme | ˌknown | as _Project Indeˋpendence | (LIBMSECCPT01: 265)

l. | ˌwhat for e°xample | is he ⁻doing to en°sure that ˋhis grip on ˌpower | is ᵛstrong e°nough | to _make the °necessary ˌchanges | (LIBMSECAPT01: 031)

m. | _Protestants how⁻ever ⁻are | a _tiny miˋnority in Argen'tina | and the ⁻delegation ᵛwon't be including | a _Roman ˋCatholic | (LIBMSECAPT01)

n. | I sup↑⁻pose the ˌpopular notion of a 'miracle is | an e_vent | unex_plained by ⁻science or 'natural ˋlaws | but the ˋscientists themˌselves | ⁻weren't having ˋany of 'that | on ᵛthis defi'nition they say | very ˋfew events | can ˋconfidently be 'called ᵛmiracles | because we have ᵛno i'dea | ˋwhat natural 'laws | may be dis_covered in the ˋfuture | more imᵛportant how'ever | is that the ⁻biblical _writers themᵛselves | ⁻thought that e_vents that ᵛfollowed natural 'laws | could ⁻still be re_garded as miˋraculous |(LIBMSECAPT01: 047-49)

o. the ᵛart 'critics how'ever | pre_sent 'rather a ˋdifferent 'picture | (LIBMSECDPT01)

5. *Topical^interpersonal*, as in:

p. | ↑ˋthis of °course was ˋnot because the ˋgovernment ˋfailed in its su°pposed ˋduty as proᵛvider | ↑but ˌlargely | because _energy prices rose conᵛsiderably | in reˌlation to ˋother prices | (LIBMSECAPT01: 199)

6. *Logico-conjunctive^topical^interpersonal*, as in:

q. | ↑and in ⁻Maraˌdona | without ˋdoubt | they °had the ˋstar of the ˍ °compe°tition | (LIBMSECJPT01: 065)

(300) *Marked pattern: interpersonal^logico-conjunctive^topical* (5.1%):
| more ᵛtypically how°ever | it's ⁻not ˌgovernments | but °business ˋenterprises ˍ which °ship the °imports |(LIBMSECCPT01: 473)

EMTs consisting of only a topical element simultaneously acting as an interpersonal or logico-conjunctive Theme (viz. interrogative, exclamative or relative pronouns), such as those included in (301) below, have not been taken into account in obtaining the patterns above. The reason is that, being realized by one and the same wording, this type of EMTs does not seem to be relevant to the elicitation of the positional tendencies of logico-conjunctive, interpersonal and topical elements within the Themes zone.

(301) a. | ˋDoster shot his ˇmother | forty-ˇfour year °old | ˇCarol °Doster | who _worked as a ˇsecretary | and _then °turned the _gun on himˏself | (LIBMSECBPT02: 013–014) (logico-conjunctive/topical Theme)
b. | ˉwho can for°get being °bowled out for °fifty-ˋthree by Pakiˋstan | I mean it's ˋjust been quite an incredible ˋyear | [change of speaker: Chris Florence] (LIBMSECFPT04: 083) (topical/interpersonal Theme)

Moreover, the tendency has also been noted that *if logico-conjunctive and/or interpersonal Themes occur before the topical element, they do not re-appear after it*, and vice versa, *if they follow the topical element, they do not appear before it*. By the same token, instances of *complex EMTs, i.e. iterative choices of topical elements* (i.e. involving paratactic or hypotactic expansions or projections) *have been found to be scarcer in the company of logico-conjunctive and/or interpersonal Themes than when occurring by themselves*. Put another way, *EMTs tend to concern simple rather than complex topical elements*.

Interestingly, our data provide ample evidence that *the boundaries between different classes or types of Themes, as well as the limits between the components of complex topical, logico-conjunctive or interpersonal Themes are normally suprasegmentally* (and typographically) *reinforced by means of a tone sequence, tone concord, or by a tone group boundary*. Some examples are included in (302) below (consider also (298), (299), (300) above):

(302) a. | yet ˏˉshe for her ˏtreasure will enˉdure | and ˏtremble | and ˉso find ˉpeace | that ˋpasseth our underˋstanding | (LIBMSECHPT04: 033) (Complex topical Themes)
b. | em | and al°though I have °ample ↑ˋtime to get through the °work I ˋwant to get through I have aˋnother problem | in that | the °students just cannot ↑ˋconcentrate for twenty °weeks | _nor can the ˋteachers | (LIBMSECJPT06: 261) (Complex logico-conjunctive Theme)
c. |often | though not ˇalways | the ˋcase for self-su°fficiency is ˇargued | with ˉreference to a °country's °need to en_sure seˇcurity | by ˉminimising deˏpendence on ˏforeign ˏsources | (LIBMSECCPT01: 249) (Complex interpersonal Theme)

Turning now to the fourth significant variable, i.e. the association between the choice of a EMT and LIBMSEC text-type, Figure 17, as well as the results derived from the Fisher's Exact Test and the χ^2 Test in Tables 50, 51, 52 demonstrate *that EMTs tend to occur in non-fictional and/or constructive texts, i.e. Lecture, Religious Broadcasts, Magazine, but also in active texts, namely Dialogues and Propaganda*. By contrast, *the non-extended class clusters around fictional and reconstructive texts, that is, Fiction stories, Commentaries, News reports and*

Poetry (contra Ghadessy 1993, 1995). As will become apparent further down, this distribution can be accounted for on the basis of the discourse function of extended multiple and non-extended multiple Theme constructions.

Table 50. *Incidence of EMTs in Fiction in LIBMSEC*

LIBMSEC text	Non-multiple Theme	Multiple Theme	Row Total
Fiction	698	321	1019
	29.1	19.3	25.1
Non-Fiction	1700	1339	3039
	70.9	80.7	74.9
Column Total	2398	1660	4058
	59.1	40.9	100.0

Fisher's Exact Test significance: .00000
Missing observations: 39

Table 51. *Rhetorical purpose of emts in LIBMSEC*

LIBMSEC text	Non-multiple Theme	Multiple Theme	Row Total
Reconstruction	1359	690	2049
	56.7	41.6	50.5
Construction	649	495	1144
	27.1	29.8	28.2
Language in action	390	475	865
	16.3	28.6	21.3
Column Total			4058
			100.0

χ^2 Test significance: .00000
Missing observations: 39

The fifth and last significant variable reported by the logistic regression test is the correlation between EMTs and β topical elements, i.e. initial dependent clauses in a hypotactic clause complex. Table 53 shows *that β Themes are more frequent in the non-extended than in the extended class*, mainly because of the high frequency of initial reported Locutions/Ideas. Yet, the remaining types of β elements are more frequent in EMTs than in the non-extended class. Thus, speaking in relative terms, it can be concluded that β topical Themes in LIBMSEC tend to be accompanied by logico-conjunctive and/or interpersonal Themes.

Table 52. *Incidence of EMTs in LIBMSEC text types*

LIBMSEC text	Non-multiple Theme	Multiple Theme	Row Total
Commentaries	374	262	636
	15.6	15.8	15.7
News	287	107	394
	12.0	6.4	9.7
Lecture	439	286	725
	18.3	17.2	17.9
Religious Broadcasts	63	55	118
	2.6	3.3	2.9
Magazine	147	154	301
	6.1	9.3	7.4
Fiction	650	282	932
	27.1	17.0	23.0
Poetry	48	39	87
	2.0	2.3	2.1
Dialogue	327	412	739
	13.6	24.8	18.2
Propaganda	63	63	126
	2.6	3.8	3.1
Column Total	2398	1660	4058
	59.1	40.9	100.0

χ^2 Test significance: .00000
Missing observations: 39

In addition, by running the χ^2 Test the following six secondary significant associations have been detected as significant for the choice of a EMT: (a)–(c) *structure, transitivity* and *syntactic* function of *topical Theme*; (d) *type of clause*; (e) *Mood* of the clause; and (f) *type of process*. Considering variable (a), *both extended multiple and non-extended multiple Themes, but especially the former, tend to have simple, rather than complex, realizations of topical Themes*: 93.6% vs. 6.4% in EMTs and 88.2% vs. 11.8% in non-extended multiple ones, respectively (Ghadessy 1993, 1995). Furthermore, although both classes of Themes typically concern *pronominal topical Themes, these are even more common in EMTs* (52.7% vs. 48% in non-extended multiple ones). The same occurs with *verbal groups*: 5.7% in EMTs vs. 1.9% in non-extended multiple ones. Conversely, non-extended topical Themes have a higher number of: common nouns (33.4% vs. 27.3%) and PPs (7.3% vs. 5%). The remaining structural expressions have a similar distribution: adverbial realizations (1.7% in EMTs vs. 1.3% in non-

Table 53. *Incidence of β Themes in EMTs in* LIBMSEC

LIBMSEC text	Non-multiple Theme	Multiple Theme	Row Total
Spatial/Temporal	44	24	68
Circumstance	24.9	27.6	25.8
Manner	17	11	28
Circumstance	9.6	12.6	10.6
Cause	8	6	14
Circumstance	4.5	6.9	5.3
Medium	74	5	79
(reported Locutions/Ideas)	41.8	5.7	29.9
Conditional	34	41	264
Circumstance	19.2	47.1	100.0
Column Total	177	87	264
	76.0	33.0	100.0

χ^2 Test significance: .00000
Missing observations: 3833

extended multiple ones), rankshifted clausal Themes (1.5% vs. 1.2%), proper nouns (6 vs. 6.6%) and adjective phrases (0.1% vs. 0.3%). Semantically, *non-extended multiple Themes have a higher proportion of Agents, Mediums* and *Circumstances*, with this order of frequency in both: 77.1% vs. 76% in EMTs, 11.2% vs. 10.8%, and 10.1% vs. 7.5%, respectively; *whereas EMTs involve more instances of processes* (5.7% vs. 1.9%). Syntactically, Subjects, Adjuncts and Objects/Complements have a slightly higher tendency to occur by themselves than to be accompanied by textual and/or interpersonal thematic elements (84% vs. 83%, 10% vs. 7.8%, and 4% vs. 3.4%). But in both non-extended multiple and EMTs these syntactic roles are first, second and third in terms of frequency, respectively. Finites/Predicators, in turn, are more often found in EMTs (5.9% vs. 1.9%).

Looking at (d), it has been observed that *EMTs predominate over non-extended multiple ones in dependent clauses* (26.6% vs. 10.5%) and in *paratactically related clauses* (26.8% vs. 12.6%), *while non-extended multiple Themes are more numerous in simple clauses, in the Head clause of hypotactic complexes* and in *rankshifted clauses* (43% vs. 21.8%, 23.7% vs. 18.1%, 10.3% vs. 6.6%, respectively). Regarding (v), the results show that *non-extended multiple Themes have a preference for declaratives*, whereas *in questions and exclamatives EMTs are more frequent*. Lastly, as regards the type of process, *extended Themes are favoured by especially material processes* (41.1% vs. 38.2%), *and the non-extended class by verbal ones* (12.1% vs. 7.7%).

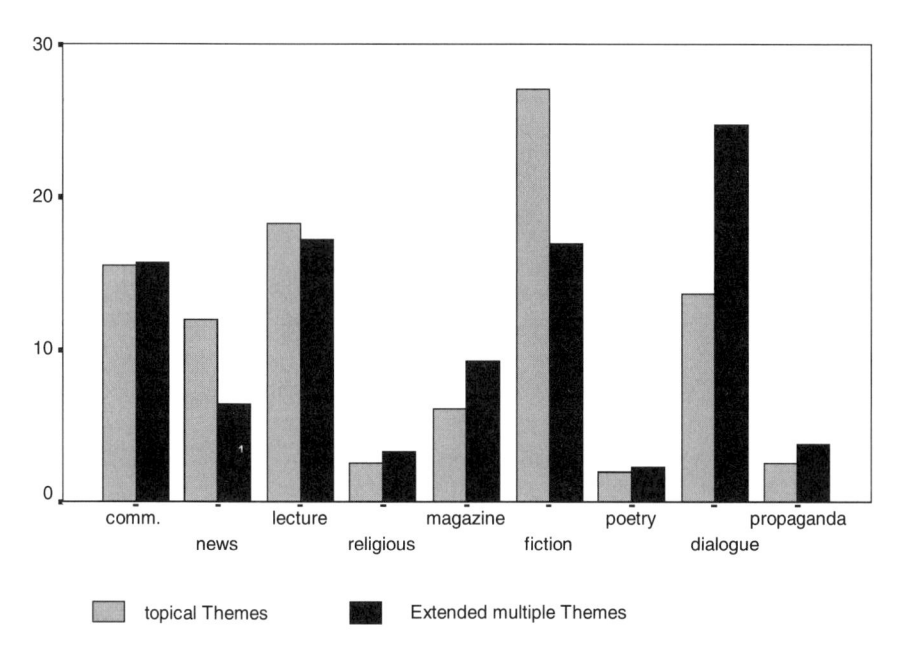

Figure 17. *EMTs vs. non-extended multiple Themes across* LIBMSEC *text-types*

7.5.2 Discourse function

We have suggested that *the unmarked centripetal organisation of elements within the Theme zone* is: (*logico-conjunctive*) ^ (*interpersonal*) ^ *topical* ^ (*interpersonal*) ^ (*logico-conjunctive*). Now we shall contend that this pattern *substantiates the layering hypothesis* as postulated in e.g. FG or RRG to explicate the positional tendencies exhibited within the clause by elements with different metafunctions (Hengeveld 1989; Fortescue et al. 1992; Van Valin Jr 1993; Vet 1998). The layering hypothesis, it should be stressed, argues for a *scopal* metafunctional organisation, rather than for a *parallel* one, as hypothesised in SFG. As represented in (303) below, within RRG the layering theory is posited that syntactic constituents are hierarchically arranged on language specific constraints, while operators display a "pure" layered structure with respect to the Nucleus in terms of their scope: the narrower the scope, the closer to the nucleus and *vice versa*, the wider the scope, the farther from the nucleus, so that inner operators are within the scope of the outer ones both between levels (e.g. core operators are in the scope of clausal operators) and within levels (e.g. tense is within the scope of IF).

(303)   Narrowest Scope
- a. Nuclear operators: Aspect   ↑
  Directionals (only those modifying orientation of action or event without reference to participants)
- b. Core operators: Directionals (only those expressing the orientation or motion of one participant with reference to another participant or to the speaker)
  Modality (root modals: ability, permission, obligation)
  Internal (narrow scope) negation
- c. Clausal operators Status (epistemic modality)
  External (wide scope) negation)
  Tense
  Evidentials
  Illocutionary Force [IF]   ↓
                                               Widest Scope

In a similar fashion, within FG Hengeveld (1989), for instance, suggests that there are three levels — representational, interpersonal and rhetorical — which contain five layers in total: a predicate and a predicational layer in the representational level, a propositional and an illocutionary layer in the interpersonal level and a textual layer in the rhetorical level (cf. Fortescue et al. 1992; Vet 1998).

SFG, admittedly, does recognise the existence of thematic scopes, but, as already noted, its discussion is mainly centred on the difference in scope between Themes spoken on a separate intonation unit and those embodied in the same information unit as the Rheme (Halliday 1967b: 214; Section 4.2.1.1 above).[131] Likewise in (IFG: 84) a case seems to be made for a scopal metafunctional organisation when the possibility is admitted that elements fulfilling a specific metafunction may fall outside the patterns of organisation imposed by that particular metafunction, and vice versa, when items not fulfilling a specific metafunction are allowed to be inside or outside the structural patterns that metafunction imposes. However, despite the occasional recognition of scopal constructs, it seems that in the current version of SFG metafunctional organisation remains a parallel one. For one thing, options from the different systems are said to be "comparatively independent" (Halliday 1968: 207; 1979: 61), an assertion that has been questioned by a number of scholars such as Butler (1985: 77–93), Berry (1982: 75–6) and Gómez-González (1998b, forthcoming), to mention but a few. And, focusing on Theme, if as systemicists claim different metafunctions have different patterns of realization, then it seems plausible to believe that topical, interpersonal and logico-conjunctive Themes can impose different patterns and/or vary with respect to their scope of influence.

The field-research carried out in this investigation and reported so far gives convincing evidence that *the array of logical and/or interpersonal and/or topical elements within the Theme zone is not "relatively independent"*. It will be claimed that *the Theme zone can entail different "orientations" depending on the kind of relationships that initial topical, textual and/or interpersonal elements have with each other within the thematic field and the nature of the relationship they have with both the subsequent predication and the overall co(n)text* (Hannay & Vester 1987; De Vries 1989; Smits 1998). Figure 16 and Figure 18 reveal a consistent tendency within the Theme zone to display *downward scopal and centripetal layering relations among classes of Themes with respect to their Nucleus, or obligatory element, i.e. the topical Theme*, which tends to be preceded or followed by logico-conjunctive and/or interpersonal Themes, the former typically preceding the latter.

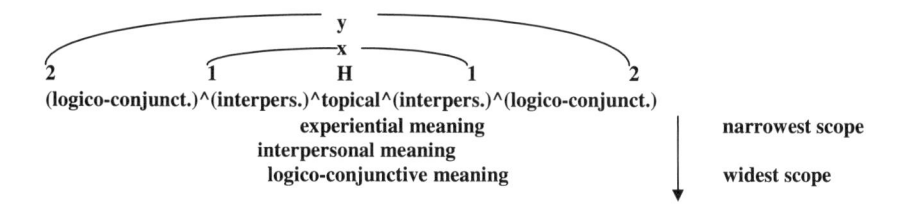

```
                       y
                ─────x─────
       2      1      H      1      2
   (logico-conjunct.)^(interpers.)^topical^(interpers.)^(logico-conjunct.)
              experiential meaning                              narrowest scope
              interpersonal meaning                                    │
              logico-conjunctive meaning                               ▼
                                                                 widest scope
```

Figure 18. *Downward scopal and centripetal relations in unmarked EMTs*

Figure 18 implies that topical Themes tend to occur in medial position because their meaning is both affected by and affects the mood of the message and the logico-conjunctive development of discourse, the functions fulfilled by interpersonal and logico-conjunctive elements, respectively. Accordingly, topical Themes attract the other two classes of Themes towards themselves, lying within the scope of both of them. Interpersonal Themes, in turn, occupy position 1, a layer external to that of topical Themes, because they exclusively affect the mood of the proposition or of the proposal, but not its logico-conjunctive development. This function is accomplished by logico-conjunctive Themes, which, as a result of their widest scope of influence, tend to occur in either pretopical or post-topical position 2, a layer external to both interpersonal and topical Themes. The scope of logico-conjunctive Themes can be said to extend over the other two classes because they establish different types of logico-semantic, conjunctive and tactic relationships between the message they introduce, with its experiential and interpersonal component, and the preceding and subsequent co(n)text.

In addition, besides the *major bi-directional orientation of the Theme zone with regard to the previous and subsequent discourse, that is to say, its backward- and forward-looking discourse potential* that has been attested throughout this book in relation to the different Theme-types, and besides the *internal downward*

Major bi-directional orientation of the Theme zone

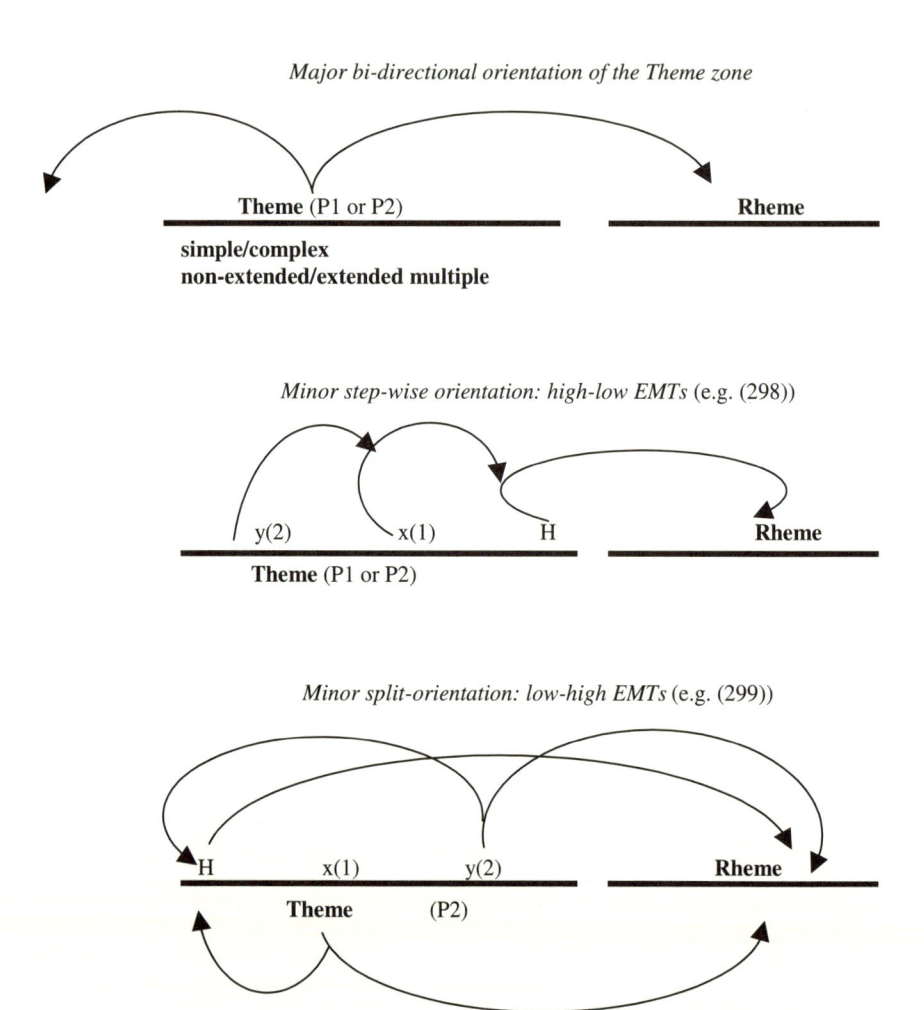

Theme (P1 or P2)   **Rheme**

simple/complex
non-extended/extended multiple

Minor step-wise orientation: high-low EMTs (e.g. (298))

y(2)   x(1)   H   **Rheme**

Theme (P1 or P2)

Minor split-orientation: low-high EMTs (e.g. (299))

H   x(1)   y(2)   **Rheme**

Theme   (P2)

Figure 19. *Major and minor orientations of the Theme zone*

centripetal scopal relations holding within the Theme zone (Figures 16, 18), *two further basic "sub-orientations" can be posited corresponding to the unmarked high-low and low-high orders of EMTs*. These I shall call *the stepwise orientation* and *the split orientation* (Smits 1998), which are illustrated in Figure 19.

Figure 19 represents that *within the overall bi-directional orientation of the Theme zone, high-low orders imply an orientation step-by-step, that is to say, in decreasing scopal span: logical, interpersonal and topical*, as in the tokens included in (298) above; *whereas in low-high orders topical elements tend to be realized in P2 because the Theme–Rheme topical continuity is "split" by interpersonal and/or textual elements, which have a bi-directional orientation and are normally arranged in increasing scopal scope*, as shown in (299) above. These two minor orientations seem to do two different jobs. My field research reveals that *high-low orders* tend to instruct for *"sameness" or "smoothness" in the progression of the text/discourse*, and as a result *the topical element of EMTs is generally "non-emphatic"* in the sense that it is not responsible for any local or global textual strategy, as in (298). By contrast, *low-high orders* in the Theme zone *have a preference for textual contexts in which the first* (simple or complex) *topical element within the Theme zone supports the textual strategy of the passage*, and thereby is *endowed with a contrastive flavour* (299). This effect is produced partly owing to processing factors, the topical Theme–Rheme continuity being disrupted causing an effect of added "emotivity", and partly because in most, if not all, instances of low-high orders, topical Themes occur in P2 before an interpersonal/logico-conjunctive boundary and are under the scope of intonational Focus and therefore are presented as newsworthy information. The same holds for the interspersed logico-conjunctive and/or interpersonal elements: they re-orientate the addressee's focus of attention which momentarily latches on to their meaning specifications bridging the existing gap between the Theme and the Rheme, typically by means of suprasegmental reinforcing. Marked extended multiple orders seem to have a similar "emotive" effect as "deviations" from CWO arrangements; however, in view of their infrequency in our corpus it seems that this question needs further empirical study.

To conclude, we have seen that EMTs in LIBMSEC are mainly obtained by the presence of initial logico-conjunctive elements, such as structural or conjunctive Themes, linking hypotactic or paratactic clause complexes, or as continuatives, punctuating an exchange and staging discourse turns. Less frequent are the instances of EMTs triggered by interpersonal elements, mainly modal Adjuncts, with which speakers express their points of view, or *wh*-words and Finites/Predicators, which are required by exclamatives and interrogatives. The frequency of these types of EMTs explains their distribution across LIBMSEC text-types.

EMTs are more likely to occur in either constructive texts, which often require the help of logico-conjunctive signposts to develop their specialised contents, or in active texts, where speakers can freely express their points of view and have to gain or maintain the discourse floor. Besides, both constructive and dialogic texts tend to involve the type of process preferred by EMTs, i.e. material processes, which, because of their informative and objective nature, readily accept logico-conjunctive connectors and interpersonal hedging. By contrast, non-extended multiple Themes normally appear in reconstructive texts; as these are mainly devoted to "projecting" reality through verbal processes by resorting to direct or free indirect speech, which disfavour interpersonal elements and keep logico-conjunctive complexity to a minimum. Lastly, the tendency of the topical element of EMTs to be weakened into pronominal realizations can reside in the fact that in this thematic class not only topical, but also interpersonal and logico-conjunctive elements compete to get the thematic ground. In other words, it has been observed that what is at issue in the majority of EMTs is not the lexical burden of the topical Theme itself, despite being the pivot of the construct, but rather its being embedded within the scopes of logico-conjunctive and/or interpersonal elements, the former typically external to the latter. It can thus be concluded that the *point of most EMTs is not (or not as much) to infuse with topical relevance a clause initial topical element, but rather to ensure the continuity of the thread of discourse and/or to foreground the speaker's perspective on it.*

CHAPTER 8

Summary, Conclusions and Further Research

This volume has attempted to fulfil a two-fold aim: (a) to *clarify the vagueness that has long pervaded the study of pragmatic/communicative functions, in particular, the analysis of Theme/Topic* (Parts I and II), and (b) to *demonstrate the functional relevance of the Theme zone, or clause-initial position, in PresE* (in Part III). The approach has been a strictly synchronic one and has sought to handle a complex interplay of factors (*Appendix I*). The theoretical foundations and evidence for this were provided in Chapters 6 and 7, resorting to parameters clarified throughout Chapter 2 (evaluating the notions of Theme/Topic and related categories) and exploiting the insights gained throughout Chapters 3 (on PS), 4 (on SFG) and 5 (on FG).

For the sake of simplicity, the conclusions of this investigation will be presented following the structure of the book. We shall summarise six new theoretical claims (Section 8.1) and twelve corpus-based findings (Section 8.2). The volume closes with a number of suggestions for further research in this field (Section 8.3).

8.1 Theoretical conclusions

This section lists six new theoretical claims made about the notions of Theme/Topic and about the Theme zone. From the first five conclusions stems the central hypothesis of this investigation, i.e. the belief that the *Theme zone acts as an orientation field across languages entailing "relational" rather than "nominal" relationships with both forward- and backward-looking potential in discourse.*

1. Chapter 1 suggested that three factors are responsible for *the lack of consensus in the study of Theme/Topic*: (a) *the general indeterminacy of functional categories* and the *non-biunique nature* of the relationships between linguistic form and function; (b) the existence of *different degrees of functionalism* (i.e. conservative, moderate, and extreme) and of *two different perspectives* (i.e. form-to-function

and function-to form); and (c) the fact that communicative functions have received *three different interpretations*, i.e. *semantic, informational* and *syntactic*.

2. The pros and cons of these three main approaches were evaluated in Chapter 2. *Syntactic accounts identifying Theme with (clause) initial position were* described as fairly homogeneous, despite the existence of some moot points, particularly, *the delimitation of the category of syntactic Theme* and *the demonstration of its (cross-)linguistic functional relevance* by means of statistically significant natural data (Section 2.4). By contrast, semantic and informational analyses were reported more heterogeneous. It was explained that *semantic interpretations* roughly *pursue the notions of discourse relevance or "aboutness" in three different ways* opening up corresponding fronts of research:

a. *relationally*, according to which Topic entails a relationship of "aboutness" with respect to a clausal predication;
b. *referentially*, describing Topic as a referent that establishes a relationship of "aboutness" with respect to the overall discourse, which is assessed with regard to the co(n)text (i.e. the contextual-referential sense) and/or the (receiver's) mind (i.e. the activated referential sense); and
c. *interactively*, treating Topic/Theme as salient/relevant information in discourse.

The insights and problems of (each trend of) this semantic approach were highlighted with the support of illustrative examples (Section 2.2). In Section 2.3 we saw that *informational approaches assimilate Theme/Topic with different types of givenness*:

a. *relational givenness*, i.e. the Given with respect to the New in individual clauses/messages;
b. *contextual givenness*, i.e. given information as rendered by the co(n)text, in terms of:
   i. *recoverability* (Giv_R): information which is recoverable from the co(n)text;
   ii. *predictability* (Giv_P): information that is predictable from the context;
   iii. *shared knowledge* (Giv_K): knowledge shared by speaker and her/his addressee;
   iv. *assumed familiarity* (Giv_F): a scalar notion of information which the speaker assumes her/his addressee can retrieve or infer from the co(n)text; and
c. *activated givenness* (Giv_S), i.e. what both speaker and/or her/his addressee have in the mind.

It was argued that by themselves, the notions of "givenness" and "aboutness", the identificational criteria applied by the informational and semantic interpretations, prove to be elusive and difficult to test.

In its turn, *Part II brought to the fore the adequacies and inadequacies of previous accounts of pragmatic functions within the frameworks of PS, SFG and FG*.

3. Chapter 3 showed that PS informational analyses assimilate "aboutness" with co(n)textually recoverable information (Giv$_R$), but, with the exception of a few examples, no co(n)textual evidence is provided to determine what should be taken as Given or New (Section 3.2). Besides, the generative-PS proposal was said to provide explanations for some data only, which renders the theory and its supporting evidence rather weak (Section 3.2.4); and CD was found to assign different degrees of communicative relevance to specific items *a priori* and in a rigid way, violating the *raison d'être* of this theory, i.e. to account for the nature of communication "dynamically" (Section 3.2.3). Lastly, PS syntactic investigations were reported to: (a) be highly "psychological"; (b) often use Given and Theme interchangeably, despite their purportedly separating approach; and (c) frequently treat as one and the same thing two different nuances of "aboutness": the relational one ("what the clause is about") and the referential one ("what the text is about") (Section 3.3).

4. In Chapter 4 it was explained that, in principle, *SFG approaches Theme from a relational-semantic perspective* ("that with which the clause is concerned"), which in *PresE is identified syntactically with clause-initial position* ("the point of departure of the message") (Section 4.2), as opposed to morpho-syntactic givenness, embodied within the system of cohesive identification, and prosodic givenness, assigned to the information structure of messages (Section 4.1). Likewise, *previous critiques of this model were reduced to three* (Section 4.3): (a) the *double-sided nature of the category of topical Theme* (Section 4.3.1); (b) the *identification of the category of Theme*, which leads us to discuss (i) some *terminological issues* in Section 4.3.2.1 (e.g. ideational elements, the label of textual Theme, the structure imposed by thematic patterns, the meaning of Theme–Rheme constructions, and the categories of substitute and reference Theme), (ii) the *profitability of the notion of "displaced" Theme* (Section 4.3.2.2), and (iii) *what should be understood by "initial position"* (Section 4.3.2.3); and (c), our last concern, *the "separating" stand of SFG as a whole* (Section 4.3.3). It was argued that many of these points of conflict could be resolved by interpreting the category of syntactic Theme "relationally" across languages, and by providing more explicit descriptions supported by quantitatively and qualitatively significant discourse evidence.

5. Focusing on FG, in Chapter 5 it was suggested that *the pragmatic functions of Theme, Tail and Topic are approached from a referential-semantic perspective.* Theme represents the initial predication-external entity that states what the subsequent predication is about, while Tails, in P3, show the reversed pattern. And Topic designates the entity about which the predication predicates something, in relation to the overall discourse and as processed by the speaker/ decoder's mind. Section 5.4 *discussed four debatable issues* raised by FG accounts: (a) the *interpretation of the semantic criterion of aboutness/relevance* (Section 5.4.1); (b) the *application of the criterion of "initial position"* (Section 5.4.2); (c) the *FG treatment of "givenness"* (Section 5.4.3); and lastly (d) the *assignment of Topic and Focus to specific constituents* (Section 5.4.4). It was concluded that *most of the controversy arises from merging syntactic, semantic and informational criteria.*

6. The foundations and supporting evidence of this corpus-based study were laid out in Chapters 6 and 7. *Theme–Rheme patterns were analysed under the structural prerequisites of PresE, in which word order is first and foremost determined by syntactic function.* It was noted that, when word order variation takes place, other levels of clausal meaning, but not the semantic and grammatical role structures, are substantially affected. On the one hand, as a result of the rigidity of the English word order system, it was claimed that *word order variation within the Theme zone, i.e. the clause-initial slot, give rise to marked, special and extended multiple thematic constructions, which represented deviations from the norm* (Section 7.3, 7.4 and 7.5), *as opposed to unmarked non-special ones* (Section 7.2). These linearisation phenomena in combination with underlying natural or cognitive principles led us to suggest that the *Theme zone is a naturally salient area that is generally used for a wide range of "urgent tasks" which profile this category as simultaneously a marker of subjectivity or subjectivification and as a marker of discourse structure* (Sections 6.1, 6.2 and 6.3).

The diversity of phenomena concerned precluded the possibility that a single syntactic or semantic criterion can be applied consistently to describe Theme–Rheme patterns. Accordingly, the *notion of syntactic Theme was first differentiated from* (a) the notion of *discourse Topic* and (b) *referential vs. relational givenness. Discourse Topics* were characterised cognitively as a prominent conceptualisations which act as a kind of *cognitive anchoring/reference points* at a given point of discourse. *Referential givenness* was interpreted in terms of *recoverability* (Giv_R) and was related to the contextual variables of field, tenor and mode. By contrast, *relational givenness-newness was associated with the speaker's choice of* (absence-presence of) *intonational Foci.* Within this framework, *a taxonomy of different classes and types of syntactic Themes was proposed with regard to 27 variables* (Appendix I), allowing *for gradual transitions from prototypical to peripheral members of individual types and classes of Theme and emphasising the need for a functional classification in terms of relevant co(n)texts*. In contrast with *unmarked non-special Themes* (Section 7.2), *marked Themes included* (a) instances of *preposings* (Section 7.3.1) and (b) the Themes of *passive processes* (Section 7.3.2). Our characterisation of special Themes involved the analysis of seven types of Theme–Rheme patterns: *existential-there constructions* (Section 7.4.1), *Subject-it Extrapositions*(Section 7.4.2), *inversions* (Section 7.4.3), *left and right detachments* (Sections 7.4.4 and 7.4.5), and *(pseudo)cleft constructions* (Sections 7.4.6 and 7.4.7). Lastly, Section 7.5 discussed *the orientation* and *patterns* displayed by a newly posited category: *EMT*, that is to say, topical Themes preceded/followed by interpersonal and/or logico-conjunctive elements.

It was shown that the use *of different classes and types of Themes underscores their affinities with specific text-types and speakers' attitudes* (Section 6.4.2), particularly: (a) the *degree of subjectivity of discourse*; (b) its *constructive, reconstructive* or *active nature*; (c) the *necessities* and *patterns of focus management*, and (d) *the speaker's role as an architect, an experiencer* or *a commentator*. Generally, it was argued that *the Theme zone provides a (re-) orientation or a grounding for what is to follow*, where any *reordering of CWO patterns involves an additional component of emotivity which is well suited for some contexts only*.

8.2 Corpus-based conclusions

This section summarises twelve corpus-based conclusions based on the evidence reported by running three statistical tests, i.e. *the Fisher's Exact Test*, the χ^2 *Test* and the *Logistic Regression Procedure* (Section 6.4.3), to my data, the *LIBMSEC* (Section 6.4.1), once *several problems of analysis* were addressed (Section 6.4.2) in relation to: the *corpus size* (Section 6.4.2.1), its *field, tenor* and *mode* characteristics (Section 6.4.2.2) and the *intricacies of corpus-based approaches* (Section 6.4.2.3).

1. In *PresE Theme choices were described as prototypically unmarked* and *non-special*: the initial Transitivity/Mood constituent demanded by each active mood pattern, expressed by a NG (usually a third person pronominal), acting as Agent/Subject of a declarative simple or complex clause, and occupying P1 (i.e. clause

initial predication-internal position), generally after a logico-conjunctive Theme (Sections 7.1 and 7.2). Besides, unmarked non-special thematic constructions were said to introduce informative messages, concerning material or mental processes, and to be associated with *no conventional implicature* (i.e. conventional meaning, as opposed to what is "literally" meant). *They tend to convey co(n)textually recoverable information*, which favours a *(Given-before)-New mapping of information* and *"thematic progressions" (TPs) with a constant Theme*.

2. *Preposings* were reported as *typically realized by prepositional, adverbial or clausal circumstantial Adjuncts*, expressing condition, place or time, or as *Verbiage/Phenomenon Objects*, in complex enhancing or projecting verbal, mental or existential processes (Section 7.3.1). Other features associated with reposings were: (a) their having a relatively high ratio of *predication-external realizations* (P2) (i.e. clause initial predication-external position) and (b) their co-occurrence with *EMTs*, typically triggered by the presence by interpersonal Themes (modal Adjuncts). Preposings were further characterised as conveying *conventional implicatures* and as tending to *contravene the (Given-before)-New principle*. For, generally, it was noted that preposed Themes conflate with Focus and precede a clausal presupposition, establishing a contrast with respect to the previous field, tenor or mode of discourse, and *thereby acting as markers of subjectivity and as markers of minor discourse shifts*. It was found that *fronted participants* normally instruct for *Topic continuity in discourse*, whereas *preposed adverbials*, by far the most common type of preposing in our corpus, typically act as focus management devices *guiding and shifting the addressee's attention in the development of discourse, foregrounding background information, highlighting extended turns, or modifying speaker-recipient roles*. In the same vein, β *Themes* (thematic dependent clause in hypotactic complex clauses) were shown to display *different types of iconic organisations* (i.e. temporal reference, non-factual nature of the subordinate clause, cause/purpose-effect sequence, the Given-before-New principle). Finally, in contrast with previous studies, my findings reported *preposings as typical of formal and planned discourse*, i.e. constructive (viz. Lectures, Magazine, Religious Broadcasts) or reconstructive texts (viz. Commentaries, Fiction, Poetry).

3. In Section 7.3.2, after a formal characterisation, passive clauses were found to typically *thematise Subject/Medium common nouns* or, *less frequently, Adjunct/ Circumstance prepositional phrases in mostly declarative material processes*. The passive voice emerged as a *device whereby, in conformity with the principles of EF and EW*, (a) *unmarked Focus* falls on a heavy final constituent *other than the Goal*, and (b) *this latter item, usually accompanied by an interpersonal Theme*

(modal Adjuncts), receives thematic highlighting as *expressing the speaker's point of view*, mainly in *constructive texts* (viz. Lectures) and in *objective reconstructive texts* (viz. Commentaries and News Broadcasts).

4. Section 7.4 reported *There-existential constructions as the most recurrent type of special Theme construction* (followed by Subject *It*-Extrapositions, Inversions, *It*-Clefts, left detachments, pseudo-clefts and right detachments). In addition, *special thematic constructions were shown to have a common core*: (a) they tend to have a *higher amount of preposings* than non-special ones Verbiages/Direct Object or conditional or spatio-temporal Adjuncts, as well as a *higher ratio of prepositional, adverbial or clausal predication-external realizations*; (b) they normally provide synoptic and subjective pictures of reality; and (c) *they generally occur in "subjective" texts*, i.e. texts in which speakers have to *reconstruct reality* (Fiction, Commentaries) or *to act upon it* (Dialogues). It was argued that the *subjective effect of these constructions lies in their conveying particular conventional implicatures*, which either *underline the PSRR, the presence/lack of an presuppositional set and/or collaborate towards some sort of thematic or rhematic highlighting*.

5. Section 7.4.1 explained that existential-*There*-constructions typically occur in declarative simple or in hypotactically complex clauses having affirmative *be* or, less frequently, other intransitive existential processes. They were described as *presentative devices used mainly in reconstructive or descriptive texts* (viz. Commentaries, Fiction and News) to introduce into the scene of *discourse a typically indefinite/irrecoverable* but sometimes *a definite/recoverable Existent*, the notional Subject, *involving a cardinal or an enumerative quantification* of entities or situations with respect to the previous co(n)texts, presenting them in the scene of discourse and within clausal Rhemes and thereby getting unmarked end-Focus and end-Weight.

6. As regards Subject *it*-extrapositions (e.g. *It is strange that the duke gave to my aunt that teapot*), they were found to be typically realized by extraposed nominal *that*-clauses or by infinitival clauses, with their Themes$_1$ usually expressed by a topical element, typically a main clause displaying the patterns: Subject-Predicator-Subject Complement, and less often Subject-Predicator (the predicator being passive), Subject-Predicator-Object, or Subject-Predicator-Indirect Object (Direct Object) (Section 7.4.2). Besides, extrapositions have been ascribed a two-fold communicative role: (a) to project within the Rheme some meaning or wording in order to avoid an unqualified claim or to ascribe it to an unspecified source; and (b) *to foreground a modal expression thematically*, i.e. degrees of modality, ± possible, ± probable, ± certain, or modulation, ± desirable, ± required. This

two-fold communicative function explained the high incidence of Subject *it*-extrapositions in *reconstructive texts* (viz. Fiction, News, Commentaries).

7. Turning to *inversions* (e.g. *Here is the teapot that the duke has given to my aunt*), they were classified into *FIs and SAIs*, which have been mainly found in *declarative paratactically projecting complex clauses* concerning *active verbal* or *relational processes* (Section 7.4.3). *The most recurrent type was FI*, especially *QFI*, i.e. inversions occurring after preposed quotations, followed *by deictic and lexical presentative/predicative inversions*, VPFIs, i.e. after preposed (past/ present) participles, SAIs, and AdjFIs. The discourse function of inversions was claimed to result from the interplay of *four factors*: (a) their *presentative function*; (b) their *behaviour as information-packaging devices*; (c) their *intonational Focus* in accordance with the *principles of EW and EF*; and (d) their role as *markers of subjectivity and discourse structure over major discourse shifts*. It was concluded that this four-fold functionality makes inversions especially suited for *reconstructive discourse* (Fiction, Lecture, Commentaries, News Broadcasts) under *conditions of displacement*, i.e. a type of discourse in which the consciousness of language producers and receivers focuses on experience that is *displaced from* the immediate environment of the speaker's mind. The effect was normally one of subjective topic construal whereby a point of reference was created, permitting the speaker to stay out of the text an to nonetheless to adopt a perspective from within it.

8. Left detachments (e.g. *As for that teapot, the duke has given it to my aunt*) was described as *prototypically consisting of a predication external (P2) NG or PP topical Theme acting as Subject or Complement or, more peripherally, as spatiotemporal circumstantial Adjuncts* (7.4.4). It was observed that, typically having a tone group of their own, LD Themes are normally presented as *new information* that introduces a discourse stage in its own right in *spontaneous and informal texts* (viz. Dialogue and Commentaries). They fulfil a *three-staged referent-(re)introduction and discourse-switching function*: they act as Topic switch devices, which establishes a contrast or parallelism with respect to the previous cotext or introduce a new participant in discourse.

9. Section 7.4.5 explained that right detachments (e.g. *The duke has given it to my aunt, that teapot*) are typically realized by *NGs* or by *finite clauses acting as either the Phenomenon of a mental process, as circumstantial Adjuncts* or as *Attributes in relational processes*. Almost restricted to *unplanned discourse* (viz. Dialogue and Propaganda), right detachments were characterised as *fundamentally re-introducers of discourse referents, which shift the "camera angle" of discourse from generic to specific reference and which also infuse their referents with forward-looking potential as discourse Topics* over the ensuing discourse span.

10. In Section 7.4.6 we saw that the *highlighted element* of *it*-clefts(e.g. *It was that teapot that the duke gave to my aunt*) is *normally realized by simple NGs, PPs or by demonstrative pronouns acting as either circumstantial Adjuncts or Agent Subjects of fundamentally material or verbal processes*. Unlike previous thematic constructions, *cleft Themes* revealed as typically *extended multiple, marking the cleavage of Theme and Rheme by means of a Tone group boundary*. It was concluded that the *discourse function* of these constructions *pivots around three hinges*: (a) their *role as thematic build-up devices of paradigmatic flexibility*, (b) their *newness-oriented nature* and (c) their *implying an implicature of exhaustiveness*. These three features made clefts a particularly suitable device for *argumentative or persuasive formal discourse* (viz. Lecture, Commentary, Dialogue and Magazine).

11. Pseudo-clefts (e.g. *What the duke gave my aunt was that teapot*) were characterised as prototypically having a *what-headed fused relative clause that invokes non-human referents with the following functions mapped onto it*: (a) *Theme*, (b) *Subject*, (c) *ID/Vl* (Identified/Value), and (d) a *logico-semantic presupposition* (Section 7.4.7). Conversely, *the highlighted element*, typically (non-)*finite noun clauses* (or NGs) was mapped onto: (a) *Subject Complement*, (b) *IR/T* (Identifier/Token) and (c) *Rheme*. In its turn, *the reversed type displayed the pattern*: *IR/T$_{typically\ a\ demonstrative\ pronoun/Theme}$-ID/Vl$_{fused\ relative/Rheme}$*, frequently involving circumstantial identification. It was found that pseudo-cleft Themes normally belong to the *complex extended multiple class* (with a majority of logico-conjunctive Themes) and are often *separated from their Rhemes by means of a tone group boundary*. Popular in *opinionative texts* (viz. Commentary, Lecture, Fiction), these constructions were reported as *thematic devices used to identify the speakers' views or to situate the thread of discourse with respect to some co(n)textual presupposition*.

12. Last, but not least, in Section 7.5 we concluded that EMTs tend to be triggered by the *presence of logico-conjunctive* (structural) *elements, rather than of interpersonal* (modal Adjunct) elements in the Theme zone, normally in either independent interrogative/exclamative clauses or in complex declarative clauses, which generally involve material processes. Crucially, it was hypothesised that the *unmarked display of EMTs* in PresE is: (*logico-conjunctive*) ^ (*interpersonal*) ^ *topical* ^ (*interpersonal*) ^ (*logico-conjunctive*), in conformity with the PCO. This suggests scopal positional tendencies of elements with different metafunctions, according to which logico-conjunctive and interpersonal Themes tend to cluster around their Nucleus, i.e. topical Themes (the obligatory element of EMTs) in decreasing potential of scope: the smaller the scope, the closer to the Nucleus, and vice versa, so that inner Themes are within the scope of the outer

Themes. Thus, it was claimed that, because they code experiential meaning intervening in choices of Mood, topical Themes are congruently within the scope of both interpersonal and logico-conjunctive Themes, which occupy outer slots within the Theme zone in conformity with their increasing scope potential. Accordingly, two unmarked orientations within the Theme zone were recognised: (a) the *stepwise orientation*, corresponding to high-low arrangements (Logico. conjunct and/or interpersonal elements preceding topical items) and (b) the *split orientation*, displayed by low-high orders (Logico.conjunct. and/or interpersonal elements following topical items). While stepwise orientations were associated with conditions of "sameness" or continuity in discourse, split-orientations were claimed to "re-orientate" the thread of discourse by disrupting the topical Theme–Rheme continuity and show an added subjectivity or subjectivification which is almost unfailingly reinforced suprasegmentally. These features accord well with the discourse conditions in which EMTs were found to cluster around: constructive and active texts (viz. Religious Broadcasts, Magazine, Dialogue, Propaganda).

8.3 Suggestions for further research

In concluding this study, it will be obvious to the reader that the discussion is incomplete in several major respects. First, further research should continue to analyse further thematic constructions (e.g. alternating complementation frames, postpositioning of Object, postpositioning of phrasal dependent, etc.), taking into account not only the interaction of the textual and interpersonal make-up of these constructions, but also their experiential semantics: what interpretation of experience do they express? In addition, further experimental research could be devoted to explore and contrast the uses to which thematic paradigms are put: (a) in different languages, (b) across a wider variety of genres, (c) in different modes of expression and (d) throughout different periods of time.

Also worth of consideration could be a deeper analysis of the interpersonal, subjective or sociolinguistic, aspects of information distribution. It would be interesting to explore, for example, how speakers "empathise" with Theme choices and thereby affect Theme–Rheme patterns and the organisation of discourse, focusing on such factors as e.g. their social, educational, geographic, age, and cultural background, or the like.

The positing of Theme at levels other than the clause is, in my opinion, also worth investigating further. Much more work needs to be done, for example, on the notions of Themes of groups and paragraphs before they can be taken as established structures of the language system. This would involve, for instance, investigating to what extent areas of thematic choice within the noun group obey the requirement for new or focused information to come last (e.g. in attributive vs. predicative constructions, in compounds using nouns as classifiers, in appositive structures, etc.), or determining to what degree nominal groups display metafunctional diversity and, if they do, what is the textual scope of their functional constituents. Likewise, the question should be addressed of whether or not paragraphs are linguistic units and so can be ascribed a Theme or a thematic progression, or whether there exists some relationship between these notions and that of discourse Topic.

The category of Rheme should also be studied in more detail. Research could be undertaken to decide whether there is such a thing as rhematic patterns and, if so, it would be necessary to establish a correlation between Rheme types and text types, as suggested by Daneš (1974b) or Ruzich (1984).

In brief, it would be most engaging to elicit whatever relationships there may be between the Theme zone and other categories in real and sufficiently representative texts in different languages, so as to evaluate the functional relevance of clause-initial position on more solid grounds and to validate its status as a linguistic universal.

Appendix

Data base structure for "A Corpus-based Analysis of Syntactic Theme in PresE"

1 Field No. 1: TEXT
1.1.1. A01-A12 Commentary
1.1.2 B01-B04 News Broadcasts
1.1.3 C01 Lecture Type I (general audience)
1.1.4 D01-D03 Lecture Type II (restricted audience)
1.1.5 E01-E02 Religious Broadcast
1.1.6 F01-F04 Magazine-Style Reporting
1.1.7 G01-G05 Fiction
1.1.8 H01-H05 Poetry
1.1.9 J01-J06 Dialogue
1.1.10 K01-K02 Propaganda
2 Field No. 2: MAJOR CLAUSE
example
3 Field No. 3: TYPE OF MAJOR CLAUSE
3.1 Simple
3.2 Complex
3.3 Paratactic (different types of expansion and projection)
3.4 Hypotactic
3.5 Rankshifted
3.6 Dependent
4 Field No. 4: ELLIPSIS
4.1 No ellipsis
4.2 Anaphoric ellipsis
4.2.1 Cataphoric ellipsis
4.2.2 Exophoric ellipsis
5 Field No 5: VERBLESS
5.1 Without verb
5.2 Elliptic verb
6 Field No. 6: MOOD
6.1 Declarative
6.2 Exclamative
6.3 Interrogative
6.4 Imperative
7. Field No. 7: PROCESS
7.1 Verbless
7.2 Behavioural
7.3 Existential
7.4 Material
7.5 Mental
7.6 Relational
7.7 Verbal
8 Field No. 8: FINITE
8.1 Finite
8.2 Non-finite
9 Field No. 9: VOICE
9.1 Active
9.2 Passive
10 Field No. 10: POLARITY
10.1 Affirmative
10.2 Negative
11 Field No. 11: THEME
Example
12 Field No. 12: CLASS OF THEME
12.1 Topical simple
12.2 Topical complex (tactic system)
12.3 Multiple simple
12.4 Multiple complex (tactic system)
13 Field No. 13: STRUCTURE OF TOPICAL THEME
13.1 Nominal group
13.1.1 Common noun
13.1.2 Proper noun
13.1.3 Pronoun
13.1.3.1 Personal
13.1.3.1.1 First person
13.1.3.1.2 Second person
13.1.3.1.3 Third person
13.1.3.2 Indefinite pronoun

13.1.3.3 Demonstrative pronoun
13.1.3.4 Numeral pronoun
13.1.3.5 Relative pronoun
13.2 Adjective group
13.3 Adverbial group
13.4 Prepositional phrase
14 Field No. 14: BETA β THEME
14.1 Temporal clause
14.2.1 Extent
14.2.2 Point
14.2.3 Spread
14.2.4 Later
14.2.5 Earlier
14.3 Spatial clause
14.3.1 Extent
14.3.2 Point
14.3.3 Spread
14.4 Manner clause
14.4.1 Means
14.4.2 Comparison
14.5 Conditional clause
14.5.1 Reason
14.5.2 Purpose
14.5.3 Positive
145.4 Negative
14.5.5 Concessive
15 Field No. 15: TRANSITIVITY FUNCTION OF TOPICAL THEME
15.1 Actor
15.2 Goal
15.3 Behaver[132]
15.4 Senser
15.5 Phenomenon
15.6 Sayer
15.7 Target
15.8 Token[133]
15.8.1 Token = Carrier
15.8.2 Token = Attribute
15.8.3 Token = Identified
15.8.4 Token = Identifier
15.9 Value
15.9.1 Value = Carrier
15.9.2 Value = Attribute
15.9.3 Value = Identified
15.9.4 Value = Identifier
15.10 Existent
15.11 Beneficiary
15.12 Initiator
15.13 Range
15.14 Extent
15.14.1 Spatial
15.14.2 Temporal
15.15 Location
15.15.1 Spatial
15.15.2 Temporal
15.16. Cause
15.16.1 Reason
15.16.2 Purpose
15.16.3 Behalf[134]
15.17 Accompaniment
15.17.1 Comitative[135]
15.17.2 Additive
15.18 Matter
15.19 Role
15.20 Angle
16 Field No. 16: SYNTACTIC FUNCTION OF TOPICAL THEME
16.1 Subject
16.2 Finite
16.3 Predicator
16.4 Direct Object
16.5 Indirect Object
16.6 Subject Complement
16.7 Extent Adjunct
16.7.1 Temporal
16.7.2 Spatial
16.8 Spatial Adjunct
16.8.1 Temporal
16.8.2 Spatial
16.9 Manner Adjunct
16.9.1 Means
16.9.2 Quality
16.9.3 Comparison
16.10 Cause Adjunct
16.10.1 Reason
16.10.2 Purpose
16.10.3 Behalf
16.11 Contingency Adjunct
16.12 Accompaniment Adjunct
16. 12.1 Addition
16.12.2 Comitation[11]
16.13 Role Adjunct
16.14 Matter Adjunct
16.15 Angle Adjunct
17 Field No. 17: SPECIAL TOPICAL THEME
17.1 *It*-cleft
17.2 *WH*-cleft
17.3 Right dislocation
17.4 Left dislocation
17.5 *There*-Existential constructions
17.6 *It*-Extraposed constructions
17. 7 Inversion
18 Field No. 18: MARKED TOPICAL THEME
18.1 Unmarked
18.2 Fronting
19 Field No. 20: POSITION TOPICAL THEME
20.1 Initial
20.2 Medial
20.3 Final
21 Field No. 21: EXTERNAL TOPICAL THEME
21.1 Internal

21.2 External
22 Field No. 22: INTER-PERSONAL THEME
Example
23 **Field No. 23: TYPE INTERPERSONAL THEME**
23.1 Modal Adjunct
23.1.1 Probability
23.1. 2 Frequency
23.1.3 Opinion
23.1.4 Admissive
23.1.5 Assertive
23.1.6 Presumptive
23.1.7 Desiderative
23.1.8 Tentative
23.1.9 Validative
23.1.10 Evaluative
23.1.11 Predictive
23.2 Vocative

23.3 Interrogative pronoun
23.4 Finite
24 Field No. 24: POSITION INTERPERSONAL THEME
24.1 Initial
24.2 Medial
24.3 Final
25 Field No. 21: LOGICO-CONJUNCT. THEME
Example
26 Field No. 26: TYPE LOGICO-CONJUNCT. THEME
26.1 Conjunctive Adjunct
26.1.1 Appositive
26.1.2 Corrective
26.1.3 Dismissive
26.1.4 Summative

26.1.5 Verifactive[136]
26.1.6 Additive
26.1.7 Adversative
26.1.8 Variative[137]
26.1.9 Temporal
26.1.10 Comparative
26.1.11 Causal
26.1.12 Conditional
26.1.13 Concessive
26.1.14 Respective
26.2 Continuative
26.3 Structural
27 Field No. 27: POSITION OF LOGICO-CONJUNCT. THEME
27.1 Initial
27.2 Medial
27.3 Final

Notes

Chapter 1. The Theme–Topic interface: Introduction

1. The term "packaging" is due to Chafe (1976: 28), but the following quote from Prince (1986: 208) reflects the view of information packaging adopted here:

   > Information in a discourse does not correspond to an unstructured set of propositions; rather, speakers seem to form their utterances so as to structure the information they are attempting to convey, usually or perhaps always in accordance with their beliefs about the hearer: what s/he is thought to know, what s/he is expected to be thinking about.

2. Upper and lower case will be employed throughout this investigation to designate functional categories (Subject, Theme, etc.) and their attributes (given information, thematic status, etc.), respectively. The categories of Theme/Topic and Focus, on the other hand, unless otherwise specified, will appear underlined and in boldtype.

3. For a contrastive study of PS, SFG, FG and *Role and Reference Grammar* (RRG), see Gómez-González (1996a).

4. Some of the scholars that distinguished between psychological and grammatical Subject and Predicate at this early stage were: von der Gabelentz (1869: 378ff., 1972 [1901]: 369ff.), Paul (1975 [1880]: 124ff.), Höffding (1910: 84ff.), Marty (1918: 31ff.), Behagel (1923: 218), Vossler (1923: 105ff.) and Kraus (1956: 289ff.). Other grammarians, however, did not differentiate these two sets of categories, such as Steinthal (1890: 235–43), Jellinek (1914: § 599ff.) and Sandman (1954: 79–105, 237).

5. Halliday's *Systemic-Functional Grammar* exemplifies the functionalist approach, which: (a) is paradigmatically-based; (b) is influenced by ethnography and rhetoric, and posits an *iconic*, or *non-arbitrary*, relation between form and meaning; (c) describes language on purely functional terms, so that the terms *functional* and *function* may be used in two senses: (i) as a *functional label*, that is, indicating a *proportional*, or paradigmatic, relation (or a term in such a relation or some means whereby such a relation is expressed) alongside classes or categories, and (ii) 1970b: 323; IFG: xxxiii); and (d) implies a historical passage from a probabilistic preference for a particular structure, based on universal tendencies, to the development of a convention that is fully determinate. By contrast, Chomsky's *Transformational-Generative* model embodies the formalist approach, which: (a) is syntagmatic in orientation; (b) posits an arbitrary relation between form and meaning; (c) rooted in logic and philosophy, focuses on universals and uses intuitions to elicit them; and (d) stratifies linguistic description in terms of syntax, semantics, pragmatics and so on.

6. Although considered as a conservative functionalist model by some analysts, FG is here regarded as "moderate" on the assumption that its later moves head towards this direction. The Prague School is also analysed for its pioneering role in communicative approaches to language, even if it does not constitute a unified programme.

Chapter 2. An evaluation of three interpretations of Theme/Topic

7. An early example of this identification is von der Gabelentz (1869: 378), who interpreted word order as a result of aboutness relationships as follows:

> Informative utterances can be divided into (1) the thing about which I am talking, and (2) what I state about it. That thing I call the *psychological* Subject, and that statement the *psychological* Predicate. The psychological Subject stands first, the psychological Predicate second. [my translation]

Paul, in turn, mixed up identificational criteria of the syntactic and the informational type. He defined (psycho)logical Subject as 'what appears first in the speaker's mind' (1975 [1880]: 124), a syntactic characterisation, but contrasted it with 'the phonetically most prominent part', the psychological Predicate (1886: 101) [my translation], an informational description. In the second part of this study we shall see that similar and other identifications reappear in later analyses arousing a number of controverted issues. See also Fries (1983) on *combining* and *separating* approaches.

8. Similar claims can be found in Magretta (1977: 126), van Oosten (1986: 29) and Hawkinson & Hyman (1975: 161), Gundel (1985: 85).

9. Equivalent accounts can be found in, for example: Hawkinson & Hyman (1975: 161), Li and Thompson (1976: 463), Magretta (1977: 126), Gundel 1985: 85), van Oosten (1986: 29), Kieras (1981: 2), Schiffrin (1992: 172), Lambrecht (1994: 127), Langacker (1993: 26). Other scholars also endorse this definition of sentence Topics but contrast it with their characterisation of *discourse Topics* (Reinhart 1982: 48; Davison 1984: 803; Witte 1983: 317; Pufahl 1992: 218–19).

10. See for instance: Bühler (1934), Halliday (1967b, 1994), Lutz (1981), Adamec (1981: 226), Kieras (1978), Vallduví (1992).

11. For further details on the analysis of Topics/Themes as perspective-taking devices see: Fillmore (1968), Kuno (1976), MacWhinney (1977), Dik (1978), Duranti & Ochs (1979) and Zubin (1979). Other labels for roughly similar approaches are: *point of view* (Owens, Dafoe & Bower's 1977); *ego perspective* (Ertel 1974) and the *me-first principle* (Cooper & Ross 1975).

12. An "evolutionary" approach to the Topic–Subject relationship is adopted in: Dragunov (1960 [1952]: 17–19), Givón (1976), Li & Thompson (1976, 1981), Schachter (1977), Hagège (1978), De Groot & Limburg (1986), Shibatini (1991), among others.

13. The examples from Chinese and Japanese are taken from Li & Thompson (1976, 1981) and Jiménez-Juliá (1995).

14. There is no established terminology to refer to "thetic" sentences (Kuroda 1972, 1984, 1985, Lambrecht 1987a, Sasse 1987). Some other labels are: *presentational sentences* (Bolinger 1954; Schmerling 1976), *neutral descriptions* (Kuno 1972a), *news sentences* (Schmerling 1976), *event reporting sentences* (Lambrecht 1986), or *sentence focus structures* (Lambrecht 1987a, 1994).

15. The examples in (9) are taken from Halliday (1967b: 212), those in (10) and (11) from Downing (1990: 123–27) and Dik (1978: 136–37), respectively; while those in (12) belong to Valldiví & Engdahl (1996: 466).
16. Examples (13)–(15) were pointed out to me by Peter Collins, personal communication.
17. Other referential-semantic analyses can be found in: Hawkinson & Hyman (1975), Perteffi & Goldman (1974: 71), Givón (1976, 1984a, 1983b, 1988, 1992), Allerton (1978), Fox (1983), Hinds (1983), Cooreman (1983), Thompson, (1985), Ramsay (1986), Dik (1989) and Downing (1991).
18. See van Dijk (1973, 1977, 1984, 1988), van Dijk et al. (1972), van Dijk & Kintsch (1983), Dressler (1972), Agricola (1979), and Brinker (1985).
19. See *inter alia* Berry (1975), Beaugrande (1980), Kieras (1981), Thorndyke (1977), Rumelhart (1975), Keenan & Schieffelin (1976), Schank (1977).
20. See Altheide's (1976: 73) *angle* in journalism, Prince's (1982: 74) *Theme* in narratology, Schank's (1977: 426) *meta-topic* in cognitive science and Polani's (1979), Fries's (1987) *point of a story* in discourse analysis.
21. "Given" (information) has been variously addressed as *Background* (Dahl 1974a, b, c; Chafe 1976), *Presupposition* (Chomsky 1971; Jackendoff 1972), *Open-proposition* (Prince 1986; Ward 1985), *Theme* (Firbas 1964; Contreras 1976; Steedman 1991) and *Topic* (Sgall et al. 1986), to name but a few labels. For different taxonomies of given information see Allerton (1978), Prince (1981a), Ariel (1985, 1996), Horn (1986), Gundel (1988), Gundel, Hedberg & Zacharschi (1993), Walker, Joshi & Prince (1997), Schwarzschild (1996a, b), Kohlhof (1997), and Section 2.3.2 in this book.
22. "Informational Focus" has also been called, among other things, *New* (Halliday 1967b, 1994), *Rheme* (Firbas 1964; Contreras 1976) and *dominant constituent* (Erteschik-Shir 1988). Cutting across the old/new dichotomy and a pragmatic characterisation, the notion of "Focus" has proved rather problematic and has been used in several senses (Rochemont 1986; Rochemont & Culicover 1990; Zubizarreta 1994). "Focus" is generally defined as a construction which marks syntactically, lexically and phonologically the new or contrastive element of a sentence. More specifically, as a purely phonological term, it designates intonational prominence in a sentence or the nuclear stress, which may be associated not only with information packaging but with other linguistic dimensions as well (e.g. illocution, string-based deaccenting) and which may also be a consequence of nonlinguistic effects. In the literature, two types of Focus are distinguished: *broad*, or presentational, and *narrow* (Selkirk 1984; Lambrecht 1994; Ladd 1996). In semantics, Focus has been used as a synonym for quantificational *nuclear* scope when analysing quantifiers, for example. And, by analogy with quantifier phrases, in syntactic analyses, Focus has been described as a constituent which substitutes into the specifier position of an extrasentential maximal projection where it binds a variable or trace in argument position. As this operation can occur either in overt syntax or in Logical Form, a Focus can be realized both fronted or *in situ*, the based-generated position being the unmarked case for economy principles (Chomsky 1971, 1976; May 1985; Hovarth 1986; Brody 1990). Lastly, as shall be shown in Section 2.3.2, in computational treatments of cognitive status and in (psycho-)linguistic analyses of reference all discourse entities are ranked according to salience in a *Focus stack*. From this perspective, the Focus is the most salient discourse entity at a given time point, that is, the one at the top of the focus stack, and referents "in focus" are those hearer-known referents that are in some sense "activated" or "salient" and that can be referred to with a pronominal form (Garrod & Sanford 1982; Gundel et al. 1993).

23. Other labels assigned to the PFSP are: *natural subjective movement* (Weil 1844), the *communicative principle* (Reszkiewicz 1966: 61ff.), the *From-Old(Given$_{k)}$-to-New Principle* (Kuno 1978a, 1980). For further details on this principle see, for example: Flesch (1946), Strunk & White (1959), Smith (1971), Prince (1978), Bock & Irwin (1980), Vande Kopple (1983, 1986).
24. Examples (22)–(25) were pointed out to me by Peter Collins, personal communication.
25. For further details on the TUP see, for instance: Givón (1983c), Fox (1983), Mithun (1987), Payne (1987).
26. Some scholars who have investigated the effects of the PFSP and the TUP on discourse structure are: Vande Kopple (1983, 1986), Daneš (1974a), Van Dijk (1977), Givón (1983b), Witte (1983) and Ruzich (1984).
27. A twofold division of labor into *relational* and *referential* readings of givenness/newness is also explicitly assumed, for instance, in: Jespersen (1924: 145), Kuno (1972a: 271–3), Dahl (1976), Reinhart (1982), Prince (1986), Adamec (1981: 226), Gundel (1988: 211–2), Gundel et al. (1993), Vallduví (1992) and Vallduví & Engdahl (1996).
28. The F-labelled brackets ([F] are used to delimit the Focus (without implying syntactic constituency of any sort), and capitalised items mark the nuclear stress.
29. The example is divided into prosodically defined intonation units, at the end of which a comma shows a nonfinal pitch contour and a period a final, falling contour. Sequences of two and three dots indicate brief and normal length pauses, and acute and grave accents, primary and secondary accents, respectively. The equals sign indicates lengthening of the preceding vowel.
30. Brown & Yule (1983) further distinguish between *current* and *displaced* textually evoked entities. They note that while "the *current evoked* entity is the one which was introduced as 'new' immediately before the current *new* entity was introduced [whereas] [d]isplaced entities were introduced prior to that" (183). Another difference is observed that while current textual entities are expressed by 'lexically attenuated' forms, either definite, pronominal or elided, displaced textual entities are usually referred to by an definite expression, often accompanied by an identifying property.
31. The notion of "file card" is related to Karttunen's (1976) *discourse referent*, Webber's (1982) *coathooks* or Heim's (1982) *file change semantics*. Referring to NPs, file cards mediate between referring expressions and real-world entities, typically denoting individuals, pluralities, substances, actions, event tokens, and event types. For further details see Chierchia & McConnell-Ginet (1990).
32. There exists a parallelism between designating a specific locus of update in the input file and linking with the "object of thought", which evokes von der Gabelentz's (1869: 378) "object of speech" or Trávníček's description of Theme as "the sentence element that links up directly with the object of thought, proceeds from it, and opens the sentence thereby" (cited in Firbas 1964: 269) (Sections 1.2, 2.3.1, 2.3.2). Similar proposals may be found in Reinhart (1982: 24), and Kuno (1972a).
33. As shall be shown in Chapter 5, the label "Tail" can also be found in the FG programme (Dik 1989, 1997), but with a different characterisation, which is closer to Chafe's (1976: 53) and Lambrecht's (1994: 203) notion of *Anti-Topics*, or to Halliday's (1967b, 1994) *Substitute Themes* (Chapter 4).
34. Vallduví & Engdahl (1996) distinguish between *link contrast* (italicised *John* in (37a)) and *focus contrast* (capitalised *John* in (37b)), which in English are accented differently:

(37) a. *John* swept (and *Mary* mopped).
b. JOHN swept (not MARY).

The underlying rationale is that while (b) conversationally implicates that no relevant person other than John swept (hence the appropriate continuation *not MARY*), (a) implicates that someone else did something other than sweeping (hence the appropriate continuation *and Mary mopped*).

35. This type of "combining" identifications can be found in e.g.: McCutchen & Pertetti's (1982: 117ff.), Bates (1976), Dahl (1976), Allerton (1978), Prince (1978, 1981b), Haviland & Clark (1974), Clark & Haviland (1977), Deyes (1978), Copeland & Davis (1983), Tejada-Caller (1988).

36. See the attention studies by Posner & Warren (1972); Schneider & Shiffrin (1977); Posner (1985); Posner et al. (1988); Posner & Petersen (1989); Gernsbacher (1985, 1989); and memory research by Jarvella (1971); Glanzer & Razel (1974); Jacoby (1974), Givón (1975), Glanzer et al. (1984), van Dijk & Kintsch (1983), Du Bois (1987), Chafe (1987).

37. See the work on English, Guarani, Russian and Turkish by Schmerling (1976), Dooley (1982), Adamec (1966) and Erkü (1983), respectively.

38. This latter stance raises the problem as to how to determine the informational status of written discourse. Most scholars argue that written discourse merely echoes the structure of spoken discourse. Thus, readers are said to derive information structure from intonational patterns residing "latently" in the text, provided by syntactic structure (for instance the correspondence, in absence of indication to the contrary, between clause and tone unit) and by punctuation (Halliday 1967a, Firbas 1992).

39. Vallduví & Engdahl (1996) find the hierarchy in (40) somewhat problematic. First, they claim that it is "interesting" that definiteness clusters at the periphery of the hierarchy if topicality is the sole underlying function driving structural realization. And secondly, the empirical problem is posed that in such languages as Catalan nonspecific indefinites can be right-detached, a totally unexpected phenomenon according to the hierarchy, since indefinite noun phrases are lowest in topicality and right-detached noun phrases are among the highest.

40. For similar function-to-form syntactic accounts see e.g.: Quirk et al. (1972, 1985), Enkvist (1974); Berry (1975), García (1979), Green (1980), Penelope (1982), Brömser (1982), McCutchen & Perteffi (1982), Habertlandt & Bingham (1982), Silva Corvalán (1984), Kies (1988).

41. A more detailed discussion of the syntactic issues raised in form-to-function approaches, i.e. where are Topics generated, which types of movement place them exactly in which syntactic positions, and what problems occur with different types of so-called Topic movements (topicalisation, left dislocation, polarity elements, etc.) can be found in: Ward (1985), Culicover (1991, 1993), Drubig (1994), Büring (1995).

42. It should be noted, however, that some primarily syntactic accounts of Topic/Theme (initial position) do show combining overtones. One example is Gundel (1988: 223-ff.), where *Topic-before-Comment* constructions (i.e. Given-before-New) are distinguished from *Comment-before-Topic* ones (i.e. New-before-Given). Likewise, Quirk et al. (1985: 1375) define marked Theme along informational lines as "a theme which is given at least as much prosodic marking as that entailed by being at the point of 'onset' (…) in a tone unit"; and, pseudo-cleft sentences are similarly described as special thematic structures which "can make explicit the division between the given and new parts of the communication" (ibid.: 1387).

Chapter 3. The Prague School

43. In this connection, ancient grammarians such as Dionysius of Halicarnassus (*De Compositione Verborum*, Roberts 1910) had already claimed that the sequence Subject-verb-Complement is the *ordo naturalis* of languages for it represents a *physei*, that is to say, it reflects the natural order of the phenomena in nature itself on the grounds that "substance" should precede "accident" or "what happens" (Jellinek 1913–14: paras. 563–78).
44. The category of *Rheme* (Mathesius's *jadró*) was incorporated by Firbas (1957) to keep the parallelism with Theme.
45. It must be noted that Mathesius interprets thetic sentences in a rather unorthodox way, classifying as thetic some strings that strictly speaking were not thetic, but did not fit into his Theme–Rheme analysis (viz. verbless clauses used as commands, suggestions, signals, or expressions of the speaker's certainty or uncertainty towards what s/he says and sequences having the infinitive as the basic element, e.g. *Auto!*, *He'll do it*, *no doubt of it*, *To think that I have always supported him*, Mathesius (1961: 87–8)) (see endnote 14 above).
46. For details on CD see e.g. Firbas (1957, 1962, 1964, 1966, 1972, 1974, 1975, 1982, 1983, 1986, 1989, 1992, 1995), Svoboda (1968, 1974, 1981, 1983), Uhlírová (1969), Chládková (1979), Golková (1987, 1995). The theory of CD shows some parallelisms with Paul's (1886) and Boost's (1955) *communicative importance*, Ertl's (1926, para. 552) *context weightiness*, Trávniček's (1937) *importance of items*, Mukarovský's (1941: 129–30) *content accumulation*, and Mathesius's (1947: 218) *relative shading of the importance*, Bolinger's (1952: 1125) *gradation of meaning* and Krushel'nitskaya's (1961) *communicative load of sentence elements*.
47. Some debatable aspects of CD have been discussed in: Francis (1966), Contreras (1976), Rybarkiewicz (1977), Adjémian (1978), Pasch (1982), among others.
48. See also Dahl (1974b: 7), Sgall (1974: 25), Benešová, Dahl (1974b: 7), Sgall (1974: 25), Benešová, Wierzbicka (1975: 73).
49. In spite of subscribing to the informational approach, Firbas (1964: 275) also admits the relevance of sentence beginning as the *starting point* (opening) of several fronts, namely: (a) the grammatical line, i.e. the line along which the sentence is being structured grammatically, (b) the line of semantic structure, (c) the intonation line, and (d) the FSP line, i.e. the line along which degrees of CD are being distributed. However, in spite of recognising that an enquiry into how sentences open in various languages may prove interesting, Firbas has not undertaken this task.

Chapter 4. Systemic Functional Grammar

50. Halliday (1994: 193) explains that "[a] sentence will be defined, in fact, as a clause complex. The clause complex will be the only grammatical unit which we shall recognize above the clause. Hence there will be no need to bring in the term "sentence" as a distinct grammatical category. We can use it simply to refer to the orthographic unit that is contained between full stops (…) a sentence is a constituent of writing, while a clause complex is a constituent of grammar."
51. We have seen that, although Beneš and Daneš also intended to use the categories of Basis and Theme as invoking the notion of "point of departure" they assimilated this concept to that of

"previous mention", and therefore did not suggest a strictly "separating" interpretation of this category, but endowed it with "combining" overtones.

52. In SFG *systems* are defined as finite sets of distinctive terms, which (a) change their meanings if a new term is added and (b) set up *networks* of relatively independent or interdependent options (if belonging to the same system(s) (or subsystem(s)), together with a condition entry, which states the environment for linguistic choice (Martin 1984a: 41ff.).

53. The choice of *Mood* refers to the presence/absence and ordering of five functional elements: (a) *Subject*, which is the element "responsible" for carrying out, a *proposal* or a *proposition*, that is to say, the performer of an action or the bearer of the argument (i.e. the one on whom its validity is made to rest) when information is exchanged (IFG: 76); (b) *Finite* element expressing the deicticity of the process by making reference to either (i) the speaker/writer-now, or *primary tense* (i.e. past, present or future at the moment of speaking) by means of *temporal operators* (viz. *did, does, will*, etc.) or (ii) the speaker's/writer's judgement of the probabilities or the obligations of what he is saying/writing by means of the *modal operators* (viz. *can, will, must*, etc.); (c) *Predicator* (i.e. verbal group minus the temporal or modal operator); (d) *Complement* (i.e. element that has the potential of being Subject but is not); and (e) *Adjunct* (i.e. element that has not the potential of being Subject.

Choices of Mood incorporate the features [imperative], [indicative], [affirmative], [interrogative], [exclamative] and [declarative]. Imperatives usually show neither Subject nor Finite, while indicative statements have both categories. Within indicatives affirmatives (including declaratives and exclamatives) display the order Subject^Finite, while interrogatives show the Finite^Subject arrangement (with the exception of *WH-interrogatives* where the wh-word is Subject, which have Subject^Finite order). Finally, exclamatives encode reactions in their syntax (WH-element).

54. There are some exceptions to the principle that unmarked (information) Focus involves nuclear stress placement on the final open class item. We have for example those cases where the nuclear stress occurs before the last open-class word (which is associated with relatively predictable, general or familiar meaning), and we can still speak of unmarked focus (e.g. *The train's arrived, Have you got any fruit to eat*). A second instance occurs in certain cases where a closed-class item which follows the first openclass item is focal (e.g. *Who's the headmaster with*). This might be used, without any of the special emphasis that occurs with marked Focus, by a speaker who wished to avoid the possibility that the addressee might interpret the headmaster as emphatic (for example, *the headmaster* in contrast to *the English master*). Similarly, in sentences containing a verb + particle idiom, the particle may occur finally with nuclear stress without attracting a marked focal interpretation (e.g. *He called the meeting off*). This exception occurs in certain cases where it is the final open-class item that is focal, and yet it carries a marked interpretation, as in *I lent the drill to **Mr Brown***. If the stress on *Brown* is produced with additional force or wider range, there will be a suggestion of special emphasis (i.e. *Of all people!, Not Mr Black, Despite my threat never to lend him my tools again*).

55. The *transitivity network* aims to present the entire lexicogrammar in terms of: (a) *processes*; (b) *participants*, that is, the linguistic representations of non-human, inanimate, abstract entities, as well as human beings, involved in the situations; and (c) any possible attending *circumstance(s)* (or qualities/attributes) of the whole situation or of the Participant(s).

56. *Projection* and *expansion* name the two types of logico-semantic structural relations holding between processes. In projection the reporting clause "instantiates" the reported clause as a *locution* ('') or as an *idea* ('). By contrast, in expansion a process "expands" another by: (a)

elaborating it (=) (i.e. re-stating it, specifying it or commenting it); (b) extending it (+) (i.e. adding some new element, and exception or an alternative to it); or (c) *enhancing* it (x) (i.e. qualifying it with some circumstantial feature). Tables 8 and 9 illustrate the different types of projections and expansions acknowledged in SFG.

57. *Embedding* is one type of constructional relationship that belongs to the system of interdependency, the *Tactic* system, and cross-classifies the logico-semantic relations of projection and expansion. It is the "mechanism whereby a clause or phrase comes to function as a constituent within the structure of a group, which itself is a constituent of a clause" (IFG: 242). The other two constructional relationships are: (a) *hypotaxis*, in which a *secondary* process (β) depends on a *primary* one (α), regardless of their sequential order; and (b) *parataxis*, in which processes have equal status, allowing internal bracketing, or *nesting*, and *branching* structures of the type e.g. *John came, but Peter didn't*.

58. Square brackets [ ] signal that a clause is functioning in an embedded way as part of another clause.

59. In (IFG: 49) the possibility is also admitted that this type of imperatives consist of Rheme only (the thematic value "I want you to" being left implicit).

60. In SFG the network of voice distinguishes *middle* voice (no feature of "agency"; process: active) from *effective* voice ("agency" implied), which, in its turn, may be *operative* (process: active) or *receptive* (process: passive).

61. Halliday explains that *who* and *which* do not occur as the Head of a nominalisation of definite human nouns, including human collectives, because being themselves definite they do not accept defining Modifiers. Rather they take such generic Heads as *the one*, (generic noun), *the person*, etc. In addition, Halliday notes that there cannot be interrogative identifying clauses with a nominalisation of the WH-item (e.g. *what who saw was the play), except in the special case of second order questions (e.g. such as *what* was what John saw? related to *what* did John see?).

62. First person in declarative or second person in interrogative, e.g. *do you reckon…?*

63. See, for instance: Verma (1976), Fries (1982, 1983, 1986, 1995a, b), Jordan (1985), Kies (1988; Francis (1989a, b, 1990), Fries & Francis (1992), Bloor & Bloor (1992), Taylor (1993), Matthiessen & Martin (1991), Martin (1992a, b, 1995), Cummings (1995), Ravelli (1995), Gómez-González (1994, 1995, 1996a).

64. Some exponents of this line of research are: Martin (1989, 1992b), Giora (1983), Eiler (1986), Du Bois (1987), Ragan (1987), Rothery (1990), Whittaker (1990), Taylor-Torsello (1992, 1996, 1997), Ravelli (1995), Consorte (1998).

65. Emblematic examples of this research area are e.g.: Berry's (1987) work on place-names Themes; Eiler's (1986) or Francis's (1989a) analyses of the TPs of a lecture chapter on physics and of three press genres, respectively, Bäcklund's (1991) study of telephone conversation, Xiao's (1991) revision of recipes and fables, Long's (1991) account of guidebooks, Wang's (1992) report on scene and line texts; and, more generally, the work by Plum (1988), Ghadessy (1993, 1995), Whittaker (1995), Yan et al. (1995), Cloran (1995), Gómez-González (1994, 1995, 1996a) on the TP of professional and popular medical texts, in news reports, and on the interaction of Theme (MOD, TP) and genre.

66. See e.g.: Francis (1989a, 1990), Nwogu & Bloor (1991: 376), Bäcklund (1991), Longacre (1981, 1989).

67. See, for instance: Berry (1987), Bäcklund (1991), Martin (1989), Francis (1989a, 1990), Xiao (1991), Wang Ling (1991, 1992), Fries (1995a), Ghadessy (1993), Gómez-González (1994, 1995, 1996a).
68. This is hypothesised in, for instance, Plum (1988), Fries (1993, 1994), Ford (1993), Prideaux & Hogan (1993).
69. See, for example: Bazell (1973: 201), Firbas (1974: 25, 212), Gundel (1974: 47, 87), Dahl (1976: 48), Kuno (1975: 326, Footnote 1), Allerton (1978: 166), Fronek (1983: 312), Fries (1983 [1981], 1987), Taglicht (1984: 14), Davidson and Lutz (1985: 33), Hudson (1986: 797, 798), Huddleston (1988, 1991, 1992), Siewierska (1991: 149 note 3) and Downing (1990, 1991).
70. A T-unit is a "minimal terminable unit, ... minimal as to length, and each ... grammaticaly capable of being terminated with a capital letter and a period" (Hunt 1965, quoted in Larsen-Freeman and Strom 1977: 128).
71. In Downing & Locke (1992: 235), however, all circumstantial Themes are described as setting up *situational* frameworks.
72. It should be noted that Downing & Locke's (1992: 231–2) classification of conjunctive and modal Themes does not totally coincide with Halliday's.
73. Exceptions to this are: (a) negative Adjuncts (e.g. *never, not often, not a soul,*); (b) directional Adjuncts (e.g. *Off* they go, Downing and Locke 1992: 228; [my emphasis]); (c) *so, neither* and *nor* introducing elliptical clauses (e.g. *Ed* passed the exam *and so* did Mary, ibid. 229; my emphasis]); (d) *such* and *so* acting as Modifiers of Objects, Complements or Adjuncts (e.g. *So* depressed did he feel that nothing would cheer him up, id.; [my emphasis]); and (e) subordinate clauses of condition and concession (e.g. *Had I know the facts*, I would not have employed him, ibid.; [my emphasis]). In spite of triggering inversion of Subject and Finite or Predicator, these Themes are regarded by Downing as Attributes of basic clause level Topics, rather than basic level Topics, because they are not Participants.
74. To the above Topic-discontinuity devices Downing & Locke (1992: 225–6) add: (a) statements that explicitly inform the hearer/reader what the Topic is going to be as in *I want to talk to you about genetic engineering*; (b) often Direct Objects or Predicator Complements when the Subject is known as in *What did you make of Elsa's behaviour?;* and (c) less frequently an initial participant (usually the Subject) which receives considerable pitch prominence as in *Eddoes, who was a driver, was admired by all the boys*. As to *Topic continuity*, Downing observes that it is achieved by means of usually thematic anaphoric (Halliday's cohesive) participants (typically Subjects), and also by such expressions as *as regards, as for, what about ...* and the conjunctive adverb *now*. Andrews (1985: 78), in turn, points out that *as for* signals a change of Topic.
75. Martin (1995: 241) mentions Matthiessen's warning about reasoning from glosses of labels instead of from proportionalitites:

> The proportionalities are primary, but the labels we use to name the members of the proportionalities (i.e. features in systems) and the proportionalities themselves (i.e. systems) are secondary. It is important to remember this when we explore the discourse-semantic motivation behind the organisation of grammar: we have to reason about the proportionalities embodied in the systems, not about the names we give them. If we reason about the names, we are only engaging in lexical semantic studies of the technical vocabulary used in the account.

76. Ambient *it*" is typically a Carrier in an attributive relational clause with an Attribute dealing with some feature of the environment such as temperature (e.g. *it's hot*), or else it appears as Actor in a material clause of qualitative change (e.g. *it's cooling down*).

77. *Congruent choices* are said to express a direct line of form to meaning to experience, in contrast with *metaphorical choices*, which are regarded to invoke an indirect line involving further meanings than congruent ones (for details on the concept and types of *metaphor* see e.g. IFG: 343–67; Martin 1992a: 406–17).

78. Downing (1991) also regards the notion of *displaced topical Theme* as unnecessary, arguing that clause level Topics need not be thematic or clause initial. Instead, she claims that initial non-Objects/Subjects do not behave as Topics, but as marked Themes, setting up emphatic points of departure which contribute to either Topic discontinuity or Topic continuity over a discourse span, as illustrated in (83) (Downing 1991: 132 [my emphasis]):

> (83) *For two hundred years* the Roman soldier-farmers had struggled for freedom and a share in the government of their state; for a hundred years they had enjoyed their privileges.

79. Despite its allegedly "separating" stand, one can find some "combining" observations in the systemic literature that seem to violate the principle of separation of categories and levels mentioned above. Note, for example, Matthiessen & Martin's (1991: 47–8) explanations that (a) the Theme of a question "is the piece of information the speaker assumes the listener can supply, i.e. information that is *recoverable* for the listener although not for the speaker, and Rheme is the rest [my emphasis]" and (b) "aboutness" is most closely associated with the topicality subtype of thematicity; or Halliday's (IFG: 38) statement that topical Theme corresponds fairly well with the category of Topic, associated in the literature with given information.

Chapter 5. Functional Grammar

80. For more details on and antecedents of the FG account of pragmatic rules/functions, see e.g. Hetzron (1975), Givón (1978), Watters (1979), Prince (1981b), Dik et al. (1981), Bossuyt (1982), Bardovi-Harlig (1983), Hannay (1983), Moutaouakil (1984), Keijsper (1985), De Vries (1985), Hannay (1985a, 1985b).

81. We could read such definitions as:

> [a] constituent with *Topic function* presents the entity "about" which the Predication predicates something in the given setting. (...) A constituent with *Focus function* presents the relatively most important or salient information with respect to the pragmatic information of the Speaker and Addressee. (Dik 1978: 130).

82. Before Dik, Prince (1981a: 233) had also stressed this important limitation as follows:

> [w]e may now word the basic problem as follows. From the point of view of the speaker/writer, what kinds of assumptions about the hearer/reader have a bearing on the form of the text being produced ...? From the point of view of the hearer/reader, what inferences will s/he draw on the basis of the particular form chosen? We are, therefore, NOT concerned with what one individual may know or hypothesise about another individual's belief-state EXCEPT insofar as that

NOTES 373

knowledge and those hypotheses affect the form and understanding of LINGUISTIC production. [emphasis in original]

83. In Dik (1989: 265) ECCs are not classified into four functional groups as in (85) above (TFG2: 379–409), but are only listed as: (a) initiators, (b) forms of address, (c) modal parenthesis, (iv) Tags, (d) clarifications, (e) Themes and (f) Tails. Despite the theoretical advance implied in (85), in (TFG2: 383) we are told that this is only a preliminary and incomplete analysis because of two facts mainly: (a) "some of these constituents may have different functions in different contexts of use; and (b) some may simultaneously have several functions in one and the same occurrence" (see Section 1.2 in this book).

84. The possibility is also admitted that individual languages may have additional special positions constrained by language-dependent restrictions, for example: in Arabic a predication external (P4) vocative position placed to the left of P2; in Basque and Hungarian a special preverbal Focus position (P0); in written Czech, Polish and Russian a clause-final Focus slot; in Dutch an extra final Topic/Focus location, etc.

85. In this connection, Fox (1987a) argues that the choice between pronominal and nominal anaphora is determined by the episode boundaries of discourse. Fox hypothesises that if the gap between two successive mentions of the same character contains another referent, not already connected in some way to the first character, then the subsequent mention will be in nominal form, and if it does not, in pronominal form.

86. In this connection Dixon (1972: 71) explains that in Dyirbal Subjects and GivTops coincide, while Bolkestein (1985a) demonstrates that Latin abides by the Given-before-New principle — which she re-labels as *backward harmony* (i.e. the Given comes first) and *forward harmony* (i.e. the New comes last).

87. Whether or not the NewTops in (existential) presentative constructions should be given Subject status has been subject of much debate. These constituents seem to have the most central properties of Subjects such as the nominative case (in case marking languages) and verb agreement. However, French existentials and English contracted equivalents serve as exceptions to this rule: the former show neither gender nor number agreement (e.g. *Les trois trains arrivaient* "the three trains arrived (plur.)" vs. *Il arrivait trois trains* (sing.) "There arrived three trains", Dik (1989: 270) [my emphasis]), while the latter may lack number agreement (e.g. *There're problems to be solved* or *There's problems to be solved*, Hannay 1985b: 187). Furthermore, the postverbal location and further distributional constraints of the NewTops are also atypical of Subjects (e.g. in English existential and presentative constructions it is *there*, not the NewTop, that occurs in question-tags and in Subject-raising constructions). In view of this irregular picture, FG opts to explain the distinct properties of NewTops not on syntactic grounds, but on the basis of their pragmatic function.

88. See also: Givón's (1984a: 411) *salient Topics* in Israeli Hebrew, Hawaii Creole, Sherpa, Persian, Romance and Germanic; or Comrie's (1981: 128) *important indefinite Objects* in Turkish.

89. Hannay (1983: 214ff.) explains that "[a]n entity that has something predicated of it can be important (foregrounded) at the same time, and this may be marked in a language by, for instance, intonational prominence" (e.g. (a) *What about **Rebecca**?* (b) *It was **to her** that John gave his most precious painting* [my emphasis].

90. Besides Barry's, I would suggest that Chafe's (1976: 50) or Li & Thompson's (1976: 461–63) notions of Topic also evoke Dik's Theme. Indeed, it has been noted (Section 2.2.1) that for

Chafe Topic limits the domain of applicability of the main predication to a certain restricted domain within which the predication holds, adding that, if resulting from a transformation of topicalisation, it may carry a *focus of contrast* and be placed in a special position in the clause or be detached from it. In a similar vein, it has been seen that Li & Thompson single out four Topic features coinciding in the main with those of Dik's Theme, namely: (a) to indicate what the sentence is about; (b) to be definite; (c) to be sentence initial; (d) to be marked by a pause or pause particles. Similar descriptions have been shown to be used also by Halliday on analysing reference Theme (Section 4.2.1).

91. See, for example, Jiménez-Juliá (1981: 340, 342), De Vries (1989: 66–71), Butler (1991: 508), Mackenzie & Keizer (1991 [1990]: 174, 183, 187ff.), Hannay (1991 [1990]: 133, 138, 140).

92. Consider, for instance: Nuyts (1983: 383; 1985: 101–2), Keijsper (1990: 45), Butler (1990: 13; 1991: 507, 511–12), Mackenzie & Keizer (ibid.: 169, 191ff.), Hannay (ibid.: 131, 146).

93. Mackenzie (personal communication) would agree with Jiménez-Juliá's observations, although he regards Theme and Tail as functionally equivalent to (and, ideally, replaceable by) *Focus* (and *Topic*) (Mackenzie 1998).

94. For FG proposals made in this area, see: Dik (1989: 265) on the functions of *initiator* and *address* and the more comprehensive view of ECCs offered in (TFG2), already sketched in Section 5.3; Hannay & Vester (1987) on the function of *Orientation*; Hannay (1991) and Buth (1994: 217) on (circumstantial) *Settings*; Bolkestein (1992) on the relative ordering of satellites relating to the text, the nature of the utterance, and the content of the utterance; and Smits (1998) on complex beginnings. Outside FG, other proposals in this field are those by Halliday (1994), Downing (1991) and Gómez-González (1998a, forthc.).

95. Other scholars outside FG that speak about *presentational Focus* constructions are: Milsark (1977), Carlson (1978), Rochemont (1986), Ward & Birner (1995), among many others.

96. Outside FG, a great deal of work has been dedicated to the intonational description of Topic constituents. See the discussion of intonational contours in e.g.: Pierrehumbert & Hirschberg (1990), Féry (1993), Ladd (1996); and the analysis of Topic and intonation in e.g.: Molnár (1997), Büring (1995), Jacobs (1996).

97. R1 places in P1 such constituents as question words, relative pronouns, and obligatory subordinators; whereas R3 puts in that same position (obligatorily so in strict verb-second languages) satellite constituents or dummy elements (e.g. English *it, there*, etc.), both cases uncovered by R1 and R2. In contrast, R2 is regarded as inherently optional. Firstly, it makes no prediction as to the ordering of the Topic with respect to the Focus, although the tendency is recognised for highly active, easily identifiable referents (Giv-, Res-, and Sub-Topics) to precede inactive or unidentifiable ones (Focus). And secondly, R2 implies that, if not placed in P1 (or some other special position), then the Topic and Focus will occur in any location consistent with their grammatical and/or semantic relation, and/or their categorical status as assigned in the *language-independent preferred order of constituents* (LIPOC); and if there is no special treatment, then the case for assigning Top/Foc collapses.

98. Mackenzie and Keizer (1991: 193) respond to Dik's proposal for P1-placement rules as follows:

> One may, of course, object that it is nowhere explicitly stated that Topic elements must go into P1; this is, however, something that must be deduced from what is stated in Dik (1989) about P1 position and from the fact that Topic assignment necessarily involves singling out elements for special treatment [there is only one

exception on p. 217 (ex. 18b) *Well, the police* (Subj.) *removed them* (Obj-GivTop) *from the platform* [my emphasis]]. Note, however, that dropping the requirement that Topics must be placed in P1 would mean losing the last possibility of giving special treatment to Topic elements in English.

Chapter 6. A corpus-based analysis of syntactic Theme in PresE: Theory and methods

99. Below clause level operate constructional relationships of parts into wholes: (a) *univariate*, or part-to-part dependency relations, or (b) *multivariate*, or part-to-whole constituency relations. Above the clause, non-constructional forms are at work which produce *co-variate* constructs, i.e. non-constructional Head-less semantic relations determined by the semantic unfolding of discourse structure (Halliday 1978: 109, 1994: xxi; Martin 1992a: 460).

100. *Field* is glossed as "what the participants in the context of situation are actually engaged in doing" and it has a recognisable meaning in the social system (Halliday 1974: 49; 1978: 222). *Tenor* refers "to the cluster of socially meaningful participant relationships, both permanent attributes of the participants and role relationships that are specific to the situation, including speech roles, those that come into being through the exchanges of verbal meanings" (Halliday 1977: 20; 1978: 143). And *mode* is concerned with "the particular status that is assigned to the text within the situation; its function in relation to the social action and the role structure, including the channel or medium, and the rhetorical mode" (Halliday 1977: 201; 1978: 143).

101. The distinction between *classes* and *types* of Themes is based on Butler (1985: 24):

    The concept of class, then, takes account of paradigmatic possibilities associated with particular elements of structure: a class is an abstraction from an inventory of items, all of which share distributional characteristics, in being able to operate at a certain structural element, in syntagmatic association with other structural elements. (…) Thus class, defined distributionally, is not to be confused with (…) "type", a grouping based on the internal structure of the unit itself.

102. As a hypothetical construct, this system network is expected to change in the light of further work in this area, in terms of adding or removing options and/or amending the dependencies between the systems.

103. For a critical evaluation of SFG as a descriptive framework see Gómez-González (1998b, forthcoming).

104. Langacker (1993: 6) describes a "cognitive reference point" as follows:

    [A] reference point has a certain cognitive salience, either intrinsic or contextually determined. It is […] owing to some kind of salience that an entity comes to be chosen as a reference point in the first place. […] To serve as a reference point, a notion must first be activated and thus established as an entity currently capable of serving in that capacity. […] However, when this potential is exploited […] it is the target thereby reached that now becomes prominent in the sense of being the focus of C's [the conceptualiser's] conception.

105. Kuno (1987: 206) characterises *empathy* as "the speaker's identification, which may vary in degree, with a person/thing that participates in the event or state that he describes in a sentence". According to Kuno (1987: 207), the beginning of a new sentence in principle allows

for a new viewpoint or empathy relation. Likewise, the "syntactic prominence principle" is considered to be at work not in terms of the assignment of Subject role, but following the other manifestation of syntactic prominence, the "word order empathy hierarchy" (p. 232); whereas the "speech act empathy hierarchy" (p. 212) refers to the strong tendency of the speaker to empathise with himself/herself.

106. LIBMSEC contains one more category, namely *Miscellaneous* ((M) 3352 words). This was discarded from this analysis because it did not refer to a specific text type, but comprised nine heterogeneous samples (viz. John Betjeman, Motoring News, two Weather Forecasts, two Programme News, Oratory, Travel Roundup), which in my view are already represented in the other ten types.

107. Unfortunately, some LIBMSEC texts have an incomplete date reference or no date at all.

108. Chafe (1992) explains that the author of a discourse is first of all the *proximal* consciousness of speech and operates in the immediacy of the speech situation, while a person who has experienced certain events at another location or time has a *displaced consciousness* of her/his own. These former kinds of — originally *immediate experience* can, later or elsewhere, be reproduced via language and then obtain the status of *events*. If an author focuses, not only on displaced matters, but also on another, displaced, consciousness, he presents events in a way similar to immediate experience, the effect of which is called *displaced immediacy*

109. Following Rosch & Lloyd (1978) and Taylor (1996), a prototypical syntactic Theme is here defined neither by the union nor by the intersection of its members, but in terms of a prototypical, or central, tendency member that contains the maximal number of features in common with members of its own set and which stands a minimum distance from members of its own set and a maximum distance from members of other sets.

110. Decimal figures given under raw figures represent percentages. In the Row Total, the decimal figures correspond to the average values against the two Row columns. Thus, in the Column Total at the bottom of the Table, the average value is 100% because it corresponds to the total amount of analysed Themes (4058), consisting of: 2398 (59.1%) instances of Topical ones and 1660 (40.9%) of Extended Multiple ones.

Chapter 7. A corpus-based analysis of syntactic Theme in PresE: Results and discussion

111. The row total is the same for both contingency Tables.

112. A number of authors have explored the differences in the discourse function between the initial, medial and final placement of adverbials, for instance: Thompson (1985) on purpose clauses, Ramsey (1987) on conditional and temporal clauses, Ford (1993) on temporal, conditional, and causal adverbial clauses, in addition to Comrie (1981), Ford & Thompson (1986), Schiffrin (1985), Backlund (1989); Downing (1991) and Downing & Locke 1992), to mention but a few. Roughly, these studies conclude that, while the framework-setting potential of fronted adverbials extends until a new circumstance is introduced in discourse, if final such elements set no span at all, whereas if medial their functional span is less than when initial, in some cases limited to modifying a process or else an attribute of a participant The implication is that, when non initial, these sequences neither raise nor respond to any discourse expectations, but restrict the scope of their meaning to the immediately preceding main clause presenting additional information. In Ford's (1993: 146) words, placed finally, adverbials "tend to work more locally

in narrowing main clause meaning without creating links or shift points in a larger discourse pattern", to which Thompson's (1985: 61) claim could be added that only the initially placed adverbial clause operates "simultaneously at the ideational and the *textual* levels" [my emphasis].

113. Examples (169) — (172) were suggested to me by Peter Collins, personal communication.
114. This *by*-phrase is to be regarded as borderline between Complement and Adjunct. It is not always omissible, as is often claimed: in a sentence such as *Lightning is often followed by thunder* it is obligatory, insofar as you can't have **Lightning is often followed*.
115. Taking the case of cleft constructions as an example, functionalists have adhered to either a *transposition* analysis (e.g. Fowler & Fowler 1906/1931: 113; Jespersen 1965 [1928]: 88–9) or to an *intercalation* analysis (e.g. Poutsma 1916: 1000; Leech et al. 1982: 126). In the first, *It* and the relative clause (e.g. "that the duke gave to my aunt" in *It was that teapot that the duke gave to my aunt*) are taken as the Subject of the main clause; whereas in the intercalation analysis the items *it be ... that/wh*-word are regarded as a kind of extraposition and as semantically empty. In contrast, generativists such as Akmajian (1970) propose that *it*-clefts be derived from *wh*-clefts (adducing such criteria as reflexivisation or person and number agreement). Others such as Higgins (1979) argue for their base-generation, while Hankamer (1974) and Pinkham and Hankamer (1975) admit both possibilities. Alternatively, Gundel (1974) analyses clefts as reduced forms of right dislocated pseudo-clefts, while Wirth (1978) derives such structures from extraposed relative clauses in copular structures and pseudo-clefts from a Restricted Nominal Reduction rule (RNR). In turn, Huddleston (1984) and Lees (1963) argue against the generativist deriving attempt. The first three conclude that, as many pseudo-clefts have plausible non-cleft counterpart, there is no basis to argue for a process of derivation (e.g. **Its richness in minerals and vitamins is unique about milk* versus *What is unique about milk is its richness in minerals and vitamins*); while Lees emphasises that there is not always an acceptable source for the dominant or for the dependent clause of clefts (e.g. *It was of him that I asked it*).
116. Conversely, a difference could be established between this type of existentials, called "presentational-*there*", from existential-*there* constructions. The presentational-*there* construction is claimed to be syntactically restricted like inversion. Compare:

(182) a. *I forgot that there appeared a ship on the horizon
       b. I forgot that there were no ships in the harbour

(183) a. *I haven't heard whether there appeared a ship on the horizon
       b. I haven't heard whether there were any ships in the harbour

(184) a. *What lives there on the other side?
       b. What is there on the other side?

(185) a. ?There never appeared a ship on the horizon
       b. There never was a ship in the harbour

(182)–(185) show that the Complement to a "non-assertive predicate", can be existential but not presentational *there*; an existential-*there* clause but not a presentational-*there* clause can be a subordinate interrogative; extraction is possible from an existential but not presentational clause; existential but not presentational clauses tolerate sentential negation (perhaps because the latter are thereby rendered "non-presentational").

117. According to Mair (1990: 42) *for* generally denotes animate experiencers, or beneficiaries, or at least entities metaphorically construed as mind-possessing. *For* may also introduce a Complement (e.g. *It was important for my mother* that the duke gave her that teapot) or a Complementiser of the superordinate clause (e.g. *It is incredible* for John to have come). No samples of these were found in LIBMSEC.
118. Green (1976), for example, notes that after negated first person matrix clauses, an FI is acceptable, while an SAI is not (e.g. *I didn't realise that standing in the corner was a black umbrella* [71b] vs. **I didn't realise that not a bite had she eaten* [70c], **I didn't realise that never before had prices been so high* [70d]).
119. The discourse conditions of CONDSAIs will not be detailed here, partly because of their relative infrequency in our corpus, and partly because they seem to follow a combination of the general principles underlying inversion and β-Themes (Section 7.3.1).
120. Other studies bar *quotation inversion* from FI status, claiming that it is "syntactically, semantically and intonationally distinguishable from other inversions, [and that it] is also functionally distinct" (Birner 1992: 29ff; Dorgeloh 1997). Here, however, we adopt a generalist view seekig to elicit the overall functional forces that lead to inversion processes and, more generally, to the placement of items within the Theme zone.
121. This construction has received various labels in the literature: *reference Theme*, *left dislocation/detachment*, *Theme*, *preposed Theme*, *Anti-Topic*, *anticipated identification* (cf. IFG; Bally 1965 [1932]; Beneš 1959; Keenan & Schieffelin 1976; Givón 1976, 1993; Kuno 1978b; Duranti & Ochs 1979, 1988; Dik 1978, 1989, 1997; Quirk et al. 1985: 1310; Zimmer 1986; Lambrecht 1986, 1994; Geluykens 1992). The more familiar, but less transparent term, "left-dislocation", is here rejected in favour of Lambrecht's (1994) term "left-detachment", which suggests — appropriately in my view — that the constituent which we are calling the "left extern" appears in a position that is "detached" from the host/governing/main clause with which it is associated, that is to say, it is in construction with, rather than a constituent of, this clause.
122. RDs have received different levels (endnote 33 above). The reason for adopting this term are in essence the same as those adduced in note 121 above to use the "left" counterpart (i.e. LD).
123. The term *cleft* (construction) was introduced by Jespersen (1965 [1928]: 251) to designate those structures with the peculiarity of being "split" or divided into two separate parts. In this work I shall refer to these constructions using this widely accepted term.
124. Ø symbolises an optional element such as markers of modality, aspect, and polarity or focusing adverbs (e.g. *only*, *just*, etc.).
125. Ball's (1994) diachronic study challenges this widely accepted view that relative clauses are a syntactic type distinct from the clause occurring in *it*-clefts.
126. The strong preference of clefts for the non-*wh* class of relative explicates the ambiguity in (256a) below (either as a cleft version of *He bought the car last week*, or as a possible answer to *What was that in the garage?*, with *it* serving as a referential rather than dummy pronoun) becomes impossible or at least highly unlikely if *which* is used, as in (256b):

    (256)   a.   It was the car (that) he bought last week
               b.   It was the car which be bought last week.

127. A possible explanation for this lack of agreement could be that the presupposition conveyed in the relative constituent of clefts generally has third person reference because the information it conveys is presented as being about "something" or "someone" that is far from the speaker/

writer's perspective and that therefore needs to be identified. This is the function fulfilled by the referent of the predicated Theme, namely: to precisely identify the actual referent of the relative presupposition, which may, but need not, be a third person referent.

128. An alternative to the analysis proposed here, with the cleft construction regarded as manifesting subordination of the non-embedded type, is to regard the relative clause as forming a constituent with its antecedent. I have been assuming that the antecedent of the relative clause of clefts is the "highlighted element" in the Head clause. It has been argued, however, that it is the dummy Subject *it* which serves as the antecedent. This suggestion gains support from the fact that proper nouns may occur as the highlighted element in clefts even though they cannot (unless accompanied by a determiner) serve as antecedent to a relative clause. Further support derives from the need to account for ambiguities of the type:

(258)   It was the car he bought last week

Whereas, on the cleft interpretation, the main stress will most likely fall on *car*, on the non-cleft interpretation (where *it* is a personal, rather than dummy, pronoun referring to a car in the linguistic or situational context) the main stress is likely to fall on *week*. In this analysis the relative clause serves as an ordinary restrictive modifier of *car*, serving to provide defining information about it. There are clearly difficulties for an account of clefts which fails to differentiate between two structures in explaining the ambiguity of the present sentence.

There are however several major difficulties with the classification of the relative clause of clefts as a postponed restrictive modifier to it. One problem is the wide range of relatives of the non-*wh* type that are found in clefts. With many of these it is difficult to suggest a plausible semantic analysis. Consider:

(259)   It is to his father that he pays attention

The proposed structure for this clause is, roughly: "*It + that he pays attention is to his father*", and the corresponding (nonsensical) semantic analysis is, roughly: "The x (such that) x pays attention is (identifiable as) to his father". A second problem is that in sentences such as the following the verb in the relative clause clearly does not agree with dummy *it*, but with the highlighted element:

(260)   It is you who   I   am
                         are in trouble
                         they are

However the evidence from such agreement patterns is not definitive. In informal usage one commonly encounters cases where the verb in the relative clause agrees with *it*, rather than the highlighted element (which is likely to be accusative in form even if the relative element functions as Subject):

(261)   It's you who's in trouble   me
                                     them

The structure of cleft clauses is thus, as one often finds with non-kernel constructions, not clear-cut. While on balance it appears more plausible to analyse the highlighted element than the *it* as the antecedent for the relative element, the evidence does not support an analysis of the relative clause as a restrictive modifier within NG structure. The most plausible solution is to regard the relative clause as an immediate constituent of the sentence as a whole (rather than as forming a constituent with its antecedent).

129. The label *pseudocleft* first appeared in the generative literature to emphasise the semantic kinship of these structures with that of cleft clauses; while Hankamer (1974) and Prince (1978) coined the term *wh-clefts*. Both being widely accepted, the two terms shall be used throughout this investigation.

130. Cf. Huddleston's (1984: 402) *fused relative*, Quirk et al.'s (1985: § 15.8) *nominal relative clause*.

131. Similar claims can be found in e.g. Magretta (1977), Backlund (1989), Thompson (1985), Lowe (1987), Fries (1983, 1987), Downing (1991).

Appendix: Data-base structure

132. *Behaver* refers to the participant who is "behaving" in *behavioural processes*, i.e. processes "of (typically human) physiological and psychological behaviour, like breathing, coughing, smiling, dreaming and staring", IFG: 139).

133. In *identifying constructions* of the type "x is y", *Value* (Vl) indicates how an entity is valued, referring to its function, meaning or status, while the *Token* (T) defines how it is recognised, specifying its form, target or holder.

134. *Behalf* (circumstance) represents "the entity, typically a person, on whose behalf or for whose sake the action is undertaken", IFG: 155).

135. *Comitative* (*comitation*) is a subtype of circumstance of Accompaniment that represents the process "as a single instance of a process, although one in which two entities are involved", as opposed to *additives* which repesents the process as two instances (IFG: 156).

136. *Verifactive* is a textual element equivalent to "actually" (Table 6).

137. *Variative* represents a textual element meaning "instead of" or "except for" (Table 6).

References

Aaronson, D. and Ferres, S.
   1983   "Lexical categories and reading tasks". *Journal of Experimental Psychology: Human Perception and Performance* 9: 675–99.

Aaronson, D. and Scarborough, H. S.
   1976   "Performance theories for sentence coding: Some quantitative evidence". *Journal of Experimental Psychology: Human Perception and Performance* 2: 56–70.

Abercrombie, D.
   1963   "Conversation and spoken prose". *English Language Teaching* 18 (1): 10–6.

Adamec, P.
   1966   *Projadok Sov v Rsskom Jazyke*. Prague: Academia.
   1981   "Theme–Rheme structure in polypropositional simple sentence in Present-day Russian". *Folia Linguistica* 15: 223–36.

Adjémian, Christian
   1978   "Rheme, and word order. From Weil to Present-day theories". *Historiografía Lingüística* 5 (3): 253–73.

Agresti, Alan
   1990   *Categorical Data Analysis*. New York: John Wiley and Sons.

Agricola, Erhard.
   1979   *Textstruktur-Textanalyse-Informationskern*. Leipzig: Verlag Enzyklopädie.

Altmann, Hans
   1981   *Formen der 'Herausstellung' im Deutschen: Rechtsversetzung, Linksversetzung, freies Thema und Verwandte Konstruktionen*. Tübingen. Niemeyer.

Allerton, David J.
   1978   "The notion of 'givenness' and its relations to presupposition and to Theme". *Lingua* 44: 133–68.

Anderson, B.
   1963   The Short-Term Retention of Active and Passive Sentences. Unpublished doctoral dissertation. Johns Hopkins University.

Anderson, R. C., Reynolds, R. E., Schaller, D. L. and Goetz, E. T.
   1977   "Frameworks for comprehending discourse". *American Educational Research Journal* 14: 367–81.

Anderson, Stephen R.
    1976   "On the notion of Subject in egative languages". In Ch. N. Li (ed.) 1976. 1–24.
Andrews, A.
    1985   "The major function of the noun phrase". In *Language Typology and Syntactic Description* I, T. Shopen (ed.), 62–154. Cambridge: Cambridge University Press.
Anisfeld, M. and Klenbort, I.
    1973   "On the functions of structural paraphrase: The view from the passive voice". *Psychological Bulletin* 79: 117–26.
Aniya, S.
    1992   "The semantics and the syntax of the existential-There construction". *Linguistic Analysis* 22 (3/4): 154–84.
Ariel, Mira
    1985   "The discourse functions of given information". In *Theoretical Linguistics* 12, Helmut Schnelle (ed.), 99–113. Berlin, New York: Walter de Gruyter.
    1996   "Referring expressions and the ± coreference distinction". In *Reference and Referent Accessibility*, F. Thorstein et al. (eds.), 13–36. Amsterdam/Philadelphia: John Benjamins.
Atlas, J. D. and Levinson, Stephen C.
    1981   "It-clefts, Informativeness and logical form". In P. Cole (ed.) 1981. 1–61.
Baart, Joan, L. G.
    1987   *Focus, Syntax and Accent Placement*. Dordrecht: Foris.
Backlund, Ingegard.
    1989   "To sum up: Initial infinitives as cues to the reader". Paper presented at the *Sixteenth International Systemic Congress*. June 12–16, 1989, Helsinki, Finland.
    1991   "Theme in English telephone conversation". Paper delivered at the *17th International Systemic Congress*. Stirling, Scotland. June 1990.
Ball, Catherine N.
    1994   "Relative pronouns in *It*-clefts: The last seven centuries". *Language Variation and Language Change* 6 (2): 179–200.
Bally, Charles
    1965   [1932] *Linguistique Générale et Linguistique Française*. Bern: Francke.
Banfield, Arm
    1982   *Unspeakable Sentences: Narration and Representation in the Language of Fiction*. London: Routledge.
Bardovi-Harlig, Kathleen
    1983   "On the claim that Topics are not stressed". In *Papers from the Parasession from The Interplay of Phonology, Morphology and Syntax*, J. F. Richardson, M. Marks, and A. Chukerman (eds.), 17–27. Chicago: University of Chicago.

Barry, N.
  1978 "Theme and Rheme as immediate constituents". *Folia Linguistica* 12: 253–65.
Barry, Roberta
  1975 "Topic in Chinese: An overlap of meaning, grammar, and discourse function". In R. E. Grossman et al. (eds.) 1975, 1–9.
Bateman, John A. and Matthiessen, Christian M. I. M.
  1991 *The Generation and Systemic-Functional Linguistics*. London: Pinter Publishers.
Bates, Elizabeth.
  1976 *Language and Context: Studies in the Acquisition of Pragmatics*. New York: Academic Press.
Bates, Elizabeth and MacWhinney, Brian
  1979 "A functional approach to the acquisition of grammar". In *Developmental Pragmatics*, E. Ochs, and B. Schieffelin (eds.), 167–214. New York: Academic Press.
Bates, Elizabeth and MacWhinney, Brian.
  1982 "Functionalist Approaches to Grammar". In *Language Acquisition: The State of the Art*, E. Wanner and L. R. Gleitman (eds.), 173–218. Cambridge: Cambridge University Press.
Bazell, C. E.
  1973 "Review of J. Lyons (ed.) New Horizons in Linguistics". *Journal of Linguistics* 9: 198–202.
Behagel, Otto
  1923–1932 *Deutsche Syntax. Eine geschichtliche Darstellung*. Heidelberg.
  1930 "Beziehungen zwischen Umfang und Reihenfolge von Satzgliedern". *Indogermanische Forschungen* 25: 110–42.
Beneš Eduard
  1959 "Zacátek N'émecké V^ety z Hledissca Aktuálního Cleneni Vetneho [The Beginning of the German Sentence from the Point of View of Topic–Comment Articulation]". *Casops pro Moderni Filologii* 41: 205–17.
  1968 "On two aspects of functional sentence perspective". *Travaux Linguistiques de Prague* 3: 267–74.
  1971 "Die Besetzung der Ersten Position im Deutschen Ausgesatz". *Fragen der Strukturellen Syntax und der Kontrastiven Grammatik* 17: 160–82.
Benešová, E. and Sgall, Petr E.
  1973 "Remarks on the Topic/Comment articulation. Part 1". *The Prague Bulletin of Mathematical Linguistics* 19: 29–58.
Benešová, E., Hajicová, Eva, and Sgall, Petr E.
  1973 "Remarks on the Topic/Comment articulation. Part II". *The Prague Bulletin of Mathematical Linguistics* 20: 3–42.
Benson, J. D. and Greaves, W. S. (eds.)
  1985 *Systemic Functional Approaches to Discourse* 26. Norwood: New Jersey.

Benson, J. D., Cummings, M. J., and Greaves, W. S. (eds.)
    1988   *Linguistics in a Systemic Perspective.* Amsterdam: John Benjamins.

Berman, R.
    1980   "The case on an (S) V O language". *Language* 56.4: 759–76.

Berman, A. and Szamosi, M.
    1972   "Observations on sentential stress". *Language* 48 (2): 304–25.

Berry, Margaret
    1975   *An Introduction to Systemic Linguistics I: Structures and Systems.* London: Batsford.
    1982   "Review of Halliday 1978". *Nottingham Linguistic Circular* 11: 120–45.
    1987   "The functions of place names". *Leeds Studies in English* XVIII: 71–88.
    1989   "Thematic options and success in writing". In *Literature and Language: Theory and Practice*, C. S. Butler, R. A. Cardwell, and J. Channell (eds.), 62–80. Nottingham: University of Nottingham.
    1992a   "Theme and variation". Plenary Address to the *1992 Conference of the Applied Linguistics Association of Australia.* University of Sydney.
    1992b   "Bringing systems back into a discussion of Theme". Plenary Address to the *19th International Systemic Functional Congress.* Macquarie University.
    1995   "Thematic options and success in writing". In M. Ghadessy (ed.) 1995. 55–84.

Berry, Margaret, Fawcett, Robin and Huang G. (eds.)
    1996   *Meaning and Form: Systemic Functional Interpretations. Meaning and Choice in Language: Studies for Michael Halliday.* Norwood, NJ: Ablex Publishing Corporation.

Berry, Margaret, Fawcett, Robin, Butler, Christopher and Huang, Guowen (eds.)
    1996   *Systemic Functional Interpretations.* Norwood, N. J.: Ablex.

Biber, D.
    1985   "Investigating Macroscopic Textual Variation through multi-feature/multi-dimensional Analyses". *Linguistics* 32(2): 337–60.
    1986   "Spoken and written textual dimensions in English: Resolving the contradictory findings". *Language* 62: 384–414.

Birner, Betty, J.
    1992   The Discourse Function of Inversion in English. Unpublished Ph. D. Dissertation. Northwestern University.
    1994   "Information status and English inversion". *Language* 70 (2): 233–59.

Birner, Betty J. and Ward, Gregory Louis
    1993   "There-sentences and inversion as distinct constructions: A functional account". *PBLS* 19: 27–39.

Blinkenberg, Andreas
    1928   *L'ordre des mots en français moderne.* Copenhague: A. F. Høst.

Bloomfield, Leonard
    1935   *Language.* London: Allen and Unwin.
    1962   *The Menomini Language.* New Haven: Yale University Press.

Bloor, Meriel and Bloor Thomas
    1992   "Given and new information in the thematic organization of text: An application to the teaching of academic writing". *Occasional Papers in Systemic Linguistics* 6: 33–43.

Blumenthal, A. R. and Boakes, R.
    1968   "Prompted recall of sentence: A further study". *Journal of Verbal Learning and Verbal Behavior* 6: 674–6.

Bock, J. K.
    1977   "The effect of a pragmatic presupposition on syntactic structure in question answering". *Journal of Verbal Learning and Verbal Behaviour* 16: 723–34.
    1982   "Toward a cognitive psychology of syntax: Information processing contributions to sentence formulation". *Psychological Review* 89: 1–47.

Bock, J. K. and Irwin, D. E.
    1980   "Syntactic effects of information availability in sentence production". *Journal of Verbal Learning and Verbal Behavior* 19: 467–84.

Bock, M., and Engelkamp, J.
    1978   "Textstrukturen aus Sprachpsychologische Sicht. Teil I: Satz, Satzkontext, Text". *Folia Linguistica* 12: 301–18.

Boguslawski, A.
    1977   *Problems of the Thematic-Rhematic Structure of Sentences*. Warsaw: Parístwowe Wydavnictwo Naukowe.

Bolinger, Dwight L.
    1952   "Linear Modification". *Publications of the Modern Language Association of America* 67: 1117–44.
    1954   "English prosodic stress and Spanish sentence order". *Hispania* 37: 152–6.
    1972a   "Accent is predictable (if you're a mind reader)". *Language* 48: 633–44.
    1972b   *That's That*. The Hague: Mouton.
    1977   *Meaning and Form*. London: Longman.
    1979   "Pronouns in discourse". In T. Givón (ed.) 1979b. 289–309.

Bolkestein, A. Machtelt
    1981   "Predication and expression". In *Predication and Expression in Functional Grammar*, Bolkestein, A. M. et al. (ed.), 1–18. London: Academic Press.
    1985a   "Discourse and case marking: Three place predicates in Latin". In *Sintaxe et Latin*, C. Touratier (ed.), 191–225. Aix en provence, Université de Provence.
    1985b   "Cohesiveness and syntactic variation: Quantitative versus qualitative grammar". In A. M. Bolkestein et al. (eds.) 1985b. 1–14.
    1992   "Limits to layering: Locatability and other problems". In Fortescue et al. (eds.) 1992, 385–407.
    1998   "What to do with Topic and Focus: Evaluating pragmatic information"". In M. Hannay & A. M. Bolkestein (eds.). 193–214.

Bolkestein, A. Machtelt, de Groot, Casper, and Mackenzie, Lachlan, J. (eds.)
    1985a   *Syntax and Pragmatics in Functional Grammar*. Dordrecht: Foris.

1985b   *Predicates and Terms in Functional Grammar.* Dordrecht: Foris.
Boomer, D. S.
   1965   "Hesitation and grammatical encoding". *Language and Speech* 8: 148–58.
Boost, K.
   1955   *Neue Untersuchungen zum Wesen and zur Struktur des Deutschen Satzes,* Berlin: Akademie.
Bossuyt, Alain
   1982   *Aspekten van de geschiedenis van de negatieve zin in het Nederlands.* Dissertation, Free University Brussels.
Brazil, D.
   1981   "The place of intonation in a discourse model". In M. C. Coulthard, and M. Montgomery (eds.) (1981). 120–45.
Brazil, D. Coulthard, M. and Johns, C.
   1980   *Discourse Intonation and Language Teaching.* London: Longman.
Brinker, Klaus. 1985. *Linguistische Textanalyse.* Berlin: Schmidt.
Brody, Michael
   1990   "Some remarks on Focus in Hungarian". UCL *Working Papers in Linguistics* 2: 201–225.
Brömser, Bernd
   1982   *Funktionale Satzperspektive im Englischen.* Tübingen: Narr. (Tübinger Beiträge zur Linguistik 171).
Brown, Gillian and Yule, George
   1983   *Discourse Analysis.* Cambridge: University Press.
Brown, R. A.
   1973   *A First Language: The Early Stages.* Cambridge, Mass.: Harvard University Press.
Bühler, Karl
   1934   *Sprachtheorie.* Jena: Gustav Fischer.
Büring, Daniel
   1995   The 59th Street Bridge Accent. On the Meaning of Topic and Focus. Unpublished Ph. D. dissertation University of Tuebingen.
Buth, Randall
   1994   "Contextualizing constituents as Topics". In *Function and Expression in Functional Grammar,* E. Engberg-Pedersen, L. Falster Jakobsen & L. Schack Rasmussen (eds.) 215–231. Berlin: Mouton De Gruyter.
Butler, Christopher S.
   1985   *Systemic Linguistics: Theory and Applications.* London: Batsford Academic and Educational.
   1988   "Pragmatics and Systemic Linguistics". *Journal of Pragmatics* 12: 83–102.
   1989   "Systemic models: Unity, diversity and change". *Word* 40 (1/2): 1–32.
   1990   "Functional Grammar and Systemic Functional Grammar". *Working Papers in Functional Grammar* 39: 1–49.

1991 "Standards of adequacy in Functional Grammar". *Journal of Linguistics* 47: 499–515.
Button, Graham and Casey, Neil
1984 "Generating Topic: The use of Topic initial elicitators". In *Structures of Social Action. Studies in Conversational Analysis*, J.M. Atkinson and J.C. Heritage (eds.), 167–90. Cambridge: Cambridge University Press.
Cadiot, Pierre
1992 "Matching syntax and pragmatics: A typology of Topic and Topiclike constructions in spoken French". *Linguistics* 30 (1): 57–88.
Cairns, H.S. and Kamerman, J.
1975 "Lexical information processing during sentence comprehension". *Journal of Verbal Learning and Verbal Behavior* 14: 170–9.
Carlson, G.N.
1978 *Referents to Kinds in English*. Ph. Dis. Amherst: University of Mass.
Carrell, P.L.
1982 "Cohesion is not coherence". *TESOL Quarterly* 16: 479–87.
Cirilo, R.K. and Foss, D.J.
1980 "Text structure and reading time for sentences". *Journal of Verbal Learning and Verbal Behavior* 19: 96–120.
Clark, Herb H. and Begun, J.S.
1971 "The semantics of sentence Subjects". *Language and Speech* 14: 34–46.
Clark, Herb H. and Card, S.
1969 "Role of semantics in remembering comparative sentences". *Journal of Experimental Psychology* 83: 545–53.
Clark, Herb H. and Haviland, Susan. E.
1974 "Psychological process in linguistic explanation". In *Explaining Linguistics Phenomena*, D. Cohen (ed.), 91–124. Washington, D.C.: Hemisphere.
1977 "Comprehension and the given-new contract". In *Discourse Production and Comprehension*, R. Freedle (ed.) 1–40. Hillside, N.J.: Erlbaum.
1995 "Defining and relating text segments: Subject and Theme in discourse"". In R. Hasan and P.H. Fries (eds.) 1995. 361–403.
Cole, Peter (ed.)
1981 *Radical Pragmatics*. New York: Academic Press.
Cole, Peter and Morgan, Jerry L. (eds.)
1975 *Studies in Syntax 3: Speech Acts*. New York: Seminar Press.
Coleman, E.
1965 "Learning of prose written in four grammatical transformations". *Journal of Applied Psychology* 49: 332–41.
Collins, Peter C.
1983 "Extern constructions in English". *Australian Journal of Linguistics* 13: 23–37.
1984 "Extraposition in English" *Functions of Language* 1 (1): 1–18.

1985 "*Th*-clefts and *all*-clefts". In *The Cultivated Australian: Festschrift in Honour of Arthur Delbridge*, J. E. Clark (ed.), 45–53. Hamburg: Buske.
1991 *Clefts and Pseudoclefts sentences in English*. London: Routledge.
Comrie, Bernard
  1972 "The ergative: Variations on a Theme". *Lingua* 32: 239–53.
  1981 *Language Universals and Linguistic Typology*. Oxford: Blackwell.
Consorte, Cesira
  1998 "Thematic structure and simultaneous interpretation". Paper presented at the *25th International Systemic Functional Congress*, Cardiff: University of Cardiff, 13th–18th July.
Contreras, Heles
  1976 *A Theory of Word Order with Special Reference to Spanish*. Amsterdam: North-Holland.
Cooper, W. E., and Ross, J.
  1975 "Word order". In R. E. Grossmann et al. (eds.) 1975, 63–111.
Cooreman, A.
  1983 "Topic continuity and the voice system of an ergative language: Chamorro". In T. Givón (ed.) 1983a, 425–89.
Copeland, James E. and Davis, Philip W.
  1983 "Discourse portmanteaus and the german Satzfeld". In *Essays in Honor of Ch. F. Hockett*, F. B. Agaro et al. (eds.), 214–45. Leiden: Brill.
Coulthard, M. C. and Montgomery, M. (eds.)
  1981 *Studies in Discourse Analysis*. London: Routledge & Kegan Paul.
Creider, Chet A.
  1979 "On the explanation of transformations". In T. Givón (ed.) 1979b. 3–21.
Croft, William.
  1990 *Typology and Universals*. Cambridge: University Press.
Culicover, Peter W.
  1991 "Topicalization, inversion and complementizers in English". In *Going Romance and Beyond: Fifth Symposium on Comparative Grammar*, D. Delfitto, M. Everaert, A. Everst, and F. Stuurman (eds.), 1–43. Utrecht: Research Institute for Language and Speech, Utrecht University.
  1993 "Focus and grammar". In *Proceedings of the Workshop on the Syntactic and Semantic Analysis of Focus*, P. Ackema and M. Schoorlemmer (eds.), 1–18. Utrecht: Research Institute for Language and Speech, Utrecht University.
Cummings, Michael
  1995 "A systemic functional approach to the thematic structure of the Old English clause". In R. Hasan and P. H. Fries (eds.) 1995a, 275–316.
Chafe, Wallace L.
  1976 "Givenness, contrastiveness, definiteness, Subjects, Topics and point of view". In Ch. Li (ed.) 1976, 26–56.

1987 "Cognitive constraints on information flow". In *Coherence and Grounding in Discourse*, R. S. Tomlin (ed.), 21–51. Amsterdam/Philadelphia: John Benjamins.
1992 "Immediacy and displacement in consciousness and language". In *Cooperating with Written Texts: The Pragmatics and Comprehension of Written Texts*, D. Stein (ed.), 231–255. Berlin: Mouton.
1994 *Discourse, Conciousness, and Time: The Flow and Displacement of Conscious Experience in Speaking and Writing*. Chicago: University of Chicago Press.
1996 "Inferring identifiability and accessibility". In *Referents and Referent Accessibility*, T. Fretheim and J. K. Gundel (eds.), 37–46. Amsterdam/Philadelphia: John Benjamins.

Chang, F. R.
1980 "Active memory processes in visual sentence comprehension: Clause effect and pronominal reference". *Memory and Cognition* 8: 58–64.

Chao, Ruen Y.
1968 *A Grammar of Spoken Chinese*. Berkeley: University of California Press.

Chesterman, Andrew
1991 *On Definiteness: A Study with Special Reference to English and Finnish*. Cambridge: Cambridge University Press.

Chierchia, Gennaro and McConnell-Ginet, Sally.
1990 *Meaning and Grammar*. Cambridge, MA: MIT Press.

Chládková, H.
1979 "English and German equivalents of the Czech adverb of manner examined from the point of view of functional sentence perspective". *Brno Studies in English* 13: 61–104.

Chomsky, Noam
1965 *Aspects of the theory of syntax*. Cambridge (Mass.): MIT Press.
1971 "Deep structure, surface structure and semantic interpretation". In *Semantics: An Interdisciplinary Reader*, D. D. Steinberg and L. A. Jakobovits (eds.). 183–216. Cambridge: Cambridge University Press.
1972 *Studies on Semantics in Generative Grammar*. The Hague: Mouton.
1975 *Reflections on language*. New York: Pantheon.
1976 "Conditions on rules of grammar". *Linguistic Analysis* 2: 303–51.

Dahl, Östen (ed.)
1974a *Topic and Comment and Contextual Boundness and Focus. Papers in Textlinguistics* 6. Hamburg: Helmut Buske.
1974b "Topic–Comment structure revisited". In Ö. Dahl (ed.) 1974, 1–24.
1974c "Topic–Comment structure in a generative grammar with a semantic base". In F. Daneš (ed.) 1974, 75–80.
1976 "What is new information?" In *Reports on Text Linguistics: Approaches to Word Order*, N. E. Enkvist and V. Kohonen (eds.), 37–50. Meddelanden från Stiftelsens för Åbo Akademi Forskningsisntitut no. 8. Åbo/Turku.

1987 "The position of Czech linguists in Theme–Focus research". In *Language Topics: Essays in Honour of Michael Halliday*, Vol. 1., R. Steele, and T. Threadgold (eds.), 47–55. Amsterdam/Philadelphia: John Benjamins.

Daneš, František
- 1960 "Sentence intonation from a functional point of view". *Word* 16: 34–54.
- 1964 "A three level approach to syntax". *Travaux Linguistiques de Prague* 1: 225–40.
- 1967 "Order of elements and sentence intonation". In *To Honor Roman Jakobson*, Vol 1, 499–512. The Hague: Mouton.
- 1970a "One instance of Prague School methodology: Functional analysis of utterance and text". In *Methods and Theory in Linguistics*, P. L. Garvin (ed.), 132–46. The Hague: Mouton.
- 1970b "Semantic considerations in syntax". *Proceedings of the Tenth International Congress of Linguists* II, 407–13. Bucharest: Rumanian Academy of Sciences.
- 1974b "Functional sentence perspective and the organization of the text". In F. Daneš 1974 (ed), 106–28.
- 1978 "De la structure semantique et thematicque du message". In *Textlinguistik. Travaux du Centre de Recherches Linguistiques et Sémiologiques de Lyon*, 177–200. Lyon: Presses Universitaires de Lyon.
- 1989 "'Functional sentence perspective' and text connectedness". In *Proceedings of the Conference on Connexity and Coherence (Urbino July 16–21)*. [*Studies in Language Comparison 16*], M. E. Conte, M. E., Petöfi, J. S. and E. Sözer, 23–32. Amsterdam/Philadelphia: John Benjamins.

Daneš, František (ed.)
- 1974a *Papers on Functional Sentence Perspective*. The Hague: Mouton.

Davidse, Kristin
- 1987 "M. A. K. Halliday's Functional Grammar and the Prague School". In *Functionalism in Linguistics*, R. Dirven, and U. Fried (eds.), 39–79. Amsterdam/Philadelphia: John Benjamins.
- 1997 "Cardinal versus enumerative existential constructions". *Preprints van het DepartmentLinguistiek-series* 160. Katholieke Universiteit Leuven: Belgium.

Davies, Martin
- 1998 "Wording without meaning and meaning without wording. Theme, information, and non-prosodic cohesion". Paper presented at the *25th International Systemic Functional Congress*, Cardiff: University of Cardiff, 13th–18th July.

Davison, Alice
- 1984 "Syntactic markedness and the definition of sentence Topic". *Language* 60 (4): 797–846.

Davison, Alice and Lutz, Richard
    1985   "Measuring syntactic complexity relative to discourse context". In *Natural Language Parsing*, R. O. Dowty, L. Kartunen, and A. Mzwickey (eds.), 26–66. Cambridge: Cambridge University Press.

De Beaugrande, Robert
    1980   *Text, Discourse and Process*. New Jersey: Ablex.
    1992   "Topicality and emotion in the economy of discourse". *Linguistics* 30 (1): 243–65.

De Beaugrande, Robert and Dressler, Wolfgang U.
    1981   *Introduction to Text Linguistics*. London: Longman.

De Groot, Casper
    1981   "On Theme in FG. An application to some constructions in spoken Hungarian". In Hoekstra et al. (eds.) 1981, 75–88.

De Groot, Casper and Limburg Machiel
    1986   "Pronominal elements: Diachrony, typology, and formalization in Functional Grammar". *Working Papers in Functional Grammar* 12.

De Jong, Jan R.
    1981   "On the treatment of Focus phenomena in Functional Grammar". In T. Hoekstra et al. (eds.) 198, 189–116.

De Schutter, Georges
    1985   "Pragmatic and syntactic aspects of word order in Dutch". In A. M. Bolkestein et al. (eds.) 1985a, 137–54.
    1987   "Pragmatic positions: The case of modifying clauses in Dutch". In J. Nuyts and G. de Schutter (eds.) 1987, 163–190.

De Vries, Lourens
    1985   "Topic and Focus in Wambon discourse". In A. M. Bolkestein et al. (eds.) 1985a, 155–80.
    1989   Studies in Wambon and Kombai. Ph. D. dissertation. Amsterdam: University of Amsterdam.

Declerk, R.
    1983   "Predicational clefts". *Lingua* 61: 9–45.
    1989   "The pragmatics of It-clefts and Wh-clefts". *Lingua* 64: 215–90.

Delis, D. and Slater, A.
    1977   "Toward a functional theory of reduction transformation". *Cognition* 5: 119–32.

Deyes, Anthony F.
    1978   "Towards a linguistic definition of functional varieties of written English". *International Review of Applied Linguistics in Language Teaching* 16: 313–29.

Dezsö, Laszló
    1970   "A Gyermeknyelv Mondattanának Elvi-modszertani Kerdesei". *Altalános Nyelvészeti Tanulmányok* 7: 77–99.

Dik, Simon C.
  1978   *Functional Grammar*. Amsterdam: North Holland.
  1980   *Studies in Functional Grammar*. London, New York: Academic Press.
  1989   *The Theory of Functional Grammar. Part 1: The Structure of the Clause. Functional Grammar Series*, 9. Dordrecht: Foris Publications.
  1997   *The Theory of Functional Grammar. Parts I and II*, Berlin/New York: Mouton de Gruyter. Edited by Kees Hengeveld.
Dik, Simon C., Hengeveld, Kees, Vester, Elseline, and Vet, Co.
  1990   "The hierarchichal structure of the clause and the typology of adverbial satellites". In J. Nuyts et al. (eds.) 1990, 25–70.
Dik, Simon C., Hoffmann, María E., de Jong, Jan R., Djiang, Sie Ing, Stroomer, Harry, and de Vries, Lourens.
  1981   "On the typology of Focus phenomena". In Hoekstra et al. (eds.) 1981, 41–74.
Dixon, Robert M. W.
  1972   *The Dyirbal Language of North Queensland*. Cambridge: University Press.
Dooley, R. A.
  1982   "Options in the pragmatic structuring of Guarani sentences". *Language* 58 (2): 307–21.
Downing, Angela
  1986   "The English modals reconsidered". *Revista Canaria de Estudios Ingleses* 12: 171–80.
  1990   "Sobre el Tema Tópico en inglés". *Revista Española de Lingüística Aplicada*. Anejo I (ed. María Teresa Turrell): 119–128.
  1991   "An alternative approach to Theme: A systemic-functional perspective". *Word* 42 (2): 119–43.
  1995   "The thematic layering and Focus assignment in Chaucer's *General Prologue* to *The Canterbury Tales*". In M. Ghadessy (ed.) 1995, 147–163.
  1996   "The semantics of *Get*-passives". In *Functional Descriptions: Theory and Practice*, R. Hasan, C. Clorann and D. G. Butt (eds.), 179–206. Amsterdam/Philadelphia: John Benjamins.
Downing, Angela and Locke, Philip.
  1992   *A University Course in English Grammar*. New York: Prentice Hall.
Downing, Pamela A.
  1995   "Word order in discourse: By way of introduction". In P. Downing & M. Noonan (eds.) 1995, 1–27.
Downing, Pamela A., and Noonan, Michael (eds.)
  1995   *Word Order in Discourse*. Amsterdam/Philadelphia: John Benjamins.
Dowty, David
  1979   *Word Meaning and Montague Grammar*. Dordrecht: Foris.
Dragunov, Alexandr A.
  1960   [1952]. *Untersuchungen zur Grammatik der Modernen Chinesischen Sprache*. Berlin (Ost.): Akademie-Verlag.

Dressler, Wolfgang U.
    1972   *Einführung in die Textlinguistik*. Tübingen: Niemeyer.
Dressler, Wolfgang U. (ed.)
    1977   *Current Trends in Textlinguistics*. New York: Walter de Gruyter.
Driven, R. and Friend, V.
    1987   *Functionalism in Linguistics*. Amsterdam/Philadelphia: John Benjamins.
Drubig, Hans Bernard
    1988   "On the discourse function of Subject-verb inversion". In *Essays in the English Language and Applied Linguistics on the Occasion of Gerhard Nickel's 60th Birthday*, J. Klegraf, and D. Nehls (eds.), 83–95. Heildelberg: Julius Groos Verlag.
    1994   "Island constraints and the syntactic nature of Focus and association with Focus". *Arbeitspapiere des Sonderforschungsbereichs 340: Sprachtheorische Grundlagen für die Computerlinguistik*, No 51.
Dusková, Libuse
    1985   "The position of the Rheme in English and Czech sentences as constituents of a text". *Philologica Pragensia* 28 (3): 128–34.
Duranti, Alessandro, and Ochs, Elinor
    1979   "Left dislocation in Italian conversation". In Talmy Givón (ed.) 1979b, 337–416.
Duszak, Anna
    1983   "Some remarks on contextual boundness and semantic relations in the thematic-rhematic structure of sentences". *Studia Anglica Posnaniensia* 16: 85–96.
    1984   "Topical sentence positions in English and Polish". *Papers and Studies in Contrastive Linguistics* 18: 55–70.
Eiler, Mary Ann
    1986   "Thematic distribution as a heuristic for written discourse function". In *Functional Approaches to Writing Research*, B. Couture (ed.), 49–68. London: Frances Pinter.
El-Menoufy, Afaf
    1988   "Intonation and meaning in spontaneous discourse". In J. D. Benson et al. (eds.) 1988, 1–26.
Enkvist, Nils Erik
    1974   "Theme dynamics and style: An experiment". *Studia Anglica Posnaniensia* 5: 127–35.
    1980   "Marked Focus: Function and constraints". In S. Greenbaum et al. (eds.). 134–52.
    1981   "Intervention de Nils Erik Enkvist à propos de la Communication du président Seiler". In *Actes du Colloque International et Multi-Disciplinaire sur la Compréhensión du Langage*, J. Barbizet, M. Pergnier, and D. Seleskovitch (eds.), 59–61. Paris: Didier Erudition.

Enkvist, Nils Erik and Kohonen, V. (eds.)
    1976   *Reports on Textlinguistics: Approaches to Word Order.* Abo: Academic Forskninginstitut No. 8, Åbo/Turko.

Erdmann, Peter
    1988   "On the principle of 'weight' in English". In *On Language, Rhetoric, Phonologica, Syntactica. A Festschrift for Robert P. Stockwell from his Friends and Colleagues*, C. Duncan-Rose, and T. Vennemann (eds.), 325–39. Routledge: London.
    1990   *Discourse and Grammar: Focussing and Defocussing in English.* Tübingen: Niemeyer.

Erteschik-Shir, Nomi
    1988   "Topic-chaining and dominance-chaining". In *The Prague School and its Legacy*, Y. Tobin (ed.), 145–55. Amsterdam/Philadelphia: John Benjamins.

Fawcett, R. P.
    1980   *Cognitive Linguistics and Social Interaction: Towards an Integrated Model of a Systemic Functional Grammar and the other Components of a Communicating Mind.* Heidelberg: Julius Groos Verlag.

Feinstein, M.
    1980   "Ethnicity and topicalization in New York City English". *International Journal of the Sociology of Language* 26: 15–24.

Fillmore, Charles J.
    1968   "The case for case". In *Universals in Linguistic Theory*, E. Bach, y R. T. Harms (eds.), 1–90. Nueva York: Holt.
    1981   "Pragmatics and the description of discourse". In Peter C. Cole (ed.) 1981. 143–66.

Firbas, Jan.
    1957   "Some thoughts on the function of word order in Old English and Modern English". *Studia Minora Facultatis Philosophicae Universitatis Brunensis* A_5: 72–100.
    1962   "Notes on the function of the sentence in the act of communication". *Studia Minora Facultatis Philosophicae Universitatis Brunensis* A_{10}: 134–48.
    1964   "On defining Theme in functional sentence analysis". *Travaux Linguistiques de Prague* 1: 267–80.
    1966   "Non-thematic Subjects in contemporary English". *Travaux linguistiques de Prague* 2: 239–56.
    1972   "On the interplay of prosodic and non-prosodic means of functional sentence perspective". In *The Prague School of Linguistics and Language Teaching*, V. Fried (ed.), 77–94. London: Oxford University Press.
    1974   "Some aspects of the Czechoslovak approach to problems of functional sentence perspective". In F. Daneš (ed.) 1974, 11–37.
    1975   "On the thematic and non-thematic section of the sentence". In *Style and Text: Studies Presented to Nils E. Enkvist*, H. Ringbom (ed.), 317–34. Stockholm: Skriptor.

1979   "A functional view of 'ordo naturalis'". *Brno Studies in English* 13: 29–59.
1982   "Has every sentence a Theme and a Rheme?" In *Current Issues in Linguistic Theory: Vol. 15. Language Form and Linguistic Variation*, J. Anderson (ed.), 97–115. Amsterdam/Philadelphia: John Benjamins.
1983   "On bipartition, tripartition and pluripartition in the theory of functional sentence perspective". In *Tekst i Zdanie [Text and Sentence]*, T. Dobrzy'nska, and J. Janus (eds.), 67–79. Wroclaw: Ossolineum.
1986   "On the dynamics of written communication in the light of the theory of functional sentence perspective". In *Studying Writing: Linguistic Approaches* [Written Communication Annual I], Ch. R. Cooper, and Sidney Greenbaum (eds.), 40–71. Beverly Hills: Sage.
1989   "Degrees of communicative dynamism and degrees of prosodic dominence". *Brno Studies in English* 18: 21–66 and Appendix.
1992   *Functional Sentence Perspective in Written and Spoken Communication.* Cambridge: Cambridge University Press.
1995   "A contribution on a panel discussion on rheme". In M. Ghadessy (ed.) 1995, 213–222.

Flesch, R.
1946   *How to Write, Speak and Think more Effectively.* New York: Harper.
1984   *Functional Syntax and Universal Grammar.* Cambridge, New York, New Rochelle, Melbourne, Sydney: Cambridge University Press.

Foley, William, A. and van Valin, Robert. D. Jr.
1985   "Information packaging in the clause". In *Language Typology and Syntactic Description, Vol 1: Clause Structure*, T. Shopen (ed.), 282–364. Cambridge: Cambridge University Press.

Ford, Cecilia
1993   *Grammar in Interaction; Adverbial Clauses in American English Conversations.* Cambridge: Cambridge University Press.

Ford, Cecilia and Sandra A. Thompson
1986   "Conditionals in discourse: A text-based study from English". In *On Conditionals*, E. Traugott et al. (eds.), 353–72. Cambridge: University Press.

Fortescue, M. P., Harder L., and Kristoffersen, L. (eds.)
1992   *Layered Structure and Reference in a Functional Perspective.* Berlin: Mouton de Gruyter.

Fowler, H. W., and Fowler, F. G.
1931   [1906] *The King's English.* Oxford: Clarendon Press.

Fox, Andrew
1983   "Topic continuity in biblical Hebrew narrative". In T. Givón (ed.) 1983a. 215–54.

Fox, Barbara A.
1985   "Word-order inversion and discourse continuity in Tagalog". In Givón (ed.) 1985, 39–54.

1987a "Anaphora in popular written English narrative". In R. S. Tomlin (ed.) 1987, 157–174.
1987b "Morphosyntactic markedness and discourse structure". *Journal of Pragmatics* 11: 359–373.

Francis, Gill
  1989a "Thematic selection and distribution in written discourse". *Word* 40: 201–22.
  1989b "Aspects of nominal group lexical cohesion". *Interface* 4: 27–53.
  1990 "Theme in the daily press". *Occasional Papers in Systemic Linguistics* 4: 51–87.

Francis, N.
  1966 "Review of Brno Studies in English". *Language* 42 (1): 142–9.

Frege, G.
  1892 "Über Sinn und Bedeutung". *Zeitschrift für Philosophie und philosophische Kritik* 100: 25–50.

Fries, Peter H.
  1978 *On the Status of Theme in English: Arguments from Discourse*. Sidney: mimeo, Dept. of Linguistics, University of Sidney.
  1982 "On repetition and interpretation". *Forum Linguisticum* 7 (1): 50–64.
  1983 [1981] "On the status of Theme in English: Arguments from discourse". In *Micro and Macro Connexity of Texts (Papiere zu Textlinguistik, 45*, J. S. Petöfi, and E. Sözer (eds.), 116–52. Hamburg: Buske Verlag.
  1986 "Language features, textual coherence and reading". *Word* 37 (1/2): 13–29.
  1987 "Towards a componential approach to text". Paper delivered at the *International Congress of Applied Linguistics*. August 17, 1987. Sydney, Australia.
  1995a "Themes, methods of development and texts". In R. Hasan and P. H. Fries (eds.). 317–360.
  1995b "A personal view of Theme". In M. Ghadessy (eds.) 1995, 1–19.

Fries, Peter H. and Francis, Gillian.
  1992 "Exploring Theme: Problems for research". *Occasional Papers in Systemic Linguistics* 6: 45–59.

Fries, Udo
  1984 "Theme and Rheme revisited". In *Modes of Interpretation: Essays Presented to Ernst Leisi*, R. Watts, and U. Weidmann (eds.), 177–92. Tübingen: Beiträge zur Linguistik.

Fronek, J.
  1983 "Some criticisms of Halliday's 'Information Systems'". *Lingua* 60: 311–29.

García, Erica C.
  1979 "Discourse without syntax". In Talmy Givón (ed.) 1979b, 23–49.

García, L. J. and Joanette, Y.
  1996 "Analysis of conversational Topic shifts: A multiple case study". *Brain and Language* 58 (1): 92–114.

Garrod, Simon and Sanford, Anthony J.
: 1982 "The mental representation of discourse in a focussed memory system: Implications for the interpretation of anaphoric noun phrases". *Journal of Semantics* 1: 21–41.

Geluykens, Ronald.
: 1987 "Tails (right-dislocations) as a repair mechanism in English conversational Discourse". In J. Nuyts, and G. de Schutter (eds.) 1987, 119–129.
: 1992 *On left dislocation in English: Studies in Discourse and Grammar* 1. Amsterdam/Philadelphia: John Benjamins.

Gernsbacher, Morton A.
: 1985 "Surface information loss in comprehension". *Cognitive Psychology* 17: 324–63.
: 1989 *Mind, Code and Context: Essays in Pragmatics*. Hillsdale, N.J.: Erlbaum.

Gernsbacher, Morton A. and Hargreaves, David.
: 1988 ""Accessing sentence participants: The advantage of first mention. *Journal of Memory and Language* 27: 699–717.

Ghadessy, Mohsen
: 1993 "Thematic development and its relationship to registers and genres". *Occasional Papers in Systemic Linguistics* 7: 1–25.

Ghadessy, Mohsen (eds.)
: 1995 *Thematic Development of English Texts*. London: Cassell.

Giora, M.
: 1983 "Functional paragraph perspective". In J. S. Petöfi, and E. Sözer (eds.) 1983, 153–82.

Giora, Rachel
: 1990 "On the so-called evaluative material in informative texts". *Text* 10: 299–319.

Givón, Talmy
: 1975 "Focus and the scope of assertion: Some Bantu evidence. *Studies in African Linguistics* 6: 185–205.
: 1976 "Topic, pronoun and grammatical agreement". In Ch. Li (ed.) 1976. 151–88.
: 1978 "Definiteness and referentiality". In *Universals of Human Language*. Vol. 4, Joseph H. Greenberg (ed.), 291–331. Stanford: University Press.
: 1979a *On Understanding Grammar*. New York: Academic Press.
: 1983b "Topic continuity in discourse: An introduction". In T. Givón (ed.) 1983a, 5–41.
: 1983c "Topic continuity and word order pragmatics in Ute". In T. Givón (ed.) 1983a, 141–214.
: 1984a *Syntax: A Functional-Typological Introduction*, vol. 1. Amsterdam/Philadelphia: John Benjamins.
: 1984b "Direct Object and dative shifting: Semantic and pragmatic case". In *Objects*, F. Plank (ed.), 151–82. New York: Academic Press.
: 1987 "Beyond foreground and background". In R. S. Tomlin (ed.) 1987, 175–188.

1988 "The pragmatics of word order: Predictability, importance and attention". In Hammond et al. (eds.) 1988, 243–84.
1992 "The grammar of referential coherence". *Linguistics* 30 (1): 5–55.
1993 *English Grammar* (vol. 2). Amsterdam/Philadelphia: John Benjamins.

Givón, Talmy (ed.)
1979b *Syntax and semantics 12: Discourse and syntax*. New York: Academic Press.
1983a *Topic Continuity in Discourse: A Quantitative Cross-Linguistic Study*. [*Typological Studies in Language* 3]. Amsterdam/Philadelphia: John Benjamins.
1985 *Quantified Studies in Discourse*. Special Issue of *Text 5.112*.

Glanzer, Muray, Fischer, B. and Dorfman, D.
1984 "Short term storage in reading". *Journal of Verbal Learning and Verbal Behavior* 23: 467–86.

Glanzer, Muray and Razel, Micha
1974 "The size of the unit in short-term storage. *Journal of Verbal Learning and Verbal Behavior* 13. 114–131.

Goatly, Andrew
1995 "Marked Themes and its interpretation in A. E. Housman's *A Shropshire Lad*". In M. Ghadessy (ed.) 1995. 164–97.

Goldman-Eisler, F.
1972 "Pauses, clauses, sentences". *Language and Speech* 15: 103–13.

Golková, Eva.
1987 "On FSP functions of the first syntactic element in the English sentence". *Brno Studies in English* 17: 87–96.
1995 "Rhema in English and Czech". *Brno Studies in English* 21: 47–57.

Gómez-González, María Ángeles
1994 "The relevance of Theme in the textual organization of BBC news reports". *Word* 45 (3): 293–305.
1995 "Theme: A heuristic method for discourse analysis". *Estudios Ingleses de la Unversidad Complutense* 3: 43–54.
1996a *A Corpus-Based Approach to Theme in Present-Day British English. Towards an Alternative Moderate Functionalist Interpretation*. Ph. D. dissertation. Compostela: University of Santiago de Compostela Microfilms [ISBN 84-8121-599-6]
1996b "Theme: Topic or discourse framework?" *Miscelanea* 17: 123–40.
1997 "On Subject *It*-extrapositions: Evidence from Present-day English". *Revista Alicantina de Estudios Ingleses* 10: 95–108.
1998a "A corpus-based analysis of extended multiple Themes in Present-day English". *International Journal of Corpus Linguistics* 3 (1): 81–114.
1998b "Some remarks on Systemic-Functional Grammar". *Interface* 12 (2): 65–80.
1998c "Aspects of Topic and topicality in Functional Grammar". *Working Papers in Functional Grammar* 65: 1–22.
1998d "The ins and outs of the notion of 'aboutness'". *Interface* 13 (1): 19–32.

Forthcoming "Some reflections on Systemic Functional Grammar: With a focus on Theme". To appear in *Word*.

Gray, A. K.
    1982   "Sequencing and staging information in explanatory discourse". Paper presented at the *Convention of the Conference on College Composition and Communication*. San Francisco.

Green, Georgia
    1976   "Main clause phenomena in subordinate clauses". *Language* 52 (2): 382–97.
    1980   "Some wherefores of English inversions". *Language* 56 (3): 582–603.
    1982   "Colloquial and literary uses of inversions". In *Spoken and Written Language: Exploring Orality and Literacy*, D. Tannen (ed.), 119–154. Norwood NJ: Ablex.

Greenbaum, Sidney, Leech, Geoffrey, and Svartvik, Jan (eds.)
    1980   *Studies in English Linguistics for Randolph Quirk*. London: Longman.

Greenberg, Joseph H.
    1966   "Some universals of grammar with particular reference to the order of meaningful elements". In *Universals of Language* J. Greenber (ed.), 73–113. Cambridge MA: The MIT Press.

Gregory, Michael J.
    1967   "Aspects of varieties differentiation". *Journal of Linguistics* 3 (2): 177–98.

Grice, H. Paul
    1975   "Logic and conversation". In P. Cole, and J. L. Morgan (eds.) 1975, 41–58.

Grieve, R., and Wales, R.
    1973   "Passives and topicalization". *British Journal of Psychology* 64: 173–82.

Grimes, Joseph E.
    1975   (3rd ed) *The Thread of Discourse*. Berlin, New York, Amsterdam: Mouton Publishers.

Grossman, R. E., San, J., and Vance, T. (eds.),
    1975   *Papers from the Parasession on Functionalism*. Chicago: Chicago Linguistic Society.

Grosz, Barbara J., Joshi, Aravind K, and Weinstein, Scott
    1995   "Centering: A framework for modelling local coherence of discourse". *Computational Linguistics* 21 (2): 203–26.

Guéron, Jacqueline
    1980   "On the Syntax and Semantics of PP Extraposition". *Linguistic Inquiry* 11: 637–78.

Gülich, Elisabeth, and Raible, Wolfgang.
    1977   *Linguistische Textmodelle*. München: Fink.

Gundel, Janette, K.
    1974   *The Role of Topic and Comment in Linguistic Theory*. Doctoral dissertation. Texas: University of Texas.
    1978   "Stress, pronominalization and the Given–New distinction". *University of Hawaii Working Papers in Linguistics* 10 (2): 1–13.

    1985   "Shared knowledge and topicality". *Journal of Pragmatics* 9 (1): 83–107.
    1988   "Universals of Topic–Comment structure". In M. Hammond et al. (eds.) 1988, 209–33.
    1994   "On the different kinds of Focus". In *Focus and Natural Language Processing* vol. 3., P. Bosch, and R. A. van der Sandt (eds.), 457–466. Heidelberg. IBM Deutschland: IBM Working Papers of the Institute for Logic and Linguistics 8.
    1996   "Relevance theory meets the givenness hierarchy. An account of inferrables". In *Referents and Referent Accessibility*, T. Fretheim and J. K. Gundel (eds.), 141–154. Amsterdam/Philadelphia: John Benjamins.

Gundel, Janette, K., Hedberg, Nancy, and Zacharsi, Ron.
    1993   "Cognitive status and the form of referring expressions". *Language* 69: 274–307.

Gunter, R.
    196   "On the placement of accent in dialogue: A feature of context grammar". *Journal of Linguistics* 2: 159–79.

Gussenhoven, Carlos
    1983   "Focus, mode, and the nucleus". *Journal of Linguistics* 19: 377–417.
    1985   "Two views of accent: A reply". *Journal of Linguistics* 21: 125–38.

Gussenhoven, Carlos, Bolinger, Dwight, and Keijsper, Cornelia
    1987   *On Accent*. Bloomington, Ind.: Indiana University Linguistics Club.

Haberlandt, Karl
    1980   "Story grammar and reading time of story constituents". *Poetics* 9: 99–118.

Haberlandt, Karl, and Bingham, Geoffrey
    1982   "The role of scripts in the comprehension and retention of texts". *Text* 2 (1/3): 29–46.

Hagège, C.
    1978   "Du Thème au Thème en Passant par le Sujet. Pour une thèorie cyclique". *La Linguistique* 14 (2): 3–38.

Haiman, John
    1978   "Conditionals are Topics". *Language* 54 (3): 564–89.

Haiman, John, and Thompson Sandra A. (eds.)
    1988   *Clause Combining in Grammar and Discourse*. Amsterdam/Philadelphia: Benjamins.

Hajicová, Eva, and Sgall, Petr E.
    1975   "Topic and Focus in Transformational Grammar". *Papers in Linguistics* 8 (1/2): 3–57.
    1987   "Topic and Focus of a sentence and the patterning of a text". In *Text and Discourse Constitution*, J. Petöfi (ed.), 70–95. Berlin: Walter de Gruyter.

Halicarnassus, Dionysius of
    1910   *De Compositione Verborum (On Literary Composition)*. Edited and translated by W. R. Roberts. London.

Halliday, M. A. K.
- 1967a *Some Aspects of the Thematic Organization of the English Clause*. Santa Monica: The RAND Corporation (Memorandum RM-5224-PR).
- 1967b "Notes on transitivity and Theme in English, Part 2". *Journal of Linguistics* 3: 199–244.
- 1967c *Intonation and Grammar in British English*. The Hague: Mouton (Janua Linguarum Series Practica 48).
- 1968 "Notes on transitivity and Theme in English, Part 3". *Journal of Linguistics* 4: 179–215.
- 1970a "Language structure and language function". In *New Horizons in Linguistics*, Vol. 1. John Lyons (ed.), 140–65. Harmondsworth: Penguin.
- 1970b "Functional diversity in language as seen from a consideration of modality and mood in English". *Foundations of Language* 6: 322–61.
- 1974 "The place of 'functional sentence perspective' in the system of linguistic description". In F. Daneš (ed.), 43–53.
- 1977 "Text as semantic choice in social contexts". In *Research in Text Theory: Vol 1. Grammars and Descriptions*, T. A. Van Dijk, and J. S. Petöfi (eds.), 176–225. New York: Walter de Gruyter.
- 1978 *Language as Social Semiotic: The Social Interpretation of Language and Meaning*. London: Edward Arnold.
- 1979 "Modes of meanings and modes of expression: Types of grammatical structure and their determination by different semantic functions". In *Function and Context in Linguistics Analysis: Essays Offered to William Haas*, D. J. Allerton, E. Carney, and D. Holcroft (eds.), 57–79. Cambridge: Cambridge University Press.
- 1981 "Options and functions in the English clause". In *Readings in Systemic Linguistics*, M. A. K. Halliday, and J. R. Martin (eds.), 138–45. London: Batsford Academic and Educational.
- 1984 "On the ineffability of grammatical categories". In *The Tenth LACUS Forum 1983*, A. Manning, P. Martin, and K. McCalla (eds.), 3–18. Columbia, SC: Hornbeam Press.
- 1989 "Towards probabilistic interpretations". Paper given at the *Sixteenth International Systemic Congress*. Hanasaari, Finland, 12–16 June 1989.
- 1994 (2nd. ed.) *An Introduction to Functional Grammar*. London: Edward Arnold. 1985a.

Halliday, M. A. K. and Hasan, Ruqaiya
- 1976 *Cohesion in English*, London: Longman

Halliday, M. A. K. and Martin, James R. (eds.)
- 1981 *Readings in Systemic Linguistics*. London: Batsford.
- 1993 *Writing Science. Literacy and Discursive Power*. London: Palmer Press.

Hammond, Michael, Moravcsik, Edith A. and Wirth, Jessica. R. (eds.)
- 1988 *Studies in Syntactic Typology*. Amsterdam/Philadelphia: John Benjamins.

Hankamer, J.
    1974   "On the non-cyclic nature of wh-clefting". *Papers from the Tenth Regional Meeting of the Chicago Linguistic Society*. University of Chicago: Chicago Linguistic Society. 221–32.

Hannay, Michael
    1983   "The Focus function in Functional Grammar: Questions of contrast and context". In *Advances in Functional Grammar*, Dik et al. (eds.), 207–23. Dordrecht: Foris.
    1985a   "Inferrability, discourse boundness and sub-Topics". In Bolkestein et al. (eds.) 1985a, 49–63.
    1985b   *English Existentials in Functional Grammar*. Dordrech: Foris.
    1991   [1990]. "Pragmatic function assignment and word order variations in a Functional Grammar of English". *Journal of Pragmatics* 16: 131–55.
    1994a   "The Theme zone." In *Nauwe Betrekkingen*, R. Boogart and I. Noordegraef (eds.), 107–117. Amsterdam: Stichting Naerlandistich vu and Münster: Nodus.
    1994b   "Pragmatic orientation in Functional Grammar." Unpublished paper.
    1998   "Message modes in a modular FG". Paper delivered to the *8th International Conference on Functional Grammar*. Amsterdam: Vrije Universiteit. 6th–11th july.

Hannay, Michael, and Bolkestein, A. Machtelt (eds.)
    1998   *Functional Grammar and Verbal Interaction*. Amsterdam/Philadelphia: John Benjamins.

Hannay, Michael, and Vester, E.
    1987   "Non-restrictive relatives and the representation of complex sentences". In J. V. der Auwera & L. Goossens (eds.), 1987, 39–52.

Harnish, R. M.
    1976   "Logical form and implicature". In *An Integrated Theory of Linguistic Ability*, T. G. Bever, J. J. Katz and D. T. Langedoen (eds.), 319–91. New York: Crowell.

Harries-Delisle, Helga.
    1978   "Contrastive emphasis and cleft sentences". In *Universals of Human Language: Vol. 4. Syntax*, J. H. Greenberg (eds.), 420–86. Stanford: University Press.

Hartvigson, Hans H., and Jakobsen, Leif K.
    1974   *Inversion in Present-Day English*. Odense: Odense University Press.

Hasan, Ruqaiya, and Fries Peter H.
    1995b   "Reflections on Subject and Theme: An introduction". In R. Hasan and P. H. Fries (eds.), xiii–xlv.

Hasan, Ruqaiya, and Fries Peter H. (eds.)
    1995a   *On Subject and Theme. A Discourse Functional Perspective*. Amsterdam/Philadelphia: John Benjamins.

Hatcher, Anna Granville
    1965a   *Theme and Underlying Question. Supplement to Word* 12. Monograph 3.
    1965b   "Syntax and the sentence". *Word* 12: 225–34.

Hausenblas, K.
    1964   "On characterisation and classification of discourses". *Travaux linguistiques de Prague* 1: 67–84.

Haviland, Susan E., and Clark, Herbert H.
    1974   "What's new? Acquiring new information as a process in comprehension". *Journal of Verbal Learning and Verbal Behaviour* 13: 512–21.

Hawkins, J. A.
    1978   *Definiteness and Indefiniteness. A Study in Reference and Grammaticality Prediction*. London: Croom Helm.

Hawkinson, Annie K., and Hyman, Larry M.
    1975   "Hierarchies of natural Topic in Shona". *Studies in African Linguistics* 5 (2): 147–70.

Heger, K.
    1982   "Nominativ-Subjekt-Thema". In *Fakten und Theorien. Beiträge zur romanishen und allgemeinen Sprachwissenschaft*, S. Heinz & U. Wandruszka (eds.), 87–93. Tübingen: Narr.

Heim, Irene
    1982   The Semantics of Definite and Indefinite Noun Phrases. Unpublished Ph. D. Dissertation, University of Massachusetts. Amherst.

Hengeveld, Kees
    1989   "Layers and operators in Functional Grammar". *Journal of Linguistics* 25: 127–57.

Hetzron, Robert
    1975   "The presentative movement or why the ideal word order is V. S. O.P". In Ch. N. Li (ed.) 1975, 345–88.

Hinds, John
    1983   "Japanese". In Talmy Givón (ed.) 1983a, 43–93.

Hockett, Charles F.
    1958   *A Course in Modern Linguistics*. New York: Macmillan.

Hoekstra, Teun, van der Hulst, Harry, and Morgan, Michael (eds.)
    1981   *Perspectives on Functional Grammar*. Dordrecht: Foris.

Høffding, H.
    1910   *Den Menneskelige Tanke. Dens Former og dens Opgaver*. Copenhagen: Nordisk.

Hopper, Paul J.
    1991a   "Functional explanations in linguistics and the origins of language". *Language and Communication* 11 (1/2): 45–47.
    1991b   "On Some Principles of grammaticalization". In E. C. Traugott and B. Heine (eds.) 1991, 17–35.

Hopper, Paul. J., and Thompson, Sandra A.
- 1984 "The discourse basis for lexical categories in universal grammar". *Language* 60 (4): 703–52.

Horn, Lawrence R.
- 1986 "Presupposition, Theme and variations". In *Papers from the 22nd Regional Meeting of the Chicago Linguistic Society*, A. M. Farley, P. T. Farley, and K. E. McCullogh (eds.) 12 (2): 168–92.
- 1989 *A Natural History of Negation*. The University of Chicago Press.

Hornby, P. A.
- 1971 "The role of Topic–Comment in the recall of cleft and pseudo-cleft sentences". *Papers from the Seventh Regional Meeting of the Chicago Linguistic Society*. University of Chicago. Chicago Linguistic Society. 445–53.
- 1972 "The psychological Subject and predicate". *Cognitive Psychology* 3: 643–54.

Horvath, B.
- 1985 *Variation in Australian English: the Sociolects of Sydney*. Cambridge: cambridge University Press.

Hovland, C. I., Mandell, W., Campbell, E. R., Brock, T., Luchins, A. S., Cohen, A. R., McGuire, W. J., Janis, I. L., and Feieraben, R. L. (eds.)
- 1957 *The order of presentation in persuasion*. New haven: Yale University Press.

Huddleston, Rodney D.
- 1984 *An Introduction to the Grammar of English*. Cambridge: University Press.
- 1988 "Constituency, multi-functionality and grammaticalization in Halliday's Functional Grammar". *Journal of Linguistics* 24: 137–74.
- 1991 "Further remarks on Halliday's Functional Grammar: A reply to Mathiessen & Martin". *Occasional Papers in Systemic Linguistics* 5: 75–129.
- 1992 "On Halliday's Functional Grammar: A Reply to Martin and Matthiessen". *Occasional Papers in Systemic Linguistics* 6: 197–211.

Hudson, Richard. A.
- 1986 "Systemic Grammar [Review article]". *Linguistics* 24: 791–815.

Huttenlocher, K, and Strauss, S.
- 1968 "Comprehension and a statement's relation to the situation it describes". *Journal of Verbal Learning and Verbal Behaviour* 7: 300–4.

Hyman, Larry
- 1975 "On the change from SOV to SVO. Evidence from Niger-Congo". In Ch. N. Li (ed.) 1975, 113–47.

Jackendoff, Ray. S.
- 1972 *Semantic Interpretation in Generative Grammar*. Cambridge, Mass.: MIT Press.

Jacobs, R.
- 1975 "Promotion and thematization processes in English, or how to get heed". In R. E. Grossman et al. (eds.), 223–31.

Jacoby, L. L.
    1974   "The role of mental continuity in memory: Registration and retrieval effects. *Journal of Verbal Learning and Verbal Behavior* 13 (2): 483–96.
Jarvella, Robert J.
    1971   "Systematic processing of connected speech". *Journal of Verbal Learning and Verbal Behavior* 10: 409–16.
Jellinek, H. M.
    1913–14 *Geschichte der Neuhochdeutschen Grammatik von den Anfängen bis auf Adelung*. Heidelberg: Winter.
Jespersen, Otto.
    1924   *The Philosophy of Grammar*. London: George Allen and Unwin.
    1965   [1927] *A Modern English Grammar on Historical Principles*. Part III. London: Allen and Unwin.
Jiménez-Juliá, Tomás
    1981   "A propósito de la gramática funcional de Simon C. Dik". *Verba* 8: 321–345.
    1986   *Aproximación al Estudio de las Funciones Informativas*. Málaga: Ágora.
    1995   "Eje temático y Tema en español". *Scripta Philologica in Memoriam Manuel Taboada Cid*, 453–92. A Coruña: Universidade da Coruña (1996).
Johnson, M.
    1967   "Syntactic position and rated meaning". *Journal of Verbal Learning and Verbal Behaviour* 6: 240–6.
Johnson-Laird, Philip H.
    1968   "The choice of the passive voice in a communicative task". *Quarterly Journal of Experimental Psychology* 20: 69–73.
Jordan, M. P.
    1985   "Non-thematic re-entry: An introduction to and extension of the system of nominal group reference/substitution in everyday English use". In J. D. Benson, and N. S. Greaves (eds.) 1985, 322–32.
Jucker, Andreas H.
    1992   *Social Stylistics: Syntactic Variation in British Newspapers*. Berlin: Mouton.
Karttunen, Laurie
    1976   "Discourse referents". In *Notes from the Linguistic Underground. Syntax and Semantics*, J. D. McCawley (ed.), 363–85. New York: Academic Press.
Keenan, Edward O., y Bambi B. Schieffelin
    1976   "Topic as a discourse notion". In C. N. Li (ed.) 1976, 335–84.
Keijsper, Cornelia, E.
    1985   *Information Structure with Examples from Russian, English and Dutch*. Amsterdam: Rodopi.
Kemmer, Suzanne
    1995   "Emphatic and reflexive — *self* expectations, viewpoint and subjectivity". In Stein Dieter, and Susan Wright (eds.), 55–82.

Kieras, David, E.
    1978   "Good and bad structure in simple paragraphs: Effects on apparent theme, reading time, and recall". *Journal of Verbal Learning and Verbal Behaviour* 17: 13–28.
    1981   "The role of major referents and sentence Topics in the construction of passage macrostructure". *Discourse Process* 4: 1–15.

Kies, D.
    1988   "Marked Themes with and without pronominal reinforcement, their meaning and distribution in discourse". In E. M. Steiner & R. Veltman (eds.) 1988, 47–75.

Kintsch, Walter
    1974   *The Representation of Meaning in Memory.* New York: Wiley.

Kintsch, Walter, and Keenan, J.
    1973   "Reading rate and retention as a function of the number of propositions in the base structure of sentences". *Cognitive Psychology* 5: 257–74.

Kitagawa, Chisato.
    1982   "Topic constructions in Japanese". *Lingua* 57: 175–214.

Kohlhof, I.
    1997   "Givenness für das Deutsche". *Arbeitspapiere des Sonderforschungsbereichs 340: Sprachtheoretische Grundlagen für die Computerlinguistik*, No. 99.

Kraus, Karl
    1956   *Die Sprache.* Munich: Kösel Verlag.

Krushel'nitskaya, K. G.
    1961   *Ocherki po Sopostavitel'no%i Grammaticke Nemeckogo i Russkogo Yazykov* [Contrastive Grammatical Studies in German and Russian]. Moscow: Izdatel'svo Literatury na Inostrannych Yazykach.

Kuno, Susumu
    1969   "Theme, contrast, and exhaustive listing -*wa* and -*ga* in Japanese". *Bulletin of the Institute for Research in Language Teaching* 289: 19–32.
    1972a   "Functional sentence perspective: A case study from Japanese and English". *Linguistic Inquiry* 3: 269–320.
    1972b   "Pronominalization, reflexivization, and direct discourse". *Linguistic Inquiry* 3 (2): 161–95.
    1975   "Three perspectives in the functional approach to syntax". In R. E. Grossman et al. (eds.) 1975, 276–336.
    1976   "Subject, Theme, and the speaker's empathy: A reexamination of relativization phenomena". In Ch. N. Li (ed.) 1976, 417–44.
    1978a   "Generative discourse analysis in America". In W. U. Dressler (ed.) 1977, 275–94.
    1978b   "Japanese: A characteristic OV language". In *Syntactic Typology: Studies in the Phenomenology of Language*, W. P. Lehmann (ed.), 58–138. Austin: University of Texas Press.

1980 "Functional syntax". In *Syntax and Semantics 13: Current Approaches to Syntax*, E. A. Moravik, and J. R. Wirth (eds.), 117–35. New York: Academic Press.

1987 *Functional Syntax: Anaphora, Discourse and Empathy*. Chicago: University Press.

Kuno, Susumu, and Kaburaki, Etsuko
    1977 "Empathy and syntax". *Linguistic Inquiry* 8 (4): 627–72.

Kuroda, S.-Y.
    1972 "The categorical and thetic judgement. Evidence from Japanese syntax". *Foundations of Language* 9: 153–85.
    1984 "The categorical and the thetic judgment reconsidered". Paper presented at the Colloquium on Anton Marty's 1988 Philosophy and Linguistic Theory. Fribourg, Switzerland.
    1985 *Japanese Grammar and Judgement Forms*. Ms. University of California. San Diego.

Ladd, D. Robert
    1996 *Intonational Phonology*. Cambridge: Cambridge University Press.

Lambrecht, Knud.
    1981 *Topic, antitopic and verb-agreement in non-standard French*. *Pragmatics and Beyond* Vol II: 6. Amsterdam/Philadelphia: John Benjamins.
    1986 *Topic, Focus, and the grammar of Spoken French*. Ph. D. dissertation. Berkeley: University of Berkeley.
    1987a "Sentence Focus, information structure, and the thetic-categorical distinction". *Berkeley Linguistic Society Proceedings of the 12th Annual Meeting* 13: 366–82.
    1987b "When Subjects behave like Objects". Paper read at the 1987 LSA Meeting in San Francisco.
    1988a When Subjects Behave like Topics: A Markedness Analysis of Sentence Focus Constructions across Languages. Unpublished ms. Texas: University of.
    1988b "Presentational cleft constructions in spoken French". In T. Haiman, and S. Thompson (eds.) 1988, 135–180.
    1994 *Information Structure and Sentence Form*. Cambridge: Cambridge University Press.

Langacker, Ronald W.
    1974 "The question of Q." *Foundations of Language* 11: 1–37.
    1990 "Subjectification". *Cognitive Linguistics* 1 (1): 5–38.
    1993 "Reference-point constructions". *Cognitive Linguistics* 4 (1): 1–38.

Larsen-Freeman, D., and Strom, V.
    1977 "The construction of a second language acquisition index of development". *Language Learning* 27 (2): 123–34.

Lautamatti, L.
   1978   "Observations on the development of the Topic in simplified discourse". In *Text Linguistics, Cognitive Learning, and Language Teaching* 22, and N. E. Enkvist and V. Kohonen (eds.), 71–104. Åbo: Åbo Akademi.

Leech, Geoffrey N.
   1974   *Semantics*. Harmondsworth: Penguin.

Leech, Geoffrey N., and Svartvik, J.
   1975   *A Communicative Grammar of English*. London: Longman.

Leech, Geoffrey N., Deuchar, M., and Hoogenraad, R.
   1982   *English Grammar for Today*. London: MacMillan.

Lehman, Christian
   1992   "Word order change by grammaticalisation". In *Internal and External Factors in Syntactic Change*, D. Stein and M. Gerritsen (eds.), 395–417. Berlin: Mouton.

Lemke, Jay L.
   1985   "Idelogy, intertextuality and the notion of register". In J. Benson and W. Greaves (eds.) 1985, 275–294.

Leonard, L., and Schwartz, R.
   1977   "Focus characteristics of single-word utterances after syntax". *Journal of Child Language* 5: 151–8.

Lesgold, A.
   1972   "Pronominalization: A device for unifying sentences in memory". *Journal of Verbal Learning and Verbal Behavior* 11: 316–23.

Levin, B., and Rappaport, H.
   1994   *Unaccusativity*. Cambridge: CUP.

Levinson, Stephen C.
   1983   *Pragmatics*. Cambridge: University Press.

Li, Charles N. (ed.)
   1975   *Word Order and Word Order Change*. Austin: University of Texas Press.
   1976   *Subject and Topic*. New York: Academic Press.

Li, Charles N., and Thompson, Sandra A.
   1981   *Mandarin Chinese. A Functional Reference Grammar*. Berkeley: University of California Press.

Linde, C., and Labov, W.
   1965   "Spatial networks as a site for the study of language and thought". *Language* 51: 924–39.

Lindner, G.
   1898   *Aus dem Naturgarten der Kindersprache*. Leipzig: Grieben.

Long, Nie.
   1991   An analysis of texts of different genres in terms of thematic selections and process types. Unpublished manuscript.

Longacre, Robert E.
   1981   "A spectrum and profile approach to discourse analysis". *Text* 1: 337–59.

1989 "Two hypothesis regarding text generation and analysis". *Discourse Processes* 12: 413–60.
Lötscher, Andreas
    1985 "Syntaktische Bedingungen der Topikalisierung". *Deutsche Sprache* 12: 207–29.
    1992 "The pragmatics of non-referential Topics in German (and other languages)". *Linguistics* 30 (1): 123–45.
Lowe, I.
    1987 "Sentence initial elements in English and their discourse function". *Occasional papers in Systemic Linguistics* 2: 5–34.
Lyons, John
    1977 *Semantics*. Cambridge: University Press.
Mackenzie, J. Lachlan
    1998 "Incremental Functional Grammar: An Application to Spoken Utterances in English". Paper Paper delivered to *the 8th International Conference on Functional Grammar*. Amsterdam: Vrije Universiteit. 6th–11th july.
Mackenzie, J. Lachlan, and M. E. Keizer
    1991 [1990]. "On assigning pragmatic functions in English". *Pragmatics* 1 (2): 169–215.
MacWhinney, Brian
    1975 "Pragmatic patterns in child syntax". *Papers and Reports on Child Language Development* 10: 153–65.
    1977 "Starting points". *Language* 53: 152–68.
MacWhinney, Brian, and Bates, Elizabeth.
    1978 "Sentential devices for conveying givenness and newness: A cross-cultural developmental study". *Journal of Verbal Learning and Verbal Behaviour* 17: 539–58.
Magretta, William Ralph
    1977 Topic–Comment Structure in Linguistic Theory: A Functional Approach. Unpublished Ph. D. disseration, University of Michigan. Univ. Microf. Internat.
Maratsos, M.
    1974 "Preschool children's use of definite and indefinite articles". *Child Development* 45: 446–55.
    1976 *The Use of Definite and Indefinite Reference in Young Children: An Experimental Study of Semantic Acquisition*. Cambridge: Cambridge University Press.
Marslen-Wilson, W. Tyler, L. K., and Seidenberg, M.
    1978 "Sentence processing and the clause boundary". In *Studies in the Perception of Language*, W. J. M. Levelt, and G. B. Flores (eds.), 219–46. London: Wiley.

Martin, James R.
- 1981 "Conjunction and continuity in Tagalog". In M. A. K. Halliday, and J. R. Martin (eds.) 1981, 310–36.
- 1984a "Functional components in a grammar: A review of deployable recognition criteria". *Nottingham Linguistic Circular* 13: 35–70.
- 1984b "Language, register and genre". In *Language Studies: Children Writing*, F. Christie (ed.), 21–30. Geelong, Vic.: Deakin University Press.
- 1984c "The development of register". In *Developmental Issues in Discourse*, J. Fine and R. O. Freeddle (eds.), 1–39. Norwood, NJ: Ablex.
- 1986b "Intervening in the process of writing development". In *Writing to Mean: Teaching Genres across the Curriculum*, C. Painter and J. R. Martin (eds.), 11–43. Applied Linguistics Association of Australia.
- 1989 (2nd ed.) *Factual Writing: Exploring and Challenging Social Reality*. London: Oxford University Press.
- 1992a *English Text: System and Structure*. Philadelphia/Amsterdam: John Benjamins.
- 1992b "Theme, method of development and existentiality: the price of a reply". *Occasional Papers in Systemic Linguistics* 6: 147–83.
- 1995 "More than what the message is about: English Theme". In M. Ghadessy (ed.) 1995, 223–58.

Martin, James R., and Matthiessen, Christian M. I. M.
- 1991 "Systemic typology and topology". In *Social Processes in Education: Poceedings of the First Australian Systemic Network Conference*, F. Christie (ed.), 345–383. Deakin University, January 1990. Darwin: Centre for Studies of Language in Education. Northern Territory University.

Martin, James R., Matthiessen, Christian M. I. M., and Painter Clare
- 1997 *Working with Functional Grammar*. London, New York, Sydney: Auckland.

Marty, Anton
- 1918 *Gesammelte Schriften*. vol. II, part I. Abteilung. Halle: Max Niemeyer Verlag.
- 1897 "Über die Scheidung von Grammatischem, Logischem und Psychologischem Subjekt resp. Prädikat". *Archiv für systematische Philosophie* 3: 174–90; 294–333.

Mathesius, Villem
- 1939 "O Tak Zvaném Aktuálním cleneni Vetném" [On the so-called functional sentence perspective]. *Slovo a Slovesnost* 5: 171–4.
- 1942 "Rec a Sloh". cteni o Jazyce a Poezii. 13–102.
- 1947 *Cestina a Obecný Jazykopzpyt* [Czech Language and General]. Prague: Melantrich.
- 1961 *Obsahový Rozbor Soucasné Anglictiny na Základe Obecne Lingvistickém, Praha* [Edited by J. Vachek; quoting from the English translation by Libuse Dusková (1975). *A Functional Analysis of Present Day English on a General Linguistic Basis*. Mouton: The Hague].

Matthiessen, Christian M. I. M.
  1988 "Representational issues in Systemic Functional Grammar". In Benson and Greaves (eds.) 1988, 87–179.
  1992 "Interpreting the textual metafunction". In *Advances in Systemic Linguistics: Recent Theory and Practice*, M. Davies and L. Ravelli (eds.), 37–81. London: Pinter.
  1995 "Theme as an enabling resource". In M. Ghadessy (ed.) 1995, 20–54.
Matthiessen, Christian M. I. M., and Bateman, J.
  1991 *Systemic Linguistics and Text Generation: Experiences from Japanese and English*. London: Frances Pinter.
Matthiessen, Christian M. I. M., and Martin, J. R.
  1991 "A response to Huddleston's review of Halliday's *Introduction to Functional Grammar*". *Occasional Papers in Systemic Linguistics* 5: 55–84.
Maynard, Douglas W.
  1980 "Placement of Topic changes in conversation". *Semiotica* 30.3: 263–90.
Maynard, S. K.
  1986 "Interactive aspects of thematic progression in English casual conversation". *Text* 6: 73–105.
McCawley, J.
  1988 *The Syntactic Phenomena of English*. Chicago: University of Chicago Press.
McCutchen, Deborah, and Perfetti, Charles A.
  1982 "Coherence and connectedness". *Text* 2: 1–3.
Milsark, G. L.
  1977 "Towards an explanation of certain peculiarities of the existential construction in English". *Linguistic Analysis* 3 (1): 1–29.
  1979 *Existential Sentences in English*. M. I. T. Dissertation (Mimeographed by the Indiana University of Linguistics Club: *Outstanding Dissertations in Linguistics*.
Mithun, Marianne
  1987 "Is basic word order universal?" In R. Tomlin (ed.) 1987, 281–328.
Montgomery, Michael
  1982 "The functions of left dislocations in spontaneous discourse". In *The Ninth Locus Forum 1982*, J. Moreall (ed.), 425–32. Columbia SC: Hornbeam Press.
Morgenthaler, E.
  1980 *Kommunikationsorientierte Textgrammatik. Ein Versuch, die Kommunikationskompetenz zur Textbildung und Rezeption aus Natürlichen Sprachvorkommen zu Erschliessen*. Düsseldorf: Schwann.
Morris, Terry
  1998 "Topic vs. thematicity: Topic prominence in impromptu Spanish discourse". *Journal of Pragmatics* 29.2: 193–204.
Moutaouakil, Ahmed
  1984 "Le Focus en Arabe: Vers une analyse fonctionnelle". *Lingua* 64: 115–76.

Mukarovský, J.
    1941   *Kapitoly z Ceské Poetiky*, Vol. I [Chapters from Czech poetics]. Prague: Melantrich.

Nichols, J.
    1984   "Functional theories of grammar". *Annual Review of Anthropology* 13: 97–117.

Novák, Pavel
    1974   "Remarks on devices on functional sentence perspective". In F. Daneš (ed-) 1974, 175–207.

Novák, Pavel, and Sgall, Petr E.
    1968   "On the Prague functional approach". *Travaux Linguistiques de Prague* 3: 291–97.

Nuyts, Jan
    1983   "On the methodology of a functional language theory". In S.C. Dik et al. (eds.). *Advances in Functional Grammar*, 369–404. Dordrecht: Foris.
    1985   "Some considerations concerning the notion of 'psychological reality' in Functional Grammar". In A.M. Bolkestein, et al. (1985a) (eds.), 91–105.

Nuyts, Jan, and de Schutter, Georges (eds.)
    1987   *Getting One's Word's into Line: On Word Order and Functional Grammar*. Dordrecht: Foris.

Nuyts, Jan, Bolkestein A. Machtelt, and Vet Co (eds.)
    1990   *Layers and Levels of Representation in Language Theory: A Functional Overview*. Amsterdam/Philadelphia: Benjamins.

Nwogu, K. and Bloor, T.
    1991   "Thematic progression in professional and popular medical texts". In *Functional and Systemic Linguistics. Trends in Linguistics: Studies and Monographs* 55, E. Ventola (ed.), 369–84. Berlin, New York: Mouton de Gruyter.

O'Shea, M.V.
    1907   *Linguistic Development and Education*. New York: Macmillan.

Ochs, Elinor and Schieffelin, Bambi B.
    1976   "Topic as a discourse notion. A Study of Topic in the conversations of children and adults". In Ch. Li (ed.) 1976, 335–84.

Olsen, Leslie, and Rod Johnson
    1988   "A discourse-based approach to the assessment of readability". *Linguistics and Education* 1: 207–231.

Olson, D., and Filby, N.
    1972   "On the comprehension of active and passive sentences". *Cognitive Psychology* 3: 361–81.

Osgood, Charles E.
    1971   "Where do sentences come from?" In *Semantics*, D. Steinberg and L.A. Jakovits (ed.), 497–529. Cambridge: Cambridge University Press.

Osgood, Charles E., and Bock, Kathryn J.
   1977   "Saliency and sentencing: Some production principles". In *Sentence Production: Development in Research and Theory*, S. Rosenberg (eds.) 89–140. Hillsdale NJ: Erlbaum.

Owens, J., Dafoe, J., and Bower G.
   1977   "Taking a point of view: character identification and attributional processes in story comprehension and memory". Paper presented to the *Meeting of the American Psychology Association*. San Francisco, August 1977.

Palková, Z., and Palek, B.
   1978   "Functional sentence perspective in textlinguistics". In W. U. Dressler (ed.) 1978. *Current Trends in Textlinguistics*. 212–27. New York: Walter de Gruyter.

Pasch, R.
   1982   "Kommunikative Dynamik. Zwei Arten der Aktuellen Gliederung von Sätzen". *Linguistische Studien* 99: 164–9.

Paul, Hermann
   1975   [1880] *Prinzipien der Sprachgeschichte*. Tübingen: Niemeyer.
   1886   (2nd ed.) *Prinzipien der Sprachgeschichte*. Halle: Niemeyer.

Payne, Doris
   1987   "Information structure in Papago narrative discourse". *Language* 63: 783–804.

Penelope, J.
   1982   "Topicalization: The rhetorical strategies and the interpretative strategies it imposes". *Linguistics* 20 (11/12): 683–96.

Petöfi, J. S., and Sözer, E. (eds.)
   1983   *Micro and Macro Connexity of Texts*. Hamburg: Buske Verlag.

Pike, K. L.
   1982   *Linguistic Concepts: an Introduction to Tagmemics*. Lincoln: University of Nebraska Press.

Pike, K. L., and Pike, E. G.
   1983   *Text and Tagmeme*. London: Pinter.

Plötz, S.
   1972   *Simple Copula Structures in English*. Frankfurt/M.: Athenaum Verlag.

Plum, G.
   1988   *Textual and Contextual Conditioning in Spoken English: A Genre-based Approach*. Ph. D. Thesis. Department of Linguistics, University of Sydney.

Portner, Paul, and Yabushita, Katsuhiko
   1998   "The semantics and pragmatic of topic phrases". *Linguistics and Philosophy* 21 (2): 117–57

Posner, M.
   1985   *Hierarchically Distributed Networks in Neuropsychology of Selective Attention*. Cognitive Science Working Papers, TR-85-1, Institute of Cognitive and Decision Sciences. Eugene: University of Oregon.

Posner, M., and Petersen, S.
  1989 *The Attention System of the Human Brain*. Cognitive Science Working Papers, TR-89–2, Institute of Cognitive and Decision Sciences. Eugene: University of Oregon.
Posner, M., Sandson, J., Dhawan, M., and Shulman, G.
  1988 *Is Word Recognition Automatic? A Cognitive-Anatomical Approach*. Cognitive Science Working Papers, TR-88–2, Institute of Cognitive and Decision Sciences. Eugene: University of Oregon.
Posner, Michael I., and Warren, Robert E.
  1972 "Traces, concepts and conscious constructions". In *Coding Processes in Human Memory*, A. W. Melton and E. Martin (eds.), 25–44. Washington, DC: Winston.
Poutsma, H.
  1916 *A Grammar of Late Modern English*. Part II. Groningen: Noordhoff.
Prentice, J.
  1966 "Response strength of single words as an influence in sentence behavior". *Journal of Verbal Learning and Verbal Behavior* 5: 429–33.
Prideaux, Gary D., and Hogan, John T.
  1993 "Markedness as a discourse management". *Word* 44: 397–411.
Prince, Ellen F.
  1978 "A Comparison of *Wh*-clefts and *It*-clefts in discourse". *Language* 54: 883–906.
  1981a "Toward a taxonomy of given-new information". In P. Cole (ed.) 1981, 223–55.
  1981b "Topicalization, Focus movement, and yiddish movement: A pragmatic differentiation". *Proceedings of the Seventh Annual Meeting of the Berkeley Linguistics Society*: 249–64.
  1982 "A comparison of topicalization and left dislocation in discourse". Paper presented at the *Linguistic Society of America annual meeting*.
  1984 "Topicalization and left dislocation: A functional analysis". In *Discourses in Reading and Linguistics*, Annals *of the New York Academy of Sciences vol 43*, Sheila J. White, and Virginia Teller (eds.), 213–225. New York: Academy of Sciences.
  1986 "On the syntactic marking of presupposed open propositions". *CLS (Parasession)* 22: 208–222.
  1997 "On the functions of left-dislocation in English discourse". In *Directions in Functional Linguistics*, A. Kamio (ed.), 117–43. Amsterdam/Philadelphia: John Benjamins.
Prince, Gerald
  1982 *Narratology*. Berlin: Mouton.
Pu, Ming-Ming, and Prideaux, Gary D.
  1994 "Coding episode boundaries with marked structures: A cross-linguistic study". *Canadian Journal of Linguistics* 39 (4): 283–96.

Pufahl, Ingrid.
    1992   "Topics in German and US television news". *Linguistics* 30 (1): 217–241.
Quirk, Randolph, and Greenbaum, Sidney
    1973   *A Concise Grammar of Contemporary English.* New York: Harcourt, Brace, Jovanovich.
Quirk, Randolph, Greenbaum, Sidney, Leech, Geoffrey, N., and Svartvik, Jan
    1972   *A Grammar of Contemporary English.* London: Longman.
    1985   *A Comprehensive Grammar of the English Language.* London: Longman.
Ragan, Peter
    1987   *Meaning in the Communication of a Set of Instructions.* Ph. D. dissertation, National University of Singapore.
Ramsey, Violeta
    1987   "Preposed and post-posed *If* and *When* clauses in English". In R. Tomlin (ed.) 1987, 383–408.
Rando, E., and Napoli, D. J.
    1978   "Definiteness in *there*-sentences". Language 54: 300–13.
Ravelli, L. J.
    1995   "A dynamic perspective: Implications for metafunctional interaction and an understanding of Theme". In R. Hasan and P. H. Fries (eds.) 1995, 187–234.
Reichenbach, H.
    1947   *Elements of Symbolic Logic.* New York: MacMillan.
Reinhart, Tanya
    1981   "Pragmatics and linguistics: An analysis of sentence Topics". *Philosophica* 27 (1): 53–94.
    1982   *Anaphora and Semantic Interpretation.* London: Cromm Helm.
Reszkiewicz, A.
    1966   *Ordering of Elements in Late Old English Prose in Terms of their Size and Structural Complexity.* Komitet Neofilologiczny Polskiej Akademii Nauk.). Wroclaw: Zaclad Narodowy Imienia Ossoli'nskich Wydawnictwo Polskiej Akademii Nauk.
Rochemont, Michael S.
    1986   *Focus in Generative Grammar.* Amsterdam/Philadelphia: John Benjamins.
Rochemont, Michael S., and Culicover, Peter William
    1990   *English Focus Constructions and the Theory of Grammar.* Cambridge: Cambridge University Press.
Romero Trillo, Jesús
    1994   "*Ahm, ehm,* you call it Theme? ... A thematic approach to spoken English". *Journal of Pragmatics* 22: 495–509.
Rosch, Eleanor, and Lloyd, C. B.
    1978   *Cognition and Categorization.* Hillsdale, N. J.: Erlbaum.
Rothery, J.
    1990   *Story Writing in Primary School: Assessing Narrative Type Genres.* Ph. D. dissertation. Department of Linguistics, University of Sydney.

Ruzich, C.
- 1984 "Writer scanning: how does it affect text cohesion?" Paper presented at the *Convention of the College on College Composition and Communication.* New York City.

Rybarkiewicz, W.
- 1977 "On the nature of the concepts of the 'Given' and 'New' in linguistic analysis". *Studia Anglica Poznaniensia* 9: 77–85.

Sandmann, Manfred
- 1954 *Subject and Predicate.* Edinburgh: Edinburgh University Press.

Sapir, Edward.
- 1921 *Language.* New York: Harcourt, Brace and World.

Sasse, Hans-Jürgen
- 1987 "The thetic/categorical distinction revisited". *Linguistics* 25 (3): 511–80.

Schachter, Paul
- 1977 "Reference-related and role-related properties of Subjects". In P. Cole (ed.) 1977, 279–306.

Schachter, Paul, and Otanes, F. E.
- 1972 *Tagalog Reference Grammar.* Berkeley: University of California Press.

Schank, Roger C.
- 1977 "Basic rules and topics in conversation". *Cognitive Science* 1: 21–42.

Schiffrin, Deborah
- 1985 "Multiple constraints on discourse options. A quantitative analysis of causal sequences". *Discourse Processes* 8 (3): 281–303.
- 1987 *Discourse Markers.* Cambridge: Cambridge University Press.
- 1992 "Conditionals as Topics in discourse". *Linguistics* 30 (1): 165–97.

Schlesinger, I. M.
- 1968 *Sentence Structure and the Reading Process.* The Hague: Mouton.

Schlobinski, Peter, and Schütze-Coburn, Stephan
- 1992 "Topic and Topic continuity". *Linguistics* 30 (1): 88–121.

Schmerling, Susan F.
- 1976 *Aspects of English Sentence Stress.* Austin: University of Texas Press.

Schmidt, Deborah Arm
- 1980 A History of Inversions in English. Unpublished Ph. D. Dissertation: The Ohio State University.

Schneider, W., and Shiffrin, R. M.
- 1977 "Controlled and automated human information processing I: Detection, search and attention". *Psychological Review* 84 (2): 127–190.

Schwarzschild, R.
- 1996a *In Defense of Givenness.* Draft: Rutgers University.
- 1996b *Givenness and Optimal Focus.* Draft: Rutgers University.

Searle, J. R.
- 1969 *Speech Acts.* London: Cambridge University Press.

Sechehaye, M. A.
    1926   *Essai sur la Structure Logique de la Phrase*. Paris: Champion.
Selkirk, Elisabeth O.
    1984   *Phonology and Syntax: The Relationship between Sound and Structure*. Cambridge, Mass.: MIT Press.
Seuren, P.
    1969   *Operators and Nucleus: A Contribution to the Theory of Grammar*. Cambridge: University Press.
Sgall, Petr E.
    1972   "Topic, Focus, and the ordering of elements of semantic representations". *Philologica Pragensia* 15: 1–14.
    1974   "Focus and contextual boundness". In Ö. Dahl (ed.) 1974, 25–51.
    1975   "On the nature of Topic and Focus". In *Style and Text: Studies Presented to Nils E. Enkvist*, H. Ringbom (ed.), 409–15. Stockholm: Skriptor.
Sgall, Petr E., Hajicová, Eva, and Benesova, E.
    1973   *Topic, Focus, and Generative Semantics*. Kronberg, Germany: Scriptor.
Sgall, Petr E. et al.
    1980   *Aktuální Clenení Vety v Cestine* [Topic and Focus in Czech]. Praha: Academia.
Sgall, Petr E., Hajicová, Eva, and Panenová, Jarmila
    1986   *The Meaning of the Sentence and its Semantic and Pragmatic Aspects*. Prague: Academia.
Shibatini, M.
    1991   "Grammaticalization of Topic into Subject". In E. C. Traugott & B. Heine (eds.) 1991, 93–133.
Siewierska, Anna
    1984   *The Passive: A Comparative Linguistic Analysis*. London: Croom Helm.
    1988   *Word Order Rules*. London: Croom Helm.
    1991   *Functional Grammar*. London: Routledge.
Silvá-Corvalán, Carmen
    1984   "Topicalización y pragmática en español". *RSEL* 14 (1): 1–19.
Simon-Vandenbergen, Anne Marie
    1987   "Left dislocations revisited". In *Studies in Honour of Rene Derolez*, A. M. Simon-Vandenbergen (ed.), 558–82. Ghent: Seminarie voor Engelse en Oud-Germaanse Taalkunde, R. U. G.
Smith, C. S.
    1971   "Sentence in discourse: An analysis of a discourse by Bertrand Russell". *Journal of Linguistics* 7: 213–35.
Smits, Aletta
    1998   "Complex beginnings in English". Paper Paper delivered to the *8th International Conference on Functional Grammar*. Amsterdam: Vrije Universiteit. 6th–11th july.

Sperber, Dan, and Wilson, Deirdre
    1986   *Relevance.* Oxford: Blackwell.
Stein, Dieter
    1995   "Subjective meanings and the history of inversions in English". In D. Stein & S. Wright (eds.) 1995, 129–150.
Stein, Dieter, and Wright Susan (eds.)
    1995   *Subjectivity and Subjectivisation.* Cambridge: Cambridge University Press.
Steiner, E. M., and Veltman, R. (eds.)
    1988   *Pragmatics, Discourse and Text.* London: Pinter Publishers.
Strawson, P. F.
    1950   "On referring". *Mind* 59: 320–44.
Strunk, W. and White, E. B.
    1959   *The Elements of Style.* New York: Macmillan.
Svartivk, Jan
    1966   *On Voice in the English Verb.* The Hague: Mouton.
Svartvik, Jan, and Quirk, Randolph (eds.)
    1980   A *Corpus of English Conversation. Lund:* Liber/Gleerups.
Svoboda, Aleš
    1968   "The hierarchy of communicative units and fields as illustrated by English attributive constructions". *Brno Studies in English* 7: 49–85.
    1974   "On two communicative dynamisms". In F. Daneš (ed.) 1974, 38–42.
    1981   "Diatheme". Brno: Masaryk University.
    1983   "Thematic elements" *Brno Studies in English* 15: 49–85.
Szwedek, A.
    1986   *A Linguistic Analysis of Sentence Stress.* Tübingen: Gunter Narr.
Taglicht, Joseph
    1984   *Message and Emphasis.* London/New York: Longman.
Taylor, Christopher
    1993   "Systemic linguistics and translation". *Occasional Papers in Systemic Linguistics* 7: 87–103.
Taylor, L. J.
    1996   (2nd ed.) *Linguistic Categorisation.* London: Clarendon Press.
Taylor, L. J., and Knowles, Dr. G.
    1988   *Manual of Information to Accompany the* LIBMSEC *Corpus: The Machine-Readable Corpus of Spoken English.* Unit for Computer Research on the English Language Bowland College, University of Lancaster. Bailrigg: Lancaster.
Taylor-Torsello, C. T.
    1992   "How Woolf creates point of view in *To the Lighthouse*". *Occasional Papers in Systemic Linguistics* 5: 159–74.
    1996   "Theme as the interpreter's path indicator through the unfolding text". *Interpreter's Newsletter* 7: 113–49.

1997 "Linguistics, discourse analysis and interpretation". In *Conference Interpreting: Current Trends in Research*, Proceedings of the *International Conference on Interpreting 'What do we Know and How?'*, August 25th–27th 1994, University of Turku, Y. Gambier, D. Gile, and C. T. Taylor Torsello (eds.), 167–86. Amsterdam: John Benjamins.

Tejada-Caller, Paloma.
1988 *Tematización y Rematización en Inglés Antiguo*. Madrid: Universidad Complutense.

Thompson, Sandra A.
1978 "Modern English from a typological point of view: Some implications of the function of word order". *Linguistische Berichte* 54: 19–35.
1985 "Initial vs. final purpose clauses in written English discourse". *Text* 5 (1/2): 55–84.

Thorndyke, Perry W.
1977 "Cognitive structures in comprehension and memory of narrative discourse". *Cognitive Psychology* 9: 77–110.

Tomlin, Russell (ed.)
1987 *Coherence and Grounding in Discourse*. Amsterdam/Philadelphia: Benjamins.

Traugott, Elizabeth C.
1995 "Subjectification in grammaticalisation". In D. Stein & S. Wright (eds.), 1995, 31–54.

Traugott, E. C., and Heine, B. (eds.)
1991 *Approaches to Grammaticalization*. Amsterdam/Philadelphia: John Benjamins.

Trávníček, František
1937 "Základy českého slovosledu [Fundamentals of Czech word order]". *Slovo a slovesnost* 3: 78–86. Prague.
1961 "O Takzvaném Aktuálním členení Vetném [On so-called functional sentence perspective]". *Slovo a slovesnost* 22: 163–71.

Tsutsui, Michio
1981 "Topic marker ellipsis in Japanese". *Studies in the Linguistic Sciences* 11 (1): 163–79.

Tyler, A., and Bno, J.
1992 "Discourse structure in non-native English discourse: The effect of ordering and interpretation cues on perceptions and comprehensibility". *Studies in Second Language Acquisition* 14 (1):71–86.

Uhlírová, L.
1969 "Aktuální členení a Styl Jazykových Projevú (na Materiále z Publicistických Textú) [Functional sentence perspective and the style of present day publicist prose]". *Slovo a Slovesnost* 44: 284–94.

1974 "O Vztahu Sémantiky Príslovečného Určení k Aktuálnímu členení [The relatinship between the semantics of adverbials and functional sentence perspective]". *Slovo a Slovesnost* 35: 99–106.
1977 "Optional constituents in Theme–Rheme structure". *Prague Studies in Mathematical Linguistics* 5: 309–20.

Ulrich, Miorita
1985 *Thetisch und Kategorisch*. Tübingen: Narr Verlag.

Uwe, Carl
1980 "Primary and secondary topicalization processes". *Central Institute of English and Foreign Language Bulletin* (CIEFL BULL.) 16 (2): 11–18.

Vachek, Josef
1958 "Some notes on the development of languages seen as a system of systems. *Proceedings of the Eighth International Congress of Linguistics*. Oslo: Oslo University Press. 418–19.

Vallduví, Enric
1992 *The Informational Component*. Ph.D. dissertation: University of Pennsylvania.

Vallduví, Enric, and Engdahl, E.
1996 "The linguistic realization of information packaging". *Linguistics* 34: 459–519.

van der Auwera, J., and Grossens, L. (eds.)
1987 *Ins and Outs of the Predication in a Functional Grammar of Spanish*. Dordrecht: Foris.

Van Dijk, Teun A.
1973 "Text grammar and text logic". In *Studies in Text Grammars*, J. Petöfi, and H. Rieser (eds.), 17–78. Dordrecht: Reidel.
1977 "Sentence Topic and discourse Topic". *Papers in Slavic Philology* 1: 49–61.
1980 *Text and Context. Explorations in the Semantics and Pragmatics of Discourse*. London and New York: Longman.
1984 *Prejudice in Discourse: An Analysis of Ethnic Prejudice in Cognition and Conversation*. Amsterdam/Philadelphia: Benjamins.
1987 "Episodic models in discourse processing". In *Comprehending Oral and Written Language*, R. Horowitz and S. J. Samuels (eds.), 161–96. London: Academic Press.
1988 *News as Discourse*. Hillsdale, N.J.: Erlbaum.

Van Dijk, Teun A., Ihwe J., Petöfi J., and Rieser, H.
1972 *Zur Bestimmung Narrativer Strukturen auf der Grundlage von Textgrammatiken*. Hamburg: Buske Verlag.

Van Dijk, Teun A., and Kintsch, Walter
1983 *Strategies for Discourse Comprehension*. New York and London: Academic Press.

Van Kuppevelt, J.
 1995 "Discourse structure, topicality and questioning". *Journal of Linguistics* 31: 109–47.
Van Oosten, Jeanne
 1986 *The Nature of Subjects, Topics and Agents: A Cognitive Explanation*. Bloomington, Indiana: Indiana University Linguistics Club.
Van Valin Jr, Robert D. Jr. (ed.)
 1993 *Advances in Role and Reference Grammar*. Amsterdam/Philadelphia: John Benjamins.
Vande Kopple, William J.
 1983 "Something old, something new: FSP". *Research in Teaching of English* 17: 85–9.
 1986 "Given and new information and some aspects of the structures, semantics, and pragmatics of written texts". In *Written Communication Annual I. Studying Writing. Linguistic Approaches*, Ch. Cooper, and S. Greenbaum (eds.), 72–111. Beverly Hills, London, New Dahli: Sage.
Vankuppevelt, J.
 1996 "Inferring from Topics — scalar implicatures as Topic-dependent inferences". *Linguistics and Philosophy* 19 (4): 393–443.
Vasconcellos, Muriel
 1992 "The Theme as message onset: Its structure and characteristics". *Linguistics* 30 (1): 147–63.
Vennemann, Theo.
 1974 "Topics, Subjects, and word order: From SXV to SVX via TVX". In *Historical Linguistics I*, J.M. Anderson, and Ch. Jones (eds.), 1339–76. North-Holland.
 1975 "Topic, sentence acent and ellipsis: A proposal for their formal treatment". In E.L. Keenan (ed.) 1975, 313–28.
Verma, S.K.
 1976 "Remarks on thematization". *Archivum Linguisticum* 7 (2): 142–151.
Vet, Co
 1998 "The multilayered structure of the utterance: About illocution, modality and discourse moves". In M. Hannay & M. Bolkestein (eds.) 1998, 1–23.
Viktor, G.A.
 1917 *A Gyermek Nyelve: A Gyermeknyelv Irodolmának Ismertetése Főként Nyelvészeti Szempontból*. Nagyvarad.
Virtanen, Tuija
 1992 "Given and new information in adverbials: Clause initial adverbials of time and place". *Joumal of Pragmatics* 17: 99–115.
von der Gabelentz, Georg
 1869 "Ideen zu einer Vergleichenden Syntax: Wort und Satzstellung". *Zeitschrift für Völkerpsychologie und Sprachwissenschaft* 6: 376–84.
 1891 *Die Sprachwissenschaft*. Leipzig: Weigel.

1972 [1901] *Die Sprachwissenschaft, ihre Aufgaben, Methoden und Bisherigen Ergebnisse*. Tübingen: Narr.

Vossler, Karl
    1923   *Gesammelte Aufsätze zur Sprachphilosophie*. Munich: Max Hueber Verlag.

Walker, Marilyn A., and Prince, Ellen F.
    1996   "A bilateral approach to givenness: A hearer-status algorithm and a centering algorithm". In *Referents and Referent Accessibility*, T. Fretheim and J. K. Gundel (eds.), 291–306. Amsterdam/Philadelphia: John Benjamins.

Walker, Marilyn A., Joshi, Aravind K., and Weinstein, Scott (eds.)
    1997   *Centering in Discourse*. Oxford: Oxford University Press.

Wang, Ling.
    1991   "Analysis of thematic bariation in *Buried Child*". Paper delivered to the *First Biennial Conference on Discourse*. Hangzhou Peoples Republic of China. 7–9 June 1991.
    1992   The Theory of Theme and its Application to Drama Analysis. MA thesis, Department of English Language and Literature: Pekin University.

Ward, Gregory Louis
    1985   *The Semantics and Pragmatics of Preposing*. Michigan: University Microfilms International.
    1988   *The Semantics and Pragmatics of Preposing*. New York: Garland.
    1990   "The discourse function of VP preposing". *Language* 66 (4): 742–63.

Ward, Gregory Louis, and Birner, Betty J.
    1992   "VP inversion and aspect in written texts". In *Cooperating with Written Texts: The Pragmatics and Comprehension of Written Texts*, Dieter Stein (ed.), 575–588. Berlin: Mouton.
    1994   "A unified account of English fronting constructions". *Penn Working Papers in Linguistics*, University of Pennsylvania 1: 159–65
    1995   "Definiteness and the English existential". *Language* 71: 722–433.

Warden, D. A.
    1976   "The influence of context on children's use of identifying expressions and references". *British Journal of Psychology* 67: 101–12.

Watters, John R.
    1979   "Focus in Aghem: A study of its formal correlates and typology". In *Aghem Grammatical Structure*, L. Hyman (ed.), 137–97. Los Angeles: University of Southern California.

Webber, Bonnie L.
    1978.   "Jumping ahead of the speaker: on recognition from indefinite descriptions". Paper presented at the *Sloan Workshop on Indefinite Reference*. Amherst: University of Massachussets, December 3th.
    1982   "So what can be talk about now?". In *Computational Models of Discourse*, M. Brady and R. C. Berwick (eds.), 331–71. Cambridge, MA: MIT Press.

Weil, H.
  1887   *The Order of Words in the Ancient Languages Compared with that of Modern Languages* (C. W. Super, Trans.). Boston: Ginn. [Original work published 1844].
Weiss, Daniel.
  1975   "Topic and an unusual comment [Topic und ein seltsamer Comment]". *Linguistische-Berichte* 36: 24–36.
Whittaker, Rachel
  1990   "Theme in cognitive processing". Paper presented at the *17th International Systemic Congress*, Stirling, Great Britain, 3th–7th July.
  1995   "Theme, processes and the realization of meanings". In M. Ghadessy (ed.) 1985, 105–128.
Wierzbicka, Anna
  1975   "Topic, Focus, and deep structure". *Papers in Linguistics* 8 (1/2): 59–87.
Williams, M. P.
  1988   "Functional sentence perspective in the context of Systemic Functional Grammar". In E. M. Steiner and R. Veltman (eds.) 1988, 76–89.
Wirth, Jessica
  1978   "The derivation of cleft sentences in English". *Glossa* 12: 58–82.
Witte, Stephen P.
  1983   "Topical structure and revision: An exploratory study". *College Compository and Communication* 34: 313–41.
Wright, R., and Glucksberg, S.
  1976   "Choice of definite *versus* indefinite article as a function of sentence voice and reversibility". *Quarterly Journal of Experimental Psychology* 28: 561–70.
Wundt, W.
  1900   (3rd ed.) *Die Sprache*. Leipzig: Engelmann.
Xiao. Qun
  1991   Toward Thematic Selection in Different Genre: Fables and Recipes. Unpublished manuscript.
Yan, Fang, McDonald, Edward, and Musheng, Cheng
  1995   "On Theme in Chinese: From clause to discourse". In R. Hasan and P. H. Fries (eds.) 1995, 235–74.
Young, David
  1980   *The Structure of English Clauses*. London: Hutchinson University Library.
Yule, George, and Mathis, Terrie
  1992   "The role of staging and constructed dialogue in establishing speaker's Topic". *Linguistics* 30 (1): 199–215.
Zimmer, Karl
  1986   "On the function of post-predicate Subject pronouns in Turkish". In *Proceedings of the Turkish Linguistics Conference, August 1984*, 195–206. Ayhan A. Koç and Eser Erguvanli (eds.). Istanbul: Bogazici University Publications.

Ziv, Yael
    1976   On the Communicative Effect of Relative Clause Extraposition in English. University of Illinois dissertation.
    1994   "Left and right dislocations: Discourse functions and anaphora". *Journal of Pragmatics* 22: 629–45.
Zubin, David A.
    1979   "Discourse function of morphology". In T. Givón (ed.) 1979b, 469–504.
Zubizarreta, María Luisa
    1994   "The grammatical representation of Topic and Focus: Implication for the structure of the clause". *University of Venice Working Papers in Linguistics* 4: 97–126.

Name Index

A
Akmajian 377
Allerton 35, 38, 48, 90, 135

B
Beneš 22, 78-80, 86, 368
Berry 50, 53, 133, 213, 342
Birner 235-237, 257, 279, 284, 374
Bolinger 67, 189, 257, 263, 275, 282, 364
Bolkestein 6, 50, 152, 157, 160, 161, 169
Brown 16, 28, 36, 49, 157, 165, 213, 366
Butler 342, 374, 375

C
Chafe 18, 23, 35, 37, 41, 45, 48, 135, 144, 201, 204, 237, 363
Clark 28, 37, 50, 150
Collins 45, 50, 177, 266-268, 271, 305, 308, 312, 324
Comrie 25, 149, 373, 376
Copeland 41, 367
Culicover 365, 367

D
Dahl 11, 62, 72-74
Daneš 22, 36, 46, 56, 80-83, 92, 98, 135, 185, 368
Davidse 90, 264
Davis 41, 367

Davison 10, 13, 24, 34, 48, 52, 117, 180, 237
De Beaugrande 29, 37, 136, 166, 391
Declerk 6
Dik 11, 13, 50, 52, 53, 140, 146-149, 152, 153, 162, 303, 329, 364, 365, 366
Dorgeloh 50, 191, 275, 283, 284
Downing 24, 50, 99, 116-118, 125, 134, 238
Dressler 29, 37, 46, 136, 166
Drubig 263, 264, 282, 367
Duranti 6, 11, 30, 294, 364

E
Enkvist 50, 53, 367

F
Fawcett 179, 384
Fillmore 50, 144, 364
Firbas 22, 35, 49, 66-72, 77, 135, 143, 281, 365-368
Foley 11, 52, 53
Ford 23, 50, 185, 371, 376
Fortescue 174, 329, 341, 342
Fries 44, 98, 99, 116, 125, 130, 133, 364, 370

G
Gabelentz 8, 363, 364, 366
Geluykens 50, 156, 288-290, 294-296, 303

Ghadessy 239, 338, 339, 370, 371
Giora 187, 286, 370
Givón 11, 24, 31, 41, 46-48, 50, 177, 180, 184, 190, 364-367, 373, 378
Gómez-González 17, 22, 50, 52, 157, 266, 329, 342, 363, 370, 374
Green 50, 144, 275, 295, 303, 367
Grice 33, 188, 228
Grimes 30, 50, 56
Grosz 6, 42, 182, 278, 282, 322, 326
Güblig 4
Gundel 11, 13, 25, 34, 40, 47, 52, 237, 364, 365, 367, 371
Gussenhoven 143

H

Halliday 11, 23, 37, 50, 89, 90, 94, 98, 100, 125, 130, 176, 299, 311, 328, 342, 363-368, 372
Hannay 50, 147, 150, 152, 157, 161, 168, 174, 189, 258, 372, 374
Hasan 90, 92, 125, 133, 176, 281, 328
Haviland 11, 37, 50, 150, 367
Hedberg 38, 365
Hengeveld 174, 329, 341, 342
Hockett 6, 17
Høffding 5, 8, 363
Hornby 6, 11, 311
Huddleston 24, 33, 54, 116, 125-127, 130, 266, 371, 377,
Hudson 54, 116, 130, 371

J

Jackendoff 6, 35, 365, 404
Jespersen 308, 366, 377, 378
Jiménez-Juliá 19, 158, 162, 364, 374
Joshi 6, 42, 365
Jucker 205

K

Karttunen 366
Keenan 11, 27, 33, 365, 378
Kemmer 176

Kuno 11, 37, 50, 135, 191, 237, 364, 375, 378

L

Lambrecht 23, 41, 52, 146, 190, 227, 288, 294, 364-366
Langacker 33, 189-191, 202, 244, 364, 375
Lautamatti 6, 50, 53, 108
Lehman 49, 185
Levinson 6, 31, 382
Li 11, 19, 25, 364, 373
Locke 116, 121, 238, 244, 263, 371, 376
Longacre 30, 370
Lötscher 29, 48, 71
Lowe 18, 49, 52, 116, 187, 380
Lyons 25, 54

M

Mackenzie 50, 159, 162-164, 167, 168, 174, 215, 374
Magretta 6, 18, 49, 364
Mair 273, 378
Martin 30, 50, 90, 98, 108, 115, 121, 124, 130, 133, 201, 213, 369, 371, 372
Mathesius 11, 43, 53, 64-66, 79, 94, 368
Matthiessen 96, 120, 121, 125, 130, 133, 370-372
McCawley 266, 267
Mithun 50, 184, 366

N

Nichols 10

O

Ochs 6, 11, 30, 294, 364, 378

P

Paul 5, 8, 53, 55, 363, 364, 368
Pike 96

Prince 11, 34, 37-39, 42, 44, 145, 150, 176, 236, 304, 318, 365-367

Q
Quirk 11, 32, 50, 195, 239, 257, 261, 268, 276, 284, 301, 305, 367, 378

R
Raible 4
Reinhart 13, 16, 25, 47, 364, 366
Rochemont 365, 374
Ruzich 357, 366

S
Schieffelin 6, 11, 33, 365, 378
Schiffrin 23, 50, 186, 364, 376
Schlobinski 4, 6, 25
Schmidt 277
Schütze-Coburn 4, 6, 25
Sgall 6, 36, 61, 75-78, 166, 365, 368
Siewierska 147, 150, 160, 165, 184, 239, 371
Simon-Vandenbergen 45
Smits 50, 174, 343, 345, 374
Sperber 29
Stein 188, 189, 277
Svartvik 195, 239

T
Taglicht 56, 130, 134, 305, 371
Thompson 11, 16, 21, 25, 50, 116, 180, 185, 364, 373

Traugott 285
Trávníček 11, 22, 49, 78-80, 366, 368

V
Vallduví 6, 36, 41, 47, 190, 215, 364-367
Van Dijk 6, 11, 31, 50, 81, 136, 365-367
Van Kuppevelt 6, 27, 28
Van Oosten 24, 30, 52, 117, 364
Van Valin 11, 13, 52, 53, 174, 329, 341
Vande Kopple 366
Vasconcellos 50, 49, 53, 133
Vennemann 11, 28, 64
Vester 50, 49, 343, 374
Vet 174, 329, 341, 342

W
Walker 6, 42, 365
Ward 34, 229, 235, 237, 284, 365, 367
Weil 53, 62-64, 87, 188
Weinstein 6, 42
Wilson 29, 50

Y
Young 50, 53, 133, 225, 231, 271, 272, 302, 325
Yule 16, 28, 50, 157, 165, 213, 366

Z
Zacharschi 38, 365
Ziv 34, 301

Subject Index

A
aboutness 15–17, 22–31, 54–58, 116–119, 125–126, 157–159, 348–350
activation 40, 43, 46, 57, 75, 144–146
 activation state 48
active 32, 41, 50, 55, 144–148, 240–245
Actor 104, 240, 243, 372
Adjunct 369
Agent 19, 21, 28, 226, 243–245,
anchoring 18, 176, 185,
architect 203–204
attention 33, 36, 40, 41, 44, 46, 52, 56, 178, 188–190
Attribute 307

B
boundness 75, 77
 contextual *see* contextual boundness

C
camera angle 203, 303, 327
categorical 23, 66, 73, 74
 categorical statement 73
centring theory 42, 43
 centring transitions 43
 forward-looking centres 43
clefting 176, 182, 378, 402
 it-clefts 248, 303–317, 377–379
 wh-clefts 248, 317–329, 377, 380
cognitive 13, 18, 29, 30, 33, 36, 39, 40, 42, 47, 107, 176, 185–191, 365, 375

cognitive schemata 117
cognitive status 36, 40, 47, 72, 146, 176, 365
cohesion 90, 92
cohesive relations 98
combining 44, 53, 63, 65, 71, 162, 367, 372
 combining approaches 44, 53
Comment 11, 17, 21–23, 28, 31, 36, 49, 56, 72–78
communicative categories 9, 10, 13, 15, 25, 57, 58, 89, 173
 communicative articulation 81
 Communicative Dynamism 66–72
 communicative functions 3, 13, 16, 52, 347, 348
Complement 324, 369, 377, 378
concern 79, 95, 131
Conjunction 90
 conjunctive items 92, 329, 331
 conjunctive Themes 108, 118, 331
 logico-conjunctive Theme 331–345
context 23, 27, 30, 32, 34, 36, 38–40, 44, 54, 71, 97, 136, 163, 193, 348
 contextual 17, 26, 27, 29, 35–39, 44, 57, 71, 93, 139, 149, 157–178, 179, 255, 325–326, 348
 contextual boundness 75, 77, 78
 contextual factor 66, 67, 71, 75
continuatives 92
contrast 23, 35–37, 41, 54, 94, 147, 176, 178, 186, 296, 326–328
 contrastive information 92, 313

430   SUBJECT INDEX

D

detachment 11, 32, 34, 48, 378
  left detachment 34, 45, 55, 287–296
  right detachment 32, 55, 297–302
discourse 23, 26, 30, 43, 140, 352–355
  discourse markers/discourse organisers 142, 179, 186, 187, 190, 287
  discourse Topics 17, 25, 26, 58, 118, 148, 175, 350

E

ellipsis 90
embedding 370
empathy 191, 375, 376
end 32, 68, 189, 328
  end Focus 31–33, 256, 352–354
  end Weight 31–33, 245, 352–354
entity 20–23, 27, 28, 39, 43, 45, 46, 148, 153, 157, 162, 372, 375
Evoked 39, 45, 187, 229, 236, 366
Existent 256–265
Existential *there*-constructions 257–265
  existentials 152, 259, 264, 373, 377
  cardinal existentials 264
  enumerative existentials 264
expansion 111, 112, 369, 370
Experiencer 202, 204
extension 257–261, 370
extrapositions 255–257, 266–273, 353

F

familiarity 37, 38, 40, 45, 57
FG 21, 22, 47, 52, 139, 143, 151, 155, 163, 169, 180, 214, 329, 342
field 68, 69, 161, 375
  communicative field 66
File 42, 43, 144, 366
  filelike data structures 41
Focus 11, 22, 23, 25, 32, 37, 39–44, 47, 54, 58, 73, 75, 93, 140, 143, 147, 166–168, 178, 236, 365, 369, 372, 374
  Focus management 190
  end *see* end Focus
  marked *see* marked Focus
  presentative *see* presentative Focus
Focus stack 29, 365
focal 32–34, 37, 46, 47, 151, 178
frames 18, 29, 30
  frames of reference 18, 283
  propositional *see* proposition
framework 29, 49, 57, 97, 118, 130, 376
  problem frames 30
front position 79, 191, 230
  fronting 11, 18, 34, 55, 275
FSP 21, 31, 33, 34, 61, 271, 279, 285
function 9, 15, 158–161, 180, 185–187
  form-to-function 10, 13, 52, 139, 367
  function-to-form 13, 49, 79, 96, 139, 367
functional 3, 4, 6, 5, 9–11, 130–133, 139, 157, 185, 357, 373
functionalism 10, 13

G

genre 30, 99, 177, 195, 197, 198, 255
Given 6, 9, 11, 15, 21, 25, 34–48, 54, 57, 58, 92–94, 176–177, 348, 365
  given Topic 148, 149, 165–166
givenness 34, 42, 46–48, 65, 66, 80, 325, 348, 366
  givenness hierarchy 39
ground 6, 22, 42, 189, 191, 238
  background 23, 44, 56, 73, 130, 185, 365
  foreground 23, 56, 75, 130, 346

H

heavy elements 135
hypotaxis 330, 370

I

identification 90, 92, 104–107, 319, 321, 378

Identified   104–106, 304, 308, 355, 379
Identifier   104, 105, 304, 355
impersonal expressions   20
implicature   255, 284, 316
Inferrable   39, 41, 45, 150, 176, 256, 302
information   6, 8, 15, 17, 20, 25, 31–48, 50, 53, 57, 71, 73, 85, 90, 92–94, 143–144, 162, 175–178, 348–349, 369
　information packaging   3, 47, 255, 363
　information structure   25, 53, 90, 92, 175, 367
　information unit   32, 93, 103
　informational bipartition   81
　informational interpretation   31
initial position   9, 15, 20, 22, 23, 33, 49–58, 65, 78–87, 96, 130, 166–167, 173, 188, 350
inversion   63, 190, 275–277, 316, 371, 377, 378

K
kinesics   30

L
layering hypothesis   174, 329, 341
left detachment   *see* detachment
linear   8, 22, 49, 65, 82, 132, 159, 178
　linear modification   66, 67, 69, 71
　linear ordering   76, 77
　linearity   8, 9
link   19, 42, 215, 366

M
markedness   103, 168, 180, 183, 184
　marked Focus   37, 93, 369
　marked tonicity   93, 120
　(un)marked   221–225
　unmarked tonality   93, 106, 311, 322
maxim   33, 188, 227

　of manner   33
　of quantity   188
message modes   168, 169, 190
metaphor   56, 115, 372
　metaphorical Themes   111
method of development   98
modalisation   109, 274
modality   109, 272, 273, 342, 353,
mode   42, 168, 177, 193, 196, 197, 375
modulation   109, 353
Mood   102, 369

N
network   27, 82, 91, 176, 369
　network approach   27
　network of isotopic relations   82
neutral description   74
New   8, 11, 15, 20, 31–39, 42, 44–47, 64–66, 85, 90, 92, 93, 145–148, 151–153, 176, 177, 365, 366
　new information   8, 15, 20, 31, 33, 34, 37, 42, 48, 58, 75, 135, 161, 176
　new Topic   11, 194
　newness   11, 34, 36, 37, 47, 73, 161, 316, 327, 366

O
Object   4, 5, 8, 9, 16, 24, 26, 49, 53, 55, 61, 66, 76, 117, 149, 180, 240, 254, 270, 275
object of thought   3, 79, 80, 366
Old   27, 29, 31, 365, 366
order of attention   33
orientation   49, 80, 139, 142, 161, 174, 185, 187, 204, 227, 274, 344, 345, 374
　orientation zone   161, 185, 215
　orientator   98
　oriented   66, 68, 69, 99, 119, 178, 179, 187, 188, 286, 316, 327
　Proper oriented elements   68, 69

P

paradigmatic 23, 119, 136, 205, 363, 375
parataxis 330, 370
passive 32, 34, 50, 55, 103, 104, 214, 240–245, 254, 277, 370
  passivisation 11, 21
Patient 21, 32, 239, 241
perspective 18, 49, 190, 191, 218, 286, 364
pragmatic 13, 16, 21, 25, 49, 52, 139, 140, 142–144, 173, 347, 365, 372, 373
  pragmatic categories 139, 173
  pragmatic functions 21, 139, 140, 147, 173, 349, 350
  pragmatic rules 139, 372
  pragmatic states 144
  Pragmatics 3, 10
Predicate 6, 17, 23, 271, 273, 288, 342, 377
  psychological Predicate 8, 363, 364
  Predicator 369
  predicated Theme 104–105, 304–317, 379
  Theme predication 100, 107, 124, 125
predictability 37, 44, 57, 92, 163
preposing 5, 230, 232, 235–237, 275
presentational 34, 46, 279–281, 364, 374, 377
  Presentation Scale 66, 69, 256
  presentative 18–20, 22–24, 151, 152, 256, 265, 279, 281
  presentative constructions 11, 20, 152, 373
  presentative Focus 162
presupposition 3, 4, 35, 73, 75, 90, 227, 255, 256, 365, 379
  presupposed 19, 35, 73, 74, 94, 103, 316
profiled relationship 190
projection 111, 112, 181, 369, 370

proposition 9, 17, 23, 27, 28, 30, 35, 73, 227, 229, 343, 365
  propositional approach 28
  propositional frames 29
  propositional Topics 27
PS 4, 13, 21, 31, 61, 70, 79, 96, 173, 363

Q

Quality Scale 66, 281
  question-based theories 27
  question-test 46, 75, 85, 165

R

recoverability 37, 44, 57, 67, 163, 176
recursiveness 53, 133
reference 18, 19, 28, 29, 49, 90, 107, 144, 148, 164, 283, 297, 302, 328, 365, 375
  reference point 176, 189, 280, 286, 375
  reference Theme 108, 128, 349, 374, 378
  referential accessibility 42, 146
  referential coherence 135
  referential-semantic interpretation 175
  referring expressions 40, 236, 366
register 87, 99, 119, 144
relational interpretation 17, 119, 126
  relational-semantic interpretation 79, 175
relevance 8, 15, 28, 49, 50, 154
retrievable information 71
Rheme 6, 22, 44, 47, 54, 56–58, 64, 68, 96, 135, 174, 180, 187, 342, 345, 365, 368
  Rheme Proper 68, 69
  Rheme Proper oriented elements 68
right detachment *see* detachment

S

salience 29, 38, 43, 173, 176, 185, 188, 365, 375
saliency 17, 28, 40, 44, 152
semantic factor 66, 67, 69, 71, 75

semantic interpretation 16, 31, 79, 87, 175
separating 54, 71, 89, 135–136, 158,
    173–175, 180, 372
  separating approaches 364
SFG 13, 21, 37, 47, 54, 89–133, 173, 183,
    329, 363, 369, 370
shared knowledge 37, 38, 44, 57, 75, 81,
    163, 348
speaker's angle 96, 119
special treatment 139, 140, 164, 173, 374
stacking 53, 133
staging 3, 15, 49, 56, 132, 135, 345
Subject 20, 26, 45, 55, 63, 66, 80, 102,
    218–220, 230, 240–241, 369
  psychological Subject 4, 5, 8, 9, 79,
    131, 364
  Subject prominent languages 18
  subjectification 286
  subjectivity 179, 188, 196–197, 200,
    229, 255, 279, 286, 350
  subjectivity scale 199, 239
subordination 89, 193, 266, 306
Substitution 90, 92
  substitute Theme 107–108
syntactic interpretation 49, 130
syntagmatic 18, 19, 23, 106, 324, 363

T

tails 153–157, 162, 373
Task Urgency Principle 31
tenor 177, 196, 200, 351, 375
text 9, 28, 37, 49, 56, 89, 90, 98, 136,
    175, 193, 195–197, 199, 204, 205,
  textual component 21, 25, 89, 135, 174
  textual pattern 77
  textual patterns 82, 96, 127, 137, 329
  textual Theme 126, 137, 331, 349
  texture 23, 89, 97, 100, 184
Theme 3–6, 9–11, 22, 28–31, 44, 47–49,
    52–58, 61, 64, 94–115, 153–160,
    173–175, 178–191, 350–356, 376–378
  (logico-)conjunctive *see* conjunction
  metaphorical *see* metaphor

predicated *see* predicate
reference *see* reference
substitute *see* substitution
textual *see* text
topical *see* topicality
Diatheme 68, 72, 418
displaced Theme 126, 129, 137, 184,
    372
extended multiple Theme 206, 299,
    329–346
interpersonal Theme 209, 250, 352, 361
multiple Theme 108, 109, 206
special Themes 121, 182, 183, 188,
    190, 246–329
syntactic Theme 49, 52, 55, 58, 79, 96,
    132, 173, 178, 180, 185, 186,
    350–356, 376
Theme system 89, 119, 120, 126
Theme zone 132, 133, 174, 183, 185,
    186, 189, 286, 329, 334, 341,
    355–357, 378
themeless 13, 65, 66, 69, 87, 215, 257
thematicity 10, 46, 48, 71, 72, 372
  thematic equative 92, 104, 106, 107,
    125, 319
  thematic importance 42
  thematic progressions 78,
  thematisation 34, 132, 135, 158, 278
thetic 20, 23, 74, 148, 151, 152, 164, 256
  thetic sentences 20, 23, 65, 69, 368
tonality 93, 106, 120, 292, 311, 322
  unmarked *see* markedness
tone 93, 94, 103, 134, 178, 330, 367
  tone group 53, 93, 96, 101, 103, 178,
    330
  tone sequence 330, 337
tonic segment 93, 178
tonicity 93, 120, 292, 311, 322
  marked tonicity *see* markedness
Topic 3–6, 9–11, 17–31, 44–58, 72–78,
    116–118, 125, 143–151, 176, 186,
    364, 367, 371, 374
  discourse *see* discourse Topic

given *see* given Topic
main Topic 26
new *see* new Topic
propositional *see* proposition
resumed Topic 150, 169
Topic *(Continued)*
   sentence Topics 17–19, 21–23, 25, 49, 162, 175, 364
   speaker's Topics 17, 29, 118, 175
   SubTopic 150, 163, 164, 169
   Topic acceptability 41, 146, 163, 169
   Topic continuity 52, 97, 165, 186, 228, 352, 371, 372
   Topic expression 46
   Topic management 194
   Topic of conversation 30
   Topic shift 30, 31
topichood 24, 45, 147, 161, 165
topicality 11, 26, 42, 46–48, 76, 143, 144, 146, 161, 175, 367
topical Theme 100–103, 182, 329, 341, 344, 372
transitivity 18, 21, 127, 129, 180, 184, 185, 369

In the PRAGMATICS AND BEYOND NEW SERIES the following titles have been published thus far or are scheduled for publication:

1. WALTER, Bettyruth: *The Jury Summation as Speech Genre: An Ethnographic Study of What it Means to Those who Use it.* Amsterdam/Philadelphia, 1988.
2. BARTON, Ellen: *Nonsentential Constituents: A Theory of Grammatical Structure and Pragmatic Interpretation.* Amsterdam/Philadelphia, 1990.
3. OLEKSY, Wieslaw (ed.): *Contrastive Pragmatics.* Amsterdam/Philadelphia, 1989.
4. RAFFLER-ENGEL, Walburga von (ed.): *Doctor-Patient Interaction.* Amsterdam/Philadelphia, 1989.
5. THELIN, Nils B. (ed.): *Verbal Aspect in Discourse.* Amsterdam/Philadelphia, 1990.
6. VERSCHUEREN, Jef (ed.): *Selected Papers from the 1987 International Pragmatics Conference. Vol. I: Pragmatics at Issue. Vol. II: Levels of Linguistic Adaptation. Vol. III: The Pragmatics of Intercultural and International Communication* (ed. with Jan Blommaert). Amsterdam/Philadelphia, 1991.
7. LINDENFELD, Jacqueline: *Speech and Sociability at French Urban Market Places.* Amsterdam/Philadelphia, 1990.
8. YOUNG, Lynne: *Language as Behaviour, Language as Code: A Study of Academic English.* Amsterdam/Philadelphia, 1990.
9. LUKE, Kang-Kwong: *Utterance Particles in Cantonese Conversation.* Amsterdam/Philadelphia, 1990.
10. MURRAY, Denise E.: *Conversation for Action. The computer terminal as medium of communication.* Amsterdam/Philadelphia, 1991.
11. LUONG, Hy V.: *Discursive Practices and Linguistic Meanings. The Vietnamese system of person reference.* Amsterdam/Philadelphia, 1990.
12. ABRAHAM, Werner (ed.): *Discourse Particles. Descriptive and theoretical investigations on the logical, syntactic and pragmatic properties of discourse particles in German.* Amsterdam/Philadelphia, 1991.
13. NUYTS, Jan, A. Machtelt BOLKESTEIN and Co VET (eds): *Layers and Levels of Representation in Language Theory: a functional view.* Amsterdam/Philadelphia, 1990.
14. SCHWARTZ, Ursula: *Young Children's Dyadic Pretend Play.* Amsterdam/Philadelphia, 1991.
15. KOMTER, Martha: *Conflict and Cooperation in Job Interviews.* Amsterdam/Philadelphia, 1991.
16. MANN, William C. and Sandra A. THOMPSON (eds): *Discourse Description: Diverse Linguistic Analyses of a Fund-Raising Text.* Amsterdam/Philadelphia, 1992.
17. PIÉRAUT-LE BONNIEC, Gilberte and Marlene DOLITSKY (eds): *Language Bases... Discourse Bases.* Amsterdam/Philadelphia, 1991.
18. JOHNSTONE, Barbara: *Repetition in Arabic Discourse. Paradigms, syntagms and the ecology of language.* Amsterdam/Philadelphia, 1991.
19. BAKER, Carolyn D. and Allan LUKE (eds): *Towards a Critical Sociology of Reading Pedagogy. Papers of the XII World Congress on Reading.* Amsterdam/Philadelphia, 1991.
20. NUYTS, Jan: *Aspects of a Cognitive-Pragmatic Theory of Language. On cognition, functionalism, and grammar.* Amsterdam/Philadelphia, 1992.

21. SEARLE, John R. et al.: *(On) Searle on Conversation*. Compiled and introduced by Herman Parret and Jef Verschueren. Amsterdam/Philadelphia, 1992.
22. AUER, Peter and Aldo Di LUZIO (eds): *The Contextualization of Language*. Amsterdam/Philadelphia, 1992.
23. FORTESCUE, Michael, Peter HARDER and Lars KRISTOFFERSEN (eds): *Layered Structure and Reference in a Functional Perspective. Papers from the Functional Grammar Conference, Copenhagen, 1990*. Amsterdam/Philadelphia, 1992.
24. MAYNARD, Senko K.: *Discourse Modality: Subjectivity, Emotion and Voice in the Japanese Language*. Amsterdam/Philadelphia, 1993.
25. COUPER-KUHLEN, Elizabeth: *English Speech Rhythm. Form and function in everyday verbal interaction*. Amsterdam/Philadelphia, 1993.
26. STYGALL, Gail: Trial Language. *A study in differential discourse processing*. Amsterdam/Philadelphia, 1994.
27. SUTER, Hans Jürg: *The Wedding Report: A Prototypical Approach to the Study of Traditional Text Types*. Amsterdam/Philadelphia, 1993.
28. VAN DE WALLE, Lieve: *Pragmatics and Classical Sanskrit*. Amsterdam/Philadelphia, 1993.
29. BARSKY, Robert F.: *Constructing a Productive Other: Discourse theory and the convention refugee hearing*. Amsterdam/Philadelphia, 1994.
30. WORTHAM, Stanton E.F.: *Acting Out Participant Examples in the Classroom*. Amsterdam/Philadelphia, 1994.
31. WILDGEN, Wolfgang: *Process, Image and Meaning. A realistic model of the meanings of sentences and narrative texts*. Amsterdam/Philadelphia, 1994.
32. SHIBATANI, Masayoshi and Sandra A. THOMPSON (eds): *Essays in Semantics and Pragmatics*. Amsterdam/Philadelphia, 1995.
33. GOOSSENS, Louis, Paul PAUWELS, Brygida RUDZKA-OSTYN, Anne-Marie SIMON-VANDENBERGEN and Johan VANPARYS: *By Word of Mouth. Metaphor, metonymy and linguistic action in a cognitive perspective*. Amsterdam/Philadelphia, 1995.
34. BARBE, Katharina: Irony in Context. Amsterdam/Philadelphia, 1995.
35. JUCKER, Andreas H. (ed.): *Historical Pragmatics. Pragmatic developments in the history of English*. Amsterdam/Philadelphia, 1995.
36. CHILTON, Paul, Mikhail V. ILYIN and Jacob MEY: *Political Discourse in Transition in Eastern and Western Europe (1989-1991)*. Amsterdam/Philadelphia, 1998.
37. CARSTON, Robyn and Seiji UCHIDA (eds): *Relevance Theory. Applications and implications*. Amsterdam/Philadelphia, 1998.
38. FRETHEIM, Thorstein and Jeanette K. GUNDEL (eds): *Reference and Referent Accessibility*. Amsterdam/Philadelphia, 1996.
39. HERRING, Susan (ed.): *Computer-Mediated Communication. Linguistic, social, and cross-cultural perspectives*. Amsterdam/Philadelphia, 1996.
40. DIAMOND, Julie: *Status and Power in Verbal Interaction. A study of discourse in a close-knit social network*. Amsterdam/Philadelphia, 1996.
41. VENTOLA, Eija and Anna MAURANEN, (eds): *Academic Writing. Intercultural and textual issues*. Amsterdam/Philadelphia, 1996.
42. WODAK, Ruth and Helga KOTTHOFF (eds): *Communicating Gender in Context*. Amsterdam/Philadelphia, 1997.

43. JANSSEN, Theo A.J.M. and Wim van der WURFF (eds): *Reported Speech. Forms and functions of the verb.* Amsterdam/Philadelphia, 1996.
44. BARGIELA-CHIAPPINI, Francesca and Sandra J. HARRIS: *Managing Language. The discourse of corporate meetings.* Amsterdam/Philadelphia, 1997.
45. PALTRIDGE, Brian: *Genre, Frames and Writing in Research Settings.* Amsterdam/Philadelphia, 1997.
46. GEORGAKOPOULOU, Alexandra: *Narrative Performances. A study of Modern Greek storytelling.* Amsterdam/Philadelphia, 1997.
47. CHESTERMAN, Andrew: *Contrastive Functional Analysis.* Amsterdam/Philadelphia, 1998.
48. KAMIO, Akio: *Territory of Information.* Amsterdam/Philadelphia, 1997.
49. KURZON, Dennis: *Discourse of Silence.* Amsterdam/Philadelphia, 1998.
50. GRENOBLE, Lenore: *Deixis and Information Packaging in Russian Discourse.* Amsterdam/Philadelphia, 1998.
51. BOULIMA, Jamila: *Negotiated Interaction in Target Language Classroom Discourse.* Amsterdam/Philadelphia, 1999.
52. GILLIS, Steven and Annick DE HOUWER (eds): *The Acquisition of Dutch.* Amsterdam/Philadelphia, 1998.
53. MOSEGAARD HANSEN, Maj-Britt: *The Function of Discourse Particles. A study with special reference to spoken standard French.* Amsterdam/Philadelphia, 1998.
54. HYLAND, Ken: *Hedging in Scientific Research Articles.* Amsterdam/Philadelphia, 1998.
55. ALLWOOD, Jens and Peter Gärdenfors (eds): *Cognitive Semantics. Meaning and cognition.* Amsterdam/Philadelphia, 1999.
56. TANAKA, Hiroko: *Language, Culture and Social Interaction. Turn-taking in Japanese and Anglo-American English.* Amsterdam/Philadelphia, 1999.
57 JUCKER, Andreas H. and Yael ZIV (eds): *Discourse Markers. Descriptions and theory.* Amsterdam/Philadelphia, 1998.
58. ROUCHOTA, Villy and Andreas H. JUCKER (eds): *Current Issues in Relevance Theory.* Amsterdam/Philadelphia, 1998.
59. KAMIO, Akio and Ken-ichi TAKAMI (eds): *Function and Structure. In honor of Susumu Kuno.* 1999.
60. JACOBS, Geert: *Preformulating the News. An analysis of the metapragmatics of press releases.* 1999.
61. MILLS, Margaret H. (ed.): *Slavic Gender Linguistics.* 1999.
62. TZANNE, Angeliki: *Talking at Cross-Purposes. The dynamics of miscommunication.* 2000.
63. BUBLITZ, Wolfram, Uta LENK and Eija VENTOLA (eds.): *Coherence in Spoken and Written Discourse. How to create it and how to describe it.Selected papers from the International Workshop on Coherence, Augsburg, 24-27 April 1997.* 1999.
64. SVENNEVIG, Jan: *Getting Acquainted in Conversation. A study of initial interactions.* 1999.
65. COOREN, François: *The Organizing Dimension of Communication.* 2000.
66. JUCKER, Andreas H., Gerd FRITZ and Franz LEBSANFT (eds.): *Historical Dialogue Analysis.* 1999.

67. TAAVITSAINEN, Irma, Gunnel MELCHERS and Päivi PAHTA (eds.): *Dimensions of Writing in Nonstandard English.* 1999.
68. ARNOVICK, Leslie: *Diachronic Pragmatics. Seven case studies in English illocutionary development.* 1999.
69. NOH, Eun-Ju: *The Semantics and Pragmatics of Metarepresentation in English. A relevance-theoretic account.* 2000.
70. SORJONEN, Marja-Leena: *Recipient Activities Particles nii(n) and joo as Responses in Finnish Conversation.* n.y.p.
71. GÓMEZ-GONZÁLEZ, María Ángeles: *The Theme-Topic Interface. Evidence from English.* 2001.
72. MARMARIDOU, Sophia S.A.: *Pragmatic Meaning and Cognition.* 2000.
73. HESTER, Stephen and David FRANCIS (eds.): *Local Educational Order. Ethnomethodological studies of knowledge in action.* 2000.
74. TROSBORG, Anna (ed.): *Analysing Professional Genres.* 2000.
75. PILKINGTON, Adrian: *Poetic Effects. A relevance theory perspective.* 2000.
76. MATSUI, Tomoko: *Bridging and Relevance.* 2000.
77. VANDERVEKEN, Daniel and Susumu KUBO (eds.): *Essays in Speech Act Theory.* n.y.p.
78. SELL, Roger D. : *Literature as Communication. The foundations of mediating criticism.* 2000.
79. ANDERSEN, Gisle and Thorstein FRETHEIM (eds.): *Pragmatic Markers and Propositional Attitude.* 2000.
80. UNGERER, Friedrich (ed.): *English Media Texts – Past and Present. Language and textual structure.* 2000.
81. DI LUZIO, Aldo, Susanne GÜNTHNER and Franca ORLETTI (eds.): *Culture in Communication. Analyses of intercultural situations.* n.y.p.
82. KHALIL, Esam N.: *Grounding in English and Arabic News Discourse.* 2000.
83. MÁRQUEZ REITER, Rosina: *Linguistic Politeness in Britain and Uruguay. A contrastive study of requests and apologies.* 2000.
84. ANDERSEN, Gisle: *Pragmatic Markers and Sociolinguistic Variation. A relevance-theoretic approach to the language of adolescents.* n.y.p.
85. COLLINS, Daniel E.: *Reanimated Voices. Speech reporting in a historical-pragmatic perspective.* n.y.p.
86. IFANTIDOU, Elly: *Evidentials and Relevance.* n.y.p.
87. MUSHIN, Ilana: *Evidentiality and Epistemological Stance. Narrative Retelling.* n.y.p.
88. BAYRAKTAROGLU, Arin and Maria SIFIANOU (eds.): *Linguistic Politeness Across Boundaries. Linguistic Politeness Across Boundaries.* n.y.p.
89. ITAKURA, Hiroko: *Conversational Dominance and Gender. A study of Japanese speakers in first and second language contexts.* n.y.p.